ISLAND INFERNOS

ALSO BY JOHN C. McMANUS

Fire and Fortitude: The US Army in the Pacific War, 1941–1943

Hell Before Their Very Eyes: American Soldiers Liberate Concentration Camps in Germany, April 1945

The Dead and Those About to Die: D-Day: The Big Red One at Omaha Beach

September Hope: The American Side of a Bridge Too Far

Grunts: Inside the American Infantry Combat Experience, World War II Through Iraq

American Courage, American Carnage: The 7th Infantry Regiment's Combat Experience, 1812 Through World War II

The 7th Infantry Regiment: Combat in the Age of Terror, the Korean War Through the Present

U.S. Military History for Dummies

Alamo in the Ardennes: The Untold Story of the American Soldiers Who Made the Defense of Bastogne Possible

The Americans at Normandy: The Summer of 1944—The American War from the Normandy Beaches to Falaise

The Americans at D-Day: The American Experience at the Normandy Invasion

Deadly Sky: The American Combat Airman in World War II

The Deadly Brotherhood: The American Combat Soldier in World War II

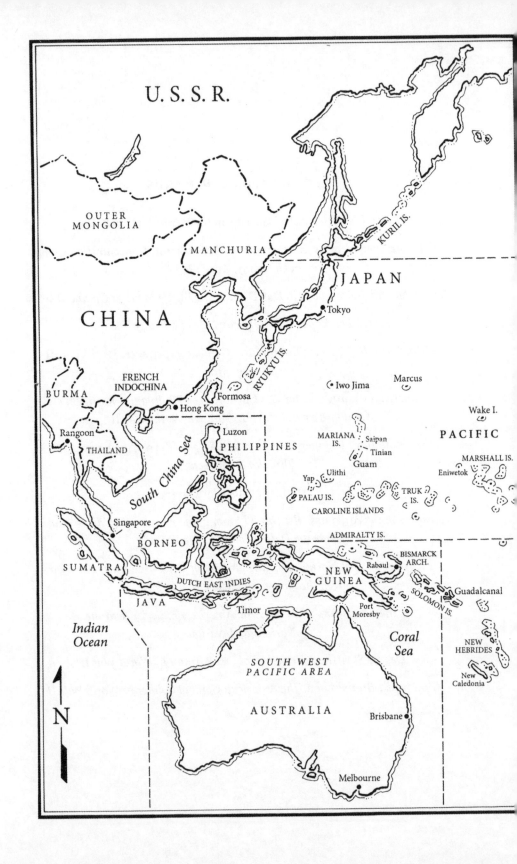

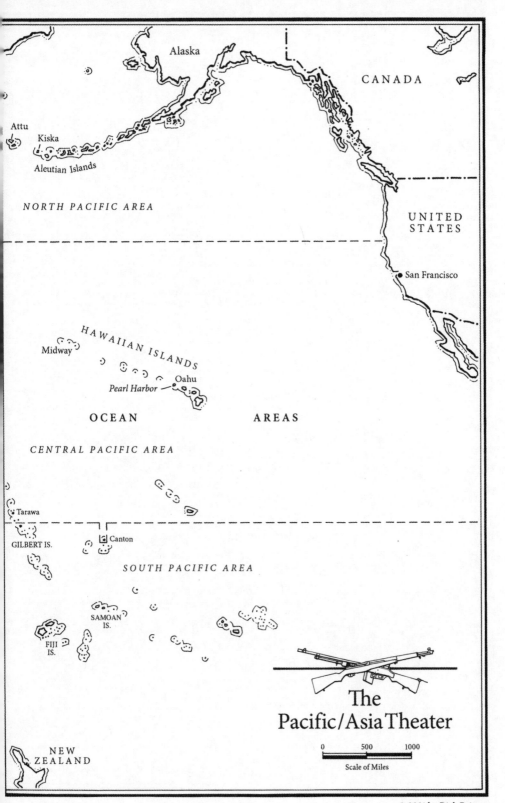

Alaska

CANADA

Attu
Kiska
Aleutian Islands

NORTH PACIFIC AREA

UNITED
STATES

San Francisco

HAWAIIAN ISLANDS
Midway
Oahu
Pearl Harbor

OCEAN   AREAS

CENTRAL PACIFIC AREA

Tarawa

Canton

GILBERT IS.

SOUTH PACIFIC AREA

SAMOAN
IS.

FIJI
IS.

The
Pacific/Asia Theater

NEW
ZEALAND

0   500   1000

Scale of Miles

ISLAND INFERNOS

THE US ARMY'S PACIFIC WAR ODYSSEY,
1944

JOHN C. McMANUS

CALIBER

CALIBER

An imprint of Penguin Random House LLC
penguinrandomhouse.com

Copyright © 2021 by John C. McManus

Penguin supports copyright. Copyright fuels creativity, encourages diverse voices, promotes free speech, and creates a vibrant culture. Thank you for buying an authorized edition of this book and for complying with copyright laws by not reproducing, scanning, or distributing any part of it in any form without permission. You are supporting writers and allowing Penguin to continue to publish books for every reader.

DUTTON CALIBER and the D colophon are registered trademarks of Penguin Random House LLC.

LIBRARY OF CONGRESS CATALOGING-IN-PUBLICATION DATA

Names: McManus, John C., 1965– author.
Title: Island infernos : the US Army's Pacific War odyssey, 1944 / by John C. McManus.
Description: New York : Dutton Caliber, Penguin Random House LLC, [2021] |
Includes bibliographical references and index.
Identifiers: LCCN 2021009801 (print) | LCCN 2021009802 (ebook) |
ISBN 9780451475060 (hardcover) | ISBN 9780698192775 (ebook)
Subjects: LCSH: World War, 1939–1945—Campaigns—Pacific Area. |
United States. Army—History—World War, 1939–1945.
Classification: LCC D767 .M36 2021 (print) | LCC D767 (ebook) |
DDC 940.54/26—dc23
LC record available at https://lccn.loc.gov/2021009801
LC ebook record available at https://lccn.loc.gov/2021009802

Printed in the United States of America
1 3 5 7 9 10 8 6 4 2

While the author has made every effort to provide accurate telephone numbers, internet addresses, and other contact information at the time of publication, neither the publisher nor the author assumes any responsibility for errors or for changes that occur after publication. Further, the publisher does not have any control over and does not assume any responsibility for author or third-party websites or their content.

To Nancy, with all my Love . . .

To the Pacific Theater veterans, so many of whom experienced far more anonymity than glory . . .

To the McManus and Woody families

To my incredible parents, Michael and Mary Jane McManus, and to Ruth and Nelson, who have treated me as their son . . .

Contents

Author's Note

Most Pacific theater events and operations took place on the other side of the International Dateline from North America. Thus, all dates and times in this series are local. To avoid confusion between morning and afternoon times, this series employs the twenty-four-hour military clock. For instance, 8 A.M. is 0800; 2 P.M. is 1400, and so on.

In the Japanese and Chinese languages, surnames are listed before given names, i.e., Tojo Hideki rather than Hideki Tojo. This is the exact opposite of Western practice. Because this is a work written in the English language, Japanese and Chinese names will be listed in the Western style, except with individuals, such as Chiang Kai-shek or Mao Zedong, whose names are widely known in their correct cultural format.

The terms "Jap" and "Nip" are viewed today as racist and offensive. However, during World War II, they were used so commonly among Americans, Australians, and Britons—even generals and policy makers—as to take on the status of mundane slang. As such, I will make no attempt to excise the terms from the quoted sources in this series. In no way does this indicate my acceptance or approval of these pejorative words.

Throughout the series, the terms Pacific War and Pacific/Asia War are interchangeable.

All rank designations are current. Many soldiers were promoted several times in the course of the war. In this series, I use the rank of the person at the appropriate time frame. For instance, Douglas MacArthur began 1944 as a four-star general. In the passages that cover this phase of his life, I refer to him as a general. Later, he was promoted to five-star rank. Thus, in subsequent chapters, I recognize his new ranks and refer to him appropriately.

The term "native" to describe peoples of Asia, Pacific islands, Melanesia, and the like is, in my view, an inappropriate, patronizing, and somewhat dehumanizing legacy of colonialism. After all, one does not refer to someone from France or Poland as a "native," so why would one use the term to describe someone from Burma or Guadalcanal? Thus, this series eschews the term "native" in favor of appropriate local or ethnic designations. The exception, of course, is in quotes from contemporary sources.

There are many versions and dialects of Chinese (Mandarin, Cantonese, etc.). Thus names, places, and terms can have strikingly different English translations, i.e., Chiang Kai-shek versus Jiang Jieshi. This series employs the most commonly known versions of names, places, and terms.

Prologue

Beneath a tropical canopy of alien and friendly places, spanning untold thousands of miles, an army waited. And languished. And planned. And trained. And plotted. And innovated. And anticipated. A coiled olive-drab machine, growing in strength and purpose, it had more than two years of campaigns already under its belt, ranging from the disastrous, as in the Philippines, to the triumphant, as at Guadalcanal. Like a young adult just beginning to feel the prodigious power of youth, this burgeoning army stood, as 1944 dawned, on the cusp of full maturity and overarching purpose. From desolate Alaskan outposts to viny, choking jungles in Burma, New Guinea, and the Solomon Islands; from Oahu to Australia and a dizzying array of otherwise insignificant little coral stepping-stone Pacific islands in between, nearly 700,000 soldiers of this growing army were spread across nearly a third of the globe's surface, answering to no single commander, a dispersion of geography and command unprecedented before or since in American history.

By the time this army had completed its monumental task a year and a half later, it would number more than 1.8 million soldiers, the third-largest land force ever fielded for an overseas war by the United States, behind only the European theater armies of World Wars I and II, and certainly the most amphibious-experienced ground force in human history, comprising some twenty-one infantry and airborne divisions, plus assorted independent combat teams whose manpower equated to three or four more divisions, in addition to accompanying service and support forces. Nearly 42,000 of these soldiers would not survive, felled as they were by combat, disease, accidents, and the terrible privation of captivity, a harvest of death that totaled more than the entirety of any previous American conflict save the Civil War and World War I. Even now, at the end of 1943, thousands of them moldered inside improvised graves in some of the most remote places on earth, many with indistinct names like Buna, Sanananda, Attu,

1

Vella Lavella, and Cabanatuan. They and their living comrades were part of a fighting force that dwarfed the Marine Corps, which, at peak strength, mobilized six divisions and, in the full expanse of the war, carried out fifteen amphibious combat landings, compared with many dozens more by the Army. Staggeringly complex, with vast capabilities seldom seen in the course of human events, this army had already by 1944 proven itself adept at performing a breathtaking variety of missions—grand strategical planning, interservice coordination, diplomacy and joint operations with allies, logistics, transportation, engineering, intelligence, guerrilla warfare, medical care on a scale unimaginable even a generation earlier, civil affairs, mortuary affairs, the struggle for survival and purpose amid horrifying conditions of captivity, and ground combat operations of nearly every type, fought in some of the world's most inhospitable locales, against a foe who recognized few Western-style rules of warfare. Plunged into an elemental death struggle whose base nature few Americans truly grasped at the time (and largely ever since), the soldiers of this army, and their opponents, had already determined that scruples mattered less than victory and survival. And many of those 700,000 US soldiers had glimpsed some troubling portents of the American postwar future—irregular warfare, moral ambiguities, rapidly modernizing, ever deadlier weapons, racial strife, postcolonial uncertainty, flawed alliances, and the labyrinthine struggle for influence in Asia and the Pacific, a crucial enterprise that the United States has never yet mastered nor relinquished.[1]

At the beginning of 1944—surely one of the most momentous, consequential years in American history—the soldiers of this army, and the generals who led them, looked to the near future with a mixture of excitement and dread. On the northeastern coast of New Guinea, where town-size logistical facilities had begun to proliferate in the wake of Allied military victories the previous year, service troops labored mightily on the mundane but crucial tasks so vital to sustain the massive enterprise of total war. No job loomed larger in importance than the loading and unloading of ships—literally the *sine qua non* of amphibious island-to-island and ocean warfare—and generally performed by a chronically understaffed coterie of port companies. Nineteen-year-old Corporal Sy Kahn and about 150 other soldiers of the 244th Port Company had spent Thanksgiving eating rubbery turkey and chasing lizards, insects, and snakes out of their makeshift tents. By Christmastime, they had managed to stave off their growing boredom and sense of isolation by scrounging half a dozen bottles of

170-proof vanilla extract that, even when mixed with fruit juice, went down with all the smoothness of liquid fire. With no real piers or port installations, they had to ferry back and forth aboard landing craft to anchored ships where they toiled for hours, hauling freight from stuffy, overheated holds onto the landing craft and then to various points onshore. Kahn and his buddies constantly speculated about future invasions and destinations. "Is this Sy Kahn going into battle, to fight the Japs?" he wondered in a private diary. "He has some vague ideas what it is all about. Sy Kahn, soldier, might have to kill men, he might be killed. Perhaps the former is worse than the latter."

But service troops like Kahn, though constantly in danger from Japanese air raids, were too scarce and too badly needed for the vast matériel requirements of the burgeoning Allied war machine to use as fighting soldiers. That job largely belonged to the combat troops whose numbers in theater were growing as the calendar turned to 1944. In a tent camp outside Rockhampton, Australia, the Jungleers of the 41st Infantry Division were readjusting their nerves and battling malarial fever after months of patrolling and episodic combat in the wilds of Papua New Guinea. The skin of many was still pockmarked with cherry-colored splotches of jungle rot and ulcerous boils. For the first time in almost a year, they enjoyed dry clothes, hot showers, hot food, and regular mail. After eighteen months overseas, the men speculated endlessly, and pointlessly, about the remote possibility of rotating home. Special Services troupes performed stage shows for them. Well-behaved soldiers received furloughs into Rockhampton, a midsize city of thirty-five thousand people. They strolled the streets aimlessly, ate local ice cream, and crowded into a movie theater carved out of a former coconut grove. "Everything seemed to be twenty years behind the times," one GI recalled. The luckiest traveled to the big cities of Melbourne and Sydney, where dates with attractive Australian women could easily be had, and a party seemingly beckoned around every corner; some even ventured to Tasmania, where they proceeded to gorge themselves on local chocolates and apples. The division band traveled to Brisbane and recorded music for a Christmas concert aired on Australian national radio.

For Americans used to a chilly yuletide season, the Southern Hemisphere's summer weather at Christmastime seemed bizarre and incongruous. Clustered inside six-man tents, the troops gamely celebrated the holiday by unwrapping presents and hanging colored wrapping twine from home onto local trees. An especially resourceful rifle company got its collective hands on eight kegs of Australian beer, "making the holiday a little more home-like in that dismal area," according to the unit history. After bingeing on the warm brew and suffering the inevitable consequences, the men soon dubbed it "Green Death." The pace and intensity of training had since picked up, ominously pointing toward an amphibious invasion, one that the veterans who had spent much of 1943 grappling with the tenacious Japanese imagined might be costly and protracted. One platoon leader gathered his men together and painted a grim portrait of the days ahead. "He acknowledged that combat was in the near future," Private First Class (PFC) Francis "Bernie" Catanzaro, a new member of the platoon, later wrote. "The important thing, he said, was not whether we were wounded or killed, but that we gain our objectives. If there was a hill to be taken, we would take it even if it cost most of us our lives." The soldiers' reaction to these dark tidings was predictably unenthusiastic, to the point where the platoon sergeant felt compelled to reassure the men, after the lieutenant had left, that they need take no unnecessary chances.

At Oro Bay, on the north New Guinea coast some fifteen miles east of Buna, where American soldiers had a year earlier won the war's hard-earned first ground victory, the mood was not quite as dreary for the rookie 1st Cavalry Division. As the modern descendants of the old mounted cavalry—once the mobile cutting edge of the Army but now obsolete in an age of global multiservice operations—the troopers had only recently relinquished their horses during a teary ceremony at Fort Bliss, Texas, before deploying overseas. "It was the end of an era for us," Lieutenant Joseph Cribbins later said. "It was a sight to see that whole field full of horses and mules with a division completely mounted with their guidons. It felt really like a different way of life." Indeed, it was precisely that. They had exchanged their cavalry bridles for infantry rifles. For some, the stark change in identity did not sit well. According to one soldier, "Many of the proud cavalrymen would rather turn [in] their stripes, bars, or stars than trade in their saddles" for the tools of their new job as infantry ground pounders. But they had done it even though they still could not bring themselves to relinquish the unique terminology of the cavalry branch. They called a company a troop, a battalion a squadron, and an individual soldier was known as a trooper, not a GI. They had spent six months in Australia, training intensively for amphibious warfare. By mid-December, when they had settled into their bug-ridden tent camp at Oro Bay and begun patrolling the adjacent jungles to get acclimated to the tropical heat, they were walking the fine line between edginess and readiness emblematic of well-trained troops before combat. In New Guinea's dense jungle, they battled malaria-bearing mosquitoes, not Japanese. "We did our best to drain swamps, sleep under nets, and kill the mosquitoes," one commander later wrote. The Army had already learned that the best way to prevail in this interspecies warfare was to mandate the taking of atabrine, a drug that suppressed the symptoms of malaria. Commanders took this order very seriously. Throughout the division, men were not allowed to eat until they took their daily pill.

Many of the troopers yearned for action after so many mundane months of dry-run invasions, road marches, night problems, and the like. Some were so eager to get into combat that they stowed themselves aboard resupply ships bound for Cape Gloucester on the western coast of New Britain, where the 1st Marine Division had landed the day after Christmas to carve out a perimeter airfield from which to bomb Japanese-held Rabaul at the opposite end of the island. The 1st Cavalry Division adventurers filtered from the ships to the front lines, where the startled Marines welcomed them to their world of jungle heat, danger, and privation. When Major General Innis Swift, the 1st Cavalry Division commander, got wind of these unauthorized expeditions, he had all his men rounded up and returned to Oro Bay. The unauthorized expedition did little to quell the impatient mood. Rumors of an imminent amphibious operation continued to preoccupy the troopers, seemingly night and day.

About forty-one hundred miles to the northeast, at Oahu, the same kind of talk swept through the ranks of the 7th Infantry Division, though these men did have a slightly better idea of where they were going next. In May 1943, on Attu, a desolate, boggy rock of an island in Alaska's Aleutian chain, they had fought America's only cold-weather battle in the war against Japan. In wet, freezing conditions, they had methodically annihilated die-hard Japanese soldiers, ridge by ridge, hill by hill. The enemy fought largely to extinction, inflicting shocking losses on the 7th Division: 549 killed, 1,148 wounded, and 2,112 men lost to trench foot, frostbite, disease, accidents, and combat fatigue, a 25 percent casualty rate. In numbers of casualties inflicted versus incurred, Attu would be exceeded in the Pacific War only by Iwo Jima. Though they had prevailed, the nightmarish struggle for this otherwise insignificant place still hung over the survivors like a mourning veil. "The Attu battle stands very much foremost in the experiences of these men," Lieutenant Gage Rodman, a replacement rifle platoon leader fresh out of officer candidate school, wrote to his parents. A Catholic chaplain one day showed Rodman a picture of seven junior officers taken before the invasion. The priest soberly related that one had been relieved, four were killed, one fell prey to combat fatigue, and only one was promoted. Attu took a toll on the senior leadership as well. Communications mishaps and the protracted, bloody nature of the fighting had led to the relief of the division commander, the luckless Major General Albert Brown, whose brusque superiors did not even bother to visit the island or speak with him before casting him aside. He had since been replaced by colorful, innovative Major General Charles Corlett, a no-nonsense westerner who had earned the unique nickname "Cowboy Pete" at West Point because of his skill at tending to horses. Survivor of a World War I mustard gas attack, Corlett had evolved into a passionate advocate for the gospel of combined arms coordination and rapid-fire amphibious operations. A relentless communicator, Corlett liked to send advice-laden memos to his troops. "Look to your physical condition," he lectured them in one missive, "train like a football player. Cut down your beer and cigarettes so you can run up or down hill to the position that will give you the greatest advantage in smashing the Jap." In another memo specially intended for his commanders, he opined, "Our men are willing and enthusiastic if their orders are clear, definite and based on common sense. In order to be worthy of the men we command, every leader must get in and push with all his might until victory is won. THINK THIS OVER AND APPLY IT."

Since arriving on temperate Oahu in September 1943—a welcome climate change from the moist, frosty Aleutians—he had put the division through months of intensive jungle and amphibious training. Their days were filled with long hikes, mock landings, live-fire exercises, and earnest orientation for newcomers. "The infantry battalions rotated through a round robin of specialized training," one staff officer later said. "They had a week on the beach learning to swim, another week in a jungle training center, *next* a week in an amphibious center where they went out to sea on landing craft and then returned, making full scale live ammunition landings. *Next* a week of intensive training in the use of explosives and the reduction of pillboxes and *finally* a week of practicing the exact tactics for this type of attack." Some of the men lived in tents on the Ewa Plain, under strict orders not to poach the adjacent local pineapple crop lest they impoverish Hawaiian farmers. Others settled into stately Schofield Barracks, where Japanese planes had strafed 25th Infantry Division soldiers on

December 7, 1941. "We just got up every day, went and trained and went back and slept," Lieutenant Gerard Radice, an artillery forward observer, quipped. Staff officers prepared realistic, life-size mock-ups of hypothetical coral atoll islands and fortifications.

By January the abstract had turned into the expectant when the commanders learned their target was the Kwajalein Atoll, in the Marshall Islands. Thorough as ever, Corlett trooped group after group into a spacious amphitheater at Schofield Barracks, where they listened to briefings and studied reams of intelligence material. "We renamed all the islands in our group giving American code names to every terrain object and shore irregularity that could be recognized," Corlett later wrote. "We had thousands of maps made, so every corporal could have one." The knowledge of their destination, conveying as it did an unmistakable whiff of inexorable momentum, energized the men to a near fever pitch of anticipation. "Detailed plans were rapidly completed," one man later recalled. "Landing teams were organized, shore parties trained, landing plans prepared, special communication teams distributed, and a multitude of other details taken care of."[2]

Many miles over the ocean horizon, sprinkled among a diversely random assortment of hellhole prison camps, stretching from the Japanese home islands to Formosa (Taiwan), Manchuria, and the Philippines, thousands of less fortunate soldiers who had been captured in the war's early months were now living a hand-to-mouth struggle for existence. Typical of many, twenty-six-year-old Private Michael Campbell greeted the new year toiling as a slave laborer in a steel mill at Yodogawa, near Osaka, on the main island of Honshu. Campbell specialized in making fifty-gallon steel barrels. Other prisoners worked in the foundry, pulled handcarts of freight to boats in canals, or loaded or unloaded the boats. Everyone worked backbreaking eight-to-ten-hour daily shifts, with only three days off per month. Campbell was more than used to hardship. His mother had been committed to a Michigan insane asylum; his father had gone to a state prison for what Michael called "a crime too heinous to describe." His seven younger siblings had been scattered all over Michigan, adopted by separate families. As the eldest, he had ended up on his own at age sixteen and had since found a home in the Army with the 31st Infantry Regiment. He had managed to survive the fighting on Bataan and Corregidor, the chaotic initial days of captivity after the surrender of the Corregidor garrison, a perilous journey by ship to Japan, and more than a year of slave labor. He had seen about a quarter of his fellow prisoners succumb to starvation, disease, and death-inducing depression. Almost out of habit, he struggled on, cheating the ubiquitous death that pervaded his dark world. "There was nothing to hide and we had lost our inhibitions," he later wrote.

The same was true for Private Lester Tenney, a Chicago native and former tank crewman who had lived through the infamous Bataan Death March, the Cabanatuan POW camp on Luzon, a horrendous sea journey to Kyushu, and now the daily grind as a slave laborer in a coal mine near a prison camp called Fukuoka Number 17. Small coke stoves, fueled by the fruits of the mine, helped Tenney and his fellow inmates stave off the winter cold. The typical day's work left him exhausted and covered in coal dust. In captivity, he had evolved from a naive, adventure-seeking kid into a canny student of human nature. He had learned how to read people and negotiate with them. He had cultivated productive relationships among friends and foe alike and he had developed a survivor's go-with-the-flow attitude. "While trying to get enough food and at the same time build his financial empire, a prisoner would trade cigarettes for rice that would be collected at some future date," he later wrote. "I played this supply-and-demand game." As the new year began, Tenney and the others looked forward to staging a theatrical production in their free time and perhaps receiving Red Cross care packages. Aside from a general sense that Japan had lost the strategic initiative, they were largely ignorant of what was happening in the war.

At Cabanatuan, home to the largest single group of American prisoners of the Rising Sun, Lieutenant Colonel Harold Johnson knew much more, thanks to a clandestine radio, contacts outside the camp, and even Japanese media sources such as the *Nippon Times*. Every evening, a trusted cluster of prisoners huddled around the radio, quietly listening to the Voice of America from San Francisco and even the BBC from London. Those who heard the broadcasts circulated the news to Johnson and thousands of others by word of mouth. Others tracked the progress of Allied armies on maps readily available in the reference section of the camp library. As commissary officer—the most trusted job among the prisoners—Johnson had developed an elaborate bartering system with outside vendors and donors to augment the meager POW rations of nearly every necessity from food to medicine to soap. His extraordinary efforts had improved Cabanatuan from a holding center of death in 1942, when hundreds died of disease and starvation, to a reasonably bearable incarceration center in 1943.

North Dakota born and raised, ten years out of West Point, Johnson exuded a sort of pioneering modesty that served him well as a military leader. For Johnson, the son of a humble lumberyard manager, the Army represented a way out of the Upper Midwest frontier, a place of self-improvement and sophistication. During the Japanese invasion of the Philippines, he had served in nearly every capacity, from staff officer to battalion commander, with the 57th Infantry Regiment, a unit composed primarily of highly professional Philippine Scouts under the tutelage of American officers and NCOs. In combat he proved himself brave and level-headed. In captivity, he emerged as arguably the most highly regarded officer among his fellow prisoners, hence his commissary job. Through the horrendous early months as guests of the Japanese—the cruelty of the Bataan Death March, the parched, callous deadliness of Camp O'Donnell, the degraded horrors of Cabanatuan—Johnson had somehow managed to become more honest, more honorable, more ethical, even as others occasionally stooped to any level of depravity just to survive. Johnson had even, by some miracle, survived O'Donnell's infamous Zero Ward, where diseased, starved, dysentery-racked prisoners had wallowed in their own excreta and green vomit until they died delirious and alone, their bodies then roughly hauled to a communal grave by their half-dead comrades.

Philosophical and religious, he had come to believe that true leadership meant total devotion to soldiers. He was determined to do everything in his power to help every last soldier survive the war. He studied the psyche of his Japanese captors. He learned how to manipulate them, accommodate them, even deceive them when necessary, all for the larger welfare of the prisoner population. He rang in the year 1944 with several Japanese interpreters who insisted on sharing liquor and food with him. "This New Year's was as strange as I ever expect to spend," he scrawled in a secret diary. "There was a great spirit of 'live and let live' and much back slapping." The incongruous comradely mood belied a deeper tension. A pair of recent typhoons had significantly curtailed Johnson's commissary operations. Some ten million pesos' "worth of prime commodities ready for distribution in Manila were destroyed," he told his diary. The price of bananas, beans, coconuts, and cigarettes had all gone up. Would the Japanese allow him to pay more or buy more items to make up the difference in supply? For that matter, how much longer would they let him run the commissary at all? For all his machinations, he knew he and the others were still dependent on their mortal enemies for their meager existence. Thanks to Cabanatuan's illicit news network, Johnson knew that the Allies were poised for major offensives in the South and Central Pacific, and Burma as well. He reckoned that American armies would eventually come back to the Philippines. Johnson worried that the Japanese, rather than permit the prisoners to be liberated by their returning comrades, would move them to Japan or perhaps just kill them outright. He could not help but contemplate whether he and his fellow POWs would live to see another new year.

At Muksaq POW camp on the island of Formosa, sixty-year-old Lieutenant General Jonathan Wainwright, the highest-ranking of all the American prisoners, worried about much the same thing. The grandson of a naval officer and the son of a West Point–trained cavalry commander, Wainwright was born to soldiering in the same way that others have farming or music or athletics in their familial DNA. At West Point, he had been a natural choice for First Captain, the most prestigious of cadet honors. Throughout the Army that he had served for nearly forty years, few referred to him by his given name. Lean and rooster-necked, with gaunt cheeks and soulful eyes, the nickname "Skinny" had followed him for decades from post to post, over much of the globe. The privation of captivity had only exacerbated his scrawniness. A cavalryman to the core, he loved horses, soldiers, and liquor in equal denominations. In combat his soldiers had universally respected him as a courageous and coolheaded commander, though his closest aides worried incessantly about his penchant for strong drink. The prisoner's life, of course, offered him no such outlet. Since reluctantly acceding to the surrender of all Allied military forces in the Philippines nearly two years earlier, he had for a time convinced himself that he would face court-martial proceedings after the war. Those fears had recently diminished when he found out that President Roosevelt had named him to a list of permanent major generals. As a prisoner, Wainwright had endured beatings, torture, near starvation, forced labor, and abject humiliation. At Muksaq, though, food and living conditions were adequate to good, especially compared to the deprivation experienced by Campbell, Tenney, Johnson, and many thousands of other American POWs. Wainwright worried incessantly over the welfare of that unseen host of prisoners, and mentally struggled with the stark reality that he could do little for them.

He and his fellow Muksaq POWs celebrated Christmas by slaughtering a hog. "On top of that the commander of the post sent us two turkeys," he later wrote. He enjoyed a quiet dinner with Sergeant Hubert "Tex" Carroll, his orderly. Behind the veneer of benevolence, the Japanese agenda was to persuade Wainwright and other high-ranking prisoners to make propaganda statements attesting to good treatment and urging the American government to end the war. Taking a cue from Wainwright, the prisoners refused. The more heavy-handed, and clumsy, the Japanese attempts at persuasive propaganda, the more Skinny came to believe that their desperation stemmed from the realization that they were losing the war. In one typical instance, they claimed to Wainwright that the Imperial Navy had sunk sixteen American battleships. But subsequently in the *Nippon Times*, an English-language newspaper published by the Japanese government, he read that the United States Navy currently had twenty serviceable battleships. "I knew therefore that we could not have lost what the Japs claimed." He stubbornly and steadfastly refused to cave in to Japanese propaganda demands. "I had resigned myself," he later said. "I didn't care what happened to me." The general had once optimistically predicted to his men that liberation would come by New Year's Day 1944. With that date come and gone, and no end to captivity in sight, he could not help but wonder how many more holidays he and his men would spend under the Japanese yoke. Wainwright knew the Allies were winning. The question was whether that meant salvation or annihilation for the prisoners. Dark rumors swirled that the Japanese would kill all prisoners in the event of Allied victory. Wainwright could do little besides watch, wait, and hope for the best.[3]

As Wainwright stewed over the uncertain future, his professional peers planned and schemed for Japan's demise. The generals who had turned the tables on the Rising Sun after a spate of early defeats now found themselves responsible for supervising operations over the largest expanse of geography and the most inhospitable conditions in the Army's long history. In northern Burma, where Nationalist Chinese and Imperial British Armies had nearly two years earlier been summarily expelled by a tougher, better-led Imperial Japanese Army expeditionary force, Wainwright's old friend Joseph Stilwell was now finally back in the field, following months of frustrating high-command inter-Allied diplomacy. At once a theater commander and military adviser to a foreign government, he actually yearned for nothing more than field command. Nearly blind in his left eye and dependent upon strong corrective lenses just to see adequately out of his right, the sixty-year-old Stilwell was a curious mixture of physical hardiness and aging dissipation. Unique for the time, he wore his salt-and-pepper hair in a high and tight style. In 1942, he had personally led several dozen subordinates and locals on a physically taxing but strategically pointless—and politically damaging to his relations with the Chinese— exodus from Burma to India, in the process negotiating his way through some of the world's most forbidding terrain. Though trumpeted in the American media as an epic event, the trek hinted at a kind of forest-for-trees myopia inherent to his makeup. Prone to nursing hatreds that ranged from the self-defeating, like his disdain for the British, to the eccentric, such as his dislike of cavalry, Stilwell nonetheless attempted to guide his every action with a sense of personal honor. Caustic, energetic, opinionated, intellectually curious, and so fundamentally honest in his personal character that he could muster no empathy or understanding for anyone who fell short of his own pristine standards, Stilwell dreamed of fostering the establishment of a modern China whose government might prove worthy of its remarkable people. The 1904 West Point graduate had spent nearly half of his forty-year career in China, including two recent years as chief of staff to Nationalist leader Chiang Kai-shek, whom he privately referred to as "Peanut" and loathed as little more than a self-interested, shortsighted despot. Fluent in Mandarin Chinese, Stilwell understood the Chinese and their culture better than anyone else in the United States Army. Yet, paradoxically, he seemed incapable of connecting with Chiang and appreciating the gravity of his tenuous situation as head of a shaky, diverse government coalition of generals, warlords, property owners, and farmers whose power to control fractured China was anything but assured in the face of Mao Zedong's growing communist shadow government and military forces, as well as Wang Ching-wei's pro-Japanese accommodationist government in Nanking.

For many months Stilwell had urged Chiang to purge the Nationalist Army of corruption and inefficiency so that it might prove more effective in combat against the Japanese. But Stilwell seemed unable to grasp that doing so might deprive the Generalissimo of the power base he badly needed to emerge as the strategic victor in China. Chiang cared little for the possibility of tactical military victories over the Japanese. He preferred instead to husband American lend-lease material largesse and weaponry for the long-term struggle against his domestic enemies. Stilwell wanted him to put those US goodies to immediate use against the common Japanese enemy. The Allied ejection from Burma in 1942 had severed China's landward ties with the outside world, necessitating an inefficient hand-to-mouth aerial resupply effort from Indian bases that did little more than maintain an uneasy status quo. Ever since, Stilwell had lobbied ferociously for a land campaign to open up a supply route from British-controlled India through northern Burma and into China. In the absence of this logistical link, Stilwell believed China might collapse, leading to a strategic disaster of the first magnitude, since victory in China would free up at least half of the Imperial Japanese Army to fight elsewhere. By embracing hostilities with China on the Asian continent and the Western powers in the Pacific, the Japanese government had essentially opted for a strength-sapping two-front war, similar to what the Germans had done in Europe. As long as Japan was forced to divide its resources to fight over such an enormous expanse of the globe, it ceded the strategic tail of the tape, in resources, manpower, economic power, and firepower, to the Allies. Hence the importance of keeping China afloat.

So, at Stilwell's insistence, a diverse force of US Army engineers, British engineers, Indian laborers, and Chinese soldiers had battled torrential rains, mud, mountains, and jungle for much of 1943 to carve out a usable road in unoccupied northwest Burma. In the meantime, Stilwell had managed to persuade the Generalissimo to let him train and equip two divisions of Nationalist soldiers at Ramgarh in northern India with the intention of using them to lead the way in clearing northern Burma. At the same time, Major General Claire Chennault, the charismatic American air commander in China and a close confidant of the Generalissimo and his savvy, manipulative wife, Mei-ling, had succeeded in selling Chiang and President Roosevelt on a simplistic plan to defeat the Japanese in China, and elsewhere, exclusively through an aerial campaign. The idea of turning up the aerial pressure on the Japanese in China made perfect sense. But the notion that this alone could produce ultimate victory was sophistry, an oversell of the worst sort. The aerial effort, in addition to the cross-purposes agenda of Chiang and the empire-minded British, who had no desire to fight in backwater places on China's behalf, siphoned resources from Stilwell's north Burma campaign, a tough blow to a commander whose theater was already at the bottom of the American government's strategic priority list. "There are times I need a strait jacket," he once wrote to his wife, Win. "Ordinary straightforward shooting and killing would be a relief, and I prefer associating with soldiers and sleeping on the ground to this bickering and dickering that I've gotten into."

Now, as the new year approached, he had at last gotten his wish, with a limited offensive underway in the Japanese-held Hukawng Valley. He established a forward headquarters at Shingbwiyang, the limit of where the engineers had succeeded in building the vital supply route (alternatively referred to by the troops as the Ledo Road or the Stilwell Road). The remote Burmese village had since matured into a growing sally base with an airstrip, a sixteen-hundred-bed hospital, tent camps, and a proliferation of construction vehicles. Like a boy freed from distasteful household chores, Stilwell embraced his return to field soldiering with an almost vindictive gusto. As the two American-trained Chinese divisions tentatively pawed their way forward into the dense Burmese jungle, Stilwell circulated among the troops in the manner of a regimental colonel rather than a theater commander, constantly urging aggressiveness. "Wherever Stilwell went, something happened," Gordon Seagrave, an American missionary surgeon who tended to patients at the hospital, later said.

Clad in grubby fatigues and leggings, with an M1 helmet obscuring his salt-and-pepper flattop, he hiked for miles over muddy trails and through thick foliage, spoke with frontline commanders and soldiers, and even supervised tactical attacks. He handed out cigarettes to the troops, slept on a cot or in a hammock, waited in line for chow, and used his helmet as a washbasin. "We eat straight rations or Chinese chow and we live where we have to and the trails are tough, and we get wet and muddy, but we sleep soundly and the food tastes good because we are usually hungry," he wrote, with an almost palpable whiff of self-satisfaction, to Win. "Once in a while the Jap patrols get ambitious but they have pulled in their horns lately and the trails to the rear are quite safe. Progress is slow; the jungle is everywhere and very nearly impenetrable. It takes a long time to locate the Japs, and a lot more to dig them out. The Chinese soldier is doing his stuff, as I knew he would if he had half a chance."

Try as Stilwell might to escape into the comparative refuge of field operations, the necessities and politics of high command made this impossible. Urgent messages from Chungking and Delhi continually streamed into his forward command post, "screaming for me to come to both places and decide on this or that." Chain-of-command issues and even the very future of his offensive still hung in the balance. The message traffic grew so insistent that he bowed to the inevitable, hopped a plane to Delhi, and made it there in time to see the city's New Year's Eve fireworks.[4]

On the South Pacific island of Bougainville, in the Solomon Islands, where the 3rd Marine Division and the Army's 37th Infantry Division had carved out a beachhead in November 1943, Major General Oscar Griswold, commander of the XIV Corps, worked to strengthen a perimeter that stretched end to end for some twenty-two thousand yards and included three nascent airstrips. The product of a Nevada cattle ranch, Griswold had logged over thirty years in the Army since graduating from West Point in 1910. He had fought at Argonne Forest, taught tactics at his alma mater and Fort Benning's Infantry School. He believed, with the intensity of an old-fashioned evangelical preacher, in the timeless importance of the infantry-man. Ambitious but unassuming in manner and speech, he disdained self-promotion and flashy leadership. "Standing over six feet and weighing 190 pounds, he had the physique of a soldier," Colonel Hugh Milton, his chief of staff, once wrote of him. "His penetrating gray eyes, topped by a high, wide forehead and gray hair bespoke of a deep knowledge of men and events." Introspective, bespectacled, unpretentious, prone to wearing olive-drab ball caps and field fatigues, Griswold had masterminded a trau-matic American victory at New Georgia a few months earlier. He had since suffered a brief health scare, having cysts removed from an eye, necessitat-ing a battery of medical tests from Army doctors. "Gave me a *thorough* going over," he scrawled in his diary. "Scared me to death, but finally gave me a clean bill of health!" He got on well with his theater commander, Admiral William Halsey, one of the Navy's most tenacious fighters, who once referred to Griswold as "a far sighted and capable planner."

Griswold, after assuming his Bougainville command on December 15, focused on strengthening the perimeter with mutually supporting pill-boxes, zeroed in artillery, machine-gun posts, mines, multilayered lines of fortified trenches, augmented by mortars, antiaircraft guns, plus naval gunfire. For Griswold, the core of it all was the individual soldier. "As re-gards my troops, I am fair bursting with pride at the way they have handled themselves," he wrote to Washington-based Lieutenant General Lesley McNair, the commander of Army Ground Forces. "It is a real privilege to command such men. My constant anxiety has been never to let them down." Griswold knew that the Japanese still maintained a substantial force on Bougainville, a largely alien, jungle-infested place whose only value lay in its geographic proximity to the major Japanese base at Rabaul some two hundred miles to the northwest. Griswold and forty thousand other Americans on Bougainville understood that their enemies were still out there somewhere in the island's thick jungles and grassy swamps. The general wondered how much more time would pass before they attempted to eliminate his perimeter. He felt confident that he would hold against whatever they threw at him, but he could not yet know for sure.[5]

In the Southwest Pacific Area (SWPA), an Army-dominated theater controlled like a fiefdom by General Douglas MacArthur, a rivalry was brewing between his two primary ground commanders, Lieutenant Generals Walter Krueger and Robert Eichelberger, whose respective personalities and backgrounds differed substantially. Among high-level Army commanders in World War II, Krueger was the rarest of birds: foreign born, commissioned from the ranks, no West Point pedigree, indeed no college degree of any kind, nor even a high school diploma. The son of a prominent West Prussian landowner and captain in the Prussian Army, Krueger spent his formative years in the newly united Germany. He had barely known his father, who died when Walter was four. (Had he lived, perhaps the son would have grown up to high command in the German Army.) When Krueger was eight, he immigrated to the United States with his mother and settled in St. Louis, where his uncle owned a brewery. His mother soon married a Lutheran minister and fellow German immigrant who tutored his stepson ceaselessly on math, languages, and the classics. From his mother, the boy learned to play the piano and love classical music, both of which would become lifelong passions for Walter. When war with Spain broke out in 1898, he left high school and joined the Army as a private. He served in Cuba (though too late to see any action) and subsequently fought in the Philippine-American War, proving himself such a fine soldier that he was commissioned in 1901, at the age of twenty. Over four subsequent decades, he had steadily climbed through the ranks, serving in nearly every capacity, including staff duty with the American Expeditionary Force in France, instructor positions, an unsuccessful attempt to transfer to the Air Corps and become a pilot at age forty-six, and eventually a high-level post in command of the Third Army during the Louisiana Maneuvers in 1941, when he was ably assisted by his chief of staff, Dwight Eisenhower. In Ike's view, "few [generals] were physically tougher or more active. Relentlessly driving himself, he had little need of driving others—they were quick to follow his example."

A remarkable autodidact, a voracious reader, and a passionate student of military history, his intellectual development eventually outpaced that of all but a few of his formally educated colleagues. Fluent in Spanish, French, and German, he proudly spoke English with little trace of an accent. He wrote scholarly articles for military journals, published translations of German Army tactics manuals, and developed into a leading authority on joint Army-Navy planning and operations, expertise that would serve him well in combat command. To a casual observer, his medium build, close-cropped gray-black hair, cold eyes, and downcast, impassive face created an impression of a business executive rather than a soldier. "[He] came from the bottom up," Brigadier General Charles Willoughby, MacArthur's formality-minded, German-born intelligence chief said of Krueger. "He was much better than he looked." Arthur Collins, an artillery officer who had many interactions with Krueger in the Pacific, later said of him, "He was a good soldier and a good strategist and very sound thinker, but he didn't have much of a personality."

An uncharismatic and brusque, even occasionally rude exterior masked Krueger's deeply complex, thoughtful personality. A naval colleague once referred to him as a "taciturn Prussian type of officer." Straightforward, cold, and no-nonsense in dealings with superiors and subordinates alike, he was a warm and loving father to his three children and a committed husband to his wife, Grace, whom he had met during his early days in the Philippines. He had little tolerance for politicking and bootlicking, nor much sensitivity to human foibles. To a man so self-effacing, humility and authority went hand in hand. "The higher up the flagpole the monkey climbs, the more his rear end shows," he often quipped. He believed mutual loyalty was the bedrock of all effective command relationships. "He clung to what he thought was right with a bulldog's grip," a friend once said of him. He cared deeply for the average soldier, in part because he had once been one and understood the experience better than most generals. Once, when he went to inspect a rifle company that was supposed to be training for an upcoming amphibious invasion, he found the troops clad only in boots and undershorts, absorbed in a contentious volleyball match. Bathed in sweat and dust, the company commander reported to him, fully expecting a reprimand. Instead, Krueger asked him for the score, sat down on a log, and said, "Get on with the game. I want to see how it turns out."

Krueger strongly believed that, even in modern warfare, the individual soldier still mattered more than weapons, no matter how destructive. "Weapons are no good unless there are guts at both ends of the bayonet," he often said. Whenever he visited a command, he made a point of speaking to privates, asking them when they had last eaten a hot meal or received clean, dry socks. "I can't control the terrain on which we fight or the weather," he was fond of saying, "but I can control the food that my men eat." Headquarters and staff officers existed to serve the troops, not the other way around. When he discovered one day that officers at a division headquarters were eating fresh eggs while the frontline troops subsisted on cold rations, he immediately buttonholed the division commander and forcefully told him that fresh eggs were for combat troops, not the rear echelon. He routinely asserted that an officer had a "cardinal duty to look after his men before he looks after himself." He took this credo so seriously that he spent much of his time looking into the actions of subordinates, making sure they followed his orders. "Sincerity in looking after the welfare of his troops must be clearly apparent," he once said of a commander's proper role. "It will not suffice for him to issue orders to have faulty conditions remedied; he must personally see to it that they are corrected."

Already past his sixtieth birthday when the war broke out, he had assumed he would be deemed by his superiors as too old for combat command. When in early 1943 MacArthur personally requested him for a new army-level command, he was pleasantly stunned. "I had about concluded that I would not get to see active service in this war," he wrote to an old friend. "I must admit that I was greatly pleased to be mistaken." By necessity in the early days of the Pacific War, American soldiers had served under Australian command, particularly during the New Guinea campaign in 1942. As MacArthur looked to the future and his expectation that he would one day lead major ground forces to liberate the Philippines, he sought to remove American soldiers from Australian command, not just for the obvious reason of sovereignty but also because he envisioned no significant role for the Aussies once the war progressed beyond New Guinea. To begin this process, he created the Alamo Force, a term that hinted at nothing more than a minor task force but was, in actuality, an army-level formation with an appropriate headquarters and corps-level subordinate units. He selected Krueger because he thought well of him— they had previously served together at Fort Leavenworth and in Washington—but also because at age sixty-two and with three stars on his shoulders, Krueger enjoyed seniority over any Australian general who might lay claim to command of Alamo Force. Moreover, MacArthur knew that the unassuming Krueger would never compete with him for publicity. The arrangement, with its curious mixture of duplicity, self-promotion, and sophisticated diplomacy, was vintage MacArthur. But it worked. Throughout 1943, with a sort of open-secret unobtrusiveness, Krueger and his staff had steadily built and trained Alamo Force for combat. Not until September 1944 would the Americans feel sufficiently safe to officially rename it the Sixth Army. But well before this, among themselves, they regularly referred to it by the latter name.

As 1943 came to an end, Krueger and his staff were at Cape Cretin, New Guinea, feverishly making last-minute arrangements for an invasion at Saidor, some 117 miles to the west along the island's north coast. Given less than ten days by MacArthur to plan a complicated amphibious operation designed to eject the Japanese from New Guinea's Huon Peninsula and set the stage for more Allied landings to the west, Krueger had reluctantly assented. Soldiers of the 32nd Infantry Division's 126th Infantry Regiment, victors at Buna the previous year, packed aboard troop ships, LCIs (Landing Craft, Infantry), and LSTs (Landing Ship, Tank). Deliberate and cautious by nature, Krueger did not like the shoestring feel of the operation. To wit, the planners had no information about the Japanese presence other than aerial reconnaissance photographs. Krueger breathed a big sigh of relief when, on the second day of the New Year, 6,779 men from the 126th, plus engineers and other supporting troops, landed smoothly against no opposition, established a beachhead, and forced the Japanese to evacuate the Huon. "A large number of them perished in the attempt," Krueger later contended. MacArthur and Krueger had already resolved never to undertake another blind landing. With many other invasions on the drawing board, the need for real-time intelligence would only increase. With MacArthur's blessing, Krueger and his staff created a training center for special all-volunteer reconnaissance units whose harrowing mission was to land on potential invasion beaches and gather pertinent information. As a nod to San Antonio, where Krueger and his wife, Grace, had decided to make their permanent home, the staff dubbed them the Alamo Scouts.[6]

At Rockhampton, fifty-seven-year-old Lieutenant General Robert Eichelberger, commander of I Corps but currently little more than a sidelined troop trainer, watched the expanding war at a distance, with the worried anxiety of one who felt himself increasingly left behind. To a man driven by a powerful need for distinction and achievement, this separation from the center of the action was hard to endure. As the underestimated baby of a prosperous Ohio family run like a reality show competition by a father who had served in the Union Army during the Civil War, Eichelberger had found in the Army a place to cultivate his many talents. While his four older siblings chased financial success in the civilian world, young

"Bobby" attended West Point and graduated in 1909 as an infantry officer. Over three subsequent decades of service, he had earned an Army-wide reputation as a charming, reliable, and courageous officer who deeply understood the mindset of soldiers and how to prepare them for combat through intense, realistic training. As a young officer, he quickly learned from his sergeants the importance of leading by personal example, especially in difficult circumstances. "There was a certain courage and pride which made [soldiers] march to exhaustion rather than fall out on long hikes or night forced marches," he later asserted.

Professional, considerate, and extraordinarily adept at social relationships, Eichelberger was universally well-liked, with friends in every corner of the service (including Eisenhower and George Patton, the latter of whom was a classmate) and, quite remarkably, no enemies. "General Eichelberger had a rare way with people," historian Jay Luvaas, who came to know him well, once commented. "He enjoyed people . . . all kinds of people." A colleague once described him as "good looking, smooth, polished." Another referred to him as "a soldierly man, dignified, with a rather appealing personality. He did not give . . . the impression of a very forceful man, but I think he was. I had the impression that he knew his business." His leadership style favored cordiality and personal rapport over coercion and intimidation. "He wore his rank like a comfortable, well-fitted garment," Colonel Harold Riegelman, his chemical officer, once wrote of him. "In conversation, there were few subjects he did not illumine from a storehouse of rich and colorful incident in the four quarters of the globe. His responsiveness and geniality were sparked by a fine sense of humor, his stories on the subtle side, his talent for listening attentive and appreciative."

At six foot one and 190 pounds, with smooth facial features, a prominent brow, piercing gray-blue eyes, a full head of black hair (though now whitening at the edges), and an athletic build, he cut an impressive figure. Over his career, he had served in a long sprinkling of command, staff, student, instructor, and supervisory positions, including the superintendency of West Point. A voracious reader who believed in professional development with an almost religious intensity, Eichelberger thought that preparation and self-improvement set the foundation for good leadership. While many of his peers had served on the Western Front in World War I, he instead participated in the Siberian Expedition from 1918 to 1920, an ill-fated attempt by Japan, France, Britain, and the United States to intervene in the Russian Civil War and squelch Bolshevism. As intelligence officer and key aide to the American commander, Major General William Graves, who mentored him like a son, he proved himself quite valorous in combat as well as an adept analyst and mediator. In Russia, Eichelberger earned the Distinguished Service Cross and the Distinguished Service Medal. He also studied the Japanese intently, accruing firsthand knowledge he would put to good use many years later. "Out of my Siberian experiences came a conviction that pursued me for the next twenty years," he wrote. "I knew that Japanese militarism had as its firm purpose the conquest of all Asia." During a posting in the Panama Canal Zone, he had met and married Emmaline Gudger, the good-looking, vivacious daughter of the zone's chief magistrate. The marriage only increased Bob's determination to succeed, not just to impress his own family but also his elitist in-laws and the wife whom he respected more than anyone else on earth. He held her in some level of awe, often just referring to her as "Miss Em" rather than by her given name. Most everyone else called her Emma. Her sheltered North Carolina upper-middle-class background prepared her well for life with an ambitious young soldier. Bright, polite, and witty, she moved smoothly within the protocol and seniority-minded world of early twentieth-century Army wives. The two were soul mates, partners, confidants whose bond ran to the core of their collective being. They seldom quarreled. They had no kids, only each other and the Army. They were committed to each other and to Bob's career, in a manner almost reminiscent of running a burgeoning family business. Upon deploying to the South Pacific in 1942 as I Corps commander, Eichelberger wrote to her every day, sometimes two or three times a day, even while he was in combat. She wrote back with similar frequency.

In December 1942, at Buna in Papua New Guinea, Eichelberger had engineered the first American ground victory of World War II. At MacArthur's behest, he had personally assumed command, salvaging victory from a seemingly hopeless stalemate. He fostered good relationships with Australian commanders and greatly improved coordination between the two allies. For over a month, he personally led the frontline troops, in the ferocious heat and enervating conditions of jungle combat. He regularly fought in small-unit actions, more like a sergeant leading a squad than a three-star general leading a corps. He lost thirty pounds in thirty days, dodged death more times than he or anyone else around him could ever count. He forced himself to sack an old friend and West Point classmate, who never forgave him. With almost no supporting artillery, few tanks, and little air support, he had managed to root tenacious Japanese defenders out of an extensive network of bunkers and pillboxes nestled within a suffocating jungle canopy. He engendered fierce loyalty from his staff and admiration from the combat soldiers, many of whom wondered how the crazy old man managed to survive.

By any measure, his performance at Buna had been excellent, a resounding professional triumph, the shining moment that he had prepared for his entire life. Eichelberger expected plaudits and gratitude from MacArthur for delivering him such an important victory, one that effectively turned the tide of the ground war in the South Pacific. Instead, after a brief intoxicating surge of publicity—glib and friendly, Eichelberger got along well with war correspondents—he found himself back in Australia for the rest of 1943, anonymously training troops for battle, consigned to the SWPA bench. Shocked and chastened, Eichelberger soon learned that MacArthur wanted no one else to crowd his limelight, even though he himself had released Eichelberger's name to the media and allowed him to interact with reporters. "There was no place in the Southwest Pacific for two glamorous officers," Vice Admiral Daniel Barbey, MacArthur's amphibious commander, perceptively commented. In one uncomfortable meeting, the SWPA chief even made a veiled threat to bust Eichelberger to colonel and send him home over any undue publicity. MacArthur awarded Eichelberger the Distinguished Service Cross for Buna, but in the citation, he failed to differentiate the I Corps commander's extraordinary actions from those of several other recipients who did not see any real action. Subsequently, MacArthur made a concerted effort to torpedo a Medal of Honor nomination for Eichelberger that had made it all the way to Army Chief of Staff General George Marshall, who would have approved the award if not for MacArthur's intercession. In the aftermath of Buna, Eichelberger's reputation was such that he came under serious consideration for army command in the European theater. He found out that his old friend Eisenhower probably wanted him to command First Army in the upcoming Normandy invasion. Behind the scenes, MacArthur made sure this did not happen, even as he indicated, in several face-to-face meetings, that he would not stand in Eichelberger's way. Privately, MacArthur held Eichelberger in high esteem as a quality combat commander and was loath to let him go, especially to Eisenhower, who had once served as a key aide to MacArthur but whom the SWPA commander now detested and resented as a supposedly disloyal upstart. MacArthur knew he would need

Eichelberger in many upcoming battles. Until then, he was content to keep him in mothballs until the right moment arose.

By the latter part of 1943, when Eichelberger came to realize that MacArthur had denied him the Medal of Honor and his own prominent army command while shelving him in Australia and inserting Krueger into place as head of the Alamo Force, an indignant, self-righteous anger began to boil in Bob's belly. To be sure, he was intelligent and self-interested enough to maintain good relations with his boss and he thought highly of his intellect. But he had come to resent MacArthur deeply, in the self-pitying manner of the deeply aggrieved. In letters to Emma and in private conversations with Brigadier General Clovis Byers, his able chief of staff, intimate confidant, and the kid brother he never had, he took to referring to MacArthur as "Sarah" after Sarah Bernhardt, the notoriously vain French actress. In a secret memo meant for Emma's eyes only, he sarcastically described MacArthur as "the great hero who willingly sent me to my death or the great daily risk thereof," and asserted that MacArthur "knew nothing of the jungle and how one fights there." At the end of December, he wrote her bitterly, "I have definitely given up hope of getting that other job. My disappointment is keen particularly as it would have given me the opportunity of seeing you. I am grateful to Ike who evidently kept his word to me that he would try to get me to serve with him. The fact that I slept through the night without a break last night would indicate that I have no intention of letting this get me down."

But it did get him down. For all of Eichelberger's accomplishments, his tremendous personal valor, his unimpeachable personal integrity, and his prominent reputation, he still remained insecure at heart, overly sensitive to perceived slights, prone to self-destructive overanalysis. As the months in Australia had piled up, he struggled with dark moods and resentment. He derisively dubbed himself "The Mayor of Rockhampton." He spent far too much time and energy keeping abreast of rumors and gossip. After an initial honeymoon period, he grew to dislike Krueger, who was now his boss since I Corps had come under the authority of Alamo Force. Eichelberger was justifiably leery of answering to a superior whose combat record paled in comparison to his own. Over the course of numerous conversations, he came to view Krueger as something of a pompous bore. "I always find when I am thrown with him very closely that it really amounts to hard work," he told Emma in one letter. Later, Bob asserted, "In my opinion, he was just naturally mean." Eichelberger felt uncomfortable with his military future apparently in the hands of someone whom he did not trust. In his heart, he worried that Krueger might surpass him as MacArthur's go-to ground commander. Krueger, for his part, uttered no ill words about Eichelberger, but he often kept him in the dark on plans, occasionally rebuked him for the condition of his troops during inspections, and deliberately avoided preparing any evaluation of Eichelberger's performance so as to keep him in limbo.

At Buna, Eichelberger had seen the avoidable human cost of inadequate training and preparation, so he drove his troops relentlessly with realistic, challenging field problems, mock invasions, and physical fitness exercises all designed to save lives in combat. "We were perfecting our amphibious techniques," he later wrote. "We were turning raw youngsters into tough and tenacious jungle warriors." Determined to keep himself ready for whenever Krueger or MacArthur might need him in combat, Eichelberger worked off his frustrations with a daily regimen of calisthenics, swimming, and hiking. For recreation, he played endless games of badminton with his staff, and read voluminously. He was a near fanatic about taking vitamins and eating a balanced diet. The active schedule helped him to keep his demons somewhat in check. "You would be overjoyed if you could see the enthusiasm, good humor and good health of Bob in the face of his . . . disappointment," Byers wrote to Emma. To Byers and other intimates, he often quipped, "As long as I keep my sense of humor, they can't get me down." Day by day, he waited for that indeterminate "they" to save him from the sidelines and put him back in the war.[7]

The man who controlled that decision rang in the new year at Port Moresby, New Guinea, before returning a few days later to Brisbane, where he had located his primary headquarters shortly after evacuating the Philippines for Australia in 1942. If the American war in the Pacific had a main character, undoubtedly it was Douglas MacArthur. A man of astonishing pomposity, megalomania, and egocentrism, he certainly thought in such terms. An Olympian figure, the Zeus of the theater, he powerfully believed in himself as a man of providential destiny and he unquestionably elicited an almost hypnotic sense of awe in many who encountered him. At the same time, he exuded petty vanities, a slew of insecurities, and troubling character flaws. "He is shrewd, selfish, proud, remote, highly strung and vastly vain," Lieutenant Colonel Gerald Wilkinson, a British liaison officer with his headquarters, wrote in a penetrating, insightful contemporary analysis of MacArthur. "He has imagination, self confidence, physical courage and charm, but no humor about himself, no regard for truth, and is unaware of these defects. He mistakes his emotions and ambitions for principles. With moral depth he would be a great man; as it is he is a near miss which may be worse than a mile. His main ambition would be to end the war as Pan-American hero in the form of generalissimo of all Pacific theaters."

Captivating and magnetic in social situations, MacArthur was prone to long monologues and a sort of aloofness that cultivated an oddly mystical quality about the man. Capable all at once of intimacy and remoteness, he was a man of deep complexity whom few could fully understand, no matter how close to him. "None of us knew MacArthur," Master Sergeant Paul Rogers, a longtime aide, once wrote to another staffer. "We all saw fragments of the man." When MacArthur was not the center of attention, he tended to hover on the edges of groups, looking off in the distance as if contemplating something more profound. Intuitively image-conscious, he took to clenching an emblematic corncob pipe in his mouth and wearing upscale sunglasses. He commissioned a subordinate to find him a cap with unique braiding worthy of his stentorian presence, and combed his thinning black hair over an otherwise balding pate. Once physically imposing, his physique was sliding toward middle-age flab as he approached his sixty-fourth year. Courtly and courteous in person, he nurtured sub rosa hatreds of Eisenhower, Marshall, New Dealers, Europe Firsters, and unnamed, faceless Washington conspirators whom he blamed for betraying the Philippines and sabotaging his every subsequent design. "No one will ever know how much could have been done to aid the Philippines if there had been a determined will-to-win," he once wrote bitterly. He ardently opposed the Allies' Germany First policy. He believed strongly that America's future lay in Asia and the Pacific. A first-rate student of grand strategy and geopolitics, his egocentrism nonetheless hindered his ability to see the need for the Allies to pour resources into any other theater besides his own. Always convinced that he had to make do with less, and that decision makers in Washington had deliberately starved him of resources—though he now controlled about 700,000 servicemen and -women, half of whom were Army soldiers, a larger force than any other Pacific theater commander—he portrayed himself as a general who could produce more bang for the buck than anyone else. "A classic in conservative military expenditure," one MacArthur-approved SWPA memo characterized his operations to date.

As the son of Arthur MacArthur, a Civil War Medal of Honor recipient and three-star general, Douglas was born to soldiering in the manner of a child who inherits a successful corporate empire. Like Wainwright, whom he privately disdained during much of the war, he had been First Captain at West Point, setting the stage for a singularly brilliant career now into its fortieth year. A successful, highly decorated combat commander in World War I, and promoted to one-star rank at age thirty-nine, MacArthur in 1919 had become superintendent of West Point, where he implemented vital reforms and modernized the curriculum. Unique among all World War II US Army commanders, MacArthur had once served in the top post as chief of staff from 1930 to 1935. He was the only chief of staff whose most notable and important service occurred *after* leaving the number one job. In both war and love, he had proven himself a survivor. After a disastrous marriage to wealthy socialite Louise Cromwell, he had met and married Jean Faircloth, a Tennessee heiress who became the bedrock of his personal life. Bright, considerate, good-hearted, sensible, and eighteen years his junior, Jean was Douglas's true soul mate. In 1938, she gave birth to their only child, a son whom they named Arthur IV.

Ever since Douglas's father had commanded American military forces during the Philippine-American War, the MacArthur family had developed a deep affection for the archipelago. Douglas served multiple tours in the Philippines and came to love the people and the country with an almost religious devotion. In the late 1930s, with the Philippines scheduled to receive imminent independence from the United States, Douglas had accepted an invitation from commonwealth president Manuel Quezon to establish a military force capable of defending the country, a frustrating and nearly impossible task, owing to poor infrastructure, Quezon's scarce treasury, the linguistic and cultural diversity of the people, and a paucity of military support from the American government. Recalled in 1941 to active Army service as commander of a colonial-style Filipino-American military force, MacArthur had presided over what might well have been the most disastrous campaign in US military history. In spite of ample warning about the onset of hostilities after Pearl Harbor, he had allowed a substantial portion of his air force to be destroyed on the ground by a surprise Japanese attack. He had foolishly scrapped interwar plans to stalemate Japanese invaders with a calculated withdrawal to the Bataan peninsula in favor of spreading his meager forces around the beaches in hopes of repelling the Japanese at the waterline. MacArthur's new plan was a colossal failure. Never was the dictum "He who defends everything defends nothing" more true. Quickly overwhelmed along the beaches by an invading force half their size, Fil-American units descended into a desperate, fighting retreat, forcing MacArthur to reassemble whatever forces he could, declare the capital Manila an open city, and retreat to Bataan. The tumult compromised the logistical lifeline of MacArthur's army. Soldiers subsisted on half and then quarter rations; medical supplies began to run out; disease spread rampantly; morale buckled.

MacArthur spent most of the nightmarish campaign on Corregidor, a fortified island that stood like a sentinel astride the mouth of Manila Bay. The doom of the Bataan and Corregidor garrisons was really just a matter of time. At the behest of President Roosevelt, whom MacArthur had detested and feared since dealing with him in his days as chief of staff, the general and select members of his staff, Jean, and Arthur IV were evacuated in a clandestine ship-to-plane operation, from the Philippines to Australia. By contrast, some twenty thousand Americans and perhaps three times that many Filipinos had been consigned to the oblivion of captivity. The presence of MacArthur's family in a combat zone, when other military dependents had been ordered out by the War Department months before the onset of hostilities, hinted at a strong MacArthur tendency to flout rules he did not wish to follow. While everyone else in SWPA endured separation from family, MacArthur, unique among all American commanders in World War II (and most other wars), continued to live with his wife and son in Australia, an appalling double standard.

Lionized in the media and government propaganda as a hero, toasted nationwide in an almost frightening cult of personality, MacArthur subsequently received the Medal of Honor (surely the most political in American history) and famously pledged to return to the Philippines. Haunted by the abandonment of his troops and the Filipino population, he devoted himself to the eventual liberation of the Philippines and crafted nearly all SWPA strategy toward the fulfillment of that goal. Though egotistical, self-involved, devious, and disingenuous when it suited his ambitions, MacArthur also had an honorable, morally upright side. In his mind, the United States had a sacred duty to liberate the Philippines from what he viewed as Japanese-imposed slavery. Having learned much through intelligence sources about the abominable Japanese treatment of American prisoners, he worried constantly over their welfare, and yearned to liberate them as soon as possible. Like many an experienced warrior, he had come to detest war. Beyond the obvious goal of leading his nation to final victory over Japan, his fondest hope for the postwar world was to see the implementation of an American-led, postcolonial international system of collective security. In his view, war had become so terrible and destructive that human beings could no longer resort to it without flirting with their own extinction.

In mid-December he had met for the only time during the war with George Marshall on Goodenough Island, off the northern coast of New Guinea, where the chief of staff visited on the way back home from the recent Tehran and Cairo conferences. "I remember him as an imposing dignified figure," Paul Rogers later wrote of Marshall. "He called MacArthur 'Douglas,' something I had never heard before from anyone. Their demeanor was formal and restrained, with no show of intimacy or close friendship." The relationship between the two men was one of wary correctness, built upon a healthy mutual distrust. Though MacArthur disliked and envied Marshall, he was savvy enough to maintain a respectful, courteous facade with him. Marshall understood that MacArthur was not like his other commanders—he had once been chief of staff himself, he had once been a superior and, as such, he had to be handled differently. Indeed, when MacArthur was chief of staff, he had attempted to snuff out Marshall's career by assigning him to a dead-end National Guard job. "He is the most overrated man in the Army," MacArthur once said of Marshall. "He'll never be a general officer as long as I'm chief of staff." Yet Marshall seemed not to hold a grudge. Classy, selfless, honorable, fair-minded, and yet coldly decorous in nearly all professional dealings, Marshall had already endured two years of haranguing from MacArthur for more troops, more planes, more resources.

True to form, at the meeting, MacArthur urged the chief of staff to do all he could to advance his strategic concept to strangle Rabaul, hopscotch across the rest of the New Guinea coast as a prelude to a Philippines return, and provide him with appropriate resources. "We had a long and frank discussion," MacArthur later wrote. "I called attention to the paucity of men and materiel I was receiving as compared with all other theaters of war." Many of these decisions were out of Marshall's hands, so he could promise nothing, though he did his best to placate MacArthur by assuring him that he was doing all he could to provide him with the necessary resources to carry out his grand strategical design.

In a torrential downpour, the two men inspected some of Krueger's troops. Later the Alamo Force commander briefed them on plans for his upcoming operations. MacArthur and Marshall concluded their short visit by flying to Port Moresby for lunch at SWPA's advance headquarters. They parted as they had met—formally and inconclusively, never to see each other for the rest of the war. When Marshall returned to Washington, he immediately radioed a thank-you message to MacArthur. "I was greatly impressed by all that I saw." The chief of staff pledged to do whatever he could to augment MacArthur's air forces. An able and flowery wordsmith, MacArthur responded, "Your trip here was an inspiration to all ranks and its effects were immediate. You have no more loyal followers than here." Beneath the veneer, the SWPA commander of course felt anything but loyalty for Marshall or anyone else in Washington. For all his fulminations about poor strategic prioritization and his supposed neglect, though, he was actually something of a lone wolf, and part of him preferred the martyr role. With absolute control of SWPA at his fingertips, and a burgeoning spate of future operations on his drawing board, he knew that 1944 promised to be a make-or-break year, not just for the Allies in their struggle against Japan, but for Douglas MacArthur as well.[8]

1

Flintlock

Two years to the day after the Japanese attacked American military installations on Oahu, Admiral Chester Nimitz met with his principal subordinates and staffers at Pearl Harbor, where the decimated ruins of USS *Arizona* and USS *Oklahoma* still lay half-sunken in the shallow waters like haunted, muted monuments to the worst day in the history of the US Navy. Nimitz might have been the only American who actually benefited from the infamous attack that initiated the Pacific War, though of course he would never have thought in such terms. The disaster at Pearl Harbor had led to the appointment of Nimitz as commander in chief of the Pacific Fleet, replacing Admiral Husband Kimmel, who, fairly or not, took most of the blame and was quickly and shabbily retired away to queasy oblivion. Every bit as modest and self-effacing as MacArthur was egomaniacal, Nimitz had by the end of 1943 emerged as the leading naval officer of history's leading war. Every bit the peer of the general, and actually a bemused rival in the same manner that a gentle-tempered German shepherd endures the nips of a frisky beagle, Nimitz controlled the sort of prodigious naval power that might have made Horatio Nelson salivate. After two hard years of war, the United States Pacific Fleet had grown into a powerful beast. Nimitz had at his disposal twenty aircraft carriers, including six major fleet carriers, eight battleships, nineteen cruisers, seventy-eight destroyers, forty submarines, among many hundreds of other vessels, and with plenty more warships on the way. From the West Coast to Alaska, New Zealand, and many points in between, his vast theater of responsibility comprised some sixty-five million square miles of ocean and islands.

Because Army and Navy leaders could not hope to agree on a single commander for the American war against Japan, and since neither service was willing to subordinate itself to the other, they had, more by inertia than intent, agreed on an uneasy divided command compromise. MacArthur was the lord in SWPA, Stilwell in Asia, and Nimitz everywhere else.

In effect, this meant a two-pronged Pacific advance to Japan, with MacArthur and Nimitz as competing, and sometimes cooperating, theater commanders. The fifty-eight-year-old admiral was a Texan who had originally intended to go to West Point before ending up at the Naval Academy, where he graduated seventh in the class of 1905. As a young officer, Nimitz had fought seasickness, leading, in his later words, to "some chilling of enthusiasm for the sea." As a rookie skipper, he had once been court-martialed and reprimanded for running his ship aground, normally a mortal maritime sin but one that did not end his career because of his sterling reputation as a sagacious military thinker and fair-minded leader. The decision quickly proved sound. Nimitz subsequently saved the life of a sailor who fell overboard, taught naval science at the University of California, became a foremost expert on navigation and propulsion, and accrued years of experience in submarines and surface ships alike.

White-haired, blue-eyed, and fair-skinned, a devotee of daily walks, tennis, sunbathing, and pistol marksmanship, Nimitz's studious, patient nature somehow meshed well with the underlying urgency of a commander who demanded and expected results. Modest, open-minded, and low-key, he detested grandstanding and cared little for military glory. "No concessions should be made towards glamorizing individuals or incidents that do not deserve it," he once wrote revealingly to E. B. Potter, his main biographer. Nimitz's sense of humor was so keen that he collected a mental inventory of amusing stories and delighted in recounting them to subordinates to ease tensions at difficult or stressful times. He kept himself in excellent physical condition. "Exercise was almost a fetish with Nimitz," war correspondent Robert Sherrod once wrote. On any given day, an observer might find Nimitz holed up in his office, working round the clock, honing his considerable marksmanship skills, taking a long walk, going for a swim at one of Oahu's spectacular beaches, or standing shirtless with a group of sailors, pitching horseshoes. One of his frequent horseshoe partners, Fifth Fleet commander Vice Admiral Raymond Spruance, years later described him as a "very great man. Regardless of how tough the situation might be, I never knew him to get worried or excited. This state of mind, plus his keen intelligence and sound judgment, made his subordinates feel that any task given them could be accomplished."

Nimitz's office at Pearl Harbor exuded an informality that reflected the personality of the man. His bare walls were ringed with canvas chairs to facilitate his frequent meetings with staffers and commanders; behind his desk, he kept a weather barometer and a radio, the latter of which he often used to listen to local symphony concerts while he quietly wrote or read dispatches. A pair of black pens holstered in a stand, along with papers and ashtrays, covered his wooden desktop. As a theater and fleet commander in chief, he had already shown himself to be an able and thoughtful strategist. On his cluttered desk, he kept a card close at hand with his three rules of thumb for any military operation: Is the proposed operation likely to succeed? What might be the consequences of failure? Is it in the realm of practicability in terms of matériel and supplies?

He bore these three questions in mind at every planning and strategy session, and his December 7 meeting was no different. He huddled with Spruance, Rear Admiral Richmond Kelly Turner, commander of Task Forces 51 and 52, and Major General Holland Smith, the Marine commander of V Amphibious Corps, to discuss Operation Flintlock, a plan to secure the Marshall Islands. Three months earlier, the Joint Chiefs in Washington had ordered Nimitz to gain hegemony over this collection of thirty-two island groups and atolls scattered over 400,000 miles of Central Pacific ocean. Since then, Nimitz and his staff had planned the operation on the assumption that they must first capture the Wotje and Maloelap Atolls at the eastern edge of the Marshalls before taking the Kwajalein Atoll, located in the heart of the islands and home to important Japanese air bases. But Nimitz's thinking had recently evolved. The November seizure of the Tarawa Atoll in the Gilbert Islands, where the 2nd Marine Division had suffered a staggering three thousand casualties in four bloody days of combat and the Army's 27th Infantry Division had fought a difficult battle for the Makin Atoll, had made Nimitz leery of assaulting similar Pacific island fortresses when other options might exist. The imperative of attacking Wotje and Maloelap rested on the assumption that the Americans must negate the Japanese aerial presence in these places and build their own bomber bases before they could proceed to Kwajalein. Nimitz had come to believe that his fast carrier forces, in tandem with land-based aircraft, could pummel these two spots and clear the way for an immediate invasion of Kwajalein, a concept that would advance his timetable by many months, secure useful sea and air bases, and, for the first time, imperil the inner ring of Japanese bastions in the Caroline and Mariana Island chains. As an added benefit, the lightning-quick capture of Kwajalein would provide a new layer of northern flank protection for MacArthur's ongoing advance in New Guinea and the Solomon Islands.

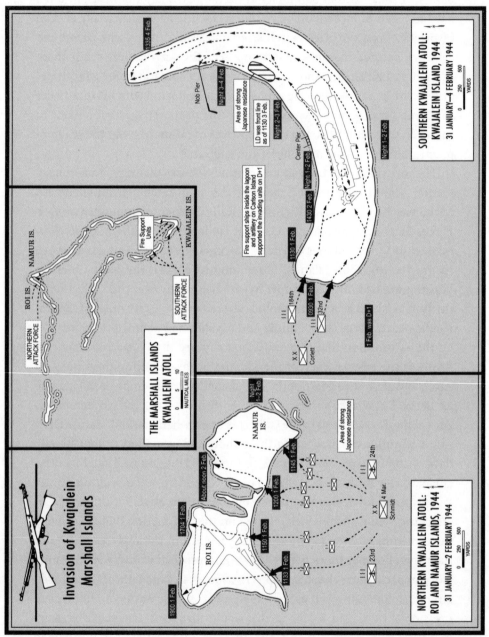

Invasion of Kwajalein
Marshall Islands

THE MARSHALL ISLANDS
KWAJALEIN ATOLL

0   5   10
NAUTICAL MILES

ROI IS.   NAMUR IS.

NORTHERN
ATTACK FORCE

Fire Support
Units

SOUTHERN
ATTACK FORCE

KWAJALEIN IS.

SOUTHERN KWAJALEIN ATOLL:
KWAJALEIN ISLAND, 1944
31 JANUARY–4 FEBRUARY 1944

0   250   500
YARDS

1335 4 Feb.

Nob Pier

Night 3–4 Feb.

Area of strong
Japanese resistance

LD was front line
as of 1130 3 Feb.

Night 2–3 Feb.

Center Pier

Night 1–2 Feb.

Night 1–2 Feb.

Fire support ships inside the lagoon
and artillery on Carlson Island
supported the invading units on D+1

1430 2 Feb.

1130 1 Feb.

0950 1 Feb.

184th

32nd

Corlett

1 Feb. was D+1

NORTHERN KWAJALEIN ATOLL:
ROI AND NAMUR ISLANDS, 1944
31 JANUARY–2 FEBRUARY 1944

0   250   500
YARDS

1900 1 Feb.

1704 1 Feb.

ROI IS.

1150 1 Feb.

1133 1 Feb.

About noon 2 Feb.

NAMUR
IS.

Night
1–2 Feb.

1145 1 Feb.

1200 1 Feb.

Area of strong
Japanese resistance

24th

4 Mar.
Schmidt

23rd

© 2021 by Chris Erichsen

The concept was so bold that all but one member of Nimitz's staff opposed it. When he proposed it to Spruance, Turner, and Smith at their December 7 meeting, the startled trio joined in the opposition. "Spruance, Smith and I all spoke against it," Turner later recalled. Normally mild-mannered and calm, almost to the point of coldness, Spruance reacted with uncharacteristic stridency and attempted to talk Nimitz out of the idea. "I argued as strongly as I could with Admiral Nimitz," he commented. "The principle [*sic*] reason for my objection to the capture of Kwajalein alone, was that units of the Fifth Fleet were scheduled, after its capture, to proceed to the South Pacific to support an operation there. This would have left our line of communications in to Kwajalein surrounded by Japanese bases . . . with no fleet support." After considerable discussion, the meeting ended in an impasse. Nimitz spent the following days mulling over the reservations of his subordinates but nonetheless decided to stick to his guns, even in the face of so much opposition, a rare experience of command loneliness for the consensus-building admiral. At heart, his appreciation for the growing importance of airpower on naval and amphibious operations was more advanced than his colleagues'. Given what he knew of Japanese defenses in the Marshalls (mainly on the basis of photo intelligence), he was confident that his aviators could negate the Japanese threat to the Kwajalein invaders, and save both time and lives.

When he met again with Spruance, Turner, and Smith on December 14, he asked them where they wanted to strike first in the Marshalls. All three advocated the outer atolls. "Well, gentlemen," he replied quietly but firmly, "our next objective will be Kwajalein." Opinionated and self-confident, especially after more than a year of leading amphibious task forces, Turner would not back down. He referred to Nimitz's plan as "dangerous and reckless." Finally, Nimitz gazed at him steadily. "This is it. If you don't want to do it, the Department will find someone else to do it. Do you want to do it or not?" Faced with such a stark choice, Turner quickly assented. Nimitz would get his way. Kwajalein it was.[1]

Located 540 miles northwest of Tarawa, 2,440 miles southwest of Oahu and 2,477 miles southeast of Tokyo, Kwajalein consists of over ninety coral- and reef-encircled islands ringed together in a rough triangle over 655 square miles of ocean and lagoon. The product of subsea volcanic activity, the coral islands tend to be small, none more than three miles in length and a few hundred yards in width, and barely above sea level, rising to an average height of just under six feet above the ocean's surface. The string of islands forms an enclosed ring that, from an aerial or map vantage point, almost assume the shape of a musket pistol. Sparsely populated by Micronesians, the place had once been loosely colonized by Spain and then Imperial Germany before the Japanese assumed control under a League of Nations mandate after World War I. By 1944, under the multiple pressures of a two-front war that was not trending their way, the Japanese had come to view Kwajalein, and the whole Marshall Islands chain, as an expendable fortified outpost. Their most important garrisons, and airfields, were located on the three largest islands. At the atoll's northern tip, the islands of Roi and Namur, connected by a narrow beach and causeway, contained an airstrip and a complex of barracks and other buildings. At the southern tip, Kwajalein Island, the largest in the atoll, was the main Japanese administrative and communications center in the Marshalls and home to a partially constructed airfield. Some forty-eight miles of lagoon and coral reef separated these key islands.

Shaped like a fishhook, Kwajalein is about two and a half miles long and eight hundred yards wide for about two-thirds of its surface before narrowing to about three hundred yards at the point of the hook. In early 1944, dense stands of palm trees, coconut trees, breadfruit trees, and thick pandani covered much of the island. Since early 1941, defense of the Marshalls had been the responsibility of the Imperial Navy's 6th Base Force under Rear Admiral Monzo Akiyama. The Japanese had partially fortified the three key islands and scores of smaller ones around the atoll. The air base at Roi contained about ninety aircraft, three concrete blockhouses, and over a dozen antiaircraft guns of varying caliber. Between Roi and neighboring Namur, there were about 3,500 men, at least two-thirds of whom were aerial personnel ill-suited for ground combat. At most, maybe about 500 of these men had any substantial training with infantry weapons and tactics. Kwajalein and several nearby islands were defended by about 5,000 troops of varying quality, the best of whom hailed from the Imperial Army's 1st Amphibious Brigade and the Navy's Yokosuka 4th Special Naval Landing Force. By one estimate, about 1,800 of the defenders were combat effective, and another 865, mainly headquarters troops, engineers, communications specialists, and grounded submariners, partially effective. The rest were Korean and Japanese laborers working on the airfields, and

Okinawan stevedores who spent their days unloading ships or hauling construction matériel. The military value of these civilians was close to nil.

Kwajalein Island bristled with six eight-centimeter dual-purpose guns, at least half a dozen antiaircraft and heavy machine guns, 160 reinforced concrete or coconut log pillboxes, a concrete seawall, a major antitank ditch, with three supporting ditches, plus a maze of rifle pits, fighting trenches, machine-guns posts, and fortified dugouts. The thickness of the concrete pillboxes ranged from fifteen inches to three feet. "In most cases, coconut logs and sand were banked around and on top of the pillboxes," wrote Colonel Syril Faine, an Army Ground Forces analyst. Around one hundred barracks, warehouses, and headquarters buildings, each of which could become a dangerous defensive position, were clustered in the northern part of the island. The American service official histories, and most all subsequent interpretations, have contended that Roi-Namur was more heavily defended than Kwajalein. But given the larger garrison of effectives and the greater number of prepared fortifications at Kwajalein, this seems to be a wrongheaded analysis. "In fact, every inch of ground was organized for defense, and because of the small size of the island, the garrison lived in its battle stations," an observer later recalled. In truth, neither the Kwajalein nor Roi-Namur garrisons were an even match for the invaders, though both were potent enough to put up a bloody fight.

For Flintlock, Nimitz amassed 297 ships, more than fifty thousand Marine and Army assault troops, and about thirty thousand garrison troops from the Army, Navy, and Marine Corps. Given the significant distance between Roi-Namur and Kwajalein, Admiral Turner split this sizable naval flotilla into a Northern Attack Force (Task Force 53) under Rear Admiral Richard Connolly and a Southern Attack Force (Task Force 52) under his own personal control. The Northern Attack Force carried the 4th Marine Division and supporting units whose mission was to seize Roi-Namur. The Southern Attack Force focused on Kwajalein and transported General Corlett's reinforced 7th Infantry Division.

Before these amphibious forces got anywhere near the Kwajalein Atoll, a steady procession of land- and carrier-based aircraft pummeled Japanese bases in the Marshalls over the course of several weeks. Nimitz had originally planned for a New Year's Day invasion. But because of the ferocity of the fighting in the Gilberts, and the necessity for more time to refit and repair ships, digest hard-learned lessons, accrue more intelligence data, and train the assault troops, he pushed the operation back a month. For nearly seven weeks, Army Air Forces B-24 Liberators, plus medium bombers and fighters, mauled the Marshalls. In December alone, they dropped 601 tons of bombs; in January they dumped another 200 tons on the Kwajalein Atoll. The raids damaged enemy installations and degraded Japanese air strength. In the final week of January, the carrier planes, flying at lower altitudes, which allowed more precision strikes, administered the coup de grace to Japanese air and sea forces. Flying thousands of sorties in a handful of late-January days, the naval aviators more than fulfilled Nimitz's strategic vision. "It was, in my opinion, a splendid decision and one characteristic of Admiral Nimitz, a man whom I admire very much," General Corlett later wrote of Nimitz's insistence on directly assaulting Kwajalein. All over the Marshalls, including Wotje and Maloelap, which had so concerned Spruance, the carrier planes wrecked enemy airfields, shot down or destroyed dozens of Japanese aircraft on the ground, and sank numerous cargo ships. "The American attacks are becoming more furious," a Japanese soldier jotted in his diary. "Planes come over day after day. Can we stand up under the strain?" The troops could and did; not so for the equipment. By the end of January, the Japanese did not have even one operational aircraft left in the entire island group. Japanese strategists were already loath to risk any naval assets in the Marshalls. With the Americans now in absolute control of the air, and consequently the waters of the island group, they no longer even had the option of naval opposition to Flintlock.[2]

Assisted mightily by this unseen benevolent fist, Turner's armada steamed steadily west during the declining days of January. The Southern Attack Force comprised a formidable bodyguard for the amphibious invaders of the 7th Division—four battleships, three heavy cruisers, twenty-one destroyers, three escort carriers, plus minesweepers and control ships. The sheer level of coordination and logistics necessary to unleash this two-division amphibious operation—modest by later standards—was daunting. The convoys originated from ports as varied as San Diego, Maui, Kauai, and Pearl Harbor. To coordinate the minutely scheduled linkups of the vast fleet, planners had to factor in the differing speed capabilities of ships as well as how to provide them constant protection during their long journey. To feed the prodigious supply needs of modern vessels, especially in the open waters of the Central Pacific, where substantial anchorages and harbors were at a premium, Navy logisticians had devised an ingenious system of forward provisioning that centered around floating repair and storage facilities and rotating support ships packed with ammunition, food, and any conceivable item of military value. The leading naval foot soldiers of this unglamorous, though incredibly vital, supporting cast were the seventeen fleet oilers that operated in three ship task groups. Each oiler could carry fifteen thousand barrels of diesel oil and 200,000 gallons of aviation gasoline. At any given time, at least half of these floating gas stations were at sea, carrying out the absorbing, occasionally dangerous job of at-sea refueling. To replenish their own stocks, they shuttled back to bases at Funafuti, where hundreds of thousands of barrels of fuel were stored in readiness for Flintlock. The oilers provided the American fleet with the great gift of continual mobility, obviating the need to depend upon forward ports to take on fuel. Their impact on the speed of naval operations was strikingly similar to the revolutionary effect of in-air refueling on aerial operations for future generations of aviators.

If the ships and other conveyances needed their unique form of sustenance, so did the men. The ten-day journey to the objective necessitated huge amounts of provisions: 5,360,850 pounds of dried food, 2,118,400 pounds of chilled food, 1,167,300 pounds of frozen food, occupying some 283,980 cubic feet of shipping space. Just to transport the 7th Infantry Division required twelve attack transport ships, three attack cargo ships, two dock-landing ships (LSDs) to carry the tanks of the supporting 767th Tank Battalion, and sixteen Landing Ship, Tanks (LSTs), possibly the most valuable support ship in the Allied arsenal—and in huge demand for operations around the globe because of their ability to haul scores of trucks, artillery pieces, and landing craft, plus large quantities of supplies. Each attack transport ship was capable of uncomfortably carrying a reinforced battalion of about fifteen hundred soldiers. Every conceivable item, from personal weapons to canteens, had to be packed, accounted for, and loaded according to a precise plan that took into account priority of value and ease of unloading. "Ships will be loaded, in principle, in the reverse order of unloading," Brigadier General Archibald Arnold, the division artillery commander, remarked. "The unloading priorities are properly based on the plan of attack ashore."

In a typical invasion, one division required, on average, 7,500 tons of cargo on the first day alone. At Attu, the 7th Division staff had invented a pallet system that ate up shipping space but greatly facilitated the speed and efficiency of landing cargo. For this invasion, the division prepared 4,174 sled- and toboggan-style pallets, each measuring four feet by six feet.

An entire pallet was required just to package a dozen and a half 155-millimeter howitzer shells. The division's inventory included 64,150 pounds of TNT, 18,000 blasting caps, 3,216 bangalore torpedoes, 101,450 feet of fuse and detonation cord, 7,000 fuse lighters, three concrete mixers, 300,000 board feet of lumber, fourteen 10,000-gallon water tanks, 1,613,600 rounds of .30-caliber M1 carbine ammunition, 2,197,019 rounds of .30-06 M1 Garand and Browning automatic rifle (BAR) bullets, 1,158,000 bullets for bolt-action Springfield rifles, 6,414,700 .30-caliber machine-gun bullets, 68,914 60-millimeter mortar shells, 26,913 81-millimeter mortar shells, 47,425 hand grenades, just under 1,000,000 gallons of fuel for the division's vehicles, 7,500 water cans, 15,000 pairs of mosquito gloves, 30,000 pairs of sunglasses, 15,000 Sterno stoves, and 1,012 tons of food, enough to sustain the division for two weeks. Division leaders had decided to beef up their automatic weapons capability by equipping each rifle squad with two Browning automatic rifles instead of one. With almost 250 rifle squads in the division, this brought the BAR total to about 500, only increasing the demand for .30-06 bullets.

Once aboard ship, every commander at the battalion level and above received a sealed envelope stamped "Secret. To be opened at sea when your ship leaves the harbor." Inside their packages, they found maps, orders, and detailed invasion plans that they used to brief their soldiers. Thanks to excellent photographs of Kwajalein taken by reconnaissance planes and the submarines USS *Seal* and *Tarpon*, the troops knew their target intimately. "Every soldier knew what he was going up against," Corlett wrote; "the mystery was gone. The men knew what to do and how to do it." The soldiers spent hours studying plaster mock-ups and granular photographs of the island. "Shipboard training consisted of debarkation drills and intensive indoctrination of every officer and enlisted man in the part they would play in the coming operation," the division after-action report declared. "Classes were organized and the field order discussed in detail. Teamwork was stressed and the part it would play in . . . the overall plan was emphasized." On a cramped stateroom table, Lieutenant Colonel Ernest Bears, a battalion commander, displayed an oversize photograph of his unit's objective, and made sure his men studied it in depth. "We could see each wave and wash, each frond of the palm trees, tire tracks on a road. A squad at a time crowded into the small space, along with the platoon sergeant and platoon leader. We talked about the steep rise up the surf . . . the supporting fires of naval guns and artillery and how that would change the landscape." In briefings, Bears and other commanders shared a minute level of detail on the invasion plan, right down to individual landing craft assignments.

Though the 7th Division was under the control of Holland Smith's V Amphibious Corps, Corlett and his staff had trained their troops and prepared their Kwajalein invasion plan with very little input from their higher headquarters, reflecting autonomy but also some level of Army uneasiness at the notion of serving under a Marine Corps commander, particularly one with a reputation for volatility and a poor opinion of soldiers. During the planning, Corlett often dealt directly with Admiral Turner rather than Smith. D-day was set for January 31. Corlett earmarked his 17th Infantry Regiment to seize the adjacent islands of Ennylabegan and Enubuj—quickly dubbed Carlos and Carlson by the tongue-tied Americans—as platforms for his artillery and quartermaster units to support the main invasion the next day. The beaches on Kwajalein's ocean coast were not well suited for landings, owing to problematic reefs and pounding surf. The lagoon-side beaches were somewhat more hospitable, but the concrete wall, the majority of the Japanese pillboxes, and other defenses were sited in that direction. So Corlett chose to land on the western end of Kwajalein. The 184th and 32nd Infantry Regiments were to land on Red Beaches 1 and 2, a narrow spit of sandy coast no more than eight hundred yards from end to end. Once ashore, they were to advance steadily inland, with the 184th on the left and the 32nd on the right. Corlett later wrote that landing on western Kwajalein "provided an ideal situation for a very strong attack with [the] two regiments abreast in a column of battalions, the narrowing dimension of the Island to the North East contributing to the strength of the attack."[3]

The night before D-day, the troops played the time-honored preinvasion waiting game of cleaning weapons, checking equipment, and talking about most anything except the upcoming battle. Many took walks on the blacked-out decks of their transport ships, breathing the salty, fresh Pacific night air. True to his nature, General Corlett prepared an aphorism-laden message for his small-unit leaders. "Each little team (the squad) is part of the big team. The big team cannot succeed if each little team does not do its part. After your men get ashore, work them as a team with other teams. Watch the ammunition, rations and water to keep your men going. The supply services will all help you but they are not mind readers. The Japs are much more afraid of us than your men are of the Japs. We have got to kill or capture every Jap. The sooner we do it with the help of Naval gunfire, Artillery, Tanks and Air attack, the fewer men we will lose. If we work together—for each other—we cannot fail."

The initial landings on January 31 worked almost perfectly. Under cover of darkness, soldiers from the division's Cavalry Reconnaissance Troop, plus troops from B Company, 111th Infantry, left the transports *Overton* and *Manley* and paddled ashore in rubber boats to capture tiny Carter, Cecil, and Chauncey Islands against feeble opposition. Control of these islands meant control of the Cecil Pass, the primary deepwater channel into the lagoon, where Admiral Turner's ships were now safe from enemy submarine attacks and could maneuver into close range to land the assault troops and provide them with close-in fire support. The 17th Infantry had little trouble capturing Carlos and Carlson Islands during the day on January 31. By nightfall, most of the division's artillery pieces were in place on Carlos; the crews even began hurling harassing fire at Kwajalein. The fire support ships added to the violence, pounding the island much of the day and night. The distant crump of explosions and the eerie glow of fires could be heard and seen aboard the troop ships, conveying an uneasy sense of impending danger. "Our time was drawing near," one company commander wrote; "only God knew what was in store for us."

With the operation proceeding smoothly, Corlett and Turner green-lighted the main landings for the next morning. Admiral Turner was committed to doing everything in his power to facilitate a smooth landing for Corlett's people. Back in Oahu, the admiral had told his skippers, "The capital ships of this fleet are the transports. The weapons of the transports are the troops they carry. It is the duty of every officer in this fleet, whether he is in an airplane, ashore or afloat, to assist and support [them] with all the resources at his disposal."

They took his words to heart. At 0618 on February 1, as rain squalls and low clouds occasionally blotted out the rising sun, the final preinvasion bombardment commenced as two battleships, two cruisers, and sixteen destroyers unleashed a torrent of shells at pre-plotted targets. In the last moment of dead calm before the shooting started, a sailor yelled in the direction of the unseen Japanese, "Reveille, you sons of bitches!" A rolling, concussive, almost physical wave of noise soon echoed over water and ships alike. To Captain Warren Hughes, a company commander, the shelling felt like being "inside of a base [*sic*] drum in the middle of a Sousa march." He watched the naval guns in awe as a "huge sheet of orange flame would leap thirty feet out of the muzzle and disappear into a billowing mass of brownish-gray smoke, which drifted lazily upward. Then a small black puff of smoke as they 'blew' their barrels in preparation for the next round."

One of the battleships, USS *Mississippi*, edged as close as fifteen hundred yards away from the Kwajalein shore and hurled fourteen-inch shells at pillboxes and other defenses along the lagoon coast and the landing beaches. The cruisers added their eight-inch projectiles, the destroyers their five-inch shells. In total, they fired 7,700 rounds, totaling 3,964 tons of ordnance. Forty-millimeter and .50-caliber gun crews added their own bullets to the maw; their tracer rounds formed impossibly straight red lines from ship to beach. The 7th Division's field artillery batteries on Carlos Island contributed another 29,000 105- and 155-millimeter shells, accounting for another 1,361 tons of explosives. Specially fitted LCIs buzzed in and disgorged thousands of rockets at Kwajalein. Half a dozen B-24 Liberators soon arrived to dump 1,000- and 2,000-pound bombs on a blockhouse and twin mounted guns at the island's northwestern end. The carrier planes had their say as well. During a lull in the naval gunfire, they zoomed in to bomb and strafe the landing area, adding another 176,600 .50-caliber machine-gun rounds, 125 rockets, and 119 tons of bombs. At 0905, just twenty-five minutes before H hour, they left and the ships resumed their relentless punching. "There was never any holiday in the gunfire," quipped Captain James Doyle, a staff officer aboard USS *Rocky Mount*, Admiral Turner's flagship. Indeed, some kind of ordnance exploded on Kwajalein every two seconds. The explosions were so continuous that a dense pall of smoke and dust, combined with an existing sea mist, hung over the island, obscuring visibility. Those who caught glimpses of Kwajalein thought it looked like it had been hit by a hurricane. "The damage is so intensive that it is difficult to determine which type of explosive missile is responsible for each sample of destruction," a naval observer recorded. "It is even impossible to visualize what 90% of the original installations consisted of."

Buildings and concrete emplacements were reduced to rubble. Trees were shattered and uprooted, coral ridges blown to bits, the ground indented with massive craters. "The entire island looked as if it had been picked up to 20,000 feet and then dropped," a witness later wrote. By design, the western and northern sections of the island suffered the worst damage; the airfield was largely untouched. The bombardment was one of the best planned and well executed of the entire war and it undoubtedly negated the possibility of significant Japanese resistance on the landing

beaches. Even so, it was more destructive of structures than enemy soldiers, since most of the Japanese had access to bunkers and shelters that
offered a reasonable level of protection. General Corlett lamented that the
bombs and shells "drove the enemy under ground but did not kill many of
them." The larger-caliber naval shells were occasionally victims of their
own stupendous power. In the recollection of Colonel George Eddy, an
Army ordnance specialist, the battleship shells tended to "bounce off and
explode out over open water because of the projectile's built-in delay fea-
ture. If it hit a hut or palm-log revetment, it would go right through, not
damaging the structure at all, and explode on the other side." Lieutenant
Colonel S. L. A. Marshall, a pioneering Army combat historian who was
attached to the 7th Division for this operation, later estimated, on the basis
of inspecting enemy corpses, that the preinvasion pounding inflicted about
4 to 7 percent of Japanese fatalities on Kwajalein.[4]

The day before all this violent preparation, the assault troops of the 32nd
and 184th Infantry Regiments had climbed down rope ladders from their
troop ships and boarded Higgins boats (LCVPs) that shuttled them to
LSTs, where they had spent a restless, crowded night waiting for the order
to invade. In the early morning hours of February 1, some enjoyed a steak
breakfast; the less fortunate had to make do with K rations. With their
meals settling queasily in their nervous stomachs, they donned their gear
and boarded Landing Vehicle Tracked (LVT) amphibious craft—usually
called alligators or amtracs—crewed by soldiers of the 708th Amphibian
Tank Battalion. Outfitted with treads, capable of functioning on land and
at sea, the LVT was a game changer for Pacific theater amphibious operations because of its ability to negotiate coral reefs and boulders. Some models were fitted with armor, others not. All could provide some sort of fire
support, usually in the form of .30- and .50-caliber machine guns or a
37-millimeter gun. In addition to a crew of six soldiers, the typical amtrac
could carry about sixteen assault troops. For Kwajalein, the 7th Division
had 174 amtracs available. Aboard the LSTs, most of those men spent several uncomfortable moments breathing the exhaust fumes of their amtracs before the forward doors of the LSTs finally opened and disgorged
the landing craft into the sea. Guided by naval control boats, the troop-
laden LVTs churned through the choppy waters, bound for Kwajalein's
west coast. Japanese mortar shells exploded intermittently and ineffec-

tively. The first wave comprised the 3rd Battalion, 184th Infantry, and the 1st Battalion, 32nd Infantry, plus engineers from the division's 13th Engineer Combat Battalion. To Captain H. B. Knowles, the transport commander watching from the bridge aboard USS *Monrovia*, the unrelenting rows of thirty-two landing craft reminded him of "traffic on Broadway at rush hour." Control boats operated on the flanks, herding the landing craft into position like maritime traffic cops. "Every thousand yards the boat waves were informed by voice radio as to how much ahead or behind schedule they were," Admiral Turner later wrote in an official report.

So much smoke and detritus still hung over the area that the curious invaders could not even see the island until they were within one hundred yards of it. Aboard the boats, the troops talked about where they would rather be at the moment. Most favored dinner at a favorite restaurant and debated, in the recollection of *Yank* magazine correspondent Merle Miller, "whether steaks would be better than chocolate malteds." As the rocket boats on either flank of the amtracs and the artillery batteries on Carlos Island shifted their fire deeper inland, the leading LVTs touched down on Red Beaches 1 and 2 at 0930, exactly on time. Because the amtracs were not equipped with ramps, the soldiers hopped off the sides, into water, onto rocks, or, for the lucky ones, on dry beach. "Some difficulty was encountered by soldiers who found themselves sprawling in shallow water or on the beach because of the high drop from the LVT," wrote Marshall. A few even plunged into water over their heads but, after floundering angrily around, emerged unscathed. The infantrymen and engineers were able to maneuver on the shattered beach, but palm stumps, the edge of the seawall, and deep, water-filled shell or bomb craters made it difficult for vehicles to move. One LVT hit a stump and bellied over, helpless until it could be extracted with a cable by another amtrac. "In the landings three medium and three light tanks were drowned out when they dropped into deep holes in the reef," wrote First Lieutenant Paul Leach, in a history of the supporting 767th Tank Battalion. "Two of the mediums were out for the duration of the campaign due to their motors being filled with salt water. The others were put back into service that night."

Japanese opposition to the landing was confined to some mortar rounds, sniping, and a belligerent pillbox or two. Within minutes, the lead battalions of the two regiments were firmly ashore and advancing inland while succeeding waves continued to land on an increasingly congested beach. Kwajalein's little west coast was soon choked with vehicles, equipment, matériel, and thousands of men. It was so crowded that LVT coxswains with orders to retrieve more troops or supplies could get back into the water only by backing straight into it. Some of the follow-on am-tracs could not get anywhere near the beach and settled for dropping their troops into chest-high water thirty or forty yards offshore.[5]

By midday, the lead troops were several hundred yards inland, attempt-ing to advance through a landscape choked with debris, branches, fallen trees, heavy foliage, and the scattered wreckage of buildings. Visibility was severely restricted. "It was possible to move into this tangle and be com-pletely out of sight of a man only a few yards away," Captain Edmund Love, the division historian, later wrote. "Movement in a straight line was impos-sible. At times infantrymen had to walk a hundred yards to reach a point only twenty yards away." In some cases, they stumbled upon pillboxes, pitched grenades, or explosive charges or shot into them only to discover nothing more than dead enemy soldiers inside. Some found more danger-ous contents. A pair of engineers threw grenades into one position, en-countered no return fire, and looked inside only to discover it was filled with several hundred rounds of mortar ammunition, prompting the two men to scramble away quickly.

Before long, the vanguard began to encounter Japanese who had either infiltrated among the ruins or weathered the bombardment in active pill-boxes or bunkers. Their fire could come from every direction in a 360-degree, disorienting battlefield. "Actions of that morning are not understandable to those who think of Kwajalein as they would of any other battlefield," com-mented Marshall, who accompanied the troops into action. "It was in a sense like fighting in the dark." The toughest resistance was on the left, in the 184th Infantry sector, near the lagoon coast, where the Japanese had prepared a thick network of defenses. Given the nature of the terrain and the Japanese tendency to fight to the death, heedless of circumstances, much of the fight-ing took place at close quarters, with the two sides usually within twenty or thirty yards of each other. "Those who consider the great principles of sincer-ity, fidelity, self-sacrifice and martyrdom to country as mere slogans, and, moreover, soldiers who disgrace the absolute trust of the Emperor, are the pinnacle of unfaithfulness," Japanese soldiers were lectured in a typical in-structional manual. "In addition, if this fact be known by the parents, broth-ers and relatives in the homeland, their condemnation and long hatred will be extremely regrettable."

With this cultural peer pressure as the norm, at least for the combat-effective ethnic Japanese on Kwajalein, the Americans had to be wary of what might greet them in every stand of trees, behind every rubble pile, and inside any trench, bunker, or pillbox. Private Parvee Rasberry and PFC Paul Roper discovered an active pillbox and lobbed fragmentation grenades at it, only to have the Japanese hurl them back. A flamethrower operator attempted to burn them out, but the flames just dissipated harmlessly against the concrete. Rasberry had to leave the relative protection of a crater, crawl to within a few yards of the aperture, and hurl a white phosphorous grenade inside. Rather than be burned by this merciless weapon, the Japanese emerged. Several were cut down by American rifle fire, but others ran back inside the pillbox. Tech Sergeant Graydon Kickul crawled forward, managed to make it atop the pillbox, and emptied his M1 Garand into the remaining defenders. To make absolutely sure they were dead, the American infantrymen brought up an LVT, which proceeded to pour flame and 37-millimeter fire into the aperture. The courageous Kickul subsequently attacked three other pillboxes in a similar manner, hurling grenades and explosives down their vents, forcing the defenders to exit and face death from American rifle and machine-gun fire. When Staff Sergeant Thomas Bentley directed tank fire and threw grenades at a box from a distance of about thirty yards, eighteen enemy soldiers suddenly boiled out of it and charged directly at a stunned Lieutenant John Erickson and one of his sergeants named Bannister as the two were talking. "I didn't know what the hell was going on," Bannister later commented. "I just stood there and watched this while these guys kept coming towards me. Everybody started shooting all around and the first thing I knew a dead Jap landed about five yards away."

One sergeant had told his men as they neared the beach in their LVT, "One time I fucked a seventy-five-year-old woman in Vancouver. I'm going to get it today for what I did." Once ashore, he almost seemed hell-bent on making his premonition come true, leading every reconnaissance and attack, peeking into the embrasures of bunkers. His luck soon ran out. As he investigated a pile of logs, he took a bullet in the jaw. Blood poured from his mouth and face. "Shit, this will ruin my good looks with the girls," he told the men who gave him first aid and put him on a stretcher. As his comrades passed him, he patted each of them on the leg and wished them luck. He died before the stretcher team could get him to the beach. The bullet had apparently severed his windpipe, slowly asphyxiating him. At one nest, called the Wolf Strong Point by the Americans, the 184th ran into substantial bomb shelters. A group of Sherman tanks soon battered it. According to the 767th's historical record, "This strong point . . . was reduced after the tanks gutted the concrete bomb shelters, in which the Japs were barricaded, with armor piercing and high explosive shell. Engineer satchel charges, thrown in breaches made by the tank shells, finished off the structures, caving in the roofs."

Commanders at every level had tried to digest the sobering lessons of the Gilberts fighting, particularly the bloodbath at Tarawa, where the need for more close-range, bunker-busting weapons had become very apparent. In addition to demolition-style explosives and grenades, the 7th Division went into Kwajalein with a generous quantity of 192 M1 flamethrowers. Each rifle company had access to two or three flamethrowers, usually wielded by attached engineers who were, in turn, supported by groups of riflemen. The terrifying contraption was awkward, heavy, and messy. The operator strapped the seventy-pound tanks to his back and needed assistance to ignite the volatile mixture of nitrogen, napalm, and diesel. A hose piped the fuel from the tanks to a nozzle manipulated and fired from the hip by the operator. At best, the weapon could reach a target twenty yards away and unleash flame for one or two bursts of ten uninterrupted seconds before depleting the tanks.

Hauling the flamethrower required guts and stamina. Private Charles Craig, a diminutive man who sported a pencil-thin mustache in the manner of Douglas Fairbanks or Clark Gable, assaulted no fewer than a dozen pillboxes, dugouts, and other shelters, usually at the range of less than five feet. His fellow soldiers who knew him well were surprised at his dedication. "He had been a fuck up all along with the company and injured his foot badly on the ship trying to climb the stairs while drunk," his sergeant commented. "Everyone worried about how he'd come along." They need not have worried. In combat, he became a different person. When Craig ran out of fuel, he jogged back to a supply dump near Red Beach 1, replenished and resumed his attacks, under the watchful fire of riflemen. Twice his weapon broke, but he simply rummaged for a new one and then continued his work. When he unleashed flame into one shelter, a Japanese soldier charged and sprayed the contents of a fire extinguisher at Craig, soaking him. But in this situation, flames overwhelmed flame retardants. Engulfed in fire, the enemy soldier crumpled dead at Craig's feet. "Excitement kept me going," he later commented to an interviewer about his resilience.[6]

The struggle for Kwajalein coalesced into an incremental slugfest, with the Americans settling into wary, occasionally embattled or infiltrated nighttime perimeters, and by day steadily advancing through the jumbled ruins against stubborn resistance. Given the strictures of terrain and space, plus the determination of disjointed groups of Japanese to fight to the death, the battle could hardly have developed in any other pattern. On the second day, the Americans secured the airfield as well as the island's two coastal roads, Will on the lagoon side and Wallace on the ocean side. Bulldozers piloted by engineers soon improved the roads, facilitating the forward movement of supplies and the installation of communication wires. For the first time, an ingenious, utilitarian, two-and-a-half-ton amphibian truck, called a DUKW, was available in numbers. Equipped with six wheels, a boat hull, a propeller, and a rudder, capable of carrying twenty-five soldiers or five thousand pounds of cargo, the DUKWs were ideally suited for amphibious operations. Over one hundred of them ferried ammunition, cargo, and troops to forward areas, and evacuated wounded men for treatment at beachside aid stations or aboard ship; most commonly they moved artillery shells and even the pieces themselves to Carlos Island.

As the two infantry regiments began the gradual left turn to secure the narrow northern end of Kwajalein, they ran into the heaviest enemy resistance at what they called the Nap strong point, once the home of Admiral Akiyama's headquarters. Battered mercilessly by aerial bombs and naval and artillery shells, the area was now coated with the husks and ruins of barracks, administrative buildings, warehouses, shattered palm trees, as well as stalwart concrete blockhouses and pillboxes. The ruins obscured a warren of tunnels, dugouts, and bomb shelters. Marshall referred to the area as in "a state of well-nigh indescribable chaos. Where there were great craters from the air bombs, sand dunes had been tossed up around them. Abutting these sand piles would be piles of rubble 5 to 15 feet high where a building had been blown apart and its corrugated sheeting and splintered timbers were sticking out at weird angles. Beyond that—only a few feet— might be smaller craters or a group of enemy dead. Then perhaps a shattered concrete pillbox or a clump of coco palms, uprooted and twisted aside so that they blocked the path. Broken concrete foundations, walls lying half over, mounds that one could not be at all sure were simply earth or the upward-jutting of an enemy underground hideout. It was like strolling in the wake of a tornado."

Here the Americans were confronted with a downside of their immense firepower. The very bombardment that had smoothed the way for the landings had ironically also created an ideal landscape for the defenders, a phenomenon experienced by the Germans a year earlier at Stalingrad, albeit on a much larger and deadlier scale. On the first day of the Kwajalein battle alone, artillery batteries on Carlos Island had fired about 21,000 shells; the output was only slightly lower ever since. They averaged 4,500 shells expended each subsequent evening. Over four days of battle, the division's artillery units fired 78,700 projectiles. The naval guns added another 6,574 rounds, including 1,342 fourteen-inch shells, and air strikes 396,500 more pounds of bombs. The typical 105-millimeter howitzer battery could unleash 100 rounds every ten minutes, and a 155-millimeter battery half that much; the crewmen fired for eight straight minutes, then rested and serviced their pieces for two minutes. Other artillerymen constantly unloaded shells from DUKWs or other conveyances and moved them into position. Commanders devised a rotation system to rest one tube per battery every ten minutes while crewmen oiled it, swabbed it, and allowed it to cool. "The men can stand more than the guns," commented Lieutenant Colonel George Preston, commander of the 145th Field Artillery Battalion. The work of those men was constant and intense. "They did a grand job at the guns under severe physical, mental, and nervous strain," lauded Brigadier General Archibald Arnold, the division artillery commander. "I never expected to see such concentration, such intensity, and such accuracy." Premature explosions killed two artillerymen and wounded several others. Forward observation teams operated on the ground and overhead in spotter planes. The air over the island was so thick with shells that a low-flying plane from USS *Minneapolis* piloted by Ensign William Strayer was hit and destroyed. "It just evaporated into a sheet of flame and, still flaming, plunged straight down into the water," Captain Hughes, an eyewitness to the plane's demise, later said.[7]

In the meantime, at the Nap strong point and all over the remnants of northern Kwajalein, Japanese fighters could be lurking anywhere or nowhere. For the American soldiers who advanced into this disorienting maze of concrete, coral, wood, and mud, every step could bring death or dismemberment. They had to be wary of every hole, every mound, every indentation, every tunnel, every door, every tree stump, every hunk of building, every tangle of ruins, at the very time when fatigue had begun to set in after three days of more or less continuous combat. "Never take anyone's word for it that any area is clear of Japs," one infantryman advised his less experienced peers. "Don't pass by any holes. Watch the trees too. They're the favorite sniper hangout." Most of the soldiers had shadow beards and red-rimmed eyes by now. More than ever, they operated in combined arms teams of infantry, tanks, engineers, and artillery observers. "Before long the front line lost all semblance of unity and the action became of squads or small groups of men attempting to reduce the Jap position that was threatening them most," Major Clark Campbell, a battalion operations officer, later wrote. The two sides routinely operated within catch-playing or even handshake distance. "Men were shooting at each other at ranges measured in a few yards," Richard Wilcox, a *Life* magazine correspondent, wrote.

Visibility was so limited that even members of the same squad often became separated and worked at cross-purposes to clear out the same positions. When a soldier tossed a satchel charge into one building, a group of cornered Japanese rushed out, firing rifles, heaving grenades, hollering, "Banzai!" or, in the memory of the Americans, making "a piglike kind of squealing." Standing nearby, Private George Nabozan screamed, "God damn, here they come! Kill the sons of bitches!" and blazed away until his rifle jammed. In addition to Nabozan, two groups of Americans, oblivious to the other's presence, fired at the Japanese in between, cutting them all down. Only by a miracle of ballistics did the GIs not hit any of their own. In a crater near the wreckage of another building, a sergeant and his BAR man were concealed behind a slag pile, keeping watch, when an infantryman joined them and asked, "Can I be of assistance? I have already killed four today and would like to make it five." The two soldiers readily agreed. Moments later, they all spotted a pair of Japanese exit the building and begin moving through the wreckage. They pitched grenades and poured rifle and BAR fire at them. When they peeked over the pile, they saw that the two enemy were dead. Before the day was done, they killed four more in this manner.

The progress of the American advance, though not swift, made little impact on the Japanese desire to fight. The bombardment and three succeeding days of combat had destroyed all Japanese communications and most of their command and control. Though fatal to their already remote chances of winning the battle, these factors did nothing to diminish the

danger posed by individual Japanese or small groups of them, regardless
of whether they were trained combat troops or auxiliaries. In one US Army
soldier's handbook on their adversaries, the GIs were correctly told, "On
the defense they are brave and determined. In prepared positions the resistance of Japanese soldiers often has been fanatical in its tenacity." In this
oddly urban landscape that stretched along Kwajalein's north shore, most
kept fighting even when they were surrounded, bypassed, cornered, or
wounded. "The mere fact that a position was being flanked or enveloped
meant nothing to the Jap soldier," Major Campbell contended. "His psychology and fanatacism [sic] dictated that he kill as many Americans as
possible before dying a 'glorious death.'" As the crew of a medium tank
called "Sad Sack" pumped 75-millimeter shells into the aperture of one
pillbox, they were stunned to see several sword-wielding Japanese soldiers
charge at them and attempt to beat the sides of the tank. The Americans
mowed them down with machine-gun fire.

To protect against sniper fire and grenades in such a constricted environment, most of the tankers buttoned up their hatches, restricting visibility to eerie glimpses of the landscape. One Sherman tank, nicknamed
"Baby Satan," rolled past the body of a Japanese soldier sprawled on his
back outside a pillbox. The commander spotted a live enemy nearby and
ordered the bow gunner to open fire. "The machine-gun tracers found
him," William Chickering, a *Time* correspondent who rode inside the tank
with the crew, later wrote. "The head and shoulders of the Jap rose up and
collapsed. Then all we could see was one leg kicking in the air, kicking,
kicking, as bullets poured relentlessly into his body. Finally it stiffened,
dropped." Coordination between tankers and infantrymen had been poor
at Tarawa and Makin, in part because of their inability to communicate
smoothly. Often, infantrymen had to resort to banging on the turret or the
side of a tank to get the crew's attention, hardly an ideal or healthy practice.
In an attempt to solve that problem, communications teams had installed
a phone inside a metal box at the rear of each tank. If an infantry commander wanted to talk to his armored counterpart, he grabbed the phone
and toggled a lever that switched on a light bulb near the tank commander's head. In theory, this was an ingenious solution. But at Kwajalein, the
phones were not suitably prepared to withstand the rigors of an amphibious landing, the terrain, and the elements. "More than half short-circuited
as a result of being doused in salt water," Lieutenant Leach, the 767th historian, chronicled. "Another thirty percent of the phones were either

crushed in landings or in heavy going in the brush, or were cut out by the tankers who feared the phones would short out the tank inter-phone system, as some of them did."

As was their wont, the Americans simply improvised as best they could. Tanks operated ahead of the lead troops as mobile firing platforms, pumping shells into apertures, buildings, holes, and shelters, shooting at any live targets spotted by their crewmen or pointed out to them either in direct communication with infantrymen or simply by watching where they were shooting. "Two or three infantrymen with M-1 rifles [fired] in the apertures of the pill boxes to prevent the Japanese firing on our troops," General Corlett, who by now had come ashore and had migrated to the front lines, wrote of a typical attack. "The tank from a distance of about 100 yards [fired] its . . . gun at one of the pill boxes. The first shot appeared to make only a niche; by boresighting they were able to fire into this niche a second, third, fourth and fifth shot. About this time a ragged hole appeared in the wall of the pill box. Infantrymen then poured rifle fire through this aperture and engineers slipped under cover of this fire and set their fifty pound satchel charges of dynamite against the structure, lighted the fuse and when this charge exploded, the pill box was pretty well disintegrated." A flamethrower operator then hurried to the opening and unleashed a jet of flame, roasting anyone who was still alive. "This was a pretty horrible way to die but the Japanese, as a general thing, refused to surrender and it was either them or our men."

Corlett had made his headquarters on Carlson Island, but spent much of his time observing the fighting. His aide-de-camp, Captain Henry "Hank" Emerson, was killed by a sniper. Eventually, a sergeant sidled up to Corlett and expressed appreciation for his presence but urged him to go back to headquarters. "This was the most tactful yet firm admonition I have ever received. My place was back at my headquarters." In a few instances, the assault troops came upon Marshallese, most of whom had gone to ground in shelters the Japanese had not used. The Americans moved the locals to an adjacent island, fed them, and dispensed medical care and housing. "They were of a fine physique and good personality, friendly," Corlett commented. "Very few of them were hurt in the attack on Kwajalein."

With the possible exception of riflemen, engineers found themselves in the greatest demand because their demolitions proved to be the most effective weapons to kill concealed enemy soldiers, no matter where they were holed up, in such a confining environment. Closely covered by infantrymen, they crawled to embrasures, openings, holes, dugouts, tunnel entrances, walls, logs, or anywhere else an enemy might take shelter. Then they set their charges, lit fuses, and dashed away. "The training we had with the combat engineers prior to the Kwajalein operation was very necessary, and we were given sufficient work together," Staff Sergeant Nello Giaccani later commented. Amid the smoking ruins, they fought together with crystalline simplicity. "The infantry holds the Japs down with their BARs and rifles and the engineers blow them out with their demolitions and flamethrowers," Staff Sergeant Danny Grothers, an engineer, explained. On occasion, when they put a satchel charge in place, the Japanese pulled out the fuses and threw the charges back. In response, the engineers simply cut the fuses, shortening the detonation time. So pronounced was the need for the engineers' services that they often ran low on explosives. The typical engineer squad carried eight bangalore torpedoes, two shaped charges, four satchel charges, and a flamethrower. A single group of engineers attached to one infantry regiment went through 300 boxes of blasting caps, 400 boxes of TNT, and 150 boxes of Composition C explosives. When they ran out of satchel charges, they took to placing Composition C inside gas mask containers.[8]

By the evening of February 3, the 7th Division, after the bitter fighting around a Nap strong point, had crushed most resistance on Kwajalein. Even so, the division needed most of another day to subdue the remaining defenders. At the same time, troops from the 17th Infantry Regiment had seized adjacent Burton Island—its real name was Ebeye—in a sharp fight, and secured a couple of smaller islands as well. At 1610 on February 4, Corlett radioed Admiral Turner. "All organized resistance has ceased." Delighted, Turner quickly replied, "I wish to express to you my great admiration for the dash, courage, and efficiency with which you have performed your tasks."

While some of the troops continued patrolling to root out any remaining holdouts, others began the grisly task of policing up and burying the remains of their adversaries, about four thousand of whom had been killed on Kwajalein. Some of the bodies were burned, some shredded by bullets or shell fragments; because many had been killed by explosives, pieces of them had to be rooted out of the debris that coated much of Kwajalein. "We'd pick up feet and arms and stuff, and it wasn't good and it all smelled . . . horrible," Lieutenant Dean Galles recalled. Indeed, the stench of putrefying and burned flesh permeated the tiny coral island. "The sight and smell of dead Japs are everywhere on this island," Sergeant Miller, the *Yank* reporter, wrote. "Puddles of water are deep red with their blood. The beaches are lined with their bodies or parts of their bodies—shoes with feet, nothing else; grinning heads, with occasional cigarettes still pinched between browned teeth, but without torsos; scattered arms and legs, far from the bodies to which they belong." Lieutenant Colonel Marshall, who had to sift through the enemy dead to determine what weapons had killed them, once referred to Kwajalein as "the most stinking piece of real estate I have ever smelled in war. The island was virtually matted with rotting flesh and drying blood. The stench was so unbearable that we were trying to mask it out with towels and handkerchiefs."

Burial parties unceremoniously sprayed sodium arsenite—for disinfection and insect-suppression purposes—on the Japanese body parts and dumped them into bulldozed communal graves, one of which contained as many as 1,265 men. "There was no method by which the Jap dead could be identified," Captain Franklin Sherman, a physician who supervised the burials, commented a few months later to an Army interviewer. "Identification tags . . . gave only the name of the unit. Some five or ten minutes were required to go through the personal effects of the Jap, because apparently there was no prescribed method of wear." The most common item they found was the Yosegaki Hinomaru or "Good Luck Flag" worn into battle by many Japanese, generally around their waists, in pockets, or inside their helmets. Made out of delicate fibers, the flags were signed, and usually inscribed with well wishes, by the soldiers' families, friends, and neighbors. Part talisman, part heirloom, and part patriotic symbol, the Yosegaki Hinomaru was a sacred item to the average Japanese serviceman. To the Americans, very few of whom had any idea of, or all that much respect for, the cultural or personal significance of the flags, their small size and fascinating images simply made for easily plundered and traded souvenirs.

The American dead were handled delicately, and with some level of reverence, either by their own divisional comrades or specially trained graves registration troops attached to the 7th for the battle. Like their former enemies, they, too, were sprayed with sodium arsenite and then prepared for burial. "Transfer and interment of remains was accomplished with due honors," an administrative Army report stated. "Each body was wrapped in a blanket and covered with an American flag for movement." The burial teams kept detailed records to identify each dead GI. They buried the remains beneath small wooden white crosses in a carefully tended cemetery on Carlos Island. When the job was done, chaplains conducted a memorial service. The mourners included Admiral Turner, Generals Holland Smith and Corlett, Marshallese leaders, many of whom were Christian, and soldiers of all ranks. Gazing at the crosses, Captain Hughes asked himself if Kwajalein had been worth the cost of "trading this ugly hunk of sand and trees for the heart's blood of life and all it promised to these men beneath the white crosses."

The losses were considerable, though not comparable with the bloody Gilberts operations. The capture of the southern half of Kwajalein Atoll cost the Army 177 dead and 1,037 wounded, of whom about 400 did not require evacuation. Gunshots accounted for about 38 percent of the wounds, fragments most of the rest. To the north, the 4th Marine Division secured Roi-Namur and several smaller islands in two days of sharp fighting. The Marines lost 313 dead, 502 wounded, and another 73 missing presumed dead. The 7th Division killed 4,938 enemy servicemen at Kwajalein and its neighboring islands while capturing 206 prisoners, only 79 of whom were ethnic Japanese. In the recollection of one witness, the captives were "small, gaunt, hungry and thirsty. None had had anything to eat or drink for two or three days." The Americans provided them with food, water, and medical care. The Marines estimated that they killed 3,563 at Roi-Namur and its environs. At the behest of Admiral Spruance, a battalion-size force from the 106th Infantry Regiment, 27th Infantry Division, had also bloodlessly captured the Majuro Atoll, securing an excellent sea and air base in the eastern Marshalls. Success there and at Kwajalein allowed Turner to unleash on February 17 a joint invasion, by the Army's 106th Infantry and the 22nd Marine Regiment, of the Eniwetok Atoll at the western edge of the Marshalls. In five days of occasionally ferocious fighting, the Americans seized the atoll but lost 262 killed, 757 wounded, and 77 missing presumed dead.

In the bigger picture, control of the Marshalls yielded significant strategic results. In addition to shattering a Japanese outpost line and clearing the way for devastating US Navy carrier strikes against Japanese naval forces at Truk in the Carolines, the American victories in the Marshalls netted them a slew of useful bases from which to continue Admiral Nimitz's Central Pacific drive. As he had anticipated, the capture of the Marshalls accelerated the war's timetable by several months, making major summertime operations in the Marianas—the fulcrum of Japanese Central Pacific defenses—not only possible but likely. Moreover, American planes now threatened the major Japanese naval base at Truk and threatened the flank of their South Pacific bases in the Solomons and, to some extent, even New Guinea. Flintlock reinforced the notion among the Joint Chiefs that Nimitz's island-hopping campaign offered the most attractive means of defeating Japan. His insistence on bypassing Wotje and Maloelap to attack Kwajalein directly was proven absolutely correct, so much so that what had once appeared to be a decision fraught with risk now seemed the obvious choice. On the tactical side, the Americans learned much about preinvasion bombardments, joint service operations, the coordination of firepower, and the best techniques to prevail in close combat against the Japanese.[9]

Not everyone on the American side was so sanguine about the outcome of Flintlock. Holland Smith believed the Army's performance had been subpar. Opinionated, truculent, tempestuous, and hotheaded enough to earn the slightly ridiculous nickname "Howlin' Mad," he had logged thirty-eight devoted years in the Corps, with little combat command experience, though he had earned a reputation as one of its leading practitioners of amphibious warfare. Just shy of his sixty-second birthday, bespectacled and jowly, with a perpetual frown on his face and a cigar in his mouth, he looked every bit his age. "He was always demanding and often profane," correspondent Robert Sherrod, who befriended him during the war, assessed. "He could be kind, too. He fumed and he scolded, but when he laughed he laughed deep in the belly. He was enthusiastic, thoughtful, stubborn, a hard driver." In Hawaii a year earlier, he had been arrested for hit-and-run and drunk driving but was released for lack of sufficient evidence, in part because he seldom drank to excess. The incident might have ended his career in a later era. Instead, he continued as commander of the V Amphibious Corps.

Holland Smith believed passionately in lightning-quick operations, even at the expense of incurring high casualties. In his view, and that of many Marine and naval officers, the longer a battle dragged on, the more vulnerable ships became to enemy air and sea attacks. Though Army officers did not necessarily disagree in concept, they often did in practice, since they tended to favor a more deliberate pace if that might save lives (and allow time to employ supporting firepower, a key tenet of all Army training). Back in November 1943 at Makin, Smith had grown impatient with what he viewed as the 27th Infantry Division's unreasonably slow pace and poor leadership. He had clashed with Major General Ralph Smith, the gentlemanly division commander whom Holland Smith thought of as lacking drive. His relations with the feisty Corlett were more respectful, but chary. When he ridiculed Ralph Smith in a conversation with Corlett one day, the 7th Division commander bristled, "Don't you dare ever talk about me that way," and stalked out of the room. In their next meeting, Smith asserted, "Corlett, you were insubordinate to me the other day." Corlett refused to relent. "I'll say the same thing again." Cowboy Pete was willing to stand up to Holland Smith in a way that the less confrontational Ralph Smith would not.

Over Holland Smith's objections, Corlett insisted that he and his staff ride aboard *Rocky Mount*, a ship equipped with state-of-the-art communications and access to Admiral Turner. Corlett felt strongly enough about the issue to go directly to Turner. He got what he wanted. He also warned Smith not to come ashore himself to supervise the Kwajalein fighting and not to send staffers as proxies. "This is my battle," he told Smith. "You may put some staff officers ashore as observers. If I find they have tried to issue any orders, I'll have them arrested." It was a remarkable, and borderline insubordinate, way for a division commander to address his nominal superior, but it indicated Smith's inability to win the allegiance of his Army subordinates, mainly due to his heavy-handed, chauvinistic contempt for the Army's fighting ability.

The Corps could hardly have selected an officer less suited in outlook and temperament to conduct joint service operations. Smith loved the Marine Corps to the exclusion of all other military mistresses. His rightful pride in the Corps seemed to stem, at least in part, from a dysfunctional disdain for the other services, especially the Army. More than anything else, he was animated by a constant need to preserve the existence of the Corps and its unique traditions. Nor was he shy about publicly disparaging the Army and its fighting acumen. On many occasions, he dressed down individual soldiers and ripped the fighting ability of their leaders. Aboard ship during the Kwajalein battle, he told a pair of newspaper correspondents, "If the Marines had been sent against Kwajalein Island, they would already have taken it." Without ever setting foot on the island or getting any sense of its terrain and the nature of the fighting, he wrote to his friend General Alexander Archer Vandegrift, the commandant of the Corps, "A midget with a popgun could have taken the first 400 yards of the beach at Kwajalein."

To Holland Smith, military operations were measured in the speed of their completion, not the larger strategic results they accrued or the damage inflicted upon the enemy in comparison to losses on the American side. When he found out that the 4th Marine Division had secured Roi-Namur in two days, he wrote Vandegrift, "The same Marine Corps spirit which has permitted us to survive for 150 years against hostile Army officers and two ex-navy presidents prevailed in the capture of ROI and NAMUR. The 4th Division attacked with vigor and elan. This is the real spirit." By contrast, "the slow progress" of Corlett's division "has tried my soul." In a revealing conversation with his Marine aide, he claimed, "It's a little different in the Army . . . as they can fail and still be alright. If we ever fail once in the Marine Corps, or if we ever slow down on one of our jobs, we are through. Our very life depends on accomplishing our missions rapidly and with plenty of spirit." When he went ashore after the conclusion of the Kwajalein battle, he convened a press conference and compared the work of the 7th Division soldiers unfavorably with what the Marines had done at Roi-Namur. Corlett overheard the remark and immediately cut in to inform the correspondents tartly that Smith had no firsthand knowledge of either battle since he had been aboard ship the entire time. Corlett later wrote to a colleague of the incident, "Holland plays any game to glorify the Marine Corps at the expense of the Army." Corlett half expected to be court-martialed for his impudence, but Smith was not the vindictive sort. He let it go. Under other circumstances, the shipboard sniping and jockeying for press adulation might have amounted to little, especially because the average combat Marine and combat soldier usually had nothing but the highest regard for the other. But in the Marshalls, the tensions among the generals revealed deeper problems, mainly between Smith and his Army colleagues more than between the Army and Marine Corps institutionally—issues that would eventually boil into a serious public breach and intrude upon the health of military operations on a larger battlefield.[10]

A few days after the fighting ended in the Kwajalein Atoll, the troops turned over control of the islands to garrison units, loaded back aboard their transports, and headed for Hawaii. For the 7th Division, the tension of combat had dissipated into a near-carnival atmosphere. The soldiers were happy to be alive and heading for home soil. The seas were calm; the weather was beautiful. By World War II standards, the casualty rate of 4 to 5 percent at Kwajalein had been light. Boxing matches were held between unit champions and then between Army and Navy. The division champion took on an overmatched sailor, carried him for three rounds, and coasted to victory rather than hurt him. When the troops spotted General Corlett at the match, they gave him a thunderous ovation. "The greatest compliment of my life," he later wrote. Corlett's Army superiors, apparently heedless of Holland Smith's opinion, were impressed with the division's performance. He was soon tapped for corps command in Europe and replaced by General Arnold, formerly the division artillery commander. Lieutenant Colonel Marshall spent much of the voyage conducting group interviews that formed the basis for the battle's historical record, and set the precedent for the methods Army historians would use for the rest of World War II and beyond. "I had sufficient proof that the new method could be applied as readily to the actions of one whole division in battle as to the fighting of one platoon," he later wrote.

When the ships arrived at their berths in Honolulu, appreciative crowds packed the docks and cheered the soldiers, who proceeded to throw handfuls of captured Japanese money at them, prompting a near stampede. Some of the revelers even fell into the water. It took several minutes for police to fish them out and restore order. The troops then debarked and trucked to Schofield Barracks, where in a matter of days they began training for future battles. Only months later did they find out that the money they had thrown away in such gobs actually still held value. "In this way welcome home became idiot's delight," Marshall joked.[11]

2

Acceleration

Lieutenant General George Kenney was a difference maker. Diminutive and squat at five foot six, with a close-cropped head of dark hair cut in a rectangle, moon-round blue eyes, and a wrinkled, squarish face seemingly decorated by a constant smirk, he did not necessarily look the part of the dashing airman. Instead, he lived it. An aviation pioneer who had studied at Massachusetts Institute of Technology, Kenney had flown seventy-five combat missions in World War I, shot down two German planes, earned the Distinguished Service Cross, and established himself as a leading doctrinal thinker and combat leader in the burgeoning Army Air Forces (AAF). Major General Richard Marshall, MacArthur's deputy chief of staff, once affectionately described Kenney as "rough appearing, but he's warm hearted and congenial when you get to know him." Another colleague referred to him as "a blustery type, but very talented as an airman." Cocksure and impatient, competent to the marrow of his small bones, Kenney had taken command of the Fifth Air Force, the main SWPA aviation component, in August 1942. Kenney had quickly forged a close working relationship with MacArthur—no small feat, since the SWPA commander thought very poorly at the time of aviators and the AAF as a whole. Kenney quickly disabused him of this self-defeating bias. He built the Fifth Air Force into a powerful weapon that enhanced Allied operational mobility and largely wrested control of the skies—and hence the seas as well—from the Japanese in the South Pacific. "We never could have moved out of Australia if General Kenney hadn't taken the air away from the Jap," MacArthur once remarked. Kenney resided two floors below MacArthur's private apartment at the Lennon's Hotel in Brisbane, where the supreme commander lived with Jean and Arthur. The two men developed such a rapport that Kenney enjoyed rare unfettered access to the otherwise aloof SWPA commander. On many evenings, the airman dropped in unannounced and ended up staying for hours, engrossed in deep professional conversation with MacArthur. "We would talk til about two in the morning, discussing some move we should make and [we] came to quite a lot of decisions that way," Kenney later recalled.

As the early weeks of 1944 unfolded, Kenney's bombers and fighters carried out a steady procession of raids against Japanese airfields in northern New Guinea and the Admiralties, a grouping of volcanic islands located near the equator, 200 miles north of the New Guinea coast. In more than a year and a half of grinding, costly operations, MacArthur's SWPA forces had advanced about 350 miles, securing only one-third of New Guinea's long north coast. At this rate, it might take him three more years to navigate the world's second-largest island and put himself in a position to return to the Philippines, an objective that was not only a strategic aim for MacArthur but something of a personal obsession. In the meantime, Nimitz's forces, by seizing the Gilberts and the Marshalls, had leaped some 2,000 miles forward in the general direction of the Japanese home islands, outshining the less glamorous, plodding SWPA advance. At this pace, the Joint Chiefs might well elect to consign SWPA to nothing more than dead-end flank protection in favor of affording full support to Nimitz in the Central Pacific.

An increasingly impatient MacArthur planned to leapfrog across the New Guinea coast in 1944. To secure his northern flank and slip a decisive noose around Rabaul, he also intended, at the suggestion of the Joint Chiefs, to invade Los Negros and Manus, the two key islands in the Admiralties. Shaped like a boomerang, imprinted by inlets, harbors, swamps, and grassy plains over twenty-five miles from tip to tip, Los Negros is actually separated from larger Manus to the west only by a narrow spit of water known as the Loniu Pasage. Manus stretches about fifty miles from west to east, with a depth of sixteen miles, and is primarily coated with dense, impassable rain forest and mountain ranges, enriched by 154 inches of precipitation per year. Of particular interest to the Americans were the Seeadler Harbor on Los Negros's west coast, the Lorengau airfield in northeastern Manus, and the Momote airfield, nestled in a coconut grove along Los Negros's east coast. Before Kenney's aviators neutralized them in early 1944, Japanese aircraft flying from these bases had been in a position to menace MacArthur's New Guinea landings and bomb General Griswold's perimeter on Bougainville. On February 3 alone, the Americans destroyed eighty enemy aircraft. Between January 22 and February 24, the Fifth Air Force flew four hundred bomber sorties and dropped 650

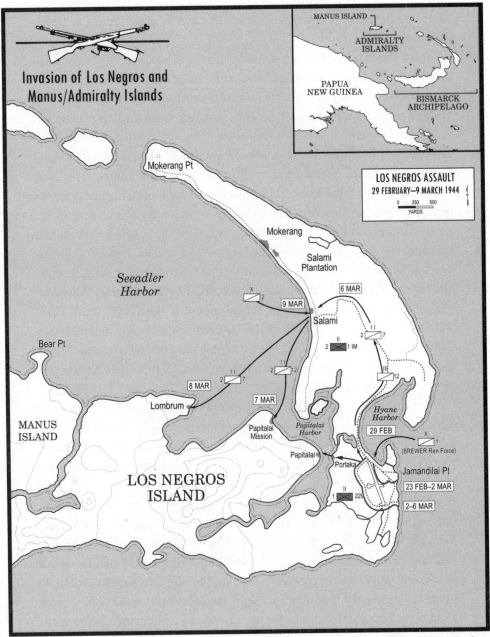

Invasion of Los Negros and
Manus/Admiralty Islands

MANUS ISLAND

ADMIRALTY
ISLANDS

PAPUA
NEW GUINEA

BISMARCK
ARCHIPELAGO

LOS NEGROS ASSAULT
29 FEBRUARY—9 MARCH 1944
0   250   500
YARDS

Mokerang Pt

Mokerang

Salami
Plantation

Seeadler
Harbor

6 MAR

X 2
9 MAR

Salami

2 7

2 1 IM

12

Bear Pt

2 7

2 12

8 MAR

Lombrum

7 MAR

Hyane
Harbor

29 FEB

MANUS
ISLAND

Papitalai
Mission

Papitalai
Harbor

Papitalai

Porlaka

X 1
(BREWER Ren Force)

LOS NEGROS
ISLAND

1 229

Jamandilai Pt

23 FEB–2 MAR

2–6 MAR

© 2021 by Chris Erichsen

tons of bombs on the Admiralties, particularly the Momote airfield. Eventually, all Japanese resistance ceased; the American planes did not even encounter antiaircraft fire.

From about mid-February onward, Japanese bases on the islands appeared deserted. On February 23, a trio of B-25 Mitchell medium bombers even flew over the area for ninety minutes at altitudes as low as twenty feet and saw no sign of any human presence, not even from the tiny population of Melanesians who lived there. What was more, the fliers noticed that the airfields were overgrown with grass, seemingly abandoned. Major General Ennis Whitehead, Kenney's able and trusted deputy commander, forwarded these reconnaissance reports and photographs to his boss in Brisbane. In late November, MacArthur had ordered Sixth Army to prepare for an April 1 invasion of the two islands. But with the Japanese apparently emasculated or in retreat from Los Negros and Manus, Kenney grew excited about the possibility of accelerating this timetable, especially because, after many a late-night conversation with MacArthur, he understood all too well his boss's anxieties about the progress of the SWPA war. "There was still a heap of dirt in front of the Jap field hospital door that had been piled there two days before by the bombing," Kenney later wrote. "There had been no washing on the lines for three days. In short, Los Negros was ripe for the picking."

Based on this information, Kenney doubted that any more than a few hundred demoralized Japanese remained in the area. He understood the potency of airpower and the development of island bases better than anyone on either side of this war. Los Negros and Manus offered nice stepping-stone bases. His office and MacArthur's were located on different floors of Brisbane's AMP Insurance building. Intrigued by the possibility of conquering valuable Los Negros easily, he rushed upstairs to see MacArthur. Relating Whitehead's reports, he urged MacArthur to authorize an immediate invasion. Kenney figured a few hundred infantrymen to seize a beachhead, plus some engineers to develop the Momote airfield, would do the trick. He argued that if he was right about Japanese weakness, a quick victory beckoned; if not, then the expeditionary force could always withdraw to ships under cover of naval gunfire and air strikes. Instead of calling it an invasion, and risking the perception of a humiliating reversal if it failed, he suggested terming it a reconnaissance in force. Since time was of the essence, he urged MacArthur to unleash the operation within the next few days. As MacArthur listened, he paced and occasionally nodded. At last, sold on the concept, he paused and said of Kenney's idea, "That will put the cork in the bottle." In other words, control of the Admiralties would permanently isolate Japanese garrisons at Rabaul, New Ireland, and other smaller South Pacific islands, thus dooming them to either starvation or strategic irrelevance. Excited about the boldness of the concept, MacArthur immediately ordered Major General Stephen Chamberlin, his operations officer (G3), and his primary naval subordinate Vice Admiral Thomas Kinkaid, commander of the Seventh Fleet, to coordinate invasion plans with Kenney and Krueger for a landing on Los Negros no later than February 29.[1]

Kenney's proposal hinged on the notion that Los Negros and Manus were largely deserted or, at best, defended by only a handful of ineffective Japanese dead-enders. He apparently based this notion exclusively on photo reconnaissance. Other than this, he did not explain to MacArthur exactly how he came up with his estimate of Japanese numerical strength. At the same time, MacArthur's intelligence officer (G2) Brigadier General Charles Willoughby reckoned that 4,050 Japanese soldiers defended the two islands. Willoughby's analytical process was more sophisticated than Kenney's. The intelligence officer had derived his appraisal from order-of-battle data he had painstakingly collected over the previous months and Ultra, the code name for top secret intelligence derived from breaking Japanese naval codes and the Imperial Army's Water Transport code. He had identified the presence of the Imperial Navy's 14th Naval Base Force and the Imperial Army's 51st Transportation Regiment, as well as the 2nd Battalion, 1st Independent Mixed Regiment, and the 1st Battalion, 229th Infantry Regiment. In his opinion, the Japanese were not gone; they were simply concealing themselves to avoid more bombing and to spring an ambush on unwitting American invaders. "Cumulative evidence does not support air observer reports that the islands have been evacuated," he wrote in a late-February intelligence summary.

Willoughby was the sort of man who took his job and himself with equal seriousness. Born Karl Weidenbach in Germany to a baron father and an American mother, he had immigrated with her to America in 1910 at the age of eighteen, became an American citizen, and took her surname. Ambitious and bright, Willoughby had entered the Army as a private soldier during World War I, earned a regular commission, and worked his way up through a series of staff and instructor positions to become a high-level staff officer. Colonel Bonner Fellers, another member of the SWPA staff who came to know him well, once described him as "a stern man . . . a professional soldier from the ground up." Handsome and physically imposing at six foot three and 220 pounds, prone to temperamental outbursts and personal intriguing, Willoughby carried himself like a European military aristocrat. Frequently, he clicked his heels and bowed deeply from the waist when introducing himself; when he met a woman, he took her hand and kissed it, the precursor to many a tryst. Behind his back, staff colleagues and intimidated subordinates from his vast intelligence section referred to him as Baron von Willoughby, Herr Hindenburg, Sir Charles, or even Bonnie Prince Charles. With acid-tongued contempt, Captain Raymond Tarbuck, a naval liaison officer attached to SWPA, once dismissively described Willoughby as a "Prussian type. All he needed was a spiked helmet. He was self opinionated, immovable and dull." Fluent in Spanish, French, and German, Willoughby was occasionally self-conscious enough about the slight German cadence in his speech to affect an Oxford accent. "Do you think I have too much of a Prussian accent?" he once asked Lieutenant Colonel Roger Egeberg, MacArthur's personal physician. "No, get rid of your accent and speak unaccented American English," the irreverent doctor replied, much to Willoughby's chagrin.

An avid military historian and extremist right in his personal politics, Willoughby had escaped from the Philippines with MacArthur. "He was basically a historian rather than an intelligence officer," judged Kenney, who considered Willoughby a friend and thought highly of him as an analyst. Jealous of any perceived slight by colleagues or encroachment on his intelligence bailiwick, an administrative empire builder par excellence, Willoughby was obsequiously loyal to MacArthur, who tended to favor sycophancy over effectiveness from staff members. For all of Willoughby's undeniable intellectual heft and curiosity, he had a disquieting propensity to misread enemy intentions and capabilities. To this point in the war, he had compiled a mixed record of semi-accurate and inaccurate estimates. MacArthur afforded due consideration to his report about enemy strength in the Admiralties, but refused to alter his plans.[2]

At Cape Cretin, New Guinea, Chamberlin paid a personal visit to show the reconnaissance photographs to Krueger. The unmoved Sixth Army commander shared Willoughby's concerns. Krueger's own intelligence section placed Japanese strength at forty-five hundred. Highly cautious by nature, and endlessly empathetic to the perilous plight of combat soldiers, Krueger did not like the idea of going into Los Negros with a makeshift force against an enemy of undetermined strength and capability. "It doesn't take a genius to fool aerial reconnaissance," he told a staffer. Yearning for a more complete picture of the Japanese presence, he decided to send his newly created Alamo Scouts on their first clandestine reconnaissance mission. In November, he had established the Alamo training center on Fergusson Island, under the command of Lieutenant Colonel Frederick Bradshaw from his intelligence section. From all over Sixth Army, hundreds of volunteers had descended on the center. Bradshaw developed an intense selection and training program. "Selectees had to possess the highest qualities of courage, stamina, intelligence and adaptability," Krueger later wrote. Prospects were subjected to extensive interviews and physical fitness tests. Anyone who did not have perfect vision and good swimming skills was immediately rejected. Bradshaw especially focused on finding even-tempered, selfless, independent thinkers. "In addition to having a solid background in ground combat, it was required to have a high sense of duty, intelligence with imagination, self discipline, common sense, good physical condition, and an unselfish and stable emotional background," wrote Major Gibson Niles, who later served as the unit's executive officer.

Those who made it through the screening process immediately underwent a grueling six-week training program personally designed by Bradshaw. They trained in map and compass reading, the mastery of infantry weapons, scouting and patrolling, intelligence gathering, jungle survival, cross-cultural communication, radio communication, and making amphibious landings from rubber boats. Almost two hours of every training day was devoted to physical conditioning, with a strong emphasis on swimming and hiking. "Each Alamo Scout was required to develop any inherent skill he possessed, such as leadership, marksmanship, knife throwing, jungle tracking, swimming, hiding, freezing," Krueger wrote. "All received intensive training in taking care of themselves in the jungle, for example, how to recognize and use edible roots and plants and how to obtain water from sling plants." Attrition rates ran as high as 40 percent. Knowing that group chemistry and personal selflessness were crucial to the survival of any Alamo Scout team operating in enemy territory, trainers kept a keen eye out for character flaws. Loud talkers, braggarts, rebels, and egotists were quickly culled out. Trainees even turned in secret ballots listing which of their classmates they most trusted to serve with on a team and which officers they would follow. Bradshaw wanted adaptive, resourceful team players, and he could afford to be choosy. Many of those who made it through selection and the six-week training course were never actually assigned to an operational team, though they did earn the coveted title of Alamo Scout. Of the 325 soldiers who became an Alamo Scout in the course of the war, only 138, or 42 percent, ever served on a team. The others took their skills back to their original units.

The first four teams of six men apiece had graduated on February 5. Interestingly, over 20 percent of the original selectees were Native Americans. For the Los Negros reconnaissance, Bradshaw selected a team led by Lieutenant John McGowen, a hard-charging twenty-five-year-old Texan with a master's degree from Texas A&M. McGowen had carefully chosen all five of his team members—Tech Sergeant Cesar Ramirez, Sergeant Walter McDonald, Sergeant John Roberts, PFC John Lagoud, and Private Paul Gomez. They received an extensive briefing from Bradshaw and Colonel Horton White, Krueger's G2. They were to go into Los Negros under cover of an air raid on the Momote airfield. They studied photographs and detailed maps, blackened their faces, geared up, and, in the dark early morning hours of February 26, boarded a Navy PBY Catalina amphibious flying boat piloted by Lieutenant Walter Pierce.

True to form, Krueger personally saw them off and stressed the importance of their mission. "This is our first mission," he told them, "our first time at bat. You know how important it is."

"Don't worry, General, we'll hit a home run," McGowen replied.

Each man wore a camouflaged jungle suit and carried a poncho, two grenades, and a couple days' supply of K rations. The team was equipped lightly with one SCR-300 walkie-talkie-style radio, four M1 carbines, and a couple of Thompson submachine guns. Their mission and purpose were strikingly similar to the long-range reconnaissance patrols (LRRPs) that would become so ubiquitous a generation later in Vietnam. Though their combat skills were superb, fighting was not their job. They were information gatherers, steely-nerved observers who thrived on stealth, field craft, secrecy, and teamwork.

The plane took off from Finschhafen, but a heavy storm forced Lieutenant Pierce to abort the mission and return to base. After enduring this adrenaline surge and letdown, the team reboarded the plane the next night in calmer weather and made it to Los Negros later than planned but otherwise without incident. The plane landed at 0645 in broad daylight on choppy waters about half a mile off the southeastern coast, farther away than McGowen wanted. Less than pleased, he and the team manhandled a rubber boat into the water and took thirty minutes to paddle ashore, an eternity under the circumstances. McGowen figured their chances of making it ashore undetected in full daylight were nonexistent, and he was right. Unbeknownst to the Americans, a patrolling Japanese soldier spotted them and excitedly reported their presence to Colonel Yoshio Ezaki, the Japanese commander in the Admiralties, who dispatched search patrols and began shifting troops away from the Momote airfield and the eastern coast of Los Negros in the direction of the McGowen team's landing site. What's more, the air strike did not materialize until a couple of hours later, after the team had already been spotted.

Meanwhile, in the tropical stillness, under full noise discipline, the six Americans deflated their boat as quietly as possible. "The hiss of air as it escaped from the rubber boat sounded to the team as if a thousand locomotives were letting off steam," Major Niles later wrote. With the boat safely hidden, they plunged into the welcome concealment afforded by the thick jungle inland from the beach, where they began patrolling in the direction of the Momote airfield. Within a few hours, they found trench systems, camouflaged vines, and voices indicative of an extensive Japanese troop presence. Through the jungle muffle, they heard the sound of the delayed bombing raid and enemy antiaircraft fire. At one point, a patrol of some fifteen Japanese soldiers materialized only about fifteen feet away, moving perpendicular to them. McGowen and the others immediately froze in place. One of the Japanese soldiers seemed to look right at the team leader. It took all the discipline in his constitution to keep still. Several excruciating seconds passed. Somehow the Japanese did not see him and the enemy patrol moved on, oblivious to how close they had come to finding their quarry. After this spine-tingling close call, McGowen decided he had found all the evidence he needed that the enemy was present in strength on Los Negros and intended to defend it. He saw no need to go all the way to Momote, jeopardize the safety of his men, only to confirm what he already knew. With the unanimous consent of the whole team, he opted to go back to the beach, hunker down for the night, and arrange for extraction the next morning. "I don't know who said the Japs were gone from this island, but I wish the bastard was here with us," Ramirez whispered indignantly.

They reconnoitered the southeastern coast some more, set up a security perimeter, and spent a tense night on watch, unmolested by the Japanese. Shortly after daybreak, they called for extraction, and in case something went wrong with the pickup, McGowen made sure to relate the information he had gathered. By radio, he passed along a cryptic, ominous report that Los Negros was "lousy with Japs." When Lieutenant Pierce's PBY arrived, he was so anxious to take off that he kept the aircraft in motion. McGowen's team struggled aboard as best they could, wet, angry, tired, but relieved to be headed back to base. They had seen the evidence with their own eyes. The idea that the Japanese were gone from Los Negros or too weak to defend it was wishful thinking.[3]

When Kenney received the McGowen team's report, he reacted with patronizing skepticism. Though he had never set foot on Los Negros, he was confident he knew it better than the Alamo Scouts who had been there and lived to tell about it. "The report meant nothing," he scribbled in his diary. "The scouts landed right where the Japs should be to keep away from the airdrome area where they have been bombed. If there are 25 nips in those woods, at night, the place would be 'lousy with Japs.'" Here was a prime example of an airpower evangelist so persuaded of his faith that he momentarily lost touch with the commonsense reality that firsthand, on-the-ground human intelligence tends to trump information gathered at a distance. Undoubtedly, McGowen and his men were parochial in their view of Japanese capabilities; the lieutenant's report was anything but detailed. However, while Kenney sat safely in his Brisbane office, confident that his aerial pictures painted a full portrait of the enemy, the Scouts were deep in enemy territory, observing him firsthand. Their experiences strongly indicated that Los Negros was occupied and defended. What's more, they hinted at the uncomfortable truth that Ezaki's men had deliberately refrained from shooting at Kenney's reconnaissance planes for the express purpose of making the Americans think Los Negros was deserted, presumably to spring an ambush against an invasion. In other words, McGowen's team had discovered that they were playing possum. (No one seems to have noticed or commented on the antiaircraft fire heard by the team.)

For all Kenney's excellence as an airpower strategist, he understood little about ground warfare and the lot of the average soldier. His dismissal of the Alamo Scout report was merely a symptom of this flaw in the makeup of an otherwise first-rate leader. By contrast, Krueger knew and understood soldiers to their core. From his days in the Philippine-

American War, he knew what it was like to patrol in a forbidding jungle, match wits with a wily enemy on his own ground, and hope to survive. So Krueger took the Alamo Scout report very seriously. His staff had personally handpicked these men and he trusted their judgment. Krueger's original plan for Operation Brewer, as the Admiralties operation was known, called for a division-size invasion of fifteen-mile-wide Seeadler Harbor on Los Negros's western coast, the most desirable landing spot. In response to MacArthur's reconnaissance-in-force order on February 24, Krueger had spent the next several days huddling with his staff and naval commanders to improvise a new, less ambitious Los Negros invasion plan. Instead of assaulting the Seeadler Harbor, they opted to hit a narrow twelve-hundred-yard-long sandy beach at lagoon-size Hyane Harbor on the island's east coast. Oval shaped, bordered by mangrove swamps, and accessible only through a fifty-yard gap between two peninsular spits of land, Hyane was anything but an ideal landing place. Only a handful of landing craft could make it through the gap at any given time, and they might be subjected to flanking fire from the peninsulas on either side. But Hyane did offer the advantage of close proximity to the Momote airfield. Plus, the Japanese did not expect an invasion there.

As always, shipping dictated the composition of the invasion force. Rear Admiral Daniel Barbey, commander of the VII Amphibious Corps, had predicated his Brewer plans on the April 1 invasion date. Due to the accelerated timetable, he could not muster any attack transports, nor any attack cargo ships, and precious few landing craft. The cerebral Barbey was fast becoming MacArthur's go-to admiral for invasions. Many in SWPA referred to him as "Uncle Dan the Amphibious Man." Like any good commander, he improvised. He scraped together a trio of high-speed transport (APD) converted destroyers, each of which could carry about a company of soldiers. Together, these three ships were capable of transporting some five hundred men, about half the size of the scratch force Krueger wanted to send in to Hyane Harbor. Barbey also had eleven conventional destroyers (DD) available for the invasion. He ordered the skippers of nine of these destroyers to carry whatever ground pounders they could. In general, about fifty-seven soldiers could fit aboard each destroyer. "It was a pretty meager force to go out on such an important mission," he later wrote. Though the plan was hardly ideal, Barbey found a way to move 1,026 men aboard these vessels.

Weeks earlier, Krueger had chosen Major General Innis Palmer Swift's

1st Cavalry Division for the job of securing the Admiralties. Eager for action and extensively trained, with a solid foundation of regular NCOs and officers, the division was unique among US Army combat units. Whereas most every other infantry division was built around a triangular structure with three regiments, the 1st Cavalry Division contained four regiments organized into a pair of brigades, both of which were commanded by a one-star general. Each regiment was composed of two squadrons, equivalent to a battalion in a conventional infantry unit. In addition to a headquarters troop, each squadron contained four troops (similar to a company in a standard unit) of about 150 soldiers apiece. The paucity of shipping and the constricted Hyane Harbor beach meant that the Americans could land only the 2nd Squadron, 5th Cavalry Regiment, plus supporting artillery, antiaircraft guns, medics, and other specialists, all of whom were officially known as the Brewer Reconnaissance Force. Their mission, according to an Army Ground Forces analyst, was to "land on the beach on the southwest shore of Hyane Harbor . . . and to make an immediate reconnaissance in force to determine enemy strength and dispositions." They were to seize the airfield so that engineers could subsequently prepare it for use by transport and combat planes. If the Brewer Reconnaissance Force encountered heavy opposition, they were to withdraw onto Barbey's ships, if such a thing was possible. If they succeeded in getting ashore and staying there, the rest of the 5th Cavalry Regiment, in addition to more medics, engineers, artillery batteries, antiaircraft batteries, and the 40th Naval Construction Battalion (known as Seabees), would land two days after D-day from LSTs and LCIs (these ships were too slow to make it to Los Negros in time for the February 29 invasion date).

The 1st Brigade commander, Brigadier General William Chase, a sturdy professional who had seen extensive combat in World War I, was the leader of the expedition. During training, Chase had met with individual units to brief them on the realities of battle. "I told them that they had to overcome the 'Thou shalt not kill' commandment because killing the enemy was now the main mission." Instead, he told them, their new motto would be "Move in on 'em and kill 'em!" To build esprit de corps, he dubbed his brigade the First Team, a moniker that ultimately stuck for the division as a whole.

Chase had seen enough combat to understand the perilous nature of his mission, but a meeting with Krueger only added to his concerns. "[He] was rather pessimistic . . . and far from encouraging, a fact which puzzled and worried me." Chase knew that both Sixth Army and 1st Cavalry Division intelligence sources agreed with Willoughby about the size of the Japanese garrison. In fact, the division G2 section thought there might be as many as five thousand Japanese on the island. With gallows humor typical of combat units, Lieutenant Colonel Roy Lassetter, the division intelligence officer, sent this estimate to Major Julio Chiaramonte, the Brewer Task Force intelligence officer, with a cynical note: "Julio, see you in heaven." Thus, the division's leaders understood—even if Kenney did not—that the Japanese were likely to outnumber the Los Negros invaders. They simply hoped the enemy could not or would not concentrate their full force at the invasion beach. On the afternoon of February 27, Chase and his troopers boarded their ships at New Guinea's Oro Bay. The invasion fleet set sail for Los Negros the next afternoon and evening. Aboard ship, Chase and his staff had the opportunity to meet with Lieutenant McGowen, who "gave us a great deal of very valuable information. We knew we had some opposition, but just what 'lousy' meant was a question."[4]

Indeed, that was the ultimate question. MacArthur may not necessarily have known the answer, but he alone possessed the power to determine whether Chase's troopers would find out firsthand. MacArthur decided to accompany the invasion fleet himself. The supreme commander had an ambivalent relationship with the beast of battle, a curious mixture of courage and distortion. To some extent, he had built his vaunted reputation on World War I battle exploits as a brigade commander, though he had probably arranged for some of his own decorations. In the Philippines, he had visited his embattled troops at Bataan only once or twice in a rear area while issuing communiqués that hinted at a fictional constant presence on the front lines. Some of his bitter troops had taken to calling him "Dugout Doug," a disrespectful and unfair nickname for a man who willingly faced many Japanese bombs and shells at his headquarters on Corregidor, one of the most heavily bombarded islands in World War II. During the nightmarish Buna campaign in 1942, he had never set foot anywhere near the battlefield, though his communiqués created an impression of frontline, hands-on leadership, when in reality Eichelberger was actually running the battle, routinely risking death. The following year, MacArthur had insisted on observing firsthand from a B-17 as paratroopers from the 503rd Parachute Infantry Regiment made the first American combat airborne jump at Nadzab, New Guinea. Though the landing turned out to be unopposed, MacArthur could not have known this beforehand. MacArthur clearly had no compunction about risking his life, but he seemed driven to exaggerate brazenly an otherwise honorable record. When Kenney found out about his intention to go along on Operation Brewer, he attempted to persuade him to opt for a safer aerial role. "I tried to talk him into going on a B24, even bribing him with the suggestion that he pull the bomb release himself," Kenney told his diary. MacArthur would not hear of it. He turned to Kenney: "I have been taking chances at being shot at all the years I have been in the Army and I am going to continue taking chances when it is advisable."

But for a man of MacArthur's complexity, his motivation for any action seldom stopped at the surface. Beyond his intrinsic courage, MacArthur probably had another reason for his participation in the operation. Nimitz had recently recommended to the Joint Chiefs that Manus should come under Navy administrative control, specifically Vice Admiral William "Bull" Halsey's South Pacific command, once the 1st Cavalry Division secured bases in the Admiralties. The territorial MacArthur's reaction had been vehement to the point of near hysteria. He argued with anyone who would listen, from Halsey to Marshall, that the Admiralties must remain under the SWPA aegis. He even threatened to turn away any naval forces not directly under his command. The matter would soon resolve in his favor, but as D-Day at Los Negros approached, it was still pending. "I think the Old Man feels that if he himself with his bare hands goes in and takes Manus they can't transfer the place to the Navy," Kenney confided to his diary a few days before the invasion. "He may not even admit that is the way he is thinking to himself, but I have a hunch it applies."

On the morning of February 27, MacArthur bid goodbye to Jean and Arthur, slipped out of the Lennon's Hotel, and was driven to Archerfield Airport on Brisbane's outskirts, where he and his entourage boarded his personal plane, a B-17 named *Bataan* (the irony of the name seemed lost on MacArthur). They flew to Milne Bay, New Guinea, deplaned, and boarded the light cruiser USS *Phoenix*. It was the first time MacArthur had been aboard a naval vessel since he had left the Philippines nearly two years earlier. The cruiser journeyed west and linked up with the troop-bearing ships at Cape Cretin near Finschhafen. The next morning, Krueger came aboard and shared McGowen's troubling, albeit cryptic, report with MacArthur. Unruffled, the SWPA commander said, "We shall continue as planned, gentlemen." He already knew the risks. If Willoughby and Krueger were right about the size of the Japanese garrison, the enemy would outnumber Chase's force by a four-to-one factor. Theoretically, Colonel Ezaki could overwhelm them, push them into the sea. Not only would this lead to a major strategic reversal for the Allies, but it might sound the death knell for MacArthur's career and any notions of a return to the Philippines. But MacArthur knew that the Japanese were unlikely to launch a well-planned, fully coordinated counterattack against the invaders. He knew of their strong propensity for mounting ill-planned, piecemeal attacks—he had seen this firsthand in the Philippines and had studied enough about the Battle of Guadalcanal to understand it even better. The protective firepower of Barbey's ships and Kenney's planes would probably keep the Japanese from snuffing out an American-held perimeter. Moreover, he was confident he could reinforce Chase well enough and soon enough to turn the manpower and matériel quotient on Los Negros in the Americans' favor. Even if Kenney's estimate of Japanese strength was dead wrong, the decision to invade was, in MacArthur's estimation, still a calculated risk, not an irresponsible gamble. The possibility of grabbing bases in a weakly held Japanese island group, isolating Rabaul, and substantially speeding up his advance through the Southwest Pacific more than justified the potential danger. As he told an aide, he had "everything to win, little to lose. I bet ten to win a million, if I hit the jackpot."

Krueger understood the decision to continue with the invasion, but he could not fathom why MacArthur insisted on personally going along. In the Sixth Army commander's estimation, it imperiled his boss's life for no appreciable purpose. "He had forbidden me to accompany our assault landings and yet now proposed to do so himself," Krueger later wrote. "I argued that it was unnecessary and unwise to expose himself in this fashion and that it would be a calamity if anything happened to him." MacArthur heard him out but said flatly, "I have to go."

That evening, as *Phoenix* and the other ships approached Los Negros, MacArthur enjoyed a nice dinner of beef and corn pudding with Vice Admiral Kinkaid, the ship's skipper, Captain Albert Noble, and others. The general liked the corn pudding so much that he got the recipe from Noble. After the meal, MacArthur spent hours on deck, silently staring at the sea, and circulated around the ship, signing autographs with sailors, chatting with aides. When one subordinate expressed concerns about the 5th Cavalry's lack of combat experience, MacArthur reassured him by pointing to the unit's proud lineage and an incident from his childhood. "I have known this 5th Cavalry for almost sixty years. When I was a little boy of four my

father was a captain in the 13th Infantry at Fort Selden, in the Indian frontier country of New Mexico. Geronimo, the Apache scourge, was loose,
and our small infantry garrison was to guard the middle fords of the Rio
Grande. A troop of this same 5th Cavalry . . . rode through to help us. I can
still remember how I felt when I watched them clatter into the little post,
their tired horses gray with desert dust. They'd fight then . . . and they'll
fight now. Don't worry about them." Outwardly calm, MacArthur nonetheless did struggle with some internal jitters. In the middle of the night,
he woke up and sent a guard to fetch Egeberg, the physician. When Egeberg arrived in the general's cabin, MacArthur proceeded to pace around
and regale him with tales from his youth, "particularly about his years at
West Point." As if compelled to give a personal testimony of his life, Mac-
Arthur progressed the narrative to his experiences in the Philippines and
then France during World War I. "We sat and talked . . . and I listened for
about half an hour while he gradually calmed down, and then rather suddenly said he would like to go to sleep."[5]

In the predawn darkness on February 29, the excited troopers of the
Brewer Reconnaissance Force gorged themselves on a meal of steak, eggs,
potatoes, pancakes, bread, butter, jam, and coffee. As the sun slowly ascended over the eastern horizon, they craned their necks for a glimpse of
their target. "The island had a flat, marshy-looking foreshore, made flatter
by the level tops and the straight white trunks of a coconut grove," Charles
Rawlings, an embedded correspondent for the *Saturday Evening Post*, later
wrote. At 0740, under cover of a bombardment from *Phoenix*, the light
cruiser USS *Nashville*, and the destroyers, the lead troops climbed into a
dozen LCPRs (Landing Craft, Personnel, Ramped), low-silhouette, early-
model Higgins boats suspended on davits. One by one, naval crewmen
lowered the boats into the choppy waters. Beneath a cloudy, gray morning
sky, the four boats of the first wave headed for Hyane Harbor. Several
troopers retched, either from seasickness or sheer nervousness. Only a
handful of the supporting Fifth Air Force bombers and fighters made it
through thick cloud cover and rain squalls to attack their planned targets
on Los Negros. Against only desultory enemy fire, the first LCPR under
Lieutenant Marvin Henshaw landed at 0817, two minutes late. Henshaw led
his people across the beach to the coconut grove, where they took cover
behind felled trees as troopers from the other first-wave boats also scrambled across the beach and inland. Henshaw saw a Japanese soldier fleeing,

drew a bead on him with his carbine, and killed him. His men killed another Japanese in the distance.

In that first hour, as the LCPRs took turns making runs onto the beach in staggered waves, the deadliest Japanese opposition was directed against the boats in the water, not the assault troops who made it ashore. From hidden positions in the land spits that flanked the harbor entrance, enemy gunners unleashed machine-gun and small-caliber shell fire at the Higgins boats. In one instance, shells tore through the front ramp of a boat, blowing the head off a sailor, killing two soldiers, wounding several others, and leaving an ugly hole in the wooden ramp. "White splashes of water were plunging through the six-inch gap in the wooden gate," Corporal Bill Alcine, a *Yank* correspondent aboard the landing craft, wrote of the damage. Seaman 1st Class William Siebieda attempted to plug the hole even as he blazed away with a tommy gun at the unseen Japanese. "The water sloshed around him, running down his legs and washing the blood of the wounded into a pink frappe," Alcine wrote. In response to the Japanese opposition, destroyers USS *Mahan*, *Flusser*, and *Drayton* pounded them with sheets of 20- and 40-millimeter fire. Four of the twelve LCPRs were damaged, though only one beyond repair. Because their numbers were so limited and they were so crucial to any potential evacuation of Los Negros, they landed later waves under protective guard by the destroyers rather than adhering to a strict schedule.

Ashore, an uneasy quiet prevailed as the Brewer Task Force landed almost entirely intact and quickly overran the Momote airfield. They found the place in total disrepair, overgrown with weeds, pocked by watery bomb craters, littered with rusty, useless equipment, and, in Alcine's recollection, "a sorry-looking Jap bulldozer." American casualties so far totaled four dead and six wounded. By early afternoon, the Americans were patrolling beyond Momote against almost nonexistent resistance. They found abandoned kitchens, officers' quarters, a warehouse full of food, and a bivouac area for a recently vacated antiaircraft unit (elements of which probably accounted for the fire against the boats). General Chase radioed Krueger, "Enemy situation undetermined." Leery of overextending himself, and knowing that a Japanese response to his successful landing was probably inevitable, he ordered Lieutenant Colonel William Lobit, the 2nd Squadron commander, to pull his troops back to the airfield. "There's something besides cockatoos in those woods," Lobit said of the area beyond the airfield. His troopers began to set up a stingray-shaped perimeter along the runway, anchored along both flanks at the beach with the southern peninsula of Hyane Harbor at their backs. Ammunition and ration boxes were already piled up on the beach; communication wires snaked through sand and mud tracks like ebony vines. A steady, driving rain poured down throughout much of the afternoon, prompting the men to don their ponchos.[6]

Aboard *Phoenix*, MacArthur had spent the day prowling back and forth between the bridge and the deck, watching the bombardment, craning his neck for any indication of how the landings were unfolding. At 1600, after an entire day of this uncertainty, he decided to inspect the newly won beachhead for himself. Clad in khaki pants and shirt, a long gray trench coat, and with a layer of protective cellophane coating his telltale braided cap, he boarded a landing craft with Kinkaid, Egeberg, and several war correspondents at his side. The downpour had given way to a drizzle. As the boat entered Hyane Harbor and neared the beach, MacArthur stood upright, reminding an admiring *Newsweek* correspondent of Washington crossing the Delaware. The boat landed safely and MacArthur began to inspect the perimeter. He personally decorated Lieutenant Henshaw, who had led the first wave ashore, with the Distinguished Service Cross. "It does me great honor to pin this medal on your breast, where, for all eyes and all time, it will be a symbol of the courage and devotion with which you have fought for your country," he told the thirty-year-old Texan. Clad in helmet and poncho, Henshaw shifted his carbine to his left hand and shook hands with MacArthur.

Word of the SWPA commander's presence spread quickly among the soldiers, prompting amazement and consternation. "I wonder if the C in C realizes we are still killing enemies here?" Lobit asked an aide. "I don't know, sir. I don't think he minds," came the reply. Though the area remained quiet, with no obvious danger, Chase shared their concerns for the theater commander's safety in such uncomfortably close proximity to the front lines. "It was a heavy responsibility to have the General visit our sector," he later wrote. In the recollection of one MacArthur aide, his presence generated significant excitement. When soldiers caught a glimpse of him, "they were astonished, but there was a great glow in their faces." The soldier glow probably stemmed from a mixture of modern military emotions—awe at being in the presence of a celebrity, the uniqueness of any encounter with a high-ranking general, respect for his willingness to face danger, and perhaps a tantalizing sense that the situation must be in hand if he felt confident enough to visit. "Golly, that makes me feel better," one GI remarked when he saw MacArthur. "I was getting worried."

At nearly every step, photographers snapped pictures and the entourage trailed along. Obviously used to being the center of attention, MacArthur seemed to give this circus-like atmosphere scarcely a thought. Instead, he was determined to get a personal feel for the terrain. With the duty of reinforcing or withdrawing his "reconnaissance in force" firmly on his shoulders, he wanted to see the situation for himself, a laudable priority. MacArthur, Kinkaid, and Egeberg, accompanied by a reluctant Chase, made their way beyond the forward positions to see the airfield. Seemingly unconcerned about the possibility of drawing Japanese fire, MacArthur studied the runway, the craters, the soil, and the general layout of the field. To get a sense of the preinvasion bombing and bombardment, he personally measured the size of the craters. When he came upon a pair of dead Japanese soldiers, he took note, with a professional eye, of their uniforms and appearance. "He wanted to see whether they were officers or men, how they were equipped, and if there was evidence of the kind of outfit to which they belonged," Egeberg mused. Turning away from the bodies, MacArthur told the others, "That's the way I like to see them."

At one point, a soldier touched his sleeve, pointed to a spot in the jungle, and warned, "Excuse me, sir, but we killed a Jap sniper in there just a few minutes ago."

"Fine, that's the best thing to do with them," an unfazed MacArthur replied.

He moved on and spoke with a wounded soldier, asking how he got hit and how he felt. Though the soldiers admired the general's courage, as his battlefront visit stretched from minutes into hours, the tension over his presence grew. "General Chase was very, very anxious to get him out of there," Private Gaetano Faillace, MacArthur's photographer, asserted. In Egeberg's opinion, Chase was hardly the only one. According to the doctor, nearly everyone around the supreme commander "was uneasy about MacArthur's safety and, more vital to them, about their own safety."

At last, when the SWPA commander was ready to leave, he grasped Chase by the shoulder and looked him in the eye. "You have performed marvelously. Hold what you have taken, no matter against what odds. You have your teeth in him now—don't let go."

After fewer than two hours on the ground, he left and reboarded *Phoenix*. With a long look back at the island, he told a reporter, "I knew that whatever was there could not be better than the Fifth Cavalry." The troopers he had visited, and some latter-year historians, tended toward hyperbole in their memories of the MacArthur visit. He seemed to have that effect on people. "There were eight hundred pairs of Jap eyes . . . looking at him," one soldier claimed. "Why they didn't kill him, nobody knows." One officer claimed that he "completely ignored sniper fire [and] departed wet, cold, and dirty with mud up to the ears," as if the latter could have been possible. In a description more appropriate for a superhero than a military leader, one journalist gushed, "He stalks a battlefront like a man hardly human, not only arrogantly but lazily."

Undoubtedly, MacArthur did face real danger on Los Negros and, as was typical of him in any combat situation, he demonstrated steady, almost dismissive courage, maintaining a masterful mask of command, the sort that made a deep impression on his soldiers and enhanced their morale. However, at the time he visited Chase's perimeter, the Japanese were in a state of confusion and disarray. Shooting had died down to a state of near quietude; no shells of any kind exploded in the area, no bullets snapped, nor has there ever been any evidence that the Japanese actually saw him. Though Los Negros was a frontline position, it was a quiet one, experiencing a lull after a couple hours of desultory shooting much earlier in the day. MacArthur probably understood the degree of danger better than anyone else. Beyond the appealing opportunity to exorcise some of his "Dugout Doug" demons and inspire the invaders, his Los Negros visit afforded him the chance to make an informed decision about whether or not to continue with the operation or withdraw Chase's men. By the time the SWPA commander boarded *Phoenix*, ate a nice dinner, and then traveled with the ship back to New Guinea later that evening, he had made up his mind to keep going with Operation Brewer. Even with the lightly opposed landing, MacArthur by now realized that Willoughby and Krueger were right about Japanese numbers (and intentions) on Los Negros and Manus, and that Kenney was wrong. But his instincts told him that with the troopers of the 1st Cavalry Division now firmly ashore, they would be very difficult for the enemy to dislodge, especially with effective air and naval support. Moreover, he had seen enough of the Momote airfield to realize its potential use for his strategic cause. He ordered Krueger to reinforce Chase as quickly as he could.[7]

At the same time, Colonel Ezaki was scrambling to put together whatever forces he could to attack the American perimeter. He had not been surprised by the invasion itself, only its location. He knew from intercepted American submarine communications that a Los Negros invasion was imminent. The Alamo Scout landing served as further proof. He also fully understood the strategic implications of American control of the Admiralties. He had ordered his men to play possum with the express goal of luring an understrength American invasion force to land and this had come to pass. But he had expected the Americans to land at Seeadler Harbor, not Hyane, so most of his defenses were oriented in the wrong direction. What's more, after the south coast Alamo Scout landing, he had moved troops away from Momote on the mistaken assumption that this had to mean the main landing would come in that area.

Though his garrison outnumbered the Americans as a whole, he was in a tough spot. The enemy controlled the air and the sea. In the absence of total victory on the ground, he could not hope for reinforcement and resupply. His combat troops were oriented away from the American perimeter, hardly in good striking position. His two battalion commanders, Major Iwakani and Captain Baba, hated each other with a passion and were not inclined to work together, at least in the absence of major strongarming from Ezaki, whose authority they at least did recognize even though he hailed from the noncombat 51st Transportation Regiment. Iwakani's 2nd Battalion, 1st Mixed Independent Regiment, was deployed considerably north of the beachhead at the Salami Plantation, on the other side of a skidway the locals had built to drag their canoes to and from the northern part of Los Negros and the Hyane area. Tunesco Baba's 1st Battalion, 229th Infantry Regiment, was arrayed closer to the Americans, but still several hundred yards to the southwest of Momote through thick jungle. Ezaki's force was part of the Eighth Area Army, headquartered at Rabaul, under the command of Lieutenant General Hitoshi Imamura, who ordered him to snuff out the American beachhead. Ezaki understood that the longer he gave the Americans to dig in, reinforce, and flex their incredible logistical muscles, the more remote the chances of ever dislodging them. He knew he had to hit them immediately even though this would not afford him enough time to amass his own full strength for a coordinated, proper attack. He fully recognized the perils of expending his limited manpower in piecemeal attacks (as other Japanese commanders had at Guadalcanal in 1942) but felt he had little other choice—mainly because he did not.

Ezaki ordered Captain Baba to attack under cover of darkness and eliminate Chase's force. "This is not a delaying action," Ezaki told Baba and his people in a poignant attack order. "Be resolute to sacrifice your life for the Emperor and commit suicide in case capture is imminent. We must carry out our mission with the present strength and annihilate the enemy on the spot. I am highly indignant about the enemy's arrogant attitude. Remember to kill or capture all ranking enemy officers for our intelligence purposes." Some of the attackers moved in position along the muck of a small jungle trail. Others donned life jackets and planned to swim ashore and hit the Americans from behind.

Chase's troopers had fortified the perimeter as best they could. The rocky coral soil made digging a backbreaking, almost hopeless task. They used picks to hack out shallow foxholes. In general, two troopers squeezed uncomfortably into each hole. The Americans had no barbed wire and few mines. They hacked at the foliage to clear fields of fire as best they could. In an attempt to forge a continuous line, commanders placed the holes as close together as five or six yards. A pair of 75-millimeter howitzers were the only artillery support. Most of the fleet had left for the evening, but a pair of destroyers remained behind to provide fire support. Waiting on station-like nautical sentinels in the harbor, they stood ready to make up for the paucity in onshore artillery. Specially trained teams, known as Joint Assault Signal Companies, maintained communication with the destroyers. A dozen .50-caliber guns from the 673rd Antiaircraft Machine Gun Battalion, sited to cover nearly every route of advance, provided heavy fire support. Chase ordered all his men to stay in their holes and "shoot to kill anything that moves, ask questions later."

The nervous troopers, experiencing their first evening in combat, maintained a constant state of alert as the sun set over the lonely tropical perimeter. "We are alone," Sergeant Lawrence Baldus scrawled in his diary. "There are plenty of Japs on the island." In the dusky shadows, Captain Baba's troops edged forward in small, poorly organized groups, cutting communication wires, hurling grenades at the Americans, infiltrating among their foxholes as best they could. "You could hear them start blowing their whistles, blowing their bugles and then they would come out of that jungle . . . right at us," Lieutenant Sam Harris later said. Steady bursts of American machine-gun and rifle fire stabbed through the air. The American artillerymen and heavy machine gunners blazed away at any targets they could pinpoint in the darkness. Japanese knee mortars sprinkled shells around the American lines, inflicting few casualties but adding to the confusion. "There were long moments of complete darkness, just the jungle night dripping and breathing," Charles Rawlings, the embedded correspondent for the *Saturday Evening Post*, later wrote. "Then there would come the stuttering crazy red neon dance of our nervous machine-gun tracer, the woodpecker 'Ta-ta-ta-ta-ta' of the enemy's automatic fire with its dazzling white pellets. Then 'P-o-o-o-ow!' the sudden, ghastly, white-hot, upward vomit of a Jap grenade somewhere on the perimeter—somewhere inside the lines." In a racially loaded description of Japanese proficiency at infiltration, he claimed they could "melt through a white man's lines like a stalking furred animal, like an invisible wraith of smoke from a Shinto sacrifice altar."

For most of the night, intimate fighting raged on and off. Though there was little coherence to Baba's attack, and he soon suffered heavy casualties, many of his soldiers breached the small perimeter; some hurried or crept past foxholes; others swam ashore, took cover in vegetation, and attacked any Americans they could find. "The only way we could see the Japs was to let them get close enough so we could make them out against the sky over our holes," one trooper remembered, "then we'd cut loose." Japanese attackers popped up anywhere and everywhere. "Individuals and small groups were most aggressive," Colonel Marion Carson, an Army Ground Forces observer, chronicled. "They attacked our automatic weapons with grenades and knives, infiltrated into all parts of the position and cut all telephone lines."

A pair of them made it to a revetment in the center of the perimeter where General Chase had placed his headquarters. They paused to arm their grenades. Major Chiaramonte, the intelligence officer, noticed them and opened fire with his tommy gun, killing one and wounding the other. Corporal Joe Hodoski heard a commotion outside his hole, popped his head up, and found himself looking straight into the face of a Japanese machine gunner. "How you doin', Joe?" the shocked enemy soldier blurted. Instead of replying, Hodoski shot and killed him. Lieutenant Colonel Lobit had located his command post inside a captured triple-logged bunker with a hard, dry floor. At one point, a Japanese machine-gun crew actually began to set up their gun atop the bunker. "There was nothing to do but freeze and pray, with cold sweat starting," he later shuddered. Inexplicably, the enemy soldiers failed to make sure that the bunker was clear of Americans. In the meantime, Lieutenant Harris and several other soldiers in an adjacent position cut the machine-gun crew down with rifle fire. To Lobit, listening tensely underneath the logs a few feet below, the impact of the bullets sounded like "sugar plums splashing into hot custard." One wayward attacker ended up in a foxhole between a pair of infantrymen. As one American held him down, the other beat him to death with a rifle butt and then, for good measure, cut his throat. They spent the entire night bathed in the blood of their enemy, with his lifeless remains between them. An Army Air Forces major who was serving as a liaison officer for the Fifth Air Force had strung a hammock between a pair of trees and told *Yank* correspondent Corporal Bill Alcine, "There's nothing like comfort," before settling in for the night. A couple of colleagues tried to persuade him, in one of their recollections, "to make himself less conspicuous." Stealthy Japanese soldiers materialized and attacked him so suddenly that the groggy officer thought he was the victim of a mistaken friendly assault. Other Americans in the area heard him cry out, "Don't boys, it's me, the major!" The Japanese cut his throat and hacked him to death, nearly severing his head with a samurai sword. "Just a bit of neck skin held his head," Rawlings, who saw his body, later wrote.

Violent though it was, the Japanese attack was far too ill supported and poorly coordinated to fulfill Colonel Ezaki's goal of destroying the American beachhead. By sunrise on March 1, Baba's survivors had withdrawn. The Americans counted sixty-six enemy dead; seven Americans had been killed and fifteen wounded, half of whom had to be evacuated to the destroyer USS *Bush*. Other Japanese, including Baba and his command group, were trapped within the American lines. The 5th Cavalry troopers spent the day hunting them down and killing them. Either completely out of touch with the reality at the front, or for deceptive purposes, Colonel Ezaki wrote to General Imamura and claimed that his men had defeated the Americans and were in the process of mopping up survivors. Instead, of course, his men were dying in isolated, lonely encounters with their enemies. Under cover of the thick foliage, Baba's group spent the day stealthily creeping toward Chase's command post, probably intending to overrun it. By 1700, they had made it to within thirty-five yards of Chase, when the Americans glanced in their direction and noticed the brush moving. "One of the Japanese in the brush fired a shot at me and we all moved in with our guns blazing," Chase recalled. Chiaramonte and four others poured fire on the brush, closed in, and killed several of the enemy holdouts. Three Japanese blew their brains out with grenades. One used his sword to stab himself to death. When the Americans overran the Japanese position, they found seventeen corpses. The dead included Captain Baba, who, in Chiaramonte's ironical estimation, "died a glorious death for the greater co-prosperity sphere of Japan, ancestors and emperor." Among the dead, the cavalrymen found fifteen ceremonial swords, the most prized souvenir among GIs. Chase later gave Baba's sword to General Swift. The rest were divvied up among the troopers who had risked their lives to destroy the Baba patrol.[8]

Worried that the Japanese might hit him with better-organized, more powerful attacks, Chase asked Krueger for as many reinforcements and as much support as he could send. For the moment, though, there was little the Sixth Army commander could do besides adhere to the preinvasion landing schedules. Even so, in the course of the day, B-25s and B-17s dropped three tons of ammunition, mines, grenades, and medical supplies to the Brewer Task Force. The reinforcement convoy was due to arrive the following morning. As such, the evening of March 1–2 represented Colonel Ezaki's last realistic chance to destroy Chase's task force, though Chase could hardly have known this. With Baba's battalion shattered, and Ezaki's other units continually harassed by bombardment from the two destroyers and Fifth Air Force raids, he could manage only an ineffective series of lunges at the American line during the late afternoon and early evening hours of March 1. American firepower ravaged these men. The 75-millimeter pieces alone fired three hundred rounds and killed an untold number of Japanese soldiers.

At 0926 the following morning, the exhausted men of the Brewer Task Force were thrilled to see half a dozen LSTs, escorted by destroyers, arrive in Hyane Harbor. "LSTs a grand sight," an exultant Sergeant Baldus scrawled in his diary. The doors of the LSTs swung open and, under covering fire from three-inch guns and .50-caliber machine guns mounted on the decks, almost two thousand men of the support force landed safely. The reinforcements included the rest of the 5th Cavalry Regiment, more artillery, medics, engineers, and signalmen, and five hundred sailors from the Navy's 40th Construction Battalion. Aided by bulldozers, the newcomers immediately built ramps that hastened the unloading of supplies and vehicles. Crates of ammunition, food, and construction equipment were soon piled head high in the beach area, ready for movement inland. Antiaircraft batteries now defended the shore against seaborne infiltrators. With this welcome infusion of combat and engineering manpower, Chase was able, by day's end, to expand his perimeter to include the entire Momote airfield.

Aided by Seabee bulldozers, the troopers constructed a new front line of trenches and log-reinforced fighting holes, dugouts, or revetments. They dug in mortars and cleared vegetation, affording better fields of fire for machine guns. "From the time they landed until dark, the construction battalion and the combat engineer troops were engaged in burying enemy dead, clearing firing areas for field artillery and mortars, demolishing enemy dugouts and fortifications within the position, constructing a road from the beach, and assisting in the preparation of defenses in rear areas," Colonel Carson wrote. The engineers even found some time to begin grading Momote's runways.

The incorporation of the support force more than doubled Chase's manpower and firepower, even as Ezaki's force had diminished by at least 20 percent. With these crucial quotients now turning against Ezaki, his chances of eradicating the American presence were almost nil, though he knew he must still try. The colonel had no choice but to admit to Imamura that not only were the Americans far from defeated, they actually controlled the airfield. Ezaki promised to attack and destroy them immediately, but his remaining units were too dispersed and he could not get them into position for any substantial offensive action until the evening of March 3, affording the Americans even more time to strengthen their perimeter. They sowed mines and sited more automatic weapons. Bulldozers cleared away more brush, improving sight lines and increasing the operating sectors of mortar units. Though the Americans lacked barbed wire, they improvised. At every logical avenue of approach, they strung taut strands of communication wire ten inches off the ground, placed coral rocks inside C ration cans, and hung them on the wire to function as a warning signal of approaching Japanese. Artillerymen scattered metal ammunition containers around their guns to trip up any enemy interlopers who might not see them at night. At the same time, artillery gun crews and destroyers spewed harassing fire throughout the day and into the early evening.

At 2100, with flickering flares only occasionally lighting up the eerie darkness, the Japanese struck. Major Iwakani's 2nd Battalion, 1st Independent Regiment, carried out the main assault across the skidway, on the northwest side of the American perimeter (Baba's survivors launched a weak parry against the southwest sector). Many of Iwakani's troops had tied bandages tightly around their arms so that they could keep fighting even if a limb was shattered or severed. They made little effort to move with stealth.

They laughed and shouted the names of American officers; some even sang "Deep in the Heart of Texas," a tune they had undoubtedly overheard their adversaries singing. Others roared nonsensical threats like "We kill you, then go six hundred miles to Frisco!" A terrified Rawlings indelicately described them as "a howling, blood-hungry crazed band of savages."

They pitched grenades and surged forward, seemingly uncaring of American mortar, artillery, and machine-gun fire. Destroyers added their own deadly firepower. The Japanese blundered into the C ration cans and the minefields. Scores of them were blown apart or wounded by the exploding mines. Machine-gun bursts laced through others. Still the survivors kept coming. They cut phone wires. The cleverest among them tapped phone lines and issued false orders. In one case, they succeeded in persuading a heavy mortar section to retreat. All night long, they assaulted or infiltrated the American lines, grappling in intimate death duels with the troopers.

The heaviest fighting raged in a sector defended by G Troop, 2nd Squadron, 5th Cavalry, where the Imperial Army soldiers and the troopers fought among dugouts and revetments, particularly one manned by Lieutenant Henshaw's platoon. He and his men leaned over an embankment and fired their rifles point-blank into the heads of the Japanese. Tracer bullets from flanking machine guns stabbed into the attackers. The fighting was so desperate that, in the course of the night, two nearby guns spewed 8,770 rounds. A company-size enemy unit assaulted an adjacent revetment defended by Sergeant Troy McGill and his squad of eight men. "There were over one hundred fifty Japs that came right at us," PFC Elmer Bense claimed. Right next to McGill and Bense, Private Alberto Moreno was shot in the head and killed instantly. "We saw we couldn't hold them and Sergeant McGill told me to pull out and drop back to another bunker," Bense recalled. Besides McGill and Bense, everyone else in the squad was now dead or wounded. He took off. McGill stayed behind and fought alone. When he exhausted his ammunition, he struggled hand-to-hand with the attackers, clubbing them with his rifle. Nearby Americans could hear him screaming desperately. For his extraordinary valor, McGill later received a posthumous Medal of Honor.

Though the American lines largely held, small groups of Japanese succeeded in breaching the forward areas. They roamed malevolently around the perimeter, materializing seemingly anywhere. "Infiltration into rear areas was worse than on any previous night," Carson wrote. They attacked artillery and antiaircraft crewmen, and smashed into a secondary defensive line held by the Seabees. Amid the confusion and danger, with bullets from both sides whizzing crazily in every direction, medics found it difficult to evacuate wounded men. In many cases, troopers died before anyone could even provide them with first aid. "A buddy of mine in the next foxhole had both legs blown off by a mortar burst, and I had to lie there listening to him call for help until he bled to death," one trooper sadly recalled. "I'll never forget that." At a makeshift canvas-covered hospital in a dugout near the beach, doctors operated on badly wounded patients while fighting raged a couple hundred yards away. Instruments were sterilized in a bucket of water over a wood fire. Parachutes from the supply drop were used as blankets. The concussion of nearby explosions occasionally threatened to tip over trays of instruments. At one point, a doctor looked up from an operation and said, "If those bastards get in here and ruin what equipment we have, I'm going to be really annoyed."

Like so many other desperate Japanese attacks throughout the Pacific War, this one followed a kind of nocturnal thunderstorm pattern. The wee hours were the most violent, with a steady diminution of Japanese strength as dawn approached. By daylight, the worst of the fighting had abated and the attackers decisively defeated. Patrols hunted down surviving Japanese, most of whom chose to take their own lives. At Henshaw's position, an officer led a squad-size group in full view of the Americans. One by one, each soldier stood at attention, pulled the pin from his grenade, armed it by rapping it against his helmet, held it to his belly, and blew out his own abdomen. "The line toppled unevenly . . . some falling stiffly, others seeming to melt in the knees," Rawlings wrote. Lieutenant Henshaw found a live Japanese lieutenant in what had been Sergeant McGill's dugout and leveled his carbine at him. The enemy lieutenant had attached a silk Japanese flag to his saber. He solemnly stared at Henshaw and waved the saber back and forth. After only a few days of combat, the Texan was already tired of killing. "I wish you'd surrender," he wearily implored the lieutenant. "Give me that sword and flag and stay alive. Surrender?" In response, the man bowed, shook his head, took out a grenade, and killed himself.

In the wake of the terrible battle, the Americans counted 750 Japanese corpses, including 168 around G Troop's sector. Wild stories had circulated among the Americans—who could not conceive of sober men fighting so self-sacrificially—that the Japanese had been drunk or doped. But the bodies revealed no evidence to support these contentions. Sixty-one Americans had been killed and another 244 wounded. Seabees accounted for 9 of the dead and 38 of the wounded. Not one Japanese surrendered. In response to new entreaties from Chase for more support, Krueger on March 4 rushed in the 2nd Squadron, 7th Cavalry Regiment, and the 82nd Field Artillery Battalion. These reinforcements, combined with the failure of Ezaki's attack and his devastating losses, swung the odds even more in favor of the Americans. Ezaki knew that he no longer had any chance, however remote, of destroying the American beachhead. By his own estimate, he was down to about 1,200 effectives. All he could do now was fight to the last man and inflict casualties upon the Americans. For the Americans, Operation Brewer soon transitioned from a defensive battle centering around protecting the airfield beachhead into an offensive campaign to secure the rest of Los Negros and eastern Manus.[9]

The stridency of Chase's reinforcement requests, in tandem with his failure to provide the Sixth Army commander with continual reports about the situation on Los Negros, prompted the brusque Krueger to wonder about Chase's state of mind. "His task was undoubtedly a difficult one, but did not, in my judgment, warrant the nervousness apparent in some of his dispatches," Krueger wrote to General Swift, the 1st Cavalry Division commander. Swift and Chase met aboard the USS *Bush* on March 5. The grizzled Chase, who had slept little in five days, was in no mood to parse words about those who had underestimated the Japanese presence in the Admiralties. Chase was imbued with the combat soldier's cynical contempt for rear-area analysts who risked the lives of fighting men on the basis of incomplete or incorrect information. "The gist of his loud talking was severe criticism of higher headquarters for assuming that there were no enemy on Los Negros," Swift later wrote to Krueger. Embarrassed and irritated at Chase for carrying on this way, especially in front of naval commanders, Swift twice had to tell him to cease and desist.

When the annoyed division commander came ashore, observed the battlefield for himself, and saw burial parties inter hundreds of dismembered Japanese bodies, he understood Chase's feelings a bit better. "I cannot have anything but sincere praise for the tactical disposition of the troops and the personal bravery of Gen. Chase and his staff, for the courageous manner in which they held Momote against a numerically superior force." What Chase lacked in diplomatic judgment, he more than made up for in combat leadership. He was, after all, correct that some of the creators of Operation Brewer had badly erred in their underestimates of Japanese strength and capabilities. He understood that he and his men could have paid a terrible price for this misjudgment. To his jaded ears, the term "reconnaissance in force" might just as well have meant pawns or bait. Like all combat soldiers, Chase knew only what he saw in front of him, with little appreciation for the bigger picture. He could not have known of MacArthur's gut-wrenching dilemma in having to choose between radically different intelligence estimates. Chase's communication issues with Krueger stemmed primarily from the necessity to shut down the generators that powered his radios and other gear during the night battles, lest their noise tip off the Japanese to the location of his headquarters. Moreover, he and his staff had personally fought the Japanese, nearly eyeball to eyeball, an uncommon experience for any general. By any measure, he had performed well. Even so, Krueger never quite appreciated these factors. On the basis of little more than his distant impressions and the incident related by Swift, the Sixth Army commander formed an opinion of Chase as too nervous and excitable, without personally taking the measure of his situation, a tendency that Krueger would exhibit again in the future.

Swift, a determined commander himself and a dedicated Krueger loyalist, now oversaw the expansion of the beachhead. Reinforced by the 12th Cavalry Regiment, he supervised throughout March a series of attacks and amphibious landings to secure the Seeadler Harbor coast, the Salami Plantation, and the balance of Los Negros. Complementary landings in mid-March on Manus by the 8th Cavalry Regiment and a squadron from the 7th Cavalry Regiment initiated several weeks of enervating fighting for Lorengau airfield and its environs. Halting advances, jungle patrols, and occasional desperate struggles to the death with hungry, cornered enemy soldiers characterized most of this action. "Tracking down these elusive and desperate groups was a hard job, made harder by the dense jungle, poor trails, rough ground and long supply lines," Krueger wrote of the fighting on Manus. "Hundreds of Japanese were killed in these minor encounters." Though strategically doomed, the Japanese gave no thought to any organized surrender, a pattern that had begun at such places as Buna and Guadalcanal and one that would hold for much of the rest of the war. They were rather like the shards of a shattered window or mirror—sharp enough and dangerous enough to require an exacting, occasionally exhausting cleanup.

MacArthur's headquarters had already invented the trivial and patronizing term "mop up" for this harrowing process. Though soldiers disliked and resented the phrase, it soon came into ubiquitous usage by most all American commanders in the Pacific. Aside from the battalion-size movements to capture the key objectives throughout March on Manus and Los Negros, the bulk of this challenging task boiled down to jungle patrolling by squad- and platoon-size units. Often guided by locals, patrols traveled light because they seldom ventured farther than a few miles from unit bases. Troopers carried ponchos, a haversack, ammunition, a rifle or tommy gun, an entrenching tool, a first aid kit, a canteen, and enough C or K rations to last a couple of days. They remained in touch by radio with their units and artillery batteries. They learned to live and move in the jungle, and deal with the tropical heat. They spent their days relentlessly hunting for Japanese in every swamp, along every trail, and in every tiny local village. "This type patrol naturally stressed a painstaking search for any evidence of previous Jap occupation, and also sought any prospective hideouts and suitable locations for ambush," a division post-battle report explained. They dealt with the elements and learned how to sniff out danger. "The Japanese were ever present and you could not spot them because they were super artists in camouflage," Lieutenant Joseph Cribbins, a frequent patrol leader, later said. "The toughest thing ever was to be on point in a patrol. We found out very quickly that if you wanted to survive as part of a patrol, you better be prepared to react very quickly." To cover every flank, they took to putting left- and right-handed men at the point. They figured out a way to shoot their 60-millimeter mortars without using the baseplate, enhancing their mobile firepower. To smooth the reloading process, they taped clips of ammunition in place on their rifles "so all you had to do was flip around the clip and slap it in. These things were not in field manuals, but the GIs devised them very quickly, and they worked very well." An 8th Cavalry post-battle report curtly noted that patrolling on Manus "for the most part necessitated digging the Jap out of his hole." The improvisations of the troopers, their patrolling techniques, the rhythm of their operations, and even the conditions in which they operated were strikingly similar to what many of their sons would experience in Vietnam over two decades later.

As General Krueger indicated, the 1st Cavalry Division troopers gradually killed off the Japanese in many hundreds of small-unit patrol engagements fought over the course of several exhausting weeks, often in torrential rain and mud. "The troopers were carrying 4 days' rations and their ammunition," Brigadier General Verne Mudge, the 2nd Brigade commander, wrote of a typical patrol he encountered. "They had nothing but a poncho, wool-knit sweater, and toilet articles with them in the way of comforts. Of all the rough, tough, muddy, ragged troops you ever saw, they were it." A tiny few of their enemies surrendered. Most died in firefights, or of disease or starvation. "It is discouraging when one thinks of how little food and ammunition remains," one of them wrote in a diary that later fell into American hands after his death. "My mind and body are both tired, due to lack of nourishment. This is the honorable defeat! Our names may remain, but it is regrettable! The lives of us . . . soldiers are diminishing to a few days! Our bodies are getting weaker and weaker, and this hunger is getting unbearable." Colonel Ezaki met his end anonymously in the middle of May, starving to death somewhere in the jungle wilds of eastern Manus. On May 18, Krueger declared an official end to the campaign.[10]

While the infantrymen were relentlessly subduing the dwindling number of Japanese holdouts, more Seabees and Army combat engineers landed. Working efficiently with bulldozers and graders, and aided by some twelve hundred local laborers, they succeeded on March 9 in turning Momote into a serviceable airfield for artillery liaison planes, fighters, and medium bombers. By the twenty-second of April, the base had matured enough to accommodate B-24 heavy bombers. Although Lorengau on Manus proved to be an unsuitable air base, the engineers simply built a new coral-surfaced strip, eight thousand feet long and one hundred feet wide, at Mokerang Plantation on the northwest tip of Los Negros. The Seabees developed Seeadler Harbor into a substantial naval installation with multiple loading docks and enough fuel storage space to accommodate nearly forty thousand barrels.

The solidification of these bases made a prospective invasion of neighboring New Ireland unnecessary and continued the steady strangulation of the Japanese garrison at Rabaul. In a larger sense, victory in the Admiralties accelerated MacArthur's timetable for his next New Guinea invasion by six weeks, and provided him with a counterweight to Nimitz's triumph in the Marshalls. This, in turn, forced the Joint Chiefs to maintain SWPA's strategic relevance and kept MacArthur's Philippine dreams alive. At an intelligence level, the operation validated the accuracy of the Ultra material upon which Willoughby's estimates had been based, building MacArthur's confidence in this remarkable source of information on Japanese plans and forces. Around the Momote airfield, Swift's troopers had found four hundred enemy bunkers, seven times the number estimated by

Kenney's photo interpreters. At the tactical level, Operation Brewer proved the value of the Alamo Scouts and the intense training that had equipped the 1st Cavalry Division to win both a defensive and an offensive battle. The Americans found and buried 3,280 Japanese bodies. They captured a mere 75 underfed enemy soldiers. Krueger estimated that another 1,100 Japanese had been buried by their own side or died somewhere in the forlorn tropical jungles. American losses were substantial: 330 killed and 1,189 wounded. They were the price MacArthur paid for the major strategic payoff of controlling the Admiralties, and he knew it. "He was always concerned about casualties," Richard Marshall, his deputy chief of staff, commented. Though the genesis of Operation Brewer was flawed, based as it was on Kenney's faulty intelligence, MacArthur had mentally sifted through the risks and rewards of the enterprise and made the right decision. In so doing, he had, for the first time in this war, demonstrated an innovative adroitness in thought and boldness of action. In particular, his understanding of air- and sea power had grown considerably from his self-pitying 1942 days in the Philippines, when he had blamed many of his woes on the Navy and the Army Air Forces. Like the man himself, his reasons for taking Brewer's risk were complicated—opportunism, appreciation for the crucial importance of naval and air bases, confidence in the cavalry troopers, impatience to speed up his personal road to Manila, and, undoubtedly, rivalry with Nimitz. Regardless, it worked and this was all that mattered. With the Admiralties in his pocket, he was now poised for bigger game to the west, on New Guinea's north coast.[11]

3

Consolidation

No one really wanted the whole island of Bougainville, and with good reason. Most of it consisted of little more than scum-crusted swamps and suffocating, mountainous rain forest. Plus, there was a lot of it. The largest island in the Solomons, it stretched 125 miles in length and between 30 and 48 miles in width. A pair of active volcanoes, Mounts Balbi and Bagana, dominated a range of high ground in the north. The latter peak frequently spewed smoky plumes of volcanic ash into the dense tropical air. Earthquakes and tremors shimmied the place almost daily. "Banyan trees of great height and diameter are found throughout the area, with low growing palms, ferns and vines constituting an impenetrable mass," a 1944 US Army report explained of the island's typical terrain. "The cover afforded by the undergrowth would permit a person to be within three feet of another without knowledge of the other." Sparsely populated by forty thousand Melanesians who lived mainly in small coastal villages of about one hundred people, the island had been listlessly batoned among a series of imperial powers during the early twentieth century until the Japanese invaded in early 1942 to establish small air and sea bases adjacent to Bougainville's harbors, primarily along the east coast. They made no attempt—and certainly did not have the resources—to control the whole island. Like latter-year Portuguese colonial settlers, the Americans decided to follow much the same coastal pattern. They knew it made no sense to invest blood and treasure to seize the whole useless landscape or even to attempt to seize the Japanese bases. Far better to find their own opening and exploit it. Aided by their growing control of the sea and air, the Americans had in November 1943 invaded at lightly garrisoned Empress Augusta Bay on the west coast and quickly forged a firm beachhead against ineffectual Japanese resistance. For the Americans, the value of Bougainville lay only in its proximity to Rabaul a couple hundred miles to the west. With secure air bases on Bougainville, American planes could

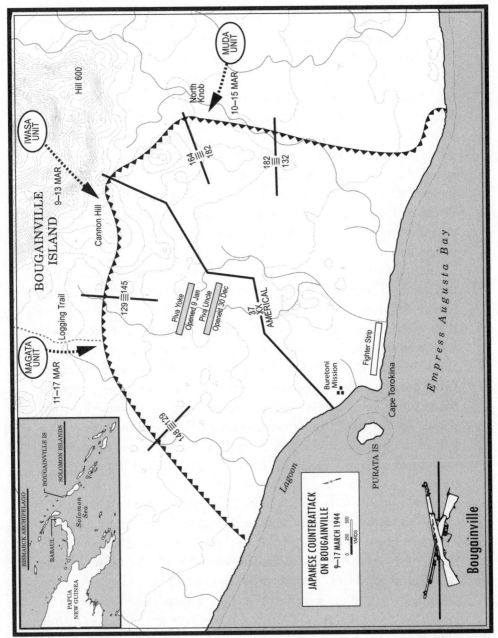

BOUGAINVILLE ISLAND

Hill 600

North Knob

Cannon Hill

Logging Trail

IWASA UNIT
9–13 MAR

MUDA UNIT
10–15 MAR

MAGATA UNIT
11–17 MAR

164 ▦ 182

182 ▦ 132

129 ▦ 145

148 ▦ 129

Piva Yoke
Opened 9 Jan

Piva Uncle
Opened 30 Dec

37 XX AMERICAL

Buretoni Mission

Fighter Strip

Cape Torokina

PURATA IS

Lagoon

Empress Augusta Bay

JAPANESE COUNTERATTACK
ON BOUGAINVILLE
9–17 MARCH 1944

0   250   500
YARDS

BISMARCK ARCHIPELAGO

BOUGAINVILLE IS
SOLOMON ISLANDS

RABAUL

Solomon Sea

PAPUA NEW GUINEA

Bougainville

© 2021 by Chris Erichsen

bomb Rabaul at will and, in effect, complete the strangulation of the once mighty Japanese South Pacific bastion.

By January 1944, this process was well under way. Within the horseshoe-shaped beachhead perimeter spanning some twenty-three thousand yards of low hills, jungle, and coastline, Navy Seabees and Army engineers had constructed three operational airfields. From these bases, a lethal blend of Marine, Navy, and Army Air Forces planes—everything from fighters to torpedo bombers, B-25 Mitchells and B-24 Liberators—sallied forth to disgorge tons of ordnance on Rabaul and other targets. The Japanese responded with pinprick nighttime raids that, however frightening to those underneath the bombs, amounted to a nuisance more than a strategic threat. As the American planes steadily degraded the remaining Japanese air and sea capability in the Solomons, the enemy raids eventually ceased altogether.

In the middle of December, Major General Oscar Griswold's XIV Corps had assumed responsibility for defense of the Allied enclave from the I Marine Amphibious Corps. "Without the ground forces, the air could not have operated from this base, and without the air, the ground forces would have been continually harassed by hostile planes and denied much valuable information," he later wrote of the symbiotic relationship between the Allied ground and air components at Bougainville. The low-key, unassuming victor of New Georgia now had two Army divisions under his command. The Americal Division of Guadalcanal fame manned the eastern half of the perimeter. The 37th Infantry Division, whose soldiers had fought well on New Georgia, anchored the western half. They were buttressed by a diverse blend of aviation units, engineers, tankers, quartermasters, signalmen, medics, and artillery outfits that ballooned XIV Corps's strength to some fifty thousand troops and growing by the day like a city in a boom phase. They busily worked to strengthen the concentric ring of defenses that defended the whole beachhead. The entire infantry complement of the two divisions, three regiments apiece, were deployed on the line. Their positions were anchored along hilltops and ridges that overlooked the low coastal ground. Griswold's combat reserve consisted mainly of two light tank companies, one medium company, and the 1st and 3rd Battalions of the Fiji Infantry Regiment, a superbly trained force of expert jungle fighters.

At the front line, the soldiers toiled daily under the hot tropical sun, performing the hard labor necessary to turn the XIV Corps perimeter into a heavily fortified citadel impervious to all but the most potent of attacks. The dreary monotony of steady, taxing manual work, with little accompanying action, prompted the troops to dub Bougainville the "Bore War." They constructed a mutually supporting line of dugouts, observation posts, rifle pits, and trenches, stretching for almost thirteen miles from end to end. "We all lived in pill boxes," Private Edward Sears, a rifleman in the Americal Division, later wrote. "That is a hole dug in the ground with layers of logs and dirt for a roof. You had an opening in front to fire through. We had trenches running from one pill box to another." Most of the pillboxes were twelve by fifteen feet square and about eight feet deep. "We left firing ports to the front and we left inclines to the rear to crawl out of," Private Howard Ellis, a rifleman in the 129th Infantry Regiment, recalled.

Many of the well-concealed pillboxes were reinforced with layers of earth-filled oil drums, sandbags, and, in the recollection of Colonel William Long, commander of the Americal's 182nd Infantry Regiment, "some were lined with mahogany with which the area abounded." The firepower of each rifle squad was beefed up with two Browning automatic rifles. Crew-served automatic weapons of nearly every type proliferated. The typical regiment was equipped with forty extra machine guns beyond its regular allotment. "Splinter proof shelters and emplacements were constructed for machine guns, 37 mm guns, and mortars," an Army combat historian wrote. "First aid stations and signal facilities were dug in under cover. Alternate positions were prepared for machine guns, mortars and artillery." At every spot, at least fifty yards of jungle and brush were cleared to open bare fields of fire for all the weapons. Minefields were sown, especially adjacent to swamps. Double aprons of barbed wire were strung into place. For illumination during potential night attacks, trip flares, flashlights, incendiary grenades, and cans full of gasoline were fastened onto tree branches. Antiaircraft searchlights were set to shine off clouds and bathe the entire area in artificial light. As at Los Negros, the Americans placed pebbles inside cans and hung them on trees or barbed wire as early-warning devices. Ingenious GIs created wicked booby traps. Wire-laden grenades were hidden in hundreds of spots along every avenue of approach. Oil drums were packed with scrap metal, wired to bangalore torpedoes, and placed in front of pillboxes.

Like nearly every other division in the US Army, Americal and the 37th enjoyed a devastating complement of organic artillery—three battalions of 105-millimeter howitzers and one 155-millimeter battalion. The artillerymen spent an untold number of hours sweeping away jungle to dig in their guns. "Clearing was a tremendous job, and continued for a week from daylight to dark," wrote Lieutenant Colonel Howard Haines, a battalion commander. "A 360 degree field of fire was required, and . . . the trees were tall and the forest dense." In the coastal areas where they operated, the water table was too high to allow for the construction of underground shelters. "Everyone lived in log-and-sand-bag huts." The artillery units were augmented by a potent blend of antiaircraft batteries, many of which dug their 90-millimeter guns into frontline positions to fire directly at potential attackers. The diminution of Japanese air raids only served to free up more antiaircraft batteries for ground defense. The 82nd Chemical Mortar Battalion deployed its 4.2-inch guns so efficiently that there were no dead spots in its coverage. "We selected, prepared, and ranged in for possible use, 26 positions, covering the entire perimeter of the beachhead," Lieutenant Colonel William Shimonek, the commander, later commented. Under his supervision, the gun crews stored forty-eight thousand mortar shells in carefully guarded dumps and warehouses. Similar to the 82nd, forward observers from the other artillery and antiaircraft units pre-sited every inch of the perimeter as well as the jungle beyond the wire. For the sake of efficiency, Griswold placed Brigadier General Leo Kreber, the 37th Division artillery commander, in charge of all these tubes as a de facto corps artillery officer. If need be, fighters and medium bombers were available for close air support. Behind it all, destroyers lurked in Empress Augusta Bay, ready to add their five-inch shells and other gunnery to the lethal mix.

The job of sustaining this formidable garrison, in a place with no intrinsic infrastructure, stretched XIV Corps logisticians to the limit. With no docking facilities, work crews unloaded freight from ships onto LCTs and then to the beach, where more strong backs manhandled everything ashore. From January to March, stevedores unloaded over 107,000 measurement tons of freight. Tiny Puruata Island just off the Bougainville coast was used extensively as a holding area, prompting Griswold to describe it as "so heavily loaded down it was about to sink." On Puruata and Bougainville, the Corps staff organized a system of dumps, from ordnance to signals and medical.

The mere act of feeding the troops required 150 tons of matériel per day. Special refrigeration buildings, powered by gasoline generators, contained 25,800 cubic feet of space to preserve meat and other perishables. Cooks baked between twenty and thirty thousand pounds of bread per day. The average soldier subsisted on a blend of C rations, K rations, and field kitchen fare, known as B rations, served either buffet-style or slopped onto mess kits from specially insulated containers. Only the truly fortunate—usually rear-area officers, headquarters personnel, or sailors—had access to refrigerated foods. Even so, on Thanksgiving every man dined on roast turkey, mashed potatoes, cranberry sauce, hot rolls, butter, creamed cauliflower, and candy. "The meal was eaten in the rain, on jungle logs, but it was still turkey and it was still Thanksgiving, so what the hell," the 37th Division's after-action report quipped.

Resourceful as ever, Griswold's troops soon cleared six hundred acres of Bougainville to cultivate their own personal gardens. Aided by nitrogen-rich fertilizers and the expertise of local farmers, the plots yielded 1,125 pounds of cucumbers, 614 pounds of collards, 3,471 pounds of Chinese cabbage, and 1,405 pounds of lettuce, plus smaller amounts of tomatoes, radishes, watermelons, sweet potatoes, yams, eggplant, and okra. Gasoline consumption ran to 125,000 gallons, or 485 tons, per day. For maximum efficiency, Griswold's service troops installed over two dozen storage tanks connected to one another by five miles of pipeline. The XIV Corps ordnance dump contained 9,200 tons of ammunition of all types. Much of this ammunition, and as many as six million individual rations, were stored among eleven separate warehouses, each of which had eighteen hundred square feet of space with floors of wood, concrete, or tamped-down sand. Engineers chlorinated and purified 350,000 gallons of water each day; the average soldier had access to about 3 gallons in a twenty-four-hour cycle. Specially constructed incinerators burned refuse round the clock, minimizing the fly population. Ice plants created ninety cakes of ice, weighing 50 pounds apiece, each day. Laundry units washed an average of sixty thousand items per week. The engineers built forty-three miles of two-way road and thirty-six miles of one-way road out of nothing but barren jungle. Tropical downpours were so frequent and the soil so unstable that the engineers spent just as much time maintaining the roads as building them. One bulldozer alone logged 310 hours of road and ditch maintenance in a single month.

Jeeps and trucks hauled some of the supplies to the forward positions; everything else had to be carried by grumbling soldiers or hired local laborers. Four sawmills were in operation almost constantly, providing building material for hospitals, mess halls, command posts, and the like.

Between early January and early March, the mills produced 1.75 million board feet of lumber. Given the circumstances, communications were highly sophisticated. Signal teams strung 6,200 miles of wire (the 82nd Chemical Mortar Battalion alone accounted for 154 miles) and built fifteen hundred telephone poles, servicing 1,590 phones. Some of the wires were even strung all the way to Guadalcanal, allowing Griswold and other commanders to converse by phone with the rear area. Seventy telegraph stations were in operation round the clock, in addition to an uncounted blend of radios from handheld walkie-talkies and heavy sets designed for headquarters units.

Medics worked assiduously to minimize the spread of malaria. Crews drained swamps, sprayed insecticide, and torched likely breeding areas. "Rigorous evening inspections were also made concerning the wearing of proper clothing for protection against malarial mosquitoes," a command history reported. Men slept beneath mosquito nets. Standing orders mandated the wearing of long sleeves at night, when mosquitoes tended most often to prey. Commanders forced their men to take atabrine, the most common malaria suppressant available to the Americans. At chow time, under the watchful eyes of sergeants and medics, each man had to swallow his pill and then wait as a clerk checked his name off a list. "This supervised administration of Atabrine often has caused a *complete cessation* of recurrent attacks of malaria in large bodies of Men . . . who previously were subjected to episodes of this disease," one physician wrote. At Bougainville, this was certainly true. In assessing the overall strength of his beachhead, Griswold opined that "the perimeter was as well organized as the personnel and terrain would permit."[1]

From the vantage point of the high hills that brooded over the Bougainville perimeter, the Japanese observed this mighty American host, but without really seeing it. Since the initial American landings in early November, Lieutenant General Haruyoshi Hyakutake, commander of the Seventeenth Army, had assumed they were diversionary in favor of a main landing elsewhere, probably on Buka, just off Bougainville's northern tip. Short and bespectacled, with more than thirty years of experience as an infantryman and some expertise in cryptanalysis, Hyakutake was surprisingly small-minded for a man with such credentials. He and his army had suffered many hard knocks on New Guinea and Guadalcanal. Hyakutake had presided over the disastrous Japanese assaults on the strongly held American perimeter around Henderson Field at Guadalcanal. When these attacks failed and the tactical situation subsequently deteriorated, he himself had been fortunate to escape to Bougainville. A few months later, he had lost New Georgia to the Americans. Humiliated and full of self-reproach, he had reported his failure to Emperor Hirohito and concluded simply, "My crime deserves more than death."

Not until early 1944 did he realize the truth that the perimeter at Empress Augusta Bay represented the main American effort on Bougainville. He was in an odd spot in that he physically occupied more of the island than the Americans and yet had less overall operational and strategic control, primarily due to the strength of the XIV Corps perimeter and Allied dominance of the air and sea. Under pressure from General Imamura, his Eighth Area Army superior, to do something about the American interlopers, Hyakutake's options were limited. Increasingly cut off from reinforcement and resupply, his best course of action was probably to harass the XIV Corps perimeter, fortify his own coastline, and coax the Americans into costly long-range patrols or even a bloody assault against his strong points (though of course Griswold had no intention of taking this kind of bait). Like most Japanese commanders at this stage of the war, Hyakutake thought in terms of an offensive battle of annihilation, almost as a point of honor. Having apparently learned nothing from his failure to overrun Henderson Field on Guadalcanal, he decided to launch a ground offensive, with almost no air and naval support and only basic artillery and mortar rudiments, to snuff out Griswold's perimeter. Somehow, in spite of extensive Japanese patrolling, Hyakutake remained under the impression that his American opponent had only one division instead of two. He earmarked 15,400 combat soldiers, out of some 40,000 Japanese on Bougainville, to make the attack, nowhere near an appropriate force for the formidable task at hand.

Blissfully unaware of these realities, he planned a three-pronged offensive designed to rupture Griswold's lines, secure the two nearest airfields, known as Piva Yoke and Piva Uncle, and push on to the coast. The 6th Division, under the command of Lieutenant General Masatane Kanda, made up the core of Hyakutake's assault force. The 6th was a tough regular outfit that had done much hard fighting in China. Recognizable by the red patches they wore on their left sleeves, the 6th Division soldiers had been major participants in the infamous 1937–1938 Nanking Massacre, a horrendous orgy of torture, executions, beatings, beheadings, and rapes. Many of the perpetrators were still with the unit in early 1944. For Operation TA, as the planners called the Bougainville offensive, they were joined by soldiers of the 53rd and 81st Infantry Regiments of the 17th Division, plus a specially organized artillery group equipped with four 150-millimeter howitzers, a pair of 105-millimeter pieces, and several dozen smaller guns.

Hyakutake divided his combat troops into three detachments (often called a *butai* in the Japanese Army). In the center, the Iwasa Unit, under Major General Shun Iwasa, consisted of 4,150 soldiers from the 6th Division's 23rd and 13th Infantry Regiments, plus engineers, mortars, and artillery. Their job was to take Hill 700, in the heart of the 37th Division defenses, at the highest point in Griswold's perimeter and thus the key to its security. Once they had taken Hill 700, they were to press on to the two airfields. On their right flank, the Magata Unit, led by Colonel Isaoshi Magata, the commander of the 45th Infantry Regiment—with the support of more engineers, mortars, and artillery, some 4,300 troops in all—was to launch a complementary assault against the low ground approaches to Hill 700, which were defended by the 37th Division's 129th Infantry Regiment. With that accomplished, they were to join in the airfield push. On the extreme Japanese left flank, 1,350 soldiers from the 13th Infantry Regiment, organized into the Muda Unit under Colonel Toyoharei Muda, were to seize Hill 260, a rocky rampart outpost in front of the main Americal Division line, overlooking the Torokina River, plus adjacent high ground to protect the Isawa Unit's flanks as it presumably advanced toward the sea.

Hyakutake chose March 6 as the launch date but postponed it for two days because he needed more time to get troops and supplies into position. He anticipated it would take just over a week to roll up the American beachhead. With food at a premium, he arranged to send his men into battle with only two weeks' rations. For weeks they had hungrily eyed American largesse at a distance. Once the offensive began, he figured they would capture plenty of American food. "The soldiers are saying that because rations are short, it will be well to begin the battle quickly," one sergeant noted in his diary. Orders stipulated that "each force will take over captured rations, weapons and ammunition only, and the MPs will handle all military secret documents." So confident was General Hyakutake of victory—and so oblivious to reality—that he and his staff even chose the exact spot where they expected to receive Griswold's formal surrender.

Had he known the truth of the situation, perhaps he would have contemplated his own surrender, though obviously such thoughts were anathema to World War II Japanese officers. Not only were the attackers outnumbered almost two to one in combat troops and on the decidedly wrong side of every firepower and logistical ratio; they did not even enjoy the advantage of surprise, either. As the Japanese, through herculean effort, hauled artillery pieces and other weapons forward, establishing trails and other bivouac areas behind hills and beneath the jungle canopy, American photo reconnaissance flights, information from locals, and ground patrols detected the buildup. "Roads . . . leading toward our perimeter showed signs of increased activity, and following our bombing of bridges and other installations, immediate repair was effected," Griswold related in a detailed contemporary report. A mood of expectation filtered throughout all of XIV Corps. "It became a waiting game now as we knew the Japanese forces would try to drive us into the ocean," Sergeant Cletus Schwab of the 37th Division later reflected.

The Japanese telegraphed their coming punch with poor operational security. On February 24, an American patrol killed a Japanese artillery survey officer who had been carrying a dispatch case full of sensitive material. At division headquarters, Japanese-American soldiers of the intelligence section—often just called Nisei—translated the case's contents and found a jackpot. The officer's documents revealed Hyakutake's entire attack plan, the names of key commanders, his order of battle, the location of his artillery, their American targets, and even the anticipated date of the offensive. The Americans noted the location of Japanese batteries and preregistered their own artillery to fire at these areas. "The first sign of enemy firing from the positions would bring a heavy series of concentrations down on the entire sector," the Americal Division's historian noted. Commanders beefed up the already formidable nest of defenses around the XIV Corps perimeter. "Defensive positions were strengthened and new defensive reserve lines were constructed," Brigadier General William "Duke" Arnold, the XIV Corps chief of staff, later said. "Supporting service troops were schooled in their duties in the event of a breakthrough in any sector; even the Seabees were given portions of the reserve line to man."

Even more corroboration of Hyakutake's plans came from a steady trickle of Japanese deserters and prisoners, an unprecedented event in the Pacific War. Once again, the Japanese-American GIs, many of whom had family members incarcerated in internment camps back home, played a key role. Most were assigned to the intelligence sections of the two divisions. When frontline troops captured an enemy soldier, he was immediately interrogated by a Japanese-American with sufficient language skills. Because the idea of surrendering was so taboo in Japanese martial culture, their soldiers were completely unprepared for how to conduct themselves while in enemy custody. "They were very free in giving information about their own troops," the Americal's Bougainville after-action report explained. "They spoke readily when they evidently saw that they were to be treated humanely." Indeed, the Americans realized immediately that, with decent treatment, almost all the Japanese were only too happy to help their captors. "Most of them were very cooperative," said Sergeant Yukio Kawamoto, a twenty-four-year-old Berkeley, California, native whose parents were interned at the Topaz Camp in Utah. "There was psychology involved. The Nisei treated them well, gave them cigarettes and tried to comfort them. If you tried . . . slapping them around, the Japanese could get pretty obstinate." In the days leading up to the offensive, he helped question several Japanese prisoners who were captured by his fellow 37th Division soldiers. "They said things that they shouldn't have said. When we interrogated these prisoners . . . we had a pretty good idea of what to expect."

Fortunately for Hyakutake, his assault troops had no idea that their adversaries knew so much about what was in the offing. On the eve of the offensive, he exhorted his men, "It is danger's whim to appear to those who are timid and fear death's embrace, so be bold in attacking. The time has come to manifest our knighthood with the pure brilliance of the sword. It is our duty to erase the mortification of our brothers at Guadalcanal! Attack! Assault! Destroy everything! Cut, slash, and mow them down. May the color of the red emblem of our arms be deepened with the blood of the American rascals. We are invincible!" General Kanda chimed in: "There can be no rest until our bastard foes are battered, and bowed in shame—till their . . . blood adds luster . . . to the badge of the Sixth Division."

To put themselves in position for the attack, many of the soldiers had already endured weeks of misery, slogging along muddy trails, hauling weapons, ammunition, and supplies, rebuilding washed-out roads, patrolling miles of featureless jungle, eating scant rations. They were eager to make their commander's dreams of victory come true, but far too many were in anything but optimum condition. Malnutrition was common. In a secret diary, a 13th Infantry squad leader noted that his unit had only enough food left for one light meal of rice, compressed barley, and powdered bean paste. The men were so hungry that anyone who left his mess kit unattended risked having the contents stolen by his comrades. "Taking that position and the enemy's rations is in everybody's mind," the sergeant noted of his unit objective in the American sector.[2]

A pre-attack artillery barrage, the largest the Japanese would ever muster in the South Pacific, began shortly after daybreak on March 8. With cart-before-horse illogic, they decided to focus their fire on the airfields instead of the frontline fortifications their soldiers would soon attempt to capture. By and large, enemy gun crews enjoyed a direct line of sight on their targets. In spasmodic waves, Japanese shells screamed in and exploded on or near runways, tents, and supply or fuel dumps. Phone lines were torn apart, disrupting communications until hard-pressed linemen could brave the shelling and make repairs. Some aviators were injured in falls or other mishaps as they ran from their cots to foxholes. Explosions divoted several of the runways. "Seabees quickly ran out amid the hail of shells and repaired them," recalled Lieutenant William Holt, a Marine aviation public relations officer. "Many of the shells in the first barrage hit the ready rooms." Fortunately, they were not occupied at the time. Fighter pilots dodged shells as they taxied for takeoff. In one instance, fragments punctured the tire on a plane's landing gear. The pilot evacuated the plane only to watch as another round completely destroyed his aircraft. Though the shell fire caused few casualties among the aircrews, it was heavy and accurate enough to destroy one B-24 bomber and three fighters, and to damage nineteen other planes, prompting the temporary withdrawal of all bombers to New Georgia, a circumstance that took a little pressure off Rabaul but did nothing to assist Hyakutake's assault troops. Probably by mere happenstance, some of the projectiles impacted in the rear areas of XIV Corps combat units. A passel of 150-millimeter rounds exploded in and around the bivouac area of a 164th Infantry Regiment rifle company. "I found our mess tent and kitchen totally destroyed," Captain Charles Walker, the commander, later wrote. "Our supply tent was gone, the area littered with broken rifles and equipment." The supply sergeant was wounded in the buttocks and trapped under debris; he had to be dug out by his comrades. A dud tore an ugly groove in the company street and, with a menacing whoosh, skidded to a halt alongside a tent.

The Americans responded to the Japanese barrage with a boiling wave of firepower, hurling shells in quantities scarcely imaginable to their adversaries. "Observations were hastily made from high points within the perimeter, from observation planes, and from destroyers standing off the coast," the Army's historian of the campaign explained. In some cases, they utilized the captured intelligence on the location of Japanese guns. But the enemy gun crews concealed their pieces quite well and they quickly learned to shoot and move. Most of the time, the Americans looked for muzzle flashes, attempted to pinpoint trajectories, or simply just showered likely enemy positions with heavy fire. The firepower imbalance was striking. Every single Japanese shell had been hauled through miles of jungle and mud by an underweight, weary, overburdened soldier. Naturally, this untenable transportation situation had the effect of limiting Japanese firepower. The Japanese shot between 500 and 2,000 rounds in the course of the day. One contemporary American analyst dismissed their use of artillery as "meager, and poorly coordinated. Judging from what he did in the Solomons, the Jap has a rather elementary concept of the employment of artillery."

By contrast, a single field artillery battalion in the Americal Division fired 3,760 shells in less than eighteen hours. "The fire direction center sounded much like a stock market or a tobacco auction," the division after-action report wisecracked. Cooks and mechanics filled in for overworked gun crewmen. A neighboring battalion belched 3,228 rounds that day; still another added 3,120 more. "Each time we fire one round, you send back a hundred in return," a dispirited prisoner complained to his interrogators. Another claimed that an entire battalion had been decimated by the bombardment as it waited for orders to go forward. Periodic air strikes added to the pounding. Marine dive bombers dropped fourteen tons of bombs on Japanese assembly areas in the hills overlooking the beachhead.[3]

The Japanese, instead of attacking in the wake of their bombardment, inexplicably held off on launching their offensive that day, ameliorating any ancillary benefit that might have come from their otherwise ineffective artillery preparation. At last, in the midst of a driving tropical rainstorm during the early morning hours of March 9, the Iwasa Unit's lead troops from the 23rd Infantry Regiment attacked Hill 700. The hill consisted of a pair of saddles, much like the humps on a camel's back. An adjoining saddle of high ground was dubbed "Pat's Nose" by the Americans. The approaches to the hill were steep, sloped at a 65 to 70 percent grade that made footing perilous. "Crags and roots became safety strirrups, often saving a man from a disastrous fall," wrote Sergeant E. R. Birnberg, in a vivid history of the 145th Infantry, the unit charged with the mission of defending the hill. The Americans had initially sustained themselves on this high ground with old-fashioned carrying parties that worked like pack mules. "Every round of ammunition, every bite of food, every drop of water had to be carried through the jungle rains and heat to the top." Engineers eventually managed to cut a small supply road through rock and jungle. Even so, a sense of isolation prevailed atop Hill 700. Most of the Americans, including the division commander, Major General Robert Beightler, the most successful National Guard officer of the Pacific War, mistakenly doubted that the enemy would attempt to seize such a dominating hunk of desolate terrain. "It is hardly conceivable that an attack would be made up so precipitous a slope," General Griswold wrote in wonderment a few months later.

In the rainy darkness they quietly emerged out of the jungle mist that hugged adjacent gullies, and climbed the steep grades as best they could. Americans on watch in their pillboxes could see barely five feet in front of them. Crawling on hands and knees, rifles slung over their backs, the Japanese either cut holes in the barbed wire or blew gaps in it with explosives. Booby traps and warning devices began to cook off, alerting the Americans to their approach, though few of the GIs could see them. Staff Sergeant Otis Hawkins pulled a set of wires that set off buckets of oil ignited by phosphorous grenades, illuminating much of the area. Aided by the light, he called down six hundred mortar rounds on the attackers. Riflemen used the light to pick off some of the enemy soldiers. With the element of surprise expended, those Japanese who made it up the slopes unleashed their pent-up fury with all-out attacks on any American pillboxes they could locate in the half-light. "The enemy stormed the hill . . . yelling like a maniac, suicidally putting everything he had into a frontal attack," Sergeant Birnberg later wrote. "Crawling and screaming, often times in English with such shouts as, 'American, you die,' . . . they tried to use nerve shattering tactics." Some of them sang American songs as they lunged forward and pitched grenades or fired their rifles or set up knee mortars or Nambu machine guns. They blew up a pillbox on the west side of the hill, killing all four Americans inside. Adjoining pillboxes opened up with a symphony of rifle, machine-gun, 37-millimeter mortar, and grenade fire. At close quarters, the infantrymen of both sides grappled in life-and-death struggles amid the sandbags, bunkers, and jungle foliage. "The fighting with hand grenades and mortars was so close that one Jap, shot repeatedly in the arm from within fifteen yards, continued to advance even after his arm had fallen off," Birnberg claimed.

Unable to call down artillery fire on Hill 700 for fear of hitting their own men, American forward observers instead saturated large swaths of territory to the east, "the low land beyond the bottom of the hill," in the recollection of one officer, limiting the Japanese capacity to reinforce their leading troops. By midday, the Japanese had captured seven pillboxes and driven a small salient about seventy yards wide and fifty yards deep at the crown of the hill, with a commanding view of the hard-built supply road. The penetration was the equivalent of a tentative foot in the door, far short of Hyakutake's ambitious design. At the same time, the Americans could not afford to let the Japanese remain in place lest they use the high ground to menace the airfields, expand their salient, or just sever resupply to the 145th Infantry Regiment defenders. The contest for the hill developed into a seesaw battle of intimate bunker-to-bunker combat, with both sides repeatedly attacking and counterattacking over the course of several days. Japanese soldiers overlooking the supply road rolled grenades down slopes into the midst of American carrying parties. PFC Offo Schwichtenburg commandeered a truck and made five round trips through heavy mortar fire to the base of the hill. When the truck wore out, he used a half-track and even managed to evacuate some wounded soldiers. Beightler eventually threw two more infantry battalions, plus some engineers, into the maw.

Iwasa filtered whatever units he could get through the curtain of American artillery fire onto the pockmarked, battered hill. Shortly after daybreak on March 11, he attempted to take Pat's Nose. Led by saber-wielding officers who yelled in Japanese such battle cries as "Damn them!," "We will do it!," and "Cut a thousand men!," they crawled up the slope, straight into a fatal funnel of point-blank machine gun, 37-millimeter canister shell, mortar, and rifle fire. Dozens were cut down; their trailing comrades literally stepped or crawled over their dead bodies before they, in turn, were torn apart. Still others kept coming. "I am absolutely convinced that nowhere on earth does there exist a more determined will and offensive spirit in the attack than that which the Japanese exhibited," an incredulous Griswold later wrote to a colleague. "They came in hard, walking on their own dead, usually on a front not exceeding 100 yards. They try to affect a breakthrough, which they attempt to exploit like water running from a hose." To the bewildered GIs, the bravery bordered on the mindless, if not quite the pointless. "The Japanese were very strange," one of them later commented. "They never seemed to think, 'The man ahead got killed there, I'll go on this side.' So our guys would just sit there and shoot them." The attack went nowhere. In a matter of only a few minutes, the Japanese lost eighty-four dead and an untold number of wounded. That evening, in a classic case of too little too late, Magata's people from the 45th Infantry crashed into the 129th Infantry Regiment line, well past time to do their comrades at Hill 700 much good (the poor coordination among Hyakutake's attacking detachments spoke volumes about the amateurish nature of his leadership and his offensive as a whole). Magata's men, too, were badly cut up by American firepower, though in an eerie reprise of the fighting at Hill 700, they managed to capture seven pillboxes and defend them tenaciously against all comers.

Whereas the Americans held most of the cards when they were hunkered down in prepared defenses and disgorging their lethal firepower on exposed waves of Japanese attackers, the dynamic was altogether different when they were on the offense, attempting to overcome stubborn enemy defenders who were usually determined to fight to the death, a disturbing pattern that had already played out in such places as Buna, Guadalcanal, New Georgia, Makin, and Tarawa and, with some exceptions, would typify much of the rest of the war. "The difficulties of retaking Hill 700 defy description," contended the 37th Division's after-action report. "The American forces had to assault enemy-held pillboxes by crawling up a slope so precipitous that a foothold was difficult to secure and maintain . . . in the face of withering machine gun fire. The enemy . . . had rapidly dug new pillboxes and new trenches, all of which were manned and supplied. His position became stronger by the hour." In one attack, a rifle squad made it over the slope only to be raked by machine-gun fire from both sides, killing eight men instantly. Owing to the steepness of the hill and the insecurity of the road, tanks were useless. Infantrymen learned to make liberal use of bazookas and flamethrowers. Protected by BAR men and other rifle-wielding soldiers, the gutsy operators climbed into position and fired their rockets or jets of flame at the enemy-held pillbox. Occasionally they used grenades, both smoke and fragmentation. With characteristic dogface sardonic wit, one bazooka gunner liked to yell, "Make way for the artillery!" before he fired.

One by one, in ferocious, costly, intimate battles, the Americans slowly retook each pillbox and Hill 700 as a whole. Thanks to more advantageous

low ground, the 129th Infantry enjoyed the support of Sherman tanks from
the 754th Tank Battalion. Working in close teamwork with the infantrymen, they hurled themselves into the disorienting jungle foliage and raked
the pillboxes with point-blank fire. "Visibility within the tank is limited at
best . . . in the dense jungle growth," Griswold wrote in a post-battle analysis. Sometimes a dogface walked in front of the tank and acted as guide.
Other times, in spite of the poor visibility, the Shermans led the way. According to Griswold, "Infantry squads stayed in position behind the tanks
and directed fire by telephone and colored smoke grenades. Tanks were
brought within 15 yards of enemy trenches and positions, and fire from
cannon and machine guns delivered at close range. At one point 18 enemy
were killed by [a] 75mm shell fired into the roots of a giant banyan tree."
During an inspection of the fighting, General Beightler, brandishing a
folding-stock carbine, personally led one of the infantry-tank assaults.
"Your husband took part in the counterattack," he excitedly wrote to his
wife. "In fact, he directed it personally on the ground and was in the leading wave. I shot Japanese at not more than 10 feet, helped capture 4 prisoners, and in fact had one h[ell] of a good time." Outside of grenades, a few
magnetic mines, and sheer courage, the Japanese had few other effective
weapons to use against the metal monsters. As at Hill 700, the Americans
steadily regained their lost ground and shattered Magata's combat power.[4]

At the same time that this fighting raged on and around Hill 700, Colonel Muda launched his supporting thrust against the Hill 260 outpost
about eight hundred yards in front of the main Americal Division lines.
An accident of proximity had turned this otherwise unremarkable patch
of jungle rise into solid-gold real estate. In the estimation of the Americal
historian, the hill was "thick with vegetation, a twin-peaked piece of high
ground which, from above, looks much like an hourglass." Situated about
7,500 yards west of the mouth of the Torokina River, and with the smaller
Eagle Creek at its back, Hill 260 was divided by two small saddles about
150 yards apart from each other, known as the North Knob and the South
Knob. Neither knob was any bigger than about half a football field. At
most, the hill measured 850 yards from end to end. A single jungle trail led
from the Americal lines to the hill. The slopes were steep enough—almost
perpendicular in spots—that the final stretch of trail consisted of revetted
steps cut into the side of the hill. In the heart of South Knob, a 150-foot-tall
banyan tree served as an ideal observation post. On this OP Tree, as the
Americans called it, the troops scrounged lumber to build a ladder and a

platform atop which mortar and artillery observers enjoyed a fine view of the entire Torokina valley and beyond. A small force of eighty soldiers from the 182nd Infantry Regiment, plus observers, held Hill 260. According to Colonel William Long, the 182nd's commander, their fortifications consisted of "combination bunkers and pill-boxes carefully sited in a perimeter . . . enclosed in tactical and protective wire. Inside the somewhat triangular perimeter the jungle was intact except near the storage point for reserve ammunition, water and rations. Outside the perimeter inner wire the hillsides had been thoroughly cleared of brush to the limit of the outer barb-wire . . . providing excellent vision for shooting." All of this was augmented by the usual array of trip flares and booby traps. Similar to Hill 700, with possession of 260, the Japanese could look down the collective throat of Griswold's perimeter, though the purpose of Hyakutake's Operation TA was obviously far more ambitious than the seizure of a good observation position. Long compared his little Hill 260 outpost to "a sore thumb stuck out into the poison ivy."

Against this half-company-size force, Colonel Muda hurled an entire battalion from his 13th Infantry. Shortly after daybreak on March 10, they quietly materialized, infiltrating over the steepest part of the slope, catching the Americans by surprise, and soon spread seemingly everywhere, cutting off the two knobs from each other. "Those Japs who attacked hill 260 that morning were good soldiers," opined a PFC Zuska, who defended a pillbox on the South Knob and got cut off. "They knew every trick of the game. They did not fire unless we fired first." He and other besieged defenders lashed back with submachine guns, rifles, machine guns, and grenades. "They kept coming, cursing at us in English as they came, stepping over their own dead," Zuska said. "I opened fire on them and saw them fall down and roll off the hill." Zuska's buddy took a bullet in the temple, spun around and staggered to his cot, "gasping for air. I grabbed my khaki towel and put it around his head. He died in a few minutes without saying a word." Zuska fought on alone, only a few feet from the dead body. Outside, a Japanese soldier bizarrely whistled a perfect rendition of "Yankee Doodle Dandy" while the fighting raged. The Japanese quickly overran several pillboxes, cut communication wires, occupied much of the South Knob, and enveloped the OP Tree, trapping the observers, one of whom reported to his 246th Field Artillery Battalion headquarters that the Japanese were all around the base of the tree. Then no one ever heard from him again.

A radio operator, almost hysterically incoherent from fear, reported the

Japanese attack to Colonel Long's command post. He dispatched two rifle companies to set out from the main line, counterattack, and retake the lost portions of Hill 260. They quickly became involved in heavy fighting against a numerically superior force. One of the companies had started out with 150 men; by the next morning, it was down to 25. Walking wounded braved the steep slopes and made their way to the rear singly or in groups; overworked and overburdened litter teams stumbled through long stretches of jungle to get their charges to battalion aid stations and the perimeter hospitals. Most often they carried patients far enough back to load them aboard jeeps or ambulances. A typical evacuation saw fifty men struggle for more than three hours to carry half a dozen wounded soldiers through a couple thousand yards of jungle. In one instance, a soldier who was bleeding heavily from the head was placed by medics on a stretcher and hauled through jungle so thick and muddy that six men were required to get him to an aid station. Still he bled profusely and it looked as if he would die. As doctors prepared him for immediate emergency surgery, they discovered, much to their delight, that he had only a minor shrapnel wound to his ear that had somehow bled like a major head injury. The rare moment of positive levity provoked a tension-relieving gale of laughter among the physicians. "I hope that those six litter bearers were never informed of the futility of their mission of sweating and hauling that patient down the mile of hill," Captain Leonard Savitt, one of the doctors, later cracked.

The most ingenious among the medics invented a buoyant packboard litter with pillow flotation devices. They strapped their patients to the packboard and simply floated them across streams, rivers, and swamps. In spite of the isolated battlefield and difficult terrain, 80 percent of wounded men reached a hospital within three hours. Wounds to the extremities, normally caused by mortar fragments, were the most common, followed by the head and thorax. Compound fractures made up the worst of the extremity wounds, sometimes necessitating amputation. Doctors on Bougainville amputated two arms, one hand, seven fingers, and eighteen legs. The deadliest place on the body to get wounded was in the abdomen. Almost 30 percent of abdomen cases died. The deadliness of these wounds usually stemmed from unchecked internal bleeding. "I am of the opinion that abdominal wounds should be operated on immediately, regardless of whether or not in shock," Lieutenant Colonel Richard Shackelford, a surgeon, asserted. "The reason is that in most instances we found that inter-abdominal hermorrhages [*sic*] developed." Far better, he felt, to go in, find the bleeders, and deal with them rather than risk missing them and have the patient go into shock and bleed to death internally.

Worried over the larger implications of losing Hill 260, General Griswold ordered it held—or perhaps a better description would have been retaken—at all cost. Thus began a protracted struggle, primal in its intimacy and violence, for the shabby outcropping, with both sides feeding reinforcements piecemeal into the chaos. "From the outset, the problem on Hill 260 was one of ejecting the Japanese from the south end of the hill," the 182nd's history chronicled. "Their positions were well dug in and defended and various American assaults to take the hill were turned back with unusually heavy casualties." Similar to Hill 700, the Americans made extensive use of flamethrowers even as the steep slopes negated the possibility of utilizing tanks. When flamethrowers proved unequal to the task, the Americans ignited gasoline cans with white phosphorous and hurled the fiery mix at Japanese positions; eventually they resorted to pumping gasoline through long pipes at the Japanese and setting the fuel afire. Soldiers fought to the death at handshake distance. Pillboxes and bunkers changed hands many times, sometimes by the hour. Americal soldiers were routinely cut off and isolated in these positions for hours, even days, at a time. At night, they took to urinating and defecating inside empty cardboard mortar-shell containers. "The cases are leakproof, odorproof, and easily disposed of on the following morning," one soldier said. With the entire Americal Division deployed along the perimeter, and the reserve battalion earmarked to assist the hard-pressed 37th Division, Major General John Hodge, the diminutive, hard-edged Americal commander, had few reserves at hand. As a result, his beleaguered infantry survivors tended to fight and refight a similar battle each day for the same ruined pillboxes or improvised dugouts, only to lose them temporarily when the Japanese gained a local advantage. The supply trail came under heavy and steady enemy mortar fire. Locals who had previously worked with the Americans as carriers understandably refused to go anywhere near the trail as long as the shooting continued.

As Muda's combat power diminished, his commanders launched numerous desperate banzai-style local attacks. The predictable result was slaughter. "Every gun, everything was zeroed . . . and they were just piled up," Private Morris Weiner recalled. English-speaking Japanese screamed American profanity words and taunted the "Yankee bastards" to leave their holes and fight face-to-face. "They kept coming and yelling," Private Zuska said. "Our machine gunners played wise, waiting til they saw the whites of their eyes, and let them have it." The terror of these near-mortal moments mounted like overdrawn credit. "Funny things go through your mind. You see your whole life before you. Many a time I could see my mother receiving a Purple Heart medal, 'posthumously.'" The fear lingered and mingled with exhaustion. When a company commander was killed in the lead of one local American counterattack, the man behind him lay down and gave in to complete hysteria. Only the intercession of a determined young lieutenant prevented a total rout. "If any soldier said they weren't scared, that's just bananas," Weiner asserted. "We were all scared." The unremitting stress was such that most of the troops lost between ten and fifteen pounds. "This was due to the nervous strain, the impossibility of regular sleep and regular meals," a regimental surgeon reported.

After several days of this mutual bloodletting, and casualties in the rifle companies piling up, Hodge and Long realized it made no sense to keep trying to dislodge the Japanese by direct assaults. They decided to back off, focus on aggressive patrolling and let artillery and mortars do the heavy lifting against the Japanese on Hill 260, focusing in particular on South Knob. Americal gun crews launched over ten thousand 105-millimeter howitzer rounds and five hundred 155-millimeter rounds against this part of the hill. Chemical mortar units added more than one thousand of their own shells. The 182nd's Cannon Company, equipped with 75-millimeter pack howitzers, added hundreds more. Some units fired a shell every two minutes for an entire night. The explosions and fragments tore trees apart and denuded the hill of any foliage, turning it into a cratered lunar-style landscape. Pillboxes were caved in or demolished. The OP Tree was blown to pieces, leaving behind only a battered, burned stub stretching just a sad twenty feet above the rest of the ruined detritus, probably the most abused tree in American warfare since the Spotsylvania Oak of Civil War fame. In a phrase whose double meaning was lost on no one, the Americans soon began referring to the fallen banyan as "the most expensive tree in the world."[5]

Ironically, just as the Americans began to persuade themselves of Hill 260's debatable value at such a cost in lives, the Japanese did the same. The place, after all, was just an observation post—it was not even a part of the main American line. To have any prayer of success, the Japanese had to breach that line. So Hyakutake and Kanda ordered the redeployment of

Muda's survivors in support of Magata's failed attacks, leaving behind only a delaying force at Hill 260. Even so, not until 1245 on March 28 did the Americans regain control of the entire hill. They counted 560 Japanese bodies around the area. Americal suffered badly as well, particularly the hard-hit 182nd Infantry. The division lost 98 killed, 24 missing (almost all of whom were dead), and 581 wounded. "A bitter cost for a hill of dubious value," Long later reflected. "Often the least valuable places carry the highest price tag in war. From my standpoint, this hill was not worth the cost to either side." After pausing a few days to regroup, Hyakutake tried one last-gasp attack against the 129th Infantry lines on March 23, with the same failed results as before. At one point, Japanese-American soldiers translated a captured diary that revealed the location and intentions of an attacking battalion. In response, the Americans unleashed a hellfire barrage of destroyer, artillery, and mortar fire. In total, seven artillery battalions, one chemical mortar battalion, and the destroyers plus infantry mortars fired for hours. "It's something you never forget," an infantryman later commented. "The big guns shooting over your head. It was all jungle in front of us and when they got done it was all cleared out." A howitzer crewman remembered, "We fired all night long and into the day. I loaded shell after shell. It sounded like thunder that lasted for hours." They spewed 14,882 shells at the Japanese. The battalion was destroyed before it could even attempt to attack. Dazed survivors wandered into captivity; others escaped eastward through the jungle to the Japanese-held portions of Bougainville. Most were killed.

Their bodies, and those of so many others who had attempted to bring Hyakutake's ignorant, flawed vision to fruition, lay strewn among the jungles and hills where the fighting had raged and where the Seventeenth Army commander's attempt to snuff out the American perimeter had ended in disastrous failure. He had brought a tactical knife to a strategic gunfight and suffered the terrible consequences. He carved out a few small, temporary, strategically meaningless salients in the American lines. In exchange, he had lost most of his combat manpower, much of it to the breathtaking deadliness of American artillery pieces and mortars, weapons he had elected to brave head-on, with little support of his own. The 37th Division's artillery units fired 161,968 rounds during the March battles; the 4.2-inch mortar units added another 257,528. The Americal's 245th Field Artillery Battalion alone shot 25,281 shells at Hyakutake's doomed men. "Reports of prisoners cited infantry companies wiped out by artillery fire, artillery batteries reduced from 130 to 30 men and all their guns knocked out," wrote Captain John Guenther, one of the Army's contemporary analysts of the fighting. The artillery was so suffocating that some Japanese soldiers ascribed to it almost mystical qualities. One captured diary revealed the belief on the part of its author—common among Axis soldiers in all theaters—that the Americans possessed automatic artillery.

Elated at the victory, but professionally contemptuous of Hyakutake's poor imagination, sloppiness, and wasteful battle management, Griswold castigated him and the other Japanese commanders as "not only dumb but suicidal." Captain Charles Henne, a company commander in the 37th Division, ascribed their monumental defeat to "overwhelming ego and the limitless [Japanese] capacity for self delusion." The Americans lost 263 dead and 1,393 wounded. American intelligence estimated enemy fatalities at 5,500 with another 3,000 wounded. Later Japanese estimates confirmed this rough number of deaths while measuring many more wounded. Major General Kanzuo Tanikawa, a staff officer with the Eighth Area Army, calculated that the attacking units lost 5,398 dead and 7,060 wounded, a nearly 100 percent casualty rate. The numbers did not include men lost in patrol actions before and after the March attacks, nor the effects of disease, malnutrition, and deaths under the care of Japanese medical units. Griswold's staff claimed that, based on an actual count of bodies, 6,474 Japanese soldiers were killed between mid-December and the end of April. But the job of counting was anything but orderly or precise. "Enemy dead were strewn in piles of mutilated bodies . . . so badly dismembered in most cases that a physical count was impossible," Sergeant Birnberg wrote. "Here and there was a leg or an arm, or a blown off hand. At one point, the Japanese formed a human stairway over the barbed wire. Five enemy were piled one on top of the other. Farther out from the perimeter, where a little stream wound its way parallel to it, Japs, killed by the concussion of thousands of mortar shells, lay with their heads, ostrich fashion, stuck under any least protection they could find." Another eyewitness remembered "bodies had been blown to pieces by the shells and scattered everywhere. The jungle reeked of fallen Japs and the horrible silence of death enveloped everything." To a 90-millimeter gun crewman who beheld the terrible carnage, "the sight was frightful. I saw Japanese soldiers stacked up four deep like cordwood. There were hundreds of them."

Grim American burial details, braving the ubiquitous stench that almost seemed liquid in the tropical heat, unceremoniously policed the remains with shovels and bulldozers, and consigned them to hasty, shallow communal graves. According to one unit after-action report, these battle-hardened soldiers "returned retching from the stench and ghastly appearance of torn and shattered bodies. Decay-caused gas in shallow-buried bodies expanded, popping them out of the ground." The soldiers learned very quickly not to puncture or drop the swollen bodies lest they burst and splash the horrified diggers with putrid black liquid and maggots. Already imbued with a tendency to view the Japanese as racially inferior or at least culturally alien, most of the GIs maintained a hard shell of emotional distance from their fallen enemies, a kind of rote dehumanization so sadly characteristic of the Pacific War, but especially at Bougainville because of the 6th Division's reputation for butchery in China. The extreme valor of the enemy soldiers and, in the view of one Americal report, "the unbelievable disregard of the value of human life by enemy commanders" was interpreted by the Americans as mindless fanaticism, and only added to the mindset. "They are not human, they are just monkey-like animals . . . without hesitation throwing their lives away," a typical Americal soldier opined to his commanding officer. Unlike most of his fellow Americans, Sergeant Kawamoto felt some sense of sympathy for them, perhaps because, under different circumstances, they might have been his comrades. As he studied "their bodies rapidly decomposing by the jungle heat or being devoured by ugly-looking insects," he could not help but think about their families back in Japan.[6]

The dismal failure of Operation TA essentially decided the strategic outcome at Bougainville, and the Solomon Islands as a whole. Japanese air and naval forces had retreated from most of the islands. Rabaul was outflanked and isolated. Covered by the relatively fresh 6th Cavalry Regiment and the 4th South Seas Garrison Unit, Hyakutake's survivors either retreated to high ground beyond the American perimeter or fled along trails to the opposite coast. American artillery pursued them much of the way. Cut off from resupply by air and sea, many focused their efforts on growing or stealing enough food from locals to stave off starvation. Occasionally, American pilots spotted their maturing crops and roasted them with napalm. A captured 13th Infantry Regiment private later told his American interrogators that "due to lack of food and isolation from other Japanese territories, troops were very discouraged and low in morale. Nevertheless, they were determined to hold out to the last."

Knowing that Hyakutake's battered forces posed no further threat to the American existence at Bougainville, Griswold had no intention of spending lives and resources to attack them in their enclaves, though he did order a limited offensive in April to capture prominent hills beyond his original perimeter. Leavened by the occasional sharp battle to take or hold a key hill, patrolling soon dominated the operational pace for Griswold's combat troops. Day after day, week after week, long-range patrols, usually ranging from squad to company size, warily trod the trails and jungles of central Bougainville, braving the tropical heat and other elements. "Those were scary," remembered Sergeant Arthur Johnson of the Americal Division patrols; "you were walking in the jungle and you don't know if a Jap walked five feet from you. And then we heard all kinds of weird sounds, the birds were singing and you would swear they [the Japanese] were whistling signals. Once in a while a boar would jump up and we thought it was a Jap so we would fire." Instead of helmets, the Americans wore soft caps and eschewed all shiny objects or clothing. The typical patroller carried a couple of grenades, a rifle, a basic load of ammunition, a couple of rations, mosquito repellent, atabrine, a knife, a poncho, a sweater, salt tablets, two canteens, extra socks, gloves, and foot powder. Point men used machetes to hack their way through thick jungle. Seldom did the patrols venture beyond the protective umbrella of friendly artillery as they sweated out this war of wits. In general, the Americans sent out two types of patrols—combat and reconnaissance. Combat patrols were large enough to sustain themselves in a substantial fight. They were, in the estimation of Tech 4 Robert Webb, an analyst with the 182nd Infantry Regiment, "a lumbering, armored giant, armed to the teeth to destroy the enemy." Reconnaissance patrols were smaller and geared mainly for scouting. In the view of the Americal Division's operations section, they "should never be less than 12 men and preferably a platoon. A group this size can move rapidly and quietly and still defend itself if necessary." Under the right circumstances, the patrollers could "play havoc with an enemy battalion and vanish into the jungle." Most commonly, though, they made no contact and nothing happened.[7]

Some of the patrolling soldiers carried more than just the burden of their own lives and deaths. They also operated under an intense political microscope that revealed much about the distorted American racial mores of the time. War Department segregation policies that mirrored racist Jim Crow customs so prevalent in much of the United States affected the composition and culture of Army units in the Pacific. The practice of segregating white and black soldiers went back many decades, as did the policy of utilizing black soldiers primarily in menial noncombat roles, such as digging ditches, hauling supplies, and waiting on their fellow troops. All of this stemmed from the spurious—and historically incorrect—idea that black troops could not, or would not, fight as well as white troops. "Black troops were just naturally suspected of cowardice, stealing, rape, the whole racial stereotype lie," Staff Sergeant Bill Stevens, a black soldier, later remarked. In truth, when given the opportunity to fight, African-American soldiers had carved out a fine combat record dating back as far as the Revolution. Nonetheless, if love is blind, so is racism. As the United States mobilized a mass army during World War II, the attitudes and practices stemming from hundreds of years of racism meant that African-American soldiers, dubbed "Negroes" or "colored" in the prevalent terms of the time, still largely served in all-black, noncombat units, often under white officers because of the poisonous assumption that blacks either could not, or should not, serve in leadership positions, especially over whites. So entrenched were separatist racial attitudes that Army surveys revealed a strong preference among most whites and even some blacks to remain apart. Some 88 percent of whites favored separate units, 81 percent a different PX, and 84 percent separate service clubs. Almost half of the black respondents wanted their own PX and service clubs. Only a minority, though, agreed with the idea of segregated units. The commanding officer of Camp Claiborne, Louisiana, would not even allow black and white athletic teams to play against one another, lest men of different races come into physical contact. The white C.O. of one all-black unit told Army surveyors who were interested in the attitude of his troops that they were wasting their time. "They are not capable of answering many of these questions for themselves. We know better than they do what their real feelings are." Another commander in a stateside training post made a point of removing black or pro–civil rights newspapers from his outfit's library.

Grotesquely, then, even as the United States struggled to defeat intensely racist, homicidal fascist regimes, it did so with armed forces segregated on the basis of race, thus putting the lie to the latter-year, saccharine-coated American cultural memory of World War II as strictly a "good war" that pitted absolute good against absolute evil. At the same time, though, a grow-ing civil rights movement, driven to a great extent by the social, demo-graphic, economic, and moral forces unleashed by the war, increasingly contested the perpetuation of racial inequalities. Labor leader A. Philip Randolph, NAACP executive secretary Walter White, along with other in-fluential civil rights advocates and media outlets, put intense pressure on the Roosevelt administration to combat segregation in wartime industries and the armed forces. Judge William Hastie, a distinguished African-American lawyer and civilian aide to Secretary of War Henry Stimson, conducted ex-tensive research into Army race relations and strongly recommended inte-gration, leadership opportunities for black soldiers, and the end of all racial profiling. "I believe the Military authorities do not comprehend the amount of resentment among soldiers and civilians, white as well as black, over the rigid pattern of racial separation imposed by the Army," he wrote in a pow-erfully worded memo. "Insistence upon an inflexible policy of separating white and black soldiers is probably the most dramatic evidence of hypoc-risy in our profession that we are girding ourselves for the preservation of democracy."

With an existential world war to win, and the resistance to mass reform so characteristic of decision makers in nearly any entrenched institution, Army leaders from George Marshall on down had little stomach for dra-matic change, especially the sort of transformation Hastie envisioned. They did, though, have to react to the occasional political pressure that eventu-ated from the tension in Washington over race. As a result, old-school, apartheid-style racism coexisted tensely alongside new-school integrationist activism in the Pacific theater. This led to the wavering deployment of a few African-American combat troops. The 24th Infantry Regiment, a tradi-tional Regular Army unit with a proud lineage and led entirely by white officers, arrived first in April 1942, followed by the 93rd Infantry Division, with a mixed officer corps, in January 1944. In spite of the growing demand for combat manpower as the pace of operations quickened, neither unit went immediately into action. At a number of South Pacific islands, the men of the 24th spent months unloading and loading ships, guarding air bases, moving supplies, spraying insecticide, draining swamps, building roads, and pulling monotonous guard duty. Most of the 93rd was parceled out among American bases on such islands as New Georgia and Bakina to work as warehouse and dock laborers. They worked at a fast pace, with little time for any sort of rest or recreation. Trained to fight as combat troops, the men deeply resented their assignment as common laborers. To many, the work carried a strong odor of a less-than-pleasant past. "It was as if we were the slaves and the white officers in our outfit were the overseers," Private Clarence Ross seethed.

Amid such a politically charged climate, this military bench duty could not continue forever. "The War Department has been under constant pressure for alleged failure to utilize Negro soldiers in a combat capacity," Marshall radioed Lieutenant General Millard Harmon, an Army Air Forces officer in administrative charge of Army forces in the South Pacific. "We are very desirous of employing them as soon as practicable and they should have a careful test to determine their battle dependability."

A battalion from the 24th Infantry landed on Bougainville at the end of January and went into corps reserve, where it saw only limited action during the Japanese offensive. The 93rd Division's 25th Infantry Regiment—another outfit with a proud heritage—plus the 593rd Field Artillery Battalion arrived on March 28, after the defeat of Hyakutake's attack. "No other units of comparable size deployed in the Pacific theater were ever subjected to such scrutiny even before they saw any significant action," the great Pacific War historian Harry Gailey asserted with succinct accuracy. Indeed, no other soldiers went into action against the Japanese with so many fellow Americans emotionally invested in their success or failure. Almost every rookie white combat outfit started anonymously. The black troops had no such luxury. They had already been singled out as separate and different by the very nature of the era's racial customs, and they could hope for nothing else once in combat. Every move they made, for good or ill, might well affect the attitudes of white decision makers about all black troops. Understanding the political glare that suffused the "Tan Yanks," as many correspondents called the soldiers, Griswold attempted to ease them into his patrol operations. From April onward, they worked under the operational control of his two white divisions, patrolling, skirmishing, fighting an occasional sharp battle, dealing with the elements, learning jungle warfare. In a letter to Harmon, Griswold assessed them as "inclined to be a bit 'trigger-happy,' but perhaps no more so than . . . any other organization which has never had its baptism of fire." General Beightler put together a combined battle force consisting of one battalion from the 25th, a Fiji battalion, and one from the white 148th Infantry, all under the command of the 148th's C.O., Colonel Lawrence White, whose nickname was "Red." The troops soon dubbed this scratch unit the "Red, White and Black

Butai" and it carried out its missions with no issues. Griswold even told Harmon that they were "the envy of the rest of the outfit!"

By any fair measure, the performance of the greenhorn black soldiers was similar to most any outfit in its first exposure to hostile fire. Friendly correspondents, most of whom were African-American, eagerly reported any semblance of success, no matter how minor. "There is a one man wave of destruction in one of the infantry units of the 93rd Division, which has now solidified the Allied perimeter on this second largest island in the South Pacific," wrote Billy Rowe, an African-American correspondent, of Private Wade Foggie, who destroyed several Japanese pillboxes with a bazooka during a patrol in early April. In another story, he quoted Sergeant Ernest Brown of the 93rd Division as contending that "white and colored men of arms pull together against the common enemy and between most of them something has been born that will add greatly to the peace that must come some day. We work, sleep and eat together out there in that sightless wasteland, happy for the added security it brings." Rowe added that "out here in the jungle a man doesn't inquire if the fellow next to him is black or white. In the jungle, the black and the white understand each other."

Though undoubtedly true in many instances, the easy frontline camaraderie prevalent among some of the soldiers could not begin to overcome the more powerful forces of politics and institutional racism. When a patrol from the 25th Infantry Regiment panicked under fire, got cut off, and suffered scores of self-inflicted, fratricidal casualties as a result of terrified, irresponsible shooting, the consequences were far-reaching. Rumors spread among white soldiers that the 25th had run away en masse. "The contrast between the American black soldier and the Fijian black soldier was beyond belief," one Americal Division soldier contended. Gloomy stories—usually shared in sotto voce or faux insider fashion—proliferated around Bougainville, and soon the South Pacific, that black soldiers would not fight. This morphed into a canard that the 93rd had caved completely and compromised the entire beachhead, leading to untold numbers of white casualties to restore it. Among the 25th Infantry Regiment enlisted men, a widely circulated rumor claimed that the white company commander, Captain James Curran, had abandoned his black soldiers, leading to many deaths, including Lieutenant Oscar Davenport, one of his African-American platoon leaders, and that Curran's fellow white officers had covered up evidence of his malfeasance. The resentment against Curran was such that a bodyguard never left his side until he was transferred out of the unit.

The incident generated multiple investigations, ranging from the Americal Division inspector general to XIV Corps and Harmon's South Pacific command. They revealed the sort of confusion, bad fortune, inexperience, leadership mistakes, and coordination issues that generally typified such tactical fiascos. Brigadier General Leonard Boyd, the 93rd's assistant division commander and a highly combat-experienced World War I veteran who led a modified brigade-size amalgamation of 25th Infantry and other divisional soldiers on Bougainville, claimed that a similar incident had befallen a veteran Americal Division patrol the previous week, "which was considered regrettable but not important." If true, this was indeed the difference: poor performance on the part of any black unit was likely to be extrapolated into larger conclusions on the part of many about the proficiency of African-American soldiers as a whole. By contrast, a white unit carried no such representative burden. Though Griswold would have preferred to avoid the headaches endemic in these racial politics, he approached his assessment of the 93rd's combat reliability with a characteristically fair mind. As he saw it, any failures stemmed from inadequate junior officer leadership. "The 25th needs pruning badly," he told Harmon's chief of staff. "They have some White Officers who leave something to be desired, and some very poor colored Officers who should be eliminated at once. In almost every instance where poor work is done it's a question of Junior leadership."

Some of the white junior officers had no wish to lead black troops and considered it a punishment or a commentary on their own poor quality; a few were intense racists who looked down on their men. Too many of the black officers, most of whom were graduates of predominantly black colleges, were not prepared for combat leadership or mistrusted their white colleagues. In the main, though, most small-unit leaders, white or black, were well intentioned and reasonably well respected among the men. Captain George Little, the 93rd Division psychiatrist, conducted an extensive series of interviews with soldiers of all ranks, mainly to assess their morale and state of mind. He found that the majority of the troops—like combat soldiers in practically any unit—were focused primarily on survival, creature comforts, and assessing the reliability of their leaders, rather than racial issues. They hoped and expected to prove that they could fight as well as whites and, in general, improve conditions at home for African-Americans. A 25 percent minority professed to have no idea what they were fighting for or voiced outright opposition to participating in the war. Those in the latter category tended to come from urban areas. "They say it is a white man's war and when things are over the Negroes at home will be worse off than before." Little concluded that "the morale of the soldiers and officers has improved due to the excitement of going into action, with its possible rewards, the friendliness of veteran troops. Racial friction continues to be the most disturbing factor, although . . . it has diminished." Boyd said of the 93rd Division to a friend in the War Department, "I urge the retention of existing negro combat units and forming new units with careful selection to insure equality in intelligence level with white divisions. Given average officers, whether white or mixed, this unit can be developed into a combat organization capable of releasing spear-head troops after initial combat and possibly developing into shock-troops themselves. I can say that in spite of the headaches peculiar to a colored unit that I enjoy serving with it and would not desire a change in a position of similar responsibility."

Unfortunately, Boyd's assessment had little impact. In spite of the exhaustive investigations, the rumors about the 93rd Division impacted perception among those whose opinions mattered in Washington. Secretary Stimson wrote to a colleague about black soldiers, "I do not believe they can be turned into really effective combat troops without all officers being white." Neither he nor any other senior leaders disseminated a definite order to withhold black soldiers from ground combat duty, but from Bougainville onward, their preference to that effect was clear, and mirrored those of far too many other white commanders in the field. For the most part, black combat troops were now relegated to the war's backwater of low-level patrolling or guarding secured islands, in addition to the traditional manual labor chores. "Those who are industriously and dangerously spreading utterly false stories concerning the Negro as combat troops do not appear to care what the record says, nor do many who appear to accept the falsehoods unquestioningly," NAACP's Walter White later wrote to President Roosevelt in a scathing memo. Undoubtedly, they did not. To be sure, the African-American combat units did have significant issues unique to their own circumstances, stemming primarily from the realities of racial inequality in the United States—the toxic sludge that led to the creation of segregated units in the first place, the poor educational levels of many African-American soldiers, the fear and mistrust endemic to race relations that could not help but affect many soldiers, the propensity for the dissemination of rumors and misinformation among blacks and whites alike, inevitably affecting perceptions and attitudes. These were the unhappy consequences that eventuated from the existence and perpetuation of a racial caste system, one that, in the end, degraded and dishonored both victim and oppressor and did much to affect the collective psychology of the races along those lines. The performance of black combat troops on Bougainville was largely similar to those of other inexperienced units throughout much of the war. But unlike the rest of the Army, they could not afford to make any mistakes. As historian Gailey aptly summarized, these soldiers "could have had no idea of the crucial role they would play in high-level policy decisions regarding the deployment of black combat units."[8]

The fact that the Americans could afford, out of irrational prejudice, to squander a substantial chunk of their manpower indicated a remarkable material largesse. Indeed, while the Japanese scrimped and scavenged just to survive on Bougainville, the mini American city that was the XIV Corps perimeter grew and flourished to the point where it accommodated something of a tropical representation of normal American life, with plentiful food and luxury items. A single supply ship disgorged 1.5 million rations. Ice cream and butter soon became available. By the fall, port companies laboring at the beach were handling over 100,000 measurement tons of matériel each month. XIV Corps possessed a backlog of extra herringbone twill uniforms, socks, underwear, and tents. The 464th Laundry Company was now washing 200,000 items of clothing each week. A solitary bakery company now churned out thirty thousand pounds of bread per day. Among the arriving tonnage were twelve thousand baseballs, ten thousand softballs, three thousand volleyballs, forty-five thousand decks of playing cards, 676 radios, 349 Ping-Pong tables, 609 harmonicas, and 157 guitars. In pyramidal tents sprinkled around the perimeter, forty separate post exchanges (PXs) soon came into being, selling a diverse array of goods, including beer, soda, watches, pens, lighters, cigarettes, dictionaries, alarm clocks, Whitman's chocolates, and even moccasins, to the tune of $160,000 in gross revenue. At the PXs, soldiers placed money orders to send Easter and Mother's Day flowers and gifts to wives and sweethearts back home. Phonograph records were common, as were weekly unit bingo games. A few soldiers found the time and the materials to build model airplanes, kites, and leather goods. Others did woodworking or clay modeling. More than one thousand 37th Division soldiers took correspondence courses. In some instances, qualified instructors offered on-site classes for high school or college credit.

By the middle of 1944, the Americans had built sixty-six houses of worship that hosted an average of 575 Sunday services per month with an aggregate attendance of 60,045, a nearly 100 percent participation rate. The typical chapel was built of wood and featured a prominent steeple. More than a dozen choirs soon came into existence and added the singing of hymns to weekly services. One chapel abutted a brand-new, beautifully maintained cemetery containing the carefully marked graves of those who had been killed in the fighting. "In the quietness of the jungle, sleep the heroes of Torokina side by side, without regard to rank, race or religious creed, intered [sic] with soft hands and reverence," Griswold wrote. The XIV Corps Special Services section operated a radio station nearly round the clock, offering live local programs, war news, including coverage of the Normandy invasion, and shortwave broadcasts of football games in America. Most notably, the station broadcast the 1944 World Series, in which the St. Louis Cardinals defeated their crosstown rivals, the Browns. A local newspaper, the *Tropical Times*, soon went into circulation. A library lent books to GIs who had a good borrowing record; other readers relied on the ubiquitous armed forces paperbacks that circulated thousands of titles to servicemen in all theaters. Some four thousand GI spectators visited an art exhibit displaying the work of 125 soldier artists.

True to American form, on-site recreation and entertainment came to dominate the lifestyle of the soldiers on Bougainville. "The movie circuit went . . . into full operation, with pictures being shown every other night in 82 areas," reported the Special Services section of the Army's South Pacific command. In all, they showed 122 different movies. Griswold estimated that about 90 percent of his men had access to a movie on any given day (the obvious exception being the dogfaces who were on patrol or manning the perimeter defense). So ubiquitous and secure were the GI theaters that a pair of new films, *It Happened Tomorrow* and *Going My Way*, actually premiered on the island. They were soon followed by *Marriage Is a Private Affair* and *Devotion*. Audiences ranged from as small as thirty-five to as large as eight thousand. Not everyone in attendance was American. At one outdoor theater, as the audience watched captured Japanese footage of the sinking of the USS *Lexington*, they heard shouts of "Banzai!" from a nearby stand of trees. "A Jap had hidden himself to watch the movie but was overcome with patriotism at the sight of his comrades . . . sending an enemy ship to the bottom," a GI witness recalled. "He was pulled from the tree with no trouble and entered the POW compound." Division bands and visiting musicians played nightly concerts. As the perimeter grew increasingly more secure, a dizzying array of USO and Hollywood talent descended on Bougainville to perform for the troops. Randolph Scott, Jack Benny, Jerry Colonna, Frances Langford, and Bob Hope all made multiple appearances on makeshift stages in front of sizable audiences, as did many lesser-known singers, comedians, and starlets. "I sure did like Bob Hope," Private Gordon Rose wrote to his mother after the show. "He looked exactly like he does on the screen." When the beautiful Langford sang "I'm in the Mood for Love" to the sex-starved soldiers of the American, her sultry performance "brought nods of agreement from each of those present," in the recollection of one officer.

By far, the most popular recreational activity was athletics. Boxing rings, basketball courts, tennis courts, volleyball courts, and softball and baseball diamonds soon proliferated. The games provided a healthy physical outlet for otherwise bored soldiers and, quite often, a chance to gamble or compete for bragging rights. Organized leagues and schedules were soon established. On any given day, four hundred volleyball courts were in use. Practically every unit had a team for one sport or another. By one estimate, there were 50 basketball teams, 120 baseball teams, and 200 softball teams on the island. A boxing tournament began with one hundred entrants. The finale drew a crowd of fifteen thousand. Bosley Field, the main baseball and softball complex, hosted two hundred games per month. In one surreal instance, players from the 37th Division noticed a ragged-looking Japanese soldier who regularly watched their games from the distant vantage point of the jungle. He soon developed into a bona fide fan. "He somehow managed to root for the 37th teams, showing his approval of hits and runs for the home team!" a 37th Division soldier later recalled. Appreciating his support, and feeling a bit sorry for him, the American ballplayers did not have the heart or inclination to go round him up. Athletic teams competed fiercely for victories and championships. The tremendous prestige of unit pride—and probably more than a few dollars—were always on the line. The results were important enough to make it into a theater-level report on morale activities on Bougainville: the 21st Evacuation Hospital won the baseball championship, the 120th Ordnance

Company prevailed in softball, Marine Air Group 24 won in basketball, and the 670th Topographical Engineering Company took the honors in volleyball.[9]

The good life on Bougainville indicated that it had become a strategic backwater, no longer of much importance to either side, with a kind of unspoken truce in lieu of any further major operations. The defeat of Hyakutake not only meant that Rabaul was doomed; it also signaled that the Americans were moving on from the Solomons to points closer to Japan— MacArthur in northern New Guinea and Nimitz in the Central Pacific. As Griswold's combat units prepared for an eventual invasion of the Philippines, the Americans by the end of 1944 handed off responsibility for Bougainville to the Australians. This, too, portended a larger meaning. For the first two years of the war, the Australians had taken a leading role, not only in the basing and defense of their own country but in MacArthur's New Guinea operations. Now, as the Americans grew in all-around military strength and advanced beyond the Solomons, closer to the Philippines and the key island chains of the Central Pacific, the Australians were consigned to strategic backfill duty, particularly on Bougainville. The war had pivoted into a new phase of American dominance. MacArthur was about to make his boldest move.

4

Informed Boldness

I n an anonymous swamp near Sio, New Guinea, exhausted, half-starved Japanese soldiers of the Imperial Army's 20th Division retreated west, fleeing from their Australian and American adversaries, who had maintained a steady advance in the wake of the successful Saidor invasion. The Japanese abandoned anything that might slow them down, including a heavy steel box they distractedly flung into a muddy pit, half-submerged in a layer of noxious water, an unappealing place they mistakenly believed no enemy would ever investigate. The box was packed with Imperial Japanese Army code books and accompanying material, all of which was too soggy from New Guinea's monsoon rains to burn. The responsible signals officer had carelessly abandoned this precious intelligence raw material. Even worse, he had torn the covers off each code book and disingenuously forwarded them with inscribed certificates of destruction to his superiors, deliberately deceiving them about his failure to destroy the books. If Americans remember with infamy Benedict Arnold, who betrayed his country for ego, then this sloppy and deceptive Japanese signals officer is fortunate he remains anonymous to history, lest his memory endure in similar fashion among his countrymen. The damage he did to his nation's cause far exceeded whatever strife Arnold's betrayal may have created for the American revolutionaries.

On January 19, 1944, Australian soldiers of the 9th Infantry Division came upon the trunk, hauled it out of the pit, investigated the contents, and quickly discerned that they had a major find on their hands. They forwarded everything to the Central Bureau, General MacArthur's elaborate cryptanalytic agency, whose members worked at Ascot Park, a racecourse outside of Brisbane. Though the pages were waterlogged and muddy, they were retrievable. The code breakers employed commercial cooking ovens to dry them out. Amazed at their good luck, the cryptanalysts soon used the captured books to decipher most of the Imperial Army's codes, greatly expanding the scope of Ultra, even as the enemy high command remained blissfully unaware that their most secret communications were now compromised—an intelligence coup for the Allies that must rank among the most significant of modern times.[1]

This remarkable turn of events had an almost immediate effect. By March, MacArthur's analysts were intercepting and decoding as many as two thousand Imperial Army messages per day. Ironically, they even found a communication from Eighteenth Army, the Japanese land command in New Guinea, to Imperial General Headquarters in Tokyo claiming that the code books had been safely burned. In a larger sense, the message traffic presented MacArthur with a valuable real-time picture of the Japanese order of battle and dispositions in New Guinea as well as the intentions of Lieutenant General Hatazo Adachi, commander of the Eighteenth Army. Adachi expected the next Allied invasion on New Guinea's north coast to come at Hansa Bay. He had placed his 41st Division at Madang to the east and the 51st Division at Wewak in the west. Once the Allies were ashore at Hansa Bay, he planned to ambush them on both flanks. Indeed, MacArthur did originally intend to strike at Hansa Bay, at least until the decoded evidence of Adachi's plans prompted reconsideration of this operation in high-level SWPA circles. Instead of walking right into Adachi's trap at Hansa Bay, why not outflank him by landing a couple hundred miles to the west at Hollandia? Lieutenant General Kenney and Brigadier General Bonner Fellers, chief of the planning section in SWPA's operations department, both later claimed some credit for devising this concept, as did Vice Admiral William "Bull" Halsey, who remembered discussing it with MacArthur during a planning conference. Kenney wrote in his memoir, "When General MacArthur came back from the Los Negros landing, I discussed with him the proposition of bypassing Hansa Bay and jumping all the way to Hollandia." Though Kenney did not refer to the proposition as his idea, he also did not mention Fellers. Nor did he originally intend to advocate invading Hollandia because it was, at that stage, located beyond the range of his fighter planes. Even so, a March 9 entry in Kenney's diary does confirm that he spoke with MacArthur about Hollandia, but little else. In 1971, Fellers told MacArthur biographer D. Clayton James that the sheer vastness of New Guinea's geography and the remaining distance to the Philippines prompted him to think of a Hollandia landing. "As I studied the operations plans to take us all the way to the Philippines, I figured we'd never get there. They took so long. I started searching to make longer hops than had been scheduled. I decided that we'd have to skip an awful lot of intermediate stations that were already planned. The search for longer hops led us to Hollandia."

Brigadier General Charles Willoughby, the intelligence chief who had used the new decrypts to compile increasingly accurate information about Japanese dispositions along the northern New Guinea coast, also apparently came to favor the idea of a leapfrog invasion of Hollandia. But very few in Fellers's own planning section agreed. Nor did his boss, Major General Stephen Chamberlin, the operations officer (G3) who dismissed the proposal as a "wild scheme" and ordered him to shelve it. Fellers had known MacArthur for over two decades. They had served together in the Philippines, where Fellers had once functioned as MacArthur's liaison to President Manuel Quezon. Fellers defied Chamberlin and got his plan to MacArthur, supposedly through an unnamed intermediary. Fellers lost the battle but won the war. When the normally mild-mannered Chamberlin found out that Fellers had disobeyed him and gone over his head, he fired him on the spot. According to Fellers, he castigated him for letting MacArthur down. "This is going to be a catastrophe. It's just going to be God awful, and it's your fault." But MacArthur kept Fellers on as his secretary of the general staff, an invented position with nebulous responsibilities. Fellers also gravitated to Willoughby's intelligence section and soon became deeply involved in psychological operations. More important, MacArthur bought into the Hollandia idea and embraced it.[2]

Regardless of the true origins of the Hollandia plan, there is no doubt that, by the first week of March, MacArthur had abandoned his Hansa Bay invasion concept and decided to launch an ambitious amphibious leapfrog to Hollandia, something that never would have happened if not for Central Bureau's success in cracking the Japanese codes. Thanks to this information, he knew that Hollandia was lightly garrisoned by a thin screen of about twelve thousand service troops who were primarily involved in maintaining coastal supply dumps and a trio of airfields near freshwater Lake Sentani, about five to ten miles inland from the sea. The opportunity to hit this soft underbelly, outflank Adachi's entrenched divisions, sever their communication and supply lines, thus consigning them to the deadly decay of the New Guinea wilds, and accelerate the Philippines timetable was irresistible for MacArthur. While studiously avoiding any reference to

Ultra, he radioed his intentions to General Marshall on March 5. "Recent seizure of a foothold in the Admiralties which will shortly be followed by complete occupation presents an immediate opportunity for rapid exploitation along the north coast of New Guinea. To this end I propose to make the Hollandia area instead of Hansa Bay my next objective." To expand his air cover for the operation, he also recommended the assistance of Nimitz's carrier forces.

On March 12, the Joint Chiefs responded with a multipoint directive for MacArthur and Nimitz, confirming the perpetuation of the two-pronged Pacific advance, MacArthur across northern New Guinea in the general direction of Mindanao or Luzon, and Nimitz across the Central Pacific. In the directive, they communicated approval for MacArthur's Hollandia proposal and set an April 15 target date for the invasion. They also approved a request by Nimitz to proceed with plans to invade the Marianas in June. Admiral William Leahy, the chairman of the Joint Chiefs, and President Roosevelt's low-key but extraordinarily effective chief of staff, later opined that the communication "greatly clarified the situation. MacArthur and the Navy would be working in harmony in the far flung areas that constituted our Pacific battlefront."

In essence, for the first time, the chiefs nudged the two leading Pacific theater commanders into mutual cooperation. MacArthur had spent much of the war resenting and fearing Nimitz as a rival, one who might well eventually lay claim to most American resources in the war against Japan, due to the inevitable influence of the Navy in a theater dominated by vast stretches of ocean. When MacArthur was especially peeved at his naval colleague, he would privately vent about him to aides and mispronounce his name as "Neee-mitz." Publicly, both men maintained a veneer of blissful cooperation, in Nimitz's case because he deeply detested public spats between senior officers, and in MacArthur's case because he understood that an open break with the Navy's leading personality might damage his long-term goal of returning to the Philippines. Even a decade and a half after the war, he claimed in a letter to Nimitz biographer E. B. Potter that "the cooperation between Admiral Nimitz and myself was one of unbroken and hearty mutuality. Any concept of rivalry between us or ill feeling is baseless." The preternaturally calm Nimitz felt no animosity toward the general. So determined was he to maintain correct relations, he resented any indication otherwise, even in speculative media circles. When the notoriously rabble-rousing columnist Drew Pearson asserted that there was tension between the two men, Nimitz fumed in a private letter to his wife, Catherine, that Pearson was trying "to stir up trouble between MacArthur and me where *none* exists. What a troublemaker he is!" In stark contrast to MacArthur, Nimitz much preferred under-the-radar anonymity to public adulation, to the point where he refused even to publish a word about his long military career. "He said that if he wrote he would have to hurt some people and he did not want to do that," Catherine remarked years later, after his death.

For almost two years, MacArthur had resisted any inclination to work more closely with Nimitz. Now, though, in the wake of the Joint Chiefs' communication, he reached out to the admiral and invited him to SWPA to coordinate their mutual plans. "I have long had it in mind to extend to you the hospitality of this area," he wrote. "The close coordination of our respective commands would be greatly furthered I am sure by our personal conference. I can assure you of a warm welcome." Nimitz accepted with alacrity. On March 25, he and members of his staff arrived in Brisbane. True to his word, General MacArthur welcomed them like long-lost friends. When Nimitz's seaplane taxied to its wharf, MacArthur and several staffers were waiting by the dock and greeted them warmly. "His cordiality and courtesy to me and my party throughout my visit was complete and genuine, and left nothing to be desired," Nimitz later wrote to his superior, Admiral Ernest King, the chief of naval operations, a tough-minded and innovative sea power strategist who loathed MacArthur.

MacArthur put Nimitz up in a private suite in the air-conditioned Lennon's Hotel, where the general had established personal living quarters with his wife, Jean, and six-year-old son, Arthur. The general appropriated the hotel ballroom to host a banquet in the admiral's honor. Some forty-eight guests attended, including every officer of general or admiral rank in the city. Nimitz gave a short speech and indicated that the most difficult aspect of his island-hopping strategy was deciding whether to "starve or bomb" Japanese garrisons. In the recollection of Rear Admiral Felix Johnson, the SWPA naval liaison officer, MacArthur "was so very friendly with him, put his arm around him, and everybody came up to meet him." The gentlemanly admiral reciprocated in kind. He presented orchids to Jean, silk playsuits for Arthur, and boxes of Hawaiian candy for the whole MacArthur family. When MacArthur invited him to his home for a private dinner the following evening, the two commanders enjoyed, in the general's estimation, "a quiet evening of congenial conversation."

In the course of two days of productive, cordial meetings, MacArthur, Nimitz, their key aides, and SWPA commanders hammered out plans to coordinate their mutual efforts. MacArthur wanted air support for the Hollandia landings from Nimitz's growing carrier forces. The admiral was concerned that the carriers would be vulnerable to attacks from New Guinea–based Japanese planes. Kenney assured him this would not be a problem. "I promised to have them rubbed out by April 5th," he later wrote of the discussion. Though Kenney's promise provoked skepticism from nearly everyone, including Nimitz, MacArthur took it at face value and, in so doing, reassured Nimitz that he would personally vouch for the destruction of the enemy planes. So the admiral agreed to loan Vice Admiral Marc Mitscher's Task Force 58 eleven major fleet carriers—the Navy's coin-of-the-realm capital ships—to support the Hollandia invasion. Even so, he insisted on removing Mitscher's carriers within forty-eight hours of the landings. He did agree, though, to leave eight smaller escort carriers in place for about a week to provide continuous air support. In return, MacArthur pledged to assist Nimitz's Marianas operations by raiding the Palau Islands with heavy bombers flying from bases at Hollandia that he would presumably develop after the landings.

The only awkward moment occurred when Nimitz made the mistake of mentioning a portion of the Joint Chiefs' directive that ordered Nimitz to prepare assault plans for Formosa and MacArthur for Luzon, if those "operations proved necessary." The admiral and the other conferees were soon treated to a uniquely MacArthur-esque diatribe about the moral imperative of returning to the Philippines. According to Nimitz, the general pontificated for several minutes on "the impossibility of bypassing the Philippines, his sacred obligations there—redemption of the 17 million people—blood on his soul—deserted by the American people etc. etc." Kenney also remembered his boss mentioning the immorality of abandoning "all the American prisoners that the Japs held in the Philippines." Nimitz understood the argument, though he did not necessarily agree with it. For the moment, the discussion was pointless since the decision hinged on the success or failure of pending operations, not to mention approval of the president and the Joint Chiefs, but it did presage the divergent visions of climactic Pacific theater strategy that the admiral and the general would lay before the president a few months later.[3]

For the moment, though, all was harmony. After a warm send-off from MacArthur, Nimitz boarded a plane on the afternoon of March 27 and flew

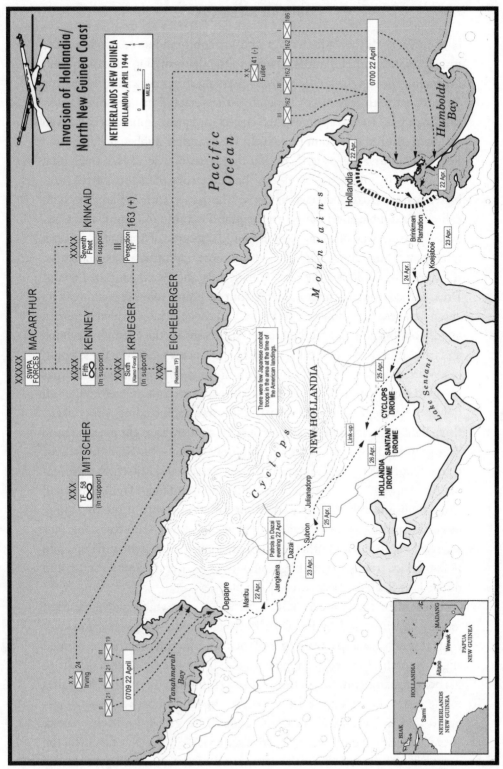

© 2021 by Chris Erichsen

back to Pearl Harbor. MacArthur and his commanders continued planning in earnest for Hollandia. Owing to the daunting logistics of compiling intelligence on the landing areas, amassing shipping, and coordinating air support within Nimitz's timetable, they elected to postpone D-Day until April 22. The invasion was the largest and most ambitious conceived by MacArthur to this point in the war. His planners dubbed it "Operation Reckless," cultivating a subtle notion that lasted for decades, namely that MacArthur, in embracing "Reckless," had taken one of history's great gambles, a masterstroke of audacious nerve. The sycophantic Willoughby later called it "a double envelopment in the grand manner of Hannibal at Cannae." The truth was, of course, less dramatic. "Because of MacArthur's secret intelligence, Sure Thing might have been more appropriate," as a name for the operation, quipped the distinguished Pacific War historian Edward Drea. Indeed, the information MacArthur received from the code breakers about Japanese intentions, dispositions, and capabilities provided him with a nice comfort zone. In football terms, he possessed the enemy's playbook and game plan. Even so, "Reckless" did hint at a new maturity in the strength of SWPA forces and MacArthur's joint planning. The amphibious landings involved eight hundred carrier- and land-based aircraft, including the full flower of Kenney's first-line strength, 217 warships, including two cruisers, three light cruisers, eight escort carriers, 55 destroyers, eight Attack Troop Transports (APAs), two Attack Cargo Ships (AKAs), 31 LCIs, 51 LSTs, four Cargo Ships (AKs), plus numerous smaller vessels and Mitscher's formidable Task Force 58. The armada carried fifty thousand tons of bulk stores and three thousand vehicles earmarked for unloading within the first three days. The landings were to be made by elements of two Army divisions, plus attached engineers and other specialists, some 37,527 combat troops and 18,184 service troops, originating from locales all over the South Pacific, and dubbed the Reckless Task Force by the planners.

Located in the western half of New Guinea, which had once been loosely administered by the Dutch, the Hollandia area was a finger of coastal beach, swamps, trails, grasslands, and mountains that protruded slightly north of the adjacent coastline into the Pacific Ocean. A pair of harbors, Tanahmerah Bay in the west and Humboldt Bay twenty-five miles to the east, bookended the area. Most of the land in between was dominated by the Cyclops Mountains, a small range whose highest peak stretched to seven thousand feet above sea level, "completely cutting off the coast from the interior," in the estimation of one Army analyst. To the south, the mountains gave way to rolling hills and then grassy plains that abutted Lake Sentani. The Japanese had already built three airfields on these plains. The Americans intended to capture and expand them into twice that number. Nestled into a cove at the northern end of Humboldt Bay was Hollandia Town, a tiny local village where European voyagers had once traded in the feathers of colorful tropical birds. The damp equatorial climate produced heavy rainfall and high humidity. In a typical year, 90 to 100 inches of rain fell on Humboldt Bay; the Tanahmerah area absorbed 130 to 140 inches. Temperatures typically hovered in the high eighties. Animal species of every type and description thrived in the warm air and rich jungle foliage. According to one Army report, "Crocodiles up to thirteen feet long are encountered in the rivers. Snakes of the constrictor type are not rare. Less dangerous but more annoying are mosquitoes, sand flies, flies and leeches."

MacArthur chose the 24th and 41st Infantry Divisions to carry out "Operation Reckless." The 24th had once been stationed at Schofield Barracks in Oahu. Many of the soldiers had been strafed and bombed by Japanese planes during the Pearl Harbor attack more than two years earlier. They had spent over a year and a half in Hawaii, training intensely under the tutelage of their division commander, Major General Frederick Irving, a decorated, hard-nosed West Pointer and former cadet boxing champion who had seen heavy combat while leading a machine-gun company in World War I. "They had a score to settle for which they had long trained," he later wrote of his troops, "and there was a long repressed desire to close with and destroy the Japanese." Irving's division deployed to Australia in August 1943 and trained for six more long months before moving to Goodenough (pronounced "good enough") Island, a major American staging base north of Papua New Guinea's easternmost coast where "the assault echelons made practice landings in a full dress-rehearsal on the north shore of New Guinea . . . during the week prior to embarkation," noted one unit history. "We had trained for so long," Sergeant Hollis Peacock, a soldier in the 19th Infantry who had experienced Pearl Harbor, later said, "so we were ready for bear." MacArthur tapped two of the division's regiments, the 19th and the 21st, to land at Red Beaches 1 and 2 on Tanahmerah Bay, with the division's other regiment, the 34th, in floating reserve. Because of the proliferation of thick underwater coral, naval planners initially objected to the landing at Red Beach 1, which was nothing more than a tiny cove inside the bay at a village called Depapre. But with little sense of the terrain around Tanahmerah Bay and uncomfortable with the idea of funneling all his men into one small beach, Irving insisted on the Red Beach 1 landing as well.

The 41st Infantry Division was perhaps the most combat experienced of any Army division in SWPA. The unit had logged nearly four months of frontline action the previous year at Gona and Salamaua, battling the elements and the Japanese in almost equal measure, earning the nickname Jungleers, though this identity would soon be eclipsed by something more colorful. Weeks of delightful rehabilitation in Australia had since given way to redeployment to Cape Cretin, the forward American base near Finschhafen, New Guinea, a sure sign for the canny veterans that combat was imminent. When a Japanese propaganda broadcast referred to them as the "Bloody 41st Division Butchers," the troops embraced the moniker, even going so far as to print up mock cards with a drawing of a GI brandishing a carving knife alongside a shivering Japanese soldier. The nickname amused the division commander, Major General Horace Fuller, a chain-smoking artilleryman who had led the outfit well the previous year in the New Guinea wilds and was almost certainly now in line for higher command. When he first heard his men referred to as butchers, he told his staff, "Nothing could make me happier."

With operational security about their ultimate destination tight, rumor-mongering among the soldiers became almost like a sport, so much so that Fuller threatened to court-martial anyone caught engaging in it. "But this served only to increase the talk of the would-be strategists," the division historian lamented. Unbeknownst—for the moment—to the artful tongue waggers, MacArthur and his planners assigned the Humboldt Bay landings to a pair of the division's infantry regiments, the 162nd and 186th. Tanahmerah and Humboldt Bays were separated by about twenty-five miles of jungle and trail. Like pincers, the assault troops of the two divisions were supposed to push gradually inland to seize the airfields at Lake Sentani, advance toward each other, then link up and bag any Japanese who failed to escape.

With this done, the focus would then change to constructing an extensive sea and air base complex in the area capable of staging half a year's worth of supplies, supporting 200,000 troops, and serving as a key logistical node for the subsequent phases of MacArthur's northwesterly advance. At a minimum, this required the construction of four million square feet of warehouse space, two hundred miles of road, enough storage area for

118,000 barrels of fuel, plus a dozen and a half Liberty ship docks. So elaborate was the basing mission and the many difficulties presented by New Guinea conditions that engineers and construction specialists made up 41 percent of the assault component. Because of Nimitz's insistence on withdrawing Task Force 58 shortly after the invasion, MacArthur also decided to authorize a supporting invasion by the 41st Division's other regiment, the 163rd, at Aitape (pronounced "A-tape"), some 120 miles to the east. The mission of this "Persecution Task Force," as the planners termed it, was to take a Japanese airfield at Tadji from which Allied fighters could provide close air support for the Hollandia beachhead. Fuller detached Brigadier General Jens Doe, his assistant division commander, to lead the Persecution Task Force. Over MacArthur's initial objections, Krueger insisted on having another regiment, the 127th Infantry from the 32nd Infantry Division, as a floating reserve for the Aitape invasion. MacArthur had wanted to earmark the whole division to follow the Hollandia invasion with a landing 112 miles to the west at Wakde-Sarmi. But the shipping situation made this problematic. Plus, he realized that the 163rd might well become vulnerable if Adachi successfully moved any of his infantry battalions west from Wewak over ninety miles of New Guinea jungle and track to Aitape, so MacArthur agreed to Krueger's design.

Similar to Operation Fortitude, a deception plan unfolding in the European theater to fool the Germans about the time and place of the coming Allied invasion of France, SWPA headquarters took elaborate measures to deceive the Japanese about MacArthur's true intentions, particularly to keep Adachi fixated on the Hansa Bay area. Allied planes flew a preponderance of missions—2,454 sorties throughout March—against Wewak and Madang, pulverizing Japanese airfields. The raids ranged from bombing to reconnaissance and even the scattering of propaganda leaflets. Kenney's aviators added dummy paratroopers to the deceitful mix. Destroyers regularly shelled the coastal areas where Adachi's formations had concentrated. Navy PT boats zipped along the coast at night, with engines at ostentatious full throttle to cultivate the sense of keen Allied interest in the beaches. In many instances, submarines scattered empty rubber boats ashore to convey the impression that landing parties were operating in advance of an invasion force. In truth, Krueger was loath to risk any Alamo Scout landings for fear that some might be captured and reveal information about Operation Reckless.

The Japanese remained completely in the dark about the pending invasion and other operational matters as well. A formidable force of about four hundred fighter planes and bombers based at the Hollandia airfields, organized into the 6th Air Division under the command of Lieutenant General Giichi Itabana, was one of their most potent assets in all of New Guinea. These fields lay beyond the range of American fighters. Even the twin-engine P-38 Lightning had only a 350-mile operating radius, too limited to escort bombers to Hollandia and back from their bases in the eastern and southern end of the vast island. Without fighter escort, the bombers would likely be decimated by enemy fighters. Knowing this, and thinking themselves impervious to Allied strikes, the Japanese parked their planes outside revetments, wingtip to wingtip in double rows along the runways. They had no idea that Kenney was in the process of preparing a work-around. His promise during the meeting with Nimitz to have these aircraft "rubbed out" well in advance of the Hollandia landings was no idle boast. Under strict secrecy, fifty-eight brand-new P38J fighters arrived in New Guinea. With an operational range of 570 miles, they had more than enough range to get to Hollandia and back. What was more, Kenney ordered the innovative engineers and mechanics at his Air Service Command to devise specially fitted external fuel tanks for his old P-38s, which immediately enhanced their range sufficiently for Hollandia missions. All the while, Kenney took steps to keep the Japanese under the misapprehension that his fighters could not range to Hollandia. He issued strict orders to his pilots not to operate west of Tadji. "Even if they were in combat, no P-38 was to remain any more than fifteen minutes before turning around and heading for home," Kenney later wrote. He authorized single-bomber night raids on Hollandia with inaccurate bombing patterns to reinforce the notion that the Americans were incapable of launching more accurate daylight raids, and even endured jeering from Tokyo radio propaganda broadcasts that accused the Yanks of splashing too much Lake Sentani water around without ever hitting anything worthwhile.

He finally unleashed his sucker punch in a series of devastating raids from March 30 to April 3. In low-level bombing and strafing strikes, B-24s and their P-38 bodyguards savaged the enemy planes, reducing them to little more than charred skeletons. By the end, 340 Japanese planes were destroyed for the loss of 4 US aircraft. The vast majority of the enemy planes met their end on the ground; only 60 were shot down in aerial duels. The beautifully conceived and executed raids destroyed the 6th Air

Division, led to the ignominious relief of Itabana, and almost completely eliminated Japanese ground-based airpower in western (or Dutch) New Guinea. After witnessing the unrelenting bombing, a Japanese sailor sardonically commented to his diary that "we received from the enemy, greetings, which amount to the annihilation of our Army Air Force in New Guinea." As Kenney had promised, Nimitz no longer needed to fear any threats to his ships from New Guinea–based planes. With an abruptness similar to the way the American fliers accomplished this feat, the jeering of the Tokyo broadcasts ceased.[4]

On January 26, well before Operation Reckless was even a gleam in the SWPA's eye, MacArthur traveled to Rockhampton, Australia, to see Lieutenant General Robert Eichelberger, who by then had spent nearly a year on the war's sidelines, intensely training his I Corps soldiers for future campaigns but otherwise morosely speculating on his future. "I was a rather glum fellow," Eichelberger later reflected about that time. By now, of course, Eichelberger knew that MacArthur had secretly maneuvered to deny him an army command in the European theater, even as he held the I Corps commander out of combat. Though Eichelberger deeply resented this—and always would—he did not let his sense of aggrievement interfere with his determination to stay ready for action. At Rockhampton, with Eichelberger behind the wheel, the two generals took a jeep ride together and inspected a training exercise while several trailing photographers snapped pictures. MacArthur was celebrating his sixty-fourth birthday and seemed to relish the opportunity to mix with soldiers. "I drove . . . down through them so they could see him," Eichelberger later wrote to his wife, Emma, of showing off his boss to the troops.

Over the course of the day, the two generals met alone for a private conversation in which Eichelberger addressed the issue of a European theater army command. "I understand, General, that you have turned me down again for a high command," he blurted.

"Yes, Bob, but I am going to get another army out here and I am going to need you," MacArthur quickly replied.

Beyond this hint of future Pacific theater army-level responsibility for Eichelberger, MacArthur let him know that, within the next couple of months, he and I Corps would go into action again. An elated Eichelberger wrote that evening to Emma of the meeting. "It was really a pleasant time. I know now when it is contemplated to use me. He hinted at armies out here—maybe I might get one some time—who knows."

In early March, he learned that he would command the Hollandia landings, with the 24th and 41st Divisions under I Corps control. He relocated his headquarters to Goodenough Island and took up residence in an exotic, tropical house with a roof made from palm fronds. Black widow spiders spun sprawling webs onto the outside of the house and, in the general's recollection, "caught enormous amounts of bugs." Using the house as a base, he commuted, throughout the rest of March and early April, all over the island and Allied-controlled New Guinea. Feeling reborn, and with characteristic energy and drive, he threw himself into invasion planning and preparations. He participated in field exercises and invasion rehearsals. He inspected everything from equipment to weapons to headquarters tents. He gave numerous speeches. Almost to the last hours before embarkation on the ships, he insisted upon rigorous physical conditioning for the soldiers. He spent untold hours in meetings. He seemingly loved every minute of the frenetic weeks leading up to the invasion. "From a *military* standpoint I guess I am more happy than I have been at any time since I declared the battle of Sanananda officially at an end [about a year earlier]. The long months with their many military and personal disappointments . . . do not affect me now." In another letter to Emma, he told her, "My mind turns away from past disappointments, ambitions and self-pity. I only want to do my duty, to gain victory, and to get back to my Doll where we can laugh and enjoy home life again. There is no low morale here—lots of hard work but plenty of good cheer." To some extent, his excitement stemmed from confidence in his two division commanders. He and Fuller were West Point classmates and old friends. Irving had been commandant of cadets at the Academy during Eichelberger's superintendency. An admiring Eichelberger later described him as "efficient, quiet, almost austere."

During the weeks leading up to the invasion, the generals, their respective staffs, and the naval commanders worked long hours to fine-tune landing plans. "Meetings with staff officers and commanders with all echelons were held," an I Corps after-action report stated. Navy representatives were constantly on hand to advise and coordinate with the Task Force staff. Before orders were issued, carefully worked-out plans were published and thoroughly digested by all. "The general training of all units was continued and included physical hardening, small-unit tactics, [and] generalized amphibious work." This was no easy job for forces and commands spread all over New Guinea and the Pacific. MacArthur's headquarters was in Brisbane, as was Kenney's, Krueger's Sixth Army was at Cape Cretin, and Eichelberger's I Corps was at Goodenough. Fuller and the 41st were at Cape Cretin, and Irving and the 24th were at Goodenough. The subordinate battalions of the 2nd Engineer Special Brigade, the main engineering support for the two assault divisions, were scattered all over eastern New Guinea from Finschhafen to Lae. Some of the brigade's amphibian engineers—units specially fitted with boats and landing craft—were based on Goodenough. On the naval side, the bulk of Rear Admiral Daniel Barbey's Seventh Amphibious Force was anchored with his flagship at Buna; Mitscher's Task Force 58 was in the Hawaiian Islands; other participating naval units were situated as far away as the Solomon Islands. The challenges of coordinating over vast distances were such that Barbey later opined, "Considering the conditions under which our own small staff worked—stifling heat, loss of time and frustrations due to the separation of the various planning staffs, utilization of borrowed ships unfamiliar with operating procedures, and the complexity of the problem—I consider it a remarkable achievement that the naval plans were completed and ready to be distributed in a period of eighteen days." Barbey's headquarters mimeographed and disseminated to the various commands eight hundred copies of the joint plans.

These documents and tens of thousands of tons of other items, everything from mess kits to communication wire spools and trucks, plus many thousands of men, all had to be loaded uncomfortably aboard the troop ships, LCIs, and LSTs over several days in mid-April. In semi-organized lines that snaked along New Guinea's north coast, troops stood for hours, in full battle gear, under an unrelenting sun, waiting to board ship. "Sunheat permeated the sand and shimmered in waves before our eyes," one of them later wrote. "Ammo belts cut off circulation of the air that might evaporate our heavy sweat. Bandoliers hung down like warm chains." One by one, first sergeants checked off the name of each relieved man as he ascended a gangway or a ramp, only to find himself now stuffed inside the hold of a cramped, foul-smelling ship.[5]

Sallying forth from all over the South Pacific, the first ships of the invasion armada—the greatest assembled thus far in MacArthur's war against Japan—got underway on the evening of April 17 and rendezvoused north of New Guinea with the faster vessels three days later. "As far as the eye could see the force stretched out," the 41st Division's historian, greatly impressed, later wrote. The convoy chugged along at nine knots per hour and extended thirty miles from end to end; radar picket ships and destroyers patrolled the flanks to provide early warning for potential enemy submarine or air attacks. In a final act of deception designed to fool enemy reconnaissance planes and other unwelcome snoopers about the fleet's ultimate destination, the ships feinted and zigzagged, mostly to the north, away from New Guinea's north coast. Puzzling over the ultimate destination of the armada, Japanese intelligence theorized wrongly, "The greatest probability is a landing between Madang and Hansa."

Many of the veteran "Butchers" remembered going into Sanananda the year before with only a handful of LCIs to transport them. Now they marveled at this prodigious display of American naval power. The same was true for new men. PFC Bernie Catanzaro, a rookie 41st Division rifleman heading into combat for the first time, gaped at the diverse array of ships that seemed to fill the ocean surface all the way to the horizon and he immediately felt better about what he would soon do. "The sight of such a powerful force gave me a feeling of confidence about the upcoming landing." Brigadier General Clovis Byers, Eichelberger's trusted chief of staff, felt the same way. In a shipboard letter to his wife, he described the fleet as stretching "in every direction as far as the eye could reach . . . ships of every type, size and description. What a picture it all made. I've never seen anything like it before." Brigadier General William Heavey, commander of the 2nd Engineer Special Brigade, claimed that "every American on that convoy was inspired. The American Eagle was beginning to show his claws." If the veterans and newbies were equally impressed by the naval power around them, their mindset about the pending invasion was hardly similar. "For the old combat men, it was just another job of hell, but many of the new men, still to have their first taste of combat, were thinking in terms of . . . heroic deeds, fear and thoughts of hatred," the war-savvy historian of A Company, 163rd Infantry, explained.

Many of the assault troops had been briefed on Operation Reckless even before boarding their ships. Once at sea, others clustered together on open decks, absorbing the cool Pacific breeze, listening to last-minute briefings from company or battalion commanders, most of whom illustrated their talks by using elaborate sand tables or pointing to fluttering maps tacked precariously onto makeshift easels. Soldiers of the 2nd Battalion, 186th Infantry Regiment, spent the voyage trying to find adequate sleeping and eating spots on a crowded LST where the main deck was packed with chain-linked trucks, and vast crates of ammunition and other supplies were stacked so high in the hold that they threatened to scrape the ceiling. Men on deck who were not lucky enough to huddle inside vehicles or under tarps were pelted with rain; those belowdecks were dry but cramped and almost overcome by the stench of body odor and fuel exhaust. "We had dire problems on this LST with too many men and too little water," the unit historian later wrote. "Water was turned on from 0600 to 0700, 1100 to 1200, and 1600 to 2100. We had just eight wash basins." Drinking water came from a few heavily used spigots. Cold saltwater showers were occasionally available. Meals, served twice a day by the LST crew, consisted of dehydrated potatoes and canned beef, "tasteless and repellent, but food anyhow." With an insufficient amount of water to wash their mess gear properly, and nauseated by the constant stench of overflowing toilets, the soldiers of I Company, 186th Infantry, soon were debilitated by diarrhea. In the pained recollection of the unit historian, about 80 percent of the company was soon "doubled up with cramps and hurriedly dashing for the foul heads." The bored troops wrote letters, read armed forces paperbacks or tattered copies of *Time*, *Newsweek*, or *Yank*, or even Superman comic books. Many passed the time by trading oft-told, lurid stories of hot dates in Australia or speculating about the possibility of home furloughs. Few discussed the immediate future.

Aboard HMAS *Kanimbla*, where conditions were markedly better, Colonel Harold Riegelman, the I Corps chemical officer, and groups of 24th Division soldiers spent the evening before the invasion crowded together in the ship's tiny bar, sipping drinks, singing anything that came to mind, from "Caissons" to "Anchors Aweigh" to "Sweet Adeline" and "Waltzing Matilda." A veteran Australian officer watched for a while, then sidled up to Riegelman and marveled, "You Yanks are simply incredible. Less than eight hours from now you are landing in a hornet's nest. You'd think [you] are going to a wedding tomorrow at daybreak. Perfectly incredible!" Aboard the destroyer USS *Swanson*, which Admiral Barbey had made his flagship, General Eichelberger shared a small cabin with General Irving. As busy as Eichelberger had been the previous weeks and soon would be again, he could do little now but wait in eager anticipation. He whiled away the hours, chatting with war correspondents, napping, reading *A Tree Grows in Brooklyn*, and writing letters to Emma. "If I were a hero of fiction I would say 'the die is cast' or some other dark fool thing," he mused breezily in one of the letters. He and Barbey had established a strong working friendship. He deeply admired his naval colleagues and the Navy as a whole. "The ship is a very efficient organization which makes me proud of our sister service—nice chaps who are on the job and friendly." He was also impressed with the higher standard of living available to sailors. "Next reincarnation I want to join the Navy," he told Emma; "good coffee, no dirt, and no bugs."

The pleasant voyage helped take his mind off the serious mission ahead, so much so that he almost appeared carefree to those around him. When a correspondent asked him if he was worried, he replied, "No, I don't worry over things which I cannot help." But knowing little about the implications of the code-breaking coup, he was privately concerned "by the ambitious scope of my orders and the brief amount of time allowed me to carry them out." Erroneous I Corps intelligence reports claimed the presence of three Japanese infantry regiments in the Hollandia area. For whatever reason, MacArthur was loath to share the complete details of Japanese weakness at Hollandia with his key operational commander. As a result, an oblivious Eichelberger wondered how he could overcome the resistance of the three phantom regiments and still fulfill the larger strategic objective of turning Hollandia into a major sea and air base. To Emma, he confided, "I am fully aware of my responsibilities and that it is no simple war game that I am engaged in."

On board the cruiser USS *Nashville*, General MacArthur spent much of the journey sitting in a chair outside his cabin, enjoying the sea breeze and the view of the fleet, chatting with aides. "Sometimes he wanted to talk and sometimes he preferred to think," Lieutenant Colonel Roger Egeberg, his personal physician, later wrote. "He even nodded, taking short naps." With a custom-made, specially adorned cap perched atop his head, and wearing sunglasses that obscured his searching eyes, MacArthur cut an impressive, almost arresting figure. Long lines of sailors waited for the opportunity to get his autograph, mostly on dollar bills they nicknamed "short snorters." MacArthur obliged them with good cheer but little expansive conversation. He ate his meals off a tablecloth in the captain's cabin with Egeberg and Lieutenant Colonel Lloyd "Larry" Lehrbas, his aide-de-camp and a former war correspondent, whom MacArthur had known since his days as Army chief of staff in the early 1930s. Like the combat soldiers, they discussed practically anything but the pending invasion.[6]

Bound for different sections of the New Guinea coast, spanning from Tanahmerah to Aitape, the three task forces soon went their separate ways. "Just as the branches of a tree spread out from its trunk toward the sky, so did the tentacles of the invasion convoy slither out toward the separated beaches in the objective area," MacArthur later wrote. Silently, under cover of darkness, they settled into place. As the sun rose on the morning of April 22, the bombardment ships, on an almost perfectly synchronized schedule, began pounding preselected target areas on and near the coast. "A flare went up and every combat ship let go with its guns simultaneously," Admiral Barbey later wrote. "In the half-light, it was a gorgeous spectacle." He was amazed at the absence of any Japanese response to the presence of the invasion force. Cruisers and destroyers hurled six hundred 8-inch and fifteen hundred 4.7- and 5-inch shells at the beach areas. Specially fitted LCIs and patrol craft added another 936 rockets to the explosive mix. Task Force 58 planes, sallying forth from such fleet carriers as USS *Hornet*, USS *Enterprise*, and USS *Belleau Wood*, among others, buzzed in and raked over the coastline. "They dove seemingly into the very jungle itself, only to rise again over the treetops like startled geese as they bombed and strafed everything in sight," the 41st Division historian wrote.

Concussion waves shimmied upward from the explosions, producing an optical illusion that the beaches were actually shaking; waves of smoke obscured visibility. More planes circled overhead, guarding against the possibility of Japanese aerial or seaborne opposition. In the wardroom aboard *Swanson*, General Eichelberger could hear the booming and feel the concussion. For some reason, he felt ravenously hungry. He devoured two ham sandwiches, a jelly sandwich, and a cheese sandwich and washed it all down with prodigious amounts of tomato juice, water, and coffee. Under a light, misty rain, the assault troops, similarly sated on a brunch of sandwiches and coffee, carefully worked their way down rope ladders into landing craft. "Boats will start for the departure line!" stentorian voices boomed over ship's loudspeakers. With the troops packed aboard in wobbly, seasick clusters, the craft plowed through the waves, bound for shore. Unmolested by any enemy resistance, the boats disgorged the soldiers into shallow coastal water or directly onto their various landing beaches. As the ensign in charge of one boat watched his load of assault troops wade ashore, he called after them, "God bless you men."

By 0700, these leading waves of the two divisions had landed safely at all three beachheads, with follow-on forces arriving soon after. Japanese resistance amounted to little more than scattered rifle and machine-gun fire. The surprise was so complete that, at Humboldt Bay, the "Butchers" found half-eaten bowls of rice, warm teapots, abandoned weapons, letters, clothing, and other evidence of a recent Japanese presence. Within a matter of moments, infantrymen, tanks, engineers, and artillery pieces all piled onto the narrow, constricted beaches from Tanahmerah Bay to Aitape. Most of the skeleton force of Japanese service troops quickly fled inland. An unlucky few were cornered by advancing Americans and either killed or captured. One dazed, wayward, ragged Japanese officer who was taken prisoner by advancing riflemen was forced to strip out of his uniform, lest he use it to conceal any weapons. "No killie please," he kept murmuring over and over to the young soldier who guarded him.[7]

The terrain presented more of an obstacle to the inland advance than did the Japanese. One of the few drawbacks to "Reckless" was that the very speed and surprise that made the plan so successful also meant that the Americans had little time to gather suitable intelligence, beyond just some inadequate photo reconnaissance images, about the landscape beyond the diminutive beaches. Once ashore, they soon realized that the Hollandia coastal rim amounted to little more than a massive maw of swampland, thick jungle, and hills, with no real avenues of advance save a few narrow, muddy trails. "The terrain was very rugged, interspersed with swamps, and generally covered with a dense growth of rain forest," the 162nd Infantry Regiment's after-action report chronicled. "No motor tracks existed, and the native trails were narrow, slippery and tortuous." Tiny spits of sandy beach, usually no more than twenty or thirty yards long, gave way to thick forest or deep swamp. Lieutenant Colonel John Clarke, the 24th Division's chemical officer, quipped that New Guinea "seemed composed of two parts dense jungle and one part swamp." Inland from Tanahmerah Bay, 24th Division soldiers soon found themselves enmeshed in a honeycomb of fetid swamps. One man even went under the water and drowned before his buddies could extract him. Another felt himself sinking in water up to his armpits. As he thrashed helplessly, his sergeant hastily held out his rifle to extract him. The desperate soldier grabbed it. When he did so, the weapon discharged, killing the sergeant. Though undoubtedly racked with guilt over the senseless death of his sergeant, the soldier made it out of the water. The invaders realized that the only way to develop a real understanding of the water-deluged areas and jungle was to experience it firsthand. Colonel Aubrey "Red" Newman, the 24th's chief of staff, who had dodged enemy bombs two and a half years earlier during the Pearl Harbor attack, personally plunged into shoulder-high water to test its depth, all in a quest to find a good spot for General Irving's command post. "We had puzzled over that possible swamp in studying air photos," he later wrote to a fellow soldier, "but could not be sure it *was* a swamp, or its possible extent."

Small columns of infantrymen slowly negotiated their way inland. But as the hours unfolded and follow-up waves landed, the beaches soon became terribly congested with troops, supplies, equipment, and vehicles. "The result was a complete mess," an officer in one of the 24th Division artillery battalions groused. The presence of massive Japanese supply dumps, particularly at Humboldt Bay and its environs, only added to the congestive stew. Tanks, trucks, and jeeps snaked in single-file horizontal columns, their drivers looking to find an opening off the beach. "Traffic was frequently at a standstill and vehicles became jammed up, bumper to bumper," a combat observer noted. LVTs ferried supplies and soldiers across swampy areas. Land-borne vehicles got bogged down easily in the soggy soil; tractors fell prey to the swamps, necessitating the use of still more tractors for retrieval, diverting engineers from constructing roads and collection points. Artillery pieces were strewn uselessly along the waterline, their crews waiting vainly for engineers to improve the trails well enough to make it possible to tow the cannons inland. Tanks threw tracks. As one horrified infantryman watched, a tank crew dismounted to fix a tread and "there was one man who tried to clean the sand out from between the drive sprocket and the track. Suddenly the tank settled in the sand, crushing his hand in between the track and sprocket. Medics had to give him shots for pain while a cutting torch was used to cut the track in order to get him loose."

LSTs ran aground, often within spitting distance of the jungle, to offload the dizzying tonnages of supplies and vehicles. In a few instances, jeeps no sooner descended ramps than they sank underneath swirling ocean waves. With orders to unload LSTs and other boats as quickly as possible and little space in which to store freight, work parties carelessly piled crates and other containers into steadily rising heaps on the beaches. The 542nd Engineer Boat and Shore Regiment alone manhandled almost five thousand tons of supplies and equipment ashore in a matter of only a few hours. "The beach was almost solidly covered with stacks of boxes and bags, vehicles, guns, and matériel of all types," an engineer historian later wrote. "Ammunition and gasoline containers were, by necessity, piled touching one another." In addition to ammo and ration dumps, cots, tents, poles, seabags, and bedrolls accumulated. Almost two thousand tons of engineering equipment and supplies lay scattered among the sea of matériel. Planners had stashed it on different ships to avoid losing it all in one sinking. But now the valuable gear was hopelessly separated and, individually, next to useless.

If not for General Irving's insistence on landing at Red Beach 1, the inundation would have been significantly worse. In fact, Depapre also provided a good jump-off point for a successful inland advance along a small trail by rifle teams of the 1st Battalion, 21st Infantry Regiment, whose dynamic commander, Lieutenant Colonel Thomas "Jock" Clifford, had once been a star center on the West Point football team. Clifford and his people advanced eight miles in the course of the day. At the same time, Irving assigned his assistant division commander, Brigadier General Kenneth Cramer, the task of untangling the considerable mess on the beach. According to the division after-action report, he started by "stopping heavy equipment in place which otherwise might have clogged the only exit road [trail] which was now churning into deep mud." It was the sort of job that would take days, not hours, to complete. What mattered most, at least for the moment, was that Reckless had come off largely as planned. The Americans had stunned the Japanese, outflanked them, and put their enemies in a nearly hopeless strategic position in New Guinea.[8]

When reports of the successful landings and negligible resistance filtered back to the command ships, a collective sigh of relief settled over the generals. MacArthur had spent the morning on the *Nashville*'s deck, watching the 41st Division landings. With cotton stuffed into his ears to protect them from the booming of the cruiser's guns, he peered through the misty sea air and periodically received the good news through fragmentary oral reports. Four hours after the lead troops went ashore, with the area secure, he boarded a landing craft and joined them. Accompanied by an entourage of aides and correspondents, he strode the beach, met with General Fuller, who looked gaunt in herringbone twill fatigues and helmet, and inspected his progress. Fuller showed him abandoned Japanese buildings and supply dumps, even an extensive stash of sake they had accumulated. Some of the newspapermen, with far less candor than hyperbole, later claimed that MacArthur landed with the second assault wave of assault troops. "At times I thought he was loping," Egeberg recounted. "He was hard to keep up with. He seemed in better shape than many of the soldiers."

Most were amazed, and a bit awed, to see the theater commander up close. As he passed by, one man turned to another and asked, "Did you see MacArthur?"

"Yes, I never thought I would see him in a hole like this."

Impressed by the successful landing, and Fuller's progress in spite of the difficult terrain, MacArthur returned to *Nashville,* told the skipper to head for Tanahmerah Bay, and summoned his high-level commanders to report to him. With Krueger and Eichelberger in tow, along with the usual coterie of aides, photographers, and reporters, he visited the 24th Division beachhead. As at Humboldt, those who accompanied the SWPA commander were amazed at the physical vitality of a man who had just celebrated his sixty-fourth birthday only three months earlier. "The sun poured down mercilessly, and my uniform was soggy and dark with wetness," Eichelberger later wrote. "I remember my astonishment that General MacArthur, despite the sweltering heat and the vigorous exercise, did not perspire at all." Like Fuller at Humboldt, Irving guided the SWPA commander around the area, related the terrain challenges, and noted Clifford's success. A pleased MacArthur turned to his group and said, "Irving's plan here was not good—it was brilliant!"

Well pleased, the supreme commander and the others boarded a landing craft and headed back to *Nashville.* On the way, MacArthur followed up on his hint of several weeks before and told Eichelberger that if the Hollandia operation continued to ultimate success, he would appoint him to army-level command once he had amassed enough troops in SWPA. At one point in the day, the ebullient SWPA leader shared chocolate milkshakes with his commanders. Eichelberger loved ice cream. When he gobbled down his shake, MacArthur "grinned and gave me his own untouched, frosted glass." A grateful Eichelberger consumed it as well. MacArthur was so buoyed by the success of Reckless that he now flirted with the idea of dramatically accelerating his plan of advance across the rest of Dutch New Guinea. The Japanese seemed in total disarray and he hoped to exploit this before they could recover. So he met with Krueger, Barbey, and Eichelberger and proposed to divert all floating reserve units for the Reckless operation to land instead in three days, to grab an airfield at Wakde Island, about 140 miles to the west of Hollandia, followed by an invasion at Sarmi, located some 10 miles west of Wakde along the New Guinea coast. The change made little difference to Barbey since these troops were already aboard his ships; he only needed to issue orders for his skippers to land them at Wakde and Sarmi rather than Hollandia and Aitape. Krueger was noncommittal. Given his deliberate and cautious nature, it is hard to imagine that he much liked the idea. Only Eichelberger spoke out clearly against MacArthur's proposal. Though the I Corps commander welcomed the successful landings at Hollandia and Aitape, and normally leaned toward aggressive moves himself, he knew that the job of establishing a major Allied base was only just beginning. His troops had not yet captured the airfields at Lake Sentani. The congestion on the landing beaches was still a thorny problem. Nor could he discount the possibility of running into stronger Japanese resistance as the 24th and 41st pincers approached each other. He still half expected to encounter the three infantry regiments his intelligence section believed were operating in the area (MacArthur apparently made no attempt to disabuse him of this mistaken notion). As Eichelberger later recalled, "I could only tell him that we should wait until we found out whether we were going to win the fight at Hollandia before going on without preparation to an entirely different place." Apparently persuaded, MacArthur dropped the notion and told his commanders to proceed as planned with Reckless. The next day, MacArthur returned to Port Moresby and then back to Brisbane.[9]

His soldiers kept advancing through the sodden jungle toward the airfields, occasionally skirmishing with groups of Japanese. The 163rd grabbed the abandoned Tadji strips on D-Day, and Australian engineers needed only a couple of days to prepare them to handle Allied fighters. From Tanahmerah and Humboldt Bays, leading troops of the 24th and 41st Divisions fanned out in long columns along narrow trails, cautiously picking their way forward over the Cyclops Mountains toward Lake Sentani. The advance was characterized by "long marches in the sun, extreme heat, but little gunfire," Sergeant William LeGro, a machine gunner in the 186th Infantry Regiment, later wrote. Flanking patrols operated off the trails, prowling through small villages and sometimes fighting wayward Japanese. The poor conditions and terrain created logistical problems. To dodge the heavy swamps beyond Red Beach 2, Irving rerouted all reinforcement and resupply to Red Beach 1 and only then just barely managed to maintain a tenuous supply line to his lead troops, mainly by the use of overburdened carrying parties slogging through thick mud, often in heavy rain. Private Bill Campbell dubbed it "the muddiest mucky trail you ever saw . . . no way of getting a vehicle over it." Nearly everything, from bullets to radios, had to be transported by hand. At least 3,500 troops, most of whom were artillerymen or medics with nothing else to do, participated in carrying parties. Signal teams strung phone wires as far forward as possible but spent much of their time repairing them or digging them out of mudbanks. "Us soldiers had to carry rations off the ships . . . for miles . . . carry them on our back," PFC Julius Siefring of the 19th Infantry later recalled. "We didn't have no road there or nothing. That was pitiful."

The turnaround time from the beach depots to the front of the advance was forty-eight hours. Some 30 percent of the food spoiled in the tropical climate or went uneaten by careless or overheated soldiers who had little appetite. Engineers dug water wells but had to choose their sites very carefully. "Too close to swamp gave reddish brown odorous water, while too close to sea gave brackish water," wrote Captain Wilbur Hayden, a medical officer who attempted to maintain the freshwater intake of troops. "The water would often change from brackish to fresh within a few feet." Purification chemicals were in constant demand and short supply. To relieve pressure on the carrying parties, Irving wangled a few C-47s from Kenney to drop supplies to his forward units. Eichelberger wisely decided to order the landing of all subsequent supplies and reinforcements—even Irving's 34th Infantry Regiment—at Humboldt Bay, where beach-area conditions were not quite as problematic.

Excessive souvenir hunting presented another sort of challenge to momentum-minded commanders. Hollandia had been a major Japanese supply depot. When they fled, they abandoned huge amounts of matériel, in huts, warehouses, barracks, and frequently even in open piles stacking more than eight feet high. "There were more than six hundred supply dumps," Eichelberger wrote. "There were clothing dumps as high as houses. There were ammunition dumps everywhere. There were pyramids of canned goods and tarpaulin-covered hills of rice which looked like Ohio haystacks." At one point, he told Krueger, "One of my biggest headaches is the question of souveniring." Indeed, the urge to pilfer was almost irresistible, especially considering that American society was (and probably still is) the most souvenir obsessed on earth. Moreover, even the humblest private could make nice money selling or trading Japanese items to sailors.

Japanese uniforms, food, equipment, utensils, candy, soda, swords, weapons, and personal items proliferated. "Looting of stores soon became the major effort of some of the troops," one observer noted. "Supplies . . . were wantonly destroyed or carried away. Numerous enlisted men and a few officers were seen wearing captured Japanese uniforms. Large stores of Japanese beer and sake were found in the dumps, much of it being consumed by our troops on the spot and resulting in many cases of intoxication." One soldier guzzled so much sake that he grabbed his weapons and set out to kill a man he detested. Fortunately, MPs intercepted him before he could make good on his drunken plan. In a particularly extreme case, a battalion commander puzzled over the slow pace of his unit's movement only to find out that a major portion of his command had absconded to Japanese supply dumps in search of liquor. PFC Catanzaro and his buddies were amazed to find Japanese books, papers, photographs, and even women's clothing and cosmetics. "I picked up some coins, a pair of ivory chopsticks, an opium pipe, a bayonet, a mandolin, a small bamboo flute, and a stack of invasion money." Eichelberger resorted to placing armed guards at any sizable enemy dump.

In spite of these many distractions, the advance proceeded well. On the afternoon of April 26, lead patrols from the two divisions secured the airfields and linked up, achieving one of the main invasion objectives. All around them were the remains of the Japanese 6th Air Division that General Kenney's aviators had destroyed. "As far as the eye could see lay blasted planes," the historian of the 21st Infantry Regiment wrote. Bulldozer-wielding engineers went to work clearing the wreckage and repairing the airdromes while infantrymen patrolled the Lake Sentani area, relentlessly hunting down and killing any enemy soldiers who had been unable to get away. Their agony might well have been less pronounced than those who had fled into New Guinea's harsh wilds—a green desert in the words of one Japanese soldier—where little awaited them besides starvation, disease, misery, and death. "These hateful bastards of the Am. Army cannot be beaten easily," one of them raged to his diary. "How can I escape from this dangerous place?" He quickly found that he could not. Instead, like thousands of others, he wandered and struggled just to exist, all the while decaying precipitously. "The fearfulness of living in the jungle cannot be expressed in words. We are beginning to hate everything in this world. We live each day sympathizing with one another. At times, we see someone in our group shedding tears. It is most pitiful. One learns the unending misery of life as it vanished into oblivion. My friends are dead. I am steadily growing lonely. To end my life at twenty-five is regrettable. This is my fate. I cannot help it. Oh God . . ." Allied planes dropped surrender leaflets along the likely routes of retreat. One of them featured a written plea from a POW, Corporal Nobuhiro Kawabe, to his countrymen, urging them to lay down arms and surrender to the Americans. "When you walk through the jungles in your unaccustomed bare feet, even though more and more wounds are suffered, there is no medicine. There would seem to be no course other than self-destruction. My dear fellow soldiers who will fall and die deep in the jungle, who will send your remains to the homeland? Your precious lives will simply vanish like the morning dew. I too am a Japanese soldier, I understand well your feelings. Fellow soldiers, come to the American Army. You need not fear the Americans at all."

Few accepted the offer. Instead, they wasted away as living skeletons, racked with disease, eating anything they could scrounge, sleeping in mud, trying to make it to Japanese bases to the west or east. Those who could no longer continue often begged their comrades to kill them. Few could bring themselves to do it. Many committed suicide by holding grenades to their abdomens or their heads. The dying sometimes gave their last few grains of rice or final letters home to anyone who happened to notice them. Many hundreds reached the point of total exhaustion, simply lay down and died, their carcasses soon devoured by jungle animals and insects. Some turned to cannibalism or struggled to stave off insanity. "I didn't really have a future while I was trudging along in those mountains," said Private Masatsugu Ogawa, a rare survivor who lived to tell about the experience. His unit went into New Guinea with 7,000 men. Only 67 ever made it out. "There was no tomorrow, no next day. I sensed that the extremes of existence could be reduced to the human stomach. Lack of protein, in particular, fostered a kind of madness in us. We ate anything. Flying insects, worms in rotten palm trees. We fought over the distribution of those worms. If you managed to knock down a lizard with a stick, you'd pop it into your mouth while its tail was wriggling."[10]

Though American engineers worked vigorously to build supply roads and establish firm bases, the beaches remained choked with supply crates, ammo dumps, vehicles, and other hastily unloaded freight. The crowded conditions smacked of chaos and vulnerability. With ample reason, General Heavey worried that "one bomb on the beach would probably have destroyed everything with the resultant fires and explosions." This very scenario came to fruition on the evening of April 23 when a lone Japanese plane overflew Humboldt Bay and dropped a stick of bombs, one of which landed on an ammo dump, igniting a massive series of fires and explosions that "spread a thousand yards up and down the beach in a matter of minutes," according to the 41st Division history. The area quaked with the tremors of sympathetic detonations, one leading to another, in a fiery, horrifying series of explosions and flashes so immense that they could be felt and seen from many miles away. Major Elmer Volgenau, watching from the deck of an LST offshore, later termed it "so awesome and terrifying as almost to defy description. Great billowing black clouds of smoke were flung thousands of feet into the air from exploding drums of gasoline, while the oil, lubricants, rations, vehicles, and hundreds of tons of miscellaneous stores and gear burned below it in a solid, hideous, frightening wall of flame five hundred feet in the air for a mile and a half along the beach." Ammunition cooked off like Fourth of July rockets. "The spitting, vicious crackle of millions of rounds of small arms ammunition, grenades, and engineer explosives permeated with increasing waves of sound the shattering, crashing, crumbling roar and rumble of barrage after barrage of heavy artillery shells. The fierce, eerie glare made faces look green in the half light. None who saw it will ever forget."

To escape death, some men fled inland, plunged into swamps, and swam to safety. Utilizing bulldozers and shovels, engineers dug firebreaks to limit the range of the conflagration, to no avail. "The fire leaped our 30-yard break and flamed new heaps of supplies," an engineer historian later wrote. "Flames raced from dump to dump. Again and again, explosions showered the beach with murderous missiles. By now, all personal gear was lost. Vehicles burned up; roller conveyors were destroyed." Bulldozers pushed fuel barrels and supply crates into the water. Individual men even rolled the barrels. Soldiers formed human chains, passing material hand to hand, out of harm's way. Quartermasters braved the fires in an attempt to save cargo or lives. In several instances, they pulled comrades away as flames licked at their boots. Soldiers of the 649th Ordnance Ammunition Company dashed into a storage depot and, according to one post-battle report, "carried by hand burned ammunition boxes, fuzes and 155-mm projectiles, some of which were too hot to handle." At one point, a 155-millimeter white phosphorous shell caught fire and exploded, but fortunately with everyone out of range.

Litter teams and medics circulated among the flames, carrying wounded men away, all the while dodging a rain of fragments, bullets, and fiery debris. Aid stations frequently relocated to avoid encroaching fire and explosions. At one point, the flames threatened to destroy the guns of two entire artillery battalions before they were narrowly contained. Firefighting LCIs hovered close to shore, laboring to extinguish the flaming debris. For two full days, the fires and sympathetic explosions raged. By the time the disastrous holocaust finally petered out, it had claimed the lives of twenty-four men and burned or wounded one hundred others. It destroyed eight million dollars' worth of matériel, equivalent to the fully discharged cargo of eleven LSTs, amounting to 60 percent of all I Corps supplies unloaded since D-Day. Even weeks later, when Corporal Sy Kahn and his comrades from the 244th Port Company arrived at Humboldt, the scars remained. "A solid black line of gutted army supplies lined the beach for a half-mile. The jungle near this stuff was scorched. Tires were burned right off the trucks, shovel handles right out of the shovels. The heat had been intense enough to melt metals. An American shoe was found, partially burned, with a foot still in it. I have never seen such a sight of utter devastation."

Though Eichelberger immediately took steps to recoup the logistical losses, the troops spent several days on half rations, or consumed captured enemy fish and rice (perhaps this accounted for some of their enthusiasm to loot). The debacle revealed the unsuitability of the Hollandia beaches for unloading operations—a necessary evil, given the element of surprise and mobility offered by Reckless—and the vulnerability of a crowded beachhead to enemy air attack. The Americans were lucky that the Japanese aerial capability was so poor. "Many more vehicles, pieces of heavy equipment, and supplies were landed on the first three days than could be cleared from the beaches," Colonel William McCreight, the I Corps supply officer, wrote soberly in an after-action report. "Had the enemy attack from the air been in force, the loss of life and property would have probably delayed the operation for a considerable period of time."[11]

Instead, the incident amounted more to a headache than a hole in the head for the fortunate Americans since it did not slow their operation in any substantial way. As it was, though, Eichelberger had a challenging job on his hands to exploit his swift tactical victory and transition Hollandia into a workable sally base to maintain the momentum for MacArthur's forthcoming operations to take Wakde-Sarmi and Biak. "As you can well imagine most of my worries now are logistical," he wrote to Emma. Rainy weather, the paucity of transportation infrastructure, and the lack of any harbor facilities presented constant obstacles. Engineers, Seabees, and support troops worked themselves ragged on an ambitious job that was tantamount to simultaneously building a large housing complex, a high-capacity harbor, several airports, and a major highway. Ships arrived faster than their cargoes could be unloaded and dispersed by overstretched work crews. In many cases, the ships did not even have cargo manifests or loading diagrams. They and their crews often waited uselessly, on their fully loaded vessels, for days on end. "The unloading capacity of a port in an objective area is limited," Krueger explained to MacArthur. To some extent, the bottleneck was also caused by the understandable desire of ground commanders to request the shipping and delivery of any conceivable item they might need once ashore. The unhappy result was overloaded ships and backlogged freight. "It was found from experience that lightly loaded ships in the assault phase often resulted in an overall gain in the delivery of supplies," Barbey later wrote. "LST's that were too heavily or improperly loaded could not approach the beach closely enough to unload their cargo over the ramp."

Aviation engineer battalions worked from dawn until midnight to improve the airfields to accommodate more frequent usages and the heavier tonnage of Allied planes. Rather than wait for the delivery of scarce construction material, much of which was still stranded aboard ships or in eastern New Guinea warehouses, they scavenged local rocks and streambeds to create improvised asphalt. "To me the stench of hot asphalt became a fragrance in a region of many worse smells," Eichelberger wrote after the war. To Krueger at the time, he described the aviation engineers "working all night with lights and the flow of gravel trucks passing by my tent." Road builders battled mud and the elements; individual men climbed steep banks to hack away at tropical trees with saws and axes while their buddies worked many feet below them. "Armed with picks and shovels . . . the men labored strenuously on corduroy roads in order to allow traffic to pass," the historian of the 339th Engineer Combat Battalion chronicled. "Soon bulldozers began climbing up the hardened trail. They cut savagely thru banks of precious gravel and 'smeared' it on the new surfaced road." Still more construction crews labored to erect prefabricated Quonset huts, warehouses, and other buildings.

Eichelberger spent his days roaming from site to site, supervising the beehive of activity, like a factory or construction foreman. "My job was to direct traffic and construction, and to demand speed, speed, speed," he later wrote. "Road construction . . . was a gigantic task. Sides of mountains were carved away, bridges and culverts were thrown across rivers and creeks, gravel and stone 'fill' was poured into sago swamps to make highways as tall as Mississippi levees." He provided Krueger, who was back at Cape Cretin, with frequent updates. "Some of our logistical problems would make you either laugh or cry," he commented in one letter while assuring the Sixth Army commander that "I shall try in every way possible to put this job over for you." All too often, heavy rains generated mudslides that undid the fruits of a day's work. Vehicles bogged down or blocked the narrow road. "Movement was slow and trucks and jeeps might be bumper to bumper for a mile," wrote Colonel Harold Riegelman, the I Corps chemical officer. "The engineers made herculean efforts to give the track more width and substance. And they succeeded slowly and painfully. The perpetual movement of traffic, rains, stifling heat, and humidity were not their only handicaps. Occasionally a small party of Japs would emerge from the jungle and open fire on the nearest work party." When that happened, the engineers put their construction tools aside, picked up their rifles, and fought back. In the course of the project, they claimed to have killed at least 108 Japanese while capturing another 28.

More important, they steadily turned the Hollandia area into a viable base. In a five-week period, they achieved significant results. They built three operational airfields near Lake Sentani, fed by seventy miles of two- and four-lane road that allowed for the movement of supplies and vehicles to the airfields and headquarters complexes around the lake. "When our tremendously heavy engineer and air equipment first hit that road during heavy rains, it just ceased to exist in places," Eichelberger later related to Lieutenant General Leslie McNair, chief of Army Ground Forces. By the time the engineers finished their work, the road could accommodate even the heaviest equipment and vehicles. They laid down 135 miles of fuel pipeline for pumping aviation gasoline to the fields, and constructed three million square feet of warehouse and building space. At the harbor, they erected one floating dock, three jetties, and multiple petroleum storage facilities. The port included a thirty-ton floating crane, half a dozen harbor tugs, nine motorboats, and twenty steel barges, each of which stretched to eighty feet in length. At its full apex, Hollandia could accommodate 140,000 troops, short of the 200,000 that SWPA planners had hoped for but remarkable nonetheless. By August, Hollandia was handling the largest amount of cargo tonnage of any Allied base in New Guinea. "Where once I had seen only a few native villages and an expanse of primeval forest, a city of one hundred and forty thousand men took occupancy," Eichelberger wrote proudly.

Krueger was considerably less impressed. He blamed Eichelberger for what he saw as a disorganized unloading situation, chaotic crowding of supplies on the beaches, the slow pace of construction, and inexcusable looting by the troops. He thought Eichelberger had been poorly served by his staff and too permissive with them. By temperament and leadership philosophy, Krueger tended to be much tougher on high-ranking officers than enlisted men, undoubtedly a by-product of his own background as a onetime private soldier. "In more than forty years as an officer I have never raised my voice to an enlisted man," he privately told Colonel Clyde Eddleman, his operations officer, after visiting Hollandia, "but a Corps commander should know better." The tension manifested itself in the exchange of strained cables between the two commanders and, after Krueger relocated his headquarters to Hollandia on May 24, several scoldings from the Sixth Army commander. General Byers remembered Krueger ripping Eichelberger "up one side and down the other." Eichelberger maintained his composure, though he seethed inside: ever since D-Day he felt that Krueger had been breathing down his neck for rapid results, without any true understanding of the real situation on the ground. He particularly believed that Krueger was too distant to appreciate the prodigious difficulties inherent in transitioning Hollandia into a usable base, especially in such a short time period. Perhaps as a way to change the culture of the I Corps staff or maybe extend an olive branch of sorts, Krueger offered Byers the chance to become the assistant division commander of the newly arrived 6th Infantry Division. Byers much preferred to stay with his close friend Eichelberger rather than become second fiddle to Major General Franklin Sibert, whom he respected but did not know as well. When Byers turned down the offer, Krueger took it as a personal affront. He told Eichelberger, "Napoleon once said the reason so few officers succeeded was that they did not recognize opportunity when it knocked." The tension over Byers's career choice and the Hollandia logistical situation blew over by June, but these incidents fostered an already growing antipathy in Eichelberger for the Sixth Army commander, a distaste that was rapidly hardening into outright dislike.

From the vantage point of the bigger picture, the Hollandia operation had clearly been successful. In one fell swoop, SWPA forces advanced farther than they had during all of 1943, accelerating MacArthur's timetable for a potential return to the Philippines (not to mention a prelude to operations in westernmost Dutch New Guinea). The Allies had, in essence, destroyed Japanese land-based aerial capacity in the South Pacific, and with few aircraft losses and almost no damage to their own shipping. The American divisions inflicted devastating casualties on the Japanese, mainly in small-unit patrol actions after the Lake Sentani linkup and through the privation of disease and the elements. The Imperial Army lost 3,300 killed, another 611 captured, and untold thousands consigned to the nightmarish desperation of jungle wandering. The Americans lost 152 dead and 1,057 wounded, many to friendly fire and other mishaps. Reckless cut off some 55,000 Japanese soldiers in the Hansa Bay/Wewak area whose only options now were either to waste away in place or brave the jungle to fight their way west in hopes of achieving a costly breakout. Tadji provided a useful airfield and the Aitape beachhead an obstacle—hard-pressed as events would unfold—to prevent their escape.

Thanks to Eichelberger's actions, imperfect though they probably were, Hollandia developed into a key base for the rest of the war. The only disappointment stemmed from the invaders' discovery that the Lake Sentani airfields, owing to soil and water table issues, could not support heavy bombers. Even before the invasion, Kenney and Major General Ennis Whitehead, his key subordinate, had suspected this, but they could not know for sure until the Americans possessed the ground. The inability to base bombers at Hollandia meant that MacArthur could not follow through on his promise to provide heavy bomber support for Nimitz's Mariana operations. On balance, Hollandia was MacArthur's finest operational moment in World War II. Though it was hardly the gutsy gamble portrayed by Willoughby and the SWPA commander himself, it did serve as a textbook example of operational imagination and efficient interservice coordination, as well as how to acquire and exploit actionable intelligence. In a conversation with a war correspondent, MacArthur triumphantly gestured with his trademark corncob pipe, pantomimed squeezing it, and exulted over the staggering defeat he had inflicted on the Japanese. "We have them like that, and we'll never let them go. They cannot get away."[12]

5

"From New Guinea No One
Returns Alive"

For General MacArthur, the Philippines now beckoned like the Emerald City of Oz. But no matter how much he yearned to be done with New Guinea, alas, New Guinea was nowhere near done with him. Though the success of Operation Reckless sped up his Philippines timetable, it did not ameliorate the necessity for subsequent operations both east and west of his growing Hollandia and Aitape bases. What was more, the myriad challenges of operating on the sprawling tropical island, and its many islet adjuncts, remained considerable. Devoid of any infrastructure, engineers and Seabees had to build from scratch every mile of road, every square foot of airfield or warehouse or building or dock, all the while making liberal use of local coral, sand, gravel, and lumber. "Storehouses, quarters, hospitals, and other structures could be made of poles bound with vines and thatched with sago leaves . . . or kunai grass," explained the Army's history of transportation and logistics in SWPA. "Buildings with light frames, roofs of corrugated iron, and floors of gravel, wood, or thin concrete were constructed. The standard pier or wharf was a pile structure 30 feet wide and 330 feet long, usually parallel to the beach and connected with it at each end by approaches 30 feet wide." In spite of the adversity, the builders succeeded mightily. At Tanahmerah Bay, the 339th Engineer Combat Battalion removed thirty-five thousand cubic yards of dirt from a hillside to make room for a long causeway. At the same, the battalion's soldiers built several ten-thousand-gallon fuel tanks and maintained the roads from the coast to Lake Sentani, including ten major bridges and twenty culverts. Oro Bay bristled with so many docks, wharves, and shipways that the harbor handled 133,000 tons of cargo in August alone; soon it was supplanted by Hollandia as the most productive port in New Guinea. By the end of the year, some 800,000 tons of matériel were arriving on the island each month. Mountains of crates lay in enclosed perimeters or packed into expanding warehouses. A pair of sawmills each cranked out twenty-five thousand board feet of lumber per day.

The productivity came with a high price tag of overwork, exhaustion, and low morale as hard-pressed service troops, many of whom were African-Americans serving in segregated units, worked daily amid squalid conditions, occasionally disrupted by Japanese air raids, to unload and disseminate mass quantities of freight. Theirs was an anonymous and thankless job of mind-numbing routine and hard physical labor, with little recognition. "The general opinion seemed to be 'There is more glory in killing Japs than there is in unloading ships,'" Colonel William Leaf, Krueger's supply officer, later wrote bitterly. Lieutenant Burton Garling-house, an observer assigned to report to higher command on unloading operations, opined in an official memorandum, "I found the morale in these groups rather low, a condition which is easily explained and understood. Living conditions . . . are unsatisfactory. Cargo handling is heavy and monotonous work. An indifferent, or even rebellious, 'What the hell' attitude is very common, as are idling and slacking on the job. There is . . . more or less continuous petty pilferage of cargo and ship's property. The military police make little serious effort to prevent this. They are far more interested in gossiping with crew members and in getting handouts from the galley. Recreational facilities in the island ports are limited, especially for colored soldiers." In his view, the troops had little time for much else besides "sleeping and eating." To keep the military machine running, stressed-out quartermasters worked at a multiplicity of jobs that included, in the recollection of one of their commanders, "maintenance and upkeep of the base cemetery, the location and removal of isolated burials and re-covery of bodies of missing personnel lost in the jungle due to airplane and other accidents; receipt, storage and disposition of all personal baggage; operation of bakeries, laundries, cold-storage plants, ice cream plants, overland refrigeration vans, sales stores, salvage and reclamation activities, petroleum drum cleaning plants, and petroleum drum filling plants."

With no indigenous waste disposal facilities, commanders resorted to burying tons of noxious garbage, burning it, or loading it onto barges and dumping it into the sea. Sewage facilities were nonexistent. Many units employed latrine trenches or simply used fifty-five-gallon drums as make-shift toilets. Luckless privates sprayed fuel onto the stinking offal and burned it (a hated task that would become quite familiar a generation later for many in Vietnam). The stench of the burning feces in the sultry heat was well-nigh suffocating. Units with more substantial latrines coated the ground around them with a mixture of oil and lime to maintain the basics of sanitation. Flytraps prevented the insects from getting inside the make-shift toilets and spreading disease.[1]

New Guinea seemed specially designed by a malicious Mother Nature to confound and harass humanity. After one visit, Lieutenant General Brehon Somerville, head of Army Service Forces, commented sagely, "The Army is really fighting two battles: one against the enemy, and the other against the jungle." The enervating tropical heat, the humidity levels that ranged between 85 and 95 percent, and frequent heavy rains practically guaranteed the spoilage and disintegration of huge amounts of food, equipment, and clothing. According to one contemporary Army study of the problem, "tentage and canvas covers molded, rotted, and were attacked by white ants. Pistons, piston rings, cylinders, carburetors, ball bearings, and transmissions were corroded by condensation. Springs, track of tanks, and brake parts and linings were 'frozen' with rust exposure to salt water or from standing in mud." Millions of dollars' worth of supplies went to waste. In one food shipment to Finschhafen, inspectors declared some 25 percent of all corned beef and 37 percent of tomato and fruit juice to be unfit for consumption. Of thirty thousand tons of ammunition stored at Oro Bay, ordnance officers considered the majority to be so degraded by the elements that it was unusable in combat. "The place was alternately mud and dust according to the vagaries of the weather," Captain Frederic Cramer, an ordnance specialist, wrote of the base at Oro Bay. The former extreme was more common than the latter. At the Finschhafen motor pool, driving rains and the resultant deep mud made fourteen hundred vehicles completely inaccessible to mechanics for a four-month period. Only by resorting to the use of tractors designed to move heavy artillery pieces did they have any success in reclaiming the vehicles from the soupy mud. Even then, many were no longer drivable. The intense heat mandated access to plenty of fresh water. "It's so hot outside, sweat comes out like water out of a squeezed wet sponge," one officer wrote to his wife.

Potable water generally came from local streams and rivers. Ingenious engineers purified millions of gallons of water and moved it through pipelines and pumping systems. Some units even had showers. The 117th Station Hospital, albeit not typical, even had troughs of water for washing and shaving. GIs subsisted on canned rations, tinned fruit, tinned vegetables, and a variety of stomach-turning dehydrated foods, most commonly milk, potatoes, and eggs. "If you have not sampled powdered eggs, you're lucky," Sergeant Paul Kinder groused in a letter home to friends. Greasy Spam, Vienna sausages, or mutton made up the meat offerings in any typical chow line. A specially designed brand of GI butter was impervious to melting in the hot weather, but in consequence maintained the consistency, and taste, of gelatinous grease. Repelled by the distasteful fare, and with appetites already diminished by the tropical heat, some men lost as much as twenty or thirty pounds; most maintained adequate nutrition while still craving any kind of fresh food. "I think anyone in New Guinea would have given their right arm for a glass of cold, fresh milk," quipped Lieutenant Colonel Milton Cloud, a physician with the 362nd Station Hospital at Oro Bay. Lieutenant Colonel William Shaw, the surgeon of the 41st Division, claimed to an Army interviewer that the men in his unit had gone "five months without seeing an egg. We had men go out and trade Japanese souvenirs to native boys for pork or beef. As soon as possible, fresh food and meat should be sent to those men." Some men grew their own vegetables or killed and ate wild game. Coconuts offered a nice distraction from mundane rations. Many soldiers relished the opportunity to gorge themselves on the milk and flesh of this unique tropical drupe. "[They] are plentiful and best when half ripe," one soldier wrote to a friend.

Troops quickly consumed the contents of care packages from home and other delicacies lest they fall prey to the ruthless New Guinea mire. "The ants are simply exasperating," Sergeant Kinder wrote to friends; "you cannot put a thing down but that they find it . . . anything that one doesn't seal air tight, and where you think of them as hundreds, I have them by millions, and from tiny pesky quarter-inch ones on up to an inch in length, and of all species and colors." In one instance, he left a candy bar on top of his bunk for a few minutes, only to return and find it inundated and consumed by a parade of ants. Rats descended on Army camps, gnawing through tent flaps, duffel bags, cots, kitchen containers, and even ammo boxes. Soldiers devoted nearly as much attention to combating rat infestations, especially in eating areas, as they did in fighting the Japanese. "The only preventative measure was to eliminate the rats," Captain Matthew Mendelsohn, an orthopedic surgeon in the 1st Evacuation Hospital, commented to an Army interviewer. "Rat poison on crackers was spread around the kitchen. Traps were set under all tents, which aided in reducing the number of rats. Another measure employed was to burn out the tall grass. That cleared out a great deal of the area." He and others learned that the only fail-safe way to keep the rats away was to seal everything as tightly as possible.

Alcohol, authorized or otherwise, offered a welcome reprieve. Some units were issued two or three cans of warm beer per soldier each week. Officers occasionally received small rations of whiskey. The best leaders willingly shared their whiskey with the troops. The issuance of these small quantities of beer and liquor was a nice gesture, but not enough to quench the collective thirst. Some traded souvenirs to sailors for cases of beer. Clever and well-connected men cut deals with air crewmen to spirit liquor back from flights to Australia. In one case, a group of men from the signals section of MacArthur's Hollandia headquarters sent one of their own on a trading expedition with the Army Air Forces and reaped some serious results. "He arrived back in Hollandia a couple days after Christmas with 55 pounds of Schenley's Black Label," Captain John McKinney later wrote. "This happy event obviously called for a party, we decided to have a Christmas Ball." Most in New Guinea had to settle for a much more humble source of alcohol—homemade liquor fermented in jerry-rigged stills made from scrounged tubing and excess containers. The usual process was to steal sugar and fruit juice from unit messing facilities, mix it with "liberated" raisins, oatmeal, apricots, potato peels, or coconut juice, let the amalgamation ferment for several days, mix it with lemonade or soda, and then imbibe. "[The] jungle juice, as nasty as it was (and it was very nasty) filled the need," Sergeant William LeGro, the machine gunner in the 186th Infantry, recalled. The hootch was typically potent, with a serious kick. The liquid fire produced in stills gave off a distinctly sweet, slightly noxious odor that could be smelled easily by anyone with a functioning nose. "One sample was enough for me and I wouldn't drink any more," PFC Joseph Steinbacher recalled of his only encounter with jungle juice. Indeed, the brew was usually so powerful that even small quantities could lead to serious drunkenness (which undoubtedly was the point). "We had to ration it because 95% alcohol can be deadly," one private later wrote. "It was a stupendous reviver after small patrol actions."[2]

The swamps and jungles teemed with so much disease that for the first two years of the war, sickness threatened to debilitate the Army, even more so than Japanese resistance. In 1943, at the height of the problem, disease caused five casualties for every one inflicted by the enemy. "Disease was a surer and more deadly peril to us than enemy marksmanship," Eichelberger once commented. Indeed, a vexing variety of maladies proliferated in New Guinea's unholy environment. "There was malaria . . . elephantiasis, scrub typhus, dysentery, tropical ulcer and a dengue-like fever," Lieutenant Colonel John Clarke, the 24th Division chemical officer, related. "Sharing the jungle with us were particularly irritating sandflies; bush mokkas, which are red insects which embed themselves in your flesh; leeches, and a small, nameless fly-like insect with an affinity for the human eye." Nonfatal skin problems, particularly for the ever-suffering infantry, bordered on the epidemic. By the estimate of one medical unit, 85 to 90 percent of combat soldiers in the Aitape perimeter were afflicted with some sort of skin issue. "Infected ulcers on the skin were slow in healing," commented Major William Davis, a physician in the 10th Evacuation Hospital. "Patients poisoned by weeds had intense itching and in that hot, moist place they didn't respond well at all."

From MacArthur on down, SWPA commanders had for many months made it a priority to combat disease, especially scrub typhus and malaria, the two most formidable maladies. Tiny chiggers that clung to blades of razor-sharp kunai grass spread scrub typhus among soldiers who moved through the grass with exposed necks and arms. In 1944, Army doctors treated nearly 4,400 cases with a 4 percent fatality rate. One wickedly virulent outbreak on Goodenough Island claimed a 25 percent death toll. Symptoms included a racking cough, red sores, swollen lymph nodes, and fatigue. A special typhus commission studied the problem but arrived at no satisfactory solution beyond the use of insect repellent and a recommendation for the dissemination of miticide-impregnated clothing, an impracticality under the circumstances. Fortunately, the disease remained uncommon enough, with only eight cases per one thousand soldiers, to keep it from wreaking more havoc. Malaria, by contrast, affected almost everyone. "[It] was our top ranking disease," Major Davis asserted. Another soldier opined in a letter to a friend, "Mosquitoes are our worst enemies." The massive mosquito population, combined with the commonality of swamps, rivers, puddles of standing water, and warm weather, pretty much guaranteed a rich growth environment for the disease. Most soldiers had some semblance of it, ranging from occasional mild fevers to full-blown cases that required hospitalization. Lieutenant Colonel Cloud's 362nd Station Hospital, typical of so many others, reported eight thousand admissions for malaria in 1944. "Quite a few cases were received in a coma," he later said.

Seldom was the disease fatal, just debilitating. The average patient required nearly two weeks in the hospital to regain his strength. Having
witnessed the mission-threatening effects of unchecked malaria proliferation earlier in the war, SWPA authorities by now had become very serious
about controlling it. By the middle of 1944, forty-seven specially formed
anti-malaria units, composed primarily of biologists, entomologists, and
epidemiologists, were operating in theater. By late September, the number
had more than doubled, to ninety-seven. Under their tutelage, engineers
drained swamps and other pools of standing water; work teams oiled and
burned mosquito breeding grounds or sprayed them with insecticide.
Through lectures, literature, and the dissemination of mosquito nets and
other useful equipment, malaria control team members schooled troops in
prevention techniques. "Another method . . . was the use of training films,"
Major Donald Patterson, a malariologist, told an Army interviewer. "Roadside signs were used to keep the men aware of the malaria hazard and
problems." Most commonly, of course, medics, sergeants, and commanders relentlessly cajoled, ordered, and forced soldiers to take their atabrine
tablets. The standard dosage was one tablet per day. Few enjoyed the experience of swallowing the bitter pill, whose unfortunate side effects included
a distinct yellowing of the skin, at least among whites. In many units, rumors swirled that atabrine caused sterility or psychosis. The sterility contention was entirely false, and the one about psychosis true only in the
rarest of cases. "Stress must be laid on the fact that atabrine is harmless,"
one division surgeon asserted. "Temporary neuroses and vomiting may
affect a very small percentage of those taking atabrine for the first time.
Less than one in 2000 persons is intolerant of atabrine." More than anything, malaria control depended upon constant, vigilant discipline. "Using
repellents, wearing leggings day and night, erecting bednets, wearing
shirts with long sleeves in the hot, humid climate after a tiresome day plus
drug prophylaxis becomes quite tiresome," commented Major John
Schwartzwelder of the 2nd Malaria Survey Unit. By the middle of 1944,
most had come to realize that complying with prevention orders was pref-
erable to developing malaria—with its recurrent fever and other unpleasant symptoms—or facing unwanted harassment and opprobrium from
superiors. Major Henry Gwynn, an SWPA medical consultant, estimated
that, while malaria remained a persistent problem, "the incidence of clini-
cal attacks had been reduced to where [the disease] is not seriously imped-
ing the military effort." To wit, in Milne Bay alone, infection rates had

declined from a staggering 3,308 cases per 1,000 men to a comparatively infinitesimal 31.[3]

Many otherwise recalcitrant GIs found motivation to ward off malaria by observing its ravages on locals, who were almost uniformly infected to some degree. Nearly universally, the Americans referred to dark-skinned New Guinea inhabitants with such colonial-tinged, dehumanizing terms as "fuzzy wuzzy" or "native." The subtle differences between the hundreds of tribes and subcultures around New Guinea were largely lost on the unschooled Americans. "The islanders have about as great a range in conduct and temperament as, say, the peoples of Europe," advised the fair-minded authors of an Army pocket guide to New Guinea. "Some groups are cheerful, approachable and talkative; others are dour and reserved. Some are trustworthy and dependable; others have a tradition of double talk and deception in dealing with outsiders. As with us, some are smart; some aren't."

The cultural gap between the tribal inhabitants of a remote corner of the planet and the products of a hustling, property-gathering, entertainment-obsessed, techno-rich industrial society was vast. Relations between the Americans and most New Guinea inhabitants were generally good, especially considering the consternation and bewilderment the people must have felt in seeing their homeland turned into bases and battlegrounds by odd-looking outsiders who possessed unimaginable power and riches. Occasionally, the Allies even moved whole villages to refugee camps away from the heaviest fighting. Locals provided a vital and cheap labor supply—they generally worked for small amounts of tobacco, money, or perhaps a cheap gadget or two—partially offsetting the paucity of service troops in theater. In a few cases, they served as a good source of intelligence gathering. "They have helped a great deal in working with our G-2 (intelligence) units," Lieutenant Colonel Stewart Yeo, an artillery commander, wrote to his father. "They often give the information on occupation of areas by the Japs that could be gotten in no other way in this jungle country." Most commonly, soldiers bartered with the inhabitants, shared meals, attempted to converse in pidgin English, or simply gawked at them from a distance. Most of the Americans seemed both repelled by their perceived backwardness and alienness (especially in relation to hygiene and medical care) and yet also fascinated with them. "The natives are not so well advanced," wrote Lieutenant Howard McKenzie to his family. "They are coal black, very small, their hair is enormously bushy, and a grey in color. Their only claim to clothing is a small rag girded about their hips. The women have rags that cover their upper bodies as well." PFC Allen Douglas, a member of an engineering unit, contended that "even though you would see them bathing naked all the time in the various water holes around the island, they still stank." Like nearly every other GI, whether white or black, Tech Sergeant Leslie Robertson had no interest in the women. "If you care to observe, the women wear no clothing from the waist up but, brother, it ain't like in the movies," he wrote with revulsion to a buddy about their appearance. At the same time, he admired and even envied their peaceful and comparatively simple lifestyle. "All the civilized people in the world are at war. These so called savages are at peace and enjoying the greatest period of prosperity they have ever known."

Though generally respectful and polite toward the local people, few GIs thought of them as equals and this was only reinforced by interaction with Dutch, British, and Australian colonials who had before the war carved out economic niches along the New Guinea coastal areas by establishing dominance over indigenous peoples. A widely circulated SWPA pamphlet, published under the imprint of General MacArthur, urged American soldiers to treat locals kindly and with forbearance, but also from an assumed position of inherent racial superiority and lordly oversight. "The native is nearly, if not quite, as good a man as you are," it intoned. "Joke with him by all means; even lark with him. But while you play the fool don't forget that you have to maintain that pose of superiority. Don't deliberately descend to his level. He has not been used to that from the white man; he will consider it unfitting and think less of you. Always, without overdoing it, be the master." Quite revealingly, the guidebook not only assumed and advised notions of Western predominance over the New Guinea islanders; it also presupposed white ubiquity and ascendance within American ranks. It contained, for instance, no advice for African-Americans or other nonwhites. The term "American" was simply assumed to be equivalent with "white," a concept typical of the time (and illuminated brilliantly after the war in Ralph Ellison's 1952 novel *Invisible Man*).

Not surprisingly, far too often, the kind of condescension that characterized the SWPA pamphlet crept into many GI dealings with locals. The Americans often saw them as childlike and related to them accordingly. In one typical encounter, Lieutenant McKenzie witnessed one of his privates approach a local man and command, "Get coconut for Great White Master." The man smiled and responded, "Certainly, sir, if it would please the

Master." As McKenzie recalled, "he shinnied up the tree, and cut several large coconuts and brought them down. The private, although he got a big kick out of it, said later he felt cheap as hell." With barely constrained bemusement and mild contempt, Lieutenant John Harrod, a young ordnance officer, wrote to his mother that "some of the natives drive jeeps and look comical as hell, with their excessively long cigarette holders, which they wear tucked behind their ears when talking." Private Joseph Adams, a member of a replacement depot unit, was highly amused to hear a local man use English swear words. "It tickled me and I laughed to beat the band. He looked at me with a silly grin and repeated it like a small child showing off." Sergeant Kinder, like so many other soldiers, avoided them if he could. "I do not mix with them. They live a very primitive and simple life, and very few of them have any idea about the outside world." Under the circumstances, the Americans and their white allies were fortunate that their rudimentary cultural understanding and notions of inherent racial superiority did not prevent the establishment of productive and cordial relations with the locals.[4]

By midyear, Hollandia had become the nerve center of the SWPA theater, not only a major logistical and staging base but now the heart of command. "Good roads were built, wooden barracks and Quonset huts sprang up overnight," Admiral Barbey later wrote. "Little tent cities dotted the landscape and the harbor filled with ships." The place teemed with brass. The cluster of huts, prefabricated buildings, and tents that served as Krueger's headquarters was located at Hollekang, right on the beach at Humboldt Bay. General Kenney's advance headquarters was located inland, adjacent to the newly refurbished airfields along Lake Sentani, where the mini fiefdoms of his colleagues proliferated. Admiral Kinkaid and his entourage were comfortably ensconced in a cluster of buildings half a mile away, on a hilltop. On the eastern shore of the lake, General Eichelberger had settled into a rambling tropical home where members of zoologist Richard Archbold's pioneering New Guinea expeditions had once slept before venturing into the nearby wilds. "The hardwood floors had not been touched and I was able to have showers, wash stands, copper screens put in for me and my aides," Eichelberger later wrote a friend. The lawns around the house were clustered with breadfruit, palm, and lemon trees. Eichelberger and his staff treated themselves to freshly squeezed lemonade and then used the surplus lemons, plus captured Japanese rifles and battle flags, to trade with sailors for the materials to improve the home's interior. The surrounding terrain and overall setting were breathtakingly attractive. "The Cyclops Mountains over 7700 feet high are on the northern shore [of the lake] and I have never seen a more beautiful view than we have from the front of this house," he wrote to McNair. The mountains and the water offered a rare respite from the otherwise sweltering high temperatures. "The cool breeze defeats the enervating effect of the tropical heat so that we are more comfortable than we have been in many months," General Byers told a friend.

On the highest ground, presiding over the whole empire, were the tents, Quonset huts, and cookie-cutter prefabricated houses of General Headquarters (or GHQ), MacArthur's forward command post. At the center of the cluster, next to a small water tower, a dirt road and patches of open, dusty ground, MacArthur's modest two-story house, dubbed the "Eagle's Nest" by the soldiers, stood like a sentinel. Engineers had hastily assembled it from prefabricated sheet metal huts. The place contained a few bedrooms, a dining room, a conference room, and office space, basically enough room to accommodate the general and some key staffers. Furniture, rugs, and a few pictures, transplanted from his apartment at the Lennon's Hotel in Brisbane, gave the Hollandia domicile the look and feel of a home. Otherwise, it served as a typical staging point for a high-level commander. More than anything, the view of New Guinea's beauty probably lent the place a resplendency it otherwise did not possess. "Across the deep blue waters of the lake, which was about twenty miles long and varied in width from half a mile to a hundred yards, the deep green hills of central New Guinea formed a backdrop of peaks, ravines, and jungle growth that was almost unreal," Kenney commented. "Little cone-shaped islands, with native houses on stilts clinging to their shores, dotted the lake. Perhaps two miles away a five-hundred-foot waterfall seemed to spring out of the center of Cyclops Mountain, dark and forbidding, with its crest perpetually covered with black rain clouds." Bizarre, erroneous rumors soon swept through the theater—surviving in popular discourse for years—that MacArthur had built a million-dollar palatial mansion for himself while most everyone else lived in the mud. The tales became ever taller with each telling. Supposedly the general had appropriated thousands of badly needed engineers to construct his Versailles-like estate, which he then adorned with expensive silver, crystal, and exotic rugs, all courtesy of the American taxpayer. One aviator breathlessly claimed to reporters that vital war supplies were diverted from a cargo plane to make room for a special load of gravel to improve the appearance of the sidewalks around MacArthur's house. When pressed for details, he sheepishly admitted that he had not witnessed the infamous diversion and could produce no evidence it had ever occurred. Anyone who saw the actual house came away mystified as to the origins of such rumors. "It was neat but not luxurious—certainly not by either Air Force or Navy standards," CBS News reporter Bill Dunn, a frequent visitor, later wrote. Master Sergeant Paul Rogers, a stenographer who now spent his days working inside the house, opined that "it had only the advantage of new construction, the smell of new wood and paint, and an unworn, unused appearance." The rumors had less to do with reality than the perception of MacArthur among his troops as a regal, self-absorbed, oddly captivating figure of faux aristocratic pretensions. This portrait was more incomplete than inaccurate. In tandem with his megalomaniacal tendencies, MacArthur also had an honorable side and a steady commitment to the welfare of the ordinary soldier under his command. Anyone who actually knew the general understood that he would never have countenanced the idea of building some sort of palace for himself at the expense of his soldiers. In fact, according to Major Egeberg, his physician and confidant, the general was actually annoyed with his subordinates "for erecting anything but the simplest structure." The irony of the matter was that MacArthur personally remained in Brisbane and ended up spending only four or five days at the Hollandia house.

Instead, the most important member of his staff was the forward leadership presence at the supposedly sumptuous house. SWPA chief of staff Richard "Dick" Sutherland, newly promoted to lieutenant general, was a man who struck more fear into the hearts of his Army peers and subordinates than did the Japanese. Yale-educated, son of a US senator from West Virginia, Sutherland had defied his father by choosing the profession of arms rather than law. He had seen combat in World War I as a company commander, but little action ever since. Bright, ruthless, conniving, cunning, hardworking, and as cold as a January evening in Siberia, Sutherland had by now logged six years with MacArthur, most as his chief of staff. Sutherland liked to circulate the story in Army circles that he had been personally responsible for running off Dwight Eisenhower when the two had served as aides to MacArthur in the Philippines before the war. Whether true or not, the claim revealed much more about Sutherland's overweening ambition and intrinsic meanness than any supposed weakness on Eisenhower's part (the latter desperately wanted out from under MacArthur's thumb anyway).

Sutherland's sharp elbows and self-interested machinations earned him far more enemies than friends throughout the Army. Eichelberger, who maintained cordial but wary relations with Sutherland, once privately wrote to Emma that the chief of staff was "one person out here . . . that I will never trust until the day he dies." Paul Rogers, his main enlisted aide, who had worked closely with him for nearly three years, both respected and feared him. "Sutherland was never a martinet. He was not unreasonable, nor was he thoughtless. There was simply no room in his prescribed duties for displays of generosity and tenderness. He had to be toughminded." Another staffer once described him as "an intense individual in everything he did." With promotion to three-star rank, Sutherland's natural brusqueness had seemingly evolved into a thirst for more power. Diminutive, solidly built, handsome, with a penchant for slicked-back hair, the fifty-year-old chief of staff was heavily devoted to MacArthur, not so much on a personal level but more in the manner of a scheming, secretly resentful son who bides his time to inherit the mantle of leadership from a chief executive father. Eventually, after the war, he would come to describe MacArthur as "an egomaniac" and privately admit to fostering great bitterness about his boss. Upon arriving at the Eagle's Nest, Sutherland installed himself, in MacArthur's absence, as a sort of alternate SWPA commander. In one instance, as Sutherland stood looking out the window of his office, taking in the sight of the mini city that now included GHQ and the other growing American bases around Lake Sentani, he summoned Rogers to his side. As Sutherland stared out the window, he said firmly, "Rogers, I am in command now. I am running the show. The General is an old man. He can't operate any more." Completely taken aback, Rogers only stammered, "Yes, sir," and stood awkwardly for several moments until realizing that his boss had nothing more to add to this bombshell.

Sutherland's growing sense of personal power now manifested itself in petty, self-defeating defiance toward MacArthur. For nearly two years, Sutherland had carried on an illicit affair with Elaine Bessemer-Clark, wife of Captain Reginald Bessemer-Clark, a British Army officer and onetime world-class tennis player whom the Japanese had captured at Malaya. Elaine was a socialite and something of an Australian aristocrat. She was the twenty-eight-year-old daughter of Sir Norman Brookes, a former Wimbledon champion whose family had made a fortune in Australian paper manufacturing and gold mining. She and Reginald had a toddler-aged son. Sutherland had a wife back home and a twenty-two-year-old daughter, Natalie, whose wedding he had recently missed. Though tongues wagged all over Australian and American military and social circles about the illicit couple, the two lovers did little to conceal their torrid affair.

The relationship was more than just a private dalliance by a lonely man far from home; it also impacted MacArthur's inner circle. Back in Australia, Sutherland had even installed his girlfriend as the main receptionist for MacArthur's headquarters. Elaine's abrasive personality, along with her high-maintenance sense of blue-blooded entitlement and a penchant for byzantine power scheming—belying in this case the notion of opposites attracting—made her a reviled, even hated figure among the troops at GHQ. Anyone who crossed her risked incurring Sutherland's wrath. She became something of a shadow authority figure, occasionally co-opting her boyfriend's power as her own. In one telling instance, when she clashed with Major John Day, the headquarters commandant, she successfully maneuvered to have him relieved. She soon conflicted with his successor and had him ushered out as well.

More recently, Sutherland had wangled a captain's commission for Elaine in the Women's Army Corps (WAC) and, in disobedience of a direct order from MacArthur, arranged for her to follow him to New Guinea. This was a deft maneuver on Sutherland's part because he knew that the Army was in the process of sending, for the first time, hundreds of WAC soldiers to New Guinea to help with administrative and clerical duties. Thus, her status as a WAC would, at least in Sutherland's mind, provide suitable cover for her presence in Hollandia. Sutherland also knew that MacArthur welcomed the assistance of the WACs. Soon a sprinkling of American women in uniform turned up at secure bases around the island (provoking the inevitable curiosity and interest of the male soldiers). But the general had a strategic reason for forbidding Elaine's presence in New Guinea. Australia's manpower was stretched to the limit; most every able-bodied man was in military service. The country was having difficulty finding labor for its many wartime industries. Increasingly, Australian leaders turned to women to relieve the scarcity. MacArthur had personally promised Australian prime minister John Curtin that he would not allow any Australian women to go to New Guinea or other forward fronts. What was more, the general almost certainly understood the poisonous effect of Elaine's presence on the men who worked in his headquarters. He himself felt anything but comfortable with her. On one embarrassing occasion in Port Moresby, at the house that served as his headquarters, he had emerged half-clothed from a nap and nearly bumped into Elaine. "Good afternoon, General," she said cheerily. Mortified and red-faced, previously ignorant of her presence, MacArthur had said nothing and stonily retreated to his room. As a faithful husband, MacArthur neither understood nor approved of Sutherland's dalliance, though he was generally inclined to stay out of the private lives of subordinates. More than anything, the SWPA commander thought it unseemly and inappropriate for Elaine to serve in such a prominent role within his headquarters and he feared it might lead to negative publicity. Subsequently, he told Sutherland in no uncertain terms that he did not want Elaine in New Guinea. "Dick, that woman must not go to the forward areas again. I want it understood. Under no circumstances is that woman to be taken to a forward area."

Instead of obeying, Sutherland, in a bold power play, had secretly arranged for her to serve alongside him in the Eagle's Nest at Hollandia. "Sutherland would control the military affairs of GHQ and [she] would control the housekeeping arrangements," Paul Rogers later wrote. "They would sit as master and mistress of a vast empire in a common exercise of command and authority. No other officer junior to Sutherland would dare complain." Their arrangement conformed to the uneven gender roles prevalent at the time. While Sutherland functioned as the overall boss, she supervised the headquarters mess and the housekeeping staff, often meting out orders to resentful soldiers. She operated as a feminine face of GHQ. Smartly turned out in a white dress, she played the role of hostess for important visitors, regularly serving them lemonade or fruit juices. Predictably, given her personality and character flaws, she soon wore out whatever welcome she might otherwise have had. "It annoyed every officer there to have that particular woman acting as a pseudo-hostess in our forward GHQ," Major Egeberg contended. Master Sergeant Rogers grew to detest her so much that he personally asked Sutherland for a transfer (the general angrily turned him down). "There were many who did not care for Sutherland and who despised [Elaine]," Rogers later reflected. "I did care for Sutherland fully as much as I despised [Elaine]." An angry rumor circulated among the engineers who had built the Hollandia headquarters that Captain Bessemer-Clark had arrived with her own personal pink-colored bathtub and commode and immediately issued orders as to exactly how she wanted her bathroom equipment installed. As a form of protest, many of the engineers decided to withhold their monthly War Bonds donations.

A man of Sutherland's intellect and cleverness must have known that Elaine's presence in Hollandia could not escape MacArthur's attention for long. The troubling details soon reached an unhappy MacArthur back in Brisbane. "This was a preposterous irritant, and the General was furious," Dr. Egeberg asserted. Sutherland's daughter Natalie later contended that her father was "one of the few not intimidated by MacArthur. [He] more than held his own in his dealing with him." She was half-right. Certainly, Sutherland enjoyed more equity with MacArthur than any other person in theater, save Jean, his wife. But Sutherland's decision to defy MacArthur's direct order not to bring Elaine forward indicated more than just the actions of an infatuated man satisfying the influence of his scheming lover. In a larger sense, it spoke to a new intention on Sutherland's part to challenge his boss's authority, one that MacArthur could not tolerate. The two engaged in an epic argument over Elaine that grew so heated that Sutherland, on the spot, asked to resign or take sick leave. Knowing Sutherland's value as a competent, knowledgeable chief of staff, MacArthur refused to let him go. Even so, Sutherland soon confided to Major Weldon "Dusty" Rhoades, MacArthur's personal pilot and probably Sutherland's only friend on the SWPA staff, that the stormy session had been "such a disagreeable event that he doubted a complete rapprochement between the two was possible." Sutherland judged the situation accurately. He had indeed inflicted irreparable damage on his relationship with MacArthur and, ironically, sowed the seeds of his own eventual demise.[5]

Even the most successful flanking maneuvers carry a sniff of danger. A bypassed or surrounded enemy can strike back hard, if only out of utter desperation. The Germans had found this out at the Battle of Arras in 1940; the Soviets during innumerable battles against encircled German formations on the Eastern Front; the Western Allies during the last stages of the Normandy breakout. At Hollandia, MacArthur had driven a powerful wedge between increasingly marginalized Japanese ground forces in New Guinea. To the SWPA commander, the godforsaken giant island—the focus of nearly all his military operations for two years—now represented only a gateway to the Philippines and he was impatient to leave it behind

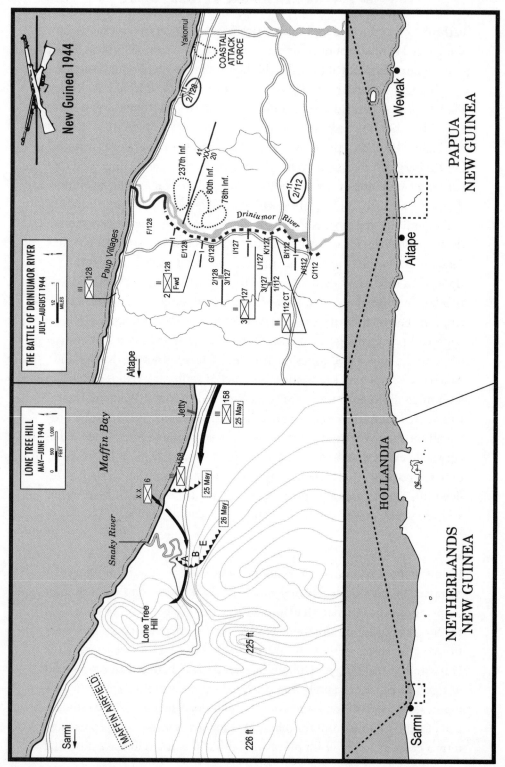

New Guinea 1944

THE BATTLE OF DRINIUMOR RIVER
JULY–AUGUST 1944

0 1/2 1
MILES

Yakomul

COASTAL
ATTACK
FORCE

2/228

41
XX
20

237th Inf.

80th Inf.

78th Inf.

11
2/112

Driniumor River

Paup Villages

III 128

F/128

E/128

II 2 128 Fwd

G/128

2/128

II 3/127

I/127

L/127

II 3

3/127

K/127

1/112

B/112

A/112

III 112 CT

C/112

Aitape

LONE TREE HILL
MAY–JUNE 1944

0 500 1,000
FEET

Maffin Bay

Jetty

III 158 25 May

III H/158 25 May

XX 6

25 May

26 May

A B E

Snaky River

Lone Tree Hill

225 ft

226 ft

MAFFIN AIRFIELD

Sarmi

PAPUA
NEW GUINEA

Wewak

Aitape

HOLLANDIA

NETHERLANDS
NEW GUINEA

Sarmi

© 2021 by Chris Erichsen

in his personal rearview mirror. He was now focused on seizing key objectives in western New Guinea to maintain his momentum; the eastern flank around Aitape represented to him little more than a strategic afterthought, a guarded back door to keep out nuisance bandits. The Japanese had other ideas. No matter how strategically compromised they might have been after the success of Operation Reckless, they remained capable of inflicting damage not just to Allied ground forces but to MacArthur's Philippines agenda. In the Wewak area, Lieutenant General Adachi still had elements of three divisions, the 20th, the 41st, and the 50th, totaling about fifty-five thousand troops, at his disposal. With the Australian Army harassing him to the east and increasingly powerful American bases at Aitape and Hollandia to his west, his options were limited. He could sit tight and consign his army to the protracted suicide of starvation and disease, or he could strike back. A 1910 Military Academy graduate, Adachi believed strongly in the Japanese warrior values of self-sacrifice, patience, and honor. His father had been an army officer; two of his brothers were major generals. He had seen much brutal combat in China. Personal tragedy had coalesced with professional triumph for him in 1942 when his wife died and he was appointed to command of the Eighteenth Army. Fanatically devoted to the emperor, a committed family man with a penchant for heavy drinking, he wrote short-verse poetry in his spare time and prided himself on sharing the many hardships of his soldiers.

To Adachi, there was no question of sitting still and waiting for a slow jungle death. Honor and pride demanded action. "I cannot find any method which will solve this situation strategically or technically," he wrote in a circular to his soldiers. "Therefore, I intend to overcome this by relying on our Japanese *Bushido*. I am determined to destroy the enemy at Aitape by attacking him ruthlessly with the concentration of our entire force in the area. This will be our final opportunity to employ our entire strength to annihilate the enemy. Make the supreme sacrifice, display the spirit of the Imperial Army." With few vehicles, a nearly disastrous logistical situation, and little in front of him but trackless, alien jungle, he had essentially decided to unleash a strategic banzai attack. Adachi had more in mind, though, than simple self-immolation. Knowing that his force could never negotiate its way past the American enclaves at Aitape and Hollandia, then through hundreds of miles of deadly jungle to link up with friendly units in western New Guinea, he decided to focus on attacking Aitape. Unlike some of his Imperial Army colleagues, whose irrational belief in the spiritual over the temporal almost made them tantamount to twentieth-century ghost dancers, Adachi was realistic enough to understand that he was unlikely to snuff out the enemy base at Aitape. Instead, he hoped to inflict heavy casualties on the Americans and force MacArthur to spend time and resources to maintain the security of the Allied eastern flank. This could ease pressure on Japanese formations in western New Guinea and all over the western Pacific, perhaps even delay or sabotage MacArthur's plan to return to the Philippines.

From early May onward, he and his men began a tortuous westward trek along confining jungle tracks, hauling nearly all their food, ammo, and equipment on their overloaded backs. Though hobbled by a hernia, Adachi insisted on walking alongside his troops. They ate half and then quarter rations. They sweltered in the heat of the day and shivered through the cooler nights. Heavy rains soaked them to the skin and turned trails into muddy quagmires that taxed all of a man's strength just to walk a few hundred yards. Medicine was scarce. Disease ravaged the ranks. "Swarms of anopheles mosquitoes abound after dusk, and it is necessary to take preventative measures other than those taken at sleeping time," an Imperial Army instructional document declared. But the soldiers had little besides mosquito netting and some quinine to ward off malaria. Most were feverish and underweight. Allied planes frequently strafed them, inflicting casualties and eroding morale. "In air superiority, to put it briefly, we are about a century behind . . . America," one bitter 41st Division officer scrawled in his diary. "If only we had air superiority!" For two awful months, even as the Americans built up their burgeoning bases and launched new operations to the west of Hollandia, Adachi's dwindling army plodded onward. They moved at a snail's pace, covering, at best, between three to seven miles per day. With every nightmarish step, the health of his command declined as soldiers died, fell out, or weakened. "Men began to use jungle plants for food," one soldier grimly told his diary. Another lamented seeing "the white bones of our comrades . . . strewn here and there."

Thanks to Ultra intelligence, aerial reconnaissance flights, reports from locals, and long-range foot patrols, the Americans knew much about Adachi's plan to attack the Aitape perimeter. But, like speculative weather forecasters who realize that a storm is coming but not much else, they struggled to pinpoint the strength of Adachi's force and the timing of his attack. In part, this was because the Japanese themselves were anything but certain about these matters. Adachi originally intended to attack in late June, but the staggered, corrosive nature of his march made it impossible to amass his strike force of about twenty thousand troops with anything like the necessary coherence. In Brisbane, Brigadier General Willoughby had collected masses of information on the Eighteenth Army's movements and intentions. Yet, in his characteristic cover-all-bases fashion, he avoided making clear assertions about Japanese strength and precise predictions about the attack timetable. Given what he knew about the near-catastrophic state of Japanese logistics, he wondered how they even had the capability of initiating any offensive action. The most definitive prediction he would make, in one intelligence summary, was that "it appears that the attack on Aitape is scheduled for some time early in July or late June." Given all the advantages at his disposal, one might understandably have hoped for more actionable intelligence. Even so, he later claimed, apparently with a straight face, that "never has a commander gone into battle knowing so much about the enemy as did the Allied commander at Aitape." Certainly this would have been news to any on-site American commander.

Lieutenant General Krueger was juggling multiple operations. Even as he oversaw MacArthur's post-Hollandia push for control of western New Guinea, he was also responsible for fending off Adachi and eliminating any threat he might pose to the momentum of the SWPA advance. The availability of increasingly more US ground combat forces in theater, including newly arrived formations, made this possible. Krueger returned the 163rd Infantry to the 41st Division but beefed up the Aitape perimeter with the entire 32nd Infantry Division. Nicknamed the Red Arrow, this National Guard outfit from Wisconsin and Michigan had fought to almost total destruction at Buna in 1942, winning the first American ground victory of World War II. So shattered was the division from its Buna death struggle that it had needed nearly a year to re-form and refit. Krueger augmented the 32nd with supporting artillery, engineers, and the 112th Cavalry Regiment, yet another equine unit that had reluctantly traded its horses for infantry rifles. With about fifteen hundred soldiers, the 112th was, by infantry standards, at half strength, and with fewer heavy weapons. Confusingly, the Sixth Army order of battle listed it as a regimental combat team, meaning that Colonel Alexander Miller commanded the regiment itself while answering to Brigadier General Julian Cunningham, who presided over both the regiment and its attachments. Eventually, Krueger fed the 124th Infantry Regiment and elements of the 43rd Infantry Division into Aitape as well.[6]

With the combat manpower equivalent of two full divisions in place, he authorized the formation of XI Corps under the command of Major General Charles "Chink" Hall, a strack Mississippian and West Pointer whose valorous combat service in World War I had earned him the Distinguished Service Cross. The laconic Hall had accrued decades of infantry service, though he was new to the Pacific War. "He was a compassionate, human man," Brigadier General Johnnie Elmore, his chief of staff, once said of him. "He was highly regarded by everyone who served on his staff. He was informal but there was never any doubt as to who was in command." Hall oversaw the establishment of a double-layered defense for Aitape. The presence of the rugged Torricelli Mountains and miles of impassable jungle essentially protected the southern flank from mass attack. Hall knew this would force Adachi to funnel his assaulting force through a relatively narrow strip of coastal low ground that stretched for about seven miles from south to north. Hall deployed a defensive line around the Tadji airstrip and its surrounding Aitape base. A few miles to the east, about three battalions from the 32nd Division, plus the 112th Cavalry, manned a defensive outpost line at the marshy, jungle-encrusted Driniumor River. The thinly held American line stretched for about five miles along the meandering river, whose depth varied from ankle- to head-high. "It was a wide, rocky riverbed . . . in some places nearly a half mile wide," Sergeant Ben Moody of the 112th Cavalry later commented. "There were no trees in the riverbed whatsoever." The span and depth of the river ebbed and flowed with rainy and dry periods. At most places, it stretched anywhere from fifty to one hundred yards wide.

On June 27, Krueger flew from Hollandia to Aitape to meet with Hall and Major General William Gill, the commander of the 32nd Division. The Sixth Army commander brought with him new indications from Willoughby's shop of an imminent Japanese attack. In fact, patrols had already fought numerous sharp small-unit engagements in the vicinity of the Driniumor. Troubled by the vulnerability of the Driniumor line, Gill suggested the idea of withdrawing the outpost battalions to the Aitape perimeter, where they could form an unassailable brick wall of a defensive line upon which the Japanese would inevitably hurl and destroy themselves (similar to Griswold's concept at Bougainville, though Gill did not describe it as such). Gill complained that the heavy jungle around the Driniumor made forward supply a nightmare and artillery support problematic. The deeper Gill's formations operated in the jungle, the more the odious terrain negated the potent American advantages of firepower and maneuver. By contrast, the close proximity of Aitape to the sea could bring more naval support in play than at the Driniumor. Krueger turned him down flat. "Although I appreciated the difficulties, I did not share that view," he later commented. "And we had naval and air support whereas the enemy had neither." Krueger neglected to take into account that the remote Driniumor terrain tended to negate those very advantages. Under pressure from MacArthur to speed up his operations east and west, he had little stomach for the notion of settling in at Aitape and waiting for the Japanese to make their move. Like almost all senior Army officers, he had been professionally indoctrinated always to seize the initiative and maintain an aggressive posture. A perceived attitude of passiveness was a mortal sin in Army culture: anyone painted with this brush soon found himself in professional oblivion. Indeed, based mainly on this conversation, Krueger formed a permanent opinion of Gill, a Virginia Military Institute graduate who had seen much combat in World War I, as lacking in aggressiveness and unsuited for potential corps command.

Not only did Krueger mandate the maintenance of the Driniumor line. He also ordered Hall and Gill to probe eastward, across the river, find the Japanese vanguard, and attack Adachi before he could strike. Under other circumstances, this notion of a spoiling attack to disrupt a pending enemy offensive would probably have made good sense. In this instance, it amounted to a fool's errand. The pair of battalion-size probes into the heavy foliage east of the Driniumor weakened the already thin American defenses along the river, penny-packeted the strength of rifle companies on the wrong side of the river, and consigned hundreds of soldiers to the enervating privation of long-range jungle patrols, desperate skirmishes, and seemingly endless days on half rations, not to mention a morale-sapping sense of isolation. "It seemed like we always had patrols going out morning and afternoon," recalled Private William Garbo of the 112th. "Sometimes we had patrols that would go out and wouldn't come back, and we would go out and try to find them. We lost some men that way." In jungle wilderness, they were immersed in "kunai grass, swamps, and leeches and lizards and just about anything," Sergeant Moody commented. "It was a miserable place. You stayed wet, continuously." Visibility was nil. "The jungle was so

dense . . . you couldn't see anything," Tech 5 Claire Ehle, a telephone lineman in the 32nd Division, commented. Long-range patrols spent massive
amounts of time and energy cutting trails, only to find them overgrown
with new foliage in a matter of just a few days. In many cases, the forward
troops had to be supplied by low-flying C-47s whose crewmen hastily
kicked boxes of medicine, ammo, or food out their side doors. Even with
the drops, the men did not have enough to eat. "Without food, in two days,
a man's fighting ability drops at least 50%," one commander contended in
a written post-battle assessment.

Hall compounded the error of Krueger's offensive-defensive strategy by
electing to apportion the majority of his combat units around Aitape
rather than reinforcing the Driniumor. By the second week of July, when
Adachi finally felt ready to attack, Hall had placed nine of his fifteen infantry battalions around Aitape, leaving not much more than a couple of battalions to screen the Driniumor. "In my opinion this force should offer
very considerable resistance and should be able to hold against anything
but a determined attack from the East or of course a determined attack in
its rear from the South," he assured Krueger in a sentence full of ominously
hedging qualifiers. In truth, Hall had done little more than satisfy Krueger's
wish to maintain the Driniumor line and go on the offensive, but without
paying the necessary price of denuding Aitape's defenses, a kind of play-it-
both-ways approach whose main consequence was to enhance the vulnerability of Driniumor. "Hall and his staff were untrained in this thing from
the top down," Gill later sniped. "They had never had any combat like
this. They didn't know anything about jungle fighting." Sergeant Moody
railed that "the decision to fight on the Driniumor was inexplicable. At
Aitape the 18th Army could have been completely destroyed."

Amazingly, even by the time Adachi had decided upon the evening of
July 10 as the launch date for his offensive, the American commanders on
the ground, in spite of all the remarkable intelligence data available to their
superiors, really had no idea that it was coming—surely a cautionary tale
about the perishable, fragile nature of even the best high-level intelligence.
"We never had any indication, no idea in the world," Moody later contended. Moreover, thanks to the decisions made by Krueger and Hall, the
Americans had weakened the very places where the Japanese intended to
push. Lean and desperate after their deadly one-hundred-mile jungle odyssey, Adachi's assault troops were ready for victory or death. For weeks they
had subsisted on an average of 330 grams of food per day. Some had taken

to consuming sago palm leaves. The numerous smokers among them had been rationed three cigarettes every ten days. Almost everyone was severely underweight, racked with diarrhea, and the fever of tropical disease. Still they pressed on and prepared to attack. "What of the Americans and the Australians?" one of them ruminated in his diary. "They can boast only of their material power. We will wage a war of annihilation. The feelings of every officer and man throughout the Army are churning with a desire to massacre all Americans and Australians." Their capacity to endure continued hardship bordered on the inexplicable. Napoleon Bonaparte had once famously contended, "The first qualification of a soldier is fortitude under fatigue and privation. Courage is only the second. Hardship, poverty and want are the best school of the soldier." By that measure, the soldiers of the Eighteenth Army had few peers in any epoch.[7]

Adachi knew much about the American dispositions, thanks to the remarkable work of his reconnaissance patrols and other infiltrators. He decided to make his main effort against the weakened center of the line, where a pair of rifle companies from the 32nd Division's 128th Infantry Regiment manned a frontage more appropriate to a regimental-size unit. During the waning moments of July 10, following a brief artillery barrage, the Japanese went forward. Massed together under the half-light of a prominent moon, screaming and cursing, they splashed across the river and struck. "Without regard for the losses our artillery, automatic weapons, mortars and small arms were inflicting upon him, the enemy came on in hordes and made a serious penetration of our lines," stated the after-action report of the 32nd Division's 128th Infantry Regiment. Hunkered down in log-reinforced bunkers, foxholes, and mortar pits, the Americans were overwhelmed with targets. Machine gunners burned out barrels. Mortar crews dropped shells down their tubes so fast that the guns became dangerously hot. Riflemen unleashed waves of bullets. A lone BAR man fired twenty-six magazines, some five hundred bullets, in a fifteen-minute period, until his overheated rifle rebelled and fired only single shots. In less than an hour, Adachi's lead battalion was scythed from four hundred to ninety survivors, many of whom spent their last energy to crawl or run back across the river. The blood of their comrades turned the shallow water red and speckled the rocks of the riverbed. Many had been snared in coils of barbed wire above the riverbank and slaughtered. Still, throughout the night, the Japanese threw more battalions into the fray. Their losses were terrible. The 78th Infantry alone lost six hundred dead and one of its battalions suffered an 80 percent casualty rate. "We just mowed them down and filled that riverbed up," one American soldier later commented.

But by weight of numbers, they overran the Americans, blasting them out of their holes with grenades and close-range rifle fire, or fighting them to the death in desperate hand-to-hand encounters. They tore a two-thousand-yard gap in the American front, fanned out assaulting infiltrators in either direction, and kept attacking. "There were Japs everywhere," Tech 5 Charles Brabham of A Troop, 112th Cavalry, later shuddered. "In front of you, in back of you, and all around you." Though the chaos made telephone and radio communications from artillery observers to their batteries spotty, American shells exploded in droves all along the riverbed and even over the friendly positions, inflicting heavy casualties on the Japanese and friendly-fire injuries on the Americans. Guided by pre-attack briefings and map study, Japanese demolition squads assaulted battery perimeters and attempted, with little success, to blow up the American fieldpieces. "Our artillery has been right up behind the infantry supporting," Lieutenant Colonel Stewart Yeo, an artillery commander in XI Corps, wrote to his father. "The batteries have been under attack at their positions and wire and observation parties have been attacked. The Jap is desperate." In a single night, the Japanese suffered about three thousand casualties. So many of their bodies choked the riverbed that American observers who glimpsed them initially thought they were looking at piles of logs.

In spite of the losses, though, the Japanese continued their relentless attacks through the gap, even as acute hunger gnawed at their bellies. "We fight while eating only grass," one junior officer bitterly commented in his diary. "Since coming to New Guinea, I fully appreciate the value of even one gram of rice." For nearly two weeks, confusing, seesaw fighting raged as the Americans sought to repair the rupture and the Japanese attempted to shatter the US front. Organized front lines became far less common than staggered or circular embattled perimeters, particularly for the two American battalions that had been operating east of the Driniumor when the attack began. Isolated American units had to be supplied by air and rescued by neighboring formations. Amid the suffocating green foliage and shattered husks of lugubrious rain forest, patrols, assaults, and counterassaults all melded together in a blur of ferocious combat between small groups of exhausted, terrified men. Between five hundred and seven hundred Japanese infiltrators roamed anywhere from Hall's Aitape line to the Driniumor, sowing terror and confusion, especially at night, when, as usual, the Americans hunkered down and fired at anything moving outside their holes. "You did not leave your foxhole at night," said Private Garbo. "If you did, you were dead, because somebody was going to shoot you." In the eerie darkness, enemy soldiers called out the names of individual Americans with such pleas as "Smitty, help, I'm wounded. Come over and get me!" At times, they cursed President Roosevelt or his wife, Eleanor. The Americans responded with the most common insult of the Pacific War, "Tojo eats shit!"

While the fighting raged, Krueger flew back to Aitape and upbraided his subordinates for what he considered to be an unjustifiable retreat. As was his tendency, he did not visit the front firsthand to form this impression—though, in fairness, the job of getting an army commander safely forward through such terrible terrain and in the midst of a very confusing tactical situation would have been challenging in the extreme. Anticipating Krueger's impatience, Hall had already prepared plans for a counteroffensive to reclaim the Driniumor line and destroy the rest of Adachi's army. The XI Corps commander proposed a two-pronged push. The Northern Force, along the coast, consisted of the 124th and 128th regimental combat teams under the command of Brigadier General Alexander Stark, the assistant division commander of the 43rd Division. The Southern Force comprised the 112th Cavalry and parts of the 127th Infantry under General Cunningham. In an irreverent nod to his paucity of hair, headquarters personnel soon began referring to these units as the "Baldy Force." Hall's aggressive restoration plan soothed Krueger's ire. The Sixth Army commander returned to Hollandia in a better mood, though for the ensuing weeks he did continue to pressure his subordinates impatiently to wrap up the Driniumor campaign, and even found time to harangue Hall for what he believed were poor patrolling techniques and slipshod discipline on the part of his men. "Our patrolling is being intensified over what has heretofore seemed adequate if properly performed," Hall responded with droll imprecision. "I am pushing commanders on patrolling. It is, as you know, extremely difficult in the jungle."

The troops of the two task forces, consigned as they were to endless days and weeks of jungle warfare, could have told Krueger much the same. The terrain, the conditions, the logistics, and the fractured, stubborn nature of Japanese resistance all mitigated against any sort of rapid conclusion to the fighting. On the southern front, the 112th Cavalry engaged in nearly three weeks of bitter seesaw fighting just to regain control of the tiny riverside village of Afua. Not until the end of July could the Americans accurately claim to have eliminated Japanese infiltrators west of the Driniumor and fully restored the original lines. In August, even as a defiant Adachi launched new but smaller attacks, the two American prongs simply lined up in columns and bulled their way into the jungles east of the river to subdue or shatter the enemy remnants. Patrols fought to the death in the anonymous foliage. Japanese infiltrators harassed tense nighttime perimeters; as usual, the Americans eschewed night patrols, outposts, and listening posts and passively hunkered down, ceding night movement to their enemies. It was not unusual for a man to go more than a month without a change of clothes. Baths consisted of stripping naked in the rain, soaping up, and hoping the rain did not stop before rinsing the soap residue off. Medics and stretcher teams struggled mightily to evacuate badly wounded men, sapping the pace of an already deliberate advance. "Column moving very slowly," one battalion journal tersely recorded on a typical early August day. "Litter bearers are worn out. Rough trail. No food today. Whole battalion helping with litter cases." Overworked doctors in forward hospitals were likely to press any bystander into assisting them with emergency surgery. "Would you hold this guy's tongue while we are operating on him?" a physician once asked Lieutenant Judson Chubbuck, a young 112th Cavalry officer. In another case, he watched as a doctor rebuilt the abdomen of a man who had been slashed open by a saber-wielding Japanese soldier. "His intestines [were] scattered all over everywhere in this goddamn heat, flies, jungle, sulfa powder all over" the guts. The doctor stuffed them back in and sewed up the abdomen. The man survived.

According to regulations, the dead were supposed to be buried immediately. "Make sure the cadavers are buried deeply, especially in wet or marshy country," one memo stipulated. In most cases, though, they were unceremoniously dragged rearward by overburdened soldiers or locals. PFC Joseph Steinbacher described a typical dead soldier as "a gruesome sight. He . . . had been hit in the head. Unfortunately his head was hanging out of [a] poncho and had turned a bright . . . blue color." Amid the terrible conditions and the protracted fighting, more than a few men succumbed to combat fatigue. "Their rifles were just dropped on the ground—their equipment was discarded—helmets thrown away and with utter disregard for their own safety, these men, most of them sobbing with big tears in their eyes, started moving back to the rear," Major Edward Logan, a battalion intelligence officer, later wrote of the afflicted.

Supply trains maintained by support troops and local laborers kept up with the columns as best they could, but the voracious demands of combat formations in sustained action, combined with the alien environment, necessitated supply drops, particularly of rations, by C-47s to isolated or far-afield units. In one three-day period, the planes dropped 8.2 tons of supplies just to the 112th Cavalry. "I distinctly remember those C47s . . . and they would have their flaps down," Private Garbo later recalled. "They looked like they were just creeping along." Flying low and slow, they dropped their wares into small jungle clearings or trails marked by smoke grenades. "They had to orbit around the general locality until the panels or smoke were seen," Logan wrote. "There were only two or three planes available to make the drops and this necessitated making a number of trips." The drops were chaotic enough that, in one battalion alone, seven men were struck and killed by falling ration boxes. Often as not, pallets and crates were parachuted and lost or ended up in Japanese hands. Facing the desperation of imminent starvation, the Japanese learned to pop smoke grenades in hopes of luring unwitting C-47 crews into dropping the supplies to them; more often, enemy soldiers watched the drops and then raced the Americans to pick up the booty. "Our guys would sit there and wait for them and then shoot them," Sergeant Moody recalled. The jungle was so featureless and maps so poor that artillery observers had difficulty calling in fire with much precision. By one estimate, the North Force, in at least one engagement, suffered more casualties from friendly artillery fire than enemy ordnance.

As the Americans plodded forward, they found increasing numbers of Japanese bodies and body parts, mainly by smelling them before seeing them. A fog-like stench hung over fetid jungle. "I remember seeing one face—just the skin—plastered up against the side of a tree," Moody noted. "Boy! There was parts and pieces of every kind that you could dream of." In almost all cases, the Japanese fought to the death or anonymously succumbed to disease or starvation. Suffused with hatred and fear, the Americans were little inclined to take prisoners. "We don't capture many, we just kill the devils," Staff Sergeant Milton Sutherland of the 124th Infantry related coldly in a letter to his siblings. PFC Steinbacher's company found a badly wounded enemy soldier and subjected him to interrogation by a Japanese-American interpreter. When the interpreter finished, the battalion intelligence officer nodded to a nearby medic and said, "Okay, Doc." The medic gave the Japanese soldier multiple shots of morphine in hopes of sedating him to the point where his heart would stop. Steinbacher and several other riflemen in the meantime hacked out a shallow grave and placed him inside, but still he did not die. After a few minutes, the intelligence officer "walked up carrying an M1 carbine and aimed down at a spot between the prisoner's eyes. The Japanese soldier raised a hand up and placed it between his eyes as the officer shot down through the hand. A thin stream of blood squirted up out of the hole in the hand that flopped back down alongside the body." The Americans wordlessly shoveled dirt onto the grave and left. In a telling foreshadowing of the Vietnam War, commanders grew increasingly preoccupied with inflicting the highest possible number of deaths on the enemy for every American casualty—the popular term for this was "kill ratio"—an attitude present in the European theater but far more prevalent in the Pacific against a nonwhite enemy. In one press briefing, Willoughby emphasized that SWPA commanders were loath to "waste valuable Caucasian lives on Orientals, who prefer to die." Lieutenant Colonel Yeo, the artillery commander, enthused in a July letter to his father that "everyone is in better spirits now that we are slugging it out with the Japs and keeping great ratio of killed and wounded in our favor, usually about 10 to 1."

By mid-August, Adachi and his exhausted survivors were in headlong retreat back to Wewak, and the threat—such as it ever was—to the Aitape base had long since passed. On August 25, Lieutenant General Krueger declared the Driniumor operation over, though patrolling and skirmishes continued. Adachi had certainly caused significant consternation and loss to the Americans, who suffered 440 killed in action, 2,550 wounded, 10 missing, and an undocumented number of men lost to combat fatigue and sickness. But the Japanese general failed to disrupt the momentum of Mac-Arthur's operations in western New Guinea or the possibility of his return to the Philippines. According to Japanese records, Adachi lost 10,000 men, including nearly an 80 percent fatality rate from disease or combat. Only 98 Japanese surrendered or were captured by the Americans. The casualties especially decimated the combat formations that contained Adachi's best soldiers. For instance, all three infantry regiments of the 20th Division suffered more than a 50 percent loss rate. If anything, the "kill ratio" might have been even higher than Yeo's claim of 10 to 1. Those Japanese who escaped could look forward only to more harassment from Australian formations that took on the grim duty of patrols and containment for the rest of the war. But by far the biggest enemy of the Eighteenth Army soldiers was hunger and sickness. Many thousands simply starved to death or succumbed to disease. A mournful, sardonic phrase proliferated among these isolated souls. "From New Guinea, no one returns alive."[8]

Even as the Driniumor drama unfolded, the westward leapfrogging continued. On the heady day of the unopposed landings at Hollandia, an ebullient MacArthur had wanted to follow up with an immediate invasion of Wakde Island, 140 miles to the west and home to a key airfield. But Eichelberger had steered him away from what would likely have been an overambitious, possibly even disastrous lunge. Instead, the SWPA commander had to wait nearly another month before the necessary shipping, plans, and troops all came together. By then, Krueger and his staff had decided to launch mid- and late-May invasions of Wakde and also Biak Island, located in the Schouten Islands some 210 miles to the west off New Guinea's north coast. The planners augmented the 163rd Infantry into a regimental combat team and earmarked it to seize both Wakde and the opposite New Guinea coastline less than a mile away. As in the original Aitape operation, the combat team was placed under the independent command of Brigadier General Jens Doe. From May 17 to 19, the 163rd dutifully seized coastal bases at Arare and Toem and fought a sharp engagement with a die-hard garrison of about 800 Japanese soldiers, capturing Wakde. The fight for the little island cost Doe 40 dead and 107 wounded; the Japanese lost 759 killed, and only 4 survivors became prisoners. Within forty-eight hours, engineers had readied the airstrip for use by fighters and bombers. With a foothold along the Arare-Toem coastline, the American presence soon expanded to include more engineers, artillery, and antiaircraft units, plus another regimental combat team, the 158th, which landed in echelons from LCIs on May 21.

Krueger designated the American beachhead as the Tornado Task Force and placed it under the command of Brigadier General Edwin Patrick, who had originally served as his Sixth Army chief of staff. Mercurial, erratic, and colorful, the fifty-year-old Patrick had originally served in the Indiana National Guard and had fought in World War I as a machine gunner. While he never lacked for courage in battle, he was completely bereft of the diplomatic and administrative skills necessary to function smoothly in the chief of staff role, especially for Krueger, whose oblivious, blunt curtness tended to grate on his staff. "He didn't have the ability to get along with General Krueger, and didn't really soften the blows from on high," Brigadier General George Decker, his successor, whose contrasting demeanor was smooth as silk, later said of him; "he would more or less pass them on to the staff and this caused a bit of resentment." In any case, Krueger understood that Patrick was better suited for a combat command and happier in that role. Even so, Patrick's demeanor in combat inclined toward manic highs and lows. "He was hard to handle, alternatively in high spirits and then depressed," Lieutenant Colonel Bruce Palmer, his chief of staff, once said of him. Patrick's penchant for prodigious alcohol consumption only exacerbated his erratic tendencies. In Army circles, it was said that Patrick slurped coffee all day to negate the effects of the liquor he consumed all night. Behind his back, staffers nicknamed him "the Green Hornet" for the garish, easily visible green jumpsuit he wore in action.

Personality-wise, he was not a good match with his primary subordinate, the gentlemanly, fastidious Colonel J. Prugh Herndon, commander of the 158th, probably the most diverse infantry unit in an otherwise segregated Army. Originally established as an Arizona National Guard outfit, the 158th included Native Americans of multiple tribes, Mexican-Americans, and white frontiersmen as well as a variety of whites from all regions and social backgrounds. Herndon had presided over these latter-day Rough Riders since 1932. He had logged nearly two decades of military service but not, as yet, a day in combat. Grandson of a Confederate soldier and son of Victorian missionary educator parents who settled in Arizona, Herndon inherited his mother and father's passionate, paternalistic affinity for Native Americans and self-improvement through education. A graduate of the University of Arizona, he had once served as its comptroller and proved himself such a stickler for balanced books that faculty members took to avoiding him lest they have to account personally for every single penny of their research expense money. As an officer, he believed in strict but fair discipline. Meticulous, clearheaded, alternately kind or exacting according to circumstances, Herndon had trained his regiment to a fever pitch of physical fitness and weapons proficiency. "Colonel Herndon at all times insisted upon the highest standards of military courtesy and discipline, sanitation and personal hygiene, and individual proficiency," Major Paul Shoemaker, his operations officer, later commented.

The soldiers of the 158th had nicknamed their outfit "the Bushmasters" after a deadly snake. Herndon, like many from his social background, saw alcohol consumption as ruinous, especially for Native Americans. Once, after many of his troops engaged in a wild drinking spree, he ordered the whole regiment to carry out a forced march from Dallas, Texas, to the Louisiana border. Herndon was equally narrow-minded and innovative. Army regulations were to him like divine rules, no matter how outmoded or irrelevant to combat circumstances. Yet he was probably the first American officer to utilize Native Americans as radio operators and code talkers. The Pima, Apache, and Navajo tribesmen who proliferated in the regiment called him "the Old Sunnatabichi"; whether affectionately or not depended largely on the individual and the situation. His Mexican troops dubbed him the "Viejo Soldado," or "Old Soldier."

Though Krueger was pleased with the rapid seizure of Wakde and the Toem-Arare beachhead, he worried that Japanese possession of coastal high ground west of the Tor River would allow them to shell the beaches and the airfield. If so, they could disrupt the unloading and construction work of amphibious engineers and deprive the Americans of an important staging base for the Biak operation, sapping MacArthur's momentum. Moreover, the existence of small airfields at Maffin Bay created the possibility of Japanese air strikes against Allied shipping. With time always of the essence, Krueger ordered Patrick to immediately push west of the river and take the high ground. "My decision to enlarge the mission of the TTF [Tornado Task Force] was due to my desire to prevent the Japs from endangering our hold on Wakde, which could not be considered secure without our having more than a toe hold on the adjacent mainland of New Guinea," he later wrote to an Army historian.

The prudence of this decision was somewhat offset by the unfortunate fact that Krueger knew little about Japanese strength in the area. The Imperial Army had made modifications to its codes that temporarily disrupted the massive Allied eavesdropping operation until the SWPA Central Bureau's resourceful analysts adjusted. Willoughby knew that American submarines had inflicted major losses on Japanese convoys during a series of Ultra-aided troop ship sinkings in late April and early May that led to the deaths at sea of about forty-three hundred Japanese soldiers. The losses deprived Lieutenant General Hachiro Tagami's 36th Division in western New Guinea of badly needed reinforcements. Willoughby was buoyed by the relatively mild Japanese response to the presence of the Tornado Task Force. "If the Japanese had sufficient forces available to attack our positions, it is logical to assume that he would have done so promptly rather than allow us a week's time to consolidate our positions," he wrote in a daily summary on May 23. He reckoned that Tagami had, at most, about five thousand undernourished men in the vicinity of the task force beachhead, an underestimate by at least one-half. Willoughby's logic was incomplete. The weak Japanese response to the American invasion did not necessarily equate to absence, just surprise. Tagami had been taken off guard by both the Hollandia and Wakde landings, but like Adachi to the east, he was determined to resist to the full extent of his power. To counterattack Hollandia, he had dispatched two battalions to the east under Colonel Soemon Matsuyama, one of his regimental commanders. When Doe's men hit the beach at Wakde on May 17, these two battalions were about halfway to Hollandia and had since been absorbed in making their way back west. The rest of Tagami's men lay in wait, atop hills west of the Tor.

Willoughby's long-distance ignorance of Japanese capabilities was not necessarily surprising, even in spite of his Ultra advantage. Though adept at the collection of data and the study of history, he displayed, throughout the entire war, little understanding of how to analyze the more abstract notions of Japanese intentions and mindset. In all probability, these shortcomings stemmed from his overweening cultural arrogance against an Eastern foe. Far more shocking was that Krueger—who shared similar birth origins with Willoughby but nothing of his condescending racial views—did not elect to improve upon the limited information he received from the SWPA G2. Only a few months earlier, Krueger had created the Alamo Scouts for the express purpose of pinpointing key real-time intelligence about Japanese capabilities and dispositions, the exact sort of information that might have greatly aided Herndon and Patrick, neither of whom had any idea that their forces were outnumbered at least two to one. The Scouts had already demonstrated their great worth at Los Negros. And yet Krueger never seems to have considered using them to reconnoiter the area west of the Tor River. Surely such a mission would have yielded much valuable information about the enemy defenses. Instead, he allowed Patrick to launch an offensive with little knowledge of the enemy's strength and location, tantamount to a regimental-size reconnaissance operation in difficult terrain.

Herndon's people were tasked with the mission of seizing a swath of coastal territory that was dominated by several patches of high ground, particularly Mount Saksin, Hill 225, which was scored with ridges and especially a prominent ridge spur that sat like a sentinel astride the sea, just east of the Maffin airfield. In the long American tradition of misnamed terrain features that dated at least back to Cold Harbor during the Civil War, the Yanks dubbed this spur Lone Tree Hill because their inadequate maps symbolized it with a single tree. In truth, the hill was coated with an uncounted number of trees and splotches of viny jungle. "Lone Tree Hill is about 1200 yards long, 1200 yards wide and rises to a height of about 175 feet," a contemporary Army report explained. "It is bounded to the east by the Snaky River and to the west by Maffin Drome. On the north is a very rugged prominence, Rocky Point, which extends out into the ocean about 100 yards and which is roughly 300 yards long. A coral road extends east from the Snaky River completely around the south and west sides of the hill, coming out on the ocean between Maffin Drome and hill. This road runs through a narrow defile between Lone Tree Hill and Hill 225. Most of the northern part of the hill and Rocky Point is honeycombed with natural tunnels and crevices in the coral, many of which are interconnected and others of which open on the seaward side of the hill and Rocky Point." The place bristled with ravines, caves, craters, and rocky slopes. The Japanese camouflaged the cave openings with burlap behind which hid 75-millimeter guns and machine guns. Soldiers hunkered down in a dizzying array of log-, earth-, and coral-reinforced bunkers or fighting holes "so that the occupants had only a small aperture at the entrance from which to fire, or from which they could emerge, fire a few shots and retire to the dugout," the contemporary report continued. "Others were small holes dug under and between the roots of trees with coral piled in front."[9]

The Americans did not have enough available landing craft to outflank Lone Tree Hill with an amphibious invasion, though they would draw some fire support from destroyers and small-grade resupply efforts from individual craft. A stretch of mountains made it impossible to skirt around Lone Tree Hill from the south. The place had to be taken from the front. On May 24, Colonel Herndon's two lead battalions forged westward as best they could (Patrick used a pair of battalions from the 163rd to guard the beachhead). The Bushmasters soon became enmeshed in a savage fight just to get to Lone Tree Hill, much less take it. When, after two days of heavy combat, they reached the approaches, they found themselves in a kill zone, fighting for their lives among the bewildering sea of crevasses and razor ridges. A quartet of Shermans aided the advance until the Japanese pulled back the burlap coverings of several caves and sniped effectively enough with antitank pieces to inflict heavy damage on three of the tanks. Because the Japanese were so well dug in, and the American spotting maps so poor, artillery provided little help, even with spotter planes roaming the skies— indeed occasionally the shells were worse than useless when they exploded among friendly troops. Day after day, the Americans launched multiple attacks. Small units and patrols grappled over individual bunkers and caves. Hardy flamethrower operators hosed cave apertures, scorching or roasting the occupants, whose screams could be distinctly heard above the din of battle. Japanese mortar, machine-gun, and rifle fire saturated most any route of advance. "The fire was so terrible that it was just knocking the bark off the trees," Sergeant Ramon "Ray" Acuna later said. In a few hor- rible seconds he witnessed bullets smash through the heads and torsos of three men in his squad. An enemy bullet struck the helmet of Lieutenant Hal Braun, his company commander. "I think I just got hit in the neck," Braun blurted. Actually, the bullet had hit his helmet with such force as to push it down onto his neck; another bullet creased his helmet, but, almost miraculously, he remained unhit. Brazen Japanese infiltrators, outfitted in captured American fatigues and occasionally armed with American rifles, circulated among the GIs, prompting more than a few close-quarters death struggles. Most of the soldiers were horrified and deeply stressed by the daily struggle to survive in this world of death. A few came to enjoy the killing. A sniper who had once been a lightweight boxer stalked enemy soldiers like prey. In one instance, he spotted a man squatting with his pants down, answering the call of nature. "I hope he enjoyed that crap because it's his last," he muttered before clinically squeezing the trigger and dropping him.

After four days of this fighting, the 158th had lost three hundred men killed, wounded, missing, or debilitated by heat prostration or combat fa- tigue. The Japanese still firmly held Lone Tree Hill. "It was a very difficult situation," the 158th's after-action report understated. To make matters worse, Krueger appropriated the two battalions from the 163rd for service at Biak. Herndon now had to divert at least one of his own battalions to guard the beaches, depleting his already weakened, outnumbered attackers around Lone Tree Hill. The terrible fighting had taken a heavy toll on the colonel, who could hardly bear to see so many of his men killed or maimed. He had invested so much of his life and labor into making the 158th a smooth-running, perfectly disciplined outfit that he now had difficulty ac- cepting the natural entropy and destruction that inevitably degrades any infantry unit in protracted combat. "He was such a meticulous busybody," one of his staff officers later said of him.

In automotive terms, he recoiled at the sight of his beautifully washed and waxed car sullied by storm and road conditions. To some around him, including Patrick, he appeared frustrated and moody. Shaky hands made him seem jittery and nervous. "I do not have a steady hand and never had," Herndon later wrote sadly. "I inherited this from my father and it has been a source of embarrassment ever since I can remember." With no reinforcements available and his rifle companies ensnared in a deadly spider's web, he favored withdrawing rather than see his regiment destroyed in more futile attacks. The hard-charging Patrick, who was attempting to establish a fighting reputation in the first senior combat command of his career, did not like the idea of withdrawing. But in view of the obvious strength of the Japanese defenses at Lone Tree Hill and the loss of his reserves, the Tornado Task Force commander reluctantly agreed to Herndon's wishes. Herndon's careful attention to detail, combined with the fine discipline of his Bushmasters, resulted in a near-perfect retrograde movement, without the loss of a single man, to defensible positions about four miles east of Lone Tree Hill.

The decision to withdraw made perfect sense, and proved Herndon's judgment of the situation correct. Undoubtedly, Patrick comprehended this, but still, the retreat ate at him and for a time he considered countermanding the withdrawal and ordering another assault. Instead, he focused his frustration on Herndon, in whom he had little confidence. "My daily contact with him during this time convinced me that he was weak and wavering and indecisive and that he exercised only nominal command of his regiment," Patrick later opined. "I was convinced that this officer had no confidence in himself and in his own ability to find solutions to the numerous problems that were confronting him." Late in the afternoon of May 30, the Tornado Task Force commander arrived in a jeep at Herndon's command post with Colonel Earl Sandlin, Patrick's chief of staff and a man of similar temperament to his boss. Herndon was proud of the way he had extracted his embattled battalions and he assumed Patrick felt the same way. Only the previous day, the general had told him admiringly, "Your regiment is fighting like veterans."

As was Patrick's wont, his mood had since swung in an entirely different direction. With no preamble, he bluntly informed Herndon, "I'm relieving you of command and putting Colonel Sandlin in charge. You will report to Finschhafen immediately." Stunned and devastated, Herndon asked why. Patrick replied that Herndon had become jittery and that this nervousness had rubbed off on his battalion commanders and the rest of the regiment. Patrick later wrote in a statement intended for Krueger's eyes that he had observed "a state of bewilderment and nervousness and a defensive attitude . . . in the various headquarters of the regiment during the period of combat operations. I also observed a rapid diminution of morale and spirit of the enlisted personnel during this period." With hardly a chance to say goodbye to his beloved regiment, Herndon left, never to return to a combat command. Far too late, he realized that he had, in essence, sacrificed his own career to spare his men from needless slaughter. "The erroneous estimate of enemy strength by task force and higher headquarters was definitely proved wrong and the untimely relief of the 163rd Infantry for a more important assignment created a situation that made me a qualified goat upon whom to place blame for any mistakes," he fumed bitterly in a letter to an Army historian six years later. "If I had the same decision to make again today, I would recommend the same action even though I could see the results to me personally. I still have my own conscience to live with." When the word of Herndon's relief spread throughout the regiment, most of the men had mixed emotions. During the heavy fighting at Lone Tree Hill, many had sensed that he was not a good crisis manager. Though they did not question his courage, they wondered if he could handle the stress of combat and think clearly in such an unstable environment. On the other hand, they knew he sincerely cared for them and they deeply appreciated his loyalty. Years later, at reunions or other encounters, many proudly introduced him to family members and asserted, "I wouldn't be here today if it hadn't been for him."[10]

The irony of Herndon's relief, whether justified or not, was that Sandlin and Patrick had little other choice but to do precisely what the austere colonel had intended—hunker down, reorganize the shattered rifle companies, and wait for reinforcements before launching a renewed attempt to capture Lone Tree Hill. The 158th, along with supporting engineers, artillery, and antiaircraft units, settled into twenty-one separate perimeters along the coast. At the same time, General Tagami planned to unleash a two-pronged counterattack against the American beachhead (yet another enemy intention that had escaped the notice of US intelligence). Even as the 158th fought so hard at Lone Tree Hill, the Japanese had succeeded in slipping a force the size of two battalions under the command of Colonel Naoyasu Yoshino along trails about four miles to the south to cross the Tor River. Tagami intended for this Yoshino Force to make common cause with the Matsuyama Force, still making its way back from the aborted Hollandia expedition, to snuff out the American perimeters along the Toem-Arare coastline with a double envelopment. Communications among these various strike forces were nonexistent. General Tagami, from the remoteness of his headquarters in the bowels of Mount Saksin, could exercise no semblance of command and control. Moreover, the troops were hungry and tired; many were also sick. As a consequence, what had begun on Tagami's drawing board as a concerted counterattack concept instead manifested itself into a series of ragged, desperate individual thrusts, primarily on the evening of May 30–31 when soldiers of the Yoshino Force hit perimeters held by antiaircraft batteries and the 1st Battalion of the 158th.

Hours before the attack, the Americans sensed what was coming, in part because of poor Japanese noise discipline, possibly as a result of sake consumption. The jungle in front of the Bushmasters came alive with the sound of bizarre music—a scratchy violin, intermittent bugle blares, even a crackly recording of "The Rose of San Antone" from some unseen record player. As they rushed forward, some of the attackers could not resist unleashing a torrent of insults and taunts. "Yankee dog, tonight you die!" and "Fuck Roosevelt!" Somehow, they had determined the identity of B Company's commander, Lieutenant Hal Braun, a highly respected leader who enjoyed deep ties of kinship with the troops (he even held blood brother status in at least one tribe). In some cases, the Japanese attempted to infiltrate into the American holes by pleading, "Don't shoot, it's Braun!" Others simply screamed, "Banzai! Tonight, Braun, you die, die, die!" Some of the saltier veterans in the company, even in the middle of the fighting, joked with one another that their commander must have carried on a correspondence with the Japanese soldiers for them to know him so well.

By sheer happenstance, Braun's brother-in-law Julian, a Signal Corps soldier and engineer in civilian life who had never seen a minute of combat, was visiting him that night. The two had never gotten along particularly well. Braun had married into a devout German-American Catholic family. As the son of a man who ran a speakeasy, Braun was hardly the brother-in-law's idea of a proper mate for his sister. Braun assigned two Pima soldiers to safeguard Julian. Throughout the night, Julian helped them carry ammunition to those who needed it, while the company and the battalion fought for its collective life. "[The Japanese] shouted and fanatically charged into [our] position," the regimental after-action report chronicled. "Some were armed with rifles, some with knives, some with their bayonets tied to a stick. All seemed willing and anxious to die. They leaped into foxholes, threw grenades, fighting fiercely to the death. When they found they were in a tight spot, they would simply hold a grenade to their chests and commit suicide." Individual Japanese soldiers hurled Molotov cocktails into American supply caches or blew them up with explosives. Sergeant Acuna, who spent part of that terrible evening in a hole next to the body of an enemy soldier whom he had knifed to death, recalled that "the night was so dark, you couldn't see anything. They just kept coming in, leaving their dead, dragging their dead back, and coming in again."

The unluckiest of the Japanese touched off American mines that blew them apart. The action raged at intimate distance. In one instance, an enemy soldier bit a Bushmaster so severely, he inflicted a serious wound. "We were fighting them with trench knives, brass knuckles, bayonets, rifle butts and fists," Braun later wrote. They also blasted them point-blank with rifles and machine guns. Owing to the darkness and the swirling confusion, they pitched grenades only when they were sure they saw Japanese attackers. The enemy soldiers were so ubiquitous that Braun called for mortar fire on his own position. When the mortarmen balked, he bellowed, "Just do it!" One of the company's machine-gun nests was overrun by a group that smashed the gun and set upon the surviving crewmen in their holes. Among the dead was nineteen-year-old PFC Gus Mauzaka, a promising athlete who had lettered in football, baseball, and basketball at his New Haven, Connecticut, high school. He had recently written a poem to his worried mother, concluding, "But this the earth's dearest beauty is that wondrous mother of mine." When the Americans eventually retook the position, they found Mauzaka's corpse in a foxhole with a fatal bayonet wound in the heart. On a happier note, Julian survived the traumatic night, though he wanted no further brushes with infantry combat. At his first opportunity, he swam back to Wakde Island, from whence he had come.

The violence of the night eventually gave way to the tranquility of morning light. The Yoshino and Matsuyama Force assaults were too poorly coordinated and supported to have much chance of succeeding. The Americans lost ten dead and twelve wounded. They found fifty-two Japanese bodies. The enemy survivors melted back into the jungle or drifted west in the direction of Lone Tree Hill and its environs. The bloodied antagonists settled back into a patrolling stalemate while the Americans prepared for another go at taking the hill. In compensation for the removal of the 163rd, Krueger in early June sent the 1st and 20th Infantry Regiments of the 6th Infantry Division into the area. The newcomers had completed strenuous jungle training back in Hawaii and had been in theater for nearly half a year, but they had seen no combat. Krueger withdrew the Bushmasters for use a few weeks later to secure an airfield in the invasion of Noemfoor Island, about three hundred miles west of Sarmi, where, with the help of an effective preinvasion bombardment, they overcame a hungry but defiant, desperate garrison in a five-day battle that was highlighted by evidence of cannibalism among the Japanese, and by an unnecessary, chaotic airborne drop onto rocky, debris-strewn drop zones by the 503rd Parachute Infantry Regiment (the unit suffered 128 casualties in the jump but few in action).[11]

The 6th Division's commander, Major General Franklin Sibert, outranked Patrick and soon assumed responsibility for capture of the Lone Tree Hill area. Having seen the mauling absorbed by the Bushmasters, Sibert hoped to prepare his rookies for the task by gathering all possible information on the Japanese defenses and stockpiling plenty of supplies. He proposed a July 1 attack date to Krueger but the latter, conscious as ever of MacArthur's rapid timetable, would have none of this. He ordered Sibert to move immediately. Though advance patrols pushed west on June 18, the main assault, with the 20th Infantry assuming the lead, began on June 20. Like Patrick, Sibert's only viable option was to attack Lone Tree Hill head-on, albeit with much fire support from a destroyer, Army Air Forces fighter planes, and his divisional artillery units.

Another bloody slugfest ensued as Sibert hurled battalions forward over the course of several days. Ferocious fighting raged among the crevices, holes, and caves of Lone Tree Hill. Flamethrower teams and BAR men scorched and blasted recalcitrant Japanese defenders from their caves. An impatient rifle platoon leader personally hoisted a flamethrower and entered a cave to roast its defenders, all under the watchful eye of several BAR gunners. For Tech Sergeant Frank Caudillo, a rifle platoon sergeant, the fighting was a blur of advancing "thru snipers, mortar, artillery all day, dig in before dark, prepare our perimeter for the attack at night . . . fight most of the night with no sleep." American artillerymen disgorged hundreds of shells that burst above and sometimes directly in enemy positions. "We were firing like a mortar, almost straight up," Captain Charles Hanks of the 51st Field Artillery Battalion, later wrote. "This would drop the shells straight down onto the target." The massive firepower denuded Lone Tree Hill and Hill 225 of vegetation, leaving behind scarred stumps and ridges. Lieutenant Murven Witherel was amazed to realize this. "The hill was all coral, hard coral. There wasn't much jungle." As he led his platoon, a bullet smashed into his leg, debilitating him. Private Vincent Lidholm was firing at unseen enemy when a shell exploded at the edge of his foxhole, killing three men and shredding him with fragments. "A piece of fragment tore thru my helmet and skull and destroyed part of my brain," he later wrote. Hard-pressed litter teams hauled Witherel, Lidholm, and many like him back to the beach.

On June 24, two companies from the 1st Infantry climbed aboard LVTs and carried out an amphibious assault on the tiny beach near Rocky Point. The mini invasion, alongside the repeated attacks, put maximum pressure on Tagami's beleaguered defenders. In typical fashion, the Japanese punched back with hasty counterattacks and nighttime infiltration. The carnage was horrifying. Private Carlie Berryhill recoiled at the sight of a severed American arm lying at the edge of a trail. "It was the first time I realized that we were no longer on the rifle range." In six days of fighting, the 20th Infantry lost 83 killed, 484 wounded, and 10 missing. Sibert threw another battalion from the freshly landed 63rd Infantry into the fray.

Enemy soldiers died by the dozens and then the hundreds. Americans unceremoniously searched and stripped their shredded bodies of anything that might have fiduciary, souvenir, or intelligence value. "I just can't describe how it feels to go through the pockets of a dead man who is still warm and who just a few minutes ago was a living human (?) being," Captain Raymond Hensley wrote to his mother with an attitude characteristic of most GIs. "I of course was looking for information not the man's personal belongings. One thing about dead Japs though: they don't seem to mind being searched at all—they lie very still for you." The Japanese fought to the death. The Americans netted almost no prisoners. Staff Sergeant Minoru Hara, a Japanese-American whose job was to interrogate captives, found himself with little to do but behold the terrible waste of destruction. "Seeing dead all over the battle ground, I thought we human beings were the lowest form of life," he sadly reflected decades later. "My conscience still bothers me."

Ten days of hard fighting at last earned the Americans control of Lone

Tree Hill, Maffin Bay, the airfield, and most of the surrounding high ground. By then, Sibert's division had lost 150 killed, 550 wounded, and almost 500 more evacuated with sickness, injury, or combat fatigue. Doctors and medics of the 37th Field Hospital tended to many of these casualties. In a one-week period, the hospital admitted 325 patients, the vast majority of whom were wounded by shell fragments (only one man was treated for a bayonet wound). "Plasma and blood transfusions were used liberally as well as sulfa drugs and powders," the 37th's quarterly history chronicled. "Three operating teams worked practically continuously for 72 hours."

Weeks of enervating patrolling subsequently unfolded in July and August, but the strategic issue was decided. The exhausted Americans won themselves a valuable staging base and shattered Tagami's division, though it should be noted that the Japanese high command in Tokyo had already written off western New Guinea and its defenders as a strategic loss, in part because of the troop ship sinkings. In the Wadke–Lone Tree Hill campaign as a whole, some four hundred Americans lost their lives in exchange for these results; probably at least three thousand Japanese were killed in action and an untold number subsequently died of hunger or disease. And yet still MacArthur was not quite finished with New Guinea.[12]

As for so many other forlorn, tangential Pacific islands, airfields conferred a temporary importance upon Biak (pronounced "Bee-yak") in an otherwise lifetime of geostrategic irrelevance. Sparsely populated, covered with volcanic hills and thick rain forest, nearly bereft of fresh water, the place could appeal to no one but the most adventurous or ignorant. Indeed, an American correspondent later scornfully described it as "the most useless land ever tossed up out of the sea and one of the better haunts of malaria, dysentery, yaws, tropical ulcers, mosquitoes, flies and crocodiles." But its location within aerial striking distance of the southern Philippines, western New Guinea, the Palaus, and the Marianas made it attractive to both sides. Upon seizing it in April 1942, the Japanese had discovered suitable ground for airfields along a strip of coastal plain on Biak's southern side. They had since built three air bases—Mokmer, Borokoe, and Sorido—while busily surveying land for construction of another. In December 1943, the Japanese had successfully transferred the 36th Division's battle-hardened 222nd Infantry Regiment from China to Biak, where they formed

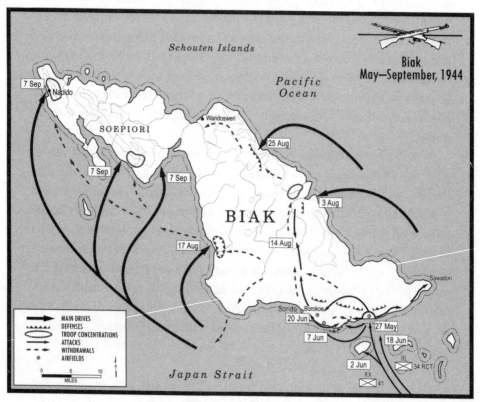

Biak
May—September, 1944

Schouten Islands

Pacific Ocean

7 Sep — Napido

SOEPIORI

Wandosweri

25 Aug

7 Sep

7 Sep

3 Aug

BIAK

17 Aug

14 Aug

Sawadori

Sorido Borokoe

20 Jun

27 May

7 Jun

18 Jun

Japan Strait

2 Jun

34 RCT

XX
41

MAIN DRIVES
DEFENSES
TROOP CONCENTRATIONS
ATTACKS
WITHDRAWALS
AIRFIELDS

0   5   10
MILES

© 2021 by Chris Erichsen

the core of the island's defensive garrison. Grand strategists at Imperial General Headquarters in Tokyo initially believed that the stunning Hollandia landings had so diminished Biak's value that they planned to write off the garrison with orders to fight a delaying, self-sacrificial action if the Americans ever did invade. But General Korechika Anami, commander of the Second Area Army, whose area of responsibility encompassed western New Guinea and included Biak, dissented. Anami, who had once served as aide-de-camp to the emperor himself, wanted to fortify Biak and, in part because of the airfields, hold on to it as long as possible. His Imperial Navy colleagues agreed. They were planning their A-Go offensive, a blueprint to fight and win a major fleet engagement with Nimitz's forces, probably in the Marianas or the Palaus, and Biak's land-based planes could provide vital air cover for their ships.

By the second half of May, Biak's garrison comprised some 11,400 men, about 40 percent of whom were combat troops. In addition to the 3,800 veteran infantrymen of the 222nd, there was a company-size detachment of light tanks, plus field and antiaircraft artillery units; the majority of the force consisted of Imperial Army aviation and construction engineers in addition to about 1,600 naval base and guard troops whose main collective mission was to service the airfields. The garrison was controlled by the 222nd's commander, Colonel Naoyuki Kuzume, a brave and efficient combat leader who neither smoked nor drank and whose bright record in China had marked him in Imperial Army circles for higher command. A seemingly endless series of rocky ridges, coral outcroppings, caves, and terraces dominated the ground overlooking the airfields. Kuzume spent much of May feverishly fortifying this highly defensible, ideal terrain. While he hoped to repel the Americans at the waterline, he intuitively understood that even if they got ashore, they could never utilize the fields as long as the high ground remained in Japanese hands. "The Biak Detachment will destroy at the water's edge any enemy force attacking this island," he wrote in a late-April operations order. "The detachment main strength will be disposed along the south coast." Kuzume and his superiors at Second Area Army understood that the airfields and Biak's location made an American invasion a near certainty, but they had no idea of their timetable.

If there had been any blemish in the otherwise beautiful complexion of the Hollandia landings, it was the fact that the spongy soil made the construction of runways for heavy bombers impossible. Biak had no such

limitations. Seizure of the place in a timely manner represented MacArthur's last opportunity to make good on his promise to support Nimitz's
mid-June Marianas landings with the heavies. To MacArthur's credit, he
valued the pledge he had made to the admiral and he was determined to
see it through. Even more, though, the general wanted bomber support for
smaller-scale valedictory operations on western New Guinea's Vogelkop
Peninsula and Morotai, not to mention the Philippine forays he hoped to
unleash. In a more subtle sense, the failure to seize bomber bases might
create a perception of stalled SWPA momentum in the minds of Washington decision makers and weaken MacArthur's strategic argument for a
return to the Philippines.

In a now familiar cycle of half-informed ignorance, the Americans underestimated the size and strength of Kuzume's garrison; nor did the invaders have a good grasp of Biak's formidable terrain. Owing to limited
Japanese radio traffic, Ultra provided little illumination on either subject.
The Americans relied exclusively on the myopic tool of aerial reconnaissance. Naturally, bad data resulted from bad process. Willoughby calculated that Biak was defended by about five thousand Japanese, including
twenty-three hundred combat troops. As at Lone Tree Hill, the Alamo
Scouts might well have offered a natural antidote for these misassumptions.
But Krueger, leery of telegraphing American intentions to the Japanese,
decided not to use them. Certainly he could not have grasped that this fear
was largely moot because the Japanese already knew of American invasion
plans. But, even so, one cannot help but wonder why Krueger had created
the Scouts in the first place if he was not willing to risk using them for their
exact purpose. Instead, Sixth Army planners relied on Willoughby's flawed
underestimate and settled on an invasion force of two reinforced infantry
regiments from the 41st Division, a bit more than half the size of Kuzume's
command. The invading units were dubbed the Hurricane Task Force. It
consisted of the 162nd and 186th Regimental Combat Teams, augmented
by two field artillery and two antiaircraft battalions, a chemical mortar
company, a company of tanks from the 603rd Tank Battalion, the 542nd
Engineer Boat and Shore Regiment, three engineer aviation battalions,
plus medics, quartermasters, and signals units, all under the command of
Major General Horace Fuller, the 41st's lean, flinty commander. Rear Admiral William Fechteler's Seventh Amphibious Force carried these troops
aboard five APD high-speed transport ships, eight LSTs, eight LCTs, and

twenty-eight LCIs and escorted them with two heavy cruisers, three light cruisers, and twenty-one destroyers, plus an assortment of smaller ships.[13]

On the morning of May 27, in a forty-five-minute preinvasion bombardment, Fechteler's fleet belched more than six thousand shells at various targets on Biak. The 186th was to land first in the Bosnek area to secure a supply harbor and the eastern flank of the landings; the 162nd would arrive next and push west to seize the airfields. The 186th encountered little opposition. But because of strong westward currents and the thick plumes of smoke and dust from the bombardment that obscured visibility, much of the regiment mis-landed in a mangrove swamp two miles to the west of their assigned areas, placing them to the left of the 162nd and closer to the airstrips. Fuller probably should have switched the missions of his two regiments since it might have led to the quick capture of the fields, if not necessarily the high ground that overlooked them. Instead, with a disappointing lack of flexibility, he ordered his regimental commanders to proceed with the original plan, leading to the bizarre spectacle of the assault troops literally passing each other in columns while their superiors complied with Fuller's wishes. "As we moved westward, we met members of the 186th Infantry coming toward us," PFC Bernie Catanzaro, a rifleman in the 162nd, later wrote. He and his buddies immediately recognized members of the 186th by the black circles stenciled onto the backs of their helmets; soldiers from the 162nd had black squares, and the 163rd troops had triangles.

A few unfortunate Japanese were trapped among the invading hordes of American soldiers. On one initial patrol, Sergeant Floyd West, a BAR man, almost physically bumped into several who had taken shelter in some bushes. "Instantly I fired first—squeezing the trigger for six shots a second. First bullet hit the Jap near the left shoulder. Other bullets then cut a strip across his body to the right ear. I felt hot blood on my own hands and face. I had beheaded the Jap, and the wind had blown the blood on me." He spotted three other Japanese soldiers and sprayed them with bullets as well. "Blood from an artery or lung squirted several feet up in the air."

The Japanese commanders, as a whole, were taken completely off guard by the landings. Though they had expected the Americans to invade, they never imagined they would come so soon. Kuzume had only partially completed his fortification plans. By sheer happenstance, Lieutenant General Takazo Numata, the Second Area Army chief of staff, was on Biak for an inspection visit. In fact, an exploding naval shell had wounded the general in the legs. Only with great difficulty and the assistance of several soldiers did he make it back to the cave that served as Kuzume's headquarters. In addition, Rear Admiral Sadatoshi Senda, commander of the naval troops, was also in residence. The presence of these two senior officers, both of whom were more than eager to exercise their authority over Kuzume, led to a jumbled Japanese command arrangement and, at least initially, a lack of any clear focus beyond the transitory objective of pushing the invaders into the sea. "The troops allocated along the water's edge die in honor," an Imperial Army report later stated with chilling finality. Neither side, then, was off to a particularly good start.

From the distant remove of SWPA headquarters some 2,072 miles to the east in Brisbane, the picture looked rosy to MacArthur. In his mind, a successful landing usually equated to a successful operation, a spurious notion of almost childlike insouciance. Carrying on with a war-long tendency to close the public book on operations well before they were anywhere near finished, he issued a triumphant communiqué stating that "our landing losses were light. The capture of this stronghold will give us command domination of Dutch New Guinea except for isolated enemy positions. For strategic purposes this marks the practical end of the New Guinea campaign."[14]

Actually, the struggle for Biak was only beginning and it quickly degenerated into a nightmare. Mindful of MacArthur's keenness to support Nimitz with bombers based on Biak, Fuller eschewed the time-consuming task of securing the many ridges and defiles of high ground in favor of a quick lunge for the airfields, but without any substantial reconnaissance. He ordered Colonel Harold Haney's 162nd to push west along a narrow coastal sliver of low ground called the Parai Defile in an effort to take the Mokmer Drome. This had the effect of funneling the troops into a small bottleneck of coastal road, under the ominous snouts of several jagged ridges. "The shoreline in this area was a vertical coral cliff, continuation of [a] terrace ledge, varying from 20 feet to 60 feet in height," the regimental after-action report expounded. "The area was covered with a small secondary growth about 15 feet high, thick enough to prevent good observation from the ground but open enough to allow excellent observation from above." One attached engineer officer remembered the coral cliffs as "just pocked with caves of all sorts." From the caves and ridges, the Japanese could rake the Americans with devastating plunging fire.

By the odd convergence of coincidence and intention that so often happens in combat, one of Kuzume's counterattacking battalions happened to be moving toward Haney's forward units. Neither adversary knew of the other's presence. Still the Yanks kept advancing, with every step fastening the figurative noose around their collective necks. In the lead, the 162nd's 3rd Battalion made it through Mokmer Village and as far as a road junction about fifteen hundred yards beyond, almost within sight of the drome, when they began taking enemy fire. "The entire area occupied by the 3rd Battalion was subjected to intense mortar, grenade discharger, machine gun, and rifle fire, and casualties were heavy," the regimental after-action report chronicled. "Communication was extremely difficult since all wire lines had been cut, and all radios except one SCR-511 set operated by a member of the Regimental Intelligence and Reconnaissance Platoon failed to function." By one estimate, the Japanese utilized twenty heavy machine guns, twenty light machine guns, and eight antiaircraft guns.

The Americans frantically pointed their weapons upward and returned fire. They found it nearly impossible to see their targets. One machine gunner remembered that "on that dizzy height in their camouflage, the Japs looked like small trees in motion. They were hard to hit." Along the sand and scrub brush, the 3rd Battalion was soon trapped in a tight perimeter, measuring some five hundred yards long and two hundred yards deep, under constant accurate fire, assisted only by a platoon of Sherman tanks whose presence proved crucial in breaking up a rare attack by outgunned Japanese armor. The unit's isolation lasted nearly two days, during which the battalion fended off at least three concentrated assaults. The naval fire support officer responsible for communication with a pair of offshore destroyers was killed, negating an otherwise powerful asset. Haney tried to place liaison officers aboard the ships to direct their fire, but his request seemingly got lost in an ether of confusion now engulfing the Hurricane Task Force. "Why we had no success with this proposition I was unable to understand as this was the all-important move," he later complained. Most likely, the poor communication and coordination stemmed from the hasty, hurried nature of the operation.

Daring LVT crews made quick runs into the perimeter to dump off ammunition and medical supplies. "When the supplies were unloaded, wounded men were loaded and evacuated," the division historian later wrote. Japanese mortar fire was so suffocating that the 3rd Battalion soldiers quickly figured out how to discern the various calibers and aeronautical tendencies of the shells. "I learned that I could usually hear the hollow 'whoomp' of the mortar as the shell left the barrel," Catanzaro explained. "I learned that a mortar shell, unlike an artillery shell, makes no noise as it travels through the air until immediately before reaching its target. Anyone unfortunate enough to be close to the point of impact could usually hear a soft 'shoosh' just before the shell landed. When you heard that characteristic sound it was too late to take evasive action." Knowing how long it took for the shell to impact, he and the others learned to keep a mental count when they heard the shell leave the tube and get well under cover before the inevitable explosion. In one terrifying instance, a 90-millimeter round landed a couple feet away, but failed to explode. A shocked Catanzaro even glimpsed the Japanese characters printed in yellow paint on the outer casing before scurrying away. Another shell exploded in a crater occupied by Tech 5 Charles Brockman and several other men. Gunpowder blackened Brockman's face, and fragments ripped a hole in the helmet of his buddy, but otherwise they were miraculously unhurt. Even so, the casualties piled up. In two days, the battalion lost 32 men killed and 183 wounded. "We had some awful wounded men," Private Thomas Smith later said, "legs and arms gone, eyes gone. Several had as many as fifteen holes in them." A shell of unknown origin—possibly even from a friendly naval vessel—exploded in the midst of a company command group, killing several men instantly. An unscathed Smith saw "men . . . seriously wounded and flailing around on the ground, screaming. Parts of their bodies were lying all around. My cousin, Quill Smith, had a big chunk gone out of his forearm."

Medics like Tech 5 Lewis Weis constantly scurried around, responding to plaintive calls for help from anyone who was hit. At one injury scene, he found a bloodied, lifeless lieutenant "gashed head to foot by fragments." Next to him lay a sergeant with a broken leg. Weis splinted the leg with a rifle, found a litter, and had the sergeant evacuated to one of the LVTs. Tech 3 William Cooley tended to a near-kaleidoscopic jumble of stricken men. "We had a lot of casualties and I went forward from . . . a wounded collection area near the battalion aid station [at Mokmer Village]. I attended to them, bandaged, did what I could, and saw that they got back to the . . . station. It seemed like it went on all day. My overwhelming impression of that day was that I wasn't going to see the sun come up the next morning. It was that intense. I guess the only way I can describe it is just brutal and frantic and confusing and noisy." In the recollection of Spencer Davis, one of the few war correspondents to go ashore at Biak, the Mokmer Village aid station "was crowded with maimed and dying American soldiers. Boys with shattered legs, bloody head wounds and faces half shot away were stretched out under every available shelter. With shocking frequency, I saw medical aides shake their heads and draw a blanket over a shattered form."

After initially temporizing over whether to reinforce the battalion for another attempt at the Mokmer airfield, Fuller and Haney in the late afternoon of May 29 instead ordered them to break out east and retreat back to division lines. Covered by artillery fire and a pair of Sherman tanks nicknamed "Murder Inc." and "Sad Sack," the survivors literally sprinted east out of their deadly perimeter and made it to safety. Along the way, the tanks rolled over the bodies of dead Japanese. "Some popped and burst like over-ripe grapes," Smith recalled, "sometimes slinging grime all over those close by."

The 3rd Battalion's difficulties indicated not only the strength of the Japanese Biak garrison but, even more so, the necessity of controlling the ridges and caves in order to have any chance of taking and utilizing the airfields. A chastened Fuller, realizing he needed reinforcements, asked Krueger to send the 163rd Infantry as soon as possible. The Sixth Army commander obliged, removing the regiment from the Arare beachhead and Lone Tree Hill fighting. The unit landed at Bosnek on June 1, assisted the 186th in fighting for the nearby hills, and assumed the role of defending the beachhead. An oblivious MacArthur, from his remote Olympian perch in Brisbane, breezily declared that Biak had entered into a mop-up phase—a statement that roughly equated to a baseball manager claiming victory in the third inning of a tie game.

The reality on the ground indicated much otherwise. Hindered by confusion and the limitations of the suffocating terrain, the two sides nonetheless tore into each other viciously, struggling in particular for control of the plateau and ridges above Bosnek. The 186th attempted to drive west along the narrow trails and brambles of high ground. To their right were mountains, and on their left, cliffs that dropped to the sea. A harried Kuzume, now out of touch with cave-bound Numata, laid hands on anyone he could to participate in a series of disjointed attacks, the worst of which hit the 186th's lines in the early morning hours of June 2. Under a shower of supporting mortar fire, screaming Japanese soldiers slammed into the jagged network of foxholes that served as the American front lines. "They opened up on us with machine gun fire, thinking it would make us keep our heads down," a rifle platoon sergeant recalled. "At the same time the riflemen, screaming and yelling, charged us. Our men waited until they were fully exposed before opening up on them."

Desperate men fought hand-to-hand with bayonets, machetes, grenades, pistols, rifles, and even rocks. Private Charles Solley, a BAR man, ran out of ammo and improvised. "A Jap was coming at me with a bayonet. My right arm was cut, so I knocked my right hand away and threw the empty BAR at the Jap. It hit him in the face." Solley's foxhole buddy then finished off the enemy soldier with a point-blank shot. A bespectacled lieutenant nicknamed Grandma, who saw one of his men slashed across the shoulder by a saber-wielding Japanese officer, became so enraged that he cornered the officer and hacked him into so many pieces that the lieutenant's soldiers had to pull him away. No one called him Grandma anymore. As the attack petered out, badly wounded enemy soldiers killed themselves with grenades or blew their own brains out. The Americans counted eighty-six dead Japanese and zero prisoners; the 186th admitted to three dead. In the wake of this and many smaller failed Japanese counterattacks, one of the regiment's battalion commanders opined that "the enemy lays too much stress on vocal noise and not enough on cover and concealment in the attack."[15]

Dependent entirely upon Bosnek as a harbor, and with the beachhead periodically harassed by Japanese air strikes, supply became a problem. The halting advance limited the amount of territory controlled by the Americans, creating congestion on the beaches, where prodigious quantities of matériel lay in diffuse dumps. Aviation engineers, who for the moment had little to occupy them with the airfields still in enemy hands, turned instead into temporary depot soldiers. "They unloaded ships, worked in the dumps, drove trucks, and even provided perimeter defense for a general dump that had to be established inland to support one of the regimental operations," Major Herbert Gerfen, a quartermaster, wrote. A bakery even went into operation within four days of the original landings.

More grimly, as fatalities from the fighting steadily rose, graves registration soldiers set to work finding suitable ground for a cemetery. Their choices were limited by the island's prevalence of coral, which made grave digging nearly impossible. They laid out neat rows of white crosses and Stars of David. Chaplains spent hours officiating over burial ceremonies while the graves registration men and other observers stood bareheaded, respectfully and silently listening. "It is a good thing to know that our government shows such rare concern for our dead," Lieutenant Russell Stroup, a chaplain with the 162nd, wrote to his family. "Everything is done that can be done under the circumstances to accord them the tender attention and respect that is their due. It shows a splendid spirit of reverence for human personality that refuses to treat carelessly these vacant temples of the Holy Spirit. I have felt that, as I assisted in this work, it is one of the hardest but finest things I can do."

Every ration can, cartridge, and shell had to be hauled forward, sometimes aboard LVTs or trucks, many of which were driven by African-American quartermasters who braved heavy enemy fire. "They have gone through hell to take men and supplies in and bring wounded out," an admiring Stroup commented. Even more often, engineers or infantrymen who were needed for other duties found themselves hauling matériel back and forth on their backs.

A paucity of water especially sapped the vitality of the American effort. With little indigenous fresh water on Biak, frontline units were almost totally dependent for sustenance on heavy, awkward cans lugged forward by groups of exhausted, sweating men. Mother Nature made the issue even worse. For the first week and a half after the invasion, temperatures never dipped below seventy-five degrees. High temperatures hovered in the eighty-eight-to-ninety-degree range, with relative humidity generally in the nineties. Soldiers were limited to the woefully inadequate quantity of one canteen of water per man per day. "The heat and humidity were intense," the 41st Division historian complained. "Thick scrub growth, about twelve feet high, covered the area and shut off any breeze." Amid the shimmering, stifling waves of tropical heat, thirst permeated the division like a malevolent shroud. "Our danger was in fainting from sunstroke, dehydration, or waterless shock," Captain Lew Turner, a company commander, later commented. For some semblance of relief, they licked morning dew from leaves or pressed cool canteen cups or even moist rifle barrels to their parched lips. PFC Catanzaro grew to be so crazed with thirst that he dipped his canteen into a mud puddle and attempted to filter out the dirt with a handkerchief. "It tasted awful; I could not drink it. In a final attempt to down the sludge, I took a packet of lemonade mix from my K rations and tried to dissolve it in the liquid in my cup. It was to no avail. I still could not swallow it." The onset of tropical rain offered some relief. On several occasions, soldiers even paused during attacks to catch rainwater with helmets and ponchos. "We drank deep again and again and filled our . . .

canteens," Captain Turner exulted. "Some men swallowed an entire can-teen!" Often bolts of lightning crackled nearby; no one cared. The gatherers even included Colonel Oliver Newman, commander of the 186th, who col-lected a helmet full of water, laughed and shouted to his men, "Game called on account of rain!" Some of the men even had enough water now to wash many layers of grime from their bodies. "We smelled like mountain goats," the author of one company history quipped.[16]

Buoyed by overoptimistic reports from General Numata of American retreats and relentless Japanese counterattacks, the Japanese in early June decided to reinforce Biak and make it the focus of their A-Go naval offen-sive. For this purpose, they loaded twenty-five hundred troops from the Imperial Army's newly created 2nd Amphibious Brigade aboard destroyers and other warships at Zamboanga in the Philippines. The escorting fleet contained an overage battleship, four cruisers, and eight destroyers, sup-ported by 166 land-based planes that raided, quite ineffectively, American LSTs at Biak and, much more effectively, Kenney's planes at the newly won base on Wakde. The latter strike heavily damaged or destroyed about two-thirds of the American aircraft, mostly on the ground, in the most serious defeat for the Fifth Air Force during the war and one so embarrassing as to merit hardly a mention in the service's official history, and outright ob-fuscation in Kenney's memoirs. Twice during the first ten days of June, the Japanese started their fleet for Biak. In the first instance, an erroneous re-port of an American aircraft carrier by a reconnaissance pilot spooked them and prompted an order to turn back. In the second episode, an Allied surface fleet of four cruisers and fourteen destroyers, called Task Force 74, under Australian rear admiral Victor Crutchley, fought them to a stand-still in a confused night engagement that inflicted little damage on either navy but once again persuaded the Japanese commanders to call off their attempt at reinforcement.

In the wake of this aborted effort, and sensing the growing desperation of the beleaguered Biak garrison, Vice Admiral Jisaburo Ozawa, com-mander of the Imperial Navy's First Mobile Fleet, decided to amass a stronger reinforcement effort. "If we should lose the island, it would greatly hinder our subsequent operations. I am therefore in favor of sending rein-forcements, especially since this might draw the American fleet into the anticipated zone of decisive battle." On June 12, he assembled *Yamato* and *Musashi*, Japan's two most powerful battleships, along with five cruisers, seven destroyers, and smaller ships, to carry the troops to Biak and then bombard the American landing craft and beachhead. Before they could get underway, though, Admiral Nimitz's fleet had begun carrier-based strikes on Japanese bases in the Marianas, and the presence of his surface ships indicated the imminent invasion of Saipan. Sensing a bigger opportunity in the Marianas, Ozawa and his colleagues called off Kon and instead reoriented their efforts to deal with Nimitz, leading to the pivotal Battle of the Philippine Sea. Ironically, given MacArthur's strident opposition to the two-pronged, divided Allied command structure in the Pacific, his operation at Biak may well have been saved by it. For the Japanese, Kon proved to be a missed opportunity and, for the hapless soldiers of the 2nd Amphibious Brigade, who were shuttled about, embarked, and disembarked throughout the dizzying drama, a serious anticlimax. The Japanese did, however, succeed in surreptitiously landing by barge on the western coast of Biak about twelve hundred 35th Division troops from Noemfoer and western New Guinea. Soldiers on both sides at Biak were well aware of the sea struggle unfolding around them. When the convoy bearing the 163rd had arrived at Bosnek, Japanese soldiers initially thought they were looking at a friendly reinforcement fleet. At the height of the Kon scare, in expectation of enemy naval bombardment, the 41st Division reoriented much of its artillery and some of its tanks to seaward. In the recollection of one eyewitness, when Crutchley's ships zipped past Biak's southern coast on the way to their showdown with the Imperial Navy, "men lined the beaches that evening and broke into spontaneous cheers. There was a feeling of relief, carelessness, and perhaps a little mightiness."[17]

Fuller, in the meantime, continued with the unglamorous, melancholy slog to subdue the 35th Division reinforcements and the other Japanese soldiers who still stood between him and control of the airfields. Day after day, the fighting raged inconclusively. He contemplated an amphibious envelopment of the Parai Defile but hoped that he might first capture the caves and ridges that brooded over the coastal plain. Worn down by sleepless nights and his relentless smoking, he knew his division had been sucked into a time-consuming, debilitating struggle for the high ground. Sticking mainly to his command post, seemingly with little inclination to visit the front, he could conceive of little else to do but continue battering the tiring Japanese, on their flanks if at all possible. By now, MacArthur had sobered from his mop-up fantasy and realized all was not well for the 41st Division on Biak, though he had little understanding of anything else about the situation. Alarmed at the lack of progress, he prodded Krueger by radio on June 5 and expressed his concern with "the failure to secure the Biak airfields. The longer this is delayed the longer our position there will be exposed to enemy air attack with the possibility of heavy loss therefrom. Is the advance being pushed with the sufficient determination? Our negligible ground losses would seem to indicate a failure to do so." Krueger shared his boss's impatience. The Sixth Army commander had already been pushing Fuller for quicker results and contemplating the viability of his leadership. Krueger in particular felt that the 41st Division commander had erred badly in his decision to send the 162nd Infantry west through the Parai Defile without thorough reconnaissance. "I considered it as imprudent, to say the least," he later commented.

In response to MacArthur's anxious message, the usually upright Krueger advised him, with an uncharacteristic whiff of buck-passing finger-pointing, "Fuller has been directed repeatedly to push his attack with the utmost vigor. Since it appeared to me some time ago that his operation was not progressing as satisfactorily as I desired, I seriously considered relieving him." Instead, the deliberative Krueger decided to gather more information. He could have, and probably should have, visited Biak himself. But with other crises to manage at Lone Tree Hill and the Driniumor, he elected to use Colonel George Decker, his chief of staff, and Colonel Clyde Eddleman, his operations officer, as his eyes and ears. Both paid visits to Biak. Neither ventured much closer to the fighting than the division command post. Colonel Kenneth Sweany, the 41st Division chief of staff who, like many other soldiers in the division, felt a fierce loyalty to Fuller, later commented that the two visitors "saw only what could be seen from the beach."

The observation visits created an odd, dysfunctional power dynamic. Because of Krueger's decision to stay at his headquarters, he essentially empowered a pair of staff colonels to decide upon not only the proper American course of action at Biak but also the career disposition of a superior officer. Fortunately for Fuller, neither colonel advocated his relief, though they were not particularly impressed by his performance. Eddleman later commented that fifty-seven-year-old Fuller was "a little too old to be commanding a division in the jungle at that time." The two staffers apprised Krueger of Biak's horrid terrain as well as the unexpectedly formidable Japanese resistance. They advised their boss to send reinforcements. Both felt that better-coordinated attacks and more aggressive leadership would be helpful as well. Krueger dutifully informed MacArthur of the unique difficulties the landscape presented. "Cliffs and ridges contain innumerable shelves and caves where the Japs have located defensive positions which dominate the coastal strip. General Fuller was faced with a most difficult task. His performance was by no means perfect, and I know several officers who, I believe, would have done better, though that is not susceptible of proof."

Goaded by a series of undiplomatic, impatient communications from Krueger, and cognizant that he was on thin career ice, Fuller decided to seize the Mokmer airfield immediately, even with the Japanese still in control of many caves overlooking it. On the morning of June 7, as the 162nd pushed west along the coastline, supported by the landing of two companies by sea, two battalions from the 186th advanced over a finger of ridges and trails and took the field against almost no resistance. Colonel Newman and his staff stood on the runway savoring their apparent victory. In an outpost nestled into the hills above, a Japanese mortar section commander peered through binoculars and could hardly believe the sight of American soldiers in the open. Like the 162nd a week earlier, they had walked straight into a trap. The mortar observer and others like him called down a spate of shells. The Japanese then unleashed withering artillery, antitank, machine-gun, and rifle fire from the caves. The Americans scrambled for the partial cover of old shell holes. They remained pinned there for nearly four hours, fortunate to avoid a complete slaughter. As it was, the regiment lost fourteen killed and sixty-eight wounded in the space of that single day. "Jap field artillery, anti-aircraft and heavy mortars sprayed us with fragments," Private Nick Wheeler recalled. "Often we moved to alternate positions to confuse gunners. Worst of all were Jap anti-aircraft; they screamed after us constantly. We feared those gunners more than anything else in the world. They fired time fuzes [sic] close to ground, and we dug like moles to save ourselves." Fortunately, muzzle flashes revealed the location of nearly every Japanese gun. Thus guided, the Americans responded with huge quantities of naval and artillery fire. "The 105s were zeroed in on the ridge and pumped thousands of rounds day and night to soften it up," a company history testified. The shells destroyed about 60 percent of Kuzume's guns, enforcing an equilibrium, though the airfield was largely useless until the Americans could eliminate them all and secure the ridges. Indeed, engineers who attempted to begin grading work were quickly forced to take cover with everyone else while the rifle companies attempted to seize the caves and ridges from the Japanese in a slow, costly process.

Frustrated and bone-weary, Fuller on June 9 informed Krueger, "each Japanese strongpoint must be pinpointed and then knocked out by artillery, tanks and infantry. Each of these positions is well covered by fire from additional Jap positions and destruction of these results in casualties for infantrymen making the final attack despite small arms, artillery and tank fire protection." He estimated that the Hurricane Task Force had suffered 1,050 casualties to date, including 145 killed in action and another 16 missing. Still, Krueger kept at him to finish the job immediately. "The slow progress of the operation and delay in gaining control and use of the airdromes had been so disturbing that I . . . dispatched several radiograms to the Task Force commander directing him to speed up the operation," he later wrote. His impatience only grew when he received a terse, uneasy message from MacArthur: "The situation at Biak is unsatisfactory. The strategic purpose of the operation is being jeopardized by the failure to establish without delay an operating field for aircraft."

At nearly the same time, Fuller asked for another infantry regiment to assist the 41st Division with the enervating job of clearing the Japanese from their caves. He estimated that the Mokmer field would be in operation for fighters as early as June 13. What mattered most, though, was the bombers, and both men knew that Mokmer could not hope to host the heavier planes for the foreseeable future. This meant that MacArthur could not possibly make good on his promise to support Nimitz's operations. Personally, Fuller felt exasperated and deeply annoyed with the Sixth Army commander, whom he felt had badgered and insulted him with overbearing missives but without having the courtesy to visit and see the situation for himself. Unaware of Fuller's anger, Krueger—whose brusque nature would hardly have led him to indulge his subordinate even had he known—pondered changes at Biak. Krueger arranged to send Fuller the help he requested. He alerted the 24th Infantry Division's 34th Infantry Regiment to board ships at Hollandia and join the Hurricane Task Force on Biak. The regiment landed and, on June 18, went into position on the western side of the American perimeter. Krueger also resolved to make some new command arrangements.[18]

Back at Lake Sentani, the increasingly idyllic locale for I Corps headquarters, Lieutenant General Robert Eichelberger had been monitoring the Biak battle from afar, with a deviousness that revealed a slightly underhanded side to his personality. Increasingly mistrustful of Krueger, Eichelberger could not help but wonder if he was sabotaging him in MacArthur's eyes. Eichelberger's suspicions only deepened during the six weeks that followed Hollandia when Krueger unwisely shared no information with him about current and future operations. So Eichelberger had authorized his signals people to secretly intercept Sixth Army communications. He found little evidence of sabotage but plenty indication of the troubles at Biak and figured he might well end up having to deal with this situation. "We knew conditions were critical," Brigadier General Clovis Byers, his chief of staff and close confidant, said decades after the war. "Bob and I, with our staff, planned what we thought we were going to be required to do." Thus, when Eichelberger received a summons late in the afternoon of June 14 to report to Krueger's headquarters, he had more than an inkling of what was in the offing.

It took the I Corps commander and Byers nearly an hour to travel by boat and jeep to Sixth Army headquarters at Humboldt Bay, near the original Hollandia landing beaches. True to form, Krueger greeted Eichelberger with little fanfare and filled him in on the worsening situation at Biak. Outside, military policemen patrolled in the darkness, on alert for Japanese infiltrators. Only a mile or two away, starving, wayward enemy soldiers regularly snuck into the burgeoning American garbage and supply dumps in hopes of finding enough food to sustain themselves. Krueger told Eichelberger to take over on Biak as Hurricane Task Force commander. Krueger felt that the job had gotten too big and too overwhelming for Fuller. He made it clear he had no wish to relieve him of division command. With Eichelberger and his I Corps staff on hand, Fuller could focus exclusively on running his own division. Krueger's meaning was clear to Eichelberger. Fuller had proved unequal to the job of Hurricane Task Force commander. So Eichelberger, as the new task force commander, would now assume responsibility for the larger job of securing Biak's strategic objectives. In other words, as quickly as possible, secure true control of every airfield. "Put some oomph into the attack and don't get yourself killed," Krueger urged. He ordered Eichelberger to leave the next morning.

Eichelberger traveled back to his headquarters that evening in a sober, reflective mood. "One can imagine the feelings in one's heart when given an order to go into a desperate situation," he later commented. "One does not call a senior officer after dark and tell him to leave early the next morning to take command in combat, unless the situation is pretty desperate."

Perhaps mindful of Eichelberger's penchant for inserting himself into frontline combat, Krueger phoned that evening with a reminder "not to get yourself killed." In fact, the situation did remind the I Corps commander of when MacArthur had summoned him to take command at Buna in December 1942 with the chilling imprecation to take the place or not come back alive. Numerous close calls during the subsequent weeks of combat had nearly fulfilled the directive. Eichelberger could not help but wonder if he would be so fortunate this time. Once again, he had been chosen by a superior officer to salvage and win a faltering battle, though now he enjoyed much more in the way of troops, fire support, and other resources. "My emotions were those of confidence in my staff, a desire to get at the Japanese military . . . and the sensations of a super-big-game hunter," he reflected years later about the evening before he went into Biak. That night, he found a little time to write a short note to Emma, apprising her of his new assignment. "Being a soldier, I am glad to go and it is something of a compliment that they reach out again and get me again when things are running crosswise. This letter will have to convey all the thousand and one things which I cannot say. You will understand . . . I'm sure."

The next morning, Eichelberger and several staffers climbed aboard a pair of Navy Catalina Flying Boats and took off, with an escort of half a dozen Army Air Forces fighters, for the flight to Biak, where they braved heavy waves to transfer from the planes to landing craft and thence to shore. At 41st Division headquarters, Fuller greeted them with all the enthusiasm of an undertaker assigned to dig his own grave. Weeks of managing the inconclusive battle, with inadequate sleep, and subsisting on untold cartons of cigarettes and considerably more than just a few sips of liquor, all had taken a heavy toll on the man who only a few weeks earlier had been earmarked by his superiors for promotion to corps command. He perceived Eichelberger's appointment as task force commander, and his own relegation solely to running the 41st, as tantamount to relief, an incorrect assumption. It was actually more equivalent to a temporary demotion. He had difficulty distinguishing between the two concepts. He burned with self-righteous anger at Krueger for what he perceived to be the egregious, insulting nature of his communications, especially without even having the courtesy to put in a personal appearance. Fuller could not help but feel that Krueger had unfairly lost confidence in him.

Fuller and Eichelberger were West Point classmates and old friends. Eichelberger sympathized with him and fully intended to work closely with him to accomplish their collective mission at Biak. "I have authority, of course, to relieve Horace but I shall hate to do that if I can avoid it," Eichelberger had written to Emma in the previous night's letter. At Buna in 1942, Eichelberger had reluctantly relieved another classmate, Major General Forrest Harding, and the genial I Corps commander had been somewhat scarred by the experience. Now Eichelberger well understood his old buddy Fuller's adverse feelings about Krueger—after all, he was not exactly a big fan of the man himself—so he was inclined to let Fuller vent his spleen. The 41st Division commander insisted on showing his comrade a file full of the offending messages, even reading aloud from what he considered to be the most egregious of them all. "Due to your slow advance which has threatened the success of future operations, I am sending General Eichelberger to take command." Indignant and emotional, Fuller sputtered, "This is a hell of a thing to happen on the anniversary of the day you graduate West Point."

He proceeded to inform Eichelberger and Byers that he had forwarded a resignation letter to higher headquarters. They both urged him to reconsider. Byers even offered to contact Colonel Decker, a close personal friend, and have him intercept the letter before it reached Krueger. Fuller adamantly refused, preferring instead the self-sabotaging martyrdom of quitting. "The dignity of man stands for something," he huffed. "I'll take no more insulting messages."

Many tried but none could persuade him to reconsider. During one such conversation with Colonel Harold Riegelman, Eichelberger's chemical officer, Fuller said, "I've been kicked out as Task Force Commander and the Division can't have the confidence in me it must have in its leader."

"The Division idolizes you," Riegelman said.

"From the beginning I begged and pleaded for one more regiment," Fuller rejoined. "I know what this operation needs. With one more regiment we would have had the airdromes a week ago. Now they send in another regiment—but not to me." A tear even streamed down his cheek.

"General, there isn't a man in the Division or Corps that wants it this way," Riegelman pointed out, with no effect.

Indeed, they did not. They admired his earthiness and knew how deeply he cared for them. On one occasion in New Guinea, when a cook had acquired fresh eggs for Fuller's mess but not for the troops, he had ordered the man never to serve them again. Another time when a private who cut his hair relayed complaints from his buddies about indifferent mess sergeants, Fuller personally interceded to make sure they served all food the same way they would if they were cooking for the general. In the main, the 41st Division troops admired his commitment to positive reinforcement leadership. He was known to offer bottles of Scotch to his people for nearly any job well done. "[He] never actually bullied or pulled rank," one of them later summarized.

Fuller wrote the division a classy but disingenuous farewell note that encapsulated the contrasting nature of the man. "I am being relieved of command for my failure to achieve the results demanded by higher authority. This is in no way a reflection upon you or your work in this operation. I, and I alone, am to blame for this failure. You are the finest body of men that it has been my privilege to be associated with in thirty-nine years of service. I part with you with many pangs of heart."

Even with such an undeniable bond, he could not bring himself to set aside his own wounded pride and continue to lead his "Bloody Butchers" in what proved to be their toughest battle in World War II. After all, how significant were his hurt feelings when compared with the terrifying struggles of the men who were fighting and dying each day among the barren ridges of Biak? Instead of focusing so much on himself, he would have been wiser to devote his efforts to helping them succeed and then let the rest play out later. For whatever reason, he could not, or would not, do this. "He was too angry to listen to me," Eichelberger later reflected. "He would not listen to reason. I begged him to stay on and guaranteed to look after his welfare, but his hatred for Krueger was beyond belief." Fuller caught a plane back to New Guinea and never returned to the 41st or any other command. Eichelberger designated Doe to succeed him as division commander.[19]

Of course, Eichelberger had many more important matters to deal with than the bruised ego of an old friend. As at Buna, he was determined to assess the situation as thoroughly as possible before acting. He spent two full days circulating around the area by jeep, spotter plane, and on foot, observing operations, gaining an appreciation for the awful terrain and the many obstacles faced by the assaulting troops. "Nastier terrain could hardly have been found," he asserted. "There were not only caves and the raw upjutting coral cliffs, but also deep ravines and tangled jungle. It was a hell of a place in my estimation!"

He went anywhere. Clad in light khaki fatigues that contrasted with the green herringbone twill uniforms of the 41st Division soldiers, he was easy to spot and was fortunate to avoid snipers. In one instance, Eichelberger, with Byers and Doe at his side, perched atop a ridge and watched Japanese soldiers emerge from caves and attack several Sherman tanks. "We . . . could see grenade-armed soldiers running in circles around the tanks. The tanks, roaring and clanking, began to pull out." As Eichelberger and the others descended from the hill, they had to hold on to vines. Eichelberger's broke and he fell twelve to fifteen feet, but fortunately he was not hurt. He elected to suspend operations for a day and give the troops a little rest while he reorganized the task force for a major new attack. He had done the same thing at Buna a year and a half earlier. Compared with the nearly disastrous condition of the men he had discovered in that hellish struggle, the 41st Division soldiers were in relatively good shape. "The troops are not nearly as exhausted as I had expected and I believe they can be made to fight with energy," he wrote to Krueger. The impatient Sixth Army commander, from the vantage point of his Hollandia headquarters 325 miles away, saw no need for any delays. In a radio message tinged with urgency, he advised Eichelberger of the strategic necessity of securing the airfields and getting them into immediate service. "Launch your attack . . . promptly and press it home with utmost vigor." Unlike the thin-skinned Fuller, who had been on the receiving end of such messages for over two weeks, Eichelberger kept his cool, though inwardly he burned with resentment at a man he had come to dislike and distrust. Always skilled with words, he sat down on the evening of June 17 and sent a polite but firm rejoinder. "Having arrived here 48 hours ago in almost complete ignorance of the situation, I have spent 2 days at the front. Tomorrow (Sunday) I have called off all fighting and troops will be reorganized. On Monday I propose to take the two airfields" that still remained under Japanese control. It was a courteous way of saying something to the effect of "I just got here. I'm gathering necessary information. You'll have action and results soon, so just buzz off and let me do my job." Ever savvy to the political winds of high command, Eichelberger knew his message would be seen by MacArthur and his staff at SWPA headquarters. He wanted his own circumspect actions on record alongside Krueger's distant prodding. More than this, Eichelberger simmered with the natural rancor of the frontline fighter for any distant, more secure superior. "A combat man who is risking his life takes a dim view of pontifical messages coming from those living in safety and comparative comfort," he later huffed.

His assault plan contained little subtlety. Nor was it much different from what Fuller had intended to do. Eichelberger wanted to strangle the Japanese instead of punching them in the face in a toe-to-toe fight. He ordered the 34th Infantry to push for the airfields while battalions from all three of the 41st Division's infantry regiments enveloped the Japanese-controlled high ground. This would sever their remaining line of supplies and reinforcements while placing the Americans on their flanks and in their rear areas. "After we had them closed in, we would fight it out for the cliffs and the caves and the airfields." Soldiers from the 186th drew the risky mission of swinging around behind the enemy. Doe attempted to persuade Eichelberger to discard this part of the plan. The new 41st Division commander was the hardy son of a Norwegian immigrant, and a West Point–trained combat soldier who had commanded a machine-gun battalion in World War I. By now he had led troops in combat through three World War II campaigns. He had much proclivity for bravery, but little for niceties. Frequently argumentative and prone to making acerbic, occasionally narrow comments, he was not the sort to butter up a superior, a valuable trait in a combat soldier. He did not like one particular aspect of Eichelberger's plan. In his opinion, the 186th would be devastated by enemy mortar fire. Eichelberger appreciated the concern, but he was willing to take this risk. He had the highest respect for Doe as a combat leader, though he did sometimes find his contentious nature a little tiresome. "Doe was a great fighter; he was also a stubborn, opinionated man, and our disagreements were spirited." To Eichelberger's credit, he valued and empowered this honest but abrasive subordinate rather than shunt him aside in favor of a yes man. After recommending Doe to succeed Fuller, he made sure that Doe remained in permanent command of the 41st.

The Japanese commanders were hardly immune to their own internal disagreements. Colonel Kuzume had anticipated that the Americans might cut his cave-bound forces off from Biak's interior. During one meeting with Rear Admiral Senda and Lieutenant General Numata, the colonel had argued for a fighting withdrawal into the jungle, where he could harass the enemy, resupply, and then make an eventual attempt to regain the airfields. Senda thought it foolish to abandon Biak's most defensible ground, and he knew that the notion of resupply might be little more than a fantasy. As a naval officer, he probably better understood the shaky nature of Japanese seaborne logistics that made the sustenance of the Biak garrison problematic at best. Numata agreed with the admiral. Thus, Kuzume's people had remained in place even as Numata received orders from Second Area

Army to leave. In mid-June, he escaped on a motorized barge and reunited with his commander, General Anami. Senda later made his way into the jungle and hid for a month before being rescued by a submarine.

Eichelberger's attack proceeded on the morning of June 19. Happily enough, the 186th soldiers made it to their objective without any casualties, from mortars or any other weapons, vindicating Eichelberger's plan. By late afternoon, the enveloping battalions had succeeded in circling behind many of the caves, killing some enemy soldiers in place and putting others in flight. The advance eliminated most sources of enemy fire on the Mokmer airfield, finally allowing the engineers to begin the process of preparing the runways for use by Allied aircraft. An elated Eichelberger radioed Krueger and informed him of this substantial improvement in the battle situation, including an accurate assessment that the Mokmer airdrome was now "secure from hostile ground attack." The next day, the 34th Infantry knifed ahead to take the other two fields while Doe's soldiers continued fighting ridge to ridge. "With the exception of anti-aircraft guns, most of the Detachment's [heavy] weapons were destroyed," one of Colonel Kuzume's officers reported to Second Area Army that evening. In typical fashion, Eichelberger watched much of the fighting firsthand from the vantage point of a frontline ridge or hilltop. He insisted on receiving constant real-time intelligence about the progress of the advance and the location of units. All too often, he simply went forward, toting a tommy gun, and checked for himself. "Because I wanted to know, I found out," he later wrote.[20]

The attacks not only brought the vital airfields under American control; they also splintered the Japanese into hard-pressed pockets, cut off from outside contact, with little remaining command and coordination. The tenacious Americans kept up the pressure, fighting countless small-unit actions amid hellish places they called the West Caves (or just "the Sump"), the East Caves, and the Ibdi Pocket. If the American failure to understand much of anything before the invasion about Biak's caves indicated a weakness in their intelligence gathering, the actual fighting highlighted their great ability to innovate under pressure. Colonel Riegelman, the chemical officer, roamed the island, often under fire, and prepared for Eichelberger a careful study of the caves, along with recommendations as to how to neutralize them. Riegelman identified four different cave types of varying sizes ranging from small holes a few feet deep with a couple dozen feet of tunnel behind them, to ridge-side caverns ten to thirty feet in height and facing seaward, to substantial underground galleries spanning in some cases many hundreds of yards deep, often wedged into the sides or bowels of cliffs. The West Caves were especially characterized by these huge galleries or sumps. Some of these even had electricity powered by gasoline generators. "An important characteristic of many caves is the screening by natural foliage, which in several observed instances made the port or entrance invisible at six paces," Riegelman wrote in the I Corps after-action report.

Increasingly apprised with this kind of information, commanders improvised effective combined arms teams that brought nearly every implement of firepower—another distinctive American strength—into play. The Americans did not so much attempt to take them as just nullify them. "The techniques of reduction were frontal and vertical attack, envelopment, isolation, siege and assault," the anonymous author of an Army post-battle analysis wrote. "The means included all ground fires capable of being laid on target, using HE [High Explosive] and WP [White Phosphorous], shell and grenades, air bombardment, and strafing, flamethrowers, gasoline, demolition charges, and . . . smoke. Tanks were employed to precede infantry, firing cannon and M.G. at point blank range." The typical Sherman at Biak could carry seventy-five high-explosive rounds, five smoke shells, and twelve thousand rounds of .30-caliber machine-gun ammunition. As tanks pummeled the Japanese with round after round, infantry soldiers lingered nearby to protect them from attacks by courageous and desperate Japanese. "On several occasions the Japs rushed our tanks from positions in the brush alongside the trails and attempted to set fire to them with molotov cocktails," one officer wrote in a post-battle note circulated throughout Sixth Army. "Suicide squads also attempted to place heavy demolition charges on the tanks, particularly at night by infiltrating the perimeter of the bivouac. Fortunately the infantry stopped every attempt." Captain Arthur Merrick, a company commander in the 163rd, was amazed to see his unit draw direct support from 155-millimeter guns that unleashed close-range fire at the hidden Japanese. "On target, never a stray round, and never a short round," he later wrote. "We were impressed, and grateful."

In many cases, the Americans poured gasoline into the cave mouths or crevasses and lit the fuel afire with white phosphorous grenades, an effective tactic as long as the opening sloped downward. The resulting fires consumed or asphyxiated untold numbers of enemy soldiers. Valorous flamethrower men, covered every step by riflemen, unleashed jets of fire at any opening or ravine, all the while shielding themselves as much as possible from the inevitable enemy response. "Since the flamethrower will literally 'shoot around a corner,' the operator should make use of 'bank shots' whenever possible to keep out of the line of fire from Jap weapons within the cave," advised an Army handbook on combat lessons learned. The flames usually failed to inflict much damage on the larger caves, but often succeeded in roasting individual Japanese who were fighting from foxholes or cavern entrances. Bazooka-wielding GIs crept close to the openings and, under protective BAR, machine-gun, and mortar fire, pumped rockets into the caves or supporting pillboxes. "Extensive use of the bazooka was effective against strong mutually supported enemy positions built on top of a coral-pinnacled ridge," one Army analyst wrote a few months later in *Infantry Journal*. The flash of the weapon, though, could make the gunner and his loader vulnerable to returning enemy fire.

High explosives provided the most consistently effective method of neutralizing the caves. "Demolition charges were brought up under cover of smoke or flame throwers, or lowered into cave mouths and fired electrically," a combat observer wrote; "charges were from 50 to 500 pounds of TNT or equivalent." Nor was 500 pounds the limit. One cave was destroyed by an 850-pound charge. Engineers even devised special clusters of 4.2-inch mortar shells, re-fused them, lowered the cluster into caves, and detonated them electrically. In some cases, the explosions caused rock slides that sealed off the caves to suffocate or starve the Japanese inside. Riegelman even later claimed that Eichelberger considered utilizing captured Japanese poison gas to snuff out resistance, before Riegelman succeeded in dissuading him. Eichelberger never mentioned this in his voluminous postwar writings and dictations.

The Japanese absorbed this pummeling with anything but passivity. They fought bitterly and to the limits of their considerable endurance. "Underwear of all the men is black with dirt, but none tries to wash it," one officer graphically told his diary. "I myself am one of them." American surrender leaflets adorned with images of faltering, deceptive Imperial Army warlords or mourning parents, netted few takers. Many of the cornered Imperial Army soldiers chose suicide. A veteran sergeant cried, "Let us be guardian spirits of the empire," immediately before killing himself. Another soldier stabbed himself in the throat but botched the job and lay writhing in horrible pain until a close friend reluctantly finished him off.

"I stabbed my own brother in arms," the friend mourned to his diary. "Who could understand my horrible predicament? I am determined to kill myself before I lose the power to pull the grenade pin. Father and Mother, please forgive me for dying before you do. I have done my duty to my country. My dearest parents, I am committing suicide with a hand grenade. My ashes will not reach you."

Infused with racial hatred, burning with anger over Pearl Harbor and a slew of wartime atrocities, few of the American frontline soldiers felt any enthusiasm about the notion of taking Japanese prisoners. "To the average GI, the Jap is no more than a yellow rat," Lieutenant Colonel William Shaw later candidly commented to an Army interviewer. "They have no use for them and just shoot them like anyone would kill a rattlesnake. They hunted the Japs like one would a deer, and shot them without mercy." Almost to the man, though, the Americans were impressed with their resilience. "It beats me how much punishment they can take," one platoon leader marveled. In one typical incident, a pair of 105-millimeter howitzers pumped shells into a cave from the point-blank range of 450 yards, but without successfully negating the returning fire from the Japanese inside.

Bypassed groups held their fire until they could inflict maximum damage on unsuspecting Americans. One 41st Division patrol found itself in a sharp firefight at a spot they had passed through peacefully only a day before. "Yesterday I sat right under a tree and ate a chocolate bar while that Jap monkey looked right down my neck," a rifleman imbued with the almost nonchalant racism of most GIs told one of his sergeants in the aftermath of the fight. "After this I'm going to take cover any time I stop." Rather than find themselves cornered inside the caves, the Japanese unleashed an uncountable number of counterattacks, banzai charges, and individual assaults or infiltrations. "Day after day there would be another Banzai attack," Private Charles Solley, a BAR man in the 186th Infantry, recalled. On the morning of June 22, Colonel Kuzume convened his staff and some of his survivors. He knew that the success of the American envelopment and the splintering of the Japanese-controlled pockets amounted to strategic defeat. He burned sensitive papers as well as the 222nd Infantry's regimental colors and urged any able-bodied men to fight their way out of the trap. Some accounts claim that he committed suicide right then. Others say he killed himself on July 2 in a ritualistic ceremony by washing his hands while facing in the direction of the imperial palace and using a sword to cut his carotid artery. Still others insist he was killed in action in early July. The full truth remains elusive.

In any event, the attacks of his survivors were usually motivated by a desperate attempt to escape from the encircled pockets to Biak's interior or overrun the American lines. Few, if any, succeeded at either objective. "The Japs began to yell and run at us with bayoneted rifles and grenades," a young platoon leader later told an Army interviewer about one enemy assault. "They fired scarcely at all and some rushed right down the middle of [a] road. We stopped them with rifle fire and cannister." The frantic shouting of the attackers was bloodcurdling and terrifying, but the Americans grew to welcome the noise. "Personally I hope they always scream," an infantry officer said; "it gives them away." One company-size attack focused on destroying an American roadside outpost position and breaking through the 186th Infantry lines. A pair of .50-caliber machine guns and other weapons tore through them, shattering their first two attempts. A third push led to hand-to-hand fighting, mainly with bayonets, rifle butts, and grenades. A Japanese soldier armed a grenade, jumped into a foxhole, grabbed the American defender, and blew them both to pieces. Most of the Japanese, though, were slaughtered on the road or in ditches alongside. "We could hear many of their wounded crying out and occasionally we'd hear one commit suicide by blowing himself up with a hand grenade," Sergeant Lee McCool, an attached medic, later wrote. The Americans killed 115 enemy soldiers for the loss of the unfortunate man killed in such intimate fashion inside his foxhole.

A few hours later, Eichelberger happened upon the scene in his jeep. "Abruptly we found our road blocked; there were dead Japanese everywhere. When I say the road was blocked I mean it." He later shuddered in a letter to Emma, "What a sight and what a smell." McCool confirmed that "they were piled two and three deep. Here and there, bodies were still smoldering and smoking, having been hit with tracers from the machine guns." A bulldozer unceremoniously cleared the corpses into a noxious pile under a nearby tree, where they decomposed rapidly. Before the end of that day, the general personally decorated all the defenders with Silver or Bronze Stars. Subsequently, he ordered the dissemination of captured Japanese beer, with infantrymen getting first priority.

The putrefying remains of many hundreds or thousands of other dead Japanese proliferated along the ridges, in pillboxes, scrubby ravines, foxholes, and inside caves. The merciless tropical climate and wildlife consumed them with stunning rapidity. It was not unusual for patrols to pass an intact enemy body one day, return two days later, and see nothing more than a skeleton in uniform. "There was a stench that hung over that island that you wouldn't believe," PFC Allen Douglas, an engineer, later shuddered. "There were big blowflies all over the place; most all of the bodies were all bloated because a few days in that sun was all it took for the gases in your body to blow you up like a balloon." Inured to squeamishness, some of the Americans plundered the remains with callous impunity, stripping them of valuables and flags and ripping out gold teeth. Some even strung the teeth together and wore them as grisly necklaces. The stink inside the confining, dank environment of the caves was especially noxious. As Colonel Riegelman and several other men investigated one of the larger caves in the Sump, they came upon "more than a hundred bodies in various stages of decomposition. One live Jap was promptly shot. The stench was weighted to suffocation with filth, death, and corruption." The smell was such that few Americans were willing to explore the caves. Lieutenant Paul Austin, a company commander in the 34th Infantry, later lamented that "the odor would knock you down." He once came upon an enemy corpse wedged against a tree, "completely eaten up . . . covered with a million maggots and black bugs. It was a horrible sight." Sergeant McCool found one dead Japanese in especially horrifying condition. "All around the top of his head, from eye level up, the maggots had cleaned the skin off, leaving his skull like a white billiard ball."[21]

The toll on the Americans was devastating as well. The high ground could be taken, and Eichelberger's objects fulfilled, only at the price of lives and flesh. "There is a look on the faces of men who have borne the brunt of battle like nothing I have seen," one officer wrote in a letter home. "But I shall never forget it as long as I live. Gaunt and drawn by fatigue and suffering, they stare straight ahead with the horror of men who have looked through the gates of hell." In one telltale instance, Japanese defenders sprang from a cave and ambushed a rifle squad before they could attack, killing two soldiers instantly and wounding several others. Another group led by an intelligence officer came back and clashed at handshake range with two enemy soldiers who were playing dead. A rifleman shot one of them point-blank in the head while the intelligence officer killed the other with two shots to the chest. During one small-unit action, a private in E Company, 163rd Infantry, swore that he heard his brother screaming in agony from an area attacked by a neighboring company. Sure enough, he soon received the news of his death. "The poor fellow went to pieces and was taken to the hospital," the company historian chronicled sympathetically.

Medical units operated on or near the ridges, evacuating hundreds of wounded men, mainly by litter but also by vehicle. "Day and night the jeeps and trucks pour in carrying the litters and we take them, wounded and weary, suffering from their hurts and the long difficult ride in on jolting vehicles," Stroup, the chaplain, told his family. "The blood drips from the litters as we lift them down." Like most of the spiritual leaders, he spent long hours at a field hospital caring for the stricken men. "Most of the men were incredibly, heartbreakingly cheerful. They laugh while they wince with pain. They grin through set teeth. They kid and joke in the shadow of death. My job is to cheer them up, but they cheer me." Wounds, deaths, disease, and combat fatigue ate away at the ranks. The 92nd Evacuation Hospital treated 2,575 patients, all but 38 of whom survived, mainly because of the unit's close proximity to the front lines. "Patients . . . were arriving at the hospital within the golden period of six hours in a great many cases, and it was extremely rare to get one that was over 16 hours old," Lieutenant Colonel Wilbur Dice, the hospital's chief surgeon, wrote in an after-action report. He noted that most patients had incurred multiple wounds, usually from grenades and mortar shells. Though men were most commonly hit in the extremities, Dice's surgeons performed the relatively low number of sixteen amputations, seven of which claimed a single finger or two rather than a whole limb.

Lieutenant Colonel Shaw's 41st Division medics also cared for dizzying numbers of fragment wounds, plus compound fractures, particularly to the legs. The task force lost a whopping 6,811 soldiers to disease, primarily malaria and scrub typhus. In addition, Shaw estimated that the division lost 402 men to combat fatigue, "caused by exhaustion and shock. Both officers and men break quickly when fatigue overcomes them." A typical victim in Sergeant William LeGro's M Company, 186th Infantry, lost complete control of his emotions. "One night he began moaning and crying. The squad leader, a tough, not very smart thug from Chicago tried to shake him out of it, but we eventually escorted him back to the aid station. Never saw him again." Private Robert Windlinx, a newly arrived replacement, drew the job of guarding an out-of-control psychoneurotic casualty who had broken down after pitching too many grenades into too many caves.

They boarded a boat, with Windlinx watching him closely. To his dismay, he realized that apparently no one, including himself, had thought to relieve him of his grenades. "We had no sooner left when this nut started pulling the pins on grenades and throwing them over the side of the boat. The boat operator . . . every once in a while . . . gave me an apprehensive look. I thought it would be better to let him throw all his grenades over the side than in the boat, so I did not say anything to him. I was relieved when he finally threw his last grenade." The standard procedure for combat fatigue cases at Biak was to evacuate them to an aid station and give them plenty of food and rest. If they did not get better in five days, they were evacuated from the island. According to Shaw, about two-thirds of the afflicted remained in a poor enough state that they could not be returned to duty during the battle.[22]

The rapid accumulation of tangible results provided a welcome silver lining for all these horrors. In a matter of just a few days, the I Corps commander and the soldiers in his charge succeeded in fulfilling the strategic objective of the Biak invasion. Though to be sure, patrols, small-unit fighting, and cave clearing persisted until early August. The defenders of the Ibdi Pocket held on with a special stubbornness. Here some eight hundred Imperial Army infantry soldiers held a four-hundred-yard-wide and six-hundred-yard-long warren of heavily log- and coral-reinforced pillboxes, trenches, caves, and crevices and armed themselves with eight heavy mortars, three 75-millimeter guns, three heavy machine guns, and a pair of 20-millimeter antiaircraft guns, in addition to innumerable small arms and light machine guns. The Americans simply obliterated them with overwhelming firepower. In a one-month period, the 146th Field Artillery Battalion alone hurled twenty-four thousand 105-millimeter shells at the Japanese. Mortar batteries added a similar number. Aided by precise targeting information from aerial observers, a flight of eight B-24 bombers carpeted them with sixty-four accurately dropped one-thousand-pound bombs. Doe, who watched the spectacle from the front, later wrote that the bombs "simply paralized [sic] the Japanese." Resistance evaporated. The Americans counted 154 bodies in one spot alone.

The fighting during this anticlimactic phase was surely just as intense as ever, but the strategic battle had been decided by the time Kuzume burned his colors on June 22. Eichelberger's offensive worked brilliantly, inflicting damage from which the Japanese never recovered. Undoubtedly, he had taken over the battle at an advantageous time, after the 41st

Division had already battered the enemy for more than two weeks and received the welcome infusion of the 34th Infantry. Plus, the failure of the Kon operation meant that Eichelberger did not have to worry about substantial Japanese air or sea intervention, much less the arrival of enough enemy ground reinforcements to alter the balance of power on Biak. Even so, the rapid, electrifying success of his operations was not a coincidence. Eichelberger brought to the American effort new organization, clarity of command, tactical acumen, inspirational frontline leadership, and an uncompromising, morale-boosting commitment to imminent victory that had not always been present before. He later told Emma that he had noticed in the troops "the old tendency which I found in Papua [Buna] . . . to get very sorry for themselves and to forget what a hard time the Japanese are having. As a matter of fact, I imagine that they [the Japanese] get fifty rounds of artillery and twenty-five rounds of mortar fire for every one we get from them. The boys needed a kick in the pants and I had to give it to them." Basically, the Japanese were much worse off and by attacking them so aggressively, Eichelberger had helped the entire task force appreciate this highly important point. As at Buna, Eichelberger had again thrived under pressure and helped turn around a difficult, potentially even disastrous situation. No American general in the entire Pacific theater, including Krueger and MacArthur, could equal his combination of World War II frontline combat experience and battlefield success. With the Biak situation in hand, Krueger ordered him and his I Corps staff back to Hollandia, where they arrived on June 29.

Driven as ever by the need for achievement and recognition, Eichelberger felt a tremendous sense of pride in what he had accomplished at Biak. He confided to Emma in a letter, "If I must pat myself on the back, I feel the way we had been fighting the Japanese would have ended in a victory for them or the fight would not have been over until next Christmas." Before his arrival, the Americans "were using little nibbling attacks that would not have gotten any place." In another missive, he ventured, "I think I have done fine thanks to profanity, flattery, offer of rewards, threats and Lady Luck." From several of his many friends throughout SWPA, he had heard that MacArthur intended to create a new Eighth Army and make him commander. Indeed, Brigadier General Spencer Akin, MacArthur's savvy signals chief and a man in a position to know, had visited during the Biak battle and told him as much. The prospect of army command filled Eichelberger with elation and, for the moment at least, softened his resentment against MacArthur for scheming the previous year to keep him from getting command of an army in Europe.

Back at Hollandia, though, Eichelberger received anything but a warm welcome from Krueger. If Eichelberger was the sort to crave praise for himself and dish it out in generous quantities to others, Krueger adhered to the philosophy that a job well done was an expectation, not a distinction. Upright in his personal moral code but devoid of much ability to appreciate the feelings of others, Krueger by temperament could not grasp the individual need for recognition and positive reinforcement. In that sense, he and Eichelberger were antithetical personalities. One was stern and brusque, an introspective loner imbued with a powerful sense of selfless professionalism. The other was garrulous and warm, endlessly attuned to the sensitivities of others, animated by a deep yearning for personal distinction and professional development. Thus, even though both were remarkably honest men in their personal lives and highly talented soldiers with more in common professionally than otherwise, they did not mesh well.

Eichelberger knew Krueger well enough not to expect a hero's reception. Even so, he was taken aback and forever embittered by the Sixth Army commander's demeanor during their first and subsequent meetings at Hollandia. Eager to fill Krueger in on the Biak battle, Eichelberger met Krueger upon the latter's return from a visit to Wakde. Instead of saying hello, Krueger blurted, "I didn't know you were back." With that awkward preamble, the two generals and their aides piled aboard a boat that served as Eichelberger's transportation across Lake Sentani. During the half-hour voyage to Krueger's headquarters, he barely uttered a word to the I Corps commander. When they did arrive, he briefly said, "I congratulate you on the fine job you have done," and turned to leave. Eichelberger invited him to his headquarters and offered to brief him on Biak. Krueger replied curtly, "I will be too busy to see you," and sped away in a jeep. Chastened and insulted, Eichelberger reported to Emma that night, "Walter acts as though he had been spanked."

Though pleased with the passing of the Biak crisis, Krueger nonetheless still felt miffed that Eichelberger had rebuffed his instructions for an immediate attack. Like Eichelberger, he, too, had gotten wind of the imminent creation of Eighth Army, a decision he saw as unnecessary and one that would inevitably siphon resources away from his own command. Nor did he relish the prospect of Eichelberger ascending from subordinate to equal authority. Krueger also worried that Fuller's high-profile exit from Biak reflected poorly on him, at least in MacArthur's eyes, especially because the latter had earmarked Fuller for corps command. In early July, the next time Krueger saw Eichelberger, he blamed him for Fuller's decision to resign. By now, Eichelberger was in no mood to indulge the man he had come to loathe. "To be insulted by him . . . was no novelty," he later wise-cracked. "Except when he had a saucer of cream in front of him . . . he was liable to be insulting any time." Discarding his usual restrained charm, Eichelberger shot back that Fuller had resigned only because of his white-hot anger over Krueger's unrelenting, offensive messages. At a subsequent lunch meeting, after Eichelberger learned that MacArthur had directed Krueger to set aside a New Guinea location for the new Eighth Army head-quarters, Eichelberger asked for Krueger's assistance in the matter. The Sixth Army commander demurred and even expressed skepticism that Eichelberger was in line to command the new army. When Eichelberger reminded him that he had already received confirmation of this from key people at MacArthur's headquarters, Krueger replied gruffly, "They talk too damn much." But Eichelberger, knowing that he soon needed to work with engineering units to build the headquarters, even as he assumed re-sponsibility for more than two hundred officers and seven hundred en-listed men who would comprise it, kept pressing his antagonist for help. In response, an exasperated Krueger snorted, "I don't give a goddamn if the Eighth Army sleeps in a swamp." An insulted Eichelberger never forgot the tense exchange. But Krueger's sharp words belied more honorable actions. Bereft of vindictiveness, he eventually relented and provided Eichelberger, albeit belatedly, with the necessary approval.

While relations deteriorated between MacArthur's two key ground commanders, Doe's task force finished off the Japanese at Biak, snuffing out the remnants of their garrison. By the time the last of the fighting pe-tered out at the end of August, the Hurricane Task Force had suffered 9,790 casualties, about two-thirds of them to disease, the vast majority of whom survived. In battle, the Americans lost 405 men killed, including 70 in July, and 2,150 wounded or injured. They captured only 220 ragged Japanese. Kuzume's garrison had cost MacArthur time and the ability to support Nimitz's operations, though this hardly hindered the admiral's prospects for success. However flawed, costly, and ugly, Biak marked a figurative, though not quite literal, end of the contest for New Guinea and functioned as a key gateway for MacArthur's eventual return to the Philippines. For the Japanese, it proved to be yet another South Pacific death house from which few ever returned. For the Americans, it was, like so many other unhappy tropical spots on New Guinea and its environs, a nightmarish mile marker on the road to Tokyo. In the wake of the battle, Doe wrote a moving thank-you note to his 41st Division veterans and especially lauded the infantrymen "who met in hand-to-hand combat the crack troops of the Japanese, threw him from his positions, destroyed him, and gave us our victory. To these men we are eternally grateful."

Their ultimate success could be measured, if one might even presume to term it this way, in the prodigious logistics their efforts made possible. At Biak, the Americans developed an otherwise useless hunk of checkered coral into a valuable air, sea, and logistical base that assisted their steady northward advance in the Pacific. In addition to the three major airfields, aviation engineers also built a fighter base at neighboring Owi Island. Within a few months, the two islands housed five Liberty ship docks, eight LST slots, five port jetties, two oil jetties, four drydocks, eight major cranes, 80,000 cubic feet of refrigerated space, 1,130,000 feet of storage area, a four-hundred-bed hospital, and enough quarters to house a garrison of seventy thousand troops.[23]

6

Galahad and Machiavelli

A t a remote camp near the east Indian town of Deogarh, a small group of about three thousand American soldiers was learning the dark arts of small-unit jungle warfare as the first US infantry troops in theater. Like a latter-year blended family, the men came from all over the Army. Some had languished with the 33rd Infantry Regiment on Trinidad, where, in the recollection of one of their rank, "nothing ever happened . . . except marching, maneuvers and jungle warfare training courses in which we hiked hundreds of miles but did little else." The monotony had manifested itself in a stratospheric 75 percent venereal disease rate before medics implemented successful treatment and prevention programs. The backwater nature of Trinidad had encouraged a dumping-ground personnel situation that brought a disproportionate share of misfits into the outfit—men with bone deformities or mental illnesses or low IQs or visual impairment or hearing loss, and even a few disabled World War I veterans. Among the more able-bodied, entire companies volunteered to leave Trinidad on the mere vague promise of a secret mission deployment. Other men had volunteered from training posts in the States. Hundreds more had seen jungle combat in the Solomon Islands or New Guinea, fighting with such units as the 37th, 43rd, 25th, 32nd, 41st, and Americal Divisions.

Plucked from far and wide, thrown together aboard transport ships in a forty-two-day voyage, and shunted around India before settling in at Deogarh, they had already established a colorful unit culture of hard-edged adventurism. "I felt they were good troops to command in action," Captain George Gordon Bonnyman, an officer who served through much of the war with them, later said, "but they would have been hell to fool with back in garrison duty. They were just trouble from the beginning." Lieutenant Charlton Ogburn, a communications officer who joined with the simple hope of escaping cold weather, later described his new comrades as a collection of "adventurers, musicians, drunkards, journalists, delivery boys, wealthy ne'er-do-wells, old Army hands, investment brokers, small-town Midwesterners, farm boys from the South, offspring of Eastern slums . . . Rothchilds [sic] and Indians . . . idealists and murderers."

They trained under the tutelage of the equally colorful British brigadier Orde Wingate, a pioneer in long-range penetration and guerrilla operations. Born to Christian evangelical parents who settled in India, the forty-year-old Wingate exuded unconventionality and eccentricity. Prone to moodiness and depression, deadly serious in manner and demeanor, blessed with almost hypnotic blue eyes, he was known to munch on raw onions, scrub himself with a wire brush instead of bathing, favor an unkempt beard, and even clothe himself in nothing but a pith helmet. A veteran of numerous clandestine operations, Wingate might well have been the most uniformly hated and admired officer in the British Army. The hatred stemmed from his preference for special operations, his tendency toward deceptive backbiting, his affinity for the world's downtrodden, and his antipathy toward the social conventions of military life. Most commonly, many fellow officers loathed him for his coziness with Zionist guerrillas during a previous posting in Palestine, where he had worked alongside the Jewish nationalists to attack Palestinian Arabs and even urged his Jewish friends to fight Britain as the means to independence. The admiration came from his undeniable personal charisma and mastery of unconventional warfare. In 1941, he had played a major role in mobilizing Sudanese and Egyptian fighters to eject Italian forces from Ethiopia. The next year in India, he created the 77th Brigade, better known as the Chindits, an ethnically diverse group of Britons, Gurkhas, Africans, Indians, and Burmese who carried out heralded long-range penetration operations against Japanese bases and lines of communications deep in the jungles of Burma in early 1943.

Though the strategic significance of these forays was questionable, Wingate had demonstrated the feasibility of protracted light-infantry operations in enemy-held territory, provided the foot troops could be supplied by air. Wingate's exploits appealed to the considerable imagination of Prime Minister Churchill, in whom the young man perhaps generated a nostalgia for his own onetime youthful attraction to exotic adventure. Churchill took Wingate with him to the Quadrant Conference in Quebec in August 1943 and the brigadier's presence helped prompt the Americans to agree to create a force of their own modeled after the Chindits. The grand strategists envisioned that this regiment-size unit of light infantry-men, code-named Galahad but as yet given no official unit designation, would serve under Wingate's command and participate in his ambitious plans for new long-range penetration operations in the spring of 1944. The great man himself fully expected to add them to his burgeoning empire of special operations warriors. He addressed them on one occasion and outlined his ideas of unconventional warfare, but otherwise offered little sense of what the future held for them.

Thus, the soldiers of Galahad had arrived in India with little identity beyond their own odd-duck sense of having volunteered for unusual duty. Initially, they did not even have a clear commander until Brigadier General Frank Merrill arrived in early January to lead Galahad. Bespectacled due to chronic astigmatism, Merrill had enlisted in the Army as a private and risen to the rank of staff sergeant before earning an appointment to West Point, from which he graduated as a cavalry officer in 1929. In the late thir-ties, he had served as an assistant military attaché in Japan before transfer-ring to MacArthur's staff in the Philippines to put his extensive knowledge of Japanese language and culture to work as an intelligence officer. By co-incidence, he happened to be on a liaison mission with the British in Burma at the outbreak of the war, and this saved him from the hunger, privation, disease, and captivity that befell most of MacArthur's army in 1942. Instead of ending up as one of MacArthur's martyrs, he became a key aide to the indomitable Lieutenant General Joseph Stilwell, the leading American personality in Asia, a man of incorruptible honesty and self-defeating piety. Merrill had made the trek out of Burma alongside Stilwell in 1942, though he had experienced a physical collapse that hinted at inher-ent corporeal weaknesses that made him ill-suited to deal with the many rigors of tropical jungle warfare. Trusted implicitly by Stilwell for his sound judgment, personal integrity, and keen intelligence, Merrill had functioned in the key role of operations officer and earned promotion to brigadier general at the tender age of thirty-nine. The prototypical protégé, the bespectacled Merrill looked eerily like a younger version of Stilwell and even sported the unusual high and tight hairstyle favored by his chief.

Merrill's appointment to Galahad command undoubtedly indicated Stilwell's determination to bring the unit under his personal control for his ongoing campaign in northern Burma. With Wingate, they were part of the Southeast Asia Command, a theater-level British-dominated organiza-tion under Vice Admiral Lord Louis Mountbatten (Stilwell was officially his deputy and commander of the Chinese-American China-Burma-India theater as well as chief of staff to Chiang Kai-shek). The murky command arrangement stemmed from divergent agendas among the Allies. Chiang Kai-shek was primarily concerned with biding time, staving off a complete military and political collapse, and husbanding his resources for an eventual domestic confrontation with the communists. The British cared less for recovering Burma so much as they hoped to safeguard the core of their empire in India and perhaps clear the way for a return to Malaya. The Americans wanted a self-sufficient, democratic, militarily potent China, not just to tie down Japanese resources but as a postwar Asian bulwark. The uneasy alliance diplomacy, along with the fact that in the US Army, generals were not supposed to command regiments, probably led to the bizarre official designation of Galahad as the 5307th Composite Unit (Provisional), an uninspiring moniker that, in Lieutenant Ogburn's estimation, sounded "like a street address in Los Angeles." The men grudgingly spoke the name "with indulgent exasperation." The title deprived them of owning any unit colors or heritage, a persistent morale sapper that contributed to a chip-on-the-shoulder insularity among the men. In fact, the name was so colorless and such a nondescript mouthful to utter that correspondents (and eventually generations of historians) simply took to calling the organization "Merrill's Marauders."[1]

At Deogarh they lived in tents, subsisted unhappily on British rations, and drilled on a dusty parade ground. To supplement their diet, some of the troops shot and ate vultures, under the mistaken notion that they were consuming turkeys. Throughout December and January, Wingate honed the Marauders with a relentless training regimen to prepare for deep-penetration jungle operations. They refined their skills at map and compass reading, land navigation, radio communication, and patrolling. Physical conditioning, weapons proficiency, and small-unit tactics also dominated their days. "There was scouting and patrolling, squad and platoon attacks upon entrenchments, pillboxes, roadblocks, bivouacs, practice booby-trapping, taking airdrops, evacuating wounded, trailing and trail concealment, demolition, and approaching, withdrawing from and crossing rivers," Lieutenant Ogburn later wrote. Another lieutenant, Phil Weld, a Massachusetts Brahmin, remembered interminable conditioning marches "across endless bullock-plowed grain fields, clods turning ankles, skirting mud and thatch villages rimmed by a maze of thorn hedges fencing plot gardens against jackals and monkeys. Moonlight [marches] through villages deep in sleep." One private recalled that "we were in good shape, but they worked us hard to toughen us up even more, partly because we didn't have any motorized transport." Indeed, because of northern Burma's dense terrain and the absence of much infrastructure, Galahad was to be entirely dependent on seven hundred mules, and a few horses, to transport most of its ammunition, equipment, and supplies. More than a few Marauders learned on the job the tricks of how to handle a mule, known as mule skinning. Training time was so short that the mules could not even be debrayed, a process that neutralized their vocal cords to keep them silent.

Merrill's battalion commanders created special intelligence and reconnaissance platoons, sardonically dubbed "ignorant and rugged" by the men, led by their best junior officers, that would function as probing and scouting elements in combat. Under Wingate's influence, they absorbed the lesson that the battalions had to be reorganized to operate effectively in the thick jungle. Instead of maintaining conventional companies, each battalion was split into two combat teams—or columns—named after a color and, in most cases, commanded by a major. With typical soldier consciousness of combat-oriented hierarchy, many of the experienced men who had served in the South Pacific developed a condescending attitude toward their rookie peers and even some of the training. "We were full of braggadocio because we had been in combat," Lieutenant John George later reflected. "Among ourselves we talked constantly of our experiences. The kind of fighting we had done—palm-grove-and-jungle fighting was pretty much the same." These veterans, yellowed from atabrine consumption and cliquish in outlook, were, against their wishes, parceled out all over the 5307th to disseminate their combat-savvy wisdom to their inexperienced comrades.

Wingate planned to incorporate the Marauders into a refurbished Chindit division for his ambitious new campaign. He paid them two personal visits, stressing the innovative nature of long-range jungle operations and their vital role in them. Given his vaunted reputation, the men were surprised at his unassuming, almost frail appearance, "much more the scholarly than the rugged type," in the estimation of one soldier. Tech 4 Ray Lyons found himself almost hypnotized by Wingate's unmistakable oddness. "He looked like a crazy man. I instantly got the impression that his eyes were very wild-looking. He didn't seem to be a normal person." To Captain James Hopkins, a surgeon with the 5307th, the eccentric Briton "was a very strange looking character. He looked almost as if he was in another world."

Indeed, Wingate was anything but normal. As it turned out, though, he had little subsequent opportunity to influence the Marauders beyond their training and his brief visits. For over two years, Stilwell had lobbied his superiors in Washington to send him American ground combat troops. The very presence of Galahad in India represented a minor strategic victory for the general. He had absolutely no intention of allowing them to serve under any command but his own. He badgered Mountbatten repeatedly and stridently for control of the 5307th. After nearly three decades of partnering with the Americans, dating back to Pershing's time, the wisest of Britons had begun to understand just how serious the Yanks were about controlling their own troops in any combat zone. The genteel admiral agreed to Stilwell's demands. When the undiplomatic Wingate heard this news from a pair of Galahad officers, he raged, "You tell General Stilwell he can take his Americans and stick 'em up his ass."

Anglophobic as ever, Stilwell cared not a whit for the discontent of Wingate or any other British officer. "The more I see of the limies, the worse I hate them," he once fulminated to his diary. "The bastardly hypocrites do their best to cut our throats on all occasions. The pigfuckers." Imbued with a puritan's sense of moralism, a soldier's reverence for honor, and an infantryman's zest for battle, Stilwell after two years in theater had nearly reached the end of his already limited patience with allies whose agendas differed from his own. "He could never tolerate the slightest attack in any form against what he considered American principles and aims," Brigadier General Frank Dorn, a key aide who served with him for many years, later commented. "He seemed to believe that one's ultimate reward was simply the defense of what he believed in. He was a highly moral man in the conventional meaning of the term. He admired and respected competence, honesty and integrity above all else." In one private note Stilwell wrote for himself on the topic of what makes for a successful military commander, he asserted that 80 percent of good leadership stemmed from character. "He must have moral backbone, and this stems from high character; and he must be physically courageous, or successfully conceal the fact that he is not." Stilwell disdained, sometimes viciously and venomously, those who fell short of these standards, particularly Chiang Kaishek, whom he derided as "Peanut" and thought of as little more than a narrow-minded, minor-league despot. "What he wants to do is make grandiose plans, have the USA deliver masses of materiel . . . and hope the war will end quickly, leaving him with the means of continuing power indefinitely," Stilwell once wrote of the Generalissimo.[2]

In early 1944, Stilwell badly needed the 5307th for his ongoing offensive in northern Burma's Hukawng Valley, code-named Operation Albacore, designed to extend the Ledo Road over 160 miles from Shingbiwang to Myitkyina (incorrectly pronounced as "Michenaw" by the Americans), where Chinese traders had once peddled their wares to local Kachins alongside the waters of the winding Irawaddy River. Looming like an El Dorado in the vast Burmese jungle wilderness, Myitkyina represented the main prize of the entire campaign. Though little more than a small town of a few thousand people nestled in a bend of the river, Myitkyina featured a key airfield and was located astride the main railroad and road terminus that led into western China. For Stilwell to achieve his almost messianic mission of securing northern Burma and opening a main supply road from India to China, he had to have Myitkyina. So, even as the Marauders labored at Deogarh, the Chinese 22nd and 38th Divisions, both of which had been trained by American liaison officers, pushed south through the valley against stiffening resistance from the Imperial Army's 18th Division.

Stilwell wanted to use Galahad as a reconnaissance and striking force in Japanese rear areas, the anvil behind the hammer of the two Chinese divisions. Chiang had entrusted Stilwell with control of these divisions, and the limited resources for land operations in northern Burma, quite reluctantly, only after many months of protracted, tortuous temporizing and obfuscation. Like the arrival of Galahad, this had represented a welcome triumph for Stilwell, who hoped that the Generalissimo would now accede to a complementary offensive by eleven Nationalist divisions from China's Yunnan Province across the Salween River to threaten the eastern flank of the Japanese. These divisions, known as the "Y" or "Yoke" Force (for "Yunnan"), included a cadre of American liaison officers who worked mightily to prepare their allies for combat.

Concerned as ever about the questionable political stability of his regime, and the serious threat posed by a large Japanese military presence in China, Chiang had expressed reluctance to authorize the Salween offensive. In essence, he had to decide if the goal of opening a permanent external supply route into China warranted the potentially dangerous weakening of his domestic military posture. Back in November, at the Sextant Conference in Cairo—a seminal moment in modern Chinese history

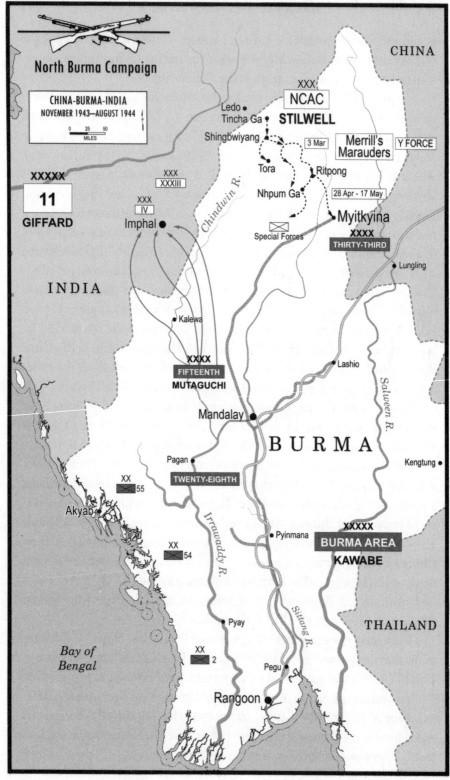

North Burma Campaign

CHINA-BURMA-INDIA
NOVEMBER 1943–AUGUST 1944

0   25   50
MILES

CHINA

XXX
NCAC
STILWELL

Ledo
Tincha Ga
Shingbwiyang
Tora   3 Mar
Ritpong   Merrill's
Marauders   Y FORCE

XXXXX
11
GIFFARD

XXX
XXXIII

XXX
IV
Imphal

Nhpum Ga   28 Apr - 17 May

Myitkyina
Special Forces
XXXX
THIRTY-THIRD

INDIA

Chindwin R.

Lungling

Kalewa

XXXX
FIFTEENTH
MUTAGUCHI

Lashio

Salween R.

Mandalay

Pagan
TWENTY-EIGHTH

B U R M A

Kengtung

XX
55

Akyab

XX
54

Irrawaddy R.

Pyinmana

XXXXX
BURMA AREA
KAWABE

Bay of
Bengal

XX
2

Pyay

Sittang R.

Pegu

THAILAND

Rangoon

© 2021 by Chris Erichsen

because Chiang met as an equal with Churchill and Roosevelt—Chiang had vacillated on the use of the Y Force. But he did indicate that he might authorize them to cross the Salween if the British and Americans agreed to launch amphibious operations in southern Burma and the Bay of Bengal. They acquiesced, only to renege in December after meeting with Soviet leader Joseph Stalin at Tehran and, at his insistence, doubling down on the Europe First policy by green-lighting the invasion of France, an operation that would consume the landing craft and other naval resources previously earmarked at Cairo for Burma.

After years of dealing with an American ally that insisted with words on his vital importance as an ally but hardly ever followed up on these sentiments with deeds—at least in the form of strategic priority for China—and a British partner whose lukewarm support and imperial ambitions were all too clear, Chiang had grown used to broken promises. He disliked the British and mistrusted the Americans. "[Roosevelt] wants to use Chinese troops to make war, otherwise he'd have to send over a million American troops to East Asia to sacrifice themselves," he once wrote resentfully of the American president in a private diary he kept throughout the war. In lieu of the amphibious operations, and as a face-saving price for his strategic abasement, Chiang instead demanded of Roosevelt a one-billion-dollar loan, an utter political and financial impossibility for the Americans. What was more, Chiang held the Y Force in place, at least for the moment, as an obvious bargaining chip. The exasperated president privately wondered if he might be better off dealing with some other Chinese leader. When Roosevelt met with Stilwell in Cairo on the way back home from the Tehran conference, he asked the general for an assessment of how long Chiang might last in power. Stilwell opined that any substantial military reversal might well topple him. "Well then we should look for some other man or group of men to carry on," the president replied.

If General Dorn is to be believed, the administration began not only to do just that but also thought of hastening the Generalissimo's demise. Dorn claimed that when Stilwell returned to China from Cairo, he ordered Dorn, under the strictest secrecy, to prepare a plan to assassinate the Generalissimo. "He emphasized that nothing was ever to be in writing; that if I was able to develop a workable plan I should explain it to him at a private meeting . . . that if such a plan should ever be carried out the order for its execution would 'come from above'; and that he doubted very much if anything would ever be done about it." When Dorn asked who had come up with the idea and who might give the fateful order, Stilwell only told him "the very top," an obvious reference to Roosevelt. One wonders how such a malevolent concept, if indeed it ever actually existed, could possibly pass Stilwell's moral muster. Surely he could not have accepted assassination as an acceptable option, especially if the idea originated from Roosevelt, whom Stilwell disliked as a "flighty fool" and mean-spiritedly referred to in his diary as "old rubberlegs" in reference to the president's disability. Was Stilwell so imbued with hatred for Chiang and the possibility of a better Chinese future in his absence to dismiss his own internal sense of right and wrong? Alas, the answer is lost to history. Fortunately, nothing ever came of the notion.[3]

By the middle of February, the two Chinese divisions had driven sixty miles south into the Hukawng Valley, the first time during the war that Chiang's men had succeeded in making any significant advance, albeit at a very deliberate pace, against the Japanese. Stilwell ordered Galahad to join them and organized his combat units into a corps-level organization called the Northern Combat Area Command. Sick to death of dealing with the Machiavellian blood sport of high-level grand strategizing, Stilwell spent as much time as he could at or near the front, far away from his respective headquarters in Delhi and Chungking. "A brief experience with international politics confirms in me my preference for driving a garbage truck," he cracked in a reflective memo he wrote to himself after the Cairo conference. In a letter to his wife, Win, he wrote that "the jungle is a refuge." Beyond his personal preferences, he sensed that his presence might prove vital to the success of Albacore. "He did not go into Northern Burma to personally take command of troops because of a personal pleasure or whim," Colonel Ernest Easterbrook, a son-in-law who served on his staff, explained years later to a historian. "He did it because of the strategic mission to open a land route as part of the over-all program," to defeat Japan.

Clad in shabby fatigues with no emblem of rank, sporting either a GI ball cap or a World War I–era doughboy hat, he looked more like an overage engineer than a high-level commander. During his frequent forays along the Ledo Road and near the front lines, few soldiers, outside of his own staffers and Chinese commanders, recognized him. In one typical instance, an African-American soldier took one look at Stilwell, shook his head sadly, and exclaimed, "Man, them draft boards are sure getting hard up for men when they bring an old 'mother' like you over here!" Stilwell just laughed and replied, "I agree with you one hundred percent." Often, the Chinese-speaking general overheard Nationalist soldiers comment to one another on his aged appearance. "They think I am about ninety years old," he wrote to Win. He tended to observe soldiers rather than engage with them. "Old Joe would walk up to where a group of us were standing around," an American sergeant commented years later; "he would stare at us vacantly as if we were from Mars. Never say a word. Next thing we knew he would be gone—like a wraith. We felt he could never come to grips with us."

When the Marauders arrived at Ledo on February 6 after an uncomfortable ten-day train ride, Stilwell was not on hand to greet them. They staged at Margherita, a lugubrious collection of thatched huts bending under the weight of jungle humidity. "They had had a hard, rough trip but were in good spirits and glad to have their feet on the ground again even though it was wet ground," the unit diary commented. Merrill and his extraordinarily competent second-in-command, fellow West Point classmate Colonel Charles Hunter, decided to order the 5307th to road march the remaining one hundred miles to the front at Ningbyen. "Although trucks were available to haul the outfit . . . I felt strongly that, from the standpoint of breaking in the animals and men, the long hike would solve several primary deficiencies." He believed that the hiking would condition the troops and their animals and break in their equipment, too. In this decision, Merrill and Hunter disregarded some sage advice from Lieutenant Colonel William Peers, commander of the Office of Strategic Services (OSS) Detachment 101, an Allied-controlled force of several hundred Kachin guerrillas who excelled at jungle patrolling, reconnaissance, and ambush operations. "An individual has only so much stamina in the jungle and after periods of exertion must rest to recoup his strength," Peers wrote.

Having personally participated in deep-penetration jungle operations alongside the Kachins, Peers knew what he was talking about. In tandem with Wingate and others, he had by now built a remarkable irregular force that established a friendly political environment for the Allies in north Burma. The Kachins dominated the northern Burma wilds, detested the lowland Shans and Burmese from whom the country took its name, and had enjoyed good relations with the British for generations. When the Japanese ejected the Allies from Burma in 1942, the lowlanders had cast their lot with Japan, mainly as a means to independence. With assistance from these locals, the Japanese had ravaged numerous Kachin villages, earning permanent enmity, tantamount to a blood feud, from the tribes-men. "Development of guerrilla activities using the Kachins was a natural," Peers later commented; "the Kachins had the knowledge of the jungles and the will to resist, while directions, leadership, arms, ammunition, and the communications equipment could be supplied to them." A GI guidebook to Burma gravely advised the soldiers about relations with the Kachins. "It's a military necessity for you to get along with them. If the majority were sympathetic to the Japs, they could cause us a lot of trouble. Don't make the mistake of thinking they are no more than simple savages. The Kachins know the Burma jungle. And they know how to fight in it. If you go a little out of your way to make friends with them, your job in Northern Burma will be a whole lot easier."

Though Merrill and Hunter intended to use OSS Detachment 101 as guides and a screening force, they dismissed Peers's concerns about the road march and went ahead with it. The paucity of any storage areas and the haste with which they departed forced them to leave duffel bags and other personal belongings behind with the age-old empty assurance that all of this cargo would eventually catch up with them. "Our baggage re-mained there in the jungle, uncovered in a light rain," wrote Lieutenant Colonel George McGee, the 2nd Battalion commander. "It would be thor-oughly looted by rear area troops." The Marauders needed ten enervating days, hiking along the muddy, winding road, often over steep grades, to make their way to Ningbyen, where they arrived in staggered groups be-tween February 19 and 21. By this point, most were exhausted and hobbled, more than a little annoyed, and far from ready for the rigors of light infan-try jungle combat. "This is the way I expected to feel on the last day of the campaign . . . instead of the first," Lieutenant Ogburn exclaimed to a col-league. Another man vowed to have ten children after the war, regale them all with every detail of the miserable march, and if they did not cry, "he was going to beat hell out of them," according to a unit diarist. One of the few highlights during the march occurred when the Galahad troops passed by African-American engineers who greeted them warmly. Their unit band stayed up all night and, as the Marauders walked by, played them a variety of tunes, including "God Bless America" and even "Dixie." One of the Galahad soldiers later wrote admiringly, "It lifted the spirits of the 5307th and the engineers seemed to get a lot of pleasure out of doing it. It was a fine gesture of good will and good luck and the men of the 5307th appreciated it."

As the Marauders arrived at Ningbyen, Stilwell characteristically sat in a jeep with a couple of aides and watched them from afar rather than mix with them. They impressed him as a "tough-looking lot of babies." Though almost every 5307th soldier had heard of the general, few recognized him in person. Clad in his usual baggy fatigues and soft cap, with thick spectacles and a wrinkled face, he hardly looked the part of high command. One sour, exhausted soldier halted next to the jeep, looked right at Stilwell and his similarly turned-out aides, and said, "My God, duck hunters!" Stilwell and the others just laughed. He later told Merrill, "I don't care what they call me as long as they will fight." Private John Egan, equally ignorant of the general's identity, strode by and wearily asked him, "Hey, old man, how far is bivouac?"

Instead of addressing the 5307th as a group, Stilwell embraced his anonymity, thus missing a valuable opportunity to establish the personal rapport that often solidifies when a senior officer looks his soldiers in their faces, speaks to them as a flesh-and-blood human being, and outlines their collective purpose and objectives. As a result, he remained little more than an abstract figure in their minds, one who appeared to become progressively crueler and more insensitive to their plight during the many challenging days that lay ahead of them.[4]

Stilwell ordered his protégé Merrill to launch wide eastward encircling movements through thick jungle terrain, cut the Kamaing Road, and establish roadblocks behind Japanese lines in the vicinity of Walawbum, a key crossroads village deep in the enemy rear, while the two Chinese divisions were to keep pushing the enemy in that direction. In this way, Stilwell hoped to trap them in a vise of sorts. With the intelligence and reconnaissance (I&R) platoons in the lead, searching carefully for mines and enemy ambushes, the Marauders hiked along narrow jungle trails and through thick foliage, past the abandoned remnants of tiny Kachin villages whose dwellings consisted of thatched roofs atop bamboo skeletons. "Near them were built up grave mounds where the bodies were burned," one soldier commented sadly. "A ditch around the mound was dug to keep the spirit in." The heavy foliage restricted their visibility to almost nothing. "The light that seeped through the tangled mass of vines, banyan trees, and verdure was hardly enough to make a tree visible two feet away," Captain Fred Lyons later remarked. Often they battled insects more than the Japanese. "My feet are now swathed in bandages from leech bites," Tech Sergeant Dave Richardson, a hardy *Yank* correspondent who embedded with the 5307th for the entire campaign, wrote to a friend. "At every ten minute break in a day's march we usually search our bodies for these blood-suckers and make them drop off by burning their fanny with a hot cigarette butt. In our poncho and blanket at night we are subject to attack by enough insects to fill an entomologist's manual—red ants being the chief menace because of their sting."

The typical I&R platoon employed five mules to carry ammo and equipment, usually at or near the front of the column. A pair of scouts led the whole unit, followed by the platoon leader and a rifle squad. BAR men and machine gunners covered the flanks. The platoon sergeant and a pair of riflemen guarded the rear of the column. Often these leading elements might range as far as a mile or more ahead of the main force. When the terrain allowed, they could look back and see the larger formations moving steadily on trails far behind them. "[They] looked like a huge serpent several miles in length," one reconnaissance soldier recalled. As the Americans moved east and then south, Lieutenant General Shinichi Tanaka, the 18th Division commander, decided to screen the slowly advancing Chinese formations and move as many combat units as he could to hit the Marauders before they could lay their trap. "The cautious movement of the Chinese forces engaged in the frontal attack made it possible for the 18th Division to save itself," he commented after the war.

With the Americans making their way to Walawbum and the Japanese withdrawing in that general direction, the two sides first bumped into each other in small-unit clashes, one of the first of which involved an I&R platoon from the 2nd Battalion. Private Robert Landis, a South Pacific veteran who had left law school to join the Army just before the Pearl Harbor attack, caught a burst of machine-gun fire, died instantly, and became the first American infantryman to lose his life on the Asian continent in World War II. His squad could not recover his body until the following day. "Robert was our only child, and it has been a great loss to us, but we are trying to be half as good a soldier as Robert was," his mother sorrowfully wrote several months later to Colonel Easterbrook. In a separate action, Corporal Werner Katz, a New Yorker who had fought with the International Brigade in the Spanish Civil War and the Americal Division on Guadalcanal, was walking point, moving along a small trail layered with elephant grass, daydreaming about his hometown, when he saw a soldier whom he mistakenly took to be Chinese. The man signaled for machine guns to open up. Bullets swept along the trail. Katz dropped to the ground, took cover in a slight indentation, and opened fire with his rifle, killing either the man he had seen or another enemy soldier. Katz got creased in the nose but was otherwise unscathed. "If I didn't have that little indentation . . . I would have got killed," he told an interviewer years later. He became the first American to kill a Japanese soldier in infantry combat on the Asian landmass.

By early March, as Merrill's units moved into position and established roadblocks in the Walawbum area, Tanaka unleashed a series of disjointed but ferocious attacks. The confining terrain, in addition to poor intelligence on the location of the Americans, meant that the Japanese commander had little choice but to funnel his combat power into any usable trail or clearing, enhancing the vulnerability of his troops. Some of the most determined Japanese attacks hit an I&R platoon commanded by Lieutenant Logan Weston, a tall, lean former Bible college student nicknamed "the Fightin' Preacher" by his men. To one officer colleague, Weston seemingly "thought of himself not so much as a fighting man but as a witness of God." But as his nickname indicated, he was part killer and part evangelist. In spare moments, he studied the Bible as well as the lethality of machine-gun fields of fire. He had seen heavy combat on New Georgia with the 37th Infantry Division. In one instance, he and his platoon had held out behind Japanese lines, with little food, for several weeks, an experience that prepared him well for duty as a Marauder. He was known to kill the enemy with impunity and then shortly after express sadness and regret to his men. "I'm sorry I had to kill those Japs, fellas, but . . . it was a case of either my getting them or their getting me," he often said. His combination of modesty, mysticism, professionalism, and bravery made him a charismatic, almost captivating small-unit leader. "One of the best combat officers I ever saw," Sergeant Bernard Jezercak later commented. "He could see things, sense things."

Weston deployed his platoon into a three-point star formation, with mutually supporting foxholes and slit trenches and a river at their backs. Five separate times, a company-size force of Japanese soldiers attacked their perimeter under cover of knee-mortar fire. Several Americans were hit. Weston and Sergeant Paul Mathis left cover to drag one of them, Private Pete Leitner, back to a safer spot. "Pete called for water and we moistened his lips," Weston later wrote. "During lulls in the firing, we lay in a prone position beside him." As Weston prayed over Leitner, he "soon dropped off into unconsciousness from which he never again revived, but as his eyes closed, a brilliant smile swept across his pain-streaked face."

Still the Japanese crawled and trotted forward, straight at the Americans. Weston's men raked them with grenades and accurate, well-aimed small arms fire. Thompson submachine gunners exacted a heavy toll, their .45-caliber bullets ripping through the enemy soldiers. "They chattered among themselves," Weston later wrote of the attackers. "Some seemed to be giving orders."

To stave off the attacks, Weston made extensive use of a unique and important asset—Tech 4 Henry Gosho, a Japanese-American interpreter, one of more than a dozen in the 5307th. Gosho listened to the orders of Japanese leaders and figured out where they planned to strike next. "His warnings enabled Lt. Weston to shift automatic weapons to the point of attack," a post-battle report testified. Using the platoon radio, Weston's platoon sergeant, Alfred Greer, called for help from Lieutenant William Woomer's mortar section—nicknamed "Woomer the Boomer"—on the American-controlled opposite side of the river. A shower of 81-millimeter mortar shells exploded among the Japanese and kept them at bay. "Nice going, boys!" Weston exulted after one especially accurate series of bursts. "We just saw a couple of Japs blown out of their holes forty yards from our point man." Even so, the Japanese pressure was intense enough that Weston had to withdraw, under cover of the mortar fire, across the river. They hauled their wounded and dead on litters improvised from bamboo poles and fatigue jackets. As they waded through the chest-high water, Corporal Katz turned and saw a Japanese Nambu machine gunner siting on him. "I thought it was possible this was the end," he said. "I would die." But PFC Norman Janis, a former rodeo rider and a member of the Sioux Nation in South Dakota, picked off the enemy gunner and several riflemen. Before getting away intact, Weston's platoon cost Tanaka casualties and crucial time.

In another spot, Tech 4 Roy Matsumoto, a Japanese-American soldier whose family members were incarcerated in the Jerome War Relocation Center, an internment camp in Arkansas, tapped into enemy telephone wires to eavesdrop on their conversations. Though Matsumoto was born in the United States, he had spent part of his childhood in Japan, living with his grandparents, so he spoke good Japanese and understood the nuances of some dialects, including those prevalent throughout the 18th Division. The phone wires had been strung in trees by Japanese headquarters troops, an obvious indicator that the Marauders were operating in the 18th Division's rear area. Matsumoto climbed a tree and settled in to listen to

Japanese communications. He overheard a call from a desperate sergeant pleading with his commanding officer for help because he feared his ammunition depot might be overrun by nearby Americans. The sergeant foolishly gave away the location of the dump. Matsumoto figured out the grid coordinates from a map, wrote the information down on a pad, and dropped it to another soldier, who encoded it and passed it on to Merrill, allowing the Americans to find and destroy the depot. "His translations were accurate, complete and quickly accomplished," Lieutenant Colonel George McGee, his battalion commander, later commented. "There was no mulling over the meaning of words or expressions."

For the Americans, Matsumoto's ability to listen in on the enemy's private conversations was like having a spy at Tanaka's elbow. Not only did the young interpreter overhear and relay reams of intelligence on 18th Division troop movements and Tanaka's intentions, allowing the Americans to set up numerous roadblocks and ambushes, inflicting substantial damage; he was also able to provide McGee and Merrill, and even Stilwell, with a good feel for the enemy's morale and overall mood. Stilwell, in his diary, jotted down several of these messages that Matsumoto had intercepted. "Casualties very large, we cannot protect river crossings . . . every man in the next few days must fight hard. [We] cannot hold much longer if help does not come . . . no help available, fight to the end." Matsumoto became so valuable that he could hardly be spared from his perch for even a few moments. Targeted occasionally by sniper fire, he spent hours in the tree, "from morning to evening, and I did not even have time to dig my own foxhole. I did not even have time to take a leak . . . so my pants were wet but this was very important so I didn't want to miss anything."

Tanaka soon found that he could not hope to overrun or flank the American roadblocks. In the numerous confused small-unit engagements, soldiers often fought at such close range that they could converse. This manifested itself in trash talking and a bizarre tendency of soldiers from both sides to comment on the eating habits of national leaders. In one instance, when a Japanese soldier yelled, "Roosevelt eats shit!" a Marauder responded with the usual "Tojo eats shit!" and then followed this with the somewhat more original "Tojo eats corned beef!" The unseen enemy soldier rejoined, "Eleanor eats powdered eggs!"[5]

Having failed to crush Galahad, and under pressure from the Chinese as well as newly arrived light and medium tanks from the 1st Provisional Tank Group, an armored unit mostly made up of Chinese crewmen commanded by American Lieutenant Colonel Rothwell Brown, Tanaka decided to withdraw south rather than face the possibility of seeing his division trapped at Walawbum. Thanks to Matsumoto, the American commanders knew this before some of Tanaka's men. Even so, the Japanese general skillfully extracted his survivors and slipped south, thanks to the efforts of his proficient engineer commander, who, in Tanaka's recollection, "had previously cleared a secret jungle trail about 20 kilometers long" that allowed their survivors to escape. Companies were down to an average of fifty men apiece. The retreating Japanese left behind the bodies of some eight hundred comrades. Their remains decomposed rapidly in the heat. "You could see the maggots coming out of the eyes, the mouth, the ears," Private Joseph Robinson recalled. "You'd look at that and say, 'Is that me sometime?'" To Corporal Lester Sherry, who came upon a rice field packed with enemy corpses, the place had the look of "being planted with dead Japs, instead of rice." The whole area reeked of their putrefaction. Mountbatten paid a visit and, according to Stilwell, recoiled at the stench. "Louis has been up but didn't like the smell of the corpses," he wrote to Win. The Marauders, for their part, had lost about 250 men, mostly to disease, sickness, and injuries, out of the original 2,750 who had set out from Ningbyen.

With the Japanese gone, the Chinese and Americans made their first contact of the campaign, initially mistaking each other for the enemy in an abortive firefight that wounded three Chinese soldiers. In general, the two groups got on well, though they had to accept substantial cultural differences. The Americans, in particular, had to get used to "the Chinese soldiers' careless habit of making off with everything not tied down or personally carried," Colonel Hunter later wrote. The Chinese had a different conception of personal property than the Americans. Unattended items were fair game to them. "Those rascals would steal anything that you didn't have a good grip on," Private Ralph Pollock fumed. In the interest of inter-Allied harmony, American liaison officers who were embedded with the Chinese told the Marauders, with the concurrence of leaders from Merrill on down, to look the other way at the thievery but to keep anything valuable close at hand, under constant observation. Communication left something to be desired. Too late the Americans found out that the Chinese were urinating and defecating into a stream the Americans had been using for drinking water. Marauder medics recorded 350 subsequent cases of amoebic dysentery, including numerous evacuations. The two sides ate meals together and traded food. K rations and cigarettes changed hands for tea, bully beef, and rice. One group placed batter atop entrenching tools and prepared flapjacks for themselves over a fire. "Other perversions of K rations were to be seen on all sides such as making rice pudding by using a fruit bar chopped up in a bowl of rice and adding sugar, chocolate rice pudding by scraping a D bar [emergency ration chocolate bar] into the sweetened rice and allowing the whole thing to simmer," one officer recalled.[6]

Stilwell knew that Burma's punishing monsoon season loomed only weeks away. The forthcoming rains, in addition to perpetual political urgency, compelled him to keep up the momentum. With Tanaka giving ground and the 18th Division in flux—not unlike Confederate general Joseph Johnston's situation in north Georgia during the 1864 Atlanta campaign—Stilwell now ordered the Marauders to lunge south through the Mogaung valley and cut the Humaing road in another attempt to trap them between the 5307th and the advancing Chinese. The plan called for a fifty-mile advance in two columns, initially with the Chinese alongside until Merrill's battalions snaked around behind the Japanese to seize Shaduzup. They set out on March 12, beginning another exhausting odyssey through thick jungle, along small trails, across serpentine rivers—it was not unusual to cross the same river dozens of times in the span of a single day—and over steep hills. Kachin guides assisted them. One officer described the guides as "intelligent, hard workers and good fighters. They carry bandoliers of ammunition slung over each shoulder and most of them wear earrings and bamboo leg bracelets below the knees. Odd pieces of British and American military equipment adorn them. They think nothing of marching ten or fifteen miles in . . . mountainous country in a day." Most commonly the guerrillas operated beyond the sight or knowledge of the Marauders. They gathered important intelligence information from friendly villagers, booby-trapped Japanese-controlled trails (including the use of punji stakes similar to the deadly Viet Cong traps of a later generation), and sprung expertly conceived ambushes. "[They] turned the Japanese rear areas into chaos," Lieutenant Colonel William Peers wrote. "The Japanese had to maintain continuous guards; they could never relax; could only move troops in combat formation. It became a war of nerves. The threat of guerrilla ambush made the Japanese tense, slow, cautious and finally paranoic."

The 1st Battalion led the way deep into the enemy rear area. The commander, Lieutenant Colonel William Osborne, knew his way around soldiering. He had served as a company commander for a Philippine Scouts unit in the archipelago and had fought against the Japanese invasion in 1941–1942. He had evaded capture and, alongside another officer, made it from Luzon to Australia aboard a twenty-two-foot sailboat, a trek that captured the popular imagination of the country and earned him the Distinguished Service Cross. On March 28, with his battalion in place at a confluence of two rivers four miles south of Shaduzup, he split his unit into three columns, maneuvered them into perfect ambush positions, and, fortified with useful intelligence on Japanese dispositions from Kachin guerrillas, unleashed that rarest of birds in the World War II US Army, a night attack. They overwhelmed the Japanese, fended off a counterattack, and then dug in to establish a roadblock. "Consternation and confusion do not halfway describe the scene," one officer later wrote; "half-dressed Japs without guns ran amuck—some with guns fired wildly—the Marauders with bayonets and grenades killed many." After routing the Japanese, the hungry Americans, who had subsisted on little but K rations for almost two weeks, devoured captured stores of rice and fish.

The problem, though, with any successful incursion, including this one, was the inalterable reality that the enemy still controlled most of the surrounding ground. Instead of retreating, Tanaka chose to reorganize and, in spite of the continuing Chinese advance toward his rear areas, strike back at the Americans with a series of counterattacks that might imperil Merrill's entire 5307th if the numerically superior enemy could trap and crush his battalions in detail. Though communication with his forward units was sometimes spotty, Merrill ordered them to hunker down as best they could and block the Japanese from any northerly advance. The brunt of Tanaka's counterpunch fell upon McGee's 2nd Battalion at Nhpum Ga ("Napoom-ga"), home to a handful of basha huts, where he had established a perimeter along a mountain-like hilltop at twenty-eight hundred feet of elevation, layered by surrounding ridges. The 2nd's enclave spanned a figure eight a mere four hundred yards in length and about eighty yards in width. "McGee had selected his position carefully," Colonel Hunter, who inspected them before necessarily moving on, later wrote approvingly. "He occupied all the high ground possible with the number of men and small units at his disposal. His animals necessarily were tied on a picket line . . . and therefore were in defilade from direct fire from the south. His aid station was set up also . . . in the best defilade position available." The Japanese pounded these positions with artillery on the evening of March 28–29. One of the shells made a direct hit on a soldier and blew him to bits. "They knew we were helpless against artillery," Lieutenant Ogburn remarked. "They decided to stay up all night getting the most out of the artillery ammunition they had accumulated. Every time a shell exploded it was as if my tongue had been touched by the two poles of a dry cell. And, Christ, they were coming close! One erupted a few feet away from me, turning a small tree into a column of sparks."

Over the course of two subsequent weeks, Tanaka's 114th Infantry Regiment besieged McGee's men and hurled innumerable attacks ranging from probes and attempted infiltrations to full-out assaults against them. The 2nd Battalion Marauders crouched in their foxholes and lashed back at the enemy soldiers with withering machine-gun, mortar, and small-arms fire, defeating every Japanese attempt to snuff out the perimeter. "They attacked savagely and bravely," a post-battle report commented on the intimacy of the fighting. In one case, a dead enemy attacker fell directly into a foxhole, almost as if he had jumped in, terrifying the unwitting American who manned it. During an infiltration attempt, a Marauder heard a groggy Imperial Army soldier approaching, mumbled to him encouragingly to draw him close, and ruthlessly killed him with a single shot to the head.

Once again, Tech 4 Matsumoto proved to be a true difference maker. Each night he roamed no-man's-land alone, listening in—at great peril to himself, since his erstwhile countrymen would undoubtedly have shown him no mercy had they captured him—on the conversations of Japanese troops. On the evening of April 2–3, the Americans heard an unusual amount of talking from the enemy positions, especially near a salient held by Lieutenant William McLogan's platoon, but they could not determine what this indicated. Lieutenant Colonel McGee ordered Matsumoto to see if he could find out. Alone, with no weapon and no helmet, he slithered into position among them. "At first they were talking about . . . their wives suffering because there was no husband to help with the farming," he later recalled. Others conversed about postwar plans. Finally he heard them mention an impending attack and outline their specific plans. He crawled back and said to McLogan, "You're not going to like what I'm going to tell you. They're going to concentrate and attack this portion of the hill." When McLogan reported this to McGee, the colonel ordered his platoon to quietly vacate their holes in the salient, booby-trap them with grenades, and withdraw about fifty yards to the rear, higher on the hill, into a dozen new foxholes. He also reinforced the new position with more troops and machine guns. Just before dawn, the Japanese attacked a fully alerted adversary. "We could sense they were gathering, and then they were yelling and screaming at the top of their lungs and running forward," McLogan later told a historian.

They roared "Banzai!" and "Death to Americans!" As the Marauders held their fire, the Japanese confusedly hurled grenades into the original line of foxholes and ran straight forward. Led by a saber-wielding officer, the survivors dashed up the hill, right at McLogan's platoon. When they closed to within fifteen yards, the Americans opened up with a lethal array of firepower. "Heavy and light machine guns, BARs, Thompson submachine guns, and M-1 rifles—as well as carbines and hand grenades," Matsumoto later wrote. They went down as if they had run into an invisible wall. "Japs were falling like flies," a witness later said. As the original attackers died or attempted to regroup, a second wave tried to find cover in McLogan's original foxholes and began tripping the booby traps. Matsumoto heard one of their sergeants order a retreat. Knowing how vulnerable the enemy force was, the courageous Japanese-American stood up and, in Japanese, yelled, "Charge! Charge!" Instead of fleeing, enemy soldiers turned around and attempted to get back up the hill, only to be cut down by American bullets, adding exponentially to the disaster. Darkness proved to be the only saving grace for the Japanese. The battered, fortunate survivors managed to slink away and drag their wounded with them. After sunrise, the Americans beheld a scene of terrible carnage. They counted fifty-four enemy bodies, including two officers, strewn about the area. The Americans took no casualties. "Sergeant Matsumoto became a legendary character overnight," Galahad's journal appreciatively noted. He later received a Legion of Merit for his actions.[7]

As the siege wore on, the profusion of dead flesh, both human and animal, combined with excreta created almost intolerable conditions. Soldiers had little room or inclination for privacy inside the perimeter. They half buried their own feces within a few feet of their foxholes. Mules and horses proved especially vulnerable to firepower because, unlike the humans, they could not take cover. The carcasses of some one hundred animals lay in grotesque stages of rigor mortis and decomposition. "Their bodies . . . had already begun to stink badly," the unit diary chronicled. "Jap bodies scattered about the edges of the perimeter were also beginning to stink. After thirty-six hours in this moist, hot climate, a dead body is in terrible shape—bloated and covered with flies and maggots." The stench created an invisible curtain of filth that almost seemed to coat itself onto everyone. "The odor was so intense you had to breathe through your mouth instead of your nose," McLogan recounted, shuddering. "I remember not being able to eat, it was so intense." The men began calling Nhpum Ga "Maggot Hill." Water was so scarce that the Marauders resorted to filling their canteens from mud puddles, "purifying" the sludge with halazone tablets, and hoping for the best. Commanders limited consumption to half a canteen per day per soldier. The shortage limited the care that medics could give the wounded. They found it impossible to make plaster casts and, more dangerously, they could do little to replace body fluids from sweat and blood loss. Major Bernard Rogoff, the battalion surgeon, operated on men in their holes, frequently while under mortar and artillery fire. Wounded men lay sprawled around the battalion's tiny aid station, blankets draped over them, mostly suffering in silence as medics attended to them as best they could under the circumstances. One man had been concussed so badly by a near miss from an artillery shell that he began to urinate and defecate blood. The walking and partially wounded stayed in their foxholes, fighting alongside the more able-bodied.

Precision supply drops from transport planes, protected by fighters and covered by ground fire from the perimeter, sustained the 2nd Battalion. This capability spotlighted a major Allied advantage in the Burma campaign: control of the air. The aviators regularly dropped sufficient quantities of K rations, ammunition, and medical supplies for McGee's people to continue the fight. "The C-47 pilots were doing an outstanding job for us," he later wrote. "Each mission over Nhpum Ga was a potentially dangerous one, and each pass over the drop zone at the low altitude necessary for pinpoint accuracy undoubtedly presented a very tense situation." The aviators even found enough cargo space to send in some special treats, including a batch of fried chicken, cigarettes, and books. The reading material included the proceedings of a symposium on gynecology and other oddities. "There were . . . a number of novels in French," one man marveled; "the men got a kick out of this as the books were passed about over the perimeter." Many of the cigarette packages featured little donation labels from American Legion posts and civic clubs in America. "It made us feel that there really was such a place as the United States," Captain Fred Lyons said. "From the strain and lack of sleep, men's eyes became glazed and staring." Without the fliers, the battalion undoubtedly would have been annihilated or captured; indeed, the existence of the planes made possible the Marauders' deep-penetration flanking moves. In response to the acute water shortage, the fliers filled sturdy sausage-shaped plastic containers with five hundred gallons of fresh water and successfully dropped them to the battalion. Priority of consumption went to the wounded, who were allowed to drink their fill, probably saving many lives. "The water had a rubberish taste to it but was delicious and refreshing compared to the blackish stinking stuff we had been drinking," one soldier recalled.

The 2nd Battalion was hardly left alone by the rest of Galahad to face its ordeal. The 3rd Battalion, situated a few miles to the north, repeatedly attempted to fight its way through Japanese lines into Nhpum Ga; the 1st Battalion made an extraordinarily tiring march, lost at least 30 percent of its number to disease or exhaustion, but joined with the 250 men who were still on their feet, in the attempt to relieve the 2nd. The Americans even airdropped a pair of 75-millimeter howitzers to the 3rd. The friendly shells bolstered morale among McGee's men and inflicted damage upon the Japanese, but the enemy cordon remained intact. The stress of this desperate situation sapped Merrill's fragile constitution. On March 28, he collapsed from a heart attack. "I found [him] lying in the middle of a path in the bivouac area occupied by Galahad headquarters," Colonel Hunter later wrote. "He told me the doctors would not let him be moved." In truth, Merrill had no wish to go anywhere. When the doctors insisted on his evacuation aboard one of the L-1, L-4, or L-5 liaison planes that were lifting out sick and wounded Marauders, he insisted on last priority. Nor would he go until he could personally inform Stilwell by radio and share the doctor's recommendation with him. Merrill lay for over two days in a makeshift shelter until he finally assented to evacuation on March 31. "From my observation, it took an exceptional man to continue on under the circumstances, and he was such a man," McGee commented.

Hunter assumed command, inheriting the task of saving the 2nd Battalion. "It may take two or three days, but we *will* get through," he told his commanders. Actually, it took nearly a week of maximum-effort ferocious fighting, with vital assistance from the Kachins, along the jungle trails that led to Nhpum Ga before the 3rd Battalion Marauders finally relieved their comrades on April 9, Easter Sunday, and only then because a frustrated Tanaka had decided to withdraw when he realized he could not destroy McGee's unit. "The spirit and morale of the Japanese forces had reached a very low ebb," one of his officers wrote after the war. "Their uniforms were so tattered and worn that many were nearly naked, a great number had no shoes, all were suffering from malaria and beriberi, and most were affected with various skin diseases. Their daily ration consisted of a handful of rice. Most of the sick and injured could not be treated because of the scarcity of medical supplies. The average strength of the infantry companies dwindled to fewer than 30 men. One company consisted of 10 men commanded by a sergeant." Allied planes dropped surrender leaflets on Japanese-controlled areas in hopes of eroding morale or prompting surrenders. One leaflet provided a concise, accurate update on recent South Pacific operations—shocking to Japanese soldiers, since their government kept them largely in the dark about war news—but concluded with offensive comments on Emperor Hirohito that unwittingly motivated its readers to fight all the harder. "It aroused great resentment and morale became very high," a 55th Infantry Regiment lieutenant who later became a prisoner told his captors. He hinted that the leaflets simply turned into toilet paper. "There is a great shortage of paper [in the Imperial Army]. We make use of them in more ways than one."

The Galahad relief force troops could hardly believe the scene of carnage around the hilltop. To Lieutenant Ogburn, the area "resembled a wheat field over which a herd of cattle had stampeded. Where there were trees, a tornado seemed to have struck. The stripped remains still standing were macerated with bullet holes. Dead Japanese were sprawled as if they had dropped haphazard from the sky, and along the trail were limbs and torsos thrust helter-skelter out of smashed-in bunkers." The animal corpses were so bloated that "to our unbelieving eyes the vista was that of a field of giant melons. The defenders looked at us out of red-rimmed eyes that were unnaturally round and dark, with death in them." McGee greeted his 3rd Battalion counterpart, Lieutenant Colonel Charles "Ed" Beach, with a simple smile and a handshake: "Sure am glad to see you, Ed." Among the detritus, the Americans found on the body of a dead Japanese soldier a fantastical poem he had written about world conquest and Japanese control of the world's major cities, including Chicago. "With the blood stained flag of the Rising sun, I'd like to unify the world," he asserted. "When I die, I'll call together all devils and wreath them in a three inch Rivulet."

The Americans used flamethrowers to roast the bodies of dead mules and horses. The job was so labor intensive and nauseating that Hunter ordered a five-hundred-pound airdrop of chloride lime and consigned the men to bury the carcasses in a coating of the disinfectant, an equally gruesome task.

Japanese bodies were roughly scooped into existing holes or bunkers and unceremoniously covered with dirt. Colonel Hunter gaped at the sight of one enemy soldier whose torso had been blown apart, leaving only "the lower half of a bloated body looking forever like a pair of football pants stuffed with gear packed by a high school football player." He noticed that other bodies were missing hands or strips of skin, which he speculated must have been removed by their surviving comrades to cremate and send home to their loved ones. The American burial parties found four hundred enemy dead and assumed that countless others had either been buried by their buddies or lay decomposing in places unseen and unexplored.

In spite of the hard-fought victory, the 5307th was in a poor state, nearing the end of its combat effectiveness. At Nhpum Ga, the unit lost 52 killed, 302 wounded, and another 379 to disease, mainly amoebic dysentery and malaria. Most of the wounded and sick were jeeped, carried by cart or horse, or airlifted to field hospitals in the Ledo area. The dead were disinterred by their buddies from the places where they had fallen. Following short memorial services, they were buried in shallow plots under bamboo crosses organized into neat lines within makeshift cemeteries. "Tears streamed down the faces of those battle-weary, rugged men as we left that area saturated with the blood of friend and foe alike," Lieutenant Weston, the "Fightin' Preacher," wrote sadly. Units were down to half strength or lower. Nearly everyone was sick, feverish, and underweight from eating little besides C rations and K rations for so many weeks. "I was still on my feet, but barely hanging on," PFC Melvin Clinton, whose weight declined from 180 to 118 pounds, later commented.

Most of the men had little desire now for anything more than a redeployment to the rear for a long rest. "At this point we were in bad shape," Captain Hopkins, the doctor, later reflected. "We had lost a lot of people from malaria, dysentery, some neurosis, dengue [fever] and everything on God's earth." Upon creating the 5307th, the War Department had maintained, with hearty concurrence from Wingate, that troops could operate in the jungles for only three months at a time before needing relief to heal their bodies and minds. He and many of the 5307th leaders had publicly acknowledged this reality. This abstract notion of ninety-day relief eventually morphed into an expectation of it among the troops, especially as the jungle ordeal sapped their collective strength. In the aftermath of Nhpum Ga, having logged nearly three months in the jungle, many simply assumed that they would soon go back to India for a rest, especially after they stood down for several days, received new clothes and mail, and had the opportunity to bathe and to eat 10-in-1 rations, a considerable improvement over C rations. "That we had been granted these indulgences and a rest . . . did not arouse our suspicions," Lieutenant Ogburn wrote. "We accepted them as our due."[8]

In reality, Stilwell had no intention of relieving Galahad. He was actually in the midst of dealing with multiple strategic crises, including the tragic loss of a key Allied leader. On the evening of March 24, Brigadier Wingate died aboard an American transport plane that crashed into a mountainside during a flight from Burma to India. The untimely death of this remarkable, unconventional leader stunned the Allied command and sapped the momentum of his Chindit operations. "General Wingate's death would have been a catastrophe whenever it happened," one of his brigade commanders reflected, "but it could not have happened at a worse moment than it did," primarily because of the ensuing confusion and lack of cohesion that resulted from the sudden demise of a unique leader whose charisma could not be replaced. "The immediate sense of loss that struck, like a blow, even those who differed most from him . . . was a measure of the impact he had made," Lieutenant General William Slim, British commander of the Fourteenth Army in India, later wrote. "Without his presence to animate it, Special Force [the Chindits] would no longer be the same to others or to itself. He had created, inspired, defended it, and given it confidence; it was the offspring of his vivid imagination and ruthless energy. It had no other parent. Now it was orphaned." They were never again quite the same without him. The plane crash had been so violent that recovery crews could not hope to identify the shredded particles of Wingate and the eight Americans. They simply buried their remnants in a communal grave.

Even worse, the Japanese soon let loose their own thunderbolts. Throughout the early weeks of 1944, they had reinforced three divisions on the Burma-India frontier for an offensive designed to cross the Chindwin River, seize the transit town of Imphal, breach the Indian frontier, and isolate Stilwell's Northern Combat Area Command. Tanaka's fighting withdrawal in the Hukawng Valley, while not necessarily planned, amounted to running interference for this main effort. The British fully anticipated Japanese intentions to invade India and placed Lieutenant General Slim's Fourteenth Army, whose ranks were dominated by Indians, into appropriate blocking positions. But the Japanese push began on March 8, catching the British by surprise and not fully prepared. "Troop movements were performed during the hours of darkness and maximum concealment was achieved by dispersion and by utilizing the cover offered by the dense jungle," one Japanese officer wrote in a postwar study of the offensive. The three Imperial Army divisions ripped through the Fourteenth Army front and progressed quickly. "With ominous rapidity Kohima was besieged and Imphal cut off," Slim later wrote.

As the situation grew more critical, Stilwell deeply worried that the enemy might soon cut his lines of supply and communication or at least force him to call off his drive for Myitkyina in favor of sending help to Slim. "This about ruins everything," he kvetched to his diary in the middle of March about the situation along the Indian border. He offered to disengage the Chinese 38th Division and send it to Slim, but the Briton declined. Nicknamed "Uncle Bill," the self-made, blue-collar Slim was a rarity among British senior officers, most of whom hailed from aristocratic or privileged backgrounds. A former teacher and bank clerk, he had earned a commission through sheer merit, led troops effectively in combat during World War I while suffering terrible wounds, and ascended the ranks through his unrelenting skill and competence. Slim's obvious quality as a commander and his down-to-earth demeanor appealed to the unpretentious Stilwell, so the two got along well (making him another rarity, a British officer whom Vinegar Joe actually liked).

On April 3, as desperate fighting raged around Imphal and Kohima, the two generals, with Mountbatten alongside, met at Jorhat in eastern India. Stilwell had just celebrated his sixty-first birthday a couple of weeks earlier. To commemorate the occasion, he had dined on C rations and a makeshift cake prepared by a headquarters cook. Slim thought he looked "tired and older." Once again, the American offered to halt his push for Myitkyina and send the 38th Division west. "He was obviously bitterly disappointed, but he made no criticisms and offered no reproaches," Slim recalled. "I had the impression that, apart from his own troubles, he was genuinely out to help me in mine." Slim declined Stilwell's offer and urged him to keep after Myitkyina, in effect promising that the Fourteenth Army would defeat the Japanese at Imphal and eliminate that threat to Stilwell's lifeline. "Much to my surprise, no question of help from us," a pleasantly elated Stilwell told his diary in the wake of the meeting. The reassurance contained an inherent, albeit unvoiced, challenge, though. With Slim tying down the bulk of the enemy's combat formations in theater, and satisfied to deal with them unaided by Northern Combat Area Command, it was even more incumbent upon Stilwell to capture Myitkyina as soon as possible. To do that, he needed every available soldier.

What was more, no sooner had the Nhpum Ga drama played out, when the Japanese unleashed a massive effort that threatened to unhinge the entire Allied strategic position on the Asian continent. From the first moment of the Pearl Harbor attack, the Japanese had deliberately chosen to fight a perilous two-front war—one against the Western powers in the Pacific and Asian rim and the other against the Chinese. Knowing that the tide of war had turned against them in the Pacific, the Japanese high command decided to turn up the pressure in China, where they enjoyed a qualitative military superiority over their enemies. The Imperial Army's China Expeditionary Force amassed 400,000 soldiers organized into seventeen divisions, supported by twelve thousand vehicles, and seventy thousand horses for a massive offensive code-named Ichi-go, in east China. The scale of the operation, the largest in Japan's long history, was such that planners earmarked some 10,560,000 gallons of gasoline for the vehicles and 2,640,000 gallons of aviation fuel for supporting aircraft. The Japanese intended to seize control of key railroads and airfields, forestall the possibility of American bombing raids on the home islands, establish land links to their bases in French Indochina, and perhaps even weaken Chiang's government badly enough to knock China out of the war. With China neutralized, the Japanese could potentially apportion more resources to fight the Americans in the Pacific and perhaps force them to negotiate a settlement based on Japanese dominance in Asia and a new geopolitical balance of power. Oddly, they did not attempt to synchronize this effort with the Imphal offensive. "We received no instructions from Imperial General Headquarters about coordination or cooperation between the Japanese forces in Burma and China, and received very little information," Field Marshal Shunroku Hata, Ichi-go's commander, later commented. This oversight exemplified the Japanese tendency to neglect well-coordinated ground attacks at all levels during the war.

When Ichi-go unfolded in mid-April, the Japanese began a relentless advance and inflicted devastating losses on Chiang's hollow armies, precipitating a near panic in Chungking and throughout Allied-controlled China. "Our men are all but wiped out," one isolated commander radioed; "this is my last message." Recruitment had lagged so badly in the

Nationalist Army that new men were marched to the front as veritable prisoners lest they run away at their first opportunity. Fighting formations were pathetically armed and supported. Their uniforms were in tatters; most wore straw sandals rather than boots. They subsisted on little more than a smattering of rice each day, if they were lucky. Teddy White, an American correspondent embedded with one unit, claimed that only one-third of the soldiers even had a rifle, much less access to any vehicles or artillery pieces. "They were walking up hills and dying in the sun but they had no support, no guns, no direction. They were doomed." In an assessment of Chiang's army, Lieutenant Colonel Charles Lutz, an American liaison officer, sniffed, "These people don't want to fight, despite all the comments to the contrary by high officials, and because of that, the lowly Chinese soldier doesn't want to be in the army; isn't interested in learning to be a soldier for he wants the solitude of his rice patties [sic] and his village, and will do only what he absolutely must and no more."

A choke of refugees only added to the sense of crisis. "[They] are still pouring in," Colonel Thomas Taylor, another American liaison officer, wrote to a superior. "It is the most pitiful sight I have ever seen—cold, hungry and weary—unbelievable suffering. Estimated 1,500 men, women, children and soldiers . . . to every mile for 50 to 75 miles. The government is furnishing meager accommodations." Ominously for the future political viability of the Chiang government, civilians all too often took advantage of the chaos to attack the retreating Nationalist soldiers as payback for years of repression, corruption, and exploitation. "They surrounded our troops and killed our officers," one Chinese commander lamented. "We heard this pretty often. They took away our stored grain, leaving their houses and fields empty, which meant that our officers and soldiers had no food for many days. In the end the damages we suffered from the attack by the people were more serious than the losses from battles with the enemy." Mao Zedong and his Chinese Communist Party colleagues exulted over these people's revolts and the damage the Japanese were inflicting on Chiang. "The CCP leadership rejoices at the news of the defeat," Peter Vladimirov, a Soviet liaison officer embedded with Mao's people in Yennan, told his diary.

The previous year, Stilwell had worried about the vulnerability of Chiang's land forces when Major General Claire Chennault, the valorous and inspirational but strategically myopic American commander of the Fourteenth Air Force—and close friend of the Chiang couple—succeeded in selling the Roosevelt administration on the flawed idea that China-based heavy bombers, including brand-new B-29 Superfortresses, could single-handedly bring Japan to its knees. Stilwell correctly anticipated that, without sufficient protection from the Nationalist Army, the airfields might become vulnerable. Ichi-go made his concern a reality. Chennault lobbied Stilwell for more resources to unleash raids on Japanese supply bases in China; Stilwell had little to give and argued that without secure bases the raids could not be sustained. Their disagreement, festering and maturing for over a year before exploding over Ichi-go, solidified into a chilly impasse and an eventual pointless postwar blame game between their adherents over responsibility for the disaster. The reality was that neither man possessed enough military power to stymie Ichi-go. Nor did the Chinese. The Japanese in China were constrained mainly by the limits of their own capabilities and resources.[9]

In the context of these troubling developments, Operation Albacore seemed perilous and possibly pointless, particularly to Chiang, who often could muster little interest in Burma as huge swaths of his own country fell under Japanese control and his regime teetered on the precipice of political collapse. At the same time, though, the Japanese had neither the manpower nor the inclination to permanently control much of the territory they gained. Nor could they finish off the British-Indians at Imphal. Slim would by late spring break the siege, turn the tables on them, and send their divisions into a disastrous retreat that owed much to logistical failures stemming from Allied control of the air over the battlefield and the seeming Japanese inability to coordinate the efforts in China and Burma well enough to put maximum pressure on the Allies.

With his allies so fully engaged, Stilwell could hardly countenance the idea of aborting the drive for Myitkyina, especially given the long, arduous advance of the Northern Combat Area Command by late April. Nor could he even begin to afford removing from action the only American ground combat formation in Asia, regardless of its dissipated condition, especially while he expected his two Chinese divisions to keep fighting and their comrades back home took on Ichi-go. In a private conversation with Merrill, who by late April had recuperated sufficiently to resume command, Stilwell admitted that he could not spare the 5307th. According to the Army's official historians, the theater commander "knew he was calling on Galahad for more effort than could fairly be expected, but that he had no other option." The bold truth was that, in order to have any chance of taking Myitkyina, he needed them. He made no effort to relay this message directly to the Marauders, instead maintaining the distance that made him seem like little more than a remote, unfeeling brute to the average soldier.

Even as the men ate better and slept more in the wake of Nhpum Ga, they also kept patrolling and clashed with the Japanese in several firefights. Most of the soldiers remained underweight and feverish, their skin marred with the unsightly red blotches of "Naga sores," where leeches had sucked at their lifeblood. At Hunter's insistence, they spent at least an hour per day performing close-order drilling, an inevitably unpopular order among combat-hardened veterans who tended to see themselves as being above such basic garrison soldier activities. But Hunter firmly believed it would cement the comradeship and teamwork that they had already honed in the jungle. "At first they were pretty sore about it but soon they were counting cadence and doing fancy drill," an anonymous officer claimed in the unit journal. As one veteran sergeant watched them march and sound off, he exclaimed, "Now I've seen everything, but it's a damn good thing to whip men back into shape." The drilling and patrolling hinted at a looming mission, at least for those attuned to the unique rhythm of army life. Every day that they remained in place without reassignment to the rear increased the odds that they would soon go back into action. Moreover, once Merrill and members of his staff met with Stilwell and the Northern Combat Area Command staffers to plan the push for Myitkyina, rumors of the new mission swept through Marauder ranks. An expectant gloom soon descended over those who allowed themselves to consider any other future possibility besides evacuation. Lieutenant Ogburn compared it to "a mosquito whining around your head. You wanted to bat it away from your ears. Most of us believed the Northern Combat Area Command was either ignorant of the shape we were in or indifferent to it—or out of its mind." When anyone speculated on the imminence of going back into action, another man would reproach him. "For Christ's sake, will you lay off that story! Are you *asking* for it?"

As before, Stilwell planned to send them on yet another wide-flanking maneuver, this time over the unfriendly peaks of the Kumon Range through the Hpungin Valley some sixty-five miles south with the objective of seizing Myitkyina airfield just west of the town. With the airfield under control, he intended to fly in reinforcements and make a quick grab for the town. As a nod to Galahad's diminished strength and condition, he reinforced them with three hundred Kachin guerrillas and a pair of newly arrived Chinese infantry regiments, the 150th and the 88th, some seven thousand soldiers, whom Chiang had donated to the Burma effort before the onset of Ichi-go. American transport planes flew these men from China to bases in India where, according to one US Army Service of Supply report, "adequate supply facilities were set up to feed [them]. By afternoon of the same day they had been deloused, fed and flown to Maingkwan," in Burma on the Ledo Road from which they marched into place. Commanders reorganized the force into three main columns, each with a Galahad battalion in the lead, followed by the Chinese. The Kachins were embedded with Lieutenant Colonel McGee's 2nd Battalion, now redesignated as M Force. When Merrill briefed his commanders and spoke to his men about the upcoming operation, he made the mistake of hinting that once Galahad gained its objective, the unit would immediately be flown back to India for some serious partying, "a fling that would make history," in the recollection of one soldier, "a party to cause taxpayers a shudder." An inevitable expectation coursed through the exhausted ranks that Myitkyina represented the Marauders' last hurrah.[10]

With the I&R platoons once again leading the way, the columns moved out on April 28, beginning an odyssey that, by comparison, made the previous five hundred miles they had gained appear like a hiking expedition. The average man hauled fifty pounds of gear and ammo, including an entrenching tool, K rations, a blanket, a poncho, extra clothing and shoes, a rifle, and a fighting knife. Terrain and conditions proved a greater adversary than the Japanese. The Kumon Range rose to heights of between two and six thousand feet. No roads of any kind existed, only a few broken, muddy trails. Lead scouts slashed at the foliage with machetes, forging their own narrow pathways. Mules routinely slipped and fell hundreds of feet to their deaths, or were so badly injured that soldiers had to make their way downhill and kill them. Mountainsides were so steep that men had to dig steps into them to provide adequate footing for themselves and the animals. As often as not, they simply unloaded the mules, coaxed them up and over the hills, and then reloaded them on the opposite side. "More than once I lay on my back, pushed my battle pack over my head, and with my heels digging into the slimy, spongy soil, I wormed my way up the steepest slopes," Weston recalled. "Mist clung to every vine and leaf, giving a hazy unreality to our surroundings. In addition, the intolerable elephant leeches would attach themselves to any part of our bodies that brushed their leafy hiding places as we passed." In the recollection of one doctor, the detested leeches were "slimy, elastic-tough, brown or green and grown, snake-like insects, one to two and one-half inches long. Their bite causes a stinging sensation. The lesion itches considerably on the second and third days following the bite." On one occasion, a Kachin guerrilla fashioned tweezers from bamboo and used them to remove a leech from inside the nose of Weston's lead scout.

Debilitating, mysterious fevers soon struck down many men, many of whom were so sick that they had to be hauled to the rear by overloaded Chinese litter teams. "There is nothing more fatiguing than carrying a loaded litter through the jungle," one medical officer later wrote. "Poor footing with entangling vines, mud, thorns, leeches, combined with heat and humidity quickly exhaust the bearers." Wherever possible, the Chinese and Americans improvised travois-style sleds braced by bamboo poles and pulled by mules for later aerial evacuation. Once flown to hospitals in Assam, several patients died. Merrill lost 149 men evacuated with the mysterious sickness before his doctors determined that it was a new form of scrub typhus caused by mites in the brush. Monsoon rains doused the soldiers every day. "We were scarcely ever dry," Lieutenant Ogburn shuddered. "The land steamed. The combination of heat and moisture was smothering. You had to fight through it. Whenever we bivouacked, men who had been incapable of keeping up with the column, slowly as it moved, and were too tired to worry about the danger from any Japanese there might be lurking about, would be plodding in for hours afterward, unsmiling and clammy with sweat. There was a feeling in the organization that it was coming apart." Many were stricken with cases of dysentery of such insistence that they took to cutting holes in the seats of their trousers and letting nature take its course while they kept moving. Determination to keep going remained high, morale low. The mood improved one night when Ogburn's communication section lucked into finding an American armed forces music radio station in Australia. Troops clustered around the radio, listening to the songs, an almost eerie juxtaposition under the circumstances.

Ogburn and the others could hardly have made it a mile without the support of the Tenth Air Force aviators who braved the heavy rains, low clouds, and peaks to drop supplies. Major General Howard Davidson, the Tenth's commander, later estimated that about 150 transport planes sustained not only the Marauders but the Chinese divisions and the Chindits. "The bases from which these supplies were flown were from 250 to 300 miles from the front line troops," he marveled. When weather or enemy action occasionally prevented drops, the Marauders simply went hungry. More often, though, the aircrews found ways to resupply Merrill's men. Loadmasters packed food, ammunition, medical supplies, mail, and other provisions into special containers weighing about 100 to 120 pounds apiece, fitted them with parachutes, and placed them aboard C-47 aircraft. Guided by air liaison officers over radio, sometimes in adversarial, stressful, confused conversations, the pilots pinpointed the Marauder elements as best they could and flew as low as possible for the greatest accuracy. Owing to the rugged terrain, drop zones generally amounted to little more than a clearing or ridgeline. "The unit had to lay out, in a good sized open area, drop zone panels of various colors to identify both the drop zone's center and the various battalions receiving the supplies," Sergeant Michael Gabbett explained. In the recollection of one officer in Stilwell's headquarters, the zones "have varied from large open paddy fields in flat terrain to where pilots could pin-point drops at a few hundred feet above the ground, to the other extreme when postage stamp clearings . . . in mountainous terrain with turbulent air currents made it impossible to drop from a low altitude."

Rear detachment Galahad men, known as "kickers," stood in the plane doorways and, on a signal from the pilot, manhandled the containers out of the plane. "About three to five chutes are dropped at a time, the plane circling until the entire load is dropped," wrote Lieutenant Colonel Marcel Crombez, who accompanied them on several missions. The typical mission involved a half dozen aircraft, with 3.4 tons of cargo per plane. Stilwell's command historian compared the kicker's job "to kicking a neat field goal. The number of flying hours amassed by the kickers is tremendous. The number who have exceeded 1,000 hours is considerable." With the cargo jettisoned, the pilots took evasive maneuvers and flew as quickly as they could for their bases in India. Marauders scrambled to recover as many containers as possible. Some chutes snagged on tall trees or were lost to the jungle or to locals or even occasionally hit animals or unwitting soldiers, causing death or serious injury. The average drop had a 10 percent wastage rate, an impressive level of efficiency for the pre-helicopter era. As the pace of resupply drops quickened, a parachute shortage developed, prompting a command attempt to recycle them. All too often, ground troops—Americans and Chinese—who liked to line foxholes with the chutes or tear them apart and trade the silk to locals for food or other valuables, were reluctant to comply.

Once over the Kumon Range on May 5, the Marauders and their Chinese allies descended into the valley, where they fought a pair of sharp but brief engagements with static Japanese garrisons at Ritpong and Tingkrukawng before embarking on the final push for Myitkyina airfield. Most of the men were exhausted, almost to the point of complete breakdown. "It was like nothing I had ever experienced before," Weston later wrote of the advance. "Personal hygiene seemed a lost cause and skin rashes, fungus, and diseases plagued our feet. The continued mud and filth made any scratch or blister a potential infection. Even the healthiest men looked like the 'walking wounded,' and maintaining morale was a monumental task." Those who could still walk and fight simply kept going, drawing on reserves of energy they did not know they possessed. "Driving, driving, driving ourselves forward, we inched up one hill and down another," Captain Fred Lyons later said. "Going up, the blood pounding in my head from the strain of hauling on vines and helping pull a mule on the trail. Going down, my heels pounded right up to my backbone, and every step was like beating on an open wound."[11]

With Myitkyina so close to his grasp, Stilwell could hardly countenance any other course of action but to maintain the advance regardless of the condition of the troops. For weeks, the Americans had pestered Chiang to order Y Force across the Salween River. The US had armed these divisions with lend-lease supplies and had earmarked scores of advisers, under the supervision of Brigadier General Dorn, to train them. In exchange, the Yanks expected them to make a military contribution to Albacore. President Roosevelt himself personally contacted Chiang on April 3 with a demand for action. "We have, during the past year, been equipping and training your Yoke Forces. It is inconceivable to me that your Yoke Forces, with their American equipment, would be unable to advance against the Japanese. If they are not to be used in the common cause our most strenuous and extensive efforts to fly in equipment and to furnish instructual personnel have not been justified. I do hope you can act." Chiang finally agreed, right before the launch of Ichi-go, to order Y Force across the Salween. Even with an infusion of American equipment and months of mentoring, they were hardly ready for the complexity of carrying out major offensive operations. "The individual soldier in forward units is suffering from malnutrition," Colonel Reynolds Condon, an experienced liaison officer with Yoke Force, assessed on the eve of battle. "No training is carried on. The soldier in forward areas *may or may not be armed*. If he is, his gun probably will not fire, because no stress is placed on care and cleaning. He has not fired his weapon for many months, IF AT ALL, because no ammunition has been issued." Nonetheless, they moved out on May 11–12. Stilwell hoped that they might play a major role in Myitkyina, but their offensive effectively went nowhere.

By the second week of May, he realized it was up to Galahad and its Kachin and Chinese partners to take the objective. Day by day, Stilwell agonized over their progress, fuming in his diary about the conditions and the dark possibility of failure. "It rains," he wailed in one entry. "The resistance grows here. Will they meet a reinforced garrison? Does it mean we'll fail on both sides instead of one? Can I get them out? The die is cast and it's sink or swim. But the nervous wear and tear is terrible." To relieve the stress, and perhaps fill the endless hours as he waited for news, he wrote soul-searching, self-critical memos. "I'm a worrier," he confided in one. "I am always imagining dangers, and experiencing them mentally. Many never occur, but those that do I'm mentally prepared for, so maybe it pays. They say the coward dies a thousand deaths, the valiant dies but once. But possibly the valiant dies a thousand deaths too, if he is cursed with imagination."

On May 16, as the lead column under Colonel Hunter closed in on the objective, an anxious Stilwell radioed Merrill. "Looks like we are going into the ninth inning with the score 0-0 and you are the first batter." Merrill radioed back, "Hope to fill the bases for you. Importance of this last inning is appreciated and we will not pull a 'Casey at the Bat.'" Hunter and Merrill had worked out a series of code words with Stilwell's headquarters to convey the situation and allow Stilwell's headquarters enough time to arrange for the airlift of troops and supplies once the airfield was in friendly hands. Perhaps reflecting the hunger that pervaded the ranks, they settled on "Cafeteria Lunch" for the signal that the final attack was two days away. "Strawberry Sundae" meant one day until the attack. "In the Ring" meant that the troops were within sight of the field, and "Merchant of Venice" indicated they had captured it.

Led as ever by Kachin guides, Hunter's column covered the last miles during the late hours of May 16. With reconnaissance teams scouting Myitkyina airfield and finding it lightly garrisoned, a sense of quiet seriousness now pervaded the ranks. "The silence of a column of four thousand men marching in a cave of darkness through unknown and unfamiliar surroundings is almost deafening in its intensity," Hunter later wrote; "the absence of the usual chatter, horseplay and wisecracks emphasizes the tenseness gripping the men. Each has retreated into the sanctity of his own thoughts, respecting the silence of his comrades." Hunter planned a masterful envelopment attack, with the 5307th's 1st Battalion scheduled to converge with the Chinese 150th Infantry Regiment. The troops set out at 1000 on May 17 and encountered little opposition.

Stilwell and his staffers huddled around their radios, hungering for news. At 1050 they heard the message "In the Ring!" and primed themselves for more good results. A pilot overflew the Myitkyina area but could provide Stilwell with no more details. "We'll just have to sweat it out," the general told his diary. They waited for four more excruciating hours while Hunter's men and the Chinese methodically cleared the area and overran the runways. Stilwell smoked incessantly and hungered for news. Finally, at 1530 the joyous message arrived. "Merchant of Venice!" For a man of Stilwell's straightlaced modesty, the news represented a vindicating triumph of tantalizing sublimity. His armies had advanced five hundred miles through some of the world's toughest terrain and had outfought a tenacious adversary. After two years of struggle and frustration, he had at last produced a tangible strategic result, and, to boot, one that stemmed from his own controversial vision. So much so that he could not resist making a gloating swipe at his British partners. "WILL THIS BURN UP THE LIMEYS!" he crowed in capital letters to his diary. The Army's official historians opined that "the brilliant seizure of the Myitkyina airstrip was the height of Stilwell's career."

The moment was so delicious to this spiritually starved man that he perhaps overestimated its importance. Control of the airfield was valuable for logistics and reinforcement, but the Allies needed the town of Myitkyina itself in order to extend their growing supply road in the direction of China, the ultimate strategic purpose of Stilwell's campaign. Unfortunately, the old man's jubilation soon evaporated in the face of multiple disasters. To maintain momentum for a push into the town, Hunter's weary force needed Allied planes to fly in ammunition, food, and infantry reinforcements. Instead, as a result of poor planning and coordination by Stilwell and his staff, the transports prematurely brought aviation engineers and antiaircraft units—the latter arrived because of an unauthorized individual order given by Stilwell's air commander, Major General George

Private First Class James Mangola of the 7th Infantry Division takes cover alongside the body of a dead Japanese soldier and a captured field piece during bitter close quarters fighting at Kwajalein. Often the opposing sides were only a few yards apart.
NARA

(*Left and below*) The violent reality of Kwajalein. Tanks provided close support to infantrymen who rooted the Japanese out of well-prepared bunkers. Flamethrowers played a major role in the battle, a harbinger for most subsequent Pacific theater combat.
U.S. ARMY

General Douglas MacArthur (center, with hands in pockets), commander of the South West Pacific Area, poses for a photograph with several of his commanders and staff officers. From left to right in the front row is Major General Stephen Chamberlin, operations officer; Lieutenant General Walter Krueger, Sixth Army commander; Vice Admiral Thomas Kinkaid (to the right of MacArthur), the theater naval commander; Major General Ennis Whitehead, Fifth Air Force commander; and Major General William Rupertus, commander of the 1st Marine Division. Though MacArthur was often vainglorious and egomaniacal, he had by 1944 forged many productive interservice working relationships, most notably with Kinkaid and Lieutenant General George Kenney, his air commander.
WALTER KRUEGER PAPERS, SPECIAL COLLECTIONS LIBRARY, U.S. MILITARY ACADEMY

Major General Oscar Griswold (front row, extreme left), commander of the XIV Corps on Bougainville. Unassuming and reliable, Griswold and his troops staved off a ferocious Japanese counteroffensive in March 1944, a victory that played a major part in winning control of the Solomon Island chain for the Allies. Sensitive and thoughtful, Griswold cared little for military glory. NARA

Soldiers of the 93rd Infantry Division patrol through a Bougainville swamp in April 1944. As members of a segregated African American unit that was led by an uncomfortable mixture of white and Black officers, the men of the 93rd found themselves under an intense political glare from proponents and opponents of Jim Crow–era racism. Unlike most white combat units, the 93rd did not have the luxury of making mistakes and learning how to function well on the front line. After a single patrol ran into trouble, War Department decision makers consigned the division to Pacific rear areas, mainly unloading cargo from ships. NARA

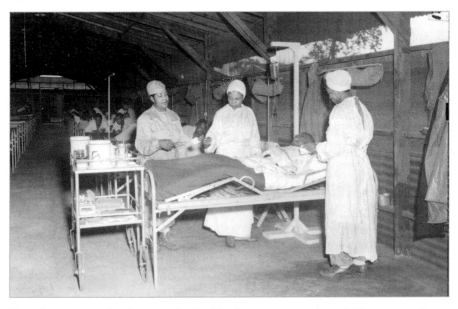

Too often even medical care in the Pacific theater was segregated. Here nurses from the all-Black 268th Station Hospital at Milne Bay, New Guinea, treat Sergeant Lawrence McKeever in the unit's surgical ward. NARA

(Above, right) The landing beaches at Hollandia were small, with no roads or infrastructure of any kind. Unloading operations were perilous and confined, as this packed column of trucks indicates. One evening, a single Japanese bomber scored a direct hit on an ammunition dump, igniting a massive explosion and a conflagration that killed twenty-four men, wounded one hundred others, and destroyed eight million dollars' worth of supplies. U.S. ARMY

(Above, left) Troops move inland through New Guinea swamps after the successful invasion of Hollandia in April 1944. At one fell swoop, the landings outflanked and cut off 55,000 Japanese troops and seized a major staging base for MacArthur's forces. His decision to invade Hollandia stemmed from an effective mixture of excellent intelligence on Japanese dispositions, a growing skill at coordinating ambitious amphibious operations, and a touch of boldness as well. U.S. ARMY

African American soldiers from a port company systematically unload and process supplies at Hollandia. Thanks largely to the efforts of these and other service troops, Hollandia in a matter of five weeks grew into the largest base in MacArthur's theater, with three airfields, seventy miles of roads, 135 miles of fuel pipeline, and three million square feet of warehouses, enough infrastructure to accommodate 140,000 troops. U.S. ARMY

Lieutenant General Robert Eichelberger (middle), mastermind of the Hollandia invasion and victor of the Biak battle, enjoys a lighthearted moment with two of his closest confidants, chief-of-staff Brigadier General Clovis Byers, on the left, and operations officer Brigadier General Frank Bowen, on the right. Brave, charming, and glib, with an easygoing demeanor and many friends throughout the army, Eichelberger proved himself to be one of the best American ground commanders of World War II. NARA

The remnants of a fortified cave on Biak, where the Japanese garrison fought elements of the 24th and 41st Infantry Divisions to a standstill for several weeks in June 1944. The battle hinted at a new prominence for cave warfare in the Pacific and a growing Japanese tendency to defend favorable inland terrain instead of attempting to repulse Allied invasions at the waterline. U.S. ARMY

Lieutenant General Walter Krueger (right), commander of the Sixth Army. Krueger emigrated from Germany to the United States as a child, joined the army as a private, earned a commission out of sheer merit, and came to control more American ground troops in the Pacific than any other operational commander. Deliberate in manner and occasionally brusque, Krueger nonetheless had a passion for interaction with the average soldier. Here he chats with troopers of the 1st Cavalry Division in March 1944 after the Los Negros invasion. NARA

Two of Krueger's most loyal lieutenants, Major General Innis "Palmer" Swift (left) and Brigadier General Edwin Patrick (right). Swift commanded the 1st Cavalry Division at Los Negros and was subsequently promoted by Krueger to command of I Corps. Patrick served as Krueger's chief of staff before taking command of the 6th Infantry Division and concluding the bitter fight for Lone Tree Hill in western New Guinea. Such was Swift's devotion to Krueger that he once commented, "If Krueger told me to cut my left arm off up to the elbow, I cut it off." NARA

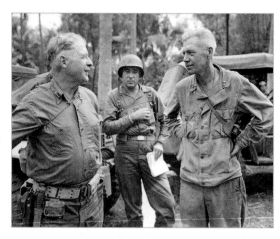

Lieutenant General Walter Krueger (left) with Major General Horace Fuller (right), commander of the 41st Infantry Division, watch troops prepare for the Hollandia invasion. In a startling contrast to Swift's high regard for Krueger, Fuller came to detest him so much for his badgering messages and micromanaging during the Biak battle that Fuller essentially quit his command. NARA

General Joseph Stilwell, commander of the China-Burma-India theater. Nineteen forty-four proved to be a year of decision for the preternaturally honest general who had such great difficulty dealing with Chinese leader Chiang Kai-shek. Even as Stilwell commanded a desperate ground campaign to open a supply route into China, he attempted to manage a rapidly deteriorating Chinese political and military situation. JOSEPH STILWELL PAPERS, SPECIAL COLLECTIONS LIBRARY, U.S. MILITARY ACADEMY

American and Chinese soldiers, with their pack animals alongside, walk through the muck of northern Burma. For nearly two-thirds of 1944, the 5307th Composite Unit (Provisional), better known as Merrill's Marauders, weathered the horrendous climate and conditions of Burma and outfought the Japanese at nearly every turn. Together the Chinese and the Americans took Myitkyina, a crucial transit point that the Allies badly needed to construct a land supply route into China. U.S. ARMY

Soldiers repair a bridge over a river in northern Burma. American engineers had a herculean task to keep bridges and roads serviceable amid some of the world's most difficult terrain. U.S. ARMY

An anonymous Nationalist Chinese soldier in Burma. Under serious and unrelenting pressure from the Japanese, and largely cut off from the outside world, Chiang Kai-shek's government had difficulty feeding, equipping, and training its armies. The Chinese 22nd and 38th Divisions in Burma represented some of Chiang's best units, and they played an important role in the ultimate success of the campaign.
U.S. ARMY

Fuel pipelines outside of Myitkyina. Army engineers built a pair of four-inch pipelines that paralleled the supply road, eventually from Ledo in India all the way to Kunming in China. The proficiency and adaptability of U.S. Army engineers proved to be a major advantage for the Allies in the war against Japan.
U.S. ARMY

Soldiers from the 27th Infantry Division come ashore on Saipan, June 1944. The 2nd and 4th Marine Divisions carried out the initial amphibious assault and ran into such tenacious resistance that the 27th Division entered the fighting sooner than American planners had expected.

NARA

GIs from the 27th Infantry Division move up to the front lines on Saipan. The well-entrenched Japanese made excellent use of Saipan's copious high ground, making any advance bloody and problematic. Over three weeks of heavy fighting, the Japanese lost nearly 30,000 killed, and the U.S. suffered 16,612 casualties. Almost one out of every four Americans who participated in the battle became a casualty.

U.S. ARMY

Major General Ralph Smith, commander of the 27th Infantry Division at Saipan. Heavily combat experienced from World War I, with a penchant for leading from the front in World War II, Smith was respected among his troops but clashed with his superior, Marine Lieutenant General Holland Smith. When Holland Smith became convinced, without ever visiting the front lines, that the 27th Division was not performing well enough at Saipan, he fired Ralph Smith, igniting a controversial interservice altercation that simmered for years. NARA

Marine Lieutenant General Holland Smith talks with Vice Admiral Richmond Kelly Turner (back to camera). Garrulous, stubborn, and disparaging of other services, Smith had little besides contempt for the average army soldier. Though historians have often pointed to doctrinal differences as the cause of army-marine tension on Saipan, the truth was that Smith's tempestuous personality and ignorance accounted for most of the trouble. In actual combat, marines and soldiers fought similarly and usually got along well. NARA

Lieutenant General Robert Richardson (right) and Major General Sanderford Jarman (center) talk with a local man on Saipan. Richardson served in an administrative position as the highest-ranking soldier in Admiral Chester Nimitz's Pacific theater command. Highly intelligent but sometimes narrow in outlook, Richardson believed that marines were ill suited for high command, and he deeply mistrusted Holland Smith. When the marine general fired Ralph Smith, Richardson ordered an immediate investigation. NARA

Riflemen from the 77th Infantry Division move inland through tall grassland beyond Agat Beach on Guam. Marines and soldiers functioned smoothly as part of a combined service team on Guam to a great extent because of the professional and competent leadership of Marine Major General Roy Geiger. U.S. ARMY

A pair of Sherman tanks hit and set afire by Japanese antitank guns during the climactic fighting at Yigo on Guam. Over three weeks of fighting in late July and early August 1944, 18,377 Japanese were killed. The Americans suffered 7,800 casualties, including 2,124 deaths. U.S. ARMY

The claustrophobic fighting on Angaur, where the 81st Infantry Division needed nearly a month to destroy a Japanese garrison of 1,600 soldiers who were hunkered down in ruins, caves, pillboxes, crags, and ridges. Two hundred sixty-four Americans died to capture what largely proved to be a useless objective. U.S. ARMY

Major General Andrew "AD" Bruce, commander of the 77th Infantry Division, pays tribute to one of his fallen soldiers. Innovative and silver-tongued, Bruce had seen heavy combat in World War I, and his valor had earned him the Distinguished Service Cross. In the invasions of Guam and Ormoc (on Leyte in the Philippines), he proved himself to be a master of combined arms warfare and a first-rate division commander. NARA

The momentous Pearl Harbor Conference in July 1944. From left to right, General Douglas MacArthur, President Franklin Roosevelt, Admiral William Leahy, and Admiral Chester Nimitz discuss the grand strategy of the Pacific theater. The meeting improved future coordination between MacArthur and Nimitz and, most important for MacArthur, paved the way for the return of his burgeoning armies to the Philippines. NARA

The remarkably effective American sinews of war. By 1944, prodigious American capacities in shipping and automation had provided the Allies with a major edge over the Japanese. Here at a New Guinea base, bulldozers, trucks, jeeps, and other vehicles abound alongside a Landing Ship Tank, or LST, arguably the most vital ship for the sustainment of amphibious invasions. NARA

A typical American base in the Pacific, bristling with LSTs, trucks, cranes, and huge amounts of freight. On New Guinea alone by the end of 1944, 800,000 tons of matériel was arriving each month. NARA

Lieutenant General Richard "Dick" Sutherland (left), MacArthur's powerful chief of staff, talks to Secretary of the Navy James Forrestal. Calculating and ruthless, Sutherland was almost universally disliked among his army brethren. In 1944, he began an effort to usurp MacArthur's authority, setting the two strong-willed men on a collision course. NARA

The invasion of Leyte, October 20, 1944. Code-named Operation King II, the assault involved four reinforced U.S. Army divisions and a total of 150,000 soldiers, a number of Americans that actually exceeded the American complement on D-Day at Normandy. This enormous Leyte invasion force brought along 1.5 million tons of equipment and 235,000 tons of vehicles, and required an armada of 420 ships to carry and protect it. U.S. ARMY

Captain William Bragg, an intelligence officer in the 127th Infantry Regiment, 32nd Infantry Division, examines one of at least 50,000 Japanese soldiers who were killed over the course of seven months of terrible fighting on Leyte. NARA

The aftermath of small-unit fighting on Leyte; soldiers from the 32nd Infantry Division examine wrecked Japanese tanks. After the successful American invasion, the Japanese chose to reinforce their garrison, leading to a protracted struggle of attrition that lasted until May 1945. Leyte was, to this point, the largest battle in the Pacific War. Because of bad weather, problematic soil, and antiquated infrastructure, the island proved to be a major disappointment as a base for future operations in the Philippines. NARA

Filipino porters carry supplies to the front lines on Leyte. The terrain was so problematic for vehicles that Lieutenant General Krueger's Sixth Army relied heavily on overworked carrying parties like this one to keep front line units supplied. In addition to the civilian carriers, Filipino resistance fighters also played a significant role in the campaign as guerrilla warriors and intelligence gatherers. U.S. ARMY

A lean, battle-hardened group of 1st Cavalry Division troopers takes a break after a two-week patrol on Leyte. Combat soldiers spent weeks and even months on the line, sometimes cut off and reliant for survival on aerial resupply. Over a two-month period, the 11th Air Cargo Resupply Squadron parachuted 1,167,818 pounds of ammunition, food, medicine, weaponry, and footgear to isolated units. NARA

Stratemeyer—whose presence added to the taut supply situation while doing little to enhance the operational potency of the Allied force. Merrill once again went down with heart troubles and had to be evacuated, this time permanently. The Chinese 150th Infantry Regiment twice attempted and failed to take the town, primarily because of bloody friendly-fire incidents that hinted at the unit's inexperience and the amateurish nature of its officers. Stilwell contemplated asking Mountbatten for the use of British reinforcements but found none available until June at the earliest. These collective issues gave the Japanese enough breathing space to send in reinforcements, eliminating any possibility for the Allies of taking Myitkyina quickly. A gloomy stalemate soon ensued.[12]

Galahad had by now reached a point of near disintegration. "None of us were really fit to go any further," Private Joe Robinson asserted. Private Frank Rinaldi added that "we were so weak . . . we couldn't even carry our rifles. We literally dragged them along on the ground." As of the third week of May, only thirteen hundred men—roughly one-third of the original unit strength—were still on their feet. Forward portable surgical hospitals clustered near the airstrip, tending to the multinational wounded and sick. One notable unit under the command of forty-seven-year-old Lieutenant Colonel Gordon Seagrave, an American physician-missionary to Burma now turned military surgeon, was crewed by a combination of Burmese nurses, American doctors, and Chinese stretcher teams. According to one command report, they worked "without adequate facilities, mired in mud, sprayed by shrapnel . . . under umbrellas held over them . . . operating on litters elevated above packing cases." In one ten-day period, they treated 1,036 patients, at least two-thirds of whom were Chinese. Overall, they treated 4,500 casualties, of whom less than 4 percent died. In the recollection of one surgeon, the blood of the wounded flowed "down the ditches, rotting, breeding maggots, flies and stench." Another medic remembered a "kaleidoscopic scene of mud, shortages, malaria, overtaxed equipment, rain, disappointments, heat, language difficulties, shifting priorities, jungle fighting . . . and homesickness."

By one estimate, Galahad medical evacuations, mainly due to sickness, were averaging forty-five per day. The ratio of combat loss to disease read like something out of a Civil War medical report. Battle casualties accounted for the loss of 424 men; a variety of diseases, such as malaria, amoebic dysentery, typhus, and the all-too-common "fever of unknown origin" claimed some 1,900 others. Northern Combat Area Command records documented the aerial evacuation of 2,625 Americans since the campaign had jumped off in February. "Transports were loaded time after time with men who could scarcely lift a hand," Captain Lyons, one of the many evacuees, marveled. "I was so sick I didn't care whether the Japs broke through [Allied lines] or not. All I wanted was unconsciousness." Some of the remaining men were so tired that they fell asleep during fire-fights. The average soldier had lost thirty-five pounds, was stricken with diarrhea and malaria, and was probably running at least a low-grade fever. Lieutenant Colonel McGee fainted three separate times but still refused evacuation. His battalion had dwindled to the squad-size strength of twelve men. Lieutenant Weston, the seemingly indestructible "Fightin' Preacher," was so racked with malaria, malnutrition, and grenade frag-ment wounds that he gave in to total exhaustion. When he fell deeply asleep in his foxhole, litter teams mistook him for dead before they dis-cerned his actual wounded and diseased condition and hauled him aboard an oxcart that carried him to the airfield. After they placed him aboard a C-47, "I bowed my head in sorrow for the loss of my buddies, and I thanked the Good Lord for sparing my life." By the assessment of Stilwell's own command history, "the Marauder Force was badly dilapidated by the cu-mulative effect of its campaign—malnutrition, disease and fatigue. It was hardly an effective fighting force any longer." Stilwell was anything but ignorant of this discomfiting truth. "Galahad is just shot," he asserted to his diary.

Galahad's deteriorated state was such that Stilwell soon worried the Japanese might actually reclaim the airfield, especially after they launched several counterattacks that the Chinese fended off. Desperate to hang on to his hard-won prize and take Myitkyina, and knowing he could not spare even one man at the front, the general bloodlessly ordered the remnants of the 5307th to remain in place alongside the Chinese regiments. "It became apparent that more stick than carrot was to be applied," Colonel Hunter later deadpanned. Fueled by Merrill's ill-advised public promise of relief after capturing the field, the bitter Marauders could not help but feel a sense of betrayal and anger toward Stilwell. Some began calling Myitkyina "our little Gallipoli." One sympathetic medical officer recalled, "They felt betrayed, lost [their] morale and the will to continue." The angry feelings only grew worse when the general put heavy pressure on the hospitals and convalescent camps to discharge any man who could still fight. Hundreds were summarily rounded up and returned to the front; few had recuperated in any meaningful way from their wounds or maladies. Sympathetic doctors immediately put 10 percent of these haggard men right back onto the planes with orders to go to the hospital and stay there. Stories, perhaps apocryphal but nonetheless stemming from eyewitness claims, circulated among the Marauders that Stilwell's staffers had brazenly removed evacuation passes from wounded and sick men at the airfield. "I can personally attest that this happened," Lieutenant Howard Garrison, a company commander, later asserted to an historian. "I received some of my medical evacs back from the airstrip."

Doctors found themselves caught between their humanitarian ethics and accountability to higher command. "The medical service was placed under unusual scrutiny of command and encouraged to withhold evacuation from all troops who were not completely incapacitated by wounds or disease," Lieutenant James Stone, the Army's theater medical historian, later wrote sadly. "Malaria cases and cases of 'fatigue' were the object of particular concern in the effort made by commanders to halt the evacuation of the Marauders. Instructions were given to retain and treat malaria in the field, restoring men to the line as soon as the frank signs of the disease had been suppressed. 'Tired' men were to be returned to their units." In one surreal instance, medical officers clambered aboard jeeps, chased down trucks evacuating stricken men away from the front, and forced them to turn around. In a postwar memoir, Dr. Seagrave commented disapprovingly, "It was clear that Stilwell wanted us to . . . get the sick into wards as rapidly as possible, cure them, and rush them out again for combat."

Over the course of months, the Marauders had proven themselves to be extremely tough, dedicated professional soldiers. Had Stilwell visited them and personally explained the desperate situation, his paucity of resources and their indispensability, they probably would have understood, assented to his actions, and rallied around him. In this sense, a little communication and personal rapport would probably have gone a long way. But he could not bring himself to do this. "I never saw him talk man to man with an American soldier or make any attempt to familiarize himself with their problems, personal or otherwise," Colonel Hunter later wrote disapprovingly. Instead, during combat the general remained distant from them, seemingly a cruel, callous figure. "I had him in my rifle sights," one soldier who saw him distantly when he visited the airfield later lamented. "I coulda squeezed one off and no one woulda known it wasn't a Jap that got the sonofabitch." After glimpsing him once—again at a distance—Lieutenant Ogburn opined in a letter to his father that Stilwell "impressed me as a small man in a big job . . . bloodless and utterly cold-hearted, without a drop of human kindness." These beliefs hardly squared with Stilwell's actual character, but, to young Marauders like Ogburn, the perception became reality. By the time he did visit and speak en masse to the Marauders months later, after the campaign, the opportunity to shape their perceptions more positively had passed, for few of the original men remained. "Many . . . talked their troubles over with him and found a sympathetic ear that before they hadn't known existed," Corporal Ferdinand Stauch later wrote of the visit. Posterity must record this incident under the "too little too late" category.[13]

With Galahad now nearing utter destruction, and the Chinese feeding five half-trained battalions into the line but otherwise few places to turn for badly needed reinforcements, Stilwell decided to order two battalions of American engineers, the 209th and 236th, to halt their work on the Ledo Road and go to the Myitkyina front to fight as infantry, in spite of far less than adequate preparation for the job. "We had been trained to build, destroy and fight, but few of us were prepared to do all three," Sergeant Lloyd Kessler of the 209th recalled. The decision, born of desperate expediency, was a symptom of the relative lack of resources afforded by American strategic thinkers to creating sufficient ground combat forces to wage global war. Stilwell's theater stood last in order of priority behind many other battlefields from Normandy to Italy to the Central and South Pacific. Galahad's destruction hardly qualified as unusual: American infantry units were almost always similarly decimated during World War II after months in combat. The difference here was that the 5307th stood alone in theater, with no other similar ground combat formations to replace it. So, like a baker who runs out of flour but must still produce a cake, Stilwell had no choice but to search for substitute ingredients. Hence the engineers. The improvisation affected others as well. At Bombay, a newly arrived boatload of twenty-six hundred replacements was hastily rushed, with little food, water, or orientation, to the Myitkyina front, where they were organized into two battalions dubbed New Galahad and placed in the lines alongside the remaining veterans of the 5307th, whom commanders now called Old Galahad. Like the engineers, the newcomers were less than prepared for their onerous new duties. A few had volunteered; most were reluctant conscripts. "They were mainly Shanghai's castoffs, misfits and men whom someone wanted rid of for one reason or another," Captain John Dunn, one of their commanders, later commented acidly. Together they became part of perhaps the most diverse Allied ground force of the war—a patchwork ring of foxhole-, trench-, bunker-, and crater-pocked small-unit perimeters along the airfield and outside the town manned by Americans, Chinese, Chindits, and Kachin guerrillas, collectively known as the Myitkyina Task Force, against a force of some four thousand Japanese.

A sprinkling of artillery and mortars, both Allied and Japanese, added just enough firepower for death to stalk men at all hours. The Allied guns fired six hundred tons of ammunition in the course of the summer. The two sides jabbed at each other with small-unit patrolling and a seemingly endless series of attacks and counterattacks. "Action was continuous as one side or the other probed for an opening or countered the efforts of the other," the Northern Combat Area Command history chronicled. "The Japanese positions were cleverly organized. Many dugouts and machine gun nests were established under great clumps of bamboo or dug under buildings on the outskirts of the town. They were interlocking and covered the entire area. Attacking through them simply courted disastrous results. On the other hand, as soon as the enemy forsook his positions and attempted an offensive, the tables were turned and he was sent back reeling, with less mouths to feed henceforth." On at least one occasion, some of the raw American soldiers ran away from attacking enemy soldiers. "They are in many cases simply terrified of the Japs," one commander sniffed. Self-inflicted wounds became so common among the new men that commanders found it necessary to print up and circulate punishment procedures so that judicial boards could save time in their deliberations.

Stilwell ruthlessly cycled through Myitkyina Task Force commanders. Initially he went with Merrill's executive officer, Colonel John McCammon, who seldom left his command tent. After a week of ineffective command, Stilwell replaced him with Brigadier General Haydon Boatner, a trusted, incorruptible, Chinese-speaking officer who had served him well for years. For all of his cultural knowledge and good intentions, though, Boatner leaned toward volatility under stress and had no ability to connect with his soldiers. One of Boatner's subordinates at Myitkyina noted that he "roared, ranted and raved in an almost hysterical manner. He was imbued with a very high sense of duty which he was able to conceal by an abrupt and oftentimes rude manner." Like McCammon, he made little effort to leave his headquarters tent and visit the frontline positions. Plus, a recurring case of malaria hobbled him. After about a month, Stilwell real-ized his protégé lacked the talent for field command and resolved on a change. To spare him the humiliation of relief in place, he arranged for a medical evacuation due to the malaria and eventually kicked him upstairs to command of the nominally higher-level but less consequential Northern Combat Area Command, essentially a functionary role. In his stead, Stil-well on June 25 appointed Brigadier General Theodore Wessels, a highly respected soldier and excellent communicator with a strong infantry back-ground who made a point of visiting every significant frontline position and quickly improved the overall condition of the task force. One subor-dinate described Wessels as "a hard and tireless worker [who] could usually be reached at some forward observation post directing the efforts of that unit. He definitely was that type of leader that men would go through hell for, and if need be die."

Seemingly at no time did Stilwell consider Colonel Hunter for task force command, though his stalwart constancy and cool, professional compe-tence through months of adversity had earned him great respect among the Marauders. Nonetheless his responsibilities were confined solely to control of the American units. Ironically, given Stilwell's own proclivities for salty honesty, he probably passed Hunter over because of the colonel's penchant for unvarnished discourse with higher command. "How to win friends and influence people was not taught at West Point during my four long years there," Hunter later quipped. During a Stilwell visit to the My-itkyina airfield on May 27, Hunter personally handed a volatile letter to the general, excoriating his staff for what he felt was their shabby, abusive treatment of the 5307th and mismanagement of the campaign. Hunter had previously cleared the letter with Colonel McCammon and gave the mis-sive directly to Stilwell rather than through channels, to spare him the embarrassment of having clerks at various headquarters eyeball the con-tents. When Stilwell read Hunter's comments, he said little else to him besides "This is a strong letter."

Hunter hoped the letter might galvanize his chief into positive action to address the mistreatment of Galahad. Instead, it backfired. Hunter failed to grasp that, to Stilwell, an attack on his staff was tantamount to an oblique, almost passive-aggressive attack on the general himself. Nor could Hunter possibly have appreciated Stilwell's extensive bigger-picture list of worries—crises at Imphal and Ichi-go, the dead-end Salween campaign, Chiang's general intransigence, delicate relations with the British, and of course the scarcity of American resources afforded to the China-Burma-India theater that had led to the seemingly callous destruction of the 5307th. Like a debater with a command of factual detail but little ability to articulate a larger interpretive theme, Hunter could not quite see that Galahad's death was a symptom of a larger disease, and not the disease itself. Though he remained in command of American forces at Myitkyina for the rest of the summer—probably owing to his valor and indispensability—he subsequently found his career vindictively dead-ended by Stilwell's loyalists, a shabby outcome for such a dedicated, honest, and brave combat soldier.[14]

For weeks the ugly stalemate wore on at Myitkyina, as neither side could make much headway. Attacks routinely failed. "Nothing of great tactical importance took place," wrote Major Robert Waters, an American liaison officer with the Chinese 30th Division. "If advances were made we counted them by yards." Allied fighter planes and medium bombers pounded the Japanese lines, but all too frequently they mistakenly strafed their own men. After one botched strike, an American commander cursed the pilot in a radio conversation: "Don't come back, you SOB. You shot my men!" Patrols clashed almost daily; a few from both sides were cut off and annihilated behind enemy lines. The vast majority returned, albeit in a state of serious dissipation. "Dirty, mud-caked, tired to the point of exhaustion, their gaunt bodies and hollow-eyed faces reflecting the physical and mental suffering they must have been going through," Captain Wonloy Chan, an intelligence officer, later wrote of them. Gobs of glutinous brown mud overwhelmed swaths of what had been grasslands and jungle. Mortar and artillery shells exploded frequently enough to require men to go to ground for survival. "Death was never very far away," Sergeant Kessler, the engineer, later wrote.

Like subterranean rats, soldiers lived in filthy, muddy trenches and dugouts. Monsoon rains poured down in sheets almost daily. Ponchos and tent shelter halves offered the only protection from the heavy downpours. To ward off flooding, troops quickly learned to dig drainage ditches away from their holes and bunkers. In between storms, steamy heat prevailed under the relentless sun. Thirst permeated the frontline soldiers. "For a glass of water, I would have been driven mad," one Japanese soldier remembered years later. "The longing for water was greater than for food, and the horrible agony was beyond expression." Waves of mosquitoes plagued the troops. Corporal Harold Seadler, a signals soldier, joked in a letter to his brother that "the mosquitoes . . . have been known to carry off a soldier while he sleeps. The mosquito takes the soldier's equipment also. It takes a little while to get used to seeing a mosquito wearing G.I. shoes or carrying a full pack."

A host of anonymous small-unit actions and attacks—most launched by the Allies—claimed an untold number of lives. By the end of June, the 236th Engineers had 336 men left; the 209th had 319. "It's really not nice, to see men get blown up, go crazy, and the bodies of American soldiers laying in front of our lines and not to be able to bury them . . . to smell and see bodies decay," Lieutenant John Jones, a New Galahad platoon leader, wrote to his family. "We're killing Japs, but they're dug in and it's hard to blow them out. I could go on with a lot more, but it would turn your stomach." As always, the Japanese generally fought to the last man rather than surrender. "It was necessary to kill each one individually and to grenade every dugout or opening that might possibly house a Jap," Captain Dunn recalled.

On the Japanese side, a paucity of supply and the ravages of disease, combined with accelerating losses, gradually wore down the potency of the garrison. Private Hideo Fujino was deeply saddened when he found out that a grenade explosion had blown the face off a good friend, killing him instantly. "He was an engineer, graduated from the Natural Sciences Division, Kyoto University. We had many opportunities to have a talk, and sometimes drank together to forget . . . the hateful life of the Army. He often told me that the best way of forgetting the painful life was to call back the scenes of his family enjoying their life. I couldn't find any words to comfort his family in their sorrow over his death. I felt deeply sorry."

Slowly the Chinese and Hunter's Americans gnawed away, bunker by bunker, at the Japanese ring of fortifications. By the end of July, only about one thousand emaciated Japanese defenders remained. Major General Genzu Mizukami, the garrison commander, gave the order to evacuate, though he himself committed suicide. Led by Colonel Fusayasu Maruyama, commander of the 114th Infantry, the core unit of the garrison, the starved survivors clambered onto makeshift rafts to float away on the Irawaddy or even, in some cases, tried to swim out. Many drowned or were killed by pursuing Allied patrols. The luckiest were rescued half-dead downriver by their comrades. In Fujino's recollection, they were "swollen with dropsy, white, and emitted offensive odors. They looked like rotted men in an advance stage of gangrene."

Finally, on August 3, the Allies took Myitkyina. After over a year of campaigning, Stilwell now controlled the key objective from which he could extend his supply road into China. When he got the news, he scrawled in his diary, with more relief than joy, "Over at last. Thank God. Not a worry in the world this morning. For five minutes anyway." His men captured 187 enemy soldiers, most of whom had been too wounded or sick to join their friends on the southeastward retreat. While the Japanese lost almost their entire garrison of 4,000 men, the Allies paid a heavy price as well for the three-month siege. The Americans lost 272 killed, 955 wounded, and 980 evacuated for sickness; 972 Chinese soldiers had been killed, 3,184 wounded, and 188 lost to disease. "It was a bitch of a fight . . . with the raw troops we had, full of anxiety, but we are sitting pretty now," Stilwell wrote to Win. The prize paid immediate dividends. With Myitkyina under control, a greater number of Allied transport planes could now fly more supply missions on shorter routes to China. By August, the tonnage of supplies delivered to the Chinese spiked from 13,836 tons three months before to 25,454 tons. Moreover, during the next couple of months alone, planes ferried some 40,000 tons of cargo, as well as reinforcements, into Myitkyina to build up for the final push to the Chinese border. "The troop carrier and combat cargo units of the 10th Air Force have done a magnificent job," the theater's air engineer summarized in an October memo.[15]

With the road expanding, a new fuel pipeline growing along with it, and much of northern Burma in his pocket, Stilwell's focus turned to the volatile political and military situation inside China, where long-standing, festering tensions now neared the boiling point. Chiang resented Stilwell's preoccupation with northern Burma while more and more of east China fell prey to the Japanese Ichi-go attackers like so many ripened fields consumed by locusts. To the Chinese leader, northern Burma operations made sense only in tandem with amphibious landings at Rangoon on the southern coast, a notion rendered impossible by the shipping and logistical demands of the Normandy landings (themselves an irritant to the Generalissimo because they stemmed from broken British and American promises made to him at Cairo of support for amphibious landings in Burma). To a man whose own home soil was under threat, fighting in a neighboring country seemed a distraction, even if it did offer him a logistical lifeline. Chiang was especially irritated that Stilwell and the Americans had strong-armed him into utilizing the Y Force in Burma rather than in China, where he felt it could have done much good. Every passing day, Ichi-go diminished the strength of Chiang's army and with it his own prestige and the perceived viability of his regime, especially in the eyes of foreigners. "Pressure has become greater every day, both internally and from abroad," he groused to his diary. Clarence Gauss, the US ambassador, had lost nearly all confidence in the Generalissimo and his Kuomintang Party. "Government's influence and control in Free China is deteriorating if not yet disintegrating," he assessed during the summer. At the same time, Mao Zedong and the Chinese Communist Party (CCP), whom Chiang correctly saw as his most dangerous enemy, grew stronger as they consolidated power, with little to fear from the overextended Japanese, over millions of Chinese in the northern part of the country.

Having poured nearly three years' worth of lend-lease supplies and military resources and endless amounts of political capital down what appeared to be a Chinese rabbit hole, the Americans were increasingly impatient for results in the form of military damage to the common Japanese enemy. The Yanks worried that even with MacArthur and Nimitz making their dramatic advances across the Pacific to threaten Japan itself, the enemy might decide to abandon the home islands and establish an enduring resistance center around the large Japanese armies in Manchuria and China proper (known respectively as the Kwantung Army and the China Expeditionary Force).

Throughout the summer of 1944, President Roosevelt strongly pressured Chiang to consummate an alliance with the communists and appoint an overall American commander, presumably Stilwell, to control the military campaign in China. Not surprisingly, the Generalissimo could muster little enthusiasm for either course of action. He understood far better than did the Americans, who had partnered with the Soviet Union and communist resistance groups in Europe and viewed these alliances as a perfectly sensible wartime expedience, that Mao would never willingly submit to his authority or enter into any sort of harmonious partnership. For months, American journalists, diplomats, and military commanders, including Stilwell—who, in spite of his personal right-wing political leanings, liked the idea of using communist divisions against the Japanese— had lobbied Chiang's government for permission to visit the communist north. The Generalissimo had allowed the correspondents to go in May, and they had generally filed favorable reports on the climate in CCP-controlled areas and the prospect of Mao as an ally.

Chiang still dragged his feet on the notion of any official contact between the US and the CCP, apparently hoping the foreigners might lose interest or the problem might somehow go away. But in late June, when President Roosevelt sent his mercurial, leftist vice president Henry Wallace to China with the mission of fostering cooperation, Chiang could stall no longer. Over four separate sessions with the vice president, he argued against the American notion of Mao and his adherents—fostered mainly by ignorance from the lack of contact enforced by the Chungking government—as agrarian democrats whose ideology amounted to a sort of "communist light" in comparison with Stalin's Soviet Union. Chiang asserted that Mao and his colleagues were "more communistic than the Russian communists" and could never be trusted. In a subsequent report to Roosevelt, Wallace described Chiang as so prejudiced against the CCP "that there seemed little prospect of satisfactory or enduring settlement."

Nonetheless, he eventually agreed to Wallace's entreaties and allowed a group of American soldiers and diplomats under Colonel David Barrett, a Chinese-speaking officer with two decades of experience in country, to visit Mao that summer. Known as the Dixie Mission because of the American penchant for referring to communist-controlled lands as rebel territory, they arrived in Yenan on July 22; another group followed a couple of weeks later. They were impressed with the contrast to Nationalist-controlled areas, riven as they were by so much corruption, chaos, and human suffering. The political environment in Yenan appeared more cohesive. People seemed better fed, healthier, the soldiers more robust, better armed and trained than Chiang's men. The Dixie Mission members were welcomed warmly by Mao and his colleagues, with whom they engaged in many convivial conversations, the general theme of which was the communist enthusiasm for an alliance with the Americans albeit without ever committing themselves to operating under the Nationalist leadership. The CCP leader emphasized the declining popular support in China for Chiang's repressive regime. "The Kuomintang will continue as the Government—without being able to be the Government," he told his visitors.

Similar to the journalists, the Dixie participants came away from the experience with a generally favorable impression of the CCP and its value as an ally. Like a fan base that is disgusted with a long-serving, increasingly hated coach, any alternative seemed better to the Americans than what they already had with Chiang. "In their rough and rumpled clothes, their earnest talk, their hard work and simple life, their energy, vitality and sincerity, they were a refreshing contrast to the world of the Kuomintang," historian Barbara Tuchman wrote sagely. "That was their chief charm." Several years later, during the self-destructive, paranoid hysteria of the McCarthy era, the Dixie Mission and its members became infamous for supposed naivete or sympathy toward the feared beast of communism. "Probably I should have known when I was in Yenan that Communists are Communists, period, and the Chinese Communists were no exception," Colonel Barrett wrote sadly in the early 1960s. "Now I can see with painful clarity that I did make some mistakes in judging the Chinese Communists. In my case, as with many other people, hindsight is so much better than foresight."

Indeed, the careers of Barrett and nearly all the unfortunate Dixie Mission members, most notably the two lead diplomats John Davies and John Service, were unfairly consumed by the fires of McCarthyite fulminations. A more sober assessment demands some fairness and empathy. Barrett and his colleagues could not possibly have anticipated the future tragic course of Chinese communism with all its terrible implications for US policy in Asia, nor the monster in the cradle that was Mao in 1944. If they fell sway to a clever CCP infomercial, as they undoubtedly did, and if they lacked Chiang's fundamental understanding of Maoist ruthlessness, this was not the result of any agenda other than the larger American goal in 1944 of defeating Japan and stabilizing China, rather than any kind of underhanded, pseudo-nefarious sympathy with Marxist ideology. From a broader point of view, their efforts were always a long shot because the differences between Chiang and Mao were largely irreconcilable, and cooperation between the two highly unlikely. Both saw themselves as the legitimate ruler of China. Chiang would only agree to communist participation under his authority for the perfectly understandable reason that anything short of this would legitimize Mao's shadow government and sow the seeds of his own undoing. Mao, for his part, could not risk setting any precedent of submitting his own political movement to Chiang, hence his refusal to commit his divisions to Nationalist or even US command.[16]

On the other issue of American command in China, the Generalissimo verbally indicated agreement but dragged out its implementation. After all, the idea of putting a foreigner in command of Chinese armies had no precedent in the country's history. It pointed to China's inadequacy and weakness, a humiliating circumstance in a culture that so valued maintaining face. It would inevitably erode Chiang's power base and leave open the possibility that the foreign commander might make common cause with the CCP, the prospect of which obviously constituted a threat to the stability of Chiang's long-term hold on power. On a personal level, Chiang found the notion of handing over so much power to Stilwell, after nearly three unhappy years of fencing with this contentious, self-righteous man, more than a little repugnant. Even so, Chiang so desired American lend-lease aid that he knew he must consider accommodating their demand. But he laid down three conditions before he would officially hand over command to Stilwell. First, the CCP could not serve under Stilwell unless they first recognized the authority of the Nationalist government. Second, the Americans' power and authority in relation to Chiang must be clearly defined. Third, the Chinese must now control the distribution and dispersal of lend-lease supplies, although under the supervision of approved American officers, a privilege the Roosevelt administration had afforded other major allies such as the British and the Soviets but not, because of corruption and US mistrust of Chiang, the Chinese.

Chiang also lobbied for Roosevelt to send him an intermediary independent of Stilwell and empowered by the president to give Stilwell orders. Roosevelt obliged the Chinese leader by sending Patrick Hurley, a self-made lawyer from Oklahoma who had served in the Army during World War I, and later as President Herbert Hoover's secretary of war. Colorful, courageous, and thoroughly attuned to domestic politics, handsome and always impeccably groomed, Hurley had already served Roosevelt well as a special envoy, helping to put a respectable bipartisan face on the administration's war policies. Hurley brought with him to China an interesting mix of military and civil authority—two-star general rank and status as the president's personal diplomatic representative. To Stilwell's credit, he welcomed Hurley with good-humored cordiality. "It takes oil and vinegar to make good French dressing," Stilwell quipped in reference to his own nickname and Hurley's history of representing oil companies. The relationship could well have been contentious or awkward, but the two got on well. Hurley deeply respected Stilwell's accomplishments, and the latter personally liked the presidential envoy.

From July through mid-September, Chiang and the Americans negotiated the particulars of Stilwell's new command arrangement in light of the

Generalissimo's three conditions. Hurley functioned as a well-meaning administration mouthpiece. In anticipation of Stilwell's ascension to control of the Chinese armed forces, the War Department promoted him to four-star rank. "I never signed a commission which has given me greater satisfaction," an admiring Secretary of War Stimson wrote of the promotion. Chiang's conditions two and three, dealing as they did with the parameters of Stilwell's power and the dispensation of lend-lease material, were resolvable, provided Chiang was truly willing to appoint Stilwell to his new post. "Peanut . . . told me that up to now my work had been 100% military," Stilwell related to his diary; "now . . . it would be 60% military and 40% political. Said I would take orders from him through the Natl. Mil. Council [National Military Council]."

All well and good, but the Americans really had no control over Chiang's first condition; only Mao could decide if he would submit his troops to Nationalist authority and, of course, he had no intention of agreeing to this. Nonetheless, by mid-September, Chiang and the Americans neared a final agreement on the latter two conditions. For a tantalizing moment, harmony seemed in the offing, but this was too good to be true. Chiang remained deeply worried about Japanese advances in China. If Stilwell did not launch a supporting attack from newly won Myitkyina to protect the Y Force position in eastern Burma, Chiang threatened to pull these troops back across the Salween to deal with Japanese advances. If this happened, the Japanese might well recapture Myitkyina and north Burma, imperiling the security of the road and undoing all the hard-won Allied gains of the spring and summer. Not surprisingly, Stilwell reacted with unvoiced fury. "The crazy little bastard," he raged to his diary of the Generalissimo. "Usual cockeyed reasons and idiotic tactical and strategic conceptions. He is impossible. The little matter of the Ledo Road is forgotten. He wants to give that up and sabotage the whole God-damn project—men, money, material, time and sweat that we have put on it for two and a half years just to help China. Unthinkable. It does not even enter into that hickory nut he uses for a head." Appalled and angered, Stilwell reported the situation to Army Chief of Staff General George Marshall, who duly relayed it to Roosevelt at Quebec, where he was meeting with the British in the Octagon conference to decide on future grand strategy.

In light of Chiang's new threats, Marshall and the president had apparently hit some sort of figurative wall in their toleration of him and his regime. The general and his staff drafted a vociferous reply, in the manner of an ultimatum, for the president's signature. Having reached a point of exasperation, Roosevelt signed it with no qualms and, quite significantly, relayed it through Marshall for Stilwell, not Hurley, to deliver to Chiang. Though procedural, the decision to route the message through Stilwell instead of Hurley was like handing a gun to an assassin rather than a pacifist. "I have urged time and again in recent months that you take drastic action to resist the disaster which has been moving closer to China and to you," Roosevelt admonished the Chinese leader. "Now, when you have not yet placed General Stilwell in command of all forces in China, we are faced with the loss of a critical area. Only drastic and immediate action on your part alone can be in time to preserve the fruits of your long years of struggle and the efforts we have been able to make to support you. It appears plainly evident to all of us here that all your efforts and our efforts to save China are to be lost by further delays."

In Chungking, Stilwell practically jumped for joy when on September 19 he received the message and instructions to deliver it personally to the Generalissimo. "Mark this day in red on the calendar of life," the new four-star general exulted. "At very long last, F.D.R. has finally spoken plain words, and plenty of them, with a firecracker in every sentence. At least F.D.R's eyes have been opened and he has thrown a hefty punch." Most likely, Stilwell assumed that the president had finally decided to make all aid to China contingent upon Chiang fighting the war in the manner the Americans wanted, a policy for which Stilwell had long argued. He could hardly wait to pass the note on to "the Peanut," whom he so loathed as a corrupt, ineffectual despot intent upon hoarding US largesse for no greater purpose than his own political power, rather than using it to defeat Japan.

Late in the afternoon that same day, the general traveled to Chiang's residence, where the Chinese leader was meeting with Hurley and several Chinese officials, including T. V. Soong, the Generalissimo's Western-savvy brother-in-law. According to Hurley's latter-year recollections, the group was working out the final details of Stilwell's appointment to head China's armed forces. Notably absent was Chiang's polished and politically adroit, glamorous English-speaking wife, Mei-ling Soong, who had wowed America the previous year during a goodwill tour and had recently left China for an international trip, possibly out of humiliation stemming from rumors of Chiang's infidelities. Though no fan of Stilwell, she had often in the past acted as a defusing intermediary between her husband and the general.

Now, in this instance, only Hurley could play that role. Out of courtesy to Hurley, Stilwell sent an aide to call him from the conference so that he could share the contents of the presidential message with him. Outside, on the veranda of the house, a horrified Hurley read the note and strongly urged Stilwell not to deliver it. "Joe, you have won this ball game and if you want command of the forces in China, all you have to do is to accept what the Generalissimo has already agreed to," Hurley counseled. Failing this, he urged the general to at least soften the tone or edit out the sharpest sentences. Anyone other than Stilwell might have heeded the advice. But he had waited far too long for this moment of vindication and, quite reasonably in light of his many previous experiences, he was far from convinced that Chiang had actually agreed to all terms as Hurley claimed. On the honesty and loyalty scale, Stilwell's character exceeded most others, but magnanimity was not among his strengths. He had been through far too much with the Peanut to throw him any sort of lifeline now. Besides, he was under direct orders from the president to deliver the note. "He wanted to embarrass and publicly humiliate the Generalissimo," Hurley opined in a 1952 letter to an Army official historian.

Stilwell entered the meeting and, after a hasty exchange of courtesies, presented the note to Chiang. "I handed this bundle of paprika to the Peanut and then sank back with a sigh," Stilwell later noted. "The harpoon hit the little bugger right in the solar plexus, and went right through him. It was a clean hit, but beyond turning green and losing the power of speech, he did not bat an eye. He just said to me, 'I understand.' And sat in silence, jiggling one foot." Chiang turned his teacup over, indicating an end to the conversation. The meeting broke up amid polite, restrained silence among all parties. A jubilant Stilwell returned to his residence and privately composed a vindictive poem whose theme was the long-overdue harnessing and humiliating of Chiang Kai-shek. "I know I've still to suffer, And run a weary race, But oh! the blessed pleasure! I've wrecked the Peanut's face," he summarized at the end of the poem.

Ironically, or perhaps even fittingly, the message that Stilwell so relished also contained the seeds of his undoing. Though Chiang studiously avoided showing his emotions in front of the foreigners, he was deeply angered and offended. A few minutes after the meeting, in a private conversation with T. V. Soong, he burst into tears and blamed Stilwell for the contents of the note, an incorrect supposition that of course seemed perfectly reasonable to the Generalissimo but really said more about the complete lack of trust between the two men than anything else. "My heart is broken," Chiang wrote in his journal; "it is difficult to go on. The humiliation . . . [has] put me in an embarrassing situation that I have never faced before."

It strains credulity to believe Hurley's later claim, offered in 1952 during the height of McCarthy's hysteria, that Chiang was just about to sign the orders appointing Stilwell to command in China when the incendiary note changed his mind and unraveled the whole deal. The Generalissimo's concerns about the communists had hardly receded, nor had the lend-lease issue been fully resolved. However, there is no doubt that the ultimatum note eliminated any possibility of Chiang appointing Stilwell, or probably any other American, to head up his armed forces. Moreover, it motivated the Generalissimo to fire back his own message to Roosevelt demanding the recall of Stilwell (Vice President Wallace had actually also recommended Stilwell's relief several weeks earlier, and Chiang knew this). Chiang made it clear that Stilwell had worn out his welcome in China and had completely lost the Generalissimo's confidence. In fact, the Chinese leader had attempted to get rid of Stilwell a year earlier, but only feverish intercession by Mei-ling and her sisters in Chungking, and Marshall in Washington, had persuaded Chiang to drop the idea. A year had changed nothing between these two antagonists, and the Generalissimo had no intention of waiting any longer to rid himself of Stilwell. "It was made manifest to me that General Stilwell had no intention of cooperating with me, but believed that he was in fact being appointed to command me," he wrote to Roosevelt after the September 19 meeting. In the Generalissimo's view, Stilwell had proven himself unfit "for the vast, complex and delicate duties which the new command will entail."

Thus began a monthlong drama in which Stilwell's fate hung in the balance, with Hurley, in his role as a go-between, attempting unsuccessfully to forge some sort of compromise or at least stall for more time. Marshall and Stimson urged the president to cut off aid to China if Chiang did not back down. Roosevelt refused. By the second week of October, when Hurley began to grasp Chiang's rock-solid determination, he reluctantly formed the opinion that Stilwell must go. The matter came to a head on the evening of October 12 when Hurley realized he must make this unvarnished, troubling recommendation to the president. After tossing and turning, he arose at 0200 and dictated a message for FDR. "My opinion is that if you sustain Stilwell in this controversy you will lose Chiang Kaishek and possibly you will lose China with him. The impasse between

General Stilwell and the Generalissimo is big with potentialities involving a prolongation of the war and increased cost to America in material and blood. If we permit China to collapse; if we fail the Chinese Army in the war all the angels in heaven swearing that we were right in sustaining Stilwell will not change the verdict of history. America will have failed in China. I respectfully recommend that you relieve General Stilwell and appoint another American general." Out of respect for the general, Hurley traveled to his residence at dawn and showed him the message before sending it to Roosevelt.

The two men sipped coffee as the general read the note. Without a hint of malice, Stilwell looked at Hurley and said, "Pat, that must have been a difficult message for you to write."

"Joe, that represents the most disagreeable service that I have ever rendered for our country."

As Stilwell's low-key reaction indicated, the news hardly came as a surprise. He had heard rumblings of his demise for weeks, writing at one point to Win, "There may possibly [be] a loud bang out here before you get this and if you look carefully in the debris which will be flying through the air you may see yours truly with his pants blown entirely off." He could not resist expressing some acrimony. "The Peanut has gone off his rocker and Roosevelt has apparently let me down completely. If old softy gives in on this, as he apparently has, the Peanut will be out of control from now on. My conscience is clear. I have carried out my orders. I have no regrets. Except to see the U.S.A. sold down the river."

Even as Stilwell wrote these lines, the president was in touch with Chiang, indicating his willingness to recall Stilwell and asking the Generalissimo for the names of acceptable generals. Chiang responded with a list that included Lieutenant General Alexander Patch, currently commanding the Seventh Army in Europe, Lieutenant General Krueger, and Major General Albert Wedemeyer, a smooth-as-silk Army strategic thinker and insider with considerable experience in theater. Roosevelt gave him Wedemeyer but stipulated that his authority would be limited to control of US forces in China and Stilwell's previous role as chief of staff to the Generalissimo, a far cry from the now bygone notion of having an American command China's armed forces. Unlike Stilwell, Wedemeyer was to have no control over the Burma operations, in effect ending the China-Burma-India theater as a command entity, pleasing Mountbatten and the British as they were thrilled to be rid of Vinegar Joe. Stilwell received the official word from Marshall on October 19, one day after the thirty-fourth anniversary of his marriage to Win. "The ax has fallen and I'll be on my way to see you within a few days," he wrote to her. "Some of the boys here were confident that F.D.R. would stand up to the Peanut. I felt from the start that he would sell out. So now I am hanging up my shovel and bidding farewell to as merry a nest of gangsters as you'll meet in a long day's march."

With more than an inkling of what would happen to him, he had circulated many goodbye missives to subordinates throughout the theater. But the order to leave came under great haste and secrecy lest he unleash his famously forked tongue and influence the pending presidential election. Marshall intended to appoint him head of Army Ground Forces, a training command, until the right moment arose to give him an army. Under orders to leave Asia in two days, Stilwell did not even have enough time to brief Wedemeyer properly or provide him with anything in the way of guidance, something the new man forever resented, without quite appreciating why it came to pass. "The thing that hurt me most . . . was the fact that Stilwell did not send me a note when I succeeded him wishing me well, or did not leave any information concerning his plans and the people who were expected to carry out plans in the theater," Wedemeyer wrote to a historian a decade and a half later.

Stilwell came home anonymously, a four-star refugee draped in a unique mixture of failure and achievement. The general's inability to set aside his antipathy for Chiang and the Kuomintang government in order to accomplish American strategic objectives in Asia would arguably haunt the US in the region for decades to come. At the same time, he had trained foreign soldiers to a reasonably high standard, held together a fractious coalition effectively enough for over two years to wreck Japanese ambitions in Burma, defeated them militarily in an innovative campaign fought amid some of the world's most difficult terrain, and reestablished a vital line of communication between China and the outside world. Dwight Eisenhower, who knew a little something about working with allies, once wrote Stilwell a note commending him as someone who truly understood the "'between the lines headaches' and the political struggles that are forever going on where so many different nationalistic interests are involved." Indeed, Stilwell grasped this well and achieved some remarkable victories in battle. But, in the end, his ability to excel tactically but without strategic results embodied a tendency among far too many modern American senior military leaders.

Before he left China, he endured one last excruciating invitation to tea with the Generalissimo at which the two men voiced platitudes about their personality clash and their mutual objective to promote China's best interests. Later, when through official channels Chiang offered to decorate Stilwell with the Order of Blue Sky and White Sun with Grand Cordon, the highest Chinese medal for a foreigner, the resentful general savored the opportunity to turn him down flat. The two men simply could not get along. More importantly, by the fall of 1944, the same might well have been true for their respective countries. Even with Stilwell gone, the Sino-American relationship remained in crisis. As yet, no one, not even Chiang or Wedemeyer, knew if that could or would change in the decisive months still to come.[17]

7

Hell on Land and at Sea

Before World War II, Japan enjoyed a reputation as a nation that treated prisoners of war quite well. In the First Sino-Japanese War in the 1890s, the Russo-Japanese War in 1904–1905, and World War I, the Japanese handled their captives with humane consideration. Though the Tokyo government had refused to ratify the 1929 Geneva Convention, which established clear rules for the proper treatment of POWs—mainly because it did not want to send an implied message to its own military personnel that surrender was acceptable—Japanese policy makers indicated at the beginning of World War II that they would afford decent treatment to captives. Buoyed by government propaganda portraying Japan as an altruistic Asian redeemer, the average Japanese soldier saw the purpose of the war as liberating fellow Asians from the repressive yoke of white colonials, a kind of racial struggle to restore Asian autonomy and honor. "We are inheriting 2600 years of glorious history," one soldier scribbled in his diary early in the war; "representing the Asiatic race we are charged with the important and honorable duty of changing world history. The true value of the Japanese must be shown, as the world is watching. Asia must be liberated. I will not regret dying for my country."

In spite of the pent-up, prevailing resentment against the white-dominated nations, a common Imperial Army soldier's handbook mandated restraint against vanquished Western enemies. "Plundering . . . or intentionally killing non-resisting people is absolutely against the good name and moral code of Japan. Control yourself so as not to spoil your reverence to the Emperor, his soldiers and his army." Imperial Army regulations commanded soldiers to behave with the highest morality toward their captives. "Prisoners of war shall be treated with a spirit of goodwill and shall never be subjected to cruelties or humiliation."

In the Japanese military of the World War II era, though, this ideal hardly conformed to reality. The vicious, almost bloodthirsty behavior of

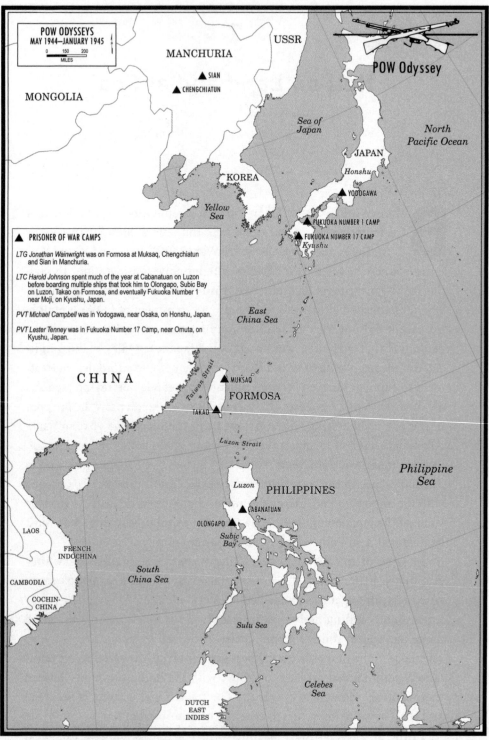

© 2021 by Chris Erichsen

Japanese soldiers in China, most notably during the infamous 1937–1938 Rape of Nanking, when Imperial soldiers raped, murdered, and plundered their Chinese victims with no official restrictions or punishment of any kind, betrayed a much darker reality that set the tone for Japanese actions after the outbreak of war with the Western powers. Almost immediately, when the Japanese captured some twenty thousand Americans and almost four times that many Filipinos in the 1941–1942 Philippines campaign, they treated their prisoners with shocking brutality, cruelty, and neglect. The infamous Bataan Death March, spanning several weeks in April and May 1942, more than hinted at a hard-core, nihilistic Japanese attitude toward prisoners of war as dishonorable subhumans who, by voluntarily surrendering, had forfeited all rights as soldiers. American and Filipino prisoners, most of whom were already diseased and malnourished from months of jungle fighting, were subjected to exhausting marches, beatings, neglect, and privation, with little food, water, or medical care. The march claimed the lives of about six hundred Americans and between five and ten thousand Filipinos.

Incredibly, most of the survivors spent the next few months in even worse circumstances at Camp O'Donnell, a converted Allied military installation with little infrastructure, where prisoners were simply left to rot in a ruthless Darwinian environment of degradation and privation reminiscent of Civil War POW camps such as Andersonville and Elmira. "You are cowards and should have committed suicide as any Japanese soldier would do when facing capture," the commandant told the prisoners in a "welcoming" speech. "It is only due to the generosity of the Japanese that you are alive." This grotesque form of "generosity" soon wore thinner than the emaciated frames of the skeletal prisoners. Dysentery, dehydration, disease, and starvation stalked O'Donnell like malevolent predators. Prisoners expired in pools of their own excreta. Billions of flies preyed on the flesh of the dead and the living alike. Food consisted of rice gruel. Water was so scarce that men stood in line all day in the tropical summer heat to fill a single canteen. Hundreds died each day, to the point where malnourished burial parties could not hope to inter them all. A secret wartime US Army report, based on intelligence gleaned from escapees, local guerrillas, and civilians, related a horrifying situation in which "a high percentage of the burial detail would be thrown into the common graves because they had died from overwork. Sometimes exhausted men were buried before they were actually dead." One American survivor remembered the camp

as a "stygian nightmare—rotting bodies stacked everywhere, flies, no water, no tools, no shelter." In a three-month period, 1,547 Americans and at
least 21,684 Filipinos died at O'Donnell. Those who survived this initiation-
like ordeal of captivity received somewhat better treatment wherever they
happened to end up among the vast array of small camps throughout the
Japanese empire, from the Philippines to Formosa (Taiwan), Manchuria,
and the home islands. Even so, most endured hunger, beatings, deprivation, and the terrible alienation that came with captivity far from home. By
and large, the Japanese did not construct permanent prison camps so
much as makeshift enclosures, either in isolated areas or near industrial
centers where they worked their prisoners as slave laborers, similar to the
labor camps that populated Nazi Germany's vast slave empire.[1]

At one of those camps, Muksaq on Taiwan, sixty-year-old Lieutenant
General Jonathan Wainwright IV spent his restless days preoccupied with
the daily responsibilities of senior leadership. Scion of a prominent military family, Wainwright knew nothing else besides army life. His grandfa-
ther had been a naval officer who was killed in the Civil War. His father
had attended West Point, become a cavalry colonel, and lost his life in the
Philippines in 1902. Jonathan had followed in his father's footsteps, both to
West Point and into the cavalry.

As an energetic combat commander in the Philippines, he had inspired
fierce admiration and loyalty among his troops, one of whom referred to
him succinctly as "a lion of a man . . . a true cavalry gentleman." Wainwright's excellence as a leader could not spare him the bitter necessity of
surrendering his starving, diseased, and isolated army in the spring of
1942, a decision that still caused him anguish two years later and for which
he initially half expected someday to face court-martial. The Japanese
hardly deferred to their three-star prisoner. At various times during his
incarceration, Wainwright endured beatings, starvation, humiliating diatribes, and backbreaking forced labor, including a stint clearing brush and
planting crops that nearly reduced him to total debilitation. Though he had
been allowed to write a few small postcard letters to his wife, Adele (or
"Kitty," as he often called her) in Skaneateles, New York, he still, as 1944
dawned, had not yet received any return mail. He could not know that she
worried constantly about him. As the daughter of a colonel and the wife of
a soldier, she, too, had known only Army life. To divert her anxiety and
contribute something to the war effort, she spent her days sewing blankets
and rolling Red Cross surgical dressings. As with her husband, the respon-

sibilities of leadership remained constant. Each week she received, in her estimation, "hundreds of letters from frantic relatives of prisoners and endless long distance calls from the press."

At Muksaq, Wainwright lived in a small barracks room with a cot, a chair, and a table, positively luxurious furnishings by the standards of most prisoners. They had books to read and they were not forced to work. "There is sufficient room for walks and outdoor exercise," reported a secret Army Military Intelligence Division memo, based on fragmentary prisoner correspondence, Japanese media accounts, and International Red Cross sources. "The prisoners have a library of 360 books, gramophone records, ping pong table, bridge, papers and magazines. The papers are usually two to three months old." They could buy cigarettes, cigars, soy sauce, ketchup, tea, and sugar. Meals were nutritious if unappetizing, a mixture of rice, vegetables, and a bit of fruit, but almost lavish by the standards of Wainwright's earlier captivity.

The decent quarters and adequate food hinted at a faintly solicitous attitude that he had recently noticed among the normally hard-edged Japanese. Colonel Hideo Sazawa, commandant of the Formosa camps, even made multiple visits, smiling, asking after the prisoners' welfare. Wainwright suspected he had an agenda, and he was right. Sazawa hoped to use Wainwright and the other high-ranking prisoners as propaganda pieces. One sunny day, he took several of them on a fishing expedition and picnic in nearby mountains. Photographers snapped pictures of guards pouring tea and serving lunch to the prisoners. After they ate, Colonel Sazawa harangued them with an anti-American speech in which he urged them to write personal letters to the Washington government testifying to good treatment and advocating an end to the war: "You have no chance of beating Japan." The prisoners simply stared at him in stony silence. After several unsuccessful attempts to get Wainwright to persuade the government to sue for peace, Sazawa sent a staffer to speak with him. "You can get the war stopped if you want to," he told Wainwright. "If you will write a letter or broadcast a statement to President Roosevelt that the United States has no chance to win the war, and that they had better stop it, the war will stop."

A defiant Wainwright refused even to hear the man out. "I do not care to continue the discussion," he replied angrily. "Now I will be pleased if you will leave this room."

Mindful always of his leadership responsibilities and the years of

Japanese perfidy he had experienced, Wainwright cared little anymore for formalities. Months of deprivation, hunger, and degradation, along with a withering contempt, bordering on hatred, for the Japanese, created a sort of simplicity to prison life for the old cavalryman. He now cared less for shaping Japanese attitudes than for simply preserving his dignity and that of his fellow prisoners. "I wasn't going to let them talk to me like that," he later said of the enemy propaganda efforts. Moreover, he knew that the Japanese entreaties betrayed the fact that they were losing the war. "We knew the Japs were beginning to worry."

Finding no cooperation from Wainwright and the other prisoners, the best the Japanese could do was attempt to shape world opinion favorably by allowing occasional, heavily supervised International Red Cross visits. "The prisoners' recreation consists largely of walking, gardening, and sports such as football and basketball, as well as indoor recreation which includes cards and chess," one representative reported to American readers in a Red Cross newsletter. But the Japanese did not allow the representatives to meet with or interact in any way with the prisoners. In that sense, almost everyone, from the Red Cross representatives to the Japanese and certainly the captives themselves, understood the sham nature of the various visits. In one instance, when a Red Cross man visited Muksaq and met only with the Japanese, an American officer defied his captors by accosting the man and rapidly relating a litany of human rights violations. "Colonel Sasawa [sic] ushered the Red Cross man off the scene and shouted that the meeting was adjourned," Wainwright later wrote of the incident.

Always mindful of maintaining the face of command, Wainwright struggled with a daily sense of melancholy. Time often seemed endless and pointless. Though his recent promotion to the Army's list of permanent major generals eased some of his previous concern over a postwar court-martial, he still felt isolated and emasculated. He worried over Adele's welfare and the safety of his son, Jack, a Merchant Marine captain. Cocooned in his remote corner of Taiwan, the general did not know that Jack had distinguished himself for bravery during the Salerno campaign when his ship was bombed and set afire and he saved the lives of several wounded crewmen. Nor did Wainwright have any intimation that *Time* featured a striking, beautifully painted portrait of him, gaunt and haggard, behind prison barbed wire, on the cover of the magazine's May 8, 1944, issue. Underneath the portrait, a succinct caption declared, "General Wainwright. Since Corregidor, two long years." Inside, a laudatory story described his valor during the 1942 Philippine fighting, cementing his status as a national hero. That same month he finally received a letter from Adele, his first in twenty-nine long months. "I read it so often that I nearly wore it out," an overjoyed Wainwright wrote. "I cannot tell you what it meant to me to hear from Adele." He also heard from Jack and "from worried parents of boys who had served under me and who were missing—terribly hard letters to which to find an adequate reply."

The mail then slowed to the usual trickle. By the fall, Wainwright had spent nearly fourteen months at Muksaq. The Japanese decided to move him and the other high-ranking Allied prisoners to Manchuria, deeper within their empire, beyond the reach of Western allied military forces. They endured an exhausting journey—albeit luxurious compared with the way the Japanese transported lower-ranking prisoners—by train and plane to Japan, where they boarded a ship that took them to Korea. At the port of Pusan, they clambered aboard yet another train that carried them to Manchuria. The trip exacerbated an old sacroiliac problem in Wainwright's pelvis, causing him to walk with a cane, reducing his posture to an awkward stoop. "Wainwright doesn't look good at all," Colonel Mike Quinn, who had served under him in the Philippines as a quartermaster officer, confided worriedly to a secret diary he kept. "He is emaciated and seems to have lost a tremendous amount of weight. He never had much to spare anyway. It seemed to me that I could see a deadening of his spirits. That can hardly be held against him."

Wainwright spent several weeks at a camp called Chengchiatun before settling in at Sian, an austere compound where the prisoners lived in crude, frigid barracks and ate a subsistence diet of cornmeal mush, gruel, raw vegetables, and soya curd with the consistency of baby food. The contents of Red Cross packages augmented the monotonous, almost starvation-level fare, though the Japanese subsequently confiscated the packages and parceled out the food parsimoniously. After years of living in a tropical climate, Skinny, as he was so aptly nicknamed, shivered from the chilly Manchurian temperatures. Fortunately for him, officers were exempt from work. The same was not true for enlisted men, whom the Japanese forced to work outside, even in bitter cold. Wainwright lent his boots and stocking cap to Tech Sergeant Hubert Carroll, his orderly. When the Japanese found out about this, they forced Carroll to return the clothing on the pretense that it was meant for officers only. As the top prisoner, Wainwright endured intense scrutiny from his captors, including routine inspections from the commandant. "He was a meticulous devil. Upon our arrival he issued to each of us an exhaustive list of instructions telling us where every object in our rooms must be placed. The waste box must be in its exact place, as must be the spittoon and the fire bucket. It was only an annoyance, but for men of our age it was so infernally picayune that it was a source of perpetual irritation. There is something degrading about being bawled out loudly in front of your men because a spittoon is a few inches out of its ordained place." On and on the drab days unfolded, with little meaning or purpose for Wainwright. At Christmastime, shivering, hungry, and miserable, he groused to his clandestine diary, "What a travesty on the day. Christmas hell! I only hope my dear ones at home are happier than I am."[2]

At Yodogawa, near Osaka on the island of Honshu, Japan, Private Michael Campbell, a hard-bitten twenty-six-year-old infantryman, had lost almost all sense of time. The Japanese had established about 175 slave labor camps sprinkled around mines, foundries, and industrial centers throughout the home islands. The steel mill where Campbell toiled eight to ten hours per day was a dystopian, hellish hothouse of casual cruelty. Prisoners worked in a superheated environment around furnaces and in foundries. Cinders from the blast furnaces coated the whole area and made the air unhealthy to breathe. Unlike at Muksaq and Sian, officers at Yodogawa were required to work (Japanese policies on this and so many other POW-related issues were seemingly random and uncoordinated throughout the empire).

Prisoners used shaky tongs to place sheets of red-hot steel in rollers, under the supervision of indifferent or overtly sadistic civilian mill employees. One POW remembered a supervisor who "tried to feed the hot stuff through the rollers so fast that I wouldn't have time to get my tongs up in time. If I was slow, the hot steel would catch me on the arm and burn me. Made this job particularly difficult." Cambpell's job was to make fifty-gallon steel barrels. He worked all but three days each month. As a survivor of heavy combat at Bataan and Corregidor, and a product of troubled foster homes, with his father in prison and his mother committed to an insane asylum, Campbell was perhaps specially inured to the horrors of POW life. He and the other prisoners lived in threadbare, drafty wooden barracks inundated with aggressive, oversize rats that chewed through shoes and clothing. "I could see and hear them at night as they fought over food," he later wrote. "They harbored fleas that lived in their fur. The fleas in turn were carried into our bedding and clothes. The fleas were blood suckers and soon infested our bodies. This caused fevers and rashes that itched terribly. They became very active at night during our sleep, crawling all over us and biting us." To combat the fleas, Private Campbell washed as often as he could.

Malnourished, overworked at hard physical labor, and miserable, many of the men were ravaged by beriberi. The dry version exposed nerve endings, especially in the feet and other extremities, making the act of walking or touching anything extraordinarily painful. In bad cases, gangrene set in, according to Campbell, "rotting the toes, turning them black. Then the toes would drop off." The horrible stench of the dead flesh saturated the barracks. Medics could do little besides administer some thiamine and hope to contain the rot. "The gangrene developed was entirely local, apparently limited to the capillaries in the toes," one hopeful medical report asserted. The wet version of the disease caused extreme swelling as body fluids reacted to starvation by collecting in the lower extremities. "The ankles would swell with the water and the swelling would continue up the knees, from there on to the testicles," Campbell wrote. "I saw . . . POW patients so puffed up with water that their legs were the size of elephant legs. Their scrotum was swollen the size of a basketball!"

Campbell focused on little else besides surviving each awful day. Harsh and cruel as his father had been, he did impart one lesson that proved extremely useful in captivity. Under pain of severe discipline, Campbell had learned to eschew tobacco in any form. For many addicted prisoners, the hunger for tobacco exceeded the hunger for food, so much so that cigarettes had become the main mode of currency at Yodogawa. "I am sorry to report that I saw many of the POWs swap away their rations of rice and other food for cigarettes," he commented sadly. Initially, he felt a tremendous reluctance to profit from his fellow prisoners in this fashion, "but I was forced to by the pressure of living under such terrible circumstances. I soon took full advantage of my issue of cigarettes and ate many an extra bowl of rice as a result."

The extra nutrition might have helped him survive a Calvary-like ordeal in May 1944, when the camp commander found out that a group of prisoners had stolen some shoes and sold them to Japanese mill workers. He convened the POWs outside, ordered them to strip their clothes off and stand at attention until the guilty parties came forward. Clouds of mosquitoes soon descended and feasted on their pasty skin. Men began to slap at the insects, but the Japanese ordered them to stay still and get eaten. Anyone who disobeyed was severely beaten. "It was sheer torture to watch the mosquitoes draw our blood until they fell away bloated." Still, no one confessed, so the commander ordered them down onto the ground, on their hands and knees, where jagged cinders from the blast furnaces dug into their legs, feet, and hands for hours, even after sunset, when the evening chill caused them to shiver violently. Campbell's father had actually punished him much the same painful way by forcing him to kneel on raw corn kernels. "I could not help but reflect on the similarity of the two cruel punishments. The mosquitoes were drinking their fill of my blood and the cinders were grinding into my bare knees. I could see the blood oozing down and the mosquitoes bathing in it." The torture did not work, so the Japanese eventually relented and ordered them to their bunks. Campbell washed his painful wounds with lye soap, but the cuts left permanent scars on his legs. He claimed that several others ended up with legs so infected that they necessitated amputation.

By now, Private Campbell had seen over one-quarter of his fellow prisoners succumb to death by disease, starvation, or just sheer hopelessness. Like him, most of the survivors were self-focused, working any socially acceptable angle they could to live another day, another week. In this sense, the Japanese had created an environment in which men felt isolated and alien from one another, with little command structure or collective sense of purpose. "No one trusts anyone else probably because they are all crooked themselves," one prisoner lamented in a secret note. "Behind the cataclysm looms the Japanese who take much pleasure in sneering at the impotence and inefficiency of the 'damned Americans.'"

Campbell sometimes felt starved not just for food but also companionship. The same was true for Captain John Olson, a West Pointer who had graduated in 1939 and served with the Philippine Scouts before his capture. Under constant stress from his attempts to establish some kind of accountability among the prisoners, and feeling terrible guilt over what he perceived as his own failure to assume the proper role of a commander, Olson felt miserable and lonely, almost suicidal. Unable to confide in anyone, Olson took some solace in writing unsent letters to his mother, whom he missed terribly. "Your little boy is so tired, lonely, and unhappy," he complained in one missive. "If I didn't have you to live for, I would end it all today." One evening when he dreamed she had died, he woke up in tears. "I wonder what is the use. If I . . . knew you were dead, I would go out and get myself killed so I could join you and Daddy. Is that too cowardly?" He struggled mightily to live up to the uncompromising ethical code he had learned at West Point and which he felt she would expect of him. "I have . . . felt so weak, worthless, and unworthy of my commission as an officer. How easy to join the throng, be one of the boys. You would never know, but my conscience, which I call 'Mother' would cry out again at such apostasy." The depravity he witnessed each day solidified a determination to be thankful for the many blessings he had once enjoyed in America. "How little we appreciate our heritage of freedom until we have lost it. To see these poor slaves fight for coke [a coal-like heating fuel] . . . bunches of dried roots, stinking dried fruit . . . is enough to rouse pity even in the hearts of men as hard as ours." He concluded one letter by identifying himself as "your lonely homesick, weary boy. He loves you so. May he live to be worthy of you."

Olson and Campbell ordinarily would have been distanced from each other by the gulf in their respective ranks. But they bonded over their mutual love of chess and became close friends. Moreover, both understood that, at terrible Yodogawa, living was actually harder than dying, and both had chosen to do all they could to live, Olson for his mother, Campbell for life's own sake. Campbell had taken to trading small items such as towels and creosote tablets—a crude medicine issued to prisoners to help calm their bowels—with his civilian overseer at the mill in exchange for food. When he ran out of his issued tablets, he asked Olson to contribute his in exchange for some of the food. "He was reluctant to go along with me. He felt that it would be aiding an enemy and also would violate his code of ethics." Facing potential starvation, though, Olson soon relented. The Japanese worker traded small amounts of chicken, fish, potatoes, and eggs to them in return for the pills. "I divided the food equally with Capt. Olson," Campbell later wrote. "He was very pleased with the arrangement."

They both yearned for news of the outside world. Campbell soon arranged to acquire Japanese newspapers and magazines. Most either spouted ludicrous propaganda or were written in characters they found difficult to translate. But in the second week of June, Campbell traded for an Osaka paper with a huge front-page headline: "Allied Forces Landed at Normandy." Tears of joy came to his eyes as he read the story. Later, back at the camp, he arranged to meet Olson secretly in the latrine and showed him the paper. "Campbell, this is terrific news!" the captain practically shouted. He congratulated the private on successfully completing the daring deed of getting hold of the paper and showing it to him. Olson then circulated it among trusted prisoners. Buoyed by the news of Allied successes, the two men soon found a shared sense of purpose by devoting themselves to establishing an undercover information network among the POWs.[3]

At Fukuoka Number 17, on Kyushu, twenty-three-year-old Private Lester Tenney, a street-smart kid from Chicago who had served as a tank crewman on Bataan with the 192nd Tank Battalion, also built his daily survival around illicit trading. He had survived the Bataan Death March and O'Donnell. Nicknamed "Ten Spot" among his comrades, he cultivated business relationships with his fellow prisoners, a few Japanese guards, and some of the civilians who oversaw him during his long days of toil inside the Matsui Coal Mine, where conditions bordered on atrocious. Major John Mamerow, the ranking prisoner, documented the privation in a postwar report. "Clothing issued was not adequate and there was a great shortage of shoes. The men were required to work in water soaked tunnels and in many cases in running water. There were many tunnel cave-ins." Mine accidents claimed the lives of six men, an almost miraculously small number under the circumstances. The laborers worked twelve-hour shifts, with only a thirty-minute lunch break, for all but three days a month. "You can't describe the conditions," Private Harold Feiner remembered, shuddering. "Some of the coal veins American miners wouldn't even consider working, the Japanese were working. We would have to wade in rivers. We'd drag beams and cross members seven feet, eight feet, nine feet long while crawling on our knees through little tiny laterals. We worked many days until we almost fell. It was indescribably hard work." They worked in groups of about a dozen or more, sometimes a half mile below the surface, under the watchful supervision of at least two Matsui employees. Privates made ten yen a day, a pittance that amounted to little more than a formality for the Japanese to claim they were not slaves. Each evening, they emerged from the mine tunnels covered in coal dust. They either washed immediately or after they made the three-mile trek back to Fukuoka 17. Few ever felt completely clean of the ubiquitous noxious dust.

Overseers from the mine company imposed daily quotas on the prisoners, usually between six and ten cars per day. A group that met its quota might earn an apple and a pack of cigarettes per man. Any group that fell

short of its quota risked a beating. Often, the beatings happened indis-
criminately or whenever the Japanese found out about an American military victory. "They would take a shovel and beat you in the face with it,"
Tenney recalled, "or a pickaxe or a hammer . . . if you didn't work hard
enough . . . or fast enough." In spite of this treatment, he remained surprisingly objective about his captors. "I do not hate the Japanese," he once told
an interviewer. "You must understand that." On one occasion, a civilian
overseer showed Tenney a ludicrous Japanese propaganda photograph that
purported to show Imperial Army soldiers rubbing elbows with Hollywood starlets in Los Angeles. Tenney could not help but laugh. In response,
the man smashed him in the face with a coal shovel, "breaking my nose,
cutting a two-inch gash under my lower lip, and knocking a couple of my
teeth loose." A beating on another day broke bones in his shoulder that
almost necessitated the amputation of his left arm. An ax also pierced his
side, just missing his hip bone but leaving him with a limp.

These injuries, and several smaller ones he inflicted on himself, did at
least get him out of the mine for short periods of time. The camp doctor,
Captain Thomas Hewlett, did the best he could, with limited supplies and
equipment, to care for Tenney and his cohorts. He performed surgeries
with little anesthetic. Bandages and surgical gauze were in such short supply that he found it necessary to clean and reuse them. "Deficiency diseases
were a continuing medical problem and despite repeated pleas to the Japanese command we were never able to obtain any dietary improvement,"
Hewlett wrote in a postwar report. His patients struggled with hunger
edema, beriberi, malaria, a local illness called Fukuoka fever, diarrhea
problems known as the benjo boogie after the Japanese word for toilet, and
even tuberculosis. Pneumonia proved to be especially menacing for malnourished, diseased prisoners who were working in wet conditions.
Hewlett described it as "our most dreaded killer . . . continuously maintaining the highest mortality rate of any infectious diseases." According to
his records, 8 percent of Fukuoka 17 pneumonia patients died during the
winter of 1943–1944. Hewlett earned a beloved reputation as a physician
who would do most anything to help his fellow prisoners. The Japanese
constantly pressured him to send injured or sick men back into the mines
and he resisted any way he could, so much so that they once put him in
solitary confinement on short rations for a week, with no effect. "He . . .
refused to compromise his medical ethics," Tenney said of him. Major
Mamerow wholeheartedly agreed. "I cannot praise to [sic] highly the

excellent work of Captain . . . Thomas H. Hewlett . . . the senior Medical officer and Surgeon of the Camp. Many men are alive and in good physical condition due to his care."

The camp housed about nineteen hundred Australian, British, Dutch, and American prisoners of war, all of whom were known to the Japanese by assigned numbers rather than their names. Yanks made up just over 40 percent of the population. They lived in an enclosed compound of a couple dozen wooden buildings surrounded by an eight-foot-high fence with electrical wires to prevent any escape attempt. According to Mamerow, "each building contained 10 rooms . . . and held 50 men. 4 men were assigned to the small rooms and 6 men to the large room. There was no crowding and everyone had plenty of sleeping space. The floors . . . were covered with Japanese Tatami Mats (approximately 3'x6'x3') these mats were soft and provided excellent sleeping accommodations." The barracks were crudely heated and drafty in the winter. One of the few pleasant aspects of working in the mine was that it tended to be warm. Prisoners did have access to adequate sleeping blankets that kept them warm in the evenings. The end of each building contained washing facilities, a urinal, and five toilets. Surprisingly, the Japanese did not require the prisoners to remove their own waste, probably so they could use it as agricultural fertilizer. Local young women, called benjo or toilet girls by the Americans, visited twice a week to transfer the nauseating offal from the latrines to a large receptacle. In one instance, a prisoner in Tenney's building propositioned a benjo girl. "He offered her an apple, which he had obtained in the mine for meeting his shoveling quota, for a few minutes of pleasure. With some giggling and a shy motion with her hands, she nodded her head yes." The two lovers retreated to the man's sleeping room for a few carnal minutes, after which the girl got dressed, politely bowed, and left. For several days Tenney and his delighted fellow prisoners joked to one another, "We screwed the Japanese!"

Most of the POWs, though, were too malnourished to think much about sexual escapades. Men who worked in the coal mine received only 700 grams of rice per day, augmented by small amounts of fish, vegetables, sweet potatoes, tomatoes, and occasional slices of bread. In addition to some of these sundries, prisoners who were on sick call or working in camp jobs got only 550 grams of rice. Most, including Private Tenney, had lost at least 20 to 30 percent of their body weight. Like Campbell, he established illicit trading networks that helped him get a little extra food and cling to life. Tenney focused intently on his long-term goal of making it home to see his wife, Laura, whom he had married in the fall of 1941 before shipping out for the Philippines. One of his best trading partners was a kindhearted, gentlemanly Japanese mine laborer who hoped one day to work as a horticulturalist in the United States and wanted to learn all he could about American flowers. Tenney knew nothing about flowers, but he feigned expertise to teach the man the English names of various plants. In exchange he gave Tenney a can of condensed milk and many packs of cigarettes, which he, in turn, traded for food. These small victories kept his body going, but his spirit, and that of so many others, needed fulfillment, too. "We were all tired of our forced labor and felt that we could not go on much longer. It was not just the work that got to the men, but the fact that we had nothing to keep our minds busy. We needed something to take our minds off of our miserable circumstances."

In an unusual gesture of humanity, the Japanese had provided the prisoners with YMCA-supplied baseball, basketball, and volleyball equipment and encouraged them to play. But most of the men were too physically weak or exhausted from their backbreaking labor to participate for any length of time. At Tenney's instigation, they turned instead to homemade entertainment. Persuasive and self-confident, he sold Major Mamerow and the Japanese camp authorities on the idea of producing stage plays. Mamerow told him, "Ten-Spot, we need to do something to break the monotony here. If we don't, the men will go berserk." Tenney canvassed the camp for singing, acting, and comedic talent, as well as volunteers to obtain instruments, build the stage, and create costumes and the like from scrap material. Collectively they threw themselves into the effort, spending any spare moment they had in the evenings and on their rare off days rehearsing and producing the "Ziegfeld Follies of 1944," as they called the show. "These were the only truly happy days of all the three and a half years I spent in prison camp," Tenney later wrote. "We felt good doing something creative, and the show got our minds off of the horrible past, the dismal present, and the uncertain future. The show was our therapy."

Immersing himself in preparing the "Follies" certainly bolstered his morale. But it also taught him something about his fellow human beings. Tenney and the others had largely distanced themselves from eight men whom they deemed to be homosexuals. "We could see a few of the gay men caressing their lovers and stroking their hair." Repulsed, Tenney had previously avoided them, but all eight men participated in the play and he got to know them as people. "My feelings about them . . . changed. I saw them and spoke to them as individuals. Once I understood what their lifestyle was all about and once I realized they were like me in every way but one, I became more tolerant." Indeed, according to Captain Hewlett, gay relationships were common enough to prompt one of his medical colleagues to "conduct a weekly marital relations clinic, in an effort to keep the couples happy in our tight society."

On the evening of the performance, Tenney, as the show's director and producer, felt "nervous as a cat on a hot tin roof." Given the hatreds and tensions of war, the audience was surprisingly diverse and the mood good-natured. The camp commandant attended, as did many of his guards, high-ranking officers from Tokyo, and even the wealthy Baron Mitsui, owner of the mine, who had once attended Dartmouth. They sat alongside the Allied POWs, rare moments of intimacy among enemies. The show included singing, skits, comedy (some of which even poked fun at the guards), and dancing "girls" who wore scanty costumes and headdresses. Tenney need not have worried about the reception. "At the end of the night, we knew the show was a hit. Everyone loved it, and they showed it with their clapping, whistling and yelling." Even the Japanese seemed to like it. Baron Mitsui arranged to meet Tenney after the show and requested that the Japanese military authorities allow the Chicagoan the special privilege of sending a personal message to his family back home. The next morning, he wrote a short note for them, though the Tenney family did not receive it for almost a year. In the aftermath of the "Follies" success, Tenney established a regular rotation of productions. He helped stage thirteen more shows, nine of which were musicals, even as he toiled on in the mine. "Although I was engrossed with the work of the entertainment program, survival was still my top priority."

In a shocking reversal of circumstances that revealed much about the perils of captivity at the hands of the Japanese, this prospect soon came into serious question when they found out about his secret trading with civilian overseers and guards. Under interrogation, Tenney readily shared the details of his trading but claimed he did not know the identities of his Japanese partners. He and seven other suspects were separated from the prison population, their hands bound behind their backs, and at morning roll call, as the other POWs watched, made to stand before the camp commander, who paced nervously to and fro. "He informed us that we had to be put to death for trading with the Japanese in the mine," Tenney later wrote. "Trading was against Japanese law, we broke the law, and we had to be punished for it." A group of Japanese soldiers immediately surrounded them, including two officers who "were swinging their samurai swords from right to left, in a full arc." The commandant told each man how he would die—some by stabbing, others by shooting. In the case of Tenney, or "Number 264" as the Japanese called him, the commandant declared, "You do good show; we honor you with head cut off!" Staring death in the face, Tenney was seized with uncontrollable terror. "At that moment I lost control over my bowels. I defecated in my pants." Even so, when the commandant asked if any of the condemned men wished to make a statement before they died, Tenney had the presence of mind and the ability to think rationally under the ultimate pressure. He had studied the Japanese closely enough to understand their idiosyncrasies and insecurities. As Private Harold Feiner once put it, "The egos of the Japanese had to be seen to be believed." Tenney understood much the same thing. He asked to make a statement, stepped forward, and, with his tears in his eyes and voice choking, exclaimed, "Men, don't try to fool the Japanese; they are very smart. Do what they say and you will live to see your families again. Do what I did, and you will die here in Japan."

The short speech struck the exact right chord with the commandant, who smiled broadly, excitedly clapped his hands, and ordered their death sentences commuted to ten days in solitary confinement with only a little water and one meal per day. Whether or not the Japanese truly intended to execute Tenney and the other illicit traders can, of course, never be known. But he fervently believed that his speech "saved my life and the lives of the other men waiting to be executed." Ironically, because he had remained loyal to his Japanese trading partners, they secretly arranged for him to receive extra food during his stint in solitary confinement. He ate better than he would have in the regular mess hall and actually gained a little weight. "I was alive, that was all I could think of," he reflected years later. "I had just met one more goal in my quest for returning home." Whether by luck or savvy, he had made it one step closer to home—and Laura.[4]

The Japanese had captured the vast majority of their American prisoners in the Philippines and most were still there. Cabanatuan, a former Philippine Army training compound about ninety-five miles north of Manila on Luzon, served as the largest repository for American POWs. About four

thousand American survivors languished there, in steadily worsening circumstances. Throughout much of 1943, the place had stabilized into a habitable, if not necessarily desirable, incarceration center. Though the
Japanese forced most of the prisoners to work, primarily tilling crops in an
ever-growing camp farm, the prisoners did make small wages, paid in the
local currency of pesos, and ate a survivable diet of about two thousand
calories a day. Deaths had slowed to a trickle and then ceased altogether.
In-house entertainment had flourished. Cabanatuan featured a prisoner
band, regular plays, musicals, singing groups, the occasional baseball
game, and even a camp library that boasted thirty-five hundred volumes,
six hundred magazines, and fifty games. Under Japanese noses, library-
going prisoners studied atlases to track the progress of Allied military
forces on fronts all over the world. Thanks to a secret prison radio fashioned from spare parts by a resourceful engineer, the inmates possessed a
treasured link to the outside world. Only a trusted few knew the location
of the radio and listened to it regularly. Once informed, they disseminated
war news by word of mouth to the others. Most everyone knew by now that
the Allies were winning the war and approaching the Philippines.

Lieutenant Colonel Harold "Johnny" Johnson, the West Pointer who
had survived the Bataan Death March and Camp O'Donnell's dreaded
Zero Ward to assume an important leadership position as Cabanatuan's
commissary officer, understood that the war had now reached a tipping
point, with the survival of the Cabanatuan inmates in the balance. His
commissary had played a major role in the improvement of the camp by
adding greatly, and economically, to the supply of food, medicine, and
many other necessities. He and others had also established special sources
of funding and food for the most impoverished of all the prisoners, creating a fair and equitable system of distribution, undoubtedly saving many
lives. Among his fellow prisoners, whether enlisted or officers, he had
earned universal respect and trust as a scrupulously honest, effective
leader. A fellow soldier once described him as "the finest man I have ever
met." Another revered him as the sort of person who "inspires a pretty
high code of behavior on the part of the people around him."

Much to his chagrin, by the middle of 1944, the Japanese had repeatedly
cut rice rations and severely restricted the amount of vegetables and other
crops that the Americans could take from the thirteen-hundred-acre farm.
"A lot of 'coolie' labor was provided by Americans involving watering,
planting and cultivation," Johnson later said. Weight records kept at the

prison hospital revealed that over a six-month period the average prisoner had lost fifteen and a half pounds. Camp doctors found that 52 percent of the POWs were now afflicted with hunger edema or pellagra. Beatings, many of them severe, became common to the point of routine. The Japanese imposed a finite quota on how many prisoners could be hospitalized at any given time. Anyone over the quota had to work a full day, usually at hard physical labor under the scorching sun, regardless of his malady or physical condition. Each day, between five hundred and one thousand prisoners were marched to an adjacent site to construct an airfield. "They worked all day with picks and shovels levelling off the field," a postwar provost marshal study reported. "The work they did was very hard, hot and heavy."

A worried Johnson was increasingly encountering great difficulty in acquiring commissary items. Prices for such life-sustaining commodities as bananas, mongo beans, eggs, peanuts, and a wheat flour called panocha were skyrocketing. Over an eight-month period, the price of mongo beans alone shot up a staggering 800 percent. To make matter worse, the Japanese had stamped out clandestine smuggling networks that were run by extraordinarily courageous Filipinos and other local civilians to help the American prisoners survive. The Japanese rounded up twenty-five American prisoners who were involved, placed them in solitary confinement, then interrogated, tortured, and beat them. They executed most of the Filipinos they apprehended, most notably Ramon Amusategui, a wealthy Filipino who had risked his own life and fortune to help the Americans. Lorenza, his equally brave wife, feigned insanity when the Japanese arrested her and managed to avoid incarceration and interrogation, but had to cease her activities.

Spiritual, thoughtful, and intensely ethical, Johnson constantly searched for an inner strength to keep him going. Privately he wondered how much longer he and his comrades could withstand the worsening loneliness, isolation, and deprivation of captivity. He missed his wife, Dorothy, and their three children so badly that it almost caused him physical pain. "I am aware each day of certain minute changes in my own mental attitude and am powerless to stop them," he confided to his secret diary. "I wish so desperately to go home [but] can see no quick end to our present conditions." In the diary, he lamented the shrinking rations, the worsening treatment, and the tense uncertainty over the future. "Our food supply grows shorter," he once noted with sad brevity. By the end of the summer of 1944, his commissary was on the verge of ceasing operations. "Our food problem is most acute. Every day sees at least 5 persons admitted to the hospital, most of them suffering from severe malnutrition."

His own weight had declined to 136 pounds, a loss of at least 40 pounds from his prewar frame. Even so, he thought of himself as fortunate compared to many who were in worse shape and now desperately scrounging for any food they could get. "They were driven to catching or trapping birds, cats, dogs, and iguanas in order to have food for their starving bodies," a postwar Army analysis of Cabanatuan stated. "The number of thefts of products from the farm increased every day." Captain Eugene Forquer attested in a private diary to the growing desperation. "We are eating anything we can get our hands on. Some people eat corn stalks and leaves, squash and pumpkin leaves, also the flowers, papaya trees, fried grub worms, dogs, cats, rats, frogs, lizards, roots of various kinds etc.—anything that can be chewed." Lieutenant Philip Meier took to his own personal diary to document an inventory of his unorthodox food intake. "Since the beginning of the war, I have eaten horse, mule, carabao . . . Dog, Monkey . . . cat and Iguana lizard. When a fellow gets hungry enough he will eat anything. I am hungry all the time and it is just about the worst feeling a man can have." Another secret diarist, Major Elbridge Fendall, poignantly summarized a typical day now as "hunger, hunger, hunger—men bringing in weeds from detail and cooking them."

Some took solace in making more frequent visits to the library, whose catalog had actually grown due to new donations from the Red Cross and local sources. An avid reader, Johnson kept a meticulous record of the books he accessed. Among the diverse array of books he devoured were *House of Exile* by Nora Wann, *The Army Wife* by Nancy Shea, *Random Harvest* by James Hilton, *Stars on the Sea* by F. Van Wyck Mason, and *The Story of Philosophy* by Will Durant. A shortage of cigarettes and a spike in hunger-related dysentery soon had consequences for the library as well. "The most serious menace . . . at the present time is the practice of using pages from books as toilet and cigarette paper," wrote Major Cecil Sanders, a librarian. "Often the value of a book is completely destroyed."

By late September, a distinct tension crackled around Cabanatuan. The prisoners knew that with American advances in the Pacific, deliverance might come at any time, but only if they could survive long enough. On the morning of September 21, they heard the unmistakable sound of airplane engines. Prisoners looked up from their places of toil on the farm or poured out of their flimsy bamboo and thatched-roof barracks to see dozens of unfamiliar aircraft in the viewable distance, heading for points unknown. As the prisoners peered intently at the unfamiliar planes, they gradually came to realize that they were American, the first they had seen in two and a half years. Throughout the day, groups of these planes materialized in the skies over or near Cabanatuan. Though the prisoners could not know it, the aircraft were dive-bombers and fighters, originating from the decks of five separate fleet carriers belonging to Admiral William Halsey's Third Fleet, to carry out the first missions designed to soften up Japanese defenses on Luzon and elsewhere.

The POWs did not have to know this to understand that their world had just changed. Excitement swept through the men like a tidal wave. The presence of the planes constituted irrefutable proof that American military forces were now within striking distance of Luzon, probably with naval and air forces superior to the Japanese. This, in turn, could mean a friendly invasion—and liberation. Some of the prisoners laughed. Some shouted. Some cried. Most waved and jubilantly watched as some of the fighters peeled off, apparently to strafe the nascent airfield upon which so many of the POWs had labored. "A Nip plane was shot down in our own backyard," Johnson scrawled in his diary. Another man recalled that "a number of fighting planes peeled off and swooped low over the prison camp firing their unexpended ammo in salute to their excited countrymen below." Major Horace Greeley was so overjoyed at this sight that he climbed onto the roof of his barracks, waved a tattered shirt, and repeatedly roared, "I told you they'd come!" That evening, Major Fendall summarized the general sentiment in his diary. "What a day for the Americans who haven't seen a friend for 30 months! It has sure boosted morale around here."

In the aftermath of the raid, optimists insisted it presaged imminent liberation. Pessimists were not so sure. They argued that the Japanese would surely move them to Japan before friendly forces could free them. They pointed to the fact that the enemy had already begun this process. Earlier in the year, several hundred prisoners had been transferred from Cabanatuan to slave labor in Japan, reducing the camp's population to thirty-two hundred by September. Johnson admitted to ambivalence over the air strikes. One the one hand, he was thrilled to see a demonstration of American military might. On the other hand, as someone who had worked so closely with the Japanese for many months, studied them, and understood their psychology, he realized how determined they were to hold on to their prisoners. More than anything, the raids might well galvanize them into taking steps to make sure of this. "You can have no idea of the mixed feeling," he noted in his diary. Regretfully, the pessimists were correct. For months, the Japanese had planned to move the American POWs from the Philippines to more secure spots in the empire. If they were liberated, Japan would suffer a propaganda disaster and an accompanying loss of prestige among peoples of the Pacific and Asia. Nor did the Japanese want tales of their horrendous mistreatment of the prisoners to circulate throughout America and the rest of the world. Plus, they wanted to continue to exploit the slave labor of the prisoners.[5]

Throughout the fall, the population of Cabanatuan steadily dwindled as the Japanese arranged to transfer prisoners elsewhere by ship. A sense of gloom and resignation set in as the truth increasingly became apparent. Only the diseased and debilitated would be left in place. Everyone else would go. The first group of one thousand left even before September ended. A couple of weeks later, time ran out for another large group that included Lieutenant Colonel Johnson. Knowing that the Japanese would search them meticulously and limit their personal items, he resolved to hide his diary—many others did the same—lest he lose it to the enemy. "This will be my last entry," he scrawled before closing with a special message for Dorothy. "I love you my darling, with all of my being, and I never did realize how much until this war started. You are all I ever want." Upon completing this entry, he sealed the diary inside a tin, found a secluded spot, and carefully buried the tin, hoping fervently that he might some day come back and reclaim it. On October 20, the night before he left Cabanatuan, he listened to the secret radio and heard the exciting news that the Americans had invaded the island of Leyte in the middle of the Philippines archipelago. As Johnson listened, General MacArthur gave a stirring address marked by an unforgettable summation of the Fil-American bond. "People of the Philippines. I have returned. By the grace of God almighty, our forces stand again on Philippine soil—soil consecrated in the blood of our two peoples." Elated but filled with almost melancholy trepidation over the impending journey, Johnson simply "hoped against hope that something would interfere with that movement."

The first leg of the trip took them by truck to Bilibid, an old Spanish-built prison in the heart of Manila, where they languished in squalor for nearly two months as American forces fought far away on Leyte. On December 13, Johnson and 1,618 others finally got the order to board the

Oryoku Maru, a 7,363-ton passenger ship armed with antiaircraft guns and bereft of any indicator of its POW cargo. Officers, many of whom had served as combat commanders at Bataan and Corregidor, made up almost two-thirds of the prisoners. Five hundred enlisted men, forty-seven civilians, and thirty-seven British soldiers rounded out the group. On the way to the ship, the bedraggled column of prisoners, stretching for nearly a quarter mile, passed the Army-Navy Club and the Manila Hotel, where in peacetime American officers had danced, swilled drinks, and consumed meals of such richness and variety as to render them unimaginable now. Filthy, malnourished, disheveled, clutching a few humble possessions in their hands, and deeply apprehensive of boarding ship, the prisoners made for a pathetic sight. "We shuffled along, no longer able to march in military manner," Lieutenant Colonel Carl Engelhart later wrote. Grim-faced, melancholy Filipinos watched them slowly walk, or even limp, along the streets. PFC Lee Davis found it "very humiliating" to shamble past the locals. Major Eugene Jacobs, a physician, remembered seeing "pity on their faces. Many stores were closed, boarded up. Many homes showed signs of looting." A few courageous Filipinos flashed the V-for-Victory sign at the Americans, who dared not acknowledge them for fear of severe reprisals from their Japanese guards. Inside some adjacent buildings, other Filipinos blared their radios as a sign of unspoken solidarity. The prisoners soon arrived at Pier 7, where many of them had bid farewell to family members half a year before the Pearl Harbor attack. With silent satisfaction, they noted bomb damage in the harbor from American air raids. The POWs waited for hours while several thousand Japanese, including merchant seamen from sunken vessels, guards, and civilian women, children, and middle-aged men boarded the above-deck passenger spaces. They carried with them the ashes of 728 Japanese war dead for interment back home. A few of the civilians scornfully laughed at the prisoners as they filed past them.

Lieutenant Junsaburo Toshino, a bespectacled former gym teacher now in charge of the prisoners, gave them the order, through Mr. Shunusuke Wada, a civilian interpreter, to board the ship. Severe in manner, devoid of any compassion, Toshino spoke little English and yielded much practical power to Wada, a querulous mediocrity whose gait was hobbled by a humpback. "His incompetence for the job would have been evident even in normal times," Lieutenant Colonel Armand Hopkins later wrote of him. "He was in a constant state of extreme irritation, and he was wild with fear.

He hated the difficulties and dangers of his job, and he hated us because we were the cause of it all."

At the behest of these two overmatched functionaries, guards divided the prisoners into three groups and prodded them with rifle butts, shovels, and brooms down steep wooden steps into a trio of cramped holds in the bowels of the ship. Lieutenant Colonel Johnson found himself in the forward hold with nearly seven hundred other men, shoehorned into a space designed for about one-third that number. Each man could sit uncomfortably only with his knees drawn to his chest, hardly able to move an inch. "It was terribly crowded," Johnson, shuddering, recalled. The hold contained no portholes and no ventilation. The hatch above the stairwell provided the only source of light and air. Temperatures in all the holds quickly rose above one hundred degrees. Prisoners had trouble breathing. Some waved their mess kits in a harried attempt to fan their buddies. Prisoners began yelling desperately for water. Wada told them to shut up and even, for a short time, closed the hatches, adding to the wretchedness. When the cries continued, he shouted, "You are disturbing the Japanese women and children. If you do not shut up I will order the guards to shoot into the hold!"

Fortunately, he relented and opened the hatches, though temperatures remained unbearable. Guards lowered buckets of fish, rice, and seaweed to the prisoners. Because of the crowded conditions, the distribution of food was uneven. Some received nothing. The holds contained no latrine facilities. At the repeated request of the Americans, the guards finally lowered five-gallon relief buckets. Orderly disposal of waste proved an impossibility in the sardine-like holds. In Johnson's recollection, "buckets were passed around initially, and then were thrown around, spilling the contents upon anyone in their path." A slimy layer of feces and urine soon lined the floors. "The stench as a result of the excrement and heat was overpowering," Captain Harry Mittenthal later said. Diarrhea-stricken men often could not wait for the bucket. PFC Lee had stored his few possessions inside a small shoebox. He left it unattended for a few moments, only to discover that "someone had defecated in [it]."

In the evening, the ship briefly got underway, then sat in the harbor while a convoy assembled, and finally put to sea under cover of darkness. At the same time, the misery worsened in the overstuffed prisoner compartments, where temperatures soared as high as 120 degrees. "It was murderously hot and stifling," Lieutenant Colonel Armand Hopkins later wrote. "The sweat of our closely packed bodies vaporized and rose to the steel beams just above our heads. There it condensed and dropped back down on us." A terrible thirst soon set in among the water-deprived men. PFC Davis "saw Americans scrape sweat off the steel sides of the ship and try to drink it." In the anonymous darkness, the packed masses wallowed together in an unimaginable state of foulness and deprivation, a closed world of horror that few could even find the words to describe. "That night was ugly," Major Dwight Gard reflected a few weeks later in a secret memo he wrote to document the experience. "*A REAL HELL ON EARTH.* Men raving, crawling naked in the darkness, covered with slime . . . making speeches, threatening to kill, shouting at the Nips . . . [defecating] in place, drinking urine, stealing canteens, slashing wrists . . . and drinking their own blood."

To a delirious Hopkins, the darkness teemed with "the constant murmur, mixed with yells, of hundreds of human voices [that] seemed to be coming from far away, in some vast cavern filled with a great multitude." Many went mad. Davis saw a nearby prisoner "cut another person's throat and was holding his canteen so he could catch the blood." Some tried to wander about aimlessly. One kept offering a mess kit full of offal to anyone he encountered. "Have some of this chow," he said repeatedly. "It's good." Finding no takers, he eventually ate it himself. Some attempted to climb the ladder out of the hold or insisted on screaming obscenities or entreaties at the Japanese. Wada threatened to close the hatches or have the guards open fire. Terrified of either prospect, men took to beating their crazed comrades into submission, even unto death, to prevent Wada from making good on his threats. Some spots were so lacking in oxygen or space that men actually suffocated. "Once you passed out, you were gone," one survivor recalled, "but only those near you could tell that you were dead." Captain Mittenthal personally witnessed the deaths of four men for lack of air and he saw prisoners "fighting in an attempt to get to the front under the hatch, stepping on one another, pushing one another and swearing at each other." Lieutenant Colonel Francis Conaty suffered a severe asthma attack, undoubtedly exacerbated by the conditions and his weakened constitution. "This was brought to the attention of the Japanese sentries at the entrance of the hatch, and repeated requests were made to permit Col. Conaty to return to the deck," Lieutenant Colonel Jack Schwartz, a physician who attempted to treat him, later testified in an official statement. "These were denied, and the officer died within an hour."

Hundreds fanned their buddies or simply kept them talking to prevent them from succumbing to thirst, suffocation, or madness. "I don't think anyone survived that first night who didn't have somebody to buddy with," Captain Marion Lawton asserted. Under the circumstances, discipline and leadership suffered. Lawton later opined that "rank and authority lost their meaning." During those long hours, though, as half-dead prisoners verged on total panic and anarchy, a few determined leaders such as Marine Lieutenant Colonel Curtis Beecher, Marine Major Reginald Ridgely, Lieutenant Commander Francis Bridget, a naval aviator, and Lieutenant Colonel Frederick Saint all took it upon themselves to maintain as much calm and order as possible. "We're in this thing together," Bridget said at one point; "if any of us are going to live, we are going to have to work together." He and the others managed to prevent abject panic. In Johnson's recollection, their efforts were "very reminiscent of talking to a herd of cattle in a lightning storm or a thunder storm . . . just keeping them soothed." Their actions doubtless saved many lives. As it was, dozens died during that terrible night.

After sunrise on December 14, the convoy proceeded north off the western coast of Bataan. Filipino guerrillas apparently attempted to get word to Halsey's fleet about *Oryoku Maru*'s precious, friendly cargo, but to no avail. Planes from the USS *Hornet* and USS *Hancock* spotted the ship and began daylong strafing and bombing attacks. "The attacks would continue for 20 to 30 minutes, cease and then would come back again," Mittenthal wrote. No bombs struck the ship, but the planes machine-gunned it constantly with .50-caliber slugs. The prisoners could do nothing but cower powerlessly belowdecks and hope for the best as the ship rocked back and forth and the sound of gunfire echoed above. Lieutenant Colonel Johnson bowed his head and silently prayed, "Lord, I am ready if you want me," and immediately felt a tremendous sense of peace. Ricochets inflicted some minor wounds among the prisoners, but they remained largely unscathed. By contrast, the attacks exacted a tremendous toll on the Japanese above decks. Windows were shattered; the deck house under the bridge of the ship was torn apart. Bullets ripped through the upper cabins and lanced into the antiaircraft gun crewmen. In Major Alva Fitch's recollection, their "blood started running down the hatch well from the deck." The Americans could hear the screams of the dying crewmen and women and children as they got hit.

Late in the afternoon, when the attacks petered out, Wada ordered

Lieutenant Colonel Schwartz and several other American physicians up to the deck to care for wounded Japanese. They found the passenger areas slicked with rivulets of blood, bodies, and parts of bodies, including a baby that had been shattered by a .50-caliber round. "The ship's salon was packed with dead and dying Japanese troops, women and children," a shaken Schwartz recalled. "Medical supplies . . . were meager, and as soon as darkness set in we were forced to discontinue our work because there were no lights due to blackout restrictions." As Schwartz and the other doctors worked, Japanese-speaking Lieutenant Colonel Engelhart climbed the hatch ladder and asked Wada, in vain, to send water down to the prisoners. "I don't care if you all die," he replied. "Shut up." Before retiring to the hold, Engelhart got a good look at the shattered upper decks. "The deck cabins were shambles of dead and wounded Japanese civilians. Fifty caliber machine gun bullets had ripped through the cabin walls everywhere, tearing up humans, luggage, and . . . Red Cross parcels."

Under cover of darkness, the ship pulled into Subic Bay, near the old US naval base at Olongapo, where small ships evacuated the Japanese casualties, the civilians, and merchant seamen, leaving aboard only the *Oryoku Maru*'s crew and Lieutenant Toshino's people. The Americans passed another hellish night of surreal, depraved horrors. To Major Eugene Jacobs, the evening was filled with "frantic screams of the crazed, curses and shouts of the agitated and excited: Don't touch me! Keep away from me! Don't kill me! Give us air! Let us out! We need water!" In spite of the best efforts of Bridget and other leaders, many deranged prisoners struggled with one another for survival. Schwartz used the word "maniacal" to describe them. "Many murders were committed, and evidence the following morning was seen of slashed throats and wrists presumably from which blood was sucked."

After daylight, the carrier planes returned to finish off *Oryoku Maru*. As a stationary target within a few hundred yards of the shore, and little room to maneuver, the ship was a sitting duck. The planes pummeled it with rockets, machine-gun fire, and bombs. One of the bombs scored a direct hit on the aft hold, killing at least one hundred Americans. "I remember the big yellow flash and the hot blast of the explosion," one survivor later recalled. "The slop buckets burst and there was excrement all over the bodies." To Lieutenant Colonel Engelhart, the ship seemed to "jerk upwards a couple of feet and then settle back down with a grinding noise." The wounded and the dead lay together in piles. Among the dead was

Major Elbridge Fendall, who three months earlier had rejoiced to his diary when he saw American planes fly over Cabanatuan; tragically he had now fallen victim to friendly aircraft.

Flames threatened to get out of control. The dying ship began to take on water. The Japanese ordered the prisoners to abandon ship, with only their mess kits, canteens, and shoes, and swim to shore. Some men climbed the steps to the deck in orderly fashion; most did not. "It was a mad scramble, sort of like a bunch of rats trying to get out of a hole," PFC Davis commented. Invigorated by the fresh air, hundreds of prisoners began to jump overboard. Some detoured to the galley and scrounged food before evacuating. Lieutenant Toshino allegedly caught one man in the act and shot him to death. Many Americans, including Lieutenant Colonel Johnson, saw the remnants of Red Cross packages that had been earmarked for the prisoners but hoarded and looted by the Japanese. In the hundreds, the weakened prisoners drifted or swam away from the ship. Japanese guards shot at anyone who did not seem to be swimming to shore. Most of the castaways held on to debris or life vests. In many cases, they frantically waved at planes that appeared ready to make strafing runs. By now, the carrier pilots must have had an inkling of their presence because they held their fire and, in at least two instances, waggled their wings.[6]

Japanese guards corralled the Americans as they came ashore. "We were rounded up into a group, in waist-deep water," Jacobs remembered. At Olongapo Point, they were herded onto the old naval base tennis court, where American sailors had once whiled away their leisure hours. Now it was surrounded by fifteen-foot-high chicken wire fencing. Once inside, the prisoners themselves took roll. Of the 1,619 men who had left Manila two days earlier, 1,333 remained. Relieved as they were to escape the horrifying depredations of the sunken *Oryoku Maru*, they found no solace. To the contrary, they now embarked upon a new odyssey of hell. For five days they sat packed together lengthwise in rows of fifty-two men apiece on the blistering tennis court, half-clothed, under a hot tropical sun. They had access to a single weak water tap. Their "hospital" consisted of nothing more than a couple of propped-up sheets and a pair of raincoats to shield one hundred patients from the sunlight. Medical supplies were nonexistent. Lieutenant Colonel Schwartz could do almost nothing for the sick and wounded. At one point, he had to amputate the gangrenous arm of a wounded Marine, Corporal Eugene Specht, by "using a mess kit knife and wrapped the stump in a dirty towel." Specht died a few days later. Beecher pleaded with Wada for proper medical treatment. "For God's sake! Hospitalize these wounded or they are all going to die."

Wada replied, "All Americans are going to die anyway."

For the first two days, the prisoners received no food because, Lieutenant Toshino claimed, the Imperial Navy headquarters presiding over the base refused to give him any. Instead, he purchased a pair of seventy-pound sacks of uncooked rice with his own money but gave just one of them to the prisoners, who ended up with only skimpy rations. "Raw rice was issued to the palm of your hand, five spoons full," Lieutenant Colonel Johnson recalled years later. "You just sort of munched on it to try to keep going."

Unreconciled to leaving the prisoners in the Philippines, the Japanese continued their efforts to keep them out of Allied hands. On December 20 and 21, they began trucking them in groups inland to San Fernando Pampanga, where some were incarcerated inside a provincial jail and the rest in a theater. The Japanese provided them with some water, and the food improved to a ration of rice balls, camotes, and kelp. On December 24, they were packed aboard a hot, poorly ventilated train for a fourteen-hour journey to San Fernando La Union, a harbor in northwest Luzon. Before they left, Lieutenant Toshino asked Engelhart and Beecher to select fifteen of the sickest men who might not survive the impending sea journey to Japan for transport instead to Bilibid. PFC Davis, like most everyone else, wanted to stay on Luzon, not just to avoid the perils of the voyage aboard ship, but in hopes that he might be liberated by advancing American forces. When he got wind of Toshino's request, he got in line with the sick men and told the guards he could not travel. "I told them I was too sick to make the journey to Japan. They shoved me back into the line of healthy prisoners." The change saved Davis's life. Unbeknownst to him and the other prisoners, Toshino and several of his soldiers marched the fifteen men to a local cemetery and had them dig their own graves. At Toshino's order, they were executed. One of his sergeants beheaded seven of the prisoners; the rest were bayoneted to death.

Oblivious to this war crime, the other prisoners endured the arduous, sweltering journey aboard a train to San Fernando La Union, where they spent Christmas Day in a schoolyard. Christmas dinner consisted of a cup of rice, a camote, and half a cup of water. Two days later, they were trooped to a beach pier, forced to jump downward twenty feet onto barges, and then loaded aboard two transport ships. The vast majority, some 1,070 men, were assigned to the *Enoura Maru*. The rest, including Lieutenant Colonel Johnson, boarded the *Brazil Maru*. Though cramped, neither ship proved to be quite as crowded as the *Oryoku Maru* had been, perhaps in part because prisoner numbers had dwindled. The *Enoura Maru* had recently transported horses. The cargo compartment housing the Americans was inundated with manure and a huge fly population.

The ships left Luzon and headed for Takao on Formosa. In addition to the prisoners, the *Brazil Maru* also transported several hundred wounded or sick Japanese soldiers who were, in the recollection of one POW, "dressed in army caps, long white gowns, g-strings, and field shoes." Amid the vastness and anonymity of the *Oryoku Maru*, Johnson had deferred a leadership role to more senior officers. Aboard the *Brazil Maru*, though, he quickly assumed command of the smaller, more manageable group. The Japanese made almost no effort to provide food and water to the prisoners. The first two days they received nothing. After that, they were fortunate to get a few teaspoons full of water, a quarter cup of rice, and a few moldy, maggot-infested rolls in the course of a day. Johnson forbade individual trading with the Formosans who guarded the hold lest any prisoner get more than his fair share of food or water. A civilian who had once made a living in Manila as a gambler defied Johnson's authority and traded with a guard to obtain rice and candy for his friends and him. When the others found out, they confiscated the goodies and distributed it among themselves.

The ships were fortunate to avoid air and submarine attacks during the voyage, but the same could not be said for hunger and thirst. In desperation, Johnson constantly appealed to the Formosan guards for more food and water. Finally, one of them looked him in the eye and said brusquely, "It is better if you all die." Taken aback, Johnson hardly knew how to answer. "There's not much you can really argue about with a reply like that," he later commented. Having failed to elicit any sense of humanity among the coldhearted guards, he decided he must bribe them. In return for the leftovers from their meals and a little water, he traded them his cherished West Point ring. He then carefully and visibly divided the food and water as fairly as possible, making sure that every man received a proper share. "It was a small amount of food and a small amount of water, but it was distributed with perfect integrity on his part," one of the other prisoners later related. "Most probably the highest tribute ever paid 'Johnnie' was the respect for and the trust manifestly shown him by the miserable, starving company whom he tended."[7]

On New Year's Eve, both of the ships arrived safely at Takao, where they sat in the harbor for over a week. The thirty-seven British soldiers were sent to a camp on the island. Johnson's group was unloaded from the *Brazil Maru* and packed with their comrades aboard the *Enoura Maru*, where they ate a little better but still lived in aimless squalor. On the morning of January 9, just as the prisoners were eating a meager rice breakfast from their mess tins, American carrier planes raided Takao. A bomb struck the *Enoura Maru*'s forward compartment and another one hit close to its rear hold. A near miss tore gaping holes in the hull. Inside the forward hold, some 250 prisoners died instantly; scores of others were killed in other spots. "A blinding and deafening explosion (tremendous orange flash) caused pandemonium," Major Jacobs wrote. "Hatch covers fell into the bilge, dropping many prisoners thirty or forty feet below. There were screams, cries, groans, and oaths. The air was full of dust and dirt." Men were blown to bits, killed by concussion, crushed to death by falling beams, ripped open by fragments. Fumes from the bilge turned the hair of the living and the dead a bizarre shade of yellow. Dozens were wounded, many seriously. "Practically all of these died," Lieutenant Colonel Schwartz, the doctor who attempted to save their lives, later related to an Army board. "There were a number of compound fractures and intestinal perforations, but there were no facilities to treat these cases. Splints and dressing materials were not available for the fractures and wounds." Lieutenant Jack Wright remembered many "broken arms, broken backs, broken legs, hemorrhages, and decapitations. Many men were badly bruised and shocked."

Right before the raid, Lieutenant Colonel Johnson had left his spot to have a conversation with a fellow field-grade officer. Just as he was returning, the bombs struck. The men on either side of his spot were hit. "One . . . had the top of his head taken off like it had been taken off by a meat cleaver, slick and clean as a whistle." The other man, who happened to be Lieutenant Colonel Schwartz, received a fragment wound in the chin. A gaping hole was torn through the hull against which Johnson had sat only moments earlier. The near-death experience added to Johnson's commitment to high ethical standards and his reverence for a spiritual mysticism. "Somebody was giving me a very real protection at this stage," he later commented. "I can only conclude that God had some purpose for me."

Schwartz asked Toshino and Wada for medicine and equipment, to no avail. For nearly three days, the Americans cleaned up, tended to their wounded, and gathered the bodies of their dead as best they could. The

Japanese sent only a token medical contingent that helped treat the lightly wounded. Inside the forward compartment, in the recollection of one survivor, "there were . . . mangled Americans piled some three deep." Volunteer burial parties hoisted the bodies into cargo nets that lowered them haphazardly, often with a grisly clatter, onto the decks of barges alongside the heavily damaged ship. "Some bodies whose arms or legs were grotesquely caught in the net's webbing were freed, often with much difficulty, by a prisoner detail on the barge," one witness recalled. Tugs towed the barges to sand spits along the harbor shore. Prisoners stood in chilly, waist-deep water, unloaded the corpses, and hauled them in twos and threes aboard crude rafts to a cremation spot about a mile and a half away. All the while, guards impatiently prodded them, bellowing "Speedo!" to keep them working quickly. The process took three laborious, enervating days, "the most demanding physically that I have ever experienced and the most horrible of any I can imagine," a member of the burial party later recollected. "We found that handling a putrescent body was most difficult. When I grasped one by the wrist or ankle and pulled to move it, I was sickened to find myself with a 'glove' or 'stocking' of skin in my hands." Few could bring themselves to look at the grotesque, distorted faces, especially the eyes staring through half-closed lids.

With the disposal of the dead, the Japanese moved the one thousand or so survivors onto the barges and loaded them, in the usual crowded fashion, into compartments aboard the *Brazil Maru*. Nonambulatory wounded were trussed onto planks and hauled aboard the ship by their medical comrades. Everyone else shuffled into place to endure yet another "floating Devil's Island," as Lieutenant Colonel Engelhart aptly put it. The ship left Takao in a convoy on January 14 and, to evade American submarines and aircraft, took a circuitous route for over two weeks along the Chinese coast to get to Japan. If possible, conditions were even more deplorable than what the prisoners had experienced aboard the *Oryoku Maru*. The Japanese issued meager rice and water rations once or twice a day. They offered no medical care for the wounded men. The weather turned frigid with subfreezing temperatures and snow. "Being cold was a new hardship," Lieutenant Colonel Hopkins wrote. "With no fat on our bones, and only thin garments on our backs and our backsides, we had to huddle close together to conserve our feeble body warmth." Icy winds whipped through the men. Snow collected on the deck, and cold rain splashed into the holds. "With the cold weather, pneumonia hit us," Captain Lawton recalled.

"When it rained, dirty water from the deck would pour down on us. Men drank it—filthy, dirty water." Discipline broke down. Some stole from others. Misery spread like a virus. Exhausted, sick, starving, and almost delirious, many could bear little more. "The men were all suffering from malnutrition, years of starvation, exposure, neglect, and no medicines," one survivor later wrote. Diarrhea proliferated. Waste buckets overflowed and spilled urine and fecal matter along the floors. "The wounded lay in a sea of liquid feces," Schwartz testified. "The cold was severe and we had very little clothes. Many prisoners froze to death." The ship was carrying a cargo of brown sugar. The Japanese threatened to severely punish or kill anyone who stole from the load. Nonetheless, prisoners figured out how to pilfer from it and ate the sugar raw, perhaps helping many of them survive, but adding to their diarrhea problem.

Chaplains bolstered morale as best they could, praying with men, comforting them. Major John Duffy, a Catholic priest, had been wounded in the bombing and had no shirt, but he carried on, tending to the men. "He seemed . . . totally unaware of himself, or of the cold, the hunger, the thirst," a fellow officer wrote of him. Duffy later explained his selfless actions as "treating your neighbor as yourself. It is one of the greatest goods that comes from human suffering and want. Reduced to the least common denominator you realize you need your brother and he needs you."

In spite of the sugar and the ministrations of clerics like Duffy, prisoners began to die in droves—as many as two dozen a day—from starvation, disease, exposure, and untended wounds. "Bodies were stacked like logs against the bulkhead," PFC Davis recalled. Most were so degraded as to make them look almost inhuman. "It is impossible to recognize your best friend on the death pile due to emaciation etc.," Major Arthur Peterson told his diary. With sunken jaws and protruding ribs, they looked to Captain Mittenthal "like skeletons." Some of the living almost envied them. "The actual process of dying did not seem so unpleasant, on the contrary, it oftentimes seemed easier to die than to live," Lieutenant Colonel Irvin Alexander later mused. To keep warm, the living unceremoniously stripped them of their clothes. In Schwartz's recollection, the garments were "usually so filthy and full of feces that [they] could not be used, because even sea water was not obtainable to wash them." Prisoner undertakers circulated through the compartments and, shorn by now of any compassion, simply asked, "Got any stiffs in there?" One of them later commented sadly, "Death meant nothing to us. If you made it, you made it. If not, you died." The undertakers dragged the naked corpses up ladders, onto the deck, and, sometimes with no fanfare, dumped them overboard.

At one point, when the convoy was almost within sight of Shanghai, the ship's captain suggested, for the sake of the prisoners' welfare, that they put into port, where they might have access to medical care and more food. Toshino had no idea where he would house them. He assured his colleague that the Americans were fine. The hellish journey continued until they at last reached Moji on Kyushu on January 29. About 550 survivors had made it to Japan out of the original 1,619 who had left Manila six weeks earlier. Another 110 died within a month. Many of the others barely had the strength to stay on their feet. Japanese authorities at Moji were aghast at their appearance. Under their supervision, the prisoners were marched onto the deck, into the icy cold, given Imperial Army clothing, and then herded off the ship into a theater. "We remained here for about five hours, were fed and were divided into four groups, one a hospital group of the serious patients and the other groups to be sent to different camps," Lieutenant Colonel Schwartz remembered. In the short time this took, one prisoner dropped dead on the spot and another six died in the hospital.

Lieutenant Colonel Johnson and 192 other survivors were assigned to Fukuoka Number 1. His physical condition had deteriorated badly. He weighed less than one hundred pounds. He could hardly raise his arms or walk evenly. Captain Walter Kostecki, a camp physician who examined Johnson upon his arrival, later opined, "There was no medical reason why he should have been alive." The doctor wept at the appearance of Johnson and the other hell ship veterans. One of the other survivors later contended that those who lived were usually morally bankrupt. "If we had not been devils, we could not have survived. The generous men, the unselfish men, are the men we left behind." However true that might have been for some, it did not apply to Johnson. Somehow, through sheer force of will, he had lived through hell with his honor intact. "That's the measure of Johnny Johnson," a friend later commented. "He could have died any time he felt like it. He decided not to die." Still, as the pensive colonel slowly recuperated and settled into his new camp in Japan, he could not help but wonder which would end first, the war or his life and the lives of his fellow prisoners.[8]

8

Triumph and Travesty

A t Schofield Barracks on Oahu, where Japanese fighters had once strafed targets of opportunity during the Pearl Harbor raids, the mild Hawaiian weather and idyllic, lush tropical setting now seemed to belie the ugly realities of the war raging thousands of miles away. But even with the fighting so distant, the war remained ever present. Hawaii's population had, since the onset of war, lived under martial law, with authority vested in a military governor, and habeas corpus rights suspended. If the civilians lived daily with this reminder of ongoing war, the many thousands of soldiers based at Schofield, including those of the 27th Infantry Division—a New York National Guard outfit—remained even more immersed in the conflict, training, and planning for their next operation.

In late March, inside an innocuous office at Quadrangle 1, Major General Ralph Smith, the division commander, met privately with members of his staff to discuss the future. The fifty-year-old Smith had originally joined the Army as a National Guard private and earned a regular commission through his innate intelligence and natural leadership traits. Adventurous and curious, he once earned a pilot's license from Orville Wright. In World War I, he had served with the 1st and 4th Divisions, received multiple decorations for valor, and survived wounds he received at Argonne Forest. Part soldier, part intellectual, Smith became fluent in French and matured into one of the Army's leading experts on Great War history and European armies. His affinity for France was every bit as much personal as scholarly. His wife, Madeleine, hailed from the city of Valence in the southern part of the country. During the 1920s and 1930s, he logged several years in instructor positions—including a stint teaching French at West Point—and served in numerous infantry command slots. Given his language skills and knowledge of European geopolitics, Smith seemed a cinch for service in the war against Germany. But with the Army's legendary propensity to wedge square pegs into round holes, he instead ended up in command of the Pacific-bound 27th. Once in place as the 27th's leader, his background mattered little. His open mind, calm demeanor, and self-assured professionalism quickly earned him respect throughout a division populated mainly by post–Pearl Harbor draftees instead of prewar Guardsmen. "You were the finest person I've ever known, and ever anticipate knowing," one of his NCOs once wrote to him. "You taught me not only of war, but of people and humility." Another 27th Division soldier described him as "a very warm, down to earth type of person, unimpressed with himself or rank." Tall, gentlemanly, and popular with his soldiers, General Smith had led them successfully through the November 1943 capture of Makin with courage and forbearance. This battle had lasted only a few days, though, against an overmatched Japanese garrison.

As Smith sat down with his staff in late March, he knew that a greater challenge lay ahead for the 27th. With the office door firmly closed, they sat in chairs around the general's desk, eager to hear whatever information he could share with them. "In a quiet voice General Smith informed us that once more the Division was to enter an operation," wrote Lieutenant Colonel William Van Antwerp, his intelligence officer. "The objective, Saipan and Tinian Islands in the Marianas group."[1]

Smith indicated that the 27th was to play a part in Operation Forager, a massive air, sea, and land effort aimed at seizing the Mariana Islands to penetrate the vital inner ring of Japan's Pacific defenses. Admiral Ernest King, chief of naval operations and commander in chief of the US fleet, had long advocated for the seizure of key islands in the Marianas, particularly Saipan, Tinian, and Guam. President Roosevelt had once described the prickly admiral as so unflappable that "he could chew spikes for breakfast." Arrogant, brusque, and condescending but high-minded and completely dedicated to his country's welfare, King understood, arguably better than did any other Allied strategist, that the Central Pacific offered the most direct route to Japan. By the same token, King knew that control of the Marianas meant control of the Central Pacific. With the Marianas in hand, the Americans could sever Japanese lines of communication throughout much of the Pacific, presenting the enemy with a threat so profound as to provoke the decisive fleet engagement that had eluded Nimitz for two years, as the Imperial Navy, after the Midway debacle, had generally avoided major combat on the high seas, though Japanese naval leaders still planned and also yearned themselves for just this sort of showdown.

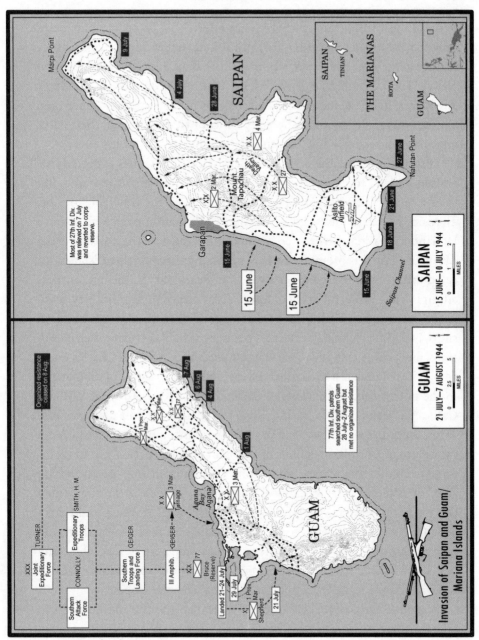

THE MARIANAS

SAIPAN

TINIAN

ROTA

GUAM

SAIPAN

Marpi Point

9 July

4 July

28 June

Mount Tapochau

Death Valley

4 Mar.

Garapan

2 Mar.

15 June

XX 27

27 June

Aslito Airfield

21 June

18 June

15 June

15 June

Nafutan Point

Saipan Channel

15 June

Most of 27th Inf. Div. was relieved on 7 July and reverted to corps reserve.

SAIPAN
15 JUNE–10 JULY 1944

0   1   2
MILES

GUAM

7 Aug

6 Aug

4 Aug

3 Mar.

1 Prov. Mar.

Aug

3 Mar.

Agana Bay
Agana

3 Mar.

XX Tumage

77th Inf. Div. patrols searched southern Guam 28 July–2 August but met no organized resistance

Organized resistance ceased on 8 Aug.

XXX
Joint Expeditionary Force

TURNER

Southern Attack Force

CONNOLLY

Expeditionary Troops

SMITH, H. M.

Southern Troops and Landing Force

GEIGER

III Amphib.

GEIGER

XX
77
Bruce
(Reserve)

Landed 21–24 July

29 July

1 Prov. Mar.
Shepherd

21 July

GUAM

21 JULY–7 AUGUST 1944

0   2.5   5
MILES

Invasion of Saipan and Guam/
Mariana Islands

© 2021 by Chris Erichsen

Perhaps most important, the Marianas offered the prospect of air bases only some thirteen hundred miles from Tokyo, well within the range of the forthcoming American heavy bomber, the B-29 Superfortress. General Henry "Hap" Arnold, the genial but calculating commander of the Army Air Forces, liked the idea of basing the B-29s in the Marianas rather than China, where Ichi-go and inherent political instability made their bases anything but secure. King thus enlisted a powerful ally for his concept.

Originally, he and the other members of the Joint Chiefs expected Operation Forager to take place in the October–November time frame. But the success of the Marshall operations speeded up the timetable to June. The same March 12 Joint Chiefs directive that had authorized MacArthur's Hollandia invasion also ordered Nimitz to proceed with the invasion of the Marianas. For this momentous task of seizing three fortified islands located thirty-five hundred miles away from Pearl Harbor, the circumspect admiral had a powerful array of forces at his disposal. Admiral Raymond Spruance's mighty Fifth Fleet was composed of more than six hundred ships, including eight major fleet carriers, seven light carriers, seven battleships, and twenty cruisers of varying tonnage. Vice Admiral Charles Lockwood's Task Force 17 added nineteen marauding and scouting submarines to the potent mix. They were all maintained by Vice Admiral William Calhoun's Service Force Pacific Fleet, a vast flotilla of oil tankers, store ships, ammunition ships, and the like. Spruance's warships required a minimum of 1.4 million gallons of fuel per two-week period just to maintain the momentum of basic operations. Calhoun had only nine provision ships outfitted to carry cargoes of fresh and dry foods, so he augmented this force with several Merchant Marine vessels, each of which could carry 348,000 cubic feet of refrigerated food, enough to feed ninety thousand men for a thirty-day period. The typical store ship carried forty thousand items, everything from vital spare parts to seemingly mundane—but, to sailors and troops, no less important—items like toilet paper.

A ground force of 105,859 troops was available to the commanders to take the three islands, of which 66,779 were earmarked to capture Saipan and Tinian; the rest were to seize Guam. The ground combat formations consisted of three Marine divisions, the 2nd, 3rd, and 4th, the 1st Provisional Marine Brigade, composed of two regimental combat teams, plus the Army's 27th and 77th Infantry Divisions. The 2nd and 4th Marine Divisions and the 27th Infantry Division were organized collectively into the V Amphibious Corps, and the rest into the III Amphibious Corps. The

V Amphibious Corps, plus attached amphibian, artillery, armor, and engineer units were known as the Northern Troops and Landing Force. Their mission was to take Saipan and Tinian. The III Amphibious Corps and its augmentations, under the command of Marine Major General Roy Geiger, were dubbed the Southern Troops and Landing Force and earmarked to take Guam. Technically, all the ground troops were commanded by Marine lieutenant general Holland Smith, the senior leatherneck in theater. He even had two staffs to oversee planning. In effect, though, Geiger conducted his operation independently and Smith focused on control of the Northern Troops and Landing Force.[2]

Feisty as ever, Holland Smith remained a relentless advocate for rapid amphibious operations, and he expected Forager to conform to that blueprint. By the middle of 1944, he had become a world leading authority on amphibious training and doctrine, the result of many years of erudition and practice over a nearly four-decade career. But mastery of doctrine does not always equate to mastery of combat command. Smith was keen to present himself as a grizzled, battle-wise combat Marine. In Hawaii, he made a point of wearing informal khaki utilities around naval officers clad in dress whites, as if he had little time for anything else but combat. "I . . . earned the reputation of being a cranky individualist who believed that in war we should dress like soldiers," he later wrote. A naval colleague once referred to him as "basically a show off. A great talker, he liked to dominate a conversation—and usually did so in a very loud voice." Garrulous and opinionated, with no apparent appreciation for how his incendiary words could adversely affect his working relationship with senior Navy and Army officers, Smith attempted to convey the notion that he felt more at ease in action than circulating among his fellow brass. "All I want to do is kill some Japs," he often growled ferociously to Captain Charles Moore, Spruance's chief of staff. "Just give me a rifle. I don't want to be a commanding general. I'll go out there and shoot some Japs. I want to fight the Japs."

Behind the facade, the actual record did not quite match up to this persona. Unlike almost all the Marines in whom he took such justified pride, he had never endured boot camp, nor any other strenuous training. Son of an affluent Alabama lawyer, he had originally followed his father into the profession before realizing that he possessed little talent or passion for the law. He earned his Marine Corps commission by passing a competitive written examination, as opposed to attending the United States Naval Academy or Officer Candidate School (the latter a practice that came into place several years after Smith became an officer). In thirty-eight years of consistently honorable and productive service, he had nonetheless logged very little time under fire, much less combat command. Invested with no actual command powers during the Gilbert campaign in November 1943, he had instead played the gadfly part of an informed, and extremely frustrated, observer. By contrast, Smith had commanded the ground formations for Operation Flintlock, the lightning campaign to seize control of the Marshall Islands. But the fighting had lasted only a few days, most of which Smith spent aboard ship. He could play the part of the gruff, world-weary combat Marine, in essence appropriating the extraordinary valor of the typical Marine in theater, but he had not really paid the price for this distinction. He blew hot and cold with his Army colleagues, sometimes engaging in convivial, jovial conversations, other times lashing them with fits of temper. Deep in his heart, he nursed a steady, corrosive, self-defeating germ of contempt for the Army as a whole, a scorn he generally expressed by touting Marines as akin to supermen by comparison. This chauvinistic attitude seeped through even during moments of levity— whatever his flaws, Smith had a keen, entertaining sense of humor—as when he told a joint group of Army, Navy, and Marine officers at a farewell dinner before leaving Hawaii, "It's nice of you Twenty-Seventh men to come along but you'll only come for the ride. The Marines can handle this job without any help."[3]

For the Saipan invasion, Smith opted for a two-division assault on the island's southwest coast by the 2nd and 4th Marine Divisions with the 27th Infantry Division as a floating reserve. All three units had battle experience. D-day was set for June 15. The job of moving three reinforced, combat-loaded divisions across thirty-five hundred miles of ocean required prodigious quantities of shipping, a total of 110 vessels, including 37 troop transports and 47 LSTs. They were to haul nearly seventy-five thousand tons of cargo, almost one-third more than for the Marshall invasions, occupying 7,845,194 cubic feet of space, a remarkable shipping total, given the nearly concurrent demands of the Normandy invasion, and a mute indicator of the US Navy's rise to global preeminence.

A tragic accident only added to the shipping pressures. On the afternoon of May 21 at Pearl Harbor's West Loch, where crews were feverishly loading ammunition and other stores onto berthed LSTs, a catastrophic chain reaction of explosions and fires swept through the closely moored vessels. Men were consumed by flames, drowned, blown to pieces, and shredded by waves of fragments and bullets as ammo cooked off. "I saw men drowning and pieces of steel hitting and killing them instantly," Marine private Charles Richardson later wrote to his sister. "I didn't even get a scratch but liked to have drowned helping a sailor." By the estimate of Samuel Eliot Morison, the Navy's official historian, the disaster cost 163 dead and 396 wounded, many of whom were badly burned. For days, bodies floated in the harbor. Retrieval parties fished them out and collected them at nearby Aiea Heights Naval Hospital for burial.

From a logistical standpoint, LSTs were the most precious vessels in the Allied inventory, owing to their considerable cargo and unloading capabilities. Six of them were destroyed and two others damaged too extensively to participate in Forager. Three Landing Craft, Tank (LCT) vessels, plus seventeen amphibious tractors (amtracs) and eight howitzers were destroyed. A naval investigation board could not precisely determine the cause of the explosions, primarily because most everyone who might have shed any light was killed. Undoubtedly, though, irresponsible smoking, fuel vapors, and the close proximity of volatile ammunition all played a role. One historian aptly commented that the LSTs had been "floating ammunition dumps, floating gasoline storage tanks, floating vehicle garages, floating ship repair yards, and floating overcrowded hotels." Incredibly, despite this disaster, American commanders and planners were still able to cobble together enough shipping to keep Operation Forager on the same schedule, a remarkable testament to the resilience and strength of the American armed forces by the summer of 1944.[4]

American intelligence gathering on Saipan and its garrison proved somewhat less robust. The Japanese had controlled the island since World War I, when as a member of the Allied coalition they had seized it and the rest of the Marianas, except Guam, from the Germans, something of an irony given their subsequent Second World War alliance with Germany. Further invested, in the postwar era, with control of the island chain by a League of Nations mandate, the Japanese had focused especially on colonizing Saipan. By the eve of World War II, the Japanese government had invested about 4.2 million dollars into the development of industry, infrastructure, and modernization of the island. Ethnic Japanese colonists, hailing primarily from Okinawa, and augmented by some Koreans, descended on Saipan in numbers, primarily to work in the sugarcane fields, to the point where they outnumbered the indigenous Chamorros and Carolinians. By 1941 the Asian newcomers made up three-quarters of the island's population of twenty-nine thousand people. Under their influence, the west coast village of Garapan grew into a Japanese-style modern town with schools, churches, temples, small businesses, and even forty-seven houses of prostitution. A statue of sugar expert Haruji Matsue stood proudly in the town's self-consciously named Central Park. Matsue had presided over the rise of an island industry that eventually produced twelve hundred tons of sugar per day. In this sense, the Japanese had come to view Saipan as not just the fulcrum of their Central Pacific defensive line but akin to their own soil.

The Americans knew very little about the place. For three decades, the Japanese had forbidden visits from Westerners, creating a kind of mysterious aura around Saipan. In America, febrile rumors—tantamount to the more modern phenomenon of urban legend—still swirled that the missing aviatrix Amelia Earhart had been incarcerated there, and perhaps executed, by the Japanese. On February 23, when naval aviators from Vice Admiral Marc Mitscher's powerful Task Force 58 flew the first American raids against Saipan, briefers could not even tell them the number and location of Japanese airfields. This strike and a subsequent raid by Eniwetok-based Navy PB4Ys and Army Air Forces B-24s on April 18 yielded only rudimentary photographs. The submarine USS *Greenling* took some coastal pictures but unfortunately not of the landing beaches. Subsequent aerial photo-reconnaissance missions flown between mid-April and mid-June, in addition to maps and other material captured during previous operations, did provide some useful information for the planners. They now knew that Saipan contained the major Aslito Airfield in the south, plus a small strip in the central part of the island, and another field under construction at Marpi Point on the north coast. Even so, the American battle maps for the invasion were inaccurate, almost to the point of uselessness, especially in relation to the topography. "Clouds, trees, and the angle at which the photos were taken helped hide the true nature of the terrain, so that many a cliff was interpreted on the map as a gentle slope," declared a post-battle intelligence report. The pictures largely failed to capture the reality of Saipan's rugged landscape. Given the paucity of tangible on-site information, the Americans struggled to determine the size and strength of Japanese forces on Saipan, a common problem in the Pacific War, owing primarily to the remoteness and exotic nature of many objectives, the paucity of on-the-ground human intelligence sources, and the resultant overreliance on information gathered by air and sea. In this case, Holland

Smith's intelligence section seriously underestimated enemy opposition. As of May 24, they estimated that Saipan was defended by, at most, eighteen thousand Japanese, of whom just over half were combat troops.

In truth, the garrison consisted of at least thirty thousand men, a polyglot force assembled over many months through adversity, chance, and sheer determination. For the first couple of years of the war, Saipan had been a backwater with only a skeletal military force. By early 1944, as the Allies advanced ever northward in the Pacific, the Japanese hurriedly began to reinforce Saipan as best they could. The ubiquity and effectiveness of American submarines along the sea-lanes from China and Japan greatly hindered these efforts. Troop ships were fortunate to make it through at all. About 10 percent of the forty thousand soldiers dispatched by the Tokyo government to the Marianas did not survive the trip. Many thousands of others survived sinkings but lost their weapons, equipment, key leaders, and at least some of their fighting effectiveness. In one cautionary example, submarines over a three-day period from May 30 to June 1 sank five of seven convoy ships carrying elements of the Imperial Army's 43rd Division, killing about 20 percent of the soldiers. The 118th Infantry Regiment alone lost 850 men beneath the waves. The two surviving vessels and other ships rescued the division's survivors and got them to Saipan, but as traumatized castaways in poor condition to fight rather than as a cohesive combat force. Major Takashi Hirakushi, a staff officer, saw many of them arrive and later described them as "almost all wounded, burned. Some died after being picked up."

Even those who made it through intact had to endure the protracted tension of negotiating circuitous routes to avoid the subs, as well as the privation of spartan conditions aboard ship. "We were laid out on shelves like broiler chickens," Sergeant Takeo Yamauchi, a former university student who had once studied Russian, later commented. "You had your pack, rifle, all your equipment with you. You crouched there, your body bent. Water dripped on you, condensation caused by human breathing. The hold stank of humanity. A few rope ladders and one narrow, hurriedly improvised stairway were the only ways out. We expected the ship to sink at any moment. We had little food to nibble for survival at sea." Japanese authorities attempted to evacuate civilians from Saipan to Japan, but many of them also fell victim to the marauding submarines. The USS *Nautilus*, for instance, torpedoed and sank the ironically named *America Maru*, a former hospital ship, en route to Japan with Japanese nationals, including the wife of Saipan's police chief. Of the 642 people aboard, only 43 survived. The deadly submarines made the job of fortifying Saipan and the other islands exponentially more difficult. Cargo ships carrying cement, building materials, ammunition, and weaponry had as much difficulty getting through as the troop ships. "The current freight shortage which is caused by shipping losses, has deprived the area of much needed materiel," a May 10 memo on the state of Japanese logistics in the Marianas complained. "One ship out of three is sunk, and a second damaged, by enemy action." Around the same time, another officer fumed that "we cannot strengthen the fortifications appreciably now unless we can get materials suitable for permanent construction. No matter how many soldiers there are, they can do nothing in regard to fortifications but sit around with their arms folded, and the situation is unbearable."

In spite of all the adversity, though, the Japanese still found a way to convene a large, diverse garrison of combat troops on Saipan, including most of the Imperial Army's 43rd Division, the 47th Independent Mixed Brigade, the 9th Tank Regiment, the 7th and 16th Independent Engineer Regiments, the 25th Antiaircraft Artillery Regiment, and the 3rd Mountain Artillery Regiment. They were augmented by the Imperial Navy's 5th Base Force, the 55th Naval Guard Force, a coastal artillery outfit, and the Yokosuka 1st Special Naval Landing Force, the latter the equivalent of an infantry battalion. Some of these units, such as a scratch battalion attached to the 47th Independent Mixed Brigade, were composed of survivors from sunken ships originally bound for other islands. The Imperial Navy's force totaled around six thousand men. They were charged with defending Garapan, the headquarters location of the Central Pacific Area Fleet, their parent unit (they were also assisted by a battalion from the 43rd Division's 136th Infantry Regiment). The Imperial Army's forces, totaling about twenty-five thousand soldiers under the command of the newly created 31st Army, were responsible for everything else. The improvised, diffuse nature of the garrison confounded American efforts to compile an accurate order of battle before and during the event.

Tension and hostility between the Imperial Army and Navy—a devastating handicap for Japan throughout the entire war—led to a nebulous, counterproductive command arrangement. Vice Admiral Chuichi Nagumo commanded the Central Pacific Area Fleet, whose misleading name obscured the reality of an administrative headquarters with no warships, few aircraft, and only the asset of ground combat manpower. Nagumo had once commanded the powerful Japanese strike forces that attacked Pearl Harbor and had subsequently fought at Midway and Guadalcanal. But his failure to inflict fatal damage on the US Pacific Fleet at Pearl Harbor, combined with bitter defeat at Midway and poor performance at Guadalcanal, had sent his career on a downward spiral that consigned him to this dead-end figurehead post. His army colleague of equivalent rank, Lieutenant General Hideyoshi Obata, was responsible for the defense of the Marianas, Bonins, Carolines, and Marshalls and yet had no authority over Nagumo. Obata and Nagumo concurred on autonomous control over their own service forces, but little else. As events progressed, Obata played no part in the Saipan battle because he happened to be on an inspection tour of the Palaus when the Americans invaded. Army seniority descended to Lieutenant General Yoshitsugu Saito, the 43rd Division commander, an Academy graduate and cavalry officer of sketchy health and average reputation. Saito outranked Obata's chief of staff, Major General Keiji Igeta, who remained on Saipan. Igeta technically answered to Saito, but their two headquarters often remained physically apart, prompting something of a parallel command situation. This lack of one undisputed commander created a tendency toward poor coordination and disorganization in the coming battle.

All these senior leaders did agree on the prevailing Japanese doctrine of defending at the waterline against amphibious invasions, a holdover from the fighting on small coral atoll islands, where it might actually have been possible to destroy the invaders in the water or on the beaches, when they were most vulnerable. But on the larger landmass islands of the Western and Central Pacific, bristling with caves, jungles, mountains, and valleys, and quite commonly expansive landing beaches as well, it made less sense. What was more, as long as the Americans enjoyed control of the air and sea, the chances of repelling them on the beaches remained minimal.

Claw-shaped Saipan was actually a volcanic mountain, most of which remained underwater. It was fourteen and a half miles long and six and a half miles wide, a seventy-two-square-mile space ringed partially by coral reefs and bordered mostly with impassable cliffs. A dizzying central spine of ravines, ridges, cliffsides, valleys, and hills, most notably 1,554-foot-high, steep-sided Mount Tapochau in the central southern area, presented much ideal defensive ground, almost as if volcanic nature had designed it as such. With the possible exception of crescent-shaped Magicienne Bay on the southeast coast, a six-thousand-yard strip of flat beaches from Afetna Point south of Garapan to Agingan Point on the southwestern coast were

the obvious landing areas for any invader. The Japanese naturally prioritized the defense of these beaches. A defense plan, circulated on May 10,
declared, "It is expected that the enemy will be destroyed on the beaches
through a policy of tactical command based on aggressiveness, determination and initiative. The main fire-power will be directed at the enemy landing forces prior to their arrival on the beach. Taking advantage of the
confusion, the enemy will be rapidly destroyed by counterattacks, mounted
from all sectors, wherever the opportunity presents itself." With even less
ambiguity, another planning document stated succinctly, "All the fighting
strength of the Army and Navy garrison will be combined to annihilate
the enemy on the beaches." If somehow the Americans did get ashore, a
doctrinal memo on island defense commanded that they be "destroyed at
the beach on the same day and not allowed to establish a foothold, as at
Dieppe." Following this vision, Saito deployed much of his first-line infantry at or near the beaches and his heavily camouflaged artillery inland,
dug into hills or caves, with forty-eight light and medium tanks of the 9th
Independent Tank Regiment positioned to react to landings on either
coast.

Though he preferred a layered defense, he had nowhere near enough
resources or time to bring this about. As May turned to June, his troops
labored intensively to build pillboxes, bunkers, mortar pits, gun pits, and
other fighting positions. Though unprepared as a whole for the invasion
and hampered by the inability to draw reliable reinforcements and supplies, Saito's force remained distressingly potent, especially in machine
guns, antitank and antiaircraft weapons, large coastal guns, and heavy
artillery. The landing beaches, for instance, were defended by thirty
machine-gun posts, plus multiple gun batteries ranging from 25 to 75 millimeters in caliber. The inland artillery ranged dramatically from
75-millimeter pieces to 200-millimeter high-trajectory guns capable of
savaging landing craft and armor. With the possible exception of the Philippines in 1941–1942, this was undoubtedly the most formidable array of
Japanese artillery that Americans had yet faced in the Pacific War. By early
June, American intelligence had detected a one-third increase from only a
few weeks earlier in the presence of medium and heavy antiaircraft guns
and crew-served machine guns, as well as the presence of thirty-seven pillboxes. The willingness of Saito's men to lay down their lives, come what
may, probably represented his greatest asset. "Despite the apparent deficiencies of the defensive installations and plans, one vital characteristic of

a good defense was present," the leading Marine historian of the battle insightfully wrote. "The individual defender was determined to hold the island and was willing to give his life to realize this end." Indeed, in light of how the battle unfolded, one shudders to imagine the kind of damage that Saipan's defenders might have inflicted had they not been so tormented by American submarines and, in general, naval and air power.[5]

All over the impossibly vast American-controlled Pacific, from Guadalcanal to Hawaii, the US armada set sail and began to assemble throughout late May. The V Amphibious Corps left the Hawaiian Islands in staggered waves, with the two Marine divisions leading the way on May 29, and the 27th Division following on June 1. The soldiers were impressed by the sobering sight of USS *Oklahoma,* a victim of the Pearl Harbor attack, now under salvage. "We could read her name plainly on the fantail and her big guns were all in sight," PFC Seymour Krawetz later recalled. Once at sea, the troops learned their destination. "Each day was spent with all hands studying maps, charts, intelligence reports, plans of attack, alternate plans, and even the customs of the natives of Saipan," Major Max LaGrone, a staff officer with the 2nd Marine Division, wrote. Aboard the attack transport USS *Cavalier,* forty-four-year-old Lieutenant Colonel William O'Brien, commander of the 1st Battalion, 105th Infantry Regiment, briefed his troops over the ship's loudspeaker, repeatedly emphasizing the phrase "Target Saipan!" On June 6, they were excited to hear news of the Normandy invasion. The 27th Division briefings were especially complex because, as the floating reserve, the unit had to prepare for many potential missions. "By the time this trip is over, we should know Saipan as we know our own home town," quipped Tech 3 Vincent Donnolo, a medic with the 105th Infantry Regiment, 27th Infantry Division, to his diary. Major General Ralph Smith and his staff drew up nineteen separate operational plans covering nearly every possible landing contingency on Saipan, plus potential participation in invasions of Tinian and Guam.

As the voyage proceeded over the course of two weeks, the novelty of the briefings gave way to the monotony of shipboard life. Enlisted men spent most of their time belowdecks, lying in bunks that stretched five high. "Packed sardines have nothing on us," Donnolo moaned. Some bored Marines stole yeast, potato peels, and sugar from the galley and fermented the mixture into a powerful booze that they disseminated among members of their unit. Most men filled the endless hours with card games, dice games, reading, and bull sessions. "The holds always smelled terrible," PFC Charles Hilbert of the 27th Division later wrote, comparing them to "a cattle ship." Officer staterooms were more comfortable but still crowded. No privacy of any kind existed anywhere. Space was at such a premium that seldom could any commander convene more than a platoon-size group for briefings or training. Drinking water came from fifty-five-gallon drums affixed with spigots. Bathing was confined to saltwater showers. "The Navy furnished us a special soap to use, but it didn't work," Hilbert said. "The soap stuck to our skin. It was better to just run the salt water over us and dry off with a towel." Men attempted to keep their uniforms clean by tying them to ropes and letting them flap in the wind from ships' sterns. The troops stood in line twice a day for meals, more than a few of which were then regurgitated due to inevitable seasickness. The lavatories—or "heads" in Navy parlance—of all too many troop ships were slicked with a bubbled coating of vomit, salt water, and urine. At one point aboard the attack transport USS *Arthur Middleton*, food poisoning swept through the ranks of the 2nd Battalion, 2nd Marine Regiment, crowding the ship's heads so badly that many of the afflicted were forced to throw up wherever they could. "The smell above and below decks was worse than the stench from my uncle's pig farm," PFC Red Butler commented. Medics dispensed paregoric to hundreds of sailors and Marines. Anyone who avoided the food poisoning, officers included, was pressed into duty hosing vomit off the decks. No matter the ship, the ground troops had nowhere near enough space to maintain any sort of training or physical fitness program. "There was a noticeable deterioration in the physical condition of the men," a Canadian Army observer later reported to his superiors. "Transports were crowded, deck space being limited by the landing craft and deck cargo carried. Below deck, the quarters were quite warm and humid." A post-operation report by one 27th Division regiment observed more succinctly that "the troops were rather softened up."[6]

The original Forager plan called for Vice Admiral Mitscher's Task Force 58 carrier planes to hit targets in the Marianas after dawn on June 12. But due to good weather and the ensuing speed of the convoy, he asked Admiral Spruance for permission to strike on the afternoon of June 11, when Mitscher anticipated he might catch the Japanese by surprise, since most previous American carrier-based strikes had occurred in the early morning. Spruance readily assented. Hard-edged and aggressive, a fighter to the core, Mitscher sent a fiery message to his aviators. "Cut their damned throats. Wish I could be with you." At 1300 on June 11, the first of 225 planes took off from their carriers. They spent the afternoon strafing and bombing airfields on Rota, Guam, Tinian, and Saipan, achieving near total surprise. On Saipan, they focused primarily on the Aslito Airfield, Tanapag Harbor, Marpi Point on the north coast, and Garapan. Air raid sirens wailed. Antiaircraft guns whomped in a steady cadence. Bombs exploded. Opposing planes grappled in deadly dogfights. A group of Japanese staff officers was so confused by the melee that they cheered the sight of several burning planes plummeting to earth, wrongly thinking them American. They realized the truth when a low-flying F6F Hellcat fighter plane zoomed in overhead and strafed a nearby communications unit.

Elsewhere, Sergeant Tarao Kawaguchi and his fellow NCOs were preparing a meal "and didn't have a chance to take cover in the air raid shelter." Standing guard at his battalion headquarters, Sergeant Takeo Yamauchi watched as American fighters shot down multiple Japanese planes and seemingly strafed at will. "Whole sections of the mountains were burned black and the island was dark with smoke." Though some soldiers fired rifles or machine guns at the American planes, most, like Private Tokuzo Matsuya of the 9th Tank Regiment, felt powerless to do anything to stop them. "All we could do was watch helplessly," he lamented to his diary. Watching the strange planes from his family ranch, eighteen-year-old Gregorio Cabrera, like many other locals, was terrified by the onslaught and took shelter anywhere he could. "The Japanese said they were going to the mountains, so my whole family went with them . . . to Mount Topatchau." A shaken Sergeant Kawaguchi told his diary, "Although our AA [antiaircraft] put up a terrific barrage and our planes intercepted them, it seems that the damage was considerable." In the raids, the Americans lost 11 fighters with 6 pilots killed or missing. The fliers destroyed or damaged 147 Japanese planes, a crippling blow to Japanese aviation in the Marianas. "Control of the air had been effected by the original fighter sweep on 11 June," Admiral Nimitz correctly asserted in a postinvasion action report. Mitscher's predators followed this up with two more days of intensive attacks, degrading Japanese aerial capability and resistance all the more. "Practically all of [our aircraft] were wiped out," Captain Mitsuo Fuchida, an air staff officer with the Combined Fleet, admitted to American interrogators after the war.

Enjoying freedom of movement to approach the Saipan coast without fear of losing ships from Japanese air attacks, the invasion fleet closed to within bombardment distance by June 13. Invasion commanders hoped to find out more about the coral reefs that ringed the landing beaches, creating a potentially perilous lagoon that the landing craft must traverse to get to shore. For this mission of reconnoitering the reefs, removing mines and obstacles, and gathering information on the depth of lagoon waters, the Navy had created the Underwater Demolition Teams (UDTs), composed of intensively trained specialists who excelled at swimming, scouting, and the handling of explosives.

Colloquially known throughout the American armed forces as "frogmen," their professional Moses was Lieutenant Commander Draper Kauffman, a resourceful, courageous 1933 Naval Academy graduate with vision so poor that he came to rely on colleagues to identify objects in the water for him, no small matter for a man whose job depended, in part, on the gathering of data through observation. The son of a vice admiral, Kauffman had established a training center for frogmen at Fort Pierce, Florida, personally overseeing the selection and preparation of many of the men he led into combat. At Saipan, he controlled a pair of ninety-six-man UDTs, with another in reserve. Staging from destroyer transports, clad only in swimming fins and trunks, two teams clambered aboard eight landing craft just after sunrise on the morning of June 14. To facilitate the measuring of accurate water depth, each man's body was painted head to toe with thick black rings and smaller lines at intervals of one foot or less over a blue base. Thus turned into flesh-and-blood yardsticks, they needed only to stand in the water to measure its depth. Kauffman had reservations about the obvious dangers of a daylight mission. But Vice Admiral Richmond Kelly Turner, the tempestuous but brilliant and highly experienced commander of Task Force 51, the Joint Expeditionary Force that transported and would land the troops, insisted that only in daylight could Kauffman's people see well enough to gather any useful information.

Beneath the steel umbrella of a friendly bombardment from at least half a dozen battleships, six heavy cruisers, five light cruisers, and over two dozen destroyers, plus machine guns from the landing craft, the UDTs hit the reefs shortly after daylight. The Japanese responded with machine-gun, rifle, and mortar fire. "The bullets would only zip into the water a couple of feet and then just sink to the bottom," one of the frogmen later recalled. Heavier-caliber Japanese guns fired at the bombardment ships, forcing many of them, including the USS *California*, which got hit and lost one man killed and nine wounded, to take evasive maneuvers. Kauffman's swimmers calmly set to work, gathering crucial information on tides, beach defenses, water depth in the lagoon and over the reefs, and even the beaches themselves. Watching from the vantage point of the bridge aboard the cruiser USS *Birmingham*, Captain Thomas Inglis, the skipper, formed the opinion that "their work was about as hazardous as anything that can be imagined." A planned air strike from carrier planes at 1000 failed to materialize—they were diverted to other targets—but the frogmen continued undeterred. In the course of the day, they placed tetratol explosives in some spots over reefs to make them easier to traverse for amphibious vehicles, and gathered a wealth of information.

By the time the landing craft returned them to their ships, Kauffman had lost four men killed and five wounded, significantly lighter casualties than he had anticipated. Kauffman brought largely good news to his superiors. Though the water was a bit deeper than planners expected, the fleet of seven hundred LVTs scheduled to ferry the assault troops ashore could still easily make their way over the reefs and across the lagoon. The lagoon distance varied from five hundred to one thousand yards. The Japanese had placed no mines or obstacles in the path of the invaders. Visual observation by the frogmen confirmed the location and composition of numerous pillboxes, trench lines, and fighting positions on the landing beaches that aerial reconnaissance photographs had previously revealed. "Their skill, determination and courage are deserving of the highest praise," an admiring Vice Admiral Turner wrote of the UDT swimmers.

Not all their discoveries boded well, though. They found that the planned route through the lagoon for the 2nd Marine Division's specially waterproofed tanks was two feet deeper than photographs had indicated. Lieutenant Commander Kauffman knew that few if any would make it through the deeper water, so he staked out a different route slightly to the south. One might have expected the division commander, Major General Thomas Watson, to commend an officer who had risked his life to prevent the useless loss of numerous tanks and lives. Instead, the abrasive Watson sharply questioned Kauffman. "What the hell is this I hear about your changing the route for my tanks?" Watson stubbornly insisted on maintaining the original route.

"General, they'll never get through there," Kauffman calmly rejoined, and showed him the water depth on charts that one of his draftsmen had just prepared.

Fortunately, Watson had the good sense to yield to reality. "Well, all right," he replied. "But, young man, you're going to lead that first tank in, and you'd better be damned sure that every one of them gets there safely, without drowning out." And so he did.[7]

On June 15, D-day, the bombardment began at 0530. To Sergeant Yamauchi, staring with bulging eyes at the American ships, the enemy fleet looked like "a large city had appeared offshore. When I saw that, I didn't even have the strength to stand up." Vice Admiral Turner had carefully divided Saipan and neighboring Tinian into seven firing sectors and organized his bombardment ships to shell targets inside these tightly prepared windows. For an hour and a half, they showered their targets with a variety of ordnance, ranging from the five-inch shells of destroyers to sixteen-inch projectiles from USS *Maryland*'s main guns, a breathtaking spectacle of firepower. "There are few things prettier than a naval bombardment, provided one is on the sending not the receiving end and (as in this case) has lost all feeling of compassion for the human victims," Morison, the naval historian, wrote sagely. "Nearby ships belch great clouds of saffron smoke with a mighty roar. Distant ones are inaudible, but their flashes of gunfire leap out like the angry flick of a snake's tongue." Sergeant David Dempsey, a Marine Corps combat correspondent, watched "the shells bite into the coral sand and shred the palm trees that lined the shore." Explosions pulverized buildings in Garapan and Charan Kanoa, a sugar mill town located in the heart of the 4th Marine Division landing area. Flames raged all over the island. Mount Topatchau boiled with so many fires as to obscure it with smoke. The ships ceased firing and yielded to air strikes from 0700 to 0800. As Dempsey watched, transfixed, the planes "peeled off, and plummeted savagely down, dropping their bombs a few hundred feet from the ground. As they began their climb the explosions threw bursts of fire, rubble and a talcum-fine dust into the air. In a few minutes the beach was obscured."

When the planes finished, the ships resumed their fire against beach targets while hundreds of LVTs, all packed with Marines, headed for the coast. A gray-brown pall of smoke and dust had settled over Saipan like a veil. "The flames are miles high," Seaman William Schmidt, a crewman aboard LST 120, later wrote to his parents, with a touch of exaggeration. "It's a reassuring sight." On the receiving end, Japanese defenders clustered into trenches, pillboxes, dugouts, bunkers, caves, and holes to weather the firepower storm as best they could. "There was no way of coping with the explosions," Private Matsuya of the 9th Tank Regiment noted in his diary. "We could do nothing but wait for them to stop." Another soldier described the shelling as "too terrible for words" but took solace in the notion that he would "die in true Samurai style." In hopes of soothing shattered nerves, one young naval officer took solace in alcohol. "There is something indescribable about a shot of liquor during a bombardment," he told his diary with a surreal honesty that might have been funny under less dangerous circumstances. Sergeant Kawaguchi's medical unit set up an aid station at a Shinto shrine, where they began to care for men who were wounded by the shells. He admired his commanding officer, who "performed bravely and courageously treating the patients under terrific naval barrage and he should be considered an ideal model for the medics section." Most of the locals fled inland away from the obvious targets or took shelter in caves. Twelve-year-old Felipe Ruak's family could find nowhere to hide until charitable strangers welcomed them into a small cave. "They gave us water and some ripe bananas. I don't remember their names, but they were a Chamorro family and they were very nice."

The punishing barrage restricted Japanese mobility, disrupted their communications, and caused casualties but did not inflict as much damage, especially along the beaches, as the Americans might have hoped. "Those observation posts and gun emplacements that were protected by splinter-proof bomb shelters were able to withstand the bombardment," a Japanese artillery captain assessed in a report to higher headquarters. "Dummy positions proved very effective. During bombardment, both day and night, movement to alternate positions was very difficult. The need for repairs and messengers was great." Major General Igeta sent a message to Tokyo assuring the high command that "units are prepared for the enemy landing, morale is high and we are in complete readiness." Vice Admiral Nagumo urged his sailors to make every sacrifice to stop the invasion in its tracks. "Every man will mobilize his full powers to annihilate the enemy on the beach, to destroy his plan and to hold our country's ramparts." Typical of so many determined Japanese defenders, one young soldier told his diary in a last-minute notation, "We are waiting with 'Molotov cocktails' and hand grenades ready for the word to rush forward recklessly into the enemy ranks with our swords in our hands. All that worries me is what will happen to Japan after we die."

Between 0830 and 0840, the LVTs carrying the assault troops closed in on Saipan's southwest coast. Many of the men had bellies full of steak, eggs, bacon, pancakes, and other goodies from generous preinvasion feasts. Chaplains had conducted last-minutes services, heard confessions, and broadcast sober prayers over ships' loudspeaker systems. Robert Sherrod, the war correspondent, heard one of them say, with tone-deaf insensitivity, "Most of you will return, but some of you will meet the God who made you. Repent your sins." A lieutenant colonel standing next to Sherrod turned to him and cynically quipped, "Perish-the-thought department." Aboard one LVT, or amtrac, a distressed Marine, undoubtedly dwelling on that very terrifying thought, panicked and began screaming, "We'll all be killed!" over and over, prompting three men to hold him down while his sergeant finally calmed him.

The leading waves of the two Marine divisions made it over the reefs in reasonably good order. The pummeling by American ships and planes had nonetheless left far too many beachside pillboxes, trench lines, and bunkers in action, not to mention most inland gun positions. From the lagoon to the beaches, the LVTs soon ran into a maelstrom of fire. "The Nips were very upset about the whole thing and before our boat hit the beach, they started throwing everything they had at us," Private Charles Harvey of the 2nd Marine Division later wrote, with a whiff of dry derision, to his family. "Artillery shells and mortars and machine guns and I think some old shoes went over my head." In a matter of twenty minutes, some seven hundred LVTs—almost half of which came from Army amphibian units—landed eight thousand Marines along a crowded six-thousand-yard expanse of beach, a powerful invasion force but one that presented the Japanese with an incredible volume of nearly unmissable targets. "Hidden guns on hill and shore opened up to pour destruction such as none had seen before," Army sergeant Frank Madzey, a crewman in D Company, 708th Amphibian Tank Battalion, later wrote with poetic flair. "The Jap defenses in the town of Charan Kanoa were a lot tougher than we had anticipated and their artillery and mortar fire was too accurate," Sergeant Charles Kohler, a tanker in the 4th Division, commented. Watching from the perspective of LST 120's bow ramp, Seaman Schmidt saw assault troops go down in droves. "All hell breaks loose and the crossfire is terrific." To Private Carl Matthews, "the beach was a madhouse with individual Marines trying to find cover." He watched in horror as a retreating LVT ran over the leg of one of his squad mates.

Shells scored hits on a few amtracs. In Sergeant Dempsey's recollection, the burning vehicles "were flopped over like pancakes on a griddle." Marines scrambled over the sides of their amtracs, splashed their way through hip-deep water, hid in shell craters and hastily dug foxholes, or crawled along the sand and bramble, dodging clouds of fragments and bullets. "Shells were exploding all around me," Private Charles Richardson, who had survived the West Loch disaster three weeks earlier, wrote to his sister. "I saw several of my best friends get blown to pieces. Still I hadn't gotten a scratch. Of course, I was scared." To another Marine survivor, the shells seemed to explode "in an almost rhythmical patter, every twenty-five yards, every fifteen seconds." The 4th Marine Division's after-action report described shelling of such volume that "its intensity never varied in the slightest amount." In many instances, small groups of Americans and Japanese clashed face-to-face, usually in trenches or inside pillboxes, fighting to the death with rifles, pistols, grenades, and even knives or bayonets. Accurate enemy rifle fire tore into individual Marines. "The whole beachhead was alive with snipers," Major LaGrone later wrote.

Armored tractors, many of which hailed from the Army's 708th Amphibian Tank Battalion, helped the Americans lash back. Known as LVT(A)s, or amtanks, and specially fitted with 37- or 75-millimeter guns, they supported the beleaguered assault troops as best they could. The amtank crewmen were mostly tankers retrained for this amphibious-centered job. Their vehicles consisted of LVTs fitted with a quarter to half an inch of protective armor, at least one .50- or .30-caliber machine gun, and of course a main gun turret. Of the 708th's sixty-eight first-wave amtanks earmarked to assist the 4th Marine Division, all but three made it ashore and plunged into the beachhead fight alongside small groups of Marines. "Observation was limited to about fifteen yards," one platoon leader recalled, "and it is a frightening thing to go into something you cannot see, so the tanks stopped momentarily. The beach . . . was receiving a lot of shellfire, and it was urgent that the tanks move inland."

Typically, they fired a few shots, advanced ten yards, halted, and then fired again, progressing at something of a crawl. The amtanks provided this welcome fire support but proved vulnerable to enemy artillery fire and close-quarters attacks from Japanese infantrymen wielding grenades or machine guns. Some became separated from the infantry and, in the recollection of one commander, "those elements which were engaged in cleaning up behind the first three waves found themselves pinned down by heavy mortar and artillery fire." Every bit as commonly, they experienced engine trouble or became bogged down in the craters or marshes of the jagged landscape, or simply got swamped by the onrushing surf. In the course of the day's fighting, the 708th lost eight amtanks destroyed by enemy fire, another six damaged, and seven from other causes. Crew losses amounted to twelve killed, eighty-three wounded, and five missing.

Against the furious, persistent Japanese resistance, the two Marine divisions succeeded in carving out a lodgement about one thousand yards inland and ten thousand yards in length. They also defeated a poorly coordinated but determined Japanese nighttime counterattack, with tanks, that Lieutenant General Saito hoped might snuff out the nascent US beachhead. The courageous Marines paid a heavy price to avert this crisis and establish the Americans firmly ashore. The 2nd Marine Division alone lost at least 238 killed, 315 missing, many of whom were dead, and 1,022 wounded, a steeper price than the 1st Infantry Division had paid nine days earlier to take its three-mile sector of Omaha Beach in Normandy. The commanders of all four of the 2nd Division's first-wave assault battalions were wounded. The 4th Marine Division added another 800 casualties to the sobering toll. By a conservative estimate, D-day at Saipan cost the Americans about 2,500 men killed, wounded, and missing. Artillery and mortars did most of the damage. Nor did this include the uncounted number of combat fatigued who, in the recollection of one observer, "hid behind trees and cowered at each new shell burst. Some could not remember their names." Given the terrible losses, the two hard-pressed divisions had needed a maximum effort just to establish themselves ashore and fend off the fierce enemy attacks. African-American Marines from support units fought bravely alongside whites from line outfits. "Their prime mission was to unload ammunition and supplies on the beach but they were needed," Sergeant Kohler, the tanker, told his parents in a post-battle letter.

The sheer volume of casualties was so shockingly heavy that it overwhelmed the evacuation capacity of the landing fleet. A quartet of dedicated hospital ships was not scheduled to arrive until June 18. In the meantime, Navy corpsmen and doctors tended to wounded men as best they could and piled them aboard LVTs that shuttled them to the reef where hard-pressed LCVP and LCM crewmen transferred them to their own craft and thence to overwhelmed LSTs or transports. The huge numbers of wounded men forced the caregivers to work quickly to save as many lives as possible. Sergeant Dempsey, the correspondent, watched in horrified fascination as a doctor amputated a man's leg "without removing him from the stretcher." PFC Carl Carlson, an amtank driver, survived a direct hit on his vehicle that killed the majority of his crewmates. The ship where he was treated seemed to him "worse than a butcher shop. They had to wash the deck down with a hose all the time from the blood and stuff." Many of those who expired aboard the ships were then simply committed to the deep. "Just a quick simple burial," Seaman Schmidt related to his parents, "the bodies lying on the [forecastle] in canvas bags weighed with anchor chain links. A flag covered each body. The captain read the funeral service while all of the crewmembers who could be spared attended in deep reverence. The bugler blew 'taps' and the men were consigned to their watery graves."[8]

By daylight on June 16, about twenty thousand Americans were ashore on Saipan. That morning, Admiral Spruance met with General Holland Smith and Admiral Turner aboard the USS *Rocky Mount*, Turner's flagship. During the night, Spruance had received reports from the submarines USS *Flying Fish* and USS *Seaborne* that a powerful Japanese fleet was steaming east from the Philippines, heading straight for the Marianas. The admiral immediately sensed that the Japanese intended to seek out his fleet for a major engagement, and he was correct. The day before, Admiral Soemu Toyoda, commander of the Imperial Navy's Combined Fleet, had formally issued the directive for A-Go, the plan to seek out a decisive battle with the US Navy in the Pacific. Originally, the Japanese had intended to carry out this fight at Biak, but the Fifth Fleet's movement to the Marianas and the landings at Saipan offered the prospect of bigger game, so they reoriented in this direction, albeit at the expense of the Kon reinforcement operation at Biak.

The developing naval situation, along with the intense Japanese resistance to the invaders at Saipan, prompted Spruance to reorient, with the concurrence of Turner and Smith, his own plans. They postponed the Guam landings, originally scheduled to take place on June 18, for some unspecified later date. Leaving in place some of Turner's older battleships, cruisers, and destroyers off Saipan's west coast to provide cover fire for the ground troops and fend off the possibility of a flanking enemy end run for Saipan, Spruance now detached most of his remaining strike assets, including Mitscher's potent Task Force 58, to sail west to take on Toyoda's approaching forces. The unloading of supplies and reinforcements from LSTs and other vessels would continue through the end of daylight on June 17. Then these ships were to move east of the Marianas beyond the reach of the Japanese. At the same time, escort carriers positioned safely to the east of the islands would provide air cover for the Marines. Quite sensibly, Holland Smith suggested landing as many troops as possible before the exit of Turner's ships. "My policy regarding reserves is that it always is better to get them on the beach rather than have them sitting out at sea on ships," he later wrote. Indeed, aboard ships they remained uncomfortable, marginalized, always vulnerable to enemy air or sea attacks. Onshore, they were in their true element as ground combat troops. Spruance and Turner agreed on this issue with Smith. Both accepted the wisdom of getting all ground troops ashore as soon as possible. So the V Amphibious Corps commander set in motion plans to begin landing the 27th Infantry Division. Before he and Spruance parted that morning, the admiral correctly opined of the Japanese, "They are out after big game. The attack on the Marianas is too great a challenge for the Japanese Navy to ignore."

All this, of course, served as preamble for the Battle of the Philippine Sea, fought primarily on June 19–20, when Spruance's forces destroyed at least 426 Imperial Navy planes, nearly annihilating the enemy's aviation arm, and sank two of Japan's major carriers plus one light carrier, a one-sided victory that eliminated any possibility that the Japanese might reinforce their beleaguered Mariana garrisons.[9]

Major General Ralph Smith, meanwhile, received orders from corps around midday on June 16 to land his 165th and 105th Infantry Regiments, and as much of the division's artillery as possible. At this point, his other infantry regiment, the 106th, was unavailable, floating far away as a reserve with the southern landing forces the commanders had earmarked to invade Guam. Though the six transport ships bearing the 165th and 105th had by now closed to within sight of Saipan's southwest coast, the reality of the circumstances made a smooth, coordinated landing unlikely, if not impossible. Communication among the various headquarters, much less ship to ship, was spotty and fragmentary. Commanders needed several hours to organize their units, coordinate egress with landing craft crewmen, move the troops from ship to craft, and get them going.

This confused process consumed most of the remaining daylight hours of June 16. As a consequence, much of the ship-to-shore movement, particularly for the 165th, took place in darkness, adding substantially to the natural disarray of such a hasty, uncertain enterprise. To make matters worse, the beachhead remained under the intense pressure of Japanese counterattacks. Few areas could be considered by the Americans as secure. Cryptic warnings had circulated among the Marines of imminent nocturnal Japanese amphibious landings. Holland Smith's headquarters had alerted, by radio, both Marine divisions that the 27th was coming ashore, but the news barely traveled much beyond headquarters. "The coxswains and boat crews were as unfamiliar with routes of approach to the beach as the troops they were carrying," Captain Edmund Love, a combat historian attached to the 27th, and probably the finest chronicler of the Saipan battle, later wrote. "A stretch of water [was] filled with hundreds of craft of all types. Fire support ships were stationed along the route and were pouring fire at enemy installations ashore. Complete darkness enveloped everything, and no one seemed to know exactly what the situation was towards shore. Traffic was in a continual jam."

Any semblance of organization disintegrated. Boats wandered for hours, trying to make their way to the reef, sometimes narrowly averting collisions or friendly-fire incidents with other vessels. Soldiers huddled together in misery, nauseous from seasickness and fumes. "I will never forget the smell of diesel fuel as the air was pretty heavy with it," Sergeant John Domanowski recalled. Once at the reef, weary crewmen simply deposited the GIs into waist-deep water with a curt "Good luck, Soldier," and vague instructions to wade the rest of the way to the beach. Unit cohesion and organization were either fragmentary or nonexistent. To the Marines ashore, straining their eyes in the inky blackness with only the light of an occasional flare as illumination, the approaching soldiers seemed like menacing phantoms emanating from the waves. If not for the discipline of one alert sentry, who verbally challenged an Army captain, they might well have opened fire and decimated the better part of one especially vulnerable arriving battalion.

Once ashore, and added to the embattled Marine perimeter, the prospect of attempting to move inland in the darkness bordered on lunacy. Many of the soldiers simply hunkered down wherever they could find openings along the beach. "In some cases infantrymen were forced to lie there with their feet in the water," Love wrote. "Every wave that came ashore soaked them from the waist down." Another battalion commander, who somehow managed to organize most of his outfit, spent the night carefully leading his column of soldiers southward along the beach, past innumerable Marine fighting holes, each time taking cover rapidly and identifying himself and his outfit in response to their challenges, an excruciating and exhausting process. By the estimate of one rifleman, the battalion "hit the dirt at least three hundred times" during the night. Company guides called out unit identifications softly in the blackness, hoping to corral the many individuals who were wandering lost, separated from their chains of command. "No man present will forget that night," one officer later wrote; "there will be more than the memories of blackness and the unknown. There will be the memory of crunching on sand and [of] the inland darkness, the voices of Marines who had been through hours of hell." In one encounter typical of many others, when one Marine greeted a newly arrived group of soldiers, he exhaled with relief and said, "Thank God, we been needing you bad."

As the hours unfolded and darkness gave way to the half-light of a new morning, many of the soldiers began to see grisly remnants of the invasion. Charan Kanoa lay in smoldering ruins; the sugar mill smokestack poked defiantly through the maze of demolished stone buildings. Smashed weapons, wrecked equipment, burning vehicles, and much worse detritus littered the area. "There were bodies floating around in the water," Sergeant Felix Giuffre recalled with a shudder. "Some of them were Japanese and some were Marines." Private Frank Standarski claimed that he and his squad mates actually had to push bodies aside to get off the beach. Already, maggots coated the bloated corpses. Surveying the ghastly scene, a horrified Tech 3 Donnolo took a moment to scrawl in his diary, "Boy, they stink. What holds true of the Jap dead holds true of our own dead. Saw quite a few Marine bodies litter the beach. The dead all smell the same. Felt like vomiting." He was not alone. According to Lieutenant Colonel Van Antwerp, "the smell . . . was so bad that at times men in close proximity to the cause became actively ill." The carcasses of cows, pigs, dogs, goats, and horses only added to the stench. "They were all bloated, stinking to high heaven," PFC Hilbert later wrote. So suffocating was the odor that it seemed to infuse the C ration meals consumed by many of the arriving soldiers for breakfast or lunch, leaving, in the recollection of one man "a bad taste in the mouth." Heaps of ammunition and food crates, water cans, vehicles, and other supplies, all landed seemingly at random in the midst of the fighting, choked the beaches. "It is a thundering wonder that some of our piled-up ammunition didn't 'go' because of all the shelling," Tech 5 James Warthen, a radioman, later wrote. Supply sergeants from newly arrived 27th Division units stalked the area, brazenly stealing food, ammunition, and water from Marine dumps. As one sergeant made off with several drums of water and searched for more, "half of *his* water had been stolen by other supply parties out on the prowl," Captain Love recorded.

By midafternoon on June 17, most of the two infantry regiments, plus three artillery battalions, division headquarters, and assorted attachments, were ashore and organized into some semblance of cohesion, though much of the 27th's motor transport, communications equipment, supplies, and other necessities remained aboard ship. Regardless, the newly arrived units moved into place on the 4th Marine Division's southern flank. Together, they thrust inland toward the Aslito Airfield. Having tried and failed to push the Americans into the sea, Lieutenant General Saito had little in southern Saipan to place in their way. Japanese resistance was sharp but fragmentary, reflecting the reality that the Americans had penetrated the hard crust of Saito's coastal defenses. After less than a day of fighting, Colonel Gerard Kelley's 165th Infantry Regiment took the airfield intact at 1016 on June 18. According to Lieutenant Colonel John Lemp, an Army Ground Forces observer, Aslito "was taken so fast it was found in relatively good condition with some Zero planes behind revetments in perfect condition." Kelley's people renamed it "Conroy Field" after Kelley's predecessor, Colonel Gardiner Conroy, who had been killed in the Battle of Makin. However, bowing to a newly established tradition of naming airfields after fallen aviators, the Americans subsequently renamed the base "Isely Field" after Lieutenant Commander Robert Isely, who had been killed several days before while strafing it.[10]

A nihilistic mood, undoubtedly stemming from the growing realization among Japanese senior leaders of the crisis they now faced in the Marianas, prevailed among high-command circles. Prime Minister Hideki Tojo, the Imperial Army general who more than anyone else had led Japan into war, and whose bespectacled visage represented to the American public the embodiment of aggressive Japanese militarism, sent a fiery message to the Saipan garrison: "Because the fate of the Japanese empire depends on the result of your operation, inspire the spirit of the officers and men and to the very end continue to destroy the enemy gallantly and persistently, thus alleviate the anxiety of our Emperor." Emperor Hirohito himself chimed in with his own blunt message. "You must hold Saipan." Major General Igeta replied with a similar mix of flowery patriotism and self-sacrificial determination so characteristic of Japanese military leaders in this war. "We are grateful for boundless magnanimity of the Imperial favor. By becoming the bulwark of the Pacific with 10,000 deaths we hope to requite the Imperial favor."

With Saipan's key objective now in American hands and Spruance's Fifth Fleet in the process of inflicting a devastating defeat on the Imperial Navy, the Japanese were ensnared in serious strategic dire straits. Even so, their courageous commitment to fight ferociously to the death and inflict heavy casualties upon the Americans remained a potent asset. The menacing motto "Shichisei Hokoku," loosely translated as "Seven Lives for the Fatherland"—meaning that every soldier must kill at least seven enemy before sacrificing himself—circulated among the ranks.

Saito cobbled together a new defensive line from Garapan across the slopes of Mount Tapochau to Magicienne Bay on the east coast, all defended by 15,000 men. About 1,250 other survivors from a mishmash of units, including the 317th Independent Infantry Battalion and the 25th Antiaircraft Artillery Regiment, found themselves behind American lines when the 2nd and 4th Marine Divisions swung northwest to assault Saito's new line. Heedless of being cut off, these military orphans simply took to the jagged cliffs, caves, and hills of Nafutan Point—a peninsula of ideal defensive terrain—on Saipan's southeastern coast to hold out as long as possible. One of Saito's men, exemplifying the attitude of so many others, confided to his diary that "if I see the enemy, I will take out my sword and slash, slash, slash at him as long as I last, thus ending my life at twenty-four years." According to one 27th Division report, the Nafutan area was characterized by "steep ridges, deep gulches with cliffs, ground broken with coral pinnacles, and thick jungle type underbrush which . . . made observation impossible." Sherrod, the correspondent, wrote that the "coral rock formations provided natural caves." According to a Canadian Army observer, the caves varied "in size from just large enough to hold a man and gun to large stalagmite caverns many hundreds of yards in depth and sometimes with multiple entrances. Natural vegetation obscured the entrances to a large proportion of these caves." Captain Warner McCabe, aide-de-camp to Ralph Smith, referred to the area as a "maze of conflicting ground." Most of the approaching cane fields were studded with sharp rocks and offered no cover or concealment. So rock-hard was the coral soil that digging foxholes became untenable, forcing men to move or gather in uncomfortably open ground. In the recollection of one GI, they felt "like pins on a bowling alley."

Neither the 27th Division nor the V Amphibious Corps had an accurate read on enemy capabilities at Nafutan, nor the true number of Japanese defenders sprinkled around the dizzying maze of caves, ledges, holes, and outcroppings. Holland Smith figured that there might be around two hundred holdouts in there; the 27th Division intelligence section estimated the presence of three hundred to five hundred Japanese, both gross underreckonings. Ralph Smith believed, erroneously as it turned out, that he must clear the Japanese from Nafutan's high ground for the Army Air Forces to get any use of Isely Field. He earmarked three battalions for this purpose and supported them with some preparatory artillery and mortar fire, plus a handful of tanks. Instead of a quick mop-up operation, they found themselves enmeshed in a bitter, casualty-intensive, cave-to-cave, hill-to-hill, ledge-to-ledge struggle that raged for days rather than hours. The Japanese may have been disjointed, desperate, and ultimately doomed, but they made excellent use of the terrain, and fought to the death, proving the enduring lesson that, in modern war, committed defenders ensconced in good defensive ground can wreak havoc on a superior attacking force. "Visibility was no more than a few yards in any direction," Captain Love, an eyewitness to the fighting, wrote. "The Japanese had prepared positions and tremendous firepower. A gain of a few feet was an accomplishment." In the thick brush or amid the boulders—"bigger than car tires," in the estimation of one soldier—plus the caves, tankers had no choice but to forge ahead blindly. Often they acted as impromptu bulldozers, breaking pathways through the mush to allow infantry soldiers to follow behind. "Tank operations there [were] difficult and hazardous," wrote Captain Roy Appleman, the Army's historian of armor on Saipan. "Frequently the brush extended above the tank periscope. At times the tanks would stand on end in trying to get over some coral obstacle. In such terrain and cover, it was difficult to destroy enemy machine gun nests, which were cleverly placed." In the typical confusion, infantry soldiers did well to stay within twenty or thirty yards of the tanks, much less maintain any sustained visual contact with them; this made the armor especially vulnerable to potentially deadly grenade and Molotov cocktail attacks from individual Japanese. "God, but the boys that were burned were the worst off," Tech 3 Donnolo, the medic, wrote of treating the survivors of burning tanks. "The flesh just rolled off their bodies."

Far too often, the foot troops assembled and attempted to move forward while under direct observation from well-hidden Japanese soldiers who raked them with machine-gun, mortar, and rifle fire. When Captain Frank

Olander's G Company, 105th Infantry Regiment, moved one morning beyond a perimeter they had maintained the previous evening, "all hell broke
loose, small arms and mortar fire just rained in on us." In a matter of seconds, he lost five men killed and fifteen wounded. By nightfall, after a day
full of abortive attacks, he had lost thirty-three wounded and nine killed,
and gained almost no ground. A mistaken shelling of the battalion command post and aid station by a Navy destroyer killed eight men and
wounded another thirty-two, only adding to the carnage.

The presence of civilians who had taken refuge in caves and other hiding places, sometimes alongside the Japanese soldiers, created more confusion. "Many . . . were killed as they were intermingled with Japanese troops
and would not come out to surrender when called upon to do so by interpreter and loud speaker," Appleman wrote sadly. The Americans captured
some civilians by force; others willingly surrendered, especially when
coaxed by Japanese-American translators. The average soldier or Marine
had little grasp of the significant ethnic and linguistic differences among
the local population. In an opinion reflective of many, Sergeant Charles
Kohler condescendingly referred to them as "nothing but mere savages
slightly tamed."

The dismissive racism did not prevent the Americans from caring for
the locals as well as conditions permitted. Confronted for the first time in
the Pacific War with a major civil affairs responsibility, the Americans set
up a holding center, Camp Susupe, in which they separated the main ethnic groups—Chamorros, Koreans, and Japanese or Okinawans—into different compounds. "Young or old, they carried bundles of belongings and
followed our directions with no question and no apparent fear," Lieutenant
Colonel Van Antwerp observed. "Curiosity appeared to overcome any
emotion." Safe from the fighting now but hardly comfortable, the refugees
initially lived a spartan existence before the Americans could provide
much in the way of amenities. "It was hard in Camp Susupe," Gregorio
Cabrera later commented. "There really wasn't much of a place to sleep.
Some of us men had to sleep on the ground with just a blanket, but under
a tent."

The Americans at first fed them C and K rations. Eventually, the GIs
were able to scrounge rice, canned fish, soy sauce, crackers, and a few other
items from captured Japanese stores. "Canned milk diluted with water was
made available for babies and children requiring it," the 27th Division civil
affairs officer wrote in a report on the internment of civilians. Japanese

troops in the pocket, meanwhile, held on as long as they could, hoping desperately for rescue or relief. "I wish I can fulfill my duty," one of them scribbled in his diary. "No reinforcements came. No food or water. It's quite a hardship. Everyone is saying that there are no reinforcing planes. Also, no naval reinforcement to aid us."

As the savage fighting raged around Nafutan, the two bloodied Marine divisions reoriented north to assault Lieutenant General Saito's main defensive line. For this new push, Holland Smith wanted to utilize the 27th Division. He had already successfully asked Vice Admiral Turner to divert the 106th Infantry from the Southern Troops and Landing Force for duty on Saipan with the rest of their 27th Division brothers. By the evening of June 20, they had safely landed on the island. Laboring under the incorrect assumption that only a couple hundred ragged dead-enders defended Nafutan, the corps commander in the early afternoon of June 21 ordered Ralph Smith to leave behind a single battalion to finish up at Nafutan while he made the rest of his division available to participate in the new offensive. "It will mop up the remaining enemy detachments, maintain antisniper patrols . . . and protect installations within its zone of action with particular attention paid to Aslito airfield," the orders stipulated.

By now, Ralph Smith had come to understand the formidable nature of the Nafutan. He knew that one battalion could not hope to take it. At 1700 he called Holland Smith at his newly established headquarters inside an intact bungalow in Charan Kanoa. Over the course of a cordial conversation that belied months of building tension between the two men, Ralph Smith described the terrain and requested that the 105th Infantry remain in place to secure the Nafutan area. Holland Smith reluctantly acquiesced but insisted on maintaining one of the regiment's battalions at the airfield as a corps reserve. During a personal meeting at 1500 the next afternoon between the two Smiths, following yet another day of bloody, ineffectual fighting, Holland Smith rescinded his permission and insisted that only one battalion from the 105th remain at Nafutan. At the same time, the Marine general expressed some impatience with the 27th Division's seeming inability to snuff out Japanese resistance. "I pointed out the difficult terrain and Jap positions in caves and said rapid advance was impracticable if undue losses were to be avoided and if Japs were to be really cleaned out," Ralph Smith wrote a few weeks later in an official report. He promised to continue the pressure and secure the area within a couple of days. Holland Smith claimed to have heard that the 105th's commander, Colonel

Leonard Bishop, a closet diabetic who was struggling to maintain his stamina for combat command, had expressed an intention to pull back and simply starve the Japanese out, a concept that clashed with the Marine commander's preference for rapid operations. Ralph Smith reassured his boss that Bishop had probably used the term "driven out" rather than "starved out," and promised to stress to him the necessity for continued attacks.

Bishop later denied making any such statement about starving the enemy out. In retrospect, though, perhaps he should have. The main justification for clearing the Japanese from all of their deadly caves and cubbyholes seems to have been to make sure they could not hinder the operation of the airfield. Hours before the generals Smith conversed, though, twenty-two P-47 Thunderbolts of the 19th Fighter Squadron had landed at Isely. By the end of that day, they had already flown a strike mission against Tinian. Within a couple more days, they were reinforced by the rest of their unit, as well as the 77th Fighter Squadron and seven P-61 Black Widows of the 6th Night Fighter Squadron. Unmolested by the Japanese at Nafutan, they flew combat air patrols and close air support missions. Thus, by this time, the mission of clearing out every inch of Nafutan was largely unnecessary and self-defeating. It reflected a myopic "see the hill, take the hill" mentality prevalent among too many American tactical commanders (and one that survived quite unprofitably into the Vietnam era).

By and large, the Japanese tended to be most potent on defense, in prepared positions, where they could use terrain, firepower, and their remarkable self-sacrificial valor to degrade and frustrate the Americans. On offense, they were vulnerable to American firepower and tenacity, and completely out of their tactical depth, owing to serious weaknesses in combined arms capabilities and coordination. Saito's abortive attempts to snuff out the beachhead, squandering most of his armor, attested to this fact. So the wisest course of action for the Yanks would have been to leave enough troops in place to make sure the enemy could not threaten the airfield, forcing them either to starve in place or launch a suicidal attack. In fact, Holland Smith's own chief of staff, Brigadier General Graves Erskine, apparently contemplated doing just this. "[He] felt that, if necessary, we should merely contain them in the Nafutan area with a minimum of force and put all our strength to the north," Ralph Smith later wrote of one conversation with Erskine. But neither he nor Holland Smith took this sensible advice well enough to heart. The attacks continued even as Holland Smith weakened the power of the attacking force by removing all but one battalion, reducing their ability to complete the misbegotten mission. A steady drumbeat of casualties only dissipated them all the more, reducing their capability of protecting the airfield. Ralph Smith repeatedly warned corps headquarters and Holland Smith personally, to no avail, that the Japanese might now well infiltrate through his thinly held lines at Nafutan and perhaps even attack the airfield. "He asked that Seabee and Air Force personnel take steps to provide security against such an eventuality," Captain Love wrote.

As the Nafutan fighting boiled on with no end in sight, Holland Smith, whose actions had actually contributed to just this circumstance, became increasingly impatient with what he saw as a lack of Army aggressiveness and competence. In the absence of the results he wanted, his inherent prejudices against the Army, and disdain in particular for the 27th Division, an outfit he viewed as little more than an incompetent militia force, began to surface. "I was reluctant to use them . . . in the Marianas, but when the operation was planned they were the only troops available in Hawaii and I had to take them," he later wrote scornfully. For a man so worried about their supposed deficiencies, though, he had taken little interest in their training back in Hawaii. Outside of staff planning, he made almost no effort to forge V Amphibious Corps into one cohesive team. In reality, he thought of himself not so much a corps commander as a Marine expeditionary commander burdened with Army troops. This toxic attitude even manifested itself in the way he talked. He routinely referred to his men as "my Marines" instead of more inclusive terms like "my men" or "my troops" or even "my Marines and soldiers."

The sheer logic of events at Nafutan would have persuaded a more open-minded man that he had underestimated the challenges of terrain and enemy resistance. Instead, Holland Smith, having never visited the Nafutan front himself, simply clung to his own preconceived, incorrect notions, blaming Ralph Smith and his division for abject failure against nothing more than a skeleton force. When the Japanese in the early morning hours of June 26 made a last-ditch breakout attempt, sweeping through thinly held 105th Infantry outposts to attack the airfield and other adjacent units—the very scenario Ralph Smith had warned of—Holland Smith's attitude only hardened. In his postwar memoir, he made the absurd claim that the 105th had "even permitted . . . a column of some 500 well-armed and organized Japanese, to march, *in column of twos*, right through its line with hardly a shot fired." Needless to say, the practice of advancing into combat in column of twos had gone out with the Civil War. In point of fact, the night and early morning daylight hours were filled with violent encounters. The enemy soldiers succeeded in destroying one plane at Isely but were largely decimated by the combination of the airfield personnel, the 2nd Battalion, 105th Infantry, and Marine and Army artillery units. The desperate Japanese actions had little to no impact on the operations of the airfield. Some 409 Japanese soldiers had participated; only a handful survived.[11]

The unsuccessful breakout attempt hastened the end of the fighting in the Nafutan pocket, where the Americans found approximately 500 bodies and captured 175 prisoners. But the bad blood between Holland Smith and the Army was only just starting to curdle. For the new offensive against Saito's line, he placed the 2nd Marine Division on the left and the 4th Marine Division on the right, with the 27th Division in between them. Portions of the 106th and 165th Regiments were to drive northward in the center, along the eastern side of Mount Tapochau, whose edges sloped steeply downward six hundred feet, into a rolling valley three-quarters of a mile wide, bordered on the right by a range of low-lying hills, ominously dubbed "Purple Heart Ridge" by the Americans. From Mount Tapochau to Saipan's east coast, some 4,000 enemy soldiers fortified and held this ideal defensive ground. The 4th Marine Division had already experienced sharp fighting in the area. "This is the toughest position we've hit yet," a Marine battalion commander wearily informed Colonel Kelley, commander of the 165th, when his unit moved into place. The Americans had started to refer to this terrible place as "Death Valley." The 27th Division assault units had little time for personal reconnaissance or even informal briefings from the Marines. "It is my opinion that the initial orientation that battalion and company commanders received did not give enough information on the impending action," Captain Charles Hallden, commander of L Company, 106th Infantry, later commented.

Not surprisingly, the GIs made little headway on June 23. The combination of confusion, hastiness, Japanese resistance, and coordination problems among 27th Division commanders led to a late launch. Some units had to fight their way to the planned start line. Once in place and moving forward, Japanese fire bracketed them from the high ground on either side of Death Valley. Hidden enemy soldiers could see practically every move the Americans made. "Japanese installations proved both difficult to find and impossible to reduce by small arms fire," Lieutenant Colonel Lemp, the Army Ground Forces observer, later reported to his superiors in an official analysis. When the Japanese opened fire, they could hardly miss. One officer remembered "fire from several machine guns, hundreds of rifles, two or three high-velocity guns, and mortars." Bullets and fragments ripped through dozens of men. One company lost the better part of two platoons in a matter of minutes. Ambulatory wounded men sprinted for the shelter of a nearby ditch. The desperate battalion commander called on a chemical mortar unit to lay down a smoke screen lest the entire company get killed or debilitated. The 27th Division was almost completely stymied. In a twenty-four-hour period, it suffered six hundred casualties.

A more successful advance by the two Marine divisions on the less well-defended flanks created the beginnings of a horseshoe in the American lines that could have made the Marines vulnerable to flanking counterattacks. As it was, the 27th Division's debacle at Death Valley robbed the two Marine divisions of any further momentum. Already exasperated from the Nafutin fiasco, though not admitting to himself his own role in fostering it, Holland Smith was in no mood to cut the 27th Division any slack. "The Twenty-Seventh won't fight and Ralph Smith will not make them fight!" he sputtered to his staff. Ever since the Makin invasion in November 1943, he had viewed Ralph Smith as a weak officer who could not inspire others to fight. The Marine general now erroneously believed that Ralph Smith had defied and countermanded an order to press his attack forward. Frustrated and deeply worried about the possibility of seeing the Saipan battle bog down into stalemate, he sent a heated telegram to 27th Division headquarters during the night of June 23–24. "Commanding general is highly displeased with the failure of the 27th Division on June 23rd to launch its attack as ordered at K hour and the lack of offensive action displayed by the division in its failure to advance . . . when opposed only by small arms and mortar fire. The failure of the 27th Division to advance in its zone of action resulted in the halting of attacks by the 4th and 2nd Marine Divisions. It is directed that immediate steps be taken to cause the 27th Division to advance and seize the objectives as ordered."

Smith also enlisted Army major general Sanderford Jarman, who was scheduled to assume command of the Saipan garrison upon the battle's conclusion, to visit Ralph Smith as a de facto emissary and communicate the corps commander's concerns. According to Jarman, Holland Smith told him that the 27th "had suffered scarcely no casualties and in his opinion he didn't think they would fight." Efficient, dedicated, an excellent organizer with more than three decades of service under his belt, Jarman nonetheless had almost no combat experience, nor much appreciation for modern battle tactics. Having been placed in an awkward position by the corps commander, who should have talked to his subordinate himself, Jarman dutifully spoke with Ralph Smith on June 23 and then reported, quite inaccurately, that the 27th Division commander acknowledged "that his division was not carrying its full share . . . and stated that if he didn't take his division forward tomorrow he should be relieved." Ralph Smith later strongly denied this version of the conversation. Instead, he had merely acknowledged the difficulties of the terrain and stubborn Japanese resistance, and speculated that if the situation did not improve, then Holland Smith might decide to relieve him.

Regardless of what actually transpired during this conversation, Ralph Smith was quite correct that Holland Smith intended to fire him. The telegram and the Jarman visit amounted to more a farewell than a warning. On the morning of June 24, without even waiting to see how the day's fighting unfolded, Holland Smith, with members of his staff, visited Vice Admiral Turner aboard his flagship, the USS *Rocky Mount*, where the galley featured hot, nutritious food, and sailors the previous evening had enjoyed watching Ginger Rogers in the movie *Kitty Foyle*. Once aboard, Smith communicated to Turner his intention to sack Ralph Smith. Turner had no objections. Together they decided to visit Admiral Spruance aboard his flagship, the USS *Indianapolis*, inform him of the decision, and solicit his approval. Holland Smith pulled no punches with the Fifth Fleet commander, ripping Ralph Smith and the 27th Division as weak and ineffectual. Captain Moore, Spruance's chief of staff, remembered Smith's demeanor as "very indignant and . . . disgusted with the general performance" of Ralph Smith and his soldiers, and "irritated beyond measure with [their] failure to attack." The outcome of Holland Smith's one-sided presentation was predictable. Spruance had little choice but to accede to the wishes of his ground commander. Anything less would undercut his authority as well as his inherent command prerogative to remove subordinates in whom he had lost confidence. With Spruance's blessing, Erskine drew up orders for the relief of Ralph Smith. Jarman, of all people, would replace him, at least for the short term.

While Holland Smith spent much of June 24 aboard ship arranging to fire Ralph Smith, the latter spent the entire day risking his life on the front lines, studying the terrain, reconnoitering Japanese defensive positions, conceiving of a new attack designed to sidestep Death Valley around the right flank. "Often at great personal risk he went to exposed points to get better observation and constantly moved about in an area under observation by the enemy . . . in the cliffs and covered by enemy small arms and mortar fire," Captain McCabe, his aide who was constantly at his elbow, later wrote. Another staffer who was with Smith during the day later related that "he showed a tremendous amount of bravery—took charge in reorganizing things, talking to company and battalion commanders, and getting the front organized, primarily for the . . . attack." Captain Love, the historian, personally witnessed Smith under fire several times and claimed that he frequently came close to being killed, including in one particularly heavy mortar and artillery barrage that cost the lives of sixteen men around him. "He was right up where the fighting was." Even Smith, modest and understated almost to a fault, later admitted that "I pretty near got killed up there during the forward reconnaissance."

At 1530, an unnamed V Amphibious Corps aide—the only person from this headquarters that anyone in the 27th Division had seen at the front since the onset of the battle—caught up in a jeep with Ralph Smith. With scarcely a word, the aide handed the 27th Division commander a sealed envelope containing the orders for his relief and then drove off. Smith read the paper wordlessly, betraying no hint of emotion. He simply folded it back up, put it in his pocket, and said nothing of its contents to anyone around him. He met with his regimental commanders, briefed them on his new plans, and issued attack orders for the next day, all the while breathing not a word of his relief. He then returned to his command post, where Jarman, his reluctant successor, was waiting for him and, without a hint of any malice, apprised his colleague in detail about the tactical situation and his attack plans. "The two Generals discussed every angle of the . . . battle," Lieutenant Colonel Van Antwerp, the intelligence officer, wrote. "General Smith covered completely the heartbreak he nursed and went into minute detail . . . [about] every item of information which his successor would require." At the conclusion of the conversation, Jarman took immediate command. At 2230, Holland Smith called the division headquarters and, without speaking personally to Ralph Smith, ordered him off the island immediately. The deposed general hastily packed his gear and, with only Captain McCabe in tow, caught a plane early the next morning for Eniwetok and thence to Hawaii. The word of their commander's relief spread quickly throughout the ranks of the 27th Division, prompting bewilderment, resentment, and regret. "They were broken hearted to see General Smith go and there was not a man on the field of battle . . . that did not feel that he had been badly treated," wrote Captain Love a couple of months later. This statement qualified as more than mere hyperbole, because Love, in his capacity as a combat historian, interviewed nearly every 27th Division survivor of the battle.

From the perspective of a latter-year historian, it is striking that Holland Smith, a man who liked to portray himself as a lead-from-the-front warrior, never once visited the front lines at either Nafutan or Death Valley before relieving Ralph Smith. Confined to headquarters three miles to the rear, studying inaccurate situation maps that bore no resemblance to frontline reality, and loath even to extend the courtesy of speaking face-to-face with the man in whom he had apparently lost confidence, he nonetheless felt qualified to question the courage and competence of an entire division of soldiers and its commander. Misled by poor intelligence, a prisoner to his own self-destructive bias, he had little idea of the actual terrain, nor much understanding of enemy capabilities. Colonel Geoffrey O'Connell, an Army officer who commanded the Nafutan effort in its final stages and who heard Holland Smith utter many snide remarks about the shortcomings of the soldiers who fought there, later asserted that the general had no "conception of the nature of the terrain . . . or any details concerning the operation." Moreover, Smith remained incredibly ignorant of the price the 27th Division paid in casualties at Nafutan and Death Valley. He did not even see fit to send any members of his staff to assess the state of the 27th Division and the situation at the battlefront.

One cannot help but be struck—and even a bit troubled—by the ironic juxtaposition in the activities of the two Smiths on June 24. As one Smith spent the day safely aboard ship and at headquarters plotting the removal of the other Smith, the latter put his life on the line repeatedly in combat over the course of nearly ten continuous hours. To be sure, Holland Smith had every right to get rid of Ralph Smith. But before doing so, he should have investigated the situation *personally* and made completely sure he understood the true circumstances. Instead, he simply gave in to his prejudices and acted on them, revealing himself to be anything but a combat leader. In the wake of the firing, he doubled down on his own misconceptions. "By God, I told him [Ralph Smith] to attack and he issued an order to hold," he vented in a private conversation that night with Robert

Sherrod. "Ralph Smith is my friend but, good God, I've got a duty to my country. I've lost seven thousand Marines. Can I afford to lose back what they have gained? To let my Marines die in vain?" Apparently, the soldier casualties that had accumulated on Saipan by the evening of June 24 did not factor into his perceived duty to his country, only the losses among those he continually referred to as "my Marines."

Weeks later, in a letter to General Alexander Archer Vandegrift, the commandant of the Marine Corps, he resorted to outright defamation and falsehoods, apparently in an effort to justify what he had done. "R. Smith is a weak officer, incapable of handling men in battle, lacks offensive spirit, and tears would come into his eyes on the slightest provocation. My duty was clear. My action was approved by every Army officer with whom my staff or I discussed the situation." The final sentence had no basis in reality. Major General Jarman did not wish to see Ralph Smith go, nor did the officers of the 27th Division. The great Pacific War historian Harry Gailey, in the course of an exhaustively researched book about the problems between the two Smiths, made a point of asking 27th Division veterans if tears ever welled in the eyes of their commander "on the slightest provocation." They responded vociferously, often with colorful language, that they had never seen any tears. One former headquarters sergeant affirmed the universal respect for Ralph Smith and deadpanned, "Any tears in General Ralph Smith's eyes were probably tears of rage and frustration at having to deal with H.M.S. [Holland McTyeire Smith]."[12]

Though historical posterity still tends to see the conflict between the two Smiths as emblematic of differing doctrinal philosophies between the Marine Corps and the Army—the Marines tending toward quicker, more aggressive frontal assaults and the Army slower and more deliberative—the truth is that the core of the conflict was Holland Smith himself. Throughout the Saipan battle, Marines and soldiers tended to fight much the same way—with tremendous courage. Tactically, their similarities outweighed their differences, especially at Death Valley, where no amount of valorous, dashing assaults could make any headway, as the Marines had begun to find out on June 22 before the 27th Division relieved them. In most cases, they employed combined arms to gain ground, and commanders, whether Marine or Army, attempted to minimize losses.

Holland Smith made no effort to establish any sort of unified doctrine or training or any sense of belonging to a common team—quite the contrary, actually. His attitude of contempt for the Army did nothing but harm relations and hinder teamwork. "The Commanding General and Staff . . . held the units of the 27th Division in little esteem, actually a position bordering on scorn," one Army officer who worked with Holland Smith's headquarters lamented in a postwar letter to a historian. Had Smith established truly collegial professional ties with Army colleagues and forged a real partnership with them, his decision to sack Ralph Smith, whether merited or not, might well have incited no particular notice or rancor in Army circles. Instead, within the poisonous environment he had fostered, the firing stoked latent Marine-versus-Army rivalries and resentments that undoubtedly did exist among some, at least in senior officer and bureaucratic circles, and soon lit the fuse for a major, unnecessary conflict between the two ground-oriented services.

Back on Oahu, Lieutenant General Robert "Nellie" Richardson, the ranking Army officer in Nimitz's command, soon got wind of Ralph Smith's firing. In spite of his lofty rank, Richardson's authority was confined to an administrative and logistical scope. He was responsible for supplying Army units on Saipan, and elsewhere within Nimitz's purview, but had no command authority over them. If Holland Smith had a partisan alter ego in the Army, surely it was Richardson, an officer who saw the Corps as primarily a naval infantry beach landing force whose senior leaders had no business exercising command over soldiers or really much of anything above the regiment or division level. "Richardson is always a menace to good relations between the services," one Army general noted during the war. Richardson already had no love for Holland Smith, whom he thought of as unstable and unsuited for corps command. "My concern stemmed from my lack of confidence in him," Richardson later wrote. "It was my duty to be sure that . . . Army troops . . . should be assured competent leadership." Miffed at Ralph Smith's firing, Richardson took steps to get to the bottom of what had transpired. He ordered the sacked commander to prepare a report to this effect, a significant challenge for Ralph Smith because he had access to almost no records. In spite of this disadvantage, he managed to produce a thirty-four-page document with useful descriptions and a tone of such remarkable evenhandedness that even Holland Smith later wrote admiringly, "He never once launched into a diatribe or a sob story. Adversity, I think, became him well."

On July 4, Richardson also ordered the establishment of an all-Army investigatory board comprising four general officers and one lieutenant colonel, headed by Lieutenant General Simon Bolivar Buckner. The ostensible purpose of the Buckner Board was to ascertain the facts of Smith's relief and assess whether it was merited. Though blithely dismissed years later by Holland Smith as "an Army Kangaroo court," the board met nine times between July 7 and 26, compiled multiple eyewitness statements, and examined vast quantities of official reports, albeit almost all of which came from Army sources. Their material, though, did include the original memos prepared by Admiral Spruance and Holland Smith explaining the reasons for the relief.

In a final report issued on August 4, the board concluded sensibly, and quite accurately, that Holland Smith had a perfect right to relieve Ralph Smith but the Marine commander "was not fully informed regarding conditions in the zone of the 27th Infantry Division when he issued orders relieving Maj. Gen. Ralph C. Smith . . . from command." As such, Buckner and his colleagues believed that the sacking of Smith "was not justified by facts." With Ralph Smith essentially exonerated, at least in Army circles, Richardson immediately appointed him to command of the 98th Infantry Division in Hawaii. In a detailed statement that eventually found its way into the board's records, Vice Admiral Turner claimed that he and Holland Smith had prioritized the maintenance of effective interservice cooperation. "Both he and I have done everything within our power to promote harmonious relationships." As such, he accepted no responsibility for the tension. "In cases where harmony has been impaired, I am convinced that blame can not attach to either of us."

Holland Smith saw the Buckner Board conclusions as little more than an Army whitewash derived from incomplete sources. "I was . . . convinced that the 27th Infantry Division was not accomplishing even the minimum combat results to be expected of an organization which had had adequate opportunity for training. In brief, there existed in the 27th Division a condition inimical to its combat efficiency. The issue of battle called for immediate remedial action. I decided that the action to be taken was the relief of Major General R. C. Smith." Holland Smith saw the Buckner Board as hopelessly biased against the Navy, the Marine Corps, and, of course, himself. But some Army officers actually saw it as something of a cover-up, absolving the Marine general of the blame he richly deserved for the relief fiasco. After the war, Brigadier General Roy Blount, a member of the board, criticized Buckner and Major General John Hodge, who also served on it, for overlooking Holland Smith's misconduct in favor of maintaining smooth interservice relations for their own future command purposes,

Buckner as an army commander with Marines in his charge, and Hodge as a corps commander working closely with the Navy. "Both of these estimable officers pulled *their* punches drastically as the senior officers of the board, and permitted only such facts to be entered into the report as *they* desired," he wrote to Richardson in 1948. "They were both out to appease the Navy for their own selfish reasons." In his capacity as a member of the board, Blount actually traveled to Saipan to investigate relevant facts of the relief. He came away from the experience with a poor opinion of Holland Smith, whom he later referred to provocatively as "that stupid, egomaniac! A perfect ass if ever one lived!" Blount claimed that Buckner and Hodge did not allow him to utilize any of the damning information he had gathered on Holland Smith's actions. Nor would they let him file a minority opinion of any kind. Outranked and overruled, Blount had no choice but to back down.

Richardson, perhaps out of dissatisfaction himself with the neutral tone of the report, traveled, with Nimitz's permission, to Saipan on July 12. During his visit, he had stormy encounters with Holland Smith and Vice Admiral Turner. The Marine general claimed that Richardson lit into him about the relief of the 27th Division commander. "You had no right to relieve Ralph Smith," he allegedly told Holland Smith. "You discriminated against the Army in favor of the Marines. I want you to know that you can't push the Army around the way you have been doing. You Marines are nothing but a bunch of beach runners, anyway. What do you know about land warfare?" Richardson later vehemently denied making any such statements. Regardless of what actually happened, his visit only served to inflame the simmering tension among the services.

To make matters worse, the first inklings of the controversy appeared in the press. Media baron William Randolph Hearst, whose nose for sensationalism far outpaced his commitment to responsible journalism, had for months been pushing the War Department to unite the entire Pacific theater under General MacArthur. In pursuit of this goal, his papers had adopted a tone of pro-Army advocacy over the other services. On July 8, the Hearst-controlled *San Francisco Examiner* blared a front-page story written by Ray Richards under the headline, "Army General Relieved in Row over High Marine Losses." Based on leaked information from an unnamed officer—possibly Lieutenant Colonel Lemp, the observer—the article inaccurately contended that Ralph Smith lost his job because he had become outraged over the unnecessary loss of life that eventuated from

Holland Smith's "Marine Corps impetuosity of attack." Nine days later, Hearst's *New York Journal-American* editorialized against the supposed butchery of the Marine Corps way of fighting, portrayed Ralph Smith as something of an outraged whistleblower over the waste of American lives, and argued for MacArthur as a more responsible steward of those precious lives. Predictably and understandably, Holland Smith became indignant when he read the articles. "At times I feel like saying my piece and pack up," he vented in a private letter to Vandegrift. Anyone even remotely familiar with the circumstances of the relief and the realities of the fighting on Saipan knew that the Hearst paper contentions amounted to little more than politically charged nonsense. Probably for this reason, these irresponsible characterizations had little overall effect on policy, and the furor soon died down. But even so, the Hearst empire insinuations did hint at the potential for Holland Smith's chronic tension with the Army to boil into public controversy and spark a more politically meaningful conflict among soldiers and Marines, especially in senior officer circles.[13]

As the leaders quibbled, the soldiers and Marines continued to fight ferociously against the actual enemy, the Japanese. For a week, the Americans battered Saito's defensive line. Jarman implemented Ralph Smith's flanking plan. Though far more intelligent than the original all-purpose drive into the heart of Death Valley, the ubiquity of hills, caves, and crevasses on either side of Purple Heart Ridge prevented any possibility of a complete end run around the worst of the enemy defenses. "Well-placed, hostile guns fired only when lines had passed and striking our forces in the rear disrupted the attack," wrote Colonel Albert Stebbins, the division chief of staff who took over as commander of the 106th Infantry when Jarman fired Colonel Russell Ayers for his inability to advance his regiment sufficiently. "It was necessary to work forward taking out each gun in turn, employing tanks to draw fire so that guns could be located and destroyed."

Intimate small-unit actions raged from hill to hill, cave to cave, often with a jarring lack of visibility. The only time most GIs actually saw the Japanese was when they were dead. The Americans blasted the Japanese out of their caves and holes with explosives, grenades, bazookas, antiaircraft guns, naval gunfire, and self-propelled artillery shells, or roasted them with flamethrowers. "We knocked out . . . machine guns, shot into . . . caves, and watched as ground troops threw a grenade into one end of a culvert and bayonetted Japs as they came out the other end," wrote PFC Hilbert, a crewman on a self-propelled 75-millimeter gun. "There was a very distinct odor connected with this. It smelled just like when we butchered hogs back home on the farm. I don't think I could ever butcher a hog again." The attackers found that they had to engage the caves with heavy weapons first from a distance of at least one hundred or more yards lest they lose anyone who ventured closer to them. "Many caves were extensive in depth and contained foxholes and barriers within them," an Army Ground Forces study reported. "Direct hits into the mouth of such positions therefore failed to kill the occupants who would retire to their inner foxholes or crevasses. Frequently entrances would only permit one soldier at a time to enter thus posing an extremely difficult reduction task. Where appropriate, such positions were sealed using demolitions and bulldozers."

The personal duels to the death exacerbated an already ubiquitous climate of hate. Sergeant Kawaguchi, the Japanese medic, reported to his diary that, among his fellow soldiers, "there was a feeling of sadness, pity, and anger and we resolved to get revenge for the dead." When Staff Sergeant Felix Giuffre and a buddy came upon the body of a Japanese soldier killed by concussion, they made a point of stopping, unbuttoning their pants, and urinating on the corpse. A Catholic chaplain saw them and remonstrated, "Is that a decent thing to do? Bury him." Giuffre, unmoved, replied, "I don't know who is going to bury me." The body remained in place, devoured by the elements. Amid the enervating tropical heat, the combat soldiers subsisted from day to day on K rations and a canteen or two of water. Sergeant Kohler, the tanker, remembered seeing men "so thirsty that their tongues were actually swollen." In one typical incident, Private John O'Brien and his buddies were so parched that they enthusiastically filled their canteen cups from a cistern full of tainted water. "There were three rats floating in [it]." Heedless of any squeamishness, they guzzled the water. Fighting raged, in stops and starts, round the clock, including at night when small groups of Japanese infiltrated or attacked jumpy American perimeters under the weird half-light of flares fired periodically by naval vessels. During the perpetual daylight attacks, American rifle companies were shot to pieces in a matter of minutes. In the confusion, most had difficulty maintaining physical contact with adjacent units, especially the Marines, who often grumbled among themselves at the 27th Division's seeming inability to prevent gaps in their respective lines.

From the generals on down, commanders relentlessly pressured their subordinates to maintain contact and keep up the momentum of the advance, even into almost certain death. In one instance, a battalion commander in the 106th, Lieutenant Colonel Harold "Hi" Mizony, sadly ordered Captain William Heminway, a thirty-one-year-old company commander who had served for several years in the National Guard, to take his outfit into a suicidal attack through fire-swept ground. "Bill, I hate to do it, but I've got to send you out there," Mizony lamented. "Don't apologize, Hi," Heminway replied, "I know how it is." A sad moment passed. Then the captain looked the colonel in the eye, shook hands, and said, "So long, Hi. It's been damned nice knowing you." Predictably, the company was decimated. Within twenty minutes, seventeen men were killed, including Heminway, who caught a bullet in the head as he attempted to reorganize his wounded company. Mizony was killed a few days later during a surprise counterattack by a pair of enemy light tanks, an atypical occurrence because the vast majority of armor in the battle was American.

All over the area, US tanks pounded Japanese-occupied caves. Desperate enemy soldiers hurled themselves at the American armor, pitching grenades, flinging Molotov cocktails. In one case, a Molotov cocktail ignited the engine compartment of a Sherman, setting off an intense conflagration. "Those who saw the tank later agreed that it was the worst burned up tank they had ever seen," Captain Appleman, the armor historian, wrote. The crew abandoned the Sherman but soon found themselves engulfed by Japanese soldiers, who bayoneted two of the Americans to death and shot another as he fled. The lone surviving crewman played dead even as enemy soldiers trampled on his hands, and managed to lie absolutely still for an entire evening before finally making his way back to friendly lines "in a bad state of shock," according to Appleman.

Medics fought alongside everyone else; the Japanese made no distinction for them anyway. "God, I was scared," Tech 3 Donnolo told his diary in the wake of one enemy nighttime counterattack. "I think I never knew what fear was until then. The poor wounded had to stay without medical treatment for three hours. One fellow in [the] collecting company got his eye blown out. God! What a night of horrors. I don't think I can stand much more." Nor could the Japanese. Thirty-First Army headquarters told Tokyo, "The fight on Saipan as things stand now is progressing one sidedly since, along with the tremendous power of his barrages, the enemy holds control of the sea and air. We are menaced brazenly by low flying planes, and the enemy blasts at us from all sides with fierce naval and artillery cross-fire. Wherever we go we're quickly surrounded by fire. The attack of the enemy proceeds ceaselessly day and night as they advance with the aid of terrific bombardments." Lieutenant General Saito made a pathetically inadequate attempt to reinforce his force by arranging for an infantry company on Tinian to board barges and make a run for Saipan. The destroyer USS *Bancroft* sank one of the barges and forced the others to return to Tinian.

Fatigued and increasingly dispirited, Saito on June 27 moved his headquarters away from the advancing Americans, to a dismal cave some twenty-two hundred yards north of Mount Tapochau. Three days later his last Death Valley defenses collapsed or were overrun. His remnants retreated ever northward, with the bloodied Americans in pursuit. "Everything was desolated," Sergeant Kawaguchi lamented. As Sergeant Yamauchi, the former university student, fled with a group of survivors, American shells exploded nearby, killing several men and blowing his glasses away from his nearsighted eyes. "I desperately searched among the corpses until I found them. We could hear American soldiers exchanging their unique whistles almost right up next to us." Somehow he managed to escape. Wounded men who were too badly mangled to join in the retreat were sorrowfully left behind by the medics and told to use their last grenades to commit suicide. "Men, die an honorable death as Japanese soldiers," a doctor at one field hospital told his stretcher-bound patients. They stifled tears and promised to meet one another again in spirit at Tokyo's Yasukuni Shrine, roughly the Japanese equivalent to Arlington National Cemetery. As the ambulatory wounded and their caregivers left, they heard cries of "Goodbye, Mother!" and a chain reaction of grenade detonations.

The Yanks lost almost 4,000 men in exchange for destroying Saito's line from Garapan to Mount Tapochau, Death Valley, Purple Heart Ridge, and on to the east coast. The 27th Division suffered 1,465 casualties and undoubtedly encountered the fiercest resistance and most difficult terrain. "No one had any tougher job to do," Major General Harry Schmidt, the 4th Marine Division commander, later commented. The most common wounds were to the extremities, followed by head wounds. As Lieutenant Colonel Mizony's death had indicated, the toll among 27th Division leaders was especially heavy. Colonel Gerald Kelley, commander of the 165th Infantry, was wounded and evacuated, as was Lieutenant Colonel John

McDonough, one of his battalion commanders. McDonough's replacement soon got hit and later died of his wounds. Twenty-two company commanders were killed or wounded.[14]

By now, Jarman had returned to his regular duties as base commander. On June 28, Major General George Griner replaced him as permanent commander of the 27th Division. Ironically, Griner had come from command of the 98th, so his arrival, in tandem with Ralph Smith taking over the 98th, completed an odd trade of sorts. When Griner reported to Holland Smith, the corps commander did not necessarily brief him on the situation so much as outline his entrenched views of the 27th Division's many deficiencies. Smith repeated his incorrect notions of the Nafutan and Death Valley fighting. He contended that the Japanese at Nafutan could have been "disposed of by a handful of Marines." The Marine general even introduced a new claim, with no basis in fact, that the soldiers had en masse "frozen in their foxholes" at Nafutan. Smith later wrote about the conversation with Griner that he "expressed the hope that he would reorganize the division and develop among the men a better fighting spirit." Griner found that he actually controlled less than half of his division's infantry battalions. The entire 165th Infantry was attached to the 4th Marine Division, with one battalion of the 105th under Jarman's island command, and another in corps reserve. When Griner asked for the return of his own units, Holland Smith indicated that he would get them back only when the division "demonstrated that it could fight." Ignorant of the true situation, having seemingly taken over a stigmatized unit on probation, Griner found himself in the difficult position of accommodating Smith's prejudicial attitude while also establishing his own credibility with the men of the 27th after taking over for a popular commander whose relief had been, in their view, unjustified. The task would have challenged the abilities of a master diplomat. Predictably, Griner fell short, even though he proved to be a competent, effective commander. The soldiers of the 27th Division, especially his staff and his field-grade officers, never quite accepted him.

Freed from the worst of Saipan's terrain, the Americans in early July continued advancing north against steady but weakening resistance. Inside his austere cave, Lieutenant General Saito opted to play his final card. With his command dying a slow death under the relentless battering of American firepower, no relief force on the way, food and water supplies dwindling, and his troops now cornered on the northern end of Saipan, he knew the end was near. He decided to scrape together his last remaining troops and launch a climactic attack designed to puncture the American lines, disrupt their logistics, and perhaps find some way to turn the tide of the battle. In truth, Saito knew he had almost no chance to fulfill these objectives. Instead, the counterattack would undoubtedly lead to the annihilation of his army. To Saito, as with so many other Japanese commanders in this war, cultural concepts of personal honor and duty to the emperor—and in his person the Japanese nation—mattered more than the pragmatism of military operations, even more than life itself. To describe his attack concept, Saito used the hallowed word "gyokusai," whose literal meaning referred to a broken jewel or bead but whose concept equated to honorable extinction rather than compromising one's principles or capitulating to an enemy. Among Japanese soldiers it was said, without much in the way of corroboration, that a gyokusai attack could only be ordered by the emperor himself. Regardless, it amounted to a suicidal assault of the sort generally just dubbed "banzai" by the Americans for the boisterous interjection that attacking Japanese troops often hollered as they attacked.

Vice Admiral Nagumo initially argued for a fighting retreat to the northern tip of Saipan, in hopes that the Imperial Navy might still materialize. With the fleet nowhere in evidence and more men dying by the hour, Saito's plan carried the day. Most of his units were so gutted and scattered that Saito, Nagumo, and Igeta found the job of organizing them into a cohesive force nearly impossible. Nor were there anywhere near enough weapons for them. More than a few would soon go into battle armed with little more than swords, knives, grenades, or even bayonets affixed to poles. Fire support consisted mainly of a few mortars and machine guns, plus a couple of tanks. Nonetheless, Saito managed to weld these remnants into a dangerous attacking force more than capable of inflicting serious damage on the Americans, if not necessarily fulfilling his dreams of reversing the general tide of battle.

After several weeks of fighting, the general's physical condition had deteriorated, so much so that he could not hope to participate personally in the operation. Instead, he intended to commit hara-kiri. He had barely eaten or slept for days. "He was wearing a long beard and was a pitiful sight," Major Takashi Hirakushi, an aide who survived the battle, later wrote. Haggard, frail, and exhausted, with a bloody bandage covering a fragment wound in his one of his wrists, his weakened condition seemed to symbolize the waning Japanese fortunes in the Marianas. On the morning of July 5, he gathered his headquarters troops around him in the musty cavern that now served as his inner sanctum. He stood on a small platform. The soldiers, many of them nursing wounds of their own, sat cross-legged on the floor or stood silently around him. Behind the general, mounted on the wall, a pair of candles provided the only flickers of light. He read from a sheet of paper that he held in surprisingly steady hands. "We have fought in unison up to the present time but now we have no material with which to fight and our artillery for attack has been completely destroyed. Our comrades have fallen one after another. Despite the bitterness of defeat, we pledge, 'Seven lives to repay our country.' The barbarous attack of the enemy is being continued. Whether we attack or whether we stay where we are, there is only death. However, in death there is life. We must continue this opportunity to exalt true Japanese manhood." Saito finished by praying for the health and welfare of the emperor.

When he stepped down, an aide told the men that the attack would proceed on the morning of July 7, under the command of Colonel Takuji Suzuki, Saito's chief of staff. When Hirakushi asked Saito what would become of the Japanese civilians on Saipan, the general replied, "There is no longer any distinction between civilians and troops. It would be better for them to join in the attack with bamboo spears than be captured." Igeta sent a final message to Imperial General Headquarters in Tokyo admonishing them that "there can be no victory without control of the air. I strongly hope [you] will increase aircraft production." That evening, Saito, Nagumo, Igeta, and other officers dined on a final banquet of canned crab meat, rice balls, squid, and sake, topped off by the communal smoking of their last cigarettes, all the while reminiscing about better days. By midday on July 6, they were all dead. Nagumo, erstwhile hero of Pearl Harbor, and his chief of staff, Rear Admiral Hideo Yano, both shot themselves. Saito and Igeta embraced suicide with more ritualism. They bowed in the direction of the emperor's palace, knelt down, exclaimed, "Tenno Heika! Banzai!" and sliced open their own abdomens. Seconds later, aides shot both men in the head. The bodies of Nagumo and Yano were quickly buried in unmarked graves. Saito's was cremated but only partially, out of fear that the smoke might attract enemy fire; the remnants were simply covered with a thin layer of soil.

Their exhausted subordinates were now left to carry out their designs. Hurriedly and with ripples of confusion, the attackers organized as best they could during the evening of July 6. In addition to the natural difficulties of coordinating a night assault from the surviving remnants of multiple units, heavy American artillery fire hindered their movements and helped delay the attack for several hours until around 0445 on July 7. In the course of the evening, 27th Division artillerymen fired 2,666 rounds, mainly along the coastal road along where the Japanese planned to make their main assault. For soldiers facing the strong probability of imminent death, many confronted their own extinction with matter-of-fact, resigned equanimity. "As long as I'm going to die, I want to die with the pharmacist's section," a young lieutenant glibly told Sergeant Kawaguchi. With a chuckle, the sergeant and his friends warmly welcomed him. Sergeant Yamauchi, one of the few who saw captivity as a better option than death, later explained, "In those days, Japanese soldiers really accepted the idea that they must eventually die. If you were taken alive as a prisoner, you could never face your family." As such, a gyokusai attack "meant suicide." Even with so much outward calm and defiance, inwardly Kawaguchi and so many others sadly readied themselves for the end. "With the determination of dying for the Emperor, we passed our time by preparing for our remembrance," Kawaguchi told his diary. "My life is fluttering away like a flower petal (to become part of the soil). It is only regrettable that we have not fought enough and that the American devil is stomping on the Imperial soil. I, with my sacrificed body, will become the white-caps of the Pacific and will stay on this island until the friendly forces come to reclaim the soil of the Emperor." He concluded with a poignant goodbye to every member of his family.

Some burned regimental colors or ate their final rations. Yeoman Second Class Mitsuharu Noda, who had served as Vice Admiral Nagumo's paymaster, congregated with twenty other headquarters men for a final farewell. "We drank the best Japanese whiskey—Suntory Square Bottle, we'd saved it to the last minute. We smoked our last tobacco—Hikari brand. We were even able to smile. Maybe because we were still together as a group. Some . . . may have [gotten] drunk, just to overcome fear. It was a kind of suicide." As they prepared to move out, a heavy downpour inundated Saipan, saturating the ground and soaking the antagonists.[15]

The Americans sensed the Japanese were coming. "There was a tension in the air, a feeling on the part of all that the attack was due," Lieutenant Colonel William Van Antwerp, the 27th Division's intelligence officer, later wrote. But the Americans did not necessarily grasp the full scale of Saito's gyokusai. Holland Smith later claimed to have personally warned the 27th Division, to no avail, of an imminent enemy attack. In truth, he had no specific information to share. He simply gave blanket warnings, almost every night, of possible banzai attacks. The actual rumblings came from the bottom up, not the top down. A civilian laborer captured by an Army patrol provided the first indications of the Japanese plans. Then at 2000 on July 6, Sergeant Hoichi Jubo, a Japanese-American soldier from the 3rd Battalion, 105th Infantry, discovered a sleeping enemy sailor in a ditch and took him prisoner. Throughout the tense evening, Sergeant Jubo, Lieutenant Ben Hazard, and Sergeant Nobuo "Dick" Kishiue of the 27th Division language section, all interrogated him, as did several field-grade officers. The man disclosed, with various meanderings and deviations, the gist of what was about to occur. "With this prisoner, we knew what was up," Hazard later said. "We knew the roof was about to fall in." As yet, though, even with the prisoner's warning, the Americans had little notion of precisely when the proverbial roof might collapse. In this sense, the evening-long delay in the Japanese attack worked to their advantage, cementing confusion and a sort of frustrated, searching anticipation around the various American headquarters. Van Antwerp's 27th Division G2 section placed fourteen separate phone calls to Holland Smith's corps headquarters in the course of the night, mainly conveying a sense of unspecified alarm. In one phone call he said, "There seems to be something in the air. All units should be particularly alert."

Like the senior leaders and staffers at headquarters, the wet, shivering soldiers on the front lines sensed that the Japanese were coming, but they could do little besides stay alert and wait in their muddy foxholes. Shortly after 0400, in the wake of a heavy rainstorm, the GIs began to hear the eerie echoes of the approaching enemy. To some of the Americans, the collective noise they made sounded like swarms of bees. "We began to hear this buzz," First Sergeant Mario Occhinerio of A Company, 105th Infantry, later told an interviewer. "It was the damndest noise I ever heard. It kept getting louder and louder. I think you could describe it as a great big hive of bees." Others heard it as a kind of mass cheering with a distinct "Wah!" "Wah!" cadence. To Major Hirakushi, who had bathed in the sea to cleanse himself before facing death, the gyokusai attackers seemed like "spiritless sheep being led to the slaughter." Their officers came across to him as "guides to the Gates of Hell." Many of the men carried beer or sake bottles with them. In packed columns, making no attempt to spread out or organize into any tactical formations, they approached, mainly along the coastal road and railroad, heading straight for two battalions of the 105th that had dug in after fighting much of the previous day along the Tanapag plain.

Amid the confusion of the day's action and the ensuring diminution of combat manpower, a five-hundred-yard gap had materialized between two of the battalions, and Colonel Suzuki's advance patrols had detected it. The American battalion commanders also knew of the gap, but they found no reinforcements available to plug it and had to settle for covering the space with nothing more than automatic weapons—not a particularly unusual circumstance in modern combat but unfortunate on this particular evening. The entire front now erupted with fire. Multicolored tracer rounds stabbed through the darkness. Along a narrow spit of front about a thousand yards in size, the attackers smashed into the American lines and, in many cases, poured through the gap. Major Edward McCarthy, one of the few American officers who survived the onslaught, later commented that they were "like the . . . stampede staged in the old wild west movies. These Japs kept coming and didn't stop. It didn't make any difference if you shot one, five more would take his place. The Japs just kept coming and coming. I didn't think they'd ever stop." Another survivor, Tech Sergeant John Polikowski, said with wonderment, "It reminded me of a circus ground, or maybe . . . Yankee Stadium. The crowd just milled out on the field, pushing and shoving and yelling. There were so many of them you could just shut your eyes and pull the trigger on your rifle and you'd be bound to hit three or four with one shot." Sergeant John Domanowski saw many of them running in single file, clothed in little more than rags. "They weren't in uniform, but had tattered clothes and bandanas on their foreheads. They looked mean. We had to fight to stay alive." Another American commented bleakly that "the enemy appeared drunk with a thirst to kill." The Americans raked them with a storm of machine-gun, rifle, mortar, and artillery fire. One company commander, Captain Louis Ackerman, placed a desperate call to Captain Bernard Toth, an artillery observer friend. "For God's sake, Bernie, get that artillery closer." Toth replied that he was already placing it within one hundred and fifty yards of the company. He shortened the range to seventy-five yards. Still the Japanese kept coming.

A procession of flares from ships offshore bathed the area in half-light. Hundreds of Japanese were hit, maimed, shot to pieces, killed instantly, or wounded. Some of those who were hit simply lay down and killed themselves. Machine-gun bullets smashed into Yeoman Noda's hip and hit several nearby soldiers. Noda fell heavily to the ground. The soldiers invited him to commit suicide with them but he demurred. Seconds later, he heard one of them exclaim, "Long live the emperor!" Then he heard grenade explosions. "Several men were blown away, dismembered at once into bits of flesh," Noda, who eventually ended up in captivity, later recalled. "I held my breath at this appalling sight. Their heads were all cracked open and smoke was coming out. It was a horrific way to die." Seemingly heedless of American firepower, the massive host of survivors kept coming. "It was a raging, close quarter fight, Grenades, bayonets, fire-arms of all descriptions, fists, spears, and even feet were used," Captain Love, an eyewitness to its aftermath, later wrote with a palpable sense of awe.

In the melee, men fought to the death with rifles, pistols, bayonets, swords, knives, clubs, rocks, fists, and anything else that might kill. In less than half an hour of intense combat, the two American battalions basically ceased to exist as cohesive military organizations. Pinned against the beach, some of the Americans plunged into the lagoon and swam desperately for the reef some two hundred and fifty yards offshore. Others fought to the death in foxholes, gullies, or on foot as they retreated. Wounded and bleeding, Lieutenant John Titterington ran from machine gun to machine gun, firing belts of bullets at the enemy. "I've got to go, I guess, but if I do go, I'm going to take a lot of those sons of bitches with me," he said grimly to a soldier who urged him to seek medical help. The lieutenant died at his gun. Another platoon leader, Lieutenant Robert McGuire, unleashed deadly sheets of machine-gun fire at the charging host. Wounded and bleeding profusely, he refused to retreat as the line collapsed around him. "I'd rather stay here," he told his men. He killed an untold number of Japanese, but he had no chance to survive. Within minutes, he lay dead at his gun. "He died like a man . . . or shall I say a hero, taking as many as possible with him," Sergeant Victor Mazzeo, a member of his platoon, later wrote reverently. "He paid the supreme price for all that; his life." First Sergeant Charles Stephani collected grenades from wounded men and pitched them in droves at the Japanese. Unlike Titterington, he was fortunate enough to survive. "I had the pleasure of getting fifteen of them," he later said with almost venomous satisfaction of the Japanese he killed.

Lieutenant Colonel William O'Brien, the revered 1st Battalion commander who had already become something of a legend to his men for his earthy demeanor and inspirational bravery, brandished a pair of pistols, ran along his lines, and told his soldiers, "Don't give them a damn inch!" A bullet smashed into the back side of his right shoulder. O'Brien barely tolerated any medical attention while he desperately radioed higher headquarters for help. He jumped into a foxhole, took a rifle from a wounded man, and emptied it at the onrushing Japanese. He left the hole, climbed onto a jeep, and unleashed torrents of .50-caliber machine-gun fire as hordes of the attackers engulfed him. When he ran out of ammunition, he grabbed a Japanese saber and, according to survivors who glimpsed his actions in the half-light, hacked several enemy to pieces until he, too, was slashed and shot to death. Near the rail line, a grenade exploded in Sergeant Thomas Baker's foxhole and nearly severed his foot. Though he could only crawl and crab walk, he refused to allow other soldiers to carry him to the rear. "I'm done for," he told one of them. He propped himself against a pole, with a cigarette in one hand, a pistol in the other, and fought to the death, killing eight enemy soldiers. Both O'Brien and Baker later received the Medal of Honor.

Groups of Japanese roamed seemingly everywhere, clashing with retreating or defiant Americans. Some of the terrified Americans ran for their lives. "Men pleaded with each other to not run, but to fight," a survivor sadly recalled. "It was too late, for the rout was in progress and nothing . . . could prevent the men from running." One of those who fled had his entire mouth shot away; only the shredded remnants of his tongue remained to flop crazily as he ran. In many instances, men from both sides became intermixed—actually running alongside one another—as the fighting gravitated southward along the coast into the battery positions of the 10th Marine Regiment, an artillery unit, and eastward in the direction of the neighboring 165th Infantry Regiment. Fighting lines had ceased to exist in favor of confused, brawling, desperate groups. Frantic calls went out from 27th Division headquarters to the 762nd Tank Battalion for armored support. Platoon-size groups of Sherman tanks soon plunged into the melee, raking the Japanese with high-explosive and white phosphorous shells augmented by thousands of .30- and .50-caliber machine-gun bullets. The enemy responded with explosives, Molotov cocktails, or just sheer reckless courage. Led by a sword-wielding officer, a group of about one hundred attackers charged straight at one tank. They were soon shredded by multiple high-explosive shells. Wounded, on his knees, and unable to take another step, the officer slowly straightened himself, almost at attention, and faced the tank. "In this posture he placed the point of the sword against his abdomen and fell forward on it," one American witness remembered. "The sword ran clear through his body." Elsewhere, as another group of enemy soldiers took shelter inside a house, a Sherman tank pumped several 75-millimeter rounds into the building and completely demolished it. According to the tank gunner, "arms and legs were seen to fly into the air." A Japanese survivor, perhaps disoriented by concussion or just suicidally brave, emerged from the wrecked house and calmly walked straight at the Sherman. Streams of machine-gun bullets, including multiple tracer rounds, tore into him. Somehow, he managed to make it to within twenty-five yards of the tank before he finally succumbed to the bullets.

Medical installations were quickly inundated with wounded and dying men. "The number of casualties was appalling," the theater surgeon bluntly wrote in a post-battle report. "They were placed up and down the area between the tents on the ground, on a litter or a blanket." Inevitably, the medics and their patients came under attacks every bit as savage as the frontline foxholes. "It was insane to try to hold the line," Tech 3 Vincent Donnolo, the medic, later jotted in his diary. "Japs short of firing weapons came upon us with sticks with bayonets attached to them, pointed hard cane stalks, hand grenades, bayonets, sumari [sic] swords, rifle and small arms. Saw Japs mowed down like one would run a scythe . . . to cut wheat. I fired my carbine into a mass of Japs not a hundred feet away. To my left . . . I could see hand to hand fighting. The scene was undescribable for the howling of the Japs . . . and our wounded rent the air." He watched in horror as enemy soldiers hacked helpless wounded soldiers to death. Individual Japanese attackers swept into the crowded tent that served as an aid station for the 2nd Battalion, 105th Infantry, and attempted to kill the wounded.

Captain Ben Salomon, the acting battalion surgeon, had already treated scores of patients by the time the enemy arrived. The twenty-nine-year-old native of Los Angeles and graduate of the University of Southern California dental school had originally entered the Army through the draft as an infantryman and demonstrated considerable weapons proficiency. Salomon proved himself to be a natural and enthusiastic combat soldier, so much so that when he received orders commissioning him as an officer in the Army Dental Corps, he attempted to decline in favor of remaining an infantry sergeant or perhaps just commissioning as an infantry officer. The Army, of course, eventually had its way and he became the 105th Infantry

Regiment dental officer. Even so, he insisted before the Saipan invasion on setting aside his afternoons for participation in training with the line companies. "Ben Salomon was the best instructor in infantry tactics we ever had," his regimental commander once said of him. On June 22 the 2nd Battalion surgeon had been wounded by shell fragments. Salomon had taken over the job and immediately demonstrated great skill as a combat surgeon. He even told one friend that he intended to attend medical school after the war. Tech 3 Donnolo described him as "a swell guy. He pitched in like one of the boys in the aid-station."

When the Japanese entered the tent, Salomon immediately made the switch from physician to combat soldier. He killed four enemy soldiers— shooting one, stabbing two others, and even clubbing one with a rifle. "Captain Salomon was pretty mad," one of the wounded Americans later told a historian. "He was muttering about some sons of bitches not doing their job very well, and he charged out of the tent with his fists doubled up, like he was going to beat hell out of somebody." Outside the tent, Salomon could see that the Japanese had overrun his unit. He poked his head back inside and told his men to take care of the wounded as best they could while he attempted to hold off the Japanese. Outside, Captain Salomon took sole control of a machine gun and unleashed torrents of devastating fire into the attackers, who died in droves as his bullets tore into them. Four separate times he displaced and resumed firing. Alone and carrying on in the face of overwhelming numbers, he elected to die at his gun rather than flee the area or return to the embattled medical tent.

Later, after the battle, American soldiers found Salomon's body slumped over the gun, with ninety-eight dead Japanese around him. Salomon's remains were riddled with stab wounds, and seventy-six distinct bullet holes. In the opinion of an examining physician, at least twenty-four of the bullet wounds had occurred before Salomon's death. Captain Love, the historian, attempted to spearhead a Medal of Honor effort for the valorous dentist, but Major General Griner squelched the nomination, not from lack of respect for Salomon's actions but because he mistakenly believed that Salomon had violated the Geneva Convention by wielding weapons. In Griner's view, this could, under the wrong circumstances, become scandalous. Given the 27th's delicate relations with Holland Smith, Griner probably had little stomach for drawing any kind of unflattering attention to his division. "I am deeply sorry that I cannot approve the award of this medal . . . although he richly deserves it," he wrote on the nomination papers. In point of fact, the 1929 Convention expressly allowed medics to use weapons in defense of themselves or their patients. Not until 2002, after multiple attempts on the part of his advocates, did Salomon receive a posthumous Medal of Honor. By then, his father, Ben Salomon Senior—the captain's only next of kin—had long since died. The father's only indication of the son's remarkable stand came from Captain Love, with whom he briefly met and corresponded shortly after the war. "Awesome as it was, it is clear that he died facing and fighting the enemy and that he exacted a high toll for his life," the senior Salomon wrote to Love. "Thank you for giving recognition to his efforts."[16]

As always with self-sacrificial Japanese attacks—and this one might well have been the largest of the entire Pacific War—poor organization and coordination, combined with alert American resilience, guaranteed ultimate defeat. Even so, V Amphibious Corps headquarters initially reacted with sluggish ignorance to news of the onslaught, surprising for an organization whose commander had supposedly expected and warned of a banzai attack on that very evening. When Lieutenant Colonel Van Antwerp, the 27th Division intelligence officer, called his counterpart at corps to report a major attack from an enemy force numbering at least three thousand troops, the corps intelligence officer replied, "Take it easy, Van. You know as well as I do that at dawn fifty Japs look like five hundred."

Morning media briefings went on as usual at corps headquarters, even as fresh reports of the attack came back from what remained of the front. "There was small indication that all hell had broken loose," Sherrod, the correspondent, told his diary. In the late morning, Major General Griner estimated Japanese strength, during a conversation with Holland Smith's chief of staff, at five thousand troops. Griner requested infantry and armored reinforcements to assist a counterattack he had ordered by the 106th Infantry to relieve the remnants of the 105th and restore the lines. He received a battalion from the 6th Marine Regiment, but no tanks. "Obviously that headquarters did not accept my version of the importance of the action then in progress," Griner later claimed in a statement to the Buckner Board. Van Antwerp, the intelligence officer, concurred that "there appeared to be an impression in that headquarters during all of the Bloody 7th that the reports from the 27th were highly exaggerated."

Regardless, the 106th's attack proceeded with the sort of cautious deliberation more appropriate for a reconnaissance mission than a rescue operation to assist an embattled sister outfit. Few of the participants understood the actual situation. Sherrod, who embedded with the lead troops, later described the attack as "inordinately slow. Accompanying tanks fired thousands of rounds from their machine guns in preparation for the attack against the invisible enemy, of whom some were hidden along the railroad track and in nearby cornfields. Whenever a rifleman fired a shot, the entire line stopped advancing. Everyone felt that the battle was over and this was simply a mopup." They recaptured the battery positions of the 10th Marine Regiment. As darkness approached, Colonel Stebbins, the 106th commander, grew increasingly concerned about the threat posed by bypassed Japanese, so he halted and dug in a few hundred yards short of making contact with the survivors from the 105th. Like most American commanders of that era, the possibility of operating at night never seemed to occur to him.

With the 106th halted, Griner sent LVTs from the 773rd Amphibian Tank Battalion to evacuate by water the men who had retreated to the beach or the reefs offshore. Working in the twilight and early evening shadows, the LVT crews evacuated between three hundred and four hundred men against little opposition. "There was not a sound from any one of these men," Major James Bartholomees, the battalion executive officer, later wrote of those evacuees who remained on their feet. "They were so tired and so relieved at being pulled out of an impossible situation that the unwounded merely got to the ground and helped unload the wounded. Not a man had had a drink of water or a thing to eat all day and yet they were not interested in food or water."

Untold numbers of the evacuees had been wounded. A few died aboard LVTs. The rest made it to whatever remained of an aid station where Tech 3 Donnolo and other medics worked all night to save lives. Later, in his diary, he wrote poignantly of "men with horrible wounds that words cannot describe. Men weeping, men hollering for morphine for relief from pain. I saw the dead rolled off litters—one does not worry too much how one treats the dead for their sufferings are all over. Never did I dream to see so many wounded and half-dying boys. [I] Did things, saw things that no human person would believe." The 31st Field Hospital hurriedly treated 750 patients, mostly from the 105th Infantry, within a twenty-four-hour period. "Wounds were debrided and left open," the unit after-action report stated; "fractures were immobilized in plaster of paris casts, as were extensive wounds of the extremities. Guillotine amputations of hopelessly disorganized extremities and whenever else indicated such as with gas gangrene, were performed following the application of skin traction for the stump."

The gyokusai attack had petered out and failed by the latter hours of July 8; the Americans simply combed the area, annihilating the surviving Japanese in small groups. By now, the two unlucky battalions from the 105th were shattered. Collectively, they lost 406 men killed and another 512 wounded, out of an original complement of around 1,100 soldiers. Japanese losses were staggering. Saito's misbegotten gyokusai had basically destroyed his remaining army. The dismembered, decomposing bodies of his men covered northwestern Saipan like a macabre blanket. "The whole area seemed to be a mass of stinking bodies, spilled guts and brains," Sherrod vividly wrote. To Lieutenant Colonel Oakley Bidwell, the 27th Division's personnel officer, the area "appeared to be virtually solid dead soldiers. A creek ran through a shallow ravine, emptying into a beautiful turquoise-blue lagoon. The creek and its banks seemed filled with bodies. And while I watched, a huge crimson flower grew out of the mouth of the creek." A Marine engineer captain who had fought on Guadalcanal surveyed the terrible aftermath and told Lieutenant Colonel Antwerp, "It was kindergarten [compared] to this." The Marine shook his head with admiration and said of the 105th, "God, how those two battalions must have fought."

Billions of flies, arising like some sort of biblical plague, descended on one and all. For days, if not weeks, anyone attempting to eat a meal had to accept the fact that he would probably consume flies along with food. "Honestly, you could hardly take a bite . . . without a fly or two going with it," Sergeant Kohler, the Mariner tanker, told his parents. "And they were not the type you have at home. These had big green bodies and were so bold you would have to pick them off your chow." The flies played a role in numerous diarrhea and dengue fever cases. At one point, a single field hospital was treating 450 dengue patients. Under General Griner's close personal supervision, Bidwell and other 27th Division officers meticulously counted the enemy dead—a vile, enervating task—and arrived at the number of 4,311, including 2,295 in the 1st and 2nd Battalion, 105th Infantry Regiment sectors. Undoubtedly, as Major General Harry Schmidt, the 4th Marine Division commander, later stated in a memo to Griner, some of the dead had lost their lives before the gyokusai. No matter, there could be little doubt that the attack had cost the Japanese at least 3,000 dead and that the 27th Division had inflicted most of that damage. Once counted, the burial parties sprayed milky colored sodium arsenite solution on the remains and unceremoniously dumped them into mass graves. "Each sign on top of a mound of earth had the number of dead inscribed such as '10, 20, 30, etc' Japanese dead," Private Robert Cypher later wrote. In many cases, the Americans used bulldozers to bury the dead. Tech 3 Donnolo watched several dozers dig hasty holes, repeatedly scoop up mounds of corpses, and dump them in the pit. "What a ghastly sight—the stench was too great for me," he sadly told his diary. "The dozers just pushed the Japs into the holes with their blades." He estimated that they buried as many as four hundred this way.[17]

Nor did the dying among the Japanese conclude with defeat of the gyokusai attack. Though the Americans declared the island secured on July 9, small-unit actions against wayward or holdout Japanese soldiers and sailors continued for weeks. At Saipan as a whole, the Japanese lost at least 30,000 killed, as most of the garrison fought to the death. Of 71,000 American troops engaged, 16,612 became casualties, a 23 percent rate. Some 3,126 Americans were killed and another 326 missing, almost all of whom were dead. The 27th Division lost 960 killed, 2,493 wounded, and 73 missing. Most of the American bodies were retrieved and stacked aboard trucks, jeeps, DUKWs, or LVTs by a twenty-six-man platoon of soldiers from the 604th Graves Registration Company who worked in tandem with engineers once the latter could be spared from the battle. Bulldozers manned by engineers cleared and graded a cemetery out of Saipan wilderness. The graves registration men carried out the thankless and grisly task of burying the seemingly endless stream of bodies. "All dead were wrapped in blankets and buried six feet under ground," Lieutenant Colonel Oakley Bidwell, whose 27th Division personnel section was responsible for supervising the burials, wrote in an official report. "The difficulties of locating the bodies among the thousands of Japanese dead, of recovering bodies from shell holes which had filled with water, and the collection of bodies which had been badly shattered by mortar fire made it impossible to complete the collection of these dead in less than 4½ days, notwithstanding the amount of personnel and transportation involved." The burial details carefully painted names of the dead onto crosses and Stars of David, and maintained the graves as best they could. Another 292 27th Division men were evacuated with combat fatigue, characterized by the division neuropsychiatrist as "a state of exhaustion, disorientation, extreme fear, and a bizarre behavior to the slightest movement or sound." One of the victims told Medical Corps survey takers, "My case is one of shattered nerves, slight amnesia and nightmares. It is a disability which only the peace of mind and soul and loving of parents can give. In my state of nervousness, G.I. 'people' and regulations merely continue to shatter the nerves." By design, the Army could offer little more than its own world of treatment, heavily spiced with "GI people" and "regulations." Some 73 percent of combat fatigue cases were returned to duty.

As the end neared, hundreds of Japanese civilians chose, either voluntarily or under coercion from their military brethren, to commit suicide, most famously hurling themselves off the cliffs of Marpi Point on the island's north coast. Horrified Americans, including interpreters, attempted to dissuade them, usually in vain, from carrying out their own destruction. As PFC John Des Jarlais gestured to one young mother to stop short of the cliffs, "she ran up to the edge, turned and looked at me with such hate in her eyes. Then she and her baby disappeared over the cliff." Major Max McGlone, a staff officer with the 2nd Marine Regiment, watched as "hundreds of civilians, as well as soldiers, destroyed themselves by jumping over the cliffs . . . by wading into the surf to drown, by killing themselves with grenades. Some were shot by Japanese soldiers as they hesitated on the edge of the cliffs. Children were thrown over the cliffs into the sea and their parents joined them soon after. Mothers clasped babies to them and jumped to the rocks below." Sherrod saw one group bow in unison to the Marines, strip their clothes off, bathe in the sea, and then, one after the other, kill themselves with grenades. In many instances, hidden Japanese soldiers killed anyone who hesitated, even for a moment. One of Marine PFC Red Butler's buddies rushed from cover to save a wavering woman and her child. "A Nip soldier stepped out of the bush, turned toward [him] and threw a hand grenade in his direction. A large chunk of shrapnel nailed him and he went down fast. I brought down the bastard who threw the grenade." Butler was so enraged that he raised his rifle to shoot the woman and child, but his dying friend talked him out of it. "His 'don't do it, buddy' and strong will to save the woman and child probably spared my soul," Butler later wrote. The coastal waters were soon choked with bloated corpses. "Part of the area is so congested with floating bodies we simply can't avoid running them down," Lieutenant Emery Cleaves, an officer aboard a minesweeper, told Sherrod. "I've seen literally hundreds in the water." The dead included a pregnant mother who had drowned herself and her newborn baby just as he emerged from the womb. "The baby's head had entered this world, but that was all of him," Cleaves commented sadly.

Japanese propaganda seized upon this orgy of self-destructive, atavistic violence to paint a picture of a powerful, defiant empire impervious to defeat. "The Heroic Last Moments of Our Fellow Countrymen on Saipan," one typical newspaper headline blared, "Sublimely Women Too Commit Suicide on Rocks in Front of the Great Sun Flag. Patriotic Essence Astounds the World." Another lionized the women who had committed suicide "in front of the American devils [to] sacrifice themselves for the national exigency together with the brave men." Writing in the same paper, a female poet pledged to fight to the end "with the pride of the women who fought to the last in a sea of blood. We will battle on beside the spirits of these women who fell beside soldiers."

Beneath the defiant veneer, though, all too many Japanese, at least at the highest levels, knew that Saipan represented a watershed setback, one that ominously augured ultimate defeat. The Americans now had a base from which they could bomb the home islands, a game-changing event. As the war had steadily turned against Japan, the jushin, a powerful group of unofficial senior advisers to the emperor, had lost confidence in Hideki Tojo, the Imperial Army general who headed up a war cabinet as prime minister. With this sour mood of discontent, and even some assassination plans, in the air, Tojo soon realized that he could not hope to survive, politically or otherwise, the loss of Saipan. Indeed, his wife was upset by menacing calls to his personal residence inquiring as to when he intended to commit suicide. On July 20, even as his ally Hitler survived an assassination attempt on the other side of the world, Tojo stepped down as prime minister and left active military service. Contrary to tradition, Hirohito did not immediately invite him into the ranks of the jushin, a calculated move that conveyed the depths to which Tojo had sunk. Another general, Kuniaki Koiso, replaced him and, with the emperor's acquiescence, shared power with Mitsumasa Yonai, an admiral who had refused to serve in Tojo's cabinet but now signed on as Navy minister. Well attuned to Japan's great crisis, the new heads of government and their cabinet members were privately more receptive to the notion of suing for peace than Tojo and his minions. Even so, they were as yet unwilling to make the hard decisions, such as withdrawal from China or agreeing to Western Allied demands for unconditional surrender, that might have actually led to peace. In that sense, the change of government in Japan had little tangible effect on the present course of the war.[18]

Though nowhere near as serious as the reverberations of mutual recrimi-
nation among the Japanese, the victors were hardly immune to their own
self-defeating flagellation. Holland Smith, with his unmatched talent for
nescient, provincial rabble-rousing, accused the 27th Division of cowardice and deficiency in the face of the gyokusai attack. During the initial
hours of the fighting, he estimated the size of the Japanese force at no more
than five hundred men. He came to believe that the Army commanders
had failed to heed his warnings of an impending banzai attack, thus allowing a relatively small group of enemy to tear through the 105th Infantry
front, unnecessarily imperiling the lives of the 10th Marine Regiment artillerymen, who were then obliged to help quell the attack and save the GIs
from total disaster (only years later did he raise his estimate to between
fifteen hundred and three thousand attackers). He blamed Griner for dis-
loyalty and inefficiency. Undiplomatic as ever, he openly vented his poor
opinion of the 27th Division to corps headquarters staffers and even media
members. He ordered the 2nd Marine Division to take over for the 105th
Infantry and finish the battle. Simmering with anger, he complained to
Sherrod of the 27th Division, "They're yellow. They are not aggressive.
They've held up the battle and caused my Marines casualties. I'm sending
the Second Division through them tomorrow and I hope the Second
doesn't get into a fight passing through. I'm afraid they'll say, 'You yellow
bastards,' as they pass through."

The toxic attitude of the commander naturally rubbed off on the Marines under his direct influence. In line for breakfast one morning, Sherrod
overheard two Marine junior officers speculating as to whether any 27th
Division officers would be court-martialed for neglect of duty. "The Japs
got through without a shot being fired," one of the speculators ignorantly
claimed. In this sense, the young officer simply reflected his corps commander. For a general who was ultimately responsible for the conduct of
the Saipan battle, and one who cultivated an image as a hardened fighter,
Holland Smith proved himself consistently and stunningly ignorant of its
realities. From the post–D-day fighting through the gyokusai, he remained
out of touch with enemy capabilities and the actual conditions his men
faced in combat. Having faced no bullets or shells himself while safely
ensconced at headquarters during the attack, he nonetheless felt no

compunction about leveling the mortal sin charge of cowardice at the very men who had borne the terrifying brunt of the fighting. Instead of investigating the facts of the gyokusai assault for himself, he simply defaulted to his usual predilection to disparage the Army, almost as a convenient means to exalt "his" Marines. One might forgive a corps commander for physical remoteness from the fighting—after all, his job hardly entailed carrying a rifle at the front. One can muster much less sympathy, though, for a commander who remained mentally remote from, and as a consequence prejudicially unaware of, the battle his people were fighting. Almost by deliberate choice, Holland Smith wallowed in this ignorance and, as a result, made poor, emotion-based decisions.

Though Sherrod was cut from much braver cloth, having courageously faced death many times alongside Marines at Tarawa and Saipan, he, too, came to embrace many of his friend Holland Smith's poisonous attitudes about the Army's supposed ineptitude. "If we had sent three Army divisions to take this place we'd still be fighting for a beachhead," he huffed in a letter to a *Time* magazine editor. Sherrod spent very little time at the front with the 27th Division on Saipan and had no real idea of the conditions the unit had faced and how it actually fought. When he did have the opportunity to embed with the 27th, he elected to go "back with the real professionals," the Marines.

These personal views of a lone war correspondent would have mattered little except that, on September 18, over two months after the Saipan battle, he published an incendiary article in *Time* about the firing of Ralph Smith. He attempted to explain both the Army and Marine points of view by couching the conflict in terms of Marine aggressiveness versus Army deliberateness, perhaps unconsciously shaping most subsequent historical understanding. Had Sherrod limited his discussion to this point, the article would probably have sparked no controversy. But he erroneously claimed that, at Nafutan, "Ralph Smith's men froze in their foxholes. For days these men, who lacked confidence in their officers, were held up by handfuls of Japs in caves." Then he dropped a literary bomb, one that reverberated for years. In the gyokusai attack, he asserted falsely, the 27th's "greenest regiment broke and let some 3,000 Japs through in a suicide charge which a Marine artillery battalion finally stopped at great cost to itself."

Given *Time*'s mass national circulation, Sherrod had basically told the entire American public that the 27th was guilty of cowardice and incompetence. Not surprisingly, the piece provoked a firestorm of controversy. At Esperitu Santo, where the 27th Division survivors were recuperating from the Saipan fighting, the article exploded among the ranks like some sort of literary nuclear bomb. "The Sherrod article hurt and stung them," Sergeant John Thorburn wrote to Ralph Smith of the pain the men felt when they read the piece. "With a few biased, nasty words he cut into their very hearts." According to the historian Captain Love, who was on the island conducting after-action combat interviews, "the impact . . . was indescribable. By nightfall the soldiers had gathered in small groups to discuss it and that night, until midnight, every company and every battery in the Division had held some sort of meeting, either official or unofficial, to protest. Most of the men were indignant, some were hopping mad, others just stunned to think that anyone could allow such an article to be published about men who had recently gone through hell for their country." Many fired off angry letters to *Time* and even Sherrod himself, who had returned to the United States for a brief respite. "The names they call us (and me) are hardly fit to print," the correspondent wrote to a Marine friend. "Most of them also contain implied threats of bodily harm." Captain John Gaddis, a public relations officer who handled press liaison during the battle, ripped Sherrod as "a one-man Marine lobby . . . who passed on many slighting remarks, purporting to constitute the true picture of the 27th's allegedly 'poor performance' on Saipan. Sherrod told several correspondents that he wasn't interested in seeing the 27th or writing about it because it had 'messed up.'" An angry Colonel Gerard Kelley, commander of the 165th Infantry, denounced Sherrod in a letter to Congressman James Fay of New York, an old friend who had lost a leg while serving with the same regiment in World War I. "He was never seen by members of the Regiment during the action. His coverage of operations out this way has been notoriously inaccurate, in a not too subtle effort to belittle Army accomplishments. The bold lies published in the story literally amazed us."

Aside from the understandable tendency to lash out at *Time* or Sherrod, the distorted article had the unfortunate effect of awakening, in some 27th Division soldiers, latent resentments against the Marines, particularly with respect to their propensity to attract positive publicity. "Most anyone who knows will agree that they are publicity hounds of the first water," one angry major wrote to his family; "if just one Marine goes ashore they immediately take credit for the whole operation." After reading the article, one incensed lieutenant claimed in a letter home, "I'm here to tell you that

we did more to secure that island than the two Marine Divisions put together. Believe me, if we hadn't landed when we did, the Marines would
have been chased right off the island in another day or so. For my money
the 27th Division was the Marines' secret weapon." Another young soldier
raged to his wife, "When I'm home, honey, I'll tell you exactly what the
whole Army thinks of Marines. I wish we didn't have to fight with them."
The humiliating pain of the allegations soon affected family members, especially among the kin of dead soldiers, who began writing searching letters to 27th Division headquarters, almost in hopes of reassurance that the
lives of their loved ones had not been squandered at the altar of incompetence or negligence. In the recollection of one senior officer, "the widow of
an officer who was killed in action on 7 July has written that her concern
over the charges of cowardice in the *Time* article approaches the poignancy
of her grief at her husband's death."

The bickering spread to higher levels, with potentially more serious
consequences than simple interservice rivalry. An incensed Major General
Griner wrote a blistering, though unpublished, rebuttal to the editors of
Time with the admonition that "your distortion of the facts of this epochal
event and your circulation of an unwarranted reflection upon the valor of
the hundreds of American soldiers who gave their lives in *your* defense
deserves the condemnation of all fair minded people." To Lieutenant General Richardson, he even expressed the opinion that he could not assume
responsibility for leading the 27th into combat again unless something was
officially done at higher military and political levels to clear the name of
the division. Ever sensitive to any slight against the Army, Richardson lobbied Nimitz to repudiate the story publicly and officially expunge any whiff
of stigma against the 27th. Richardson even urged Nimitz to revoke Sherrod's credentials. Temperamentally hostile to public squabbles among senior officers, especially among different services, the fair-minded admiral
largely agreed with Richardson. Nimitz had formed a high opinion of
Ralph Smith well before the Saipan battle, and this favorable view only
solidified with Smith's classy behavior after his relief. Nimitz also personally
believed that the 27th had fought well at Saipan. Even if it had not, though,
the admiral believed no good came from the sort of public renunciation
that naturally flowed from Sherrod's article. He forwarded Richardson's
recommendations to Admiral King with the supportive comment, "I am
in complete accord with the objections raised by Lt. Gen. Robert C. Richardson, Jr to the publication of the subject articles which, in my opinion,

are contrary to best interests of the nation." Nimitz urged King to authorize publication of Griner's rebuttal letter and have the Department of the Navy issue an official statement of confidence in the 27th Division. Admiral King refused to revoke Sherrod's credentials on the grounds that he had complied with all censorship rules before publishing the article. The chief of naval operations saw no issue with Griner sending the letter to *Time*— he took no position on its publication, since that probably remained out of his control—but he had little stomach for urging Secretary of the Navy James Forrestal to issue an exculpatory statement. In King's view, this would publicly undercut Holland Smith and validate what King considered to be biased findings against the general by the Buckner Board. "The record of the Board includes intemperate attacks on the personal character and professional competence of Lieutenant General Holland M. Smith," the admiral wrote to General Marshall. Instead, King suggested that Holland Smith make a statement of confidence in the 27th Division, an idea that carried little currency with any of the other decision makers, probably because they understood that any such pronunciation would hardly exude much authenticity.

With a global war to fight, neither King nor Marshall had any desire to lock horns over an ultimately pointless interservice squabble. In the end, although both leaders felt for the 27th Division, they agreed to quell the whole sordid matter by simply shelving it and letting the public rancor dissipate over time. "I feel that harm rather than good would result from attempting to adjust the matter through the press," Marshall wrote to King. "It would also seem that any further public statements would merely aggravate the controversy." Instead, they took less obtrusive actions, mainly to make sure that no such controversy would ever happen again. Ralph Smith, having survived his relief with no prejudice against his official record, was transferred from the 98th Division to the European theater to serve as military liaison to the nascent de Gaulle government in newly liberated France, where Smith utilized his in-depth knowledge of French history and culture to become a true asset to Eisenhower.

In the privacy of senior officer correspondence, numerous Army generals expressed their lack of confidence in Holland Smith and strongly recommended that he never again be allowed to command Army troops. The list included Jarman, Brigadier General Clark Ruffner from Richardson's staff, Brigadier General Redmond Kernan, division artillery commander of the 27th, Ralph Smith, and, perhaps most notably, Griner. Kernan described Holland Smith as "obviously so antagonistic, unreasonable and harassing as to seriously endanger the efficiency and morale of the Division during combat." Ralph Smith, in a top secret memo he wrote before leaving Oahu, opined that "this Marine officer has shown . . . that so far as the employment of Army troops are concerned, he is prejudiced, petty and unstable." Griner, who had taken over for Ralph Smith with something of a neutral attitude toward the Marine commander, had since soured badly on him after serving under his command for much of the Saipan battle. In his own top secret recommendation, Griner asserted of Holland Smith, "He is so prejudiced against the Army that no Army Division serving under his command alongside of Marine Divisions can expect that their deeds will receive fair and honest evaluation."

Marshall took these recommendations to heart, as did King, who, no matter how much he might have sympathized with Holland Smith, came to realize that his poisonous relations with the Army imperiled the harmony and success of any future joint operations under his command. With Nimitz's enthusiastic consent, Holland Smith was essentially kicked upstairs, promoted to command of the Fleet Marine Force, a largely administrative post that kept him from leading troops in the field. The new job was ironically similar to that of Smith's archnemesis and alter ego Richardson. Smith could not help but feel angry about his backhanded promotion. "Good God, I work my heart out, clean up the Marianas in good style, and all I get is—Crap!" he lamented in a letter to Vandegrift. He felt especially bitter toward and resentful of Nimitz, in part for middling ratings the admiral had assigned him in a fitness report after Saipan. "He was furious," a friend of Smith's later commented. "It hit him where he lived." More than this, Smith believed that Nimitz had acted like nothing more than a petty politician by failing to stand up to the Army for him. He never quite forgave the admiral, later snidely dismissing him as "always inclined to compromise." Like King, Nimitz had vast responsibilities and he inherently understood the vital importance to the war effort of working harmoniously with Army colleagues, a concept that Smith never really grasped. Most likely, Admiral Nimitz had also come to realize that Holland Smith was nowhere near worth the considerable baggage that inevitably accompanied him. The Pacific Fleet commander was only too happy to shunt Smith aside to his administrative post and save himself the unwanted drama of any more infighting.

With the unpleasant senior-level spats shoveled into the closet by

Washington decision makers, and thus resolved to their satisfaction, the reputation of the 27th Division proved to be the primary long-term casualty. "The 27th Division will have other opportunities to vindicate its record," Marshall told King. Indeed it would, but with no official rebuttal to the Sherrod article, the soldiers of the division remained unfairly saddled with stigma of failure for the rest of the war and beyond. "We have suffered from inaccurate and scanty descriptions of our accomplishments," Colonel Kelley wrote presciently to Congressman Fay. "You and I know this Regiment and this Division need no gaudy publicity. However, suppression of the truth of the past will add credence to the lies of the future." Perhaps sensing this, Admiral Nimitz wrote a personal letter to Griner expressing full confidence in the 27th Division.

In an ironic travesty, the Sherrod story and the interservice tiff as a whole obscured the frontline reality that Marine and Army combat troops on Saipan had largely fought well together and had developed a deep mutual respect. "We have no fight with the United States Marines," Captain Love wrote a couple of months after the battle. "They are Americans like ourselves and we admire and respect them as men." The Marine Corps official historian later summarized, with sage insight, "Marines and soldiers fought a hard campaign side by side. On the battlefield itself, there was neither place nor time for interservice rivalry. The measure of value was how well each man stood his share of the common burden, not what his uniform color was when he stood clear of the mud and the dust. In truth, there could be no other answer to success in combat than interservice cooperation." Indeed, this was so very true, for the two ground services were about to fight together on an additional array of traumatic battlefields.[19]

9

Right Way and Wrong Way

The determined Japanese stand on Saipan cost the architects of Operation Forager time but not momentum. No matter how hard the Saipan garrison fought, they were powerless to thwart US plans to invade Tinian and Guam, the other two key objectives in the archipelago. American aircraft and ships pummeled Tinian, as did heavy artillery from positions on Saipan. Some 15,600 troops from the 2nd and 4th Marine Divisions assaulted the little island on July 24, initiating a bitter weeklong battle that saw the near annihilation of the garrison of 9,000 men, at the price of 328 Americans killed and another 1,571 wounded. The Japanese were tormented by practically every instrument of US firepower, including the combat debut of napalm. The Americans fired nearly 190,000 artillery shells, about a third of them from Army tubes on Saipan, at the Japanese. "You couldn't drop a stick without bringing down artillery," a Japanese prisoner later commented. Tinian became a major air base for the Americans.

The Saipan fighting, in tandem with the Battle of the Philippine Sea, delayed the III Marine Amphibious Corps's Guam invasion for a little more than a month. In early July, Admiral Turner, Lieutenant General Holland Smith, Major General Geiger, and Vice Admiral Richard Connolly, commander of Task Force 53 (or Southern Attack Force), the naval complement for the Southern Troops and Landing Force, met and decided, with Spruance's approval, upon July 21 as the invasion date.

By that time, many of Spruance's ships had been at sea for the better part of two months. The relentless operational pace stretched Vice Admiral William Calhoun's Service Force Pacific Fleet nearly to its limit, particularly in relation to fuel, the critical blood of all World War II naval operations. Already, the Navy had consumed 43 percent more fuel of all kinds than the planners had expected. Calhoun and his staff adapted by chartering forty oil tankers to augment the fleet's rather modest flotilla of six oilers. In July alone, these unglamorous but vitally important ships hauled nearly 4.5 million barrels of oil to forward staging areas and bases. The task of distributing such huge quantities of oil was time-consuming and likely would have been impossible without favorable weather and the security from enemy harassment afforded the Americans by the Battle of the Philippine Sea and other successful naval engagements. On average, a tanker could pump 250 barrels per hour into a warship. According to one naval after-action report, "a destroyer at 50% capacity therefore (requiring about 1800 barrels of fuel) will take about seven to eight hours to fill to capacity." Somehow the tankers also found time to transport 8 million gallons of aviation gasoline and 275,000 barrels of diesel oil. Store ships sailed endless round-trip voyages to Allied-controlled bases in the Pacific to maintain sufficient quantities of fresh water, food, ammunition, and other supplies. Without this logistical proficiency, Spruance might well have been forced to retire the bulk of his ships and suspend post-Saipan Forager operations. Instead, the unrelenting war machine continued unabated.

The impressive largesse of this great modern fleet proved small consolation to the leathernecks of the 3rd Marine Division and the 1st Provisional Marine Brigade who had spent much of the previous six weeks packed miserably aboard their transports and LSTs as a floating reserve—a necessary evil of blue-water amphibious operations. They endured the usual shipboard privations of crowded bunks, saltwater showers, overflowing lavatories, seasickness, rotting food, and endless briefings until they could hardly stand another day of it. "We'd have fought hell itself . . . to get off that damned ship," one Marine later said of his unit's transport vessel. At Guam, these troops of Geiger's III Marine Amphibious Corps were scheduled to land on July 21, or "W Day" in planner's lingo, and make a pincers assault on the sock-shaped island's southwestern coast, with the 3rd Marine Division landing at Agana Bay in the north and the 1st Provisional Marine Brigade at Agat Bay to the south.[1]

The Army's 77th Infantry Division made up the balance of Geiger's main combat reserve. He tapped the division's 305th Infantry Regiment to follow the 1st Brigade into Agat Bay on W Day and thereafter. Known as the Statue of Liberty Division for its New York National Guard origins, the 77th had been training for more than two years to experience its first taste of combat. The Statue of Liberty men had cycled through preparations for nearly every aspect of modern ground warfare—desert training at Camp Hyder, Arizona, mountain training in the peaks of Elkins, West Virginia, amphibious exercises at Camp Bradford, Virginia, and eventually jungle training on Oahu. In Hawaii many of the men lived at Camp Pali, a city-size perimeter of pyramid-shaped tents, some eight miles from Honolulu. The troops were subjected to long conditioning hikes, hand-to-hand combat instruction, jungle survival training, swimming classes, weapons qualifications, and new rounds of amphibious rehearsals. In the leftover hours, they plunged with gusto into the Hawaiian social scene. "As soon as the opportunity permitted, the troops familiarized themselves with the terrain and the situation," the division historian later wrote with tongue in cheek. "This necessarily included off-duty patrols to near-by small towns such as Kailua and Kahuku, and missions in force to Honolulu and the beach of Waikiki."

Military authorities established a rotation system for units to take turns exploring these pleasure spots. Off-duty khaki-clad soldiers packed into restaurants, bars, dance halls, and, for some, luaus where hula dancers mesmerized them with the chants and motions unique to Hawaiian culture. Others thronged to the YMCA, where they could eat a good meal, play games, and swim in a well-maintained pool. On the streets, souvenir merchants hawked everything from grass skirts to local clothing "at more than three times their value," in the recollection of one soldier. At Kailua Beach, lunchtime crowds of soldiers converged on the USO, where harried volunteers served ice cream and sodas to an insatiably hungry and thirsty crowd seeking refuge from Army food. On Sundays, men with passes attended baseball games to watch such erstwhile major leaguers turned soldiers as Staff Sergeant Joe DiMaggio, Corporal Walt Judnich, and Private Mike McCormick compete for Army teams.

In the endless search for women, the 77th Division men were disappointed to realize that males in the area greatly outnumbered females, especially among whites. "There was a woman shortage, caused by an influx of so many servicemen and civilian workers long before our arrival," the 305th Infantry Regiment history lamented. "The Navy . . . had got there before us, and they had the few white girls on the island already preferring blue uniforms to khaki." Houses of prostitution on Hotel Street in Chinatown offered multiracial outlets for the soldiers that attracted crowds so large as to lead to a fast-food version of sexual relief. Customers paid two dollars for the privilege of spending five minutes with whomever might be available. "Get it in, get it off, and get it out," overworked military policemen advised the long lines of men waiting for their turn. The more chaste

GIs resorted to visiting photographic studios and having their pictures taken with professional models, in part to enjoy a fleeting moment of feminine companionship, but also to send the snapshots to friends with the ubiquitous caption, "There was a pretty girl I knew in Hawaii." The long months of training had solidified unit pride and cohesion. "I get a big kick out of the men in the company," Captain Randy Seligman, a young physician who commanded C Company of the division's 302nd Medical Battalion, wrote to an Army nurse back in the States. "Their riotous sense of humor keeps me in an uproar. They are constantly needling one another . . . and the things they call one another simply ain't fit to print." The stay on Oahu ended in early July when first the 305th Infantry, followed during the subsequent weeks by the rest of the division as shipping became available, loaded onto transports bound for Eniwetok, where they waited for the word to proceed to Guam.[2]

The 77th enjoyed the good fortune of having thoughtful, competent commanders. Lieutenant General Eichelberger had once led the division for a few months in the spring of 1942 before moving on to greater command pastures. Since May 1943, fifty-year-old Major General Andrew "AD" Bruce had served as the commanding general. "This is a super outfit, but I'm going to make it a super duper outfit," he declared upon taking over. Handsome, square-faced, with a thick head of gray-black hair, he more than looked the part of a commander. "Just to look at the stern lines of his face one would not suspect that there was a great gentleness there," Brigadier General Edwin Randle, his assistant division commander and close friend, once marveled.

Bruce managed to combine an unrelenting focus on accomplishing missions with sincere concern for the welfare of his soldiers. In a conversation with an Army historian, Admiral Nimitz once referred to him as "the finest commander of troops in the Pacific." One of Bruce's sergeants told him after the war that "it was your fine leadership that really made our fine div[ision] what it is." Blessed with a prodigious military intellect and a hardy physical constitution, Bruce insisted upon high standards for his outfit, no matter the situation. A Texan to the core, he had graduated from Texas A&M in 1917, entered the Army as an infantry second lieutenant, and seen the devastating sharp end of World War I trench warfare for many months with the 2nd Division. He finished the war as a lieutenant colonel with multiple decorations for valor, including the Distinguished Service Cross.

Profoundly affected by his combat experiences, rocked by the personal tragedy of losing an infant son in 1921, Bruce developed a passion for learning and teaching as the best means to develop good leadership habits. His interwar postings read like a tour of the American military's premier educational development institutions—the Infantry School, the Field Artillery School, the Command and General Staff College, the Army War College, and the Naval War College. A two-year stint in the historical section of the Army War College imbued him with the sort of perspective that comes from a deep understanding of military history. After all his schooling and battlefield experiences, Bruce came to believe that good habits and positive comportment in training translated to high performance in combat. During the many months of training, he enforced rigid uniform and cleaning standards, earning from his soldiers the snide but distantly affectionate nickname "Old Man Leggings, Liners and Landscape." Privately, Bruce took a good-humored pride in the descriptive moniker. Under Bruce, the division earned a reputation for leaving camps, equipment, and garrison towns in better condition than it had found them. "We left behind us neat rows of tents, an area totally devoid of weeds and brush," the 305th Infantry regimental historian boasted upon leaving Camp Pali to board ships bound for Guam. The Mother Superior of a Catholic school once wrote personally to the general to commend his men for "their courtesy and gentlemanliness, their kindness and generosity. As a token of our esteem for you and your men we have named our new school building—the 77th Division Hall."

Beyond the aesthetics, Bruce possessed a keen understanding of combined-arms warfare. At the beginning of the war, he had established a major training center for the Army's tank destroyer branch, essentially converting it from a notion into tangible action. Along with combined arms, he prized interservice cooperation and joint operations to such an extent as to exceed most of his Army peers. "I want all officers and men to be especially cautious about their dealings with other arms," he ordered his antiaircraft battalion commander in the spring of 1944 about working with the Navy and Marine Corps. "In fact, I want to 'lean over backwards' in co-operation." The general made this such a priority that his people could not help but take notice. "It was not one man who cooperated," wrote Sergeant James MacGregor Burns, a historian attached to the division for the Guam operation, "it was all officers and men with few exceptions." After working closely with the 77th, a young naval officer felt compelled to write personally to Bruce and express the opinion that "I and my officers feel we have, in the 77th Division, met and served with the finest fighting outfit in the Army, and that we have been honored by that contact."

In the fifty-nine-year-old Geiger, Bruce found a boss of similar outlook and temperament. A pioneer in naval aviation and two-time recipient of the Navy Cross, Geiger had flown combat missions in World War I as one of the first-ever Marine fighter pilots. For two months during the Battle of Guadalcanal, he had led the Marine aerial contingent at Henderson Field. Calm and self-assured, Geiger performed so well that he received command of the I Marine Amphibious Corps—later renamed the III Marine Amphibious Corps—and carried out the successful invasion of Bougainville. With nearly a year of corps-level command under his belt by the summer of 1944, Geiger had forged productive, respectful relationships with colleagues from all services. Indeed, the contrast of this positive command environment with that of Holland Smith's V Amphibious Corps could not have been any more profound. Geiger viewed his corps, and Connolly's fleet, as one team, not a series of separate service components temporarily flung together for a conveniently common purpose. Bruce and Geiger got along especially well. The Army general deeply admired Geiger for his keen military mind and cordial demeanor. Neither nursed any bias against the other's service. In fact, Bruce thought highly of the Marine Corps. During his time at the Naval War College, he had befriended many Marine officers, including Brigadier General Lemuel Shepherd, commander of the 1st Provisional Marine Brigade. Moreover, in World War I, as a member of the 2nd Division, a unit that included a Marine brigade, Bruce had fought alongside many leathernecks. He understood intuitively that the common bond they shared as American warriors mattered most, not petty rivalries.[3]

Though the postponement of the Guam invasion had forced Geiger and his commanders to modify their landing plans and shipping schedules, it did buy the fleet more time to soften up the target before the troops went ashore. For more than two weeks before W Day, a formidable force of cruisers, battleships, destroyers, escort carriers, and other vessels pounded the Japanese on Guam. Aboard USS *Appalachian*, Admiral Connolly's flagship, Geiger and his staff helped their Navy brethren locate and prioritize targets. Ammunition expenditures were staggering. The battleships hurled 836 sixteen-inch rounds and 5,422 fourteen-inch shells. Cruisers fired 3,862 eight-inch and 2,430 six-inch rounds. Destroyers fired 16,214 five-inch shells. Carrier air strikes added more bombs and rockets to the carnage. On W Day, the Navy added another 18,386 shells of all calibers, plus 9,000 rounds of 4.5-inch rockets; fighters and torpedo planes added another 400 tons of ordnance. The damage tended to be greatest at the coast. The bombardment demolished coastal gun emplacements, beachside antiaircraft positions, and partially completed fortifications. "I would say that the fires were the most effective of any operation in the Pacific," Major L. A. Gilson, the III Marine Amphibious Corps naval gunfire officer, later opined. General Geiger believed it saved many casualties. Admiral Connolly had already logged nearly two years of command experience in amphibious and surface warfare operations. His diligent dedication to providing the ground services with effective fire support had earned him the affectionate nickname "Close In Connolly." To prepare for the Guam operation, he had actually relocated his headquarters next to Geiger's on Guadalcanal, working so closely with the Marines that he almost became one of their own. "He was one of the great amphibious commanders that I have met," a Marine colleague once said of him. "He was a very splendid, strong, able man who would listen. He studied and mastered the Marines' problems as well as the naval problems." Connolly contended that the Guam strikes were "as good or better than any that had been developed in any theater by any force or service *at that time*."

A Japanese survivor, reflecting with an almost palpable tremor years later on the suffocating barrage, described it as "near the limit bearable by humans." Lieutenant Colonel Takeshi Takeda, a staff officer who became the highest-ranking Japanese survivor of the battle, acknowledged that the bombardment degraded the fighting readiness of the garrison. In his view the constant attacks "carried out day after day had a very great psychological effect. After several days there were scattered outbreaks of serious loss of spirit. There were some whose spirit deteriorated so that they could not perform their duties in a positive manner. This was especially true on the landing fronts." Even so, Takeda pointed out that, in spite of the terrifying, enervating nature of the constant pounding, Japanese communications remained largely intact, as did concrete fortifications, cave positions, and command posts. Nor did it inflict many casualties. Most of the Japanese simply hunkered down in caves or bunkers and weathered the steel storm.

The Japanese defended the island with a force of 18,500 troops, about one-third of whom were Imperial Navy sailors involved in aviation or, more commonly, coastal defense batteries whose guns ranged in size from 75 to 200 millimeters. By the third week of July, the preponderance of the defenders, for several reasons, were in place near the eventual American landing beaches on the island's southwest coast. Guam's rugged reefs and coastal cliffs made sizable landings untenable most everywhere else, though Bruce, in hopes of cutting the Japanese forces in two, did unsuccessfully propose a two-regiment assault at Tumon Bay, a serviceable spot in Guam's central neck. On June 16, when the Americans still expected to land on Guam within a few days of Saipan, they had bombarded the landing beaches, in effect tipping off the Japanese to the location, if not necessarily the timing, of the invasion. The Japanese reacted accordingly and moved most of their troops, artillery, tanks, and other weapons to that part of Guam. In turn, this reflected the prevailing wrongheaded Imperial Army doctrine of investing all their resources to foil invasions at the waterline, heedless of American control of the sea and air. One mid-July command memo, reflecting this mindset, implored the troops, "The Garrison Unit will await its initial opportunity and will completely destroy the enemy landing force upon the beaches."

Most of the Imperial Army soldiers belonged to the 29th Division under the command of Lieutenant General Takeshi Takashina, a bespectacled old-schooler. Lieutenant General Obata, the 31st Army commander who had been stranded in the Palaus at the onset of the Saipan invasion, had now made it as far as Guam, but no farther, in his quest to return to his headquarters on Saipan. Once described indulgently by a naval colleague as "extremely intelligent and, for an army officer, of extremely broad vision," Obata remained on Guam functioning as part adviser, part commander, part supernumerary. "I am firmly determined to become a breakwater in the Pacific," Obata wrote defiantly. Others shared his resolve, even after weeks of bombardment. On the eve of the invasion, one of his privates scrawled in a secret diary, "I will not lose my courage, but now is the time to prepare to die! If one desires to live, hope for death. With this conviction one can never lose. We have shortened our life expectancy from 70 years of life to 25 in order to fight."

Unlike Saipan, the Japanese on Guam could count on little local support. The small population of about twenty-four thousand Chamorros remained steadfastly pro-American, owing to the island's legacy as a US colony for nearly half a century before the Japanese invaded and seized it in 1941. "Naturally nobody was welcoming the Japanese with open arms and there was always the belief that America would be sending troops back to recapture Guam," Gregorio Borja, who lived in the small village of Sumay, later reflected. The occupiers generally behaved severely toward the locals. They changed the island's name to Omiya Jima (Great Shrine Island). Schools were forced to remove English from their curricula in favor of Japanese. "Everything was controlled," Borja said. "Everything you did you had to think first because the Japanese had to agree with it. They even took inventory of our livestock." The Japanese dealt mercilessly with anyone suspected of committing everyday crimes or harboring American sympathies. "When the Japanese investigated someone, they would beat him before they asked him any questions," Henry Pangelinan, who worked for them as a jailer and interpreter, later disclosed. "So many people on Guam did nothing, but being a suspect in Japanese custody was the same as being guilty. When they were beaten they had to agree with the questions to avoid further punishment. One of the tortures the Japanese used was to lie somebody down and put a wet towel over his face so [he] couldn't breathe." Pangelinan also saw the Japanese hang victims by their thumbs and rape female prisoners. Beginning in January 1944, with the likelihood of invasion looming, the occupation became especially brutal. The Japanese confiscated property, and implemented forced-labor policies, instituted food rationing to the point of bare subsistence, and herded some of the locals away from fortified areas into internment camps where hundreds died of starvation, disease, and exposure. The survivors hung on as best they could and waited for deliverance by the Americans.[4]

As at Saipan, the Underwater Demolition Teams performed a crucial mission, working daylight and nighttime operations under a protective shield of smoke and steel provided by Connolly's fleet. Starting on July 14 and continuing through the eve of the invasion, the UDT men blew gaps in the rugged coral reefs and removed most of the mines and obstacles the Japanese had placed on the landing beaches. Aside from some occasional sniping, the Japanese proved unable to impede or even much harass their efforts, a dire harbinger for an army that had invested all in stopping the Americans at the waterline. The intrepid frogmen even found time to share a private joke with the assault troops who hit the beaches starting at 0830 on July 21. Onto one prominent tree, they nailed a sign that read, "Welcome Marines! USO that way!"

Though not quite comparable to the Saipan invasion day bloodbath, the Japanese fought hard in a vain attempt to repel the invaders at Guam.

Aside from a few Army liaison teams, the Marines carried out the entirety of the assault. At Agat, the 1st Provisional Marine Brigade suffered 350 casualties to carve out a beachhead about two thousand yards in depth. To the north, the 3rd Marine Division took a twenty-five-hundred-yard stretch of coastal beaches and, in heavy fighting on the left flank, the crucial high ground of the Chonito Cliffs. The day cost the division 105 killed, 536 wounded, and 56 missing. Similar to Saipan, the Japanese launched determined, though ultimately ineffectual, nocturnal counterattacks against the two American enclaves.

On the southern beachhead, Colonel Vincent Tanzola's 305th Infantry began landing in the midafternoon of W Day. By necessity, Geiger had earmarked all his LVTs to shuttle the Marines who led the invasion. Tanzola, and the 77th as a whole, had available to them only LCVPs and other nontracked vessels that could not negotiate their way over the reef. As a result, the nervous soldiers, laden with heavy loads of weapons, ammunition, and equipment, were dumped into chest-high water to wade hundreds of yards to shore. "Some fell into pot-holes and were completely submerged," the division historian later wrote. "Weapons could be kept dry only by following a narrow coral ridge where the water was sufficiently shallow for the men to keep their heads and shoulders above the surface." The remainder of the division landed in similar fashion at the southern beachhead over the next few days.

By and large, the 77th functioned in a supporting role as the Marines expanded the enclave and seized the Orote Peninsula in heavy close-quarters fighting, with the help of the 77th's artillery and armor from the Army's 706th Tank Battalion. Drawing heavily on their many months of quality training, the rookie soldiers steadily accustomed themselves to the horrific sights and smells of the battlefield. Decomposing Japanese corpses littered the area. The historian of Company C, 307th Infantry Regiment, described with graphic exactitude "their bloated, blackened bodies blown up like gruesome balloons. Hundreds of small, slimy, white maggots squirmed on top one another and ate their way in and out of this stinking, rotten mess; through the opened, staring eyes; through the nose and gaping holes that once were their mouths. They slithered among torn guts and an exposed brain; and through bullet holes in arms, legs, and bodies." Their overwhelming stench "made many men sick and caused them to throw up their recently eaten rations."

Steadily the 77th Division newcomers now eased into the grim rhythm of frontline combat. They fought small-unit patrol actions, manned fox-holes, and engaged in personal death duels with Japanese infiltrators. During the long, menacing nights, they struggled to keep their fertile imaginations in check. "We had heard many tales about the famed Banzai night attacks," a 305th soldier wrote. "None of us could sleep. When we weren't pulling our turn at guard we lay in our shallow holes trying vainly to relax but listening for the slightest noise that indicated the presence of the enemy." They embraced the prevailing American doctrine of hunkering down in foxhole-honeycombed perimeters at night and, under the flickering half-light of flares fired by ships offshore, shooting at anything that moved outside their holes, sometimes damaging the Americans as much as the Japanese. "There were several instances of friendly fire casualties," Corporal Richard Forse, a gun crewman in Cannon Company of the 305th Infantry Regiment, sadly wrote. "These happened because of not observing where other men in the same unit were located at night resulting in panicky firing and grenade throwing whenever there was noise." The commander of the division signals company, like his other colleagues, ordered his men to shoot at anything moving in their perimeter at night. On one tragic evening, they inadvertently killed one of their own messengers who was simply attempting to return to friendly lines in the course of doing his job. The accidental killing so traumatized the dead soldier's best buddy that he nearly killed the commander. "He was about to pull the trigger and I automatically hit the gun out of his hands," Sergeant Ernest Schichler later wrote. "He sat down in [a] slit trench and cried. He said that I was sticking up for the S.O.B. I sat next to him and told him that I couldn't blame him for the way he felt . . . but that I was trying to prevent him from being court martialed and maybe shot for killing an officer." The nighttime siege mentality struck Colonel Aubrey Smith, commander of the 306th Infantry Regiment, as wrongheaded. "The theory that at night a unit must retire to its foxholes and remain there til daylight hampers operations unnecessarily and results in almost complete lack of fire control at night," he wrote sensibly in a post-battle critique. "We cannot be tied to our foxholes. Evacuation is sometimes necessary at night to prevent loss of life. Often messages must be sent by messengers at night. Command posts often have to operate at night and personnel must be able to move without being fired on by our own troops." Nonetheless, even in a division led by the innovative Bruce, the night paralysis continued, less a commentary on the individual commander than the larger American cultural philosophy of war by firepower and in circadian phases.[5]

The Japanese, for their part, were anything but immune to their own cultural proscriptions. A telegram from Imperial General Headquarters in Tokyo ordered Obata and Takashina, "Defend Guam to the death. We believe good news will soon be forthcoming." Beyond the optimistic veneer, both generals understood the true meaning of the message: Destroy the Americans or die. By July 25, just four days after the invasion, Takashina had already lost about 70 percent of his combat troops and many of his leaders in southwestern Guam. At Agat, the Imperial Army's 38th Infantry Regiment was nearing a point of total destruction after multiple failed frontal attacks, including one that cost the life of the regimental colonel, to snuff out the perimeter collectively held by the 1st Provisional Marine Brigade and the 77th Division.

With each passing day, as the Americans landed more troops and equipment over their hard-won beaches, they grew stronger while the Japanese gradually weakened. Takashina worried that the suffocating effects of American firepower, especially strafing attacks from aircraft, might erode the remaining will of his men to keep fighting. To date, the two American beachheads had not yet joined hands, making them potentially vulnerable to enveloping attacks. As he saw the situation, he had only two options: attack the Americans or withdraw northeast to put up a defensive fight in the heavy jungle foliage prevalent in that part of Guam. On the human level, both Takashina and Obata were products of a culture that highly valued self-sacrifice, meaningful gestures, and personal honor. On the professional level, they were trained to embrace aggressive, offensive tactics to destroy Japan's enemies. On the doctrinal level, for both men, island defense equated to pushing the Americans into the sea, either at the waterline when they invaded or with subsequent counterattacks. To these generals, honor and manhood meant confronting one's enemies, not retreating from them.

Not surprisingly, then, Takashina decided, with Obata's blessing, to amass his forces for an all-out night assault designed to push the 3rd Marine Division into the sea. Takashina planned to exploit gaps that existed among the front lines of the division's three infantry regiments, envelop the Americans, roll up their rear areas, and destroy them in detail. The concept had almost no chance of succeeding and promised little besides squandering the lives of Takashina's men and weakening the Japanese hold on Guam. Nonetheless, Imperial General Headquarters sent a commendatory message to Obata: "We are deeply moved by your hard fighting continued day and night. You have decided to launch the general attack. We wish you and your men every success." The plans of the generals would have meant nothing if not for the willingness of their soldiers to carry them out. "All of the officers and men were generally prepared for their fate, because of their honor, sense of responsibility and hate for the enemy," Lieutenant Colonel Takeda, the 29th Division operations officer, later wrote.

They went forward under the cover of darkness on the evening of July 25–26. Predictably, though the Japanese did breach the lines and maraud some rear areas, their attack was crushed over the course of a savage night of elemental, traumatic combat in which some men fought to the death hand-to-hand, sometimes even wielding rocks and sticks as weapons. By midday on July 26, the Japanese had lost 3,500 of their best remaining soldiers. By Takeda's estimate, 95 percent of the NCOs and officers were killed in the space of twenty-four hours. The 3rd Marine Division lost 166 killed, 34 missing, 645 wounded, and an unstipulated number scarred forever emotionally. "Our force failed to achieve the desired objectives, losing more than 80 percent of the personnel, for which I sincerely apologize," Obata reported to Tokyo. "I feel deeply sympathetic for the officers and men who fell in action and their bereaved families." The devastated Japanese commanders ordered their survivors to retreat and carry on the fight along a new line in the jungle. During the withdrawal, Takashina was hit in the chest by an American machine-gun bullet and died instantly. Obata carried on as the commander.

The two American beachheads joined hands on July 28 as troops from the 77th Division made contact with 3rd Division Marines. Any Japanese trapped in the rear of the now solid American front were either annihilated in violent encounters with US patrols or, in a few instances, taken prisoner. Reconnaissance patrols from the 77th swept through southern Guam, encountering almost no enemy resistance. With at least half the island now under American control, Bruce and Major General Allen Turnage, his counterpart in command of the 3rd Division, coordinated an effective advance into central and northern Guam, with the Marines on the left and the Army on the right. The GIs and leathernecks had by now formed a jocular, familiar partnership of mutual respect, undoubtedly influenced by the positive, unified command culture that Geiger had fostered. The Marines were youthful; few enlisted men were over the age of twenty-five. By contrast, the 77th had large numbers of men in their thirties. General Bruce even later claimed that many of his people "were approaching 38 years old." In the time-immemorial manner that the young seem to equate any older age as tantamount to a state of elderly incapacitation, the Marines found themselves thunderstruck at the energy and effectiveness of their GI elders. "Lookit those old buzzards go!" a young Marine exclaimed as he watched the 77th one day, encapsulating the general mood of youthfully indulgent admiration. After working closely with the 305th Infantry, Brigadier General Shepherd's Marines were so impressed that they took to calling the unit "the 305th Marines," a high compliment treasured by the soldiers. "I have always been grateful for the cooperation and support you gave me," Shepherd later wrote fondly to Bruce of their battlefield partnership. Bruce responded warmly, "I feel very strongly about the wonderful cooperation we had on Guam. Certainly we had mutual respect for each other." The soldiers especially admired the bravery and resolve of their Marine partners, particularly after seeing how they fended off Takashina's desperate attack. "I got to know the Marines pretty well on Guam," Captain Seligman, the physician, wrote home shortly after the battle. "I've got the greatest respect for them. They are a fine, courageous group of fighters—they fight with a vengeance and ask no mercy."

In the waning hours of July, the two divisions advanced across the waist of the island and steadily turned northward. On the left, the 3rd Division secured Agana, Guam's shattered capital. "Rows of houses, reduced to masses of ruins by the pre-invasion blasting, were cautiously checked for snipers and remaining Jap stragglers by infantrymen while tanks followed in support," wrote the division historian. Beyond Agana, over ridges and hilltops, they smashed through Japanese holdouts in an uncounted number of no-quarter battles. Flamethrower men roasted enemy soldiers in caves, dugouts, and fighting holes. In one typical cave, a small group of cornered Japanese soldiers was engulfed in flames and killed to the last man. "A strong stench came out of that cave and someone yelled, 'Barbecued Jap!'" Sergeant Carl Coker later wrote. "After the flames went out, one guy got a tree limb and raked out five Jap bodies, so that turned out to be a big cave." An embedded war correspondent, Robert "Pepper" Martin, described their battlefield as "a shamble of reddish, churned clay, littered with half-destroyed equipment, Japs grinning balefully and obscenely in their death agony, neatly covered rows of dead Marines; the inevitable flotsam of war: snapshots of young mothers and children who would never again see their Marine husbands and fathers, a New Testament shredded by a bullet, a punctured canteen, half eaten field rations scattered about."

The 77th pushed rapidly for the eastern coast at Yona village on Pago Bay, where Spanish colonists had once cultivated a large coconut plantation and Chammoro fishermen reaped the bounty of idyllic waters teeming with fish. "The distance across the island is not far, as the crow flies, but unluckily we can't fly," one soldier wisecracked. The troops sweated their way over a seemingly endless chain of vine-packed hills. When they reached Yona, they surprised a ragged group of Japanese in various stages of undress who bolted out of dugouts, huts, and small buildings and fled north. The soldiers blasted away at them like so many flushed quail. Most of the enemy got away. The bodies of those who were less fortunate lay in twisted, shattered, half-naked heaps.[6]

Continuing north that afternoon, lead scouts discovered, with the guidance of locals, a concentration camp at Asinan, the first such liberation in the Pacific War. The Americans were stunned at the sight of some two thousand malnourished, diseased, desperate, joyful people converging on the soldiers, shaking their hands, hugging them, kissing them. A few showed off tiny American flags they had sewn and hidden, at great personal risk, for just this occasion. "We wait long time for you to come," many of the smiling civilians told the GIs. The Japanese had told the Guamanians that the Americans were never coming back. They peddled tales that the Japanese had occupied the Hawaiian Islands and sunk every American ship but one. The liberation experience—the first of any comparable size in this theater—proved to be an eye-opener for the Americans, most of whom had little previous notion of the locals' plight. Amazed and troubled by the threadbare appearance of the former prisoners, they happily plied them with all manner of American largesse, from K rations to cigarette lighters to medical care for those in immediate need. Even frontline infantrymen, who had little to give, handed over anything they could. "Men who had been complaining because rations with more cigarettes had not yet come up, now eagerly passed out what few they had," the division historian wrote. "For the first time most of the men realized the meaning of the often heard expression, 'Liberation of enslaved peoples,' for they themselves were taking part in the liberation."

The Americans were amazed and filled with admiration at the resilience and toughness of people who had survived unimaginable conditions, at least to the Yanks. "Twas a scene I shall never forget as I watched them pass with such courage and grit," Tech Sergeant Virgil Fruckey marveled in a poem he wrote shortly after encountering long columns of liberated refugees who now streamed back to their homes or to collection points behind the American lines. "There [sic] clothes tattered and torn—nothing more than rags. Many were sick, feeble, aged and gray. The sick were treated by our Medical Corps. 'Til my dying day those memories shall live of those who had to suffer and give." As he watched in emotional awe, a young girl enthusiastically cried, "God bless you, gentlemen." Another American remembered that "the youngsters ran alongside of us holding on to our rifles. Old men held our hands and the women cried and cheered and patted our backs. All the hardship and misery and wounds we had suffered melted away at that moment and I said to myself, 'It has been worth it all.' I will never forget how grateful the people were."

Many of the local men, unheeding of their poor physical condition, lobbied to fight alongside the Americans or at least dig foxholes for them. In most cases, their offers were politely declined, though a few of the liberated men did provide invaluable service as guides. Beyond providing basic necessities, the 77th Division was ill-prepared to deal with the former camp inmates and other refugees who now came under American control. "The system of handling natives and civilians was not satisfactory in all cases," commented the after-action report for the 307th Infantry Regiment, the unit that liberated the Asinan camp. "We had two thousand natives come into the regimental area just before dark, and no higher unit would aid in moving these people from the combat area, other than designating a collecting point. Personnel from this unit were absent 48 hours longer moving these people to the rear."

Beyond the growing humanitarian responsibilities for the Americans on Guam, horrendous conditions and logistical problems hampered the pace of their advance more than did the Japanese. Guam's rainy season began, seemingly with a special vengeance. Torrential daily rains swept over the island, turning the place into a humid, steamy water world of perpetual wetness. "The rain poured all night and we had to stand up in [a] slit trench with water up to our arm pits," wrote Sergeant Schichler, the signalman. "One of us would bail out the water with a helmet while the other stood guard, or tried to rest by laying his head on top of the trench." To make matters worse, enemy shells, either mortar or antiaircraft, burst nearby with alarming frequency. Thriving on the humidity, small armies of oversize frogs and rats prowled around foxholes and tents, feasting on soggy half-eaten rations. First Lieutenant Richard Spencer, the operations officer of 1st Battalion, 307th Infantry Regiment, woke with a start one evening at the sight of a rat perched atop his wrist. "Guess he was checking me out for vital signs," Spencer later joked.

If few men could stay dry for any appreciable length of time, the same held true for the landscape. Guam seemed to be little more than a vast cauldron of sodden earth the color and consistency of red clay. Oceans of reddish-colored mud engulfed men and ensnared vehicles. "Tropical rains make everything 'gushy goo goo,'" General Bruce wrote to this wife, Roberta. "We wake up in the morning covered with mud." In an article written a few months later for a military periodical, he reported that "the mud was so bad that wheeled vehicles bogged down continually and had to be towed out by tractors." A single round trip from the landing beaches to supply dumps located only three hundred yards inland took trucks an average of three hours. Jeeps and trucks sank up to their axles in the maw. Tanks got bogged down. Men were covered with gobs of soggy red earth. "With all the rain and mud," wrote Lieutenant Spencer with admirable good humor, "the red soil made us the 'red army.'"

Operational success actually bred serious logistical problems. Geiger, Turnage, and Bruce all agreed to maintain a brisk pursuit lest they give Obata time to regroup and prepare strong fortifications. The more the frontline troops progressed, though, the harder it became to supply them from the overtaxed landing beaches that grew more distant with every new advance. Guam had only one road of any note and it was located within the 3rd Marine Division sector. Initially, General Bruce hoped to supply his division over a new road built by his own 302nd Engineer Combat Battalion. Under terrible conditions, improvising culverts out of coconut logs and oil drums, they managed to carve three miles' worth of coral-packed, muddy two-lane road from the wilderness until the unrelenting sheets of rain and constant mudslides forced Bruce to order them to abandon the effort. "We could not hope to supply the division over this route," he later explained. Instead, he successfully prevailed upon Geiger and Turnage to let him utilize the road in the 3rd Marine Division sector—yet another example of the close cooperation between the two services at Guam and, from a logistician's point of view, an amazing accomplishment. "The books would say it can't be done, but on Guam it was done," Bruce affirmed. "It had to be."

Soon the entire logistic sinews of the two divisions, plus corps artillery and other supporting forces, began passing over this single, tenuous two-lane hard-surface road. At all hours of the day and night, trucks, jeeps, and DUKWs, with headlights burning brightly due to the negation of Japanese air, moved supplies and reinforcements forward and evacuated wounded men to the rear. Marine and Army military policemen worked closely together to maintain order among the sea of vehicles. The heavy traffic wore the road down quickly, necessitating constant maintenance by engineers. Once up front, combat troops manhandled heavy crates of ammunition or food and slippery cans of water as far forward as possible. The dictates of frontline combat created incredible demand for ordnance, especially for small arms. The 305th Infantry Regiment alone expended 515,342 .30-06-caliber bullets from M1 Garand and Browning Automatic Rifles, an average of about 171 per soldier, putting the lie to S. L. A. Marshall's grossly inaccurate, mythological "ratio of fire" contention that only 15 percent of American soldiers ever fired their rifles in combat. Indeed, the division as a whole fired 3.6 million such rifle bullets throughout the battle, in addition to another 750,000 rounds of .30-caliber ammunition for the M1 carbines typically carried by machine gunners, engineers, and mortar crewmen.

At the landing beaches, ringed as they were by reefs, shore parties laboriously unloaded cargo onto LVTs, DUKWs, pontoon barges, even life rafts, and floated them over the reefs for a second unloading ashore. The dictates of operations and the tremendous challenge of maintaining an entire corps over "a long tortuous route," as Bruce termed it, mandated round-the-clock unloading with no interruptions. With no fear of enemy air attack, the Americans bathed the beaches with floodlights powered noisily by 5-KVA generator units. As of late July, the daily average of freight unloaded stood at 10,000 tons. By the end of the month, the parties had unloaded 63,332.2 short tons, about 80 percent of the matériel earmarked for the combat units. It took them three weeks to unload the full complement. The heavy rains, combined with the inevitable confusion and pilferage inherent in any operation, led to the destruction and loss of an uncounted amount of tonnage. Medical units were especially affected by the wastage. One battalion lost 20 percent of its supplies. A clearing company lost 94 of 150 allotted cots. A portable surgical hospital lost 61 of its 75 cots. A field hospital lost another eighty cots. "As a result the sick and wounded often had to be placed on the ground," the historian for the US Army Forces Middle Pacific Surgeon deplored in an official report. According to this report, the field hospital also lost "one washing machine, one kitchen range, two ward tents, and two typewriters."[7]

Ironically, given the incessant downpours, a paucity of water remained the biggest supply issue for frontline troops as July turned to August. Distillation centers at the beaches were now too far from the front lines. Bruce could not sustain his entire division indefinitely by trucking five-gallon jerry cans forward and then hauling them for distribution among combat troops. The average soldier was lucky to get a canteen full per day this way. Most had resorted to filling their canteens from muddy streams and treating the water with halazone tablets before they drank the noxious mix. Some attempted to slake their thirst with coconut milk or captured sake mixed with K ration lemonade powder and sugar in a concoction that vaguely resembled a Tom Collins. Northern Guam contained few if any streams, meaning that this source of water would soon, quite literally, dry up. The troops at the front, especially infantrymen, were beginning to experience severe water shortages, especially in the 305th Infantry, whose headquarters sent an urgent plea to division for water resupply. "We haven't had any since yesterday," the regiment reported on August 2.

A reservoir and pumping station at the tiny crossroads village of Barrigada offered relief. The station could yield twenty to thirty thousand gallons per day, more than enough to support the 77th Division. A few hundred yards north of the village lay Mount Barrigada, a two-hundred-meter-high protrusion of high ground that commanded much of the area. On the morning of August 2, Bruce sent two of his regiments forward, the 307th directly toward the village and Mount Barrigada, and the 305th along the east coast around the right flank. He supported both regiments with armor from the 706th Tank Battalion. All that day and part of the evening, the American assault troops brawled with Japanese defenders in a series of vicious, disjointed battles characterized by close-quarters fighting against unseen enemy soldiers who hid in buildings or, more commonly, the heavy foliage. At one point, when American machine-gun and mortar fire hit a shack along the road east of Barrigada, setting it afire, a lone Japanese tank emerged like a hornet flushed from a nest. American riflemen quickly picked off three Japanese soldiers who were riding on the tank, but the vehicle kept on, heedless of bazooka and machine-gun fire.

The lone-wolf tank overran a machine-gun crew, shot up cowering infantrymen in a ditch, and, in the course of its odyssey, swept a battalion aid station, a battalion command post, and the 307th regimental headquarters with cannon and machine-gun fire before a pair of American light tanks chased it away. In its wake, the enemy tank left two rifle companies in disarray. "The course of the tank was marked by bleeding men and abandoned positions," wrote Burns, the combat historian attached to the 77th Division. A less fortunate, or less intrepid, hidden enemy tank stayed in place when American fire demolished the building in which it had taken shelter. A Sherman scored a direct hit on it with a 75-millimeter shell, setting off a catastrophic explosion that destroyed it.

In the course of the day, as casualties piled up, a quartet of American tanks laid down cover fire while other tanks evacuated 108 wounded men to the rear. At nightfall, the Japanese remained in possession of the pumping station and most of Barrigada as well as Mount Barrigada. The Americans anxiously hunkered down in expectation of a banzai attack. But after enduring an entire day of intense shelling from American artillery and tanks, plus unrelenting infantry attacks, most of the Japanese survivors withdrew under cover of darkness. Inexplicably, they failed to destroy the pumping station or even foul the reservoir water in any way. The 307th took the village and the station early in the afternoon on August 3. By 1430 that day, engineers had the station functioning at full capacity, effectively solving the division's water problem. Bruce's men needed another day to secure Mount Barrigada before embarking on the final push to reclaim the northern tip of Guam. In exchange for seizing the Barrigada area, the division suffered two hundred casualties, about a quarter of whom were killed in action.

By now, Obata had, at most, only about five thousand troops left, many of whom were in too poor physical condition to fight or had no modern weapons. The best the Japanese could do to defend the northern expanse of Guam was to take shelter in caves or melt into the nearly impassable jungles that covered this part of the island, and then fight to the end. "They had lost their commanding officers, men and weapons," Lieutenant Colonel Takeda later wrote. "They had not the capacity of manoeuvre and in addition they were obliged to fight in the jungle where it was very hard to cooperate and communicate with each other." With the northern village of Yigo and the coastal high ground of Mount Santa Rosa as capstone objectives, and supported by an umbrella of air strikes, naval gunfire, and

artillery, the 77th Division lunged forward as best it could into jungle foliage so thick that visibility was often limited to an arm's length. "The terrain proved to be a greater foe than the Japs as we hacked our way through
the jungle," one soldier later wrote. Tiny trails led nowhere. Maps were
either nonexistent or laughably inaccurate, a cruel surprise to commanders
who expected to access better terrain information about an American territory. Tanks plowed through the dense jungle, creating makeshift trails,
and machine-gunned enemy soldiers wherever possible, but could provide
little other assistance in the bramble. Possession of any clearing or dirt
road promised a fight against stubborn Japanese defenders who dug themselves into makeshift bunkers or trench lines. "Sometimes our advances
approached a pursuit," Bruce later reflected, "sometimes mud and jungle
slowed us up; and the Japs were always present in between." A prewar stint
in Panama had taught him much about how to fight in the jungle, as
had studying after-action reports from the South Pacific. He knew that he
could not hope to maintain continuous front lines or fight with standard
attacking tactics in the midst of the suffocating maze of foliage. "In our
training, I stressed all around defense even at night," he later wrote to a
colleague. "I pointed out that it was far better to get through the jungle
regardless of flanks until they arrived at a trail or road where liaison and
contact could be established with adjacent units. I emphasized [that] lack
of vision in woods or jungle precluded the ordinary concept of fighting in
the open."

Wielding machetes, his men battled the vines most of the time and the
Japanese some of the time, the latter usually in intimate duels to the death
among platoon- or squad-size groups. With the onset of darkness, the GIs
dug into uneasy perimeters manned by tense guards on continuous alert
for attacks from mass waves of Japanese or just individual infiltrators that
seldom came. "Digging in had a much greater significance than just those
two words would indicate," the historian of the 305th explained in world-
weary tones. "It meant coming into an area as the evening sun settled beyond the horizon, covered with sweat and grime, tired of everything but
living. It meant digging a hole which wasn't a hole at all but merely a rect-
angular depression long enough for one to lie in and doing enough to prevent one's being seen. This unique and vital excavation was done with a
shovel just large enough to plant one's feet upon and a pick with a handle
so short one almost had to be either a midget or a contortionist to swing
it." To make matters worse, the soil in northern Guam was thin with a

solid bedrock of coral underneath. "Frenzied hammering with the pick does nothing but wear down the pick and scatter white powder around the hole to make it stand out as though spotlighted," one soldier griped. Men seldom remained dry or clean for any length of time. Depending on the volume of rain, a pool of water, ranging in depth from six inches to a foot, accumulated in most foxholes or slit trenches. Exhausted soldiers looking for a few hours of nocturnal sleep had little choice but to lie uncomfortably in the water and drift off as best they could. They awoke stiff and shivering, coated in either mud or dust. "You have no idea how dirty one can get during a campaign," Captain Seligman, the doctor, wrote home. "Fellows began calling one another 'stinky' and even the closest buddies avoided close contact."

Filthy, disoriented, fighting and advancing day by day through the alien, confining jungle, far too many turned to tobacco in hopes of relieving the constant stress, so much so that even overworked carrying parties could not keep up with the enormous demand for cigarettes among the rifle companies. "It is imperative that a resupply of cigarettes be made available to the assault troops as quickly as possible after their initial landing," Major James Doyle, the division personnel officer, implored in a post-battle critique. "The amount now contained in 'K' rations is not deemed adequate for the average smoker under average conditions. Emotional stress and the excitement of battle greatly increases the desire to smoke and the rate of consumption."

The battle climaxed August 6–8 with a bitter tank-infantry fight for the crossroads village of Yigo and a lightning capture of Mount Santa Rosa. Bruce threw all three of his infantry regiments into the fight. At Yigo the Americans systematically destroyed a network of Japanese pillboxes while tanks from both sides dueled at close quarters. A shower of 105-millimeter artillery shells lanced through droves of Japanese as they desperately attempted to flee north. "My God, this is slaughter!" one American artillery observer exclaimed as he looked down on the chaos from a spotter plane.

At Mount Santa Rosa, combined arms assault squads comprising riflemen, a flamethrower operator, and a trio of demolitions experts carrying satchel charges, pole charges, and bangalore torpedoes overwhelmed the Japanese with ruthless rapid-fire assaults, shooting or blowing up any suspected enemy position, including buildings. Flamethrowers hosed down thatched huts and any other structures. Panicked Japanese emerged with their clothes and hair on fire only to be shot down by the riflemen. In one spot, a team of riflemen entered a two-story hut and saw a thick puddle of blood on the floor. Looking up, they noticed blood dripping through the ceiling into the puddle. When they investigated the second floor, they found eight dead Japanese who had been shot to pieces. Closer to the sea, the Americans cornered another Japanese group that had taken shelter in a network of tunnels and caves. The Yanks attempted to blast them out with pole charges, grenades, and white phosphorous. Between explosions, they could just make out the sound of Japanese voices chanting, probably in prayer. As the stalemate wore on, American engineers resorted to setting off a quartet of four-hundred-pound TNT blocks at the cave entrances. Cascades of earth sealed every entrance, suffocating everyone inside. Later, when the Americans excavated the site, they discovered sixty enemy bodies, and found the nauseating stench of death around them to be so overwhelming that they were compelled to wear gas masks.[8]

A steady procession of American casualties streamed to the rear. Some retreated on foot. Others were carried by heavily burdened stretcher teams. Still others were piled onto jeeps and driven by orderlies or combat medics to aid stations or hospitals. The 36th Field Hospital admitted 765 patients in the first two weeks of August. Half of the patients needed surgery. Some 321 of the wounded required evacuation to ships, while 333 others were returned to duty. Fatalities made up about one-quarter of the casualties. Among the dead was Staff Sergeant John O'Hara of the 305th Infantry, who got hit in the abdomen and faded quickly. "The medics took care of him and eased his pain as much as was possible," Captain Nathaniel Saucier, the regimental chaplain, wrote to O'Hara's mother in Georgia. "During his moments of consciousness he manifested a most heroic spirit. I think he did not realize he was dying and made no final statement." O'Hara's company commander added his own consolation, the sort of personal and yet vaguely distant words of solace that had by this time in the war become so common for officers writing to grieving loved ones of their fallen subordinates. "The thought that John served his country well may lighten your sorrows. This is the sincere wish of all of us who served with him."

Undoubtedly the most prominent American fatality of the Guam campaign was thirty-seven-year-old Colonel Douglas McNair, the 77th Infantry Division's chief of staff and a 1928 graduate of West Point. Blessed with a full head of strawberry-blond hair and the charisma that came from his exceptional competence, McNair was the son of Lieutenant General Lesley McNair, chief of Army Ground Forces. Universally beloved throughout the

77th Division for his warm, engaging personality, easygoing nature, and physical courage, Colonel McNair had just recently found out about his father's tragic death on July 25 from misdropped American bombs in Normandy during Operation Cobra, an effort to blast a massive hole in the German front line through carpet bombing by heavies from the Eighth Air Force. General Bruce had had to share the bad news with Douglas, whom he himself loved like a son. "After dark I called him over to my enlarged foxhole to tell him about it," Bruce related to Colonel Ralph Mace, Douglas's close friend who had known him since their days at West Point. "Naturally he broke down in the darkness. I know of no son who admired a man more. He loved his father intensely as a father. He admired him intensely as a professional soldier." Knowing that the Army might want to send him home, if only to assuage the grief of Clare McNair, the general's wife and Douglas's mother, the son had insisted on remaining at his post. General Bruce had assented while also attempting to rein in the chief of staff's tendency to gravitate toward the front lines. "To be perfectly honest, I was mentally hovering [over him] all of the time like a father and when I was worried I spoke sharply to him like a father would," Bruce wrote in a consolation letter to Douglas's widow. Try as the general might, he could not shield his chief of staff from every danger. An admiring Lieutenant Spencer, the young staff officer, remembered seeing the colonel during one particularly heavy shelling "walking around, calming everyone down, like a protective father."

The mobile campaign in Guam's final days necessitated the continuous displacement and relocation of the division command post, a responsibility that devolved on the chief of staff. On August 6, McNair had persuaded Bruce to let him go forward to find a new spot for the command post. In the process, McNair and two escorting soldiers from division headquarters found themselves drawn into a firefight against three Japanese soldiers who had holed up in a shack. McNair took a bullet through the throat. He collapsed into a heap, probably dead before he hit the ground. The two other Americans, Major Harry Cutting and Sergeant Alfred Cauley, survived without a scratch and managed to kill all three Japanese.

When General Bruce received the terrible news late that afternoon, he was shocked and devastated. To stave off a total emotional collapse, he threw himself into planning the final push for Guam's north coast even as his overwhelming sorrow gnawed at him from within to the point where he could hardly face the truth. For days he refused even to speak to anyone about Colonel McNair. "This is the first time, in my letter to you, that I have done so," he wrote a week later to Clare, whose emotional desolation knew no bounds after losing her husband and son in a two-week period. "I do not want to dwell on my loss because it is so small compared to yours. But let me say that when I looked across to his tent, dug in the ground . . . and saw it empty, I thought my heart would break. I knew that no one could ever replace him either professionally or in my heart. He was so calm, square, absolutely devoid of any favoritism towards any faction, so devoted to the cause of his country, and so morally unafraid of doing the right thing that it is hard to give an adequate description of what he meant to me." Later, the general told Colonel Mace of McNair, "He was unusual in his lack of selfishness in order to promote the common good of the Division. Personally, I lost the finest Chief of Staff I have ever had and a true friend." In addition to a young widow, Colonel McNair left behind an infant daughter.

By mid-August, the Guam campaign petered out in the usual manner. Organized Japanese resistance largely ceased. The few surviving Japanese servicemen, most of whom refused to surrender, instead took to the hills and caves, where they starved, died of disease, or continued on in a hand-to-mouth existence, occasionally posing a threat to American bases or patrols. "The Japanese officer does not admit, even to himself, that his forces can be defeated," one American officer claimed in a wartime analysis of the Japanese fighting soldier. "Surrender or retreat are beyond his comprehension." No matter how true this was of many in the Japanese officer corps, the contention hardly applied now to Lieutenant General Obata, who knew all too well the reality of his situation. With defeat now a certainty, Lieutenant General Obata sent a final message to Imperial General Headquarters in Tokyo. "Officers and men have been lost, weapons have been destroyed and ammunition has been expended. We have only our bare hands to fight with. The holding of Guam has become hopeless. My only fear is that the report of death with honor (annihilation) at Guam might shock the Japanese people at home. Our souls will defend this island to the very end." Soon thereafter, when the Americans overran his headquarters and killed all but three of his aides, he took out his service pistol and shot himself in the head rather than risk the humiliation and dishonor of captivity.

At Guam, the Americans had inflicted yet another monumental defeat upon the Japanese. In addition to the moral and humanitarian aspects of liberating the population, the Americans turned the island into a major naval and air base. By the fall of 1944, the island had become home to some 200,000 American military personnel whose very presence epitomized the growing momentum of the relentless Central Pacific advance to the Japanese home islands. On Guam, the Japanese lost 18,377 killed and 1,250 taken prisoner, the majority of whom were not combat soldiers. The Americans suffered 7,800 casualties including 2,124 deaths. By far the Marines paid the heaviest price for taking Guam, particularly in the invasion and fending off the massive banzai assault on July 25–26. The Marines accounted for more than 80 percent of American casualties. The 77th Division lost 248 killed and 663 wounded. Heavily influenced by the positive environment the commanders had established, soldiers and Marines on Guam worked together the right way, like true partners. Their close working relationship probably saved American lives—though it is obviously impossible to measure such an abstraction—and did much to hasten the doom of the Japanese garrison. When Hirohito's naval adviser heard the news of Guam's fall, he glumly and correctly observed, "Hell is on us."[9]

General Douglas MacArthur had his own ideas about how best to deliver hell to Japan's doorstep, and he feared, perhaps even loathed, all other visions, save his own, for a Japanese downfall. He believed, unshakably and irrevocably, that to defeat Japan the Americans must liberate the Philippines. Beyond the endless military permutations of grand strategy, MacArthur's yearning for the Philippines' redemption amounted to something much more than a means of defeating Japan, perhaps something psychological stemming from his own cherished concepts of personal honor or maybe even, for such an egocentric personality, a powerful need to redeem his name and reputation in the eyes of the Filipino people, whom he loved in something of the same manner that a patriarch loves his descendants. "MacArthur had a deep affection for the people of the Philippines and he had a feeling, having spent so much time there, that related him to them," Lieutenant Colonel Roger Egeberg, his physician, once observed. It was as if, in MacArthur's mind, an Allied final victory would mean little without the liberation of the archipelago. Anything else might be tantamount to accepting a forfeit rather than earning a true victory. Nor could he bear the thought of subjecting the Filipinos to Japanese depredations even a day longer than necessary. The SWPA commander's impatience to set foot back onto Philippine soil knew no bounds. "I tell you I'm going back there this fall if I have to paddle a canoe with you flying cover for me with that B17 of yours," he joked in one conversation with General Kenney, his air commander.

The March 12, 1944, Joint Chiefs directive had told MacArthur to prepare plans for an invasion of Mindanao, a large island in the southern part of the archipelago, a small victory for the SWPA commander in his constant quest for influence on Washington grand strategical decision makers. But a man of MacArthur's keen intelligence understood that the directive actually represented more a general intention than a specific dictate. New developments and competing ideas, especially from his nemesis par excellence Admiral Ernest King, who detested MacArthur and ardently opposed major operations in the Philippines in favor of invading Formosa and perhaps even directly the Japanese home islands, could easily evaporate past intentions. Moreover, MacArthur hankered to liberate the heart of the archipelago, and that really meant Luzon, the foremost island, where the capital, Manila, his onetime home, beckoned like a long-lost lover. In the second half of June 1944, when General Marshall had asked him for his thoughts on how best to proceed in the Pacific after Operation Forager and the conclusion of New Guinea operations, MacArthur had argued passionately for a return to the Philippines. "It is my opinion that purely military considerations demand the reoccupation of the Philippines in order to cut the enemy's communications to the south and to secure a base for our further advance." Control of the Philippines would sever the Japanese home islands from the Dutch East Indies (present-day Indonesia), depriving the Japanese of conquered resources such as oil, tin, and rubber, all of which they badly needed to continue the war. In 1941–1942, the Japanese had invaded the Philippines, not out of any particular desire for them, but because they could not tolerate an American-controlled enclave in the belly of their burgeoning empire.

If seizing the Philippines had offered the Japanese a gateway to control of the resources they wanted in the Dutch East Indies, MacArthur was absolutely correct that the inverse was now true. Control of Luzon might also provide the Americans with a useful base to sustain northerly advances to Formosa, Okinawa, and the home islands. So there were solid strategical reasons for returning to the archipelago. Still, he could not resist espousing a political and moral argument to Marshall, and with the sort of apocalyptic tone that MacArthur tended to employ when he lobbied passionately for something. "The Philippines is American territory where our unsupported forces were destroyed by the enemy. Practically all of the seventeen million Filipinos remain loyal to the United States and are undergoing the greatest privation and suffering because we have not been able to support or succor them. We have a great national obligation to discharge." If the Americans chose to bypass the Philippines, MacArthur warned, "we would undoubtedly incur the open hostility of the people; we would probably suffer such loss of prestige among all the peoples of the Far East that it would adversely affect the United States for many years."

Even-tempered and cool almost to a fault, Marshall at this stage was inclined to agree with King's strategic vision. So he was hardly moved by the SWPA commander's stentorian rhetoric. "We must be careful not to allow our personal feelings and Philippine political considerations to override our great objective, which is the early conclusion of the war with Japan," he admonished MacArthur. Marshall's clever use of the word "we" instead of "you" took the sting off his admonition while still conveying the same meaning. At the same time, the chief of staff refused to accept MacArthur's notion of what true liberation would mean for the Philippines. "In my view, 'by-passing' is in no way synonymous with 'abandonment.' On the contrary, by the defeat of Japan at the earliest practicable moment the liberation of the Philippines will be effected in the most expeditious and complete manner possible."

Accustomed to maintaining a relationship of wary correctness, the two men seldom disagreed so openly during their many wartime exchanges. MacArthur had harbored a career-long distrust and dislike of Marshall, whom he continually suspected, with no grounding in reality, of sabotaging him in Washington. "His hatred for General Marshall never changed," Lieutenant General Eichelberger once claimed, on the basis of many conversations about this with MacArthur. True to Eichelberger's congenial nature, he managed to maintain good relations with both these titans of the World War II US Army, but he later admitted to feeling as though "I was between two mill stones." The SWPA commander viewed Marshall as a man with no strategic instincts. MacArthur once fumed to Eichelberger, "I've never known Marshall to make a correct decision in his life," a remarkably wrongheaded criticism of a man who had rightfully earned a sterling reputation for his levelheaded good judgment, devoid of any personal corruption or self-serving agenda.

In spite of MacArthur's unfounded paranoia about the Army chief of staff, whose intrinsic professionalism and fairness mandated against just the sort of behavior that MacArthur attributed to him, the SWPA commander did realize that his Philippine designs remained very much in the balance if he could not persuade the head of even his own service, much less the Navy, of the wisdom of his ideas. Sensing this, and worried that the Joint Chiefs might unilaterally decide to bypass the Philippines, he even requested in one missive to Marshall "that I be accorded the opportunity of personally proceeding to Washington to present fully my views." Marshall readily assented. MacArthur had previously sent staffers to do his strategic bidding in Washington. He had not, in fact, set foot in his home country for seven years. Thus, MacArthur's willingness to travel thousands of miles to plead his case in the capital revealed much about his unshakable devotion to liberating the Philippines.[10]

As events turned out, he did not need to travel that far. In late July, President Roosevelt, fresh from his renomination by the Democratic Party for a fourth term, decided to travel to Oahu to confer with Nimitz and MacArthur. In an election year, it made all the sense in the world for Roosevelt to be photographed with these two popular commanders. The images might also solidify his image as an active commander in chief who could be trusted to see the war to a successful conclusion. Roosevelt knew all too well that only a few months earlier MacArthur had surreptitiously attempted to secure the Republican nomination and supplant him as president. Even though MacArthur's troubling bid to attain political power while still in uniform failed, the clever Roosevelt understood the general's political potency. A high-level meeting and photo opportunity with him would send a subtle message to MacArthur's Republican political base that the general remained loyal to FDR even as it also silently made clear who was the actual commander in chief.

On July 21, the president boarded the USS *Baltimore* and set sail for Pearl Harbor. The president's party did not include any of the service chiefs, a first for any of his wartime trips out of the continental United States. For the most part, he now had only political aides in tow, the lone exception being Admiral William Leahy, his sagacious, influential military chief of staff, who, as a member of the Joint Chiefs, bridged both the political and military worlds. In the meantime, Marshall sent MacArthur a cryptic telegram telling him to report to Honolulu on July 26. Surprised by the sudden summons, MacArthur asked for clarification but, under the veil of secrecy, the chief of staff could provide little illumination except to hint at high-level discussions. Marshall did mention, though, that MacArthur could expect to meet Admiral Leahy. MacArthur surely understood that Leahy's inclusion meant the presence of Roosevelt, since the two were nearly always together, at least for overseas journeys.

The SWPA commander later disingenuously claimed that he had little lead time to prepare for a conference of such import nor much indication of whom he would meet. But the original order from Marshall arrived on July 6 and he knew by July 18 of Leahy's attendance, in effect meaning Roosevelt, too. At the very least, MacArthur had a little more than a week to prepare. What was more, key members of MacArthur's staff knew what was in the offing. Major Weldon "Dusty" Rhoades, MacArthur's personal pilot, noted in his diary a revealing conversation on July 10 with Lieutenant General Richard Sutherland, the autocratic SWPA chief of staff. "He informed me in great secrecy that I am to go with General MacArthur to a world important conference a long way from here before the end of this month." Even Rhoades surmised that Roosevelt would be present. Five days later, MacArthur himself related much the same thing and discussed the details of the flight. The pilot estimated that it would take twenty-six hours, with a pair of refueling stops in New Caledonia and Canton Island, to travel from Brisbane to Honolulu. He realized that the general's B-17, the *Bataan*, was too cramped and spartan for a long journey, so he requisitioned a C-54 from Pan American, had seats removed to create space for MacArthur, and put a cot in place. On the morning of July 26—still a day earlier on the other side of the international dateline in Hawaii—the general uncharacteristically arrived fifteen minutes late for the flight, accompanied by only three nonoperational members of his staff, Brigadier General Bonner Fellers, Colonel Larry Lehrbas, and Lieutenant Colonel David Chambers, the latter of whom was a physician.

During the long flight, MacArthur seemed in a foul mood. He refused to sleep. He paced incessantly. He hardly ate. He was even occasionally abrupt with Rhoades, a rarity for the gentlemanly general. As he paced the aisles, he groused about being summoned from his command for a "political picture-taking junket." Once he settled down a bit, he unburdened himself to Rhoades in what the pilot later termed "one of his characteristic monologues, to which I was not expected to reply." In Rhoades's recollection, MacArthur told him he was "trying to prepare himself mentally for any development that might result from his meeting with Mr. Roosevelt. He could not fully comprehend why the president would pull him away from his command at this time." In MacArthur's mind, the recall away from SWPA inherently carried the scent of indignity, a bruising prospect for a man of such monumental ego. He hoped that the trip would serve some larger purpose that might yet soften the blow of what he saw as a humiliation. As Rhoades listened carefully, the SWPA commander asserted pontifically, "There are only one of three things that can happen. He's either calling me back to relieve me of my command or he might be calling me back to say that we secured New Guinea and that's it for you or he might be calling me back to give me the go ahead signal as far as going to the Philippines. The mere fact that I don't know what's going to happen . . . depresses me." Outwardly at least, MacArthur seemed not to grasp the golden opportunity before him, namely to make his case in person to the president.

On the afternoon of July 26 on Oahu, the general's C-54 landed safely at Hickam Field. Greeted by Vice Admiral John Towers of Nimitz's staff and Brigadier General Clark Ruffner from Lieutenant General Richardson's staff, MacArthur proceeded to Richardson's quarters at Fort Shafter. Meanwhile, the USS *Baltimore* glided majestically into Pearl Harbor, past numerous ships lined with sailors clad in dress whites standing at attention. The cruiser moored at pier 22-B, alongside the fleet carrier USS *Enterprise*. The day was beautiful, with sunny skies and temperatures in the mid-seventies. At 1505, Admiral Nimitz, resplendent in dress whites, General Richardson, and dozens of other high-ranking luminaries boarded *Baltimore* for a welcoming reception with the president. On deck, they socialized under the warm rays of Hawaiian sunshine.

The president wondered about MacArthur's whereabouts, but no one among the embarrassed senior officers knew. Forty minutes later, according to the presidential log, a luxurious open-top car, driven by a khaki-clad chauffeur and accompanied by motorcycles with screaming sirens, pulled up to the pier. In the back sat MacArthur by himself, a gold-braided cap perched atop his head, and wearing a leather flying jacket and khaki trousers. The general hopped out of the car and jauntily began ascending the gangplank. An excited crowd had gathered to cheer the various leaders. When they saw MacArthur, they gave him a rousing ovation, "to the obvious annoyance of the admirals," MacArthur later ungraciously related to Eichelberger. For a moment, MacArthur turned away from the crowd. "He dashed up the gangplank, stopped halfway up to acknowledge another ovation, and soon was on deck warmly greeting the President," Sam

Rosenman, a presidential aide, later wrote. "He certainly could be dramatic—at dramatic moments." Leahy, who had known MacArthur for better than forty years, could not resist jibing him about his leather jacket: "Douglas, why don't you wear the right kind of clothes when you come up here to see us?" MacArthur pointed to the blue sky and rejoined, "Well, you haven't been where I came from, and it's cold up there in the sky." MacArthur and Roosevelt had not seen each other for almost a decade, dating to the general's tenure as Army chief of staff. They chatted convivially about the old days, "when life was simpler and gentler, of many things that had disappeared in the mists of time," in MacArthur's later wistful recollection. The conversation reestablished some common ground out of what had often been a contentious, even underhanded relationship.

True to form, the group posed for newsreel and still photographs with Nimitz and MacArthur sitting on either side of the president. At the conclusion of the photo session, they went their separate ways for the evening. Roosevelt settled into a mansion on Waikiki owned by Christopher Holmes, who had donated it to the Navy to use as a rest and recreation center for aviators. MacArthur enjoyed a quiet dinner with Richardson. The next morning, MacArthur, Roosevelt, and Nimitz all squeezed into the back seat of the same car that had conveyed MacArthur to pier 22-B. They spent a hectic day inspecting military posts around Oahu. They drove past huge stores of military equipment and weaponry neatly arrayed in open fields, waiting for deployment somewhere in the Pacific. When the car passed a Japanese POW compound, the curious occupants flocked to the wire and gawked at them. At Schofield Barracks, Richardson conjured up a stirring reception for the special car. "We had the road lined for 7½ miles with troops, shoulder to shoulder," he reported to Marshall in a letter a few days later. "They looked extremely well and the sight was impressive. You would have been proud of the Army, as was I." In all, some forty thousand soldiers turned out in their parade uniforms and light field packs, each of them presenting arms as the car passed.

Nimitz did not know the president well. MacArthur did. The unassuming admiral found himself a bit overmatched in this setting. MacArthur traded on his long association with Roosevelt to monopolize the conversation with him, occasionally even urging him to acknowledge the soldiers. "Each time I gave him an idea of what to say and he did very well with it," MacArthur later claimed to Eichelberger. At one point, MacArthur even felt comfortable enough to ask Roosevelt to assess the prospects for Thomas

Dewey, the president's Republican challenger in the coming general election. Roosevelt professed to be too busy to worry about politics. MacArthur laughed skeptically, prompting the president to laugh self-consciously, but good-naturedly, in response. "If the war in Germany ends before the election, I will not be reelected," Roosevelt said, at least according to MacArthur. The SWPA commander assured Roosevelt that the troops favored him, an ironic pronouncement from the man who had hoped only a few months earlier to capture the White House on a wave of soldier ballots. "So went the conversational game played by the master politician and his most politically minded general," MacArthur's greatest biographer, D. Clayton James, wrote with penetrating insight into this interaction. Privately, the general was shocked at the president's ashen, sickly appearance. Roosevelt seemed a shell of the man MacArthur once knew, almost as if he already had one foot in the grave. "When he was animated he looked familiar, but otherwise his jaw sagged down and he looked to be in very poor physical condition," MacArthur related a few weeks later to Eichelberger. "At no time did he stand up as he used to do with the use of leg braces. He was carried every place he went. He will not live through another term if he is reelected." To Egeberg, MacArthur later opined that "the mark of death is on him. In six months he'll be in his grave."[11]

After dinner that evening at the Holmes mansion, the president retired to the comfortable living room to discuss grand strategy with Leahy, Nimitz, and MacArthur. They sat in wicker chairs in front of an expansive, board-mounted map of the Pacific, with a long bamboo pointer as the only visual aid. Thick folded maps were piled onto an oversize coffee table at their knees. The three military officers all wore dress uniforms with ties fastened into place. MacArthur wore no hat. The bald spot at the back of his head gave way to thin tufts of black hair plastered neatly from right to left. Roosevelt wore a bow tie and puffed on cigarettes. As Leahy and Roosevelt listened and asked questions, Nimitz and MacArthur presented their differing views. The admiral dutifully advocated for King's vision of bypassing Luzon for Formosa. In fact, King had visited Nimitz only a few days earlier to outline this strategy. Rather than hang around Oahu and call attention to the fact that FDR had not invited him to attend the conference, King had flown home before the president arrived (the admiral's plane might well have flown over the very seas traversed by USS *Baltimore*, the two craft heading in opposite directions).

In the collective view of Nimitz and King, the Formosa invasion could accomplish the key objective of severing Japan from its East Indies resource lifeline but without becoming enmeshed in a bloody, protracted struggle to liberate the Philippines, an archipelago that contained more than seven thousand islands. Better to blockade and bombard them from the sea and air. Formosa might provide a nice springboard to link up with the Chinese on the Asian continent or stage for operations in Japan itself. When MacArthur had the floor, he spoke with his typical eloquence and passion, recapitulating the same arguments he had espoused in his communications with Marshall. He railed against the notion of leaving unmarked in the Philippines powerful Japanese air, sea, and land forces that might well menace the rear areas of the Allied advance. "I can land in the Philippines in three months and have the task completed six months thereafter," he promised. "The blockade which I will put across the line of supply between Japan and the Dutch East Indies will so strangle the Japanese empire that it will have to surrender shortly thereafter." He also made the salient point that an American blockade of the Philippines would probably lead the Japanese to tighten the archipelago's food supply, leading to extensive starvation among the Filipinos. As always, MacArthur could not resist making an ethical argument, in almost metaphysical terms, for liberating the Philippines. "Promises must be kept," he declared, no doubt alluding to his now famous "I shall return" vow to the Filipino people. MacArthur later remembered telling the president that "it was not only a moral obligation to release this friendly possession from the enemy now that it had become possible but that to fail to do so would not be understandable to the Oriental mind. Not to do so . . . would jeopardize the thousands of prisoners, including American women, children and men civilians held in the Philippines. I assured the president I felt confident of success if he adopted the plan."

In spite of the clear differences, a respectful, friendly tone prevailed among all parties. Nimitz even later admitted to sympathizing fully with the transcendent morality of liberating the Filipinos. In a private postwar letter to a Naval Academy midshipman, he referred favorably to "the psychological effect of liberating the P.I. [Philippine Islands] from the Japanese. This was important." MacArthur, in his postwar memoir, lauded Nimitz for showing "a fine sense of fair play." Leahy was impressed with the forbearance of both commanders. "It was both pleasant and very informative to have these two men who had been pictured as antagonists calmly presenting their differing views to the Commander-in-Chief,"

Leahy wrote. Throughout, the president maintained a neutral posture, simply acting in the role of a chairman guiding the discussion and weighing competing ideas. The session ended around midnight. The next morning, they convened again in the living room for several more hours of collegial discussion. Roosevelt continued to steer the conversation dispassionately. At some point, though, either on this morning or during the previous evening, he began to warm to MacArthur's arguments. In a private moment, the general spoke of political realities to Roosevelt by using stark, almost impertinent terms. "Mr. President, the country has forgiven you for what took place on Bataan. You hope to be reelected . . . but the nation will never forgive you if you approve a plan which leaves eighteen million Christian American citizens to wither in the Philippines under the conqueror's hell, until the peace treaty frees them. You might do it tactically and strategically but politically it would ruin you." According to MacArthur, the president stuck out his hand and said, "Douglas, you have nothing to worry about." In another version of the story, MacArthur claimed that the president assured him, "We will not bypass the Philippines. Carry on with your existing plans. And may God protect you." Still another MacArthur version had the president exclaiming, "Well, Douglas, you win! But I'm going to have a hell of a time over this with that old bear, Ernie King!" Regardless of the truth—and no transcript of any kind survives from any of these momentous meetings—there is no doubt that when MacArthur took his leave of the president after lunch that afternoon of July 28 and boarded his C-54 to return to Australia, he understood that FDR supported his concept. Major Rhoades, the pilot, never saw MacArthur so ebullient. "He was just like a kid with a new toy. I could tell he was in rare good humor." When Rhoades asked him if he had gotten what he wanted, MacArthur confirmed that he had and indicated that his troops would soon return to the Philippines. During the flight, the upbeat general remained in a chatty mood, philosophizing to Rhoades, "You know, Dusty, if you reach for the stars you may never quite grasp them, but you'll never come up with a handful of mud."

Roosevelt had once referred to MacArthur as one of the most dangerous men in America. MacArthur loathed the New Deal and harbored little personal affection for the president. The two had sometimes butted heads during MacArthur's tenure as Army chief of staff in the early 1930s. During one stormy meeting, as they argued over FDR's intention to cut the Army's budget, MacArthur had reputedly accused Roosevelt of putting the

country's security so much at risk that it would lose a future war. He predicted that a defeated, dying American soldier "lying in the mud with an
enemy bayonet through his belly and an enemy foot on his dying throat"
would curse Roosevelt's name. And yet, somehow, the experience of meeting face-to-face for a couple days—the last time they would ever see each
other—brought them closer together than ever before. At a press conference shortly after the meetings, Roosevelt more than hinted at a Philippine
return. "We are going to get the Philippines back and without question
General MacArthur will take place in it. Whether he goes direct or not, I
can't say." Upon returning to the West Coast, the president wrote warmly
to MacArthur, "You have been doing a really magnificent job. Some day
there will be a flag-raising in Manila—and without question I want you to
do it." In a particularly odd twist, Roosevelt even intimated that he wished
he and MacArthur could switch jobs. "I have a hunch that you would make
more of a go as President than I would as General in retaking the Philippines." MacArthur replied effusively, "Nothing in the course of the war has
given me quite as much pleasure as seeing you again." The general invited
Roosevelt to preside personally over the Manila flag-raising ceremony. "It
would mark the highest drama of the greatest of wars." James, MacArthur's biographer, speculated that the two leaders, both of whom were gold-
medal-caliber connivers, cut a deal whereby MacArthur agreed to trumpet
battlefield successes that owed much to Washington's excellent support, a
political win for Roosevelt, in exchange for the president's advocacy for
liberating the Philippines. Alas, with no evidence for this notional deal
beyond the circumstantial speculation of a first-rate historian, the truth
remains elusive.

Without question, Roosevelt's support mattered a great deal, but he
hardly had absolute power to implement whatever plans he wanted. "At the
present time . . . all I have won out on is the agreement that we will go up
to and including Leyte," MacArthur, upon his return to Australia, told
Eichelberger of pending operations in the Philippines. "The question of
whether or not the route will be by Luzon or Formosa has not yet been
settled in Washington." As FDR's statement about Admiral King indicated,
the Joint Chiefs still had much to say in these matters. King remained an
unrepentant advocate of Formosa. Marshall leaned that way though his
mind remained open to MacArthur's vision. With fighting still ongoing in
the Marianas, General Henry "Hap" Arnold, chief of the Army Air Forces,
coveted B-29 bases on Formosa.[12]

Every bit as much as the Hawaii meetings, the course of events in September 1944 determined the outcome of this grand strategic argument. MacArthur and Nimitz, with their respective theaters approaching each other geographically, had closely coordinated their plans. By the time they parted ways in Hawaii, they had agreed to a set sequence of operations. MacArthur was to invade Morotai, about 500 miles west of Biak, on September 15, and the Talaud Islands, some 167 miles to the northwest, a month later. Both invasions were designed to seize air bases in support of a Mindanao invasion on November 15. MacArthur hoped to land on Leyte a little over a month later. Nimitz's forces were scheduled on September 15 to invade Peleliu, and perhaps subsequently Angaur, in the Palau Islands, to take airfields and eliminate any threat to MacArthur's southern flank as he advanced to the Philippines. To strangle the Japanese base at Truk and capture sea and air bases to feed the ultimate advance to Japan, Nimitz planned to assault Yap Island and the Ulithi Atoll on October 5.

Starting on September 8, Admiral Halsey's Third Fleet unleashed air strikes to soften up these targets. They raided the Palaus and Yap that day, Mindanao and the central Philippines for the next two days. On September 12 and 13, the American planes flew twenty-four hundred sorties, many over Leyte. Hundreds of American aircraft marauded the skies, sweeping enemy aircraft away, shooting up targets with near impunity. The Americans claimed 250 Japanese planes destroyed, mostly on the ground. Japanese opposition to the American strikes was feckless, almost to the point of nonexistence. In one instance, Filipino guerrillas on Leyte recovered a downed pilot and claimed that no Japanese were on the island. Safely returned to his ship, the aviator related this information to Halsey aboard his flagship USS *New Jersey* in a personal meeting.

The Third Fleet commander had been skeptical of the need for the Yap and Palaus invasions since their inception. He and Vice Admiral Mitscher, whose aviators flew the raids, had both expected a stronger Japanese response. But the one-sided air battle prompted Halsey to rethink the pending operations. For an hour he sat in his leather-backed chair and contemplated this new turn of events. Once he had mulled all this over in his mind, he discussed the situation with key members of his staff. In light of the apparent Japanese weakness on Mindanao, an invasion of the island now seemed pointless if the Americans could get ashore safely farther north at Leyte. In a postwar memoir, he described the central and southern Philippines as "the vulnerable belly of the Imperial dragon." Moreover, with no invasion of Mindanao, the capture of Yap, the Talaud Islands, and the Palau Islands would all be rendered superfluous. Only Ulithi, whose natural anchorages the Navy needed for any northward advance, still made sense. Leyte seemed wide-open and Halsey now favored taking it as quickly as possible. He excitedly cabled Nimitz to recommend cancellation of the Yap, Talaud, Palau, and Mindanao invasions. "Halsey was sobered by the significance of what he was recommending," Commander Harold Stassen, former governor of Minnesota and a wartime member of the admiral's staff, later reflected. "We had our marching orders. Now we were asking the joint chiefs to change their script."

With enormous expanses of ocean and island under the purview of Nimitz's theater, the commander in chief of the Pacific Fleet put a high premium on judging which objectives his forces had to take and which could be bypassed. He kept a sign over his desk that read, "Is the proposed operation likely to succeed?" Only when he felt confident of the answer did he green-light any invasion. Nimitz deliberated for several hours before deciding on Halsey's proposals. He concurred with the notion of scrubbing Yap, Talaud, and Mindanao but refused to cancel the Palau operations. He cabled these recommendations to the Joint Chiefs in Quebec, where they were meeting with Roosevelt and British prime minister Winston Churchill at the Octagon conference. He also radioed MacArthur, asking for his thoughts on the new direction, and offered to make the Army's XXIV Corps, composed of the 7th and 96th Infantry Divisions, currently earmarked to invade Yap, available instead for invading Leyte on an accelerated timetable.

When Nimitz's message arrived in Quebec, the intrigued Joint Chiefs decided to consult MacArthur before making any final decisions. But the SWPA chief was aboard the USS *Nashville* on the way to Morotai, and for security reasons the ship remained under complete radio silence. With MacArthur incommunicado, it fell to Sutherland, SWPA's chief of staff, to make this important decision. No one could have been more mindful of the stakes, both strategic and personal, than a man of Sutherland's byzantine proclivities. In effect, he had to divine the intentions of his chief and do his bidding in absentia while taking care not to usurp his power. For a more purehearted chief of staff, such as Eisenhower's Bedell Smith or FDR's William Leahy, the task would probably have been straightforward. But Sutherland's recent defiance of MacArthur's authority to wangle a WAC commission for Elaine Bessemer-Clark, his abrasive Australian mistress, and station her, against MacArthur's express instructions, at Hollandia must have hung like a heavy cloak over the chief of staff's shoulders. Perhaps in an effort to muster political cover, or at least line up knowledgeable witnesses, he consulted key SWPA staffers, including Major General Stephen Chamberlin, the operations officer, and Lieutenant General George Kenney, the air commander. "I think he wants moral support," opined Kenney to his diary, of Sutherland's nervous demeanor. Writing more sympathetically after the war, the airman explained sensibly that "quite naturally everyone was reluctant to make so important a decision in General MacArthur's name without his knowledge of what was going on, but it had to be done."

Fortified by input from his colleagues, Sutherland made his decisions. He concurred with the proposed cancellations. On the subject of Leyte, Sutherland and the others knew that Halsey was wrong to assume that the Japanese had no presence on the island. Brigadier General Charles Willoughby's intelligence section estimated that some twenty-one thousand Japanese, belonging mostly to the Imperial Army's 16th Division, currently defended Leyte. So the island hardly loomed as easy pickings. At the same time, Sutherland understood that if he turned down the opportunity to speed up the timetable by invading Leyte, he might well jeopardize his boss's chances of persuading the Joint Chiefs to favor an ultimate invasion of Luzon rather than Formosa. He could never risk this. So he agreed, with the support of Kenney and Chamberlin, to an invasion of Leyte on October 20, as long as Nimitz did transfer control of the XXIV Corps to MacArthur. In MacArthur's name, Sutherland radioed the chiefs in Quebec, "Subject to completion of arrangements with Nimitz, we shall execute Leyte operation on October 20."

The Joint Chiefs received this message, seemingly from MacArthur himself, during a Canadian state dinner. The four chiefs excused themselves, conferred for ninety minutes, and disseminated new orders to Nimitz and MacArthur, formally canceling Yap, the Talauds, and Mindanao, and solidifying the October 20 Leyte invasion date. In time, the chiefs and many other senior officers throughout the Pacific came to understand that Sutherland had drafted the messages. MacArthur found out a couple of days later, after returning from the walkover Morotai invasion in which the 31st Infantry Division quickly seized a useful base against little enemy opposition. Delighted with the accelerated timetable for the return to the

Philippines, the SWPA commander heartily supported Sutherland's call. Still, even though Sutherland had clearly acted correctly and appropriately under difficult circumstances, an unpleasant aftertaste, emanating mainly from self-conscious egocentrism, lingered in the aftermath of this episode. Some MacArthur confidants, including Major Rhoades, believed that the common knowledge of Sutherland's role in making such a key decision rankled MacArthur. It is possible that MacArthur might have accepted the fact that Sutherland had made the strategic decision on his own but for the fact that all high-level commanders, including those in the navy, knew that Sutherland and not MacArthur was the source of the decision. This made it appear that Sutherland was usurping some of the commander-in-chief's authority. Sutherland's daughter Natalie, who discussed the incident with her father several times after the war, contended in a letter to a historian, "Everyone knew it was daddy who gave the order. MacArthur didn't forgive him for years."

Regardless of MacArthur's worsening relationship with his chief of staff, the big-picture permutations of the Pacific theater were now breaking his way. The Joint Chiefs' decision to invade Leyte on October 20 substantially increased the probability that they would ultimately support his designs for retaking Luzon. Nimitz came to realize that he could not muster anywhere near the two hundred thousand support troops necessary to develop Formosa as a useful air and sea base. As the Ichi-go offensive raged in China, and American relations with Chiang Kai-shek deteriorated, even as American forces developed B-29 bases in the Marianas, General Arnold lost interest in Formosa.

Like a silver-tongued salesman who knows when and how to close a big order by telling the customer anything that promises to resonate, MacArthur relentlessly pressed his Luzon case. He emphasized the assistance he could expect from Filipinos, who could fight as guerrillas, provide him with intelligence, and play much the same role as the scarce American service troops. Formosa's hostile, pro-Japanese population offered no such advantages. He pledged to invade Luzon by December 20. In conferences with a liaison officer for General Marshall, a member of General Arnold's staff, and War Department planners, he estimated that the Luzon campaign would take, at most, six weeks. According to one set of conference minutes, MacArthur promised that he "could accomplish the Luzon campaign faster and cheaper than we have ever possibly imagined and that his losses would be inconsequential." He claimed to have studied Formosa in depth and arrived at the conclusion that it "was probably the most heavily fortified point in the Japanese Empire." A SWPA staff study of Luzon versus Formosa, doubtless guided heavily by the commander, pointed to the logistical advantages of Luzon's infrastructure. The study contended, with no supporting evidence, that Manila's docks could handle twenty-one thousand long tons of matériel per ten-hour period and fifty thousand every twenty-four hours. The authors concluded that "if all military considerations are equal then Luzon should be developed as a base rather than Formosa." King made one last attempt to kill the Luzon invasion by claiming that it would involve the Navy's fleet carriers for an unreasonably long period of time. MacArthur easily parried King's concerns by pointing out that, after the initial invasion, he would only need escort carriers for a short time until he secured airfields ashore. The Joint Chiefs bowed to the seeming inevitable and, in an October 3 directive, opted for MacArthur's Luzon invasion over Formosa.

Lost for the moment in all these high-level deliberations was Nimitz's decision—wastefully tragic as events proceeded, and certainly the worst of his distinguished career—to carry on with the invasion of Peleliu. Because Nimitz never spoke publicly of his reasoning, the thinking behind his decision remains mysterious. With Mindanao bypassed, the invasion of Peleliu now seemed pointless. Certainly, Halsey thought so. It is possible that with the invasion fleet nearing Peleliu in the Palau Islands, Nimitz thought it too late to cancel the landings, at least without handing Japanese propagandists an opportunity to claim that they had chased away American invaders. With no ability to contact MacArthur, and having promised him support for Morotai by landing in the Palaus, the admiral might well have been reluctant to go back on his word. Ironically, even though MacArthur had originally agreed with Nimitz on the necessity of securing bases in the Palaus, he did in one August 1944 conference tell SWPA and War Department planners that "the elimination of the Palau operation would have no effect on the . . . Morotai operation or in speeding up the Leyte . . . operation." Neither the admiral nor any other American senior officers had a clear appreciation of Japanese strength in the Palaus, especially at Peleliu. They also had no understanding of the ideal defensive terrain available to the Japanese. Most likely, Nimitz simply saw the invasion as a way to checkmate Truk, maintain momentum for eventual operations in the central Philippines, and keep faith with MacArthur.[13]

The Japanese, in the meantime, had finally revised their thinking on how best to defend islands, especially after their monumental setbacks in the Marianas. From Imperial General Headquarters on down, a growing number of senior officers now viewed banzai attacks as pointless and wasteful. Stemming as they did from the high esteem that Japanese culture placed on a martial spirit and soldierly self-sacrifice, and harkening to an earlier time in the war when Japan was on the offensive against tactically over-matched opponents, banzai assaults no longer made any sense now. The disastrous Guam and Saipan attacks, contrasted by the more successful layered cave defense of Biak, taught thoughtful Japanese commanders that their strategic designs were much better served by eschewing banzai at-tacks. These suicidal charges only played into prodigious American strengths in firepower and tenaciousness. Put simply, the Japanese soldier was more potent on defense than offense. His almost universal willingness to fight to the death might be utilized, in tandem with sophisticated forti-fications and friendly terrain, to bleed the Americans badly enough to sap the will of the United States to win the war.

To be sure, the Japanese still hoped to defeat invasions at the waterline. Failing this, though, they resolved to settle into good terrain and fight as long as possible, costing the Americans time and lives. "I had been opin-ionated, with reservations, against the banzai attack for some time," Lieu-tenant General Sadae Inoue, commander of the Palau Sector Group, told American interrogators after the war. "I had tried to indoctrinate my of-ficers against the use of such tactics. I issued strict orders that the banzai attack was not to be employed because it wasted manpower which could be put to more effective use. I ordered that the men fight a delaying action from prepared positions, causing as many enemy casualties as possible." He urged his men not to be intimidated by American naval and air bom-bardments. If they fortified properly, the American ordnance could do them little harm, after which they could vanquish the Americans in a close-quarters mano a mano fight. "It is certain that if we repay the Amer-icans (who rely solely upon material power) with material power it will shock them beyond imagination," he wrote to his men in a conceptual document he titled "Palau Sector Group Training for Victory."

Indeed, in late May, Inoue had defended these principles during a vol-canic argument with Lieutenant General Obata, the unapologetic advocate of waterline defense and conceptual architect of the Mariana banzai disasters. The altercation had grown so heated that staff officers separated them before they came to blows. Heedless of this incident, Inoue inculcated his command with his concept. Colonel Taokuchi Tada, his fine chief of staff, later ruminated that "the situation closely resembled a contest between a large man armed with a long spear and a small man armed with a short sword. The man with a short sword must crowd in close to the large man so that his spear is useless." The Palaus provided ample opportunity to do just this.[14]

For the Palau invasions, ominously dubbed by the planners as Operation Stalemate, Nimitz chose Geiger's III Amphibious Corps, now composed of the 1st Marine Division and the Army's 81st Infantry Division. Commanded by Major General Paul Mueller, a 1915 graduate of the US Military Academy, the 81st had trained nearly two years in preparation for its first taste of combat. Nicknamed the Fighting Wildcats, the unit had developed a strong cohesion, even composing a fight song with lyrics that appealed more to bravado than imagination: "On we go! We're Wildcats. On we go! There's no stopping us. Because we know we're the fighting infantry and bound for victory! On we go, Eighty-First, on we go!" The unabashed Wildcats had once proudly sung the anthem at full throat as they marched past a reviewing stand of politicians during a parade in Montgomery, Alabama. "I am sure that I caught the spirit of the Division in the singing of the officers and men," Alabama senator J. Lister Hill subsequently wrote to General Marshall. "It was the spirit of resolution and victory." The job of transporting Mueller's fully matured division required a substantial array of shipping: twelve attack transports, three attack cargo ships, two dock-landing ships (known as LSDs in that more innocent era), and twenty-one of the all-important LSTs. They took with them thirty days' worth of combat rations, ten gallons of water per individual, and enough ammunition to last for about a week of operations.

The Americans chose to bypass Babelthaup and Koror, the two largest and most heavily defended islands in the archipelago, and the latter home to Inoue's headquarters. Instead, they targeted Peleliu, home to a well-developed airfield. If necessary, they also planned to invade Angaur, some six miles to the south. For the Peleliu assault, Geiger chose the 1st Marine Division, one of the finest combat units in the entire American armed forces. Nicknamed the Old Breed, the division had earned legendary status by fighting the Japanese to a standstill at Guadalcanal and subsequently

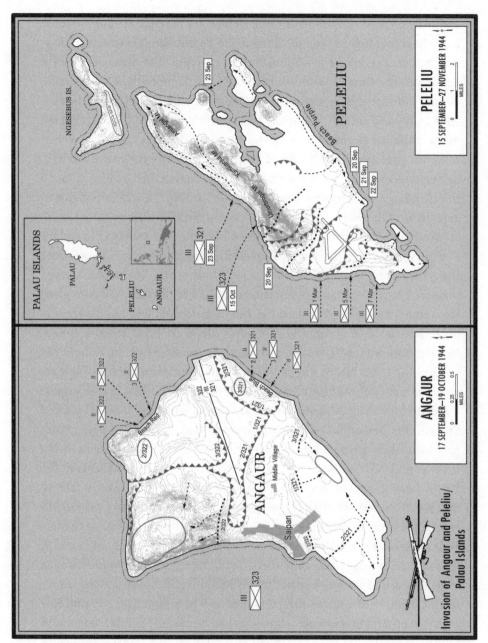

PELELIU

15 SEPTEMBER–27 NOVEMBER 1944

0   1   2
MILES

PALAU ISLANDS

PALAU

PELELIU

ANGAUR

NGESEBUS IS.

23 Sep

20 Sep
21 Sep
22 Sep

III 321   23 Sep

III 323   15 Oct

20 Sep

III   1 Mar.
III   5 Mar.
III   7 Mar.

ANGAUR

17 SEPTEMBER–19 OCTOBER 1944

0   0.25   0.5
MILES

Beach Red

II 322 2
II 322 1

II 322
3/ 322

2/322

III 322
321

3/322

2/321

III 323

ANGAUR

Middle Village

Saipan

2/321

3/321
1/321

II 321
II 321
III 321

Beach Blue

1 3 2

1/321

3/321

1/321

2/321

Invasion of Angaur and Peleliu/
Palau Islands

© 2021 by Chris Erichsen

enduring terrible conditions at Cape Gloucester on New Britain to secure an airfield that helped strangle Rabaul. No Pacific theater American division had endured more privation, even in garrison. The division's base on Pavuvu in the Russell Islands amounted to little more than a sweltering swamp inundated by heavy rains and teeming with rotten coconuts, rats, land crabs, and insects, a tropical cesspool where the Marines struggled just to maintain normal life, much less train for the next campaign. When someone later asked an Old Breed veteran what was wrong with Pavuvu, he responded archly, "What wasn't?" Private Eugene Sledge, who came to the island as a replacement, later shuddered, saying, "It was impossible to explain after the war what life on Pavuvu was like."

Well used to hardship, the Old Breed Marines had managed to endure Pavuvu with admirable aplomb. Regretfully, though, they could not escape the harmful by-products of poor senior leadership. The division commander, Major General William Rupertus, had performed well enough in the number two job at Guadalcanal, but he possessed few qualities necessary to succeed in command. Taciturn, aloof, moody, closed-minded, fiercely contemptuous of the Army, and distressingly prone to bouts of self-pitying melancholy, Rupertus hardly fit the high standard of leadership that such outstanding combat troops deserved. "[He] was a very opinionated, difficult man to serve with and for," Lieutenant Colonel Harold Deakin, his personnel officer, later commented. Rupertus's personality problems likely stemmed from the terrible personal catastrophe of losing his wife and two children to scarlet fever during a posting to China in the 1930s. Few, if any, of his young Marines knew of this tragedy. Tiring quickly of Rupertus's abrasive personality, his young officers referred to him, sotto voce, as "Rupe the Dupe." Before the invasion, he made the terrible mistake of predicting in a division-wide pronouncement that the capture of Peleliu would take only three days. During a training exercise, he broke his ankle, severely restricting his mobility, but concealed the injury from Geiger, who upon finding out later said he would have relieved Rupertus of command for medical reasons had he known. Similar to Holland Smith, Rupertus did not see himself as a member of a larger interservice team. He kept the 81st Division at arm's length during the planning phase, as he saw no meaningful role on Peleliu for the Army. Under the corps plan, the 81st was to remain aboard ship while the entire 1st Marine Division invaded Peleliu on September 15. By the next day, if the situation called for reinforcements, then Mueller would send in troops from the 81st.

Otherwise, the plan called for him to land his 321st and 322nd Infantry Regiments on Angaur, while his 323rd Infantry Regiment remained afloat as corps reserve.

From the first moment of the invasion, the Marines encountered powerful enemy resistance. The Japanese commander at Peleliu, forty-six-year-old Colonel Kunio Nakagawa, devoted his garrison of nearly eleven thousand troops to a brilliantly conceived layered defense. He personally held no illusions about the mortal seriousness of his mission. Before deploying to the Palaus, he had bluntly told his wife, "I am training for eternity." On D-day, Nakagawa's defenders fiercely resisted the invasion and attempted unsuccessfully, with three counterattacks, to push the Marines into the sea. Though the 1st Marine Division prevailed and seized a beachhead about three thousand yards deep, it suffered thirteen hundred casualties on that day alone. The toll was so terrible that the Wildcats, waiting nervously aboard their ships for news, could actually observe grim evidence of the desperate battle the Marines were fighting. "Looking out, we could see bodies floating," PFC Ed Frazer, an artilleryman, sadly recounted years later, "bodies of dead Marines."

In spite of these ominous undertones, a curious mood of triumphant inevitability prevailed, at least among the ship's crewmen, who that evening prepared steak and chicken meals, topped off by frozen strawberries, as a special invasion eve treat before an anticipated Angaur landing on the morrow. But the next day, September 16, nothing happened. Even though the costly Peleliu fighting continued unabated, and the intensity of the violence actually swelled by the hour, Rupertus never considered asking for reinforcements, in effect implying that the situation ashore was in hand, with victory imminent. In reality, the Marines were just about to run into Nakagawa's most difficult defenses, amid the seemingly endless ridges and caves on the high ground overlooking the airfield. Almost as bad, a shortage of fresh water, combined with soaring temperatures, added to the general misery and led to the loss of men from heat prostration. Nevertheless, taking his cue from Rupertus, Geiger authorized Mueller to invade Angaur on September 17, a fateful decision that deprived the hard-pressed Marines of vital air cover, naval gunfire, and reinforcements at just the time when they would most need this help. With the 81st Division now nearing its combat baptism, Mueller circulated a rapturous message to his men: "We are on the eve of seizing an important strategic area from the Japanese. On our shoulders rest grave responsibilities. What we do in this battle will be no small contribution to the glory of our country. To do the job we must cast off sentiment and restraint. To win this fight we must kill every Jap on the island except the ones we are sure are surrendering. That is the job! We are ready!"[15]

The Americans had already spent parts of two days pounding Angaur with naval ordnance. Most dramatically, cruiser fire had toppled the island's concrete lighthouse tower like a heap of children's blocks. Underwater Demolition Team 10, operating daily from the morning of September 14 onward, reconnoitered Angaur's coastline and found, in the stilted recollection of the unit after-action report, "no signs of underwater obstacles of any sort . . . in the area." Beaches were sprinkled with a few obstacles consisting, according to one post-battle report, "of light angle iron or ½" steel cable from tree to tree." On September 17, under cloudless, sunny skies, a powerful group of surface vessels, including one battleship, three cruisers, and four destroyers, bludgeoned the little island one last time. "We hear the blast of the big guns and the ripping-silk sound of the heavy shells sailing to their targets," war correspondent John Walker reported in *Time* magazine. "We see the warships with halos of yellow smoke and the bursts of fire and black smoke back of the beach." Standing next to Walker, a baby-faced, redheaded ensign muttered, "If I was a Jap in there and I wasn't scared, I'd get scared now." In the recollection of PFC William Somma, huddled aboard a landing craft heading inexorably ashore, "the island became a mass of smoke and fire." Air strikes from carrier planes, and rocket salvos from specially equipped LCI gunboats, plus more concentrated fire on the landing beaches from the cruises and destroyers, topped off the bombardment. As usual, though, the preinvasion explosive bark was worse than the bite. "It seems probable it had little other effect beyond a small degree of confusing and limiting Japanese movement," wrote Major Nelson Drummond, a combat historian attached to the 81st Division.

The Japanese commander, Major Ushio Goto, had at his disposal only one reinforced infantry battalion, totaling about sixteen hundred men, to defend a limestone and coral island measuring about three square miles. Home to little more than a phosphate mine, teeming with jungle, hills, and caves, Angaur had no roads and no airfield. The Americans hoped to build a bomber base on this desolate island. One American soldier compared the shape of it to "a triangular kite." Well trained and dedicated, Goto's troops hailed from the Imperial Army's 59th Infantry Regiment, a hardened combat unit that had redeployed from Manchuria to the Palaus only a few months earlier. A coterie of a couple dozen artillery and antiaircraft guns, ranging in size from 37 to 75 millimeters, plus 150-millimeter mortars, mines, explosives, and barbed wire, augmented this light infantry force. With limited manpower, Goto had no other option but to guess at the American landing site and fortify accordingly. He reasoned that the Americans would invade in the southeast, location of the most spacious, inviting beaches, and invested the critical mass of his strength to hold them. Indeed, that part of Angaur teemed with such a vexing array of pillboxes, fortified bunkers, antitank guns, trench lines, rifle pits, and the like that General Mueller and his commanders noticed the buildup as they studied aerial reconnaissance photographs and chose to land on more constricted beaches to the north.

Similar to many other Pacific theater invasions, the 81st Division employed a pincer concept. Mueller earmarked the 322nd to land at Red Beach on Angaur's northeast coast while the 321st hit Blue Beach on the east coast. At the same time, landing craft bearing soldiers from the 323rd feigned a landing on the island's western expanse. The combination of firepower, amphibious power, and an intelligently planned flanking invasion negated any remote possibility of the Japanese halting the American landings. Both the 321st and 322nd got ashore against minimal opposition. Initially, the Wildcats found themselves restricted more by the thick terrain and cratering from the naval bombardment than by Japanese resistance.

Having guessed incorrectly about American intentions, Goto recovered as best he could. He left only a token force in southern Angaur and moved as many troops as possible to the north to counter the American push inland. He launched two feckless counterattacks that accomplished little besides costing him soldiers he could not replace. By September 18, the two American beachheads had joined hands and, with armored support from the 710th Tank Battalion, begun moving westward. Inland from Blue Beach, bulldozers from the 1884th and 1887th Aviation Engineer Battalions were already clearing brush in preparation for construction of an airfield. With few Japanese in their way, the Americans knifed across the southern portion of the island and secured the demolished phosphate plant as well as the confusingly named village of Saipan Town, the only settlement of any size. The division historian vividly described a shattered landscape marked by "scattered machinery, narrow-gauge railroad cars, and steam and diesel locomotives. Most of the buildings were shambles. Debris was scattered throughout the area that had once provided a quiet, tropical life for Japanese overseers and natives engaged in the production of phosphate, the vital fertilizer product which was very essential for Japanese food production." Soldier scavengers found feminine Japanese clothing that they draped over their sweat-soaked fatigues, and flashy headgear that they perched atop their helmets.

In some instances, as the Americans picked through the ruins, they discovered die-hard Japanese soldiers who were determined to fight to the finish. Near the lighthouse and a splotch of high ground the Americans called Shrine Hill, Lieutenant Bob Guitteau's platoon discovered a log-and-earth bunker. When his platoon sergeant tossed a white phosphorous grenade inside, the Japanese responded with desperation. "Out they came. The first guy was swinging a samurai sword." The platoon sergeant parried the sword with his rifle, suffering a cut to the ear, as Guitteau opened fire. "I shot the sword bearer and then . . . went to a squatting position and fired away as the Japs came out of the bunker. My guys behind me were also firing." They killed at least eight enemy soldiers. Others remained inside the bunker. A bulldozer drove up and sealed the bunker with mounds of dirt. Demolition teams exploded charges in an attempt to collapse the bunker or kill the Japanese by concussion. Still the Americans heard grenade explosions as the trapped soldiers committed suicide. "This was pretty grim stuff the likes of which I had never come close to experiencing before," Guitteau later reflected.[16]

In spite of these successes, the majority of Goto's troops remained in fighting condition and determined to stymie the US advance. For the better part of three days, the two sides grappled with each other in a series of fierce engagements amid a baffling network of coral-reinforced pillboxes, bunkers, and trench lines inland from Red Beach. "In order to make any progress pill-boxes had to be bypassed," Lieutenant Colonel P. L. Elliott, an Army Ground Forces observer, related in an official report. "Assault detachments consisting of 18–20 men in each rifle company apparently were not able to cope with all the pillboxes." Commanders resorted to appropriating men from shore parties to help reduce the pillboxes. A friendly-fire bombing and strafing by Navy fighters killed or wounded thirty men from the 3rd Battalion, 322nd Infantry, "with many others badly demoralized by the unexpected blow from their own forces," one officer recalled. An unwounded survivor curled up under the cover of an embankment and exclaimed a sentiment shared by many others: "We've had enough American fire for today."

Uneven ground and thick jungle restricted mobility and provided hiding places for the Japanese. Enemy artillery and mortar fire inflicted casualties. American machine gunners wielded their weapons from the hip and fired generous quantities of ammunition in any direction ahead of cautious riflemen, demolition teams, and flamethrower operators who paced forward through thickets and bushes. "They encountered many pillboxes and dugouts," Major Drummond wrote. "Each was attacked with flamethrowers and satchel charges on the general principle of shooting first and questioning Japanese presence later." Any approach to a manned pillbox sparked machine-gun, rifle, and mortar fire. "Destruction had to be complete, since enemy patrols would infiltrate, rebuild, and reoccupy the position," the division after-action report chronicled. "Excellent results were obtained by attacking pillboxes from the rear as enemy weapons were generally sited to cover the limited avenues of approach." Covered by friendly mortar shells, grenades, and occasionally satchel charges, infantrymen sprinted or low-crawled forward as best they could, sometimes even stumbling intimately into the remnants of their enemies. "A Japanese soldier had been blown in half, legs to the right of me, torso and head on the left," PFC Keith Axelson later said. "His body and head appeared to be standing in a foxhole. I was lying on his viscera, still connected to both body parts. Moving forward I saw another Japanese to my right lying face-up with flies in his eyes."

A single stubborn pillbox could tie down a company or more for hours. "They were tough monkeys," an anonymous 81st Division narrator asserted in a graphic wartime film that reflected predominant American racial attitudes about the Japanese. "There'd still be some of them firing in there even after you'd put a twenty-five pound satchel charge under 'em." Casually referring to the enemy as "the little apes," the narrator explained that "they know how to hide like the murdering weasels they are." The rocky soil precluded digging in; men simply found indentations and stacked coral rocks around themselves for protection. The usual nighttime Kabuki dance of Japanese infiltration and prodigious American firepower led to more than a few death struggles in the darkness. Mueller's well-disciplined infantrymen knew better than to fire at shadows; landing craft crewmen, shore party members, and engineers had no such compunctions.

By late morning on September 20, the Americans had taken all but the hilly, rugged, coral cave–pocked northwest sliver of the island. Mueller radioed corps headquarters, "All organized resistance ceased on Angaur at 1034. Island secured." The general's statement contained a curious mixture of falsehood and truth. It reflected an American tendency to shape a battle narrative—like some sort of martial three-act play—that later marked US operations in Vietnam and even survived into the twenty-first century. Major Goto had lost about half of his command, but he remained alive and in full control of the survivors, whom he wisely hunkered into the ideal defensive terrain around Romauldo Hill, the adjacent Angaur Bowl, and other jags of high ground in the northwest. Goto's troops populated well-camouflaged caves and holes, most of which were impervious to naval gunfire and aerial ordnance. Almost all his men were determined to fight to the death in spite of American efforts to broadcast surrender messages over loudspeakers. So the Japanese major would have been surprised to hear Mueller's contention that he and his charges were not organized.

The 81st Division commander was absolutely correct, though, that his troops had secured everything that actually mattered on Angaur. With the habitable part of the island under control, and the engineers busily constructing the airfield, and the Japanese absolutely powerless to reverse this, the Americans already had what they needed. They had attained their strategic objectives to the extent that tactical fighting no longer benefited them. In that sense, Mueller would have done well to believe his own message. Angaur was secure, at least in the ways that mattered most. Cornered into a remote area, confined largely to caves, the Japanese now posed little threat to the American presence beyond their capability of harassing them with small-caliber mortar, artillery, and small-arms fire of limited range. American artillery, air strikes, and patrols could easily contain these hold-outs while they grew inevitably weaker from starvation, thirst, and diminished morale. If they grew restive and decided to attack, then American firepower would destroy them, as at Saipan and Guam. Far better to let them waste away in their fortified lairs than spend lives and time to root them out one by one. Instead, Mueller bought into the prevailing notion among American leaders that on a small island he must capture every last inch of ground and eradicate every last enemy soldier. "Initiate measures to make sure that not a single Jap is left unattended in your zone," he instructed his regimental commanders. "Active steps will be taken to investigate all caves, dugouts, trees and other possible hiding places."

American commanders favored the trite term "mopping up" to describe this pointlessness, as if soldiers were performing janitorial duties rather than engaging in deadly combat identical to what they had experienced in landing and securing Angaur—the previous two acts of this self-structured play. Just as banzai attacks played into American strengths, so, too, did purposeless "mopping up" attacks in ideal defensive terrain negate those very same strengths, especially in relation to firepower. Instead of stepping back and rethinking the wisdom of venturing into the enemy's daunting den, Mueller ordered the 322nd Infantry to clear the area. In response, the regiment's popular commander, bald-headed Colonel Benjamin Venable, raised a verbal caution flag. "The place is so honeycombed, I don't see how we will ever get it cleaned out. Too many crevices, caves, protected passageways . . . some underground. [We will] never get all the snipers out."[17]

Heedless of Venable's concerns, the attacks proceeded. Predictably, the Americans soon found themselves enmeshed in a bloody, tortuously slow death struggle amid an endless bramble of crags, caves, and ridges. Major Drummond referred to the area as "a nightmare of deep fissures and vertical jagged crags, no five square feet on the same level." The Japanese had already run low on food and water. Most understood that they were doomed, with no hope of relief. One NCO noted in his diary a conversation with a friend "about the food situation, homeland situation . . . there is no good news." No matter how desperate, dispirited, or hungry, they proved themselves deadly adversaries in defending such ideal terrain. Spread among the numerous caves and armed with little more than machine guns, rifles, grenades, knee mortars, and a few antitank guns, they held their fire until attackers came into close range, where they inflicted maximum damage upon them. Visibility was generally limited to only a few yards. "The underbrush made it practically impossible to recognize caves until troops were actually upon them," the division after-action report lamented. "Even after the foliage had been stripped away, it was not easy to distinguish between the opening of a cave and shadow cast by a ground projection upon . . . white coral rock."

The Americans often blundered into their adversaries rather than spotted them. In one almost comical instance, a sergeant attempted to cross a tangle of undergrowth on the trunk of a fallen tree trunk, when the trunk collapsed onto a fighting hole occupied by a Japanese soldier. The frightened sergeant scrambled away. "He heard an explosion close behind but felt no ill effects," one witness later recalled. "After considerable breathing space he cautiously investigated and found the Japanese had killed himself with a grenade." Lieutenant Guitteau nearly had his head blown off as he directed the fire of a Sherman tank. As he stood talking with the tank commander on a phone affixed to the outside of the vehicle, "an armor piercing round hit the tank not more than 10 inches from my head. It carved a groove in the tank's armor. I suspect the Jap gunner had me boresighted and when I dropped to the ground, he figured he got his man. I was scared half to death."

Most Americans were not so lucky. The Japanese could hardly miss their targets at such close quarters. Snipers reaped a grisly harvest. "Since American soldiers are large in stature, it is easier for the sniper to get a good aim and inflict heavy losses," a Japanese survivor told his American interrogators. Concealed positions and smokeless gunpowder made Japanese riflemen very difficult to see. "It was almost impossible to detect the firing position of the Jap sniper," Captain Jerry Keaveney, a company commander, later wrote. "Even from close range, detection of the fire was seldom made." Sergeant Lyle McCann arrived at one embattled spot only to find "one of my best friends dead, shot in the head." Another sniper spotted Lieutenant James Rodgers and shot him through a lung. Though medics evacuated him, he later died aboard ship. Company E of the 322nd Infantry lost no fewer than four men, including two squad leaders, killed by sniper fire, most from head shots, an indication that all too often the Japanese enjoyed unhindered visibility and fields of fire. In a single day's fighting, the regiment's I Company lost every one of its officers, including the commander, Captain Gerard Marnell, who took a bullet to the chest and, just before dying, looked at his soldiers and said, "That's all for me boys, so long." The anonymous author of the company history acknowledged that "the loss of the company commander and the other officers . . . caused the company to be disorganized. The non-coms did a good job of quickly getting control of the men."

American fatalities piled up relentlessly. PFC Frederick Burtch walked right up on a perfectly concealed machine gun that sprayed him at close range, killing him instantly. PFC John Bradshaw got hit as he attempted to negotiate his way forward over a rocky patch of nearly impassable jungle. Medics evacuated him to an aid station, where he soon died. PFC Bird Walker went forward as a litter bearer and simply disappeared, never to be seen again. Colonel Venable himself became a casualty as he observed the frontline action and directed an attack. As he took cover near a Sherman, several antitank rounds exploded. His radioman, Sergeant William Sherman, was killed. Fragments tore into the colonel's chest and left arm, nearly severing it. "I had ordered the troops into the attack in a dangerous location," he later wrote. "My purpose in going forward was to let the troops see me. Unfortunately, the Japs saw me too." Medics saved his arm and evacuated him off the island. According to Major Drummond, the historian, the loss of Colonel Venable was like a "heavy blow to the attack force. [He] was a deeply respected and warmly liked leader, who was close to his troops and in whom they had the greatest confidence." Venable's less esteemed executive officer, Lieutenant Colonel Ernest Wilson, assumed command of the regiment.

Heavy firepower had little effect on the well-ensconced enemy soldiers. The Americans pounded the area with air strikes, naval gunfire, and artillery. The division's artillery battalions hurled at the enemy over twenty thousand rounds of 105-millimeter high-explosive shells and nearly five thousand rounds of 155 fire, to little purpose. "Artillery lost its effect against the type of terrain encountered in the northwest part of the island," Brigadier General Rex Beasley, the division artillery commander, wrote in the unit after-action report. "The innumerable deep caves and crevices, usually facing away from the direction of the attack, afforded excellent protection from artillery fire. About all artillery could do was to increase visibility by stripping foliage, keeping enemy personnel under cover, and affording great morale value to the infantry." Tanks, bazookas, and 81-millimeter mortars provided some fire support, but, by and large, only small groups of terrified infantrymen could take the tattered ground and subdue enemy resistance. The close-quarters fighting negated almost every American advantage of firepower, conforming almost precisely to Inoue and Tada's vision of the man with the short sword hugging close to the man with the long spear. A battle status document produced by Inoue's headquarters claimed to have "repulsed and [driven] back with heavy casualties" the American attacks. "The close-quarters combat carried out by our forces each night kept the enemy restless and on edge." Major Drummond, the historian who observed this fighting firsthand, later commented that it occurred "so close and under such terrain conditions that the division's great superiority in heavy support fire was of little use. Automatic weapons and, above all, the individual infantryman with rifle and grenade carried the battle."

The 81st Division needed weeks of brutal fighting to subdue the entire area. "The nerve shattering combat at close quarters when a grenade might be dropped from directly overhead or an unseen enemy machine gun open up at a range of a few yards was exceedingly exhausting and nerve wracking," the division historian wrote. "Climbing, crawling, hoisting oneself over coral masses under the debilitating tropical sun in airless chasms was enervating to the strongest." The combination of the unhealthy jungle conditions, the unclean drinking water, and the prevalence of flies in pestilential numbers produced an almost universal plague of dysentery, known as the "Angaur Amble," among the frontline soldiers. Typical of most, Lieutenant Guitteau felt the need to eliminate nearly anywhere and everywhere. At night, rather than venture out of his platoon's tense, buttoned-down perimeter, he took to doing his business in hand grenade canisters. "Each grenade came in a short, round tube with a slip-off lid. You took out the grenade, pooped in the tube, put on the lid and tossed it all aside. Not much fun." He lost so much weight that he soon had to tape his wedding ring in place lest it slip off his shrinking finger.

By the first week of October, with the Japanese cordoned into an area no greater than a few hundred yards in width and depth, General Mueller finally scaled down the pace of the attacks, though he did not end them altogether. Engineers strung barbed wire around the cordon to prevent the Japanese from escaping. Patrols and demolition teams carefully scouted caves and fought intimate battles to the death with anyone they found inside. The Americans wisely began to bait the Japanese from their hideouts with booby-trapped food and water or they simply lay in wait to ambush anyone who walked into the kill zone where they had placed these enticements. On the evening of October 19–20, Major Goto collected his few remaining survivors and attempted to slip through the American lines to the shore, where he hoped to build an escape raft that might get them to an island controlled by friendly forces. All were either killed or captured. Goto was killed by a burst of machine-gun bullets fired by Private Joe Abreu. The rounds disintegrated the major's fingers and peppered his torso. Abreu did not know the identity of his victim until he saw the body in the morning light.

On the corpse, Abreu and his buddies found sketches of the area, good luck charms, a farewell note from Goto's wife, photographs, a pocket notebook, and a saber, the latter by far the most prized item. As the trigger puller, Abreu had dibs on the sword. When Abreu's battalion commander offered him one thousand dollars for it, the machine gunner replied unambiguously, "Sir, this sword is not for sale and it never will be." The

Americans snuffed out the last resistance three days after Goto's death. The major and his men had more than done their grim job of costing the Americans time and lives. Only 45 Japanese survived to become prisoners of war. In the course of the battle, the Wildcats counted 1,338 enemy dead. In exchange, the 81st Division lost 264 men killed and 1,355 wounded. The 322nd Infantry suffered about 80 percent of the battle casualties, most of which were incurred during the "mopping up" phase. The division also lost 244 men evacuated with combat fatigue and another 696 to sickness. Of the total 2,559 American casualties, about 54 percent eventually returned to duty. As a strategic objective, Angaur proved small compensation for these losses. The aviation engineers completed by October 19 a pair of six-thousand-foot runways that proved modestly useful as a minor B-24 base. Otherwise, American control of Angaur had little impact on the war.[18]

Tragically, Peleliu's extensive network of high ground was far more formidable than northwest Angaur. An impossibly jagged jumble of steep ridges and caves riddled the northern part of Peleliu, just beyond the airfield that the Marines had captured within the first twenty-four hours of the invasion. Neither the photo reconnaissance images nor the maps provided any real indication to the Americans of what this terrain, generally known as the Umurbrogol Pocket or more informally Bloody Nose Ridge, was really like. Before the invasion, Rear Admiral Jesse Oldendorf, commander of the surface ships scheduled to soften up Peleliu, had actually shortened the duration of the bombardment for lack of targets. Oldendorf had supported several invasions. He understood naval gunnery and fire support like few others, and yet even he could not truly appreciate the proficiency with which the Japanese fortified the Umurbrogol and concealed themselves.

To a great extent, the same held true for the 1st Marine Regiment under the legendary Colonel Lewis "Chesty" Puller. His regiment went into Peleliu with 3,251 Marines. Even before commencing frontal attacks against the Umurbrogol on September 17, the unit had already suffered 900 casualties, including numerous cases of heat prostration, just to carve out the beachhead. The horrific realities of Peleliu's high ground stunned the Marines of this fine outfit. "[It] was the worst ever encountered by the regiment," the unit history asserted. "Along its center, the rocky spine was heaved up in a contorted mass of decayed coral, strewn with rubble, crags, ridges and gulches were thrown together in a confusing maze. There were no roads, scarcely any trails. The pock marked footing offered no secure footing even in the few level places. It was impossible to dig in; the best the men could do was pile a little coral or wood debris around their positions. The jagged rock slashed their shoes and clothes, and tore their bodies every time they hit the deck for safety." Sergeant George Peto, a forward observer for an 81-millimeter mortar squad, aptly described the ground as "twisted coral with trees grown up through it. If you lost your footing you would end up in a fifteen foot crevice and no one would miss you. If the devil would have built it, that's about what he would have done. That was the worst place I was ever in." Another horrified Marine shuddered as he recounted, "Our language just does not contain words that can adequately describe the horrible inaccessibility of the central ridge line on Peleliu. It was a nightmare's nightmare if there ever was one."

On a scale several times the magnitude of what Major Goto did on Angaur, Colonel Nakagawa had turned the large variety of caves into well-hidden resistance nests bristling with machine guns, antiaircraft guns, antitank guns, mortars, low-caliber artillery pieces, and thousands of soldiers willing to fight to the death. The 1st Marine Division after-action report described the Umurbrogol defenses as "a series of interlocking caves . . . blasted into almost perpendicular coral ridges. The caves varied from simple holes large enough to accommodate two men to large tunnels with passageways on either side which were strong enough to contain artillery or 150mm mortars and ammunition. All of the Japanese defensive positions were carefully chosen, well-camouflaged, and had excellent fields of fire. Naval gunfire, artillery, mortars, bombing and strafing had little effect on these positions." By contrast, the jagged ground enhanced Japanese firepower substantially. "Each blast hurled chunks of coral in all directions, multiplying many times the fragmentation effect of every shell," the 1st Marine Regiment campaign history lamented. "Into all this the enemy dug and tunneled like moles: and there they stayed to fight to the death." According to the division intelligence officer, the Japanese had improved one-third of the caves "by cutting fire ports and secondary entrances and escape routes, enlarging the inside, and concreting the walls both with a rough mix of rock and concrete and with a finished cement." Some caves even featured sophisticated electrical and ventilation systems, stairways, and vast storage rooms.

For all of Colonel Puller's fabled and well-earned reputation for valor, the hard-edged veteran of many previous battles seriously misjudged this one. Day after day, he hurled the 1st Marines into the hard muscle of these Japanese defenses in a series of disastrous frontal assaults. He eschewed the opportunity to fly over the Umurbrogol to observe the horrid terrain, unknowingly worked from inaccurate maps, coordinated supporting fire poorly, and seemingly never considered the possibility of enveloping the ridges from along Peleliu's coastal areas. "He believed in momentum," Brigadier General Oliver Smith, the assistant division commander, later said of Puller. "He believed in coming ashore and hitting and just keep on hitting and trying to keep up momentum until he'd overrun the whole [island]. No finesse." As Smith's comments indicated, Puller tended to think like an amphibious assault commander charged with seizing a beachhead, rather than a combined arms commander working to achieve a strategic objective. Puller was hobbled by a badly infected leg wound he had received at Guadalcanal, was sweaty and feverish, so his natural toughness and aggressiveness became, in this circumstance, a liability. A Marine combat correspondent opined that he "crossed the line that separates courage and wasteful expenditure of lives." Puller himself later admitted of his unambiguous attempts to seize the Umurbrogol ridges, "It was more or less of a massacre."

Indeed, his regiment was dying a rapid death along those terrible jumbled ridges. "You have no idea how it hurts to see American boys all shot up, wounded, suffering from pain and exhaustion, and those that fall down, never to move again," Lieutenant Richard Kennard, an artillery forward observer, sadly wrote to his family. "It just seems impossible to get the Japs out of those coral caves." Rifle companies were down to a dozen men. Most of the regiment's officers and noncoms had become casualties. Privates now led platoons. In an attempt to keep the regiment in continuous action, Puller combed his rear areas of cooks, signalmen, headquarters troops, litter bearers, engineers, and anyone else who could carry a rifle. He sent them forward, only to see them added to the casualty rolls. "There was no such thing as a continuous attacking line," one battalion commander later wrote. "Elements of the same company, even platoon, were attacking in every direction of the compass. There were countless little salients and counter salients." By September 21, Puller had lost nearly two thousand men to gain only a few hundred yards of blood-soaked hills and caves. Still, he thought of little else to do besides continue the attacks.

In this, his outlook mirrored that of Major General Rupertus, the division commander, whose unceasing attack orders Puller simply followed to the letter. If ever lions were led by a donkey in modern American warfare, surely this was true of the Marines who had the misfortune to serve under Rupertus at Peleliu. Confined to division headquarters by his broken ankle, Rupertus had little understanding of Nakagawa's defenses nor of the forbidding terrain the Japanese troops defended. Straitjacketed by his ill-advised preinvasion prediction of a three-day battle, Rupertus seemed caught off guard when Japanese resistance continued unabated. At first he reacted with denial. When a war correspondent returning from the front lines one day told him of seeing scores of dead Marines, Rupertus refused to believe this could be true. Challenged again by the reporter, he simply muttered, "You can't make an omelet without breaking the eggs." As the battle wore on unabated, and the losses piled up, Rupertus came close to suffering a nervous breakdown. On one occasion he sat atop his bunk, head in hands, next to Lieutenant Colonel Deakin, the division personnel officer, and groaned, "This thing has just about got me beat." Deakin put his arm around the general and consoled him, "Now, General, everything is going to work out." Another time, Rupertus summoned Colonel Harold "Bucky" Harris, commander of the 5th Marine Regiment, and, with tears streaming down his cheeks, suggested that he take command of the division. The mood passed and Rupertus remained in charge.

Troubling as these stress-induced moments of weakness undoubtedly were to those around Rupertus, his greatest and most inexcusable mistakes—at least in the view of historical posterity—centered around two issues. First, with the airfield firmly under American control, he seemed never to have contemplated bypassing the Umurbrogol, cordoning off the Japanese, and simply starving them out or, failing this, at least trying something else besides obliging Nakagawa with precisely the kind of bloody, frontal, cave-to-cave fighting he wanted. Granted, Japanese fire from the caves might have hindered the security of the airfield, but almost certainly not enough to prevent the planes from operating, especially with plenty of American ordnance available to pound the cave openings. "We had the beaches, we had the airfield, we were using everything that we ever wanted to use," General Smith, the assistant division commander, later commented. Second, and perhaps worst of all, Rupertus proved willing to see his Marines get killed or wounded in larger numbers than necessary rather than accept help from the Army, thus demonstrating a level of interservice chauvinism and anti-Army enmity so pronounced that it might even have made Holland Smith blush. When Major General Mueller declared Angaur secure on September 20, the 321st Infantry became available for service on Peleliu (his division's third regiment, the 323rd, was in the process of seizing Ulithi against no resistance). Rupertus, even in the midst of one of the war's most violent, bloody battles, with devastating losses piling up, refused to consider allowing the 321st to reinforce his division. "This reluctance to use Army troops . . . was very noticeable to the Corps staff," wrote Colonel Walter Wachtler, Geiger's operations officer. Even rank-and-file Marines sensed Rupertus's self-destructive, toxic attitude. "Our high priced help would never call in the Army like this, for it would hurt the name of the Marine Corps, I suppose, to let the world know that 'doggie' reinforcements had to be called in so early!!" Lieutenant Kennard, the artillery forward observer, told his family in a letter.

Sensing this dysfunctional situation, Geiger intervened. During a visit to Peleliu on September 21, he met with Puller at his command post and, though the colonel foolishly denied that he needed any help, Geiger saw for himself the gravity of the situation. Shocked at Puller's exhaustion and his poor physical condition, Geiger became convinced that he had lost touch with reality. The corps commander visited division headquarters and ordered Rupertus to replace the 1st Marine Regiment with the 321st Infantry. "At this General Rupertus became greatly alarmed and requested that no such action be taken," one of Geiger's staff officers later wrote, "stating he was sure the island could be taken in another day or two." Geiger would have none of it. As Coleman remembered the stormy conversation, "General Geiger told General Rupertus that in his estimation the 1st Marines were finished. General Geiger was critical of the way the 1st Marines had handled the situation. He felt that efforts should have been made to exploit the easy going along the regimental left to . . . bypass the resistance in the hills for the purpose of getting at it from the flank or rear."[19]

Undoubtedly, Geiger should have stepped in sooner, but better late than never. The 321st loaded aboard LSTs that carried the regiment from Angaur to Peleliu, where the troops landed on the afternoon of September 23. They immediately relieved the shattered 1st Marines on their hard-earned frontline ridges. Puller's regiment had suffered 1,878 killed, wounded, or missing, a nearly 58 percent casualty rate. This sobering statistic did not even convey the level of devastation suffered by the rifle companies, most of which lost about three-quarters of their Marines. "We're not a regiment," one of the survivors commented darkly, "we're the *survivors* of a regiment." Another later mused sadly, "We were no longer even human beings."

The Wildcats were taken aback by their exhausted, tattered appearance and vacant eyes. As at Guam, the Marines were generally younger than the soldiers, but here they hardly looked it. They were coated in coral dust; cuts and sores, sustained while diving for cover in the Umurbrogol's rocky shambles, peppered their arms and legs. Their faces were wrinkled, and covered with shaggy whiskers. To Sergeant Thomas Climie, a member of the 321st Infantry Regiment's Service Company, they looked like "dirty, scared kids. I felt so sorry for them. They were in shock." When Climie circulated among them and asked how many were left in their respective companies, the usual answer was between ten and fifteen. A gloomy sense of foreboding settled over the soldiers, as if gazing at the Marines revealed clairvoyant glimpses into their own future. Sergeant Peto, the mortar observer, keenly remembered the scrubbed appearance of a burly, well-dressed, healthy-looking Wildcat captain when his company relieved the remnants of Peto's unit. As the reality of the situation dawned on the captain, "his face turned pale and he reminded me of a man that was told he was about to be shot and there was a good possibility that that is exactly what happened to him."

The shattered 1st Marine Regiment rotated back to Pavuvu. The rest of the 1st Marine Division remained in action. The 321st Infantry took a place in the western section of the line alongside the 7th Marine Regiment and fought under Rupertus's control. Tension between the two services soon flared when K Company of the 321st failed to take a key knoll from which the Japanese showered adjacent Army and Marine units with devastating fire. The knoll could only be taken frontally and the company commander, Captain Thomas Jones, refused to order his soldiers to do this, mainly because his unit had lost several men in an abortive direct attack on a pillbox at Angaur. The battalion commander relieved Jones as well as his successor when he also promptly refused. A Marine company had to take the knoll but suffered sixteen casualties, including the death of a well-regarded commander. The story spread like wildfire among the Marines, some of whom harbored doubts about the Army's fighting acumen. "Only the finest Army troops could fight on these islands," one Marine junior officer commented in a letter home; "the type of warfare we wage . . . is a do or die job, not fit for the Army." In the wake of the incident, General Rupertus, with a pettiness that revealed much about his narrowness of mind, raged, "That's the Wildcat Division of pussycats all the way. Now I can tell Geiger, 'I told you so.' That's why I didn't want the Army involved in this in the first place." In stark contrast to most every other commander in recorded military history, Rupertus apparently preferred not to have reinforcements! The historical record reveals no evidence that he ever shared his "I told you so" sentiments with Geiger.

The knoll fiasco proved an outlier. The soldiers more than pulled their own weight as September turned to October and the costly fighting raged on unabated. Though the 321st and the 7th Marines did envelop the Umurbrogol from the west, isolating the Japanese in their caves and severing Nakagawa's communications to much of his command, further guaranteeing the security of the airfield, no one on the American side seems to have pondered the sensible notion of backing off and besieging the remaining enemy strongholds. Certainly not Rupertus, who circulated a fiery letter to his division ordering his men to destroy all remaining Japanese on Peleliu. "They will be killed or captured, to the last man!" he thundered. Beyond a vague allusion to "revenge our colors," nowhere in the letter did he explain why this was necessary or worth the loss of more American lives. At almost the same time, Colonel Nakagawa, whose understanding of strategic purpose far exceeded that of Rupertus or, for that matter, any other American commander, told an aide, "This isn't a campaign any more. It's a struggle between one individual and another. Insofar as a person has the power and will to fight, the fighting will not end and winning or losing makes no difference. The matter is to kill as many enemies as possible and continue to fight as long as possible."

For weeks, the Americans obliged him by fighting to clear every remaining cave of Japanese resistance within an area measuring little more than 750 yards long and 500 yards wide. Over a three-week period from September 27 to October 20, he inflicted more than 1,500 casualties on the Marines and 1,006 on the 81st Division and its supporting Army units. Among the casualties was Murphy, a canine mascot who had been part of the 321st Infantry Regiment through two years of training and in combat on Angaur. At the Umurbrogol, "Murphy was in the thick of the fighting," according to Colonel Robert Dark, the regimental commander. "A mortar shell had his number on it, and he died like the hero that he was." Enraged by the death of their dog, the troops "began to fight as they had never fought before. One man took a light machine gun off the mount and [slung] a belt load with ammunition over his shoulder, mov[ing] forward with the machine gun cradled in the crook of his arm."[20]

Marine and Army artillerymen laboriously disassembled their pieces and, either on their backs or fastened to ropes and pulleys, moved them to the front, where they were reassembled and used to provide direct fire into the caves. Vehicles had great difficulty operating amid the ubiquitous rocks and crags. "Frequently it was necessary to depend upon the engineers to build roads through impassable terrain in order to put tanks on vantage points to render direct fire support," an Armor School analysis of the campaign chronicled. Raked by the firepower of two great industrial nations, the Umurbrogol had transformed into a grotesque moonscape, shorn of vegetation, nature's equivalent to a human body bereft of anything but skin and bones. "The trees and vegetation that once covered the area had long since disappeared in parts of the area due to naval and air bombardment, artillery, mortar fire, napalm strikes, and small-arms fire, and the area, except for dead snags, was almost entirely devoid of growth," explained a terrain analysis prepared by the 323rd Infantry Regiment intelligence section.

The unit entered the fray in mid-October when Geiger withdrew the balance of the 1st Marine Division and turned the remaining fighting entirely over to the 81st Division. One Wildcat, in a letter to his family, described the Umurbrogol as "a terrible place to fight a battle. Cliffs that were straight up and down with caves in their sides. The Japs stayed in their caves and what a job it was to blast them out. We had to use every trick in the book." With no way to dig into the rocky coral, the soldiers initiated an extensive sandbagging operation. After filling the bags with sand from the beaches or soil from the low ground, carrying parties hauled the bags up the ridges to the rifle companies. At times, attacking infantrymen actually advanced by crawling forward and pushing the bags ahead of themselves. During the long nights, they surrounded themselves with the sandbags and warded off Japanese infiltrators by pitching grenades at them in liberal quantities or fighting them to the death hand-to-hand. The next day, the survivors resumed the monotonous routine of more attacks, ridge by ridge, cave by cave, in a seemingly endless series of violent small-unit actions.

The Japanese heavily booby-trapped and mined natural routes of advance. In one instance, soldiers from the 323rd ran into a deadly network of pre-positioned grenades and aerial bombs, defensive weapons eerily reminiscent of the IEDs that would plague a later generation of American soldiers. A single explosion of an electrically charged five-hundred-pound bomb savaged the ranks of the regiment's E Company. "After a deafening blast, screams of pain and fright filled the air," the company history sadly related. "The evacuation of the torn bodies of our buddies . . . was a hard, grim task. Many of our closest friends could not be recognized. Many died in the arms of those who tried to ease their pain. A feeling of sadness reigned throughout the company." For medics, the jagged ridges made the task of evacuating the wounded, especially on stretchers, seem almost impossible. "In some cases men were carried out on the back," claimed the 323rd's medical report. "In others the patient was carried out on the top of a tank." Other men were sent back on litters attached to pulleys. At one point during the fighting, it took, on average, one and a half hours to evacuate wounded men a distance of slightly more than a quarter mile. Far too often, according to the theater surgeon, "the intensity of enemy fire made evacuation impossible."

Although one spot looked pretty much like any other to the average man, the troops coined nicknames for some of the more distinct terrain features, each of which developed a horrifying identity of its own as men fought and died for them—the China Bowl, the Five Sisters, the Five Brothers, Old Baldy, and the Wildcat Bowl, to name only the most prominent. The aforementioned artillery pieces, along with flamethrowing LVTs and a handful of tanks, provided some close fire support, but really the caves could be taken only by small groups of foot soldiers wielding rifles, submachine guns, satchel charges, and flamethrowers. "The infantry was confronted with a defense against which no single supporting weapon at its disposal could be brought effectively to bear," General Geiger commented. "This posed a problem the only solution for which was a slow, methodical, and relatively costly operation for their final reduction." Captain Pierce Irby, a company commander in the 321st, later commented on the complete lack of any subtlety to this climactic fighting. "All attacks were made frontally across compartments where the enemy was strongest, thereby permitting him to use maximum fires."

The Americans finally snuffed out the last Japanese resistance on November 27. Over a five-week period during this final phase of near-pointless fighting, Mueller's division lost 110 men killed and 717 wounded. Before committing ritual suicide, Nakagawa burned the colors of his 2nd Infantry Regiment and sent a farewell message to Inoue's headquarters at Koror,

"Sakura, sakura." In a literal sense, the message translated as "cherry blossom," but it really alluded to the warrior's life as analogous to the short-lived beauty of a flower. When radio operators at Koror received Nakagawa's message, they broke down and wept. In a token of reverent esteem, his superiors in Tokyo posthumously promoted him to lieutenant general.

At Peleliu the 1st Marine Division suffered 6,526 battle casualties and the 81st Division another 3,275, totaling between them 1,792 fatalities. The Wildcats also lost 2,500 men, at least temporarily, to sickness, nonbattle injuries, and combat fatigue. Almost 15 percent of the Americans who participated became casualties. Infantrymen accounted for 79 percent of the killed, wounded, or missing. The Japanese lost about 11,000 soldiers killed, plus a handful taken prisoner. They succeeded in inflicting a one-to-one casualty ratio on the Americans, a disquieting harbinger for future battles. An anonymous diarist at Imperial General Headquarters wrote of the Peleliu garrison, "They were warriors to the end and their actions really are a model for military men."

Just as Admiral Halsey had anticipated, the Palau operations, and Peleliu in particular, accrued no strategic advantages for the Americans. Operation Stalemate proved to be the very embodiment of a Pyrrhic victory, and a sour example of the wrong way to fight this war. American victories in the Marianas, combined with the decision to bypass Mindanao, and the preeminence of Allied air- and sea power, had already isolated every Japanese serviceman in the Palaus. Nakagawa and thousands of others could just as easily and intelligently have been left to fester in their caves. The airfield on Peleliu played only a tangential role in the war, as a backwater base. As a silver lining, one might argue that the only value of the air base came about the next summer when a Peleliu-based search plane located some stricken survivors of the USS *Indianapolis*. Otherwise, the Peleliu airfield played no meaningful role in the war (and Angaur field proved almost equally ancillary). "The expedition was unnecessary," Colonel Venable bluntly wrote to a historian after the war. "It accomplished little and immobilized two divisions for six months."

In the battles for both Peleliu and Angaur, American senior leaders at the division level demonstrated little strategic or, for that matter, tactical vision. Both battles demonstrated the unsettling truth that remarkable American gallantry at the tactical level, and the capture of ground, did not automatically lead to strategic advantages—an object lesson that subsequent generations of American commanders might well have taken more to heart. As at Saipan, the egregious biases of a single senior commander at Peleliu proved to have terrible consequences. Fortunately, William Rupertus never commanded troops in combat again. Rather than fire him outright, Geiger arranged to have him transferred home as commandant of the Marine Corps Schools at Quantico, Virginia. Peleliu served as a cautionary tale for the wrong way to fight the war, a dreary monument to poor strategic decision-making, faulty intelligence, self-defeating, almost childish interservice rivalry, and lack of flexible response against a thinking and determined enemy, one who had finally embraced a strategic outlook appropriate to the circumstances.[21]

10

The Ugly Midsection

At Morotai, in the wake of the successful American invasion, General MacArthur had spent about an hour inspecting the beachhead and conversing with a group of officers. As was his tendency, the SWPA commander dominated the discussion, pontificating on the value of the island as a base for his advance to the Philippines. At the mention of the archipelago, the general quieted for a moment and gazed thoughtfully to the northwest, "almost as though he could already see through the mist the rugged lines of Bataan and Corregidor," Lieutenant Colonel Larry Lehrbas, one of his press officers, later reported in a communiqué. As MacArthur stared into the distance, he uttered to the group, with characteristic dramatic brevity and indulgent self-centeredness, "They are waiting for me there. It has been a long time." If Eisenhower saw the Normandy invasion and the campaign in Europe as a modern crusade against tyranny, MacArthur viewed the Allied return to the Philippines as something even more hallowed, something akin to the rescue of a beloved family member, an almost mystical moment of redemption and fellowship. Seldom in American military history has a general felt such a messianic sense of mission and so tight a bond with those whom he sought to liberate.

Two weeks after his wistful comments on Morotai, MacArthur flew from his headquarters in Brisbane to Canberra to meet for the last time with an old ally, Australian prime minister John Curtin. Once in the Philippines, MacArthur planned not to return to Australia, an intention that reflected the changing relationship between these two great allies. In 1942–1943, Australia had served as the main Allied base in the South Pacific against an encroaching Japanese presence. During that phase of the war, Australians had done much of the fighting and dying, especially on New Guinea. But the massive growth of American power, along with the steady northern advances far away from the island continent, had begun to marginalize Australia's role. Increasingly her troops were consigned to babysitting bypassed Japanese garrisons in the South Pacific. MacArthur envisioned no substantial role in the coming Philippine campaign for Australian military forces. MacArthur—and by proxy the United States—no longer needed Australia as badly as before. Like a bicycle cast aside for an automobile, MacArthur intended to make little more use of his Australian allies beyond the incorporation of a few ships into his fleet, now that he had access to the prodigious largesse of his own nation. For Australia, this change from full partner to backbencher whiffed of bittersweetness. No Western Allied country had mobilized its population so completely for war, and contributed so much per capita, whether in blood or treasure. And yet the relief from paying such a heavy price must have been profound, even though it came at the price of less influence and importance as the war neared an end.

The awkwardness—perhaps even melancholy—at this new reality permeated MacArthur's last meeting with Curtin, as did the fact that the prime minister was dying of heart disease. MacArthur and Curtin both understood that they would never see each other again. With Lieutenant Colonel Rhoades, the pilot, and the American ambassador observing on the tarmac next to MacArthur's plane, the general and the politician spent a last few, poignant moments together. "General MacArthur said his final farewell to Mr. Curtin . . . and it was an emotional parting," Rhoades jotted that night in his diary. In this sense, the moment that MacArthur climbed back aboard the *Bataan*, his personal B-17, it encapsulated a new, climactic phase of the Pacific War, one that had been building for much of 1944, an entirely American-dominated war raging far beyond the South Pacific, focusing now on the imminent destruction of Japan itself, albeit through operations in the Philippines and other archipelagos located within close proximity to the home islands.[1]

On October 16, with the Curtin meeting very much in MacArthur's rearview mirror, he boarded the USS *Nashville* to embark upon the invasion of Leyte, known to his staff as Operation King II, the greatest amphibious operation heretofore attempted in the Pacific War. With MacArthur safely aboard, the beautiful light cruiser, displacing a proud 9,475 tons, slipped its moorings, put to sea, and joined what was, to this point, the largest-ever American armada, an assemblage of naval power that exceeded the US contribution to the Normandy invasion. Known as the Central Philippines Strike Force and composed primarily of Vice Admiral Thomas Kinkaid's Seventh Fleet, the armada hailed almost entirely

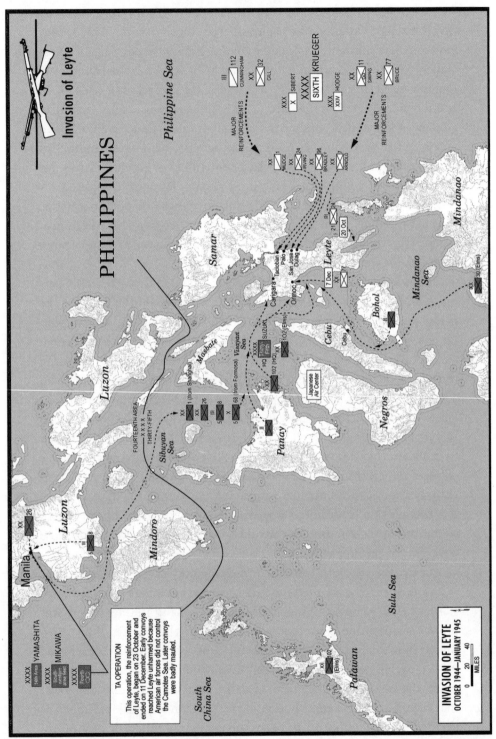

Invasion of Leyte

PHILIPPINES

TA OPERATION
This operation, the reinforcement of Leyte, began on 23 October and ended on 11 December. Early convoys reached Leyte unharmed because American air forces did not control the Camotes Sea. Later convoys were badly mauled.

INVASION OF LEYTE
OCTOBER 1944–JANUARY 1945

0 20 40
MILES

© 2021 by Chris Erichsen

from the two great SWPA bases of Hollandia and Manus. Minesweepers and the slowest of the ships had sallied forth first on October 11 and 12. In the days since, the other convoys followed on a minute, uncompromising schedule of choreographic artistry, resulting from weeks of intensive planning and close interservice coordination. "All the orders had to be cut, including, ship assignments, loading, instructions for the supplies, food, ammunition, POL [Petroleum, Oil, Lubricants], medical supplies, everything," wrote Lieutenant Colonel John Day, an operations officer in Army Support Command, or ASCOM, the enormous logistical section of MacArthur's headquarters. "Troops had to be told where to go on board the ship, what ship to board, what to bring, how many rations to bring, what to pack, how much ammo, how much medical supplies, when to expect to sail, and so on."

Over hundreds of miles of blue ocean, Kinkaid's convoys circled and rendezvoused, assembled into formations, and sailed ever northward, a mighty host of 738 warships, their varying shapes and sizes so diverse as to present nearly a complete picture of mid-twentieth-century naval hardware. There were six battleships, five heavy cruisers, six light cruisers, including *Nashville*, eighteen escort carriers, eighty-six destroyers, and twenty-five destroyer escorts, all protecting a staggering assemblage of some 420 ships needed to carry four reinforced infantry divisions, plus supporting troops, to Leyte. The attack groups earmarked for the four main landing beaches comprised five command ships, forty attack transports, 151 LSTs, ten LSDs, seventy-nine LCIs, twenty-one LCTs, and eighteen other transports. Like motorcycle cops at a parade, dozens of PT boats darted among the flanks, their crews steeling themselves every moment to the endless slap of the open-sea waves against the bows of their vessels. Far beyond the horizon, seven unseen submarines prowled the targeted waters around the Philippines, at once invisible scouts and predators. "It is difficult even for one who was there to describe the scene," MacArthur later wrote reverently. "Ships to the front, to the rear, to the left, and to the right, as far as the eye could see. Their sturdy hulls plowed the water, now presenting a broadside view, now their sterns, as they methodically carried out the zigzag tactics of evasion."

Once at sea, Kinkaid's ships could not have made it far without the sustenance of Rear Admiral Robert Glover's Service Force, a fleet of oilers, water tankers, ammunition ships, and salvage ships with unglamorous names like *Porcupine* and *Panda* and *Saranac* and *Mazama*. Round the clock, the support ships rotated their duties at preplanned meeting points, replenishing fuel, water, and frozen food. Typical of many, the USS *Ashtabula*, an oiler, provided the minesweepers with 6,350 barrels of fuel and 1,072 barrels of diesel oil one day and then, on the following day, pumped 23,728 barrels of oil and eighteen hundred gallons of gasoline into three cruisers. The freshwater needs of the fleet were voracious. Even the larger ships equipped with evaporating tanks and considerable storage space could not meet all their needs; the smaller ships had no such capacity and were totally dependent on external replenishment coming from the transportation of huge quantities of fresh water. The USS *Ponaganset*, originally commissioned as an oiler but now pressed into service as a water tanker, dispensed 43,608 barrels of purified water to 125 different vessels.

The Seventh Fleet formed nothing less than a moving American city. Kinkaid's 738 ships were crewed by some 50,000 sailors and carried about 150,000 troops of Lieutenant General Walter Krueger's powerful Sixth Army. Krueger's forces brought with them nearly every conceivable item for the coming invasion and the operations to follow. Shoehorned inside the various cargo holds and atop many windswept decks, and stored with highest-priority items packed last so that they could be accessed first, were 1.5 million tons of equipment, 235,000 tons of combat vehicles, 200,000 tons of medical supplies, and 200,000 tons of ammunition, more than one ton apiece for every man who was slated to storm the Leyte beaches. The ground units stored between ten and thirty days' worth of food, clothing, ammunition, and other sundries to sustain themselves once on Leyte. After that, they were of necessity dependent upon the fleet for maintaining their logistical lifeline. Sixth Army planners estimated that for every month of ground combat action, they would require 332,000 tons of equipment.

The cargos featured an incredible array of modern products ranging from the industrial to the mundane to the pleasurable—trucks, cranes, bulldozers, generators, chain saws, Bailey bridges, ice machines, explosives, detonation cords, fuses, wire cutters, hoses, pliers, machetes, almost 200,000 map sheets, lensatic compasses, floodlights, stereoscopes, sandbags, luminous markers, pocket combs, shaving cream, razor blades, soap, cookies, nuts, gum, candy bars, french fries, suntan lotion, playing cards, mechanical pencils, trench mirrors, bath towels, fountain pens, and assorted cans of tomato juice, grape juice, orange juice, and beer, the last of which accounted for three times the number of cans as the previous three.

The troops also found enough shipping space to store 120 cubic feet of cigarette cartons, as well as 30 more cubic feet for cigars, pipes, chewing tobacco, pipe tobacco, lighter fluid, and 720 boxes of matches. Two of Krueger's assault divisions even made room for over five hundred gallons of paint and some four hundred kegs of nails.

Nor were the Leyte invasion forces limited only to the Seventh Fleet and its copious passengers. Like an advance cavalry strike force of yesteryear, Admiral Halsey's Third Fleet continued slashing at Japanese bases from the Philippines to Formosa, Okinawa, and their environs, a mission that perfectly suited the aggressive old sea dog and his equally bellicose partner Vice Admiral Mitscher. Halsey had 105 warships at his disposal, including the capital ship cream of the Navy's aviation branch in Mitscher's Task Force 38. Mitscher had at his disposal nine fleet carriers and eight light carriers, with a collection of more than one thousand planes. A muscular complement of six new battleships, six heavy cruisers, nine light cruisers, and fifty-eight destroyers, plus submarines and support ships, rounded out the fleet. The logistical dictates of maintaining the breakneck pace demanded by these two remarkable naval commanders were eye-popping. A mini fleet of thirty-four oilers and tankers delivered practically every necessity for life at sea, including fourteen separate grades of lubricating oil, bottled oxygen for the fliers, spare-fuel belly tanks, food, new sailors, and mail. By far, fuel, the lifeblood of the fleet, was their most common item of delivery. Throughout October alone, they doled out 4.5 million barrels of fuel oil, and 7.2 million barrels of aviation gasoline.

Starting on October 10 and continuing for nearly a week thereafter, Halsey launched his strikes and engaged the Japanese in a dizzying series of air battles, some of which featured attacks by Japanese planes against his ships. The Third Fleet aviators destroyed six hundred Japanese aircraft, including many naval planes, plus aviators and instructors, that might have helped replenish the Imperial Navy's badly depleted carrier aviation forces in the wake of the Mariana disasters. In addition to the destruction of planes, the Americans sank forty merchant ships. The raids also degraded Japanese land-based air forces in the Philippines badly enough to prevent them from stopping MacArthur's invasion through air attacks. "Our fighters were nothing but so many eggs thrown at the stone wall of the indomitable enemy formation," a Japanese admiral admitted ruefully of a raid against one Formosan airfield. The Japanese inflicted damage, though. They shot down seventy-six of Mitscher's planes, costing the lives of sixty-four crewmen, and they badly damaged two cruisers that escaped only as a result of an elaborate salvaging and towing effort.

Owing to distorted, wildly optimistic damage reports by inexperienced rookie pilots, as well as a cultural tendency toward authoritarian gullibility, the Japanese convinced themselves that they had scored a major turning-point victory. The naval section of Imperial General Headquarters in Tokyo issued an October 16 communiqué that claimed massive American losses of eleven carriers, two battleships, three cruisers, and one destroyer, with eight more carriers and other surface ships badly damaged. Proving that one person's retreat is another's redeployment, the Japanese claimed that Halsey had fled in disarray, when in truth he had simply retired to begin covering the imminent Leyte landings. Emperor Hirohito issued a triumphant rescript to mark the supposed victory, prompting spontaneous waves of joyous festivities all over Japan from a worried population that had begun to sense the shadow of the American wolf approaching their door. "We celebrated the 'Glorious Victory of Taiwan,'" one Japanese general recalled with chagrin after the war. Countering this narcotic-like self-delusion, Admiral Halsey, in tandem with Nimitz's headquarters, released on October 17 a chortling statement: "Admiral Nimitz has received from Admiral Halsey the comforting assurance that he is now retiring toward the enemy following the salvage of all the Third Fleet ships recently reported sunk by Radio Tokyo." Beyond the derisive humor, the statement made it clear that the Japanese had sunk none of Halsey's ships, a true buzzkill for any Japanese observant enough to digest the message.[2]

The truth of the Japanese situation was, of course, considerably more unsettling than portrayed by Tokyo, though by no means hopeless. For the first two years of the war, the Philippines had served as little more than a backwater staging base, and a restive one due to growing guerrilla activity. The Japanese stuck mainly to their own bases and populated areas while they granted a meaningless proclamation of independence to a collaborationist regime under President José Laurel, a prominent politician who felt he could best protect his people by ingratiating himself with the occupiers. Under the pressure of fighting a vast two-front war on the Asian continent and throughout the Pacific, the Japanese could not afford to station major combat forces in the islands until circumstances dictated otherwise by the spring and summer of 1944. In May, Field Marshal Count Hisaichi Terauchi, the aristocratic, wealthy commander of the Southern Army, the equivalent of an American theater command, had transferred his headquarters from Saigon to Manila. The primary combat organization under his control included the Fourteenth Area Army, the equivalent to an American field army, under Lieutenant General Shigenori Kuroda, and the 35th Army, similar to an American corps, whose commander Lieutenant General Sosaku Suzuki was responsible for defending the Visayans, the central part of the Philippines, most notably Leyte.

Typical of the Japanese, they had no semblance of a unified command. Terauchi had no operational control over anything but his ground forces. Admiral Soemu Toyoda controlled formidable naval forces of the Combined Fleet poised to sally from bases at Lingga Roads in the Dutch East Indies across from Singapore and from the home islands to scramble to the defense of the Philippines. Fighter and medium bomber formations from the Imperial Navy's 5th Base Air Force and the Imperial Army's 4th Air Army were scattered among sixty operational airfields in the archipelago and generally answered to their own independent commands. Halsey's raids had diminished their numbers and readiness, though they still loomed as a potential threat to the security of Kinkaid's fleet, if not necessarily its ability to land invasion forces. Most of the Japanese commanders correctly anticipated an imminent powerful American offensive in the Philippines, and they fully expected Leyte landings. They knew where but not quite when. In this context, Imperial General Headquarters had conceived of the Sho, or Victory, plan, which called for massive counterstrikes by air, sea, and land against the next major American operation, for the purpose of winning a military victory that might salvage some sort of favorable negotiated peace. The supposed great victory over Halsey's fleet at Formosa had only whetted the Japanese high command's appetite for this decisive battle. So the Philippines, as the fulcrum of Japan's shrinking empire, were now central to the Sho plan. "The High Command knew that if the Americans took the Philippines the line of communications between the homeland and all the south Pacific islands would be severed," Major General Yoshiharu Tomochika, the 35th Army's chief of staff, explained after the war about the Japanese mindset.

As the Japanese grew increasingly serious about their defense of the archipelago, they channeled as many troops as possible onto the islands. By October, the Fourteenth Area Army had grown to over a quarter million soldiers. In tandem with aviation and construction units, Japanese strength in the Philippines stood at about 432,000. Some 23,000 troops of the Imperial Army's 16th Division and its attachments defended Leyte, a mountainous, marshy, sizable island measuring 115 miles in length from south to north, 45 miles at its widest, and 15 miles across at its narrowest point. The division had fought in the 1941–1942 campaign to seize the Philippines, but about one-quarter of its soldiers were draftee replacements from the Kyoto-Osaka region whom one Japanese wag snidely dismissed as producing "better businessmen than fighters." Training standards and combat readiness were, at best, mediocre, and the quality of leadership inconsistent. In one of the division's infantry regiments, an officer's duty roster that assessed the characteristics of individual junior officers contained a mixed bag of penetrating evaluations. First Lieutenant Koshi Kaneshina was said to be "straightforward, noble-spirited, gallant and courteous," and his colleague First Lieutenant Shigeo Takeuchi was "intelligent, steady and honest; able to handle affairs, [with] sound judgment." By contrast, Second Lieutenant Yasuo Ijiri was deemed by his superiors to be "not skillful in swordsmanship, lacks personality and noble spirit. Effeminate and has no dignity," while Second Lieutenant Ryuzo Yasuhisa demonstrated "poor leadership, lacks courage, and is not esteemed by his subordinates." Similar to Yasuhisa, another officer, Second Lieutenant Toyoichi Aoyama, was seen by his boss as "unable to control his men, lacks character, irresolute, and failed in punitive operations" against guerrillas. The division commander, Lieutenant General Shiro Makino, had logged barely six months in the area. He had time only to construct defenses near the obvious invasion beaches on Leyte's east coast and to begin working on inland layers near central Leyte's mountainous spine. A believer in the "Glorious Victory of Taiwan" myth, he expected mainly to defend the airfields in eastern Leyte, particularly near his headquarters at the coastal capital city of Tacloban, while friendly planes and ships savaged the remnants of Halsey's fleet and American amphibious forces.

Perhaps the greatest indicator of the importance that Imperial General Headquarters now placed on the defense of the Philippines was the decision in early October to replace Kuroda as head of the Fourteenth Area Army. During a year in command, he had earned a reputation, whether fairly or not is difficult to assess, as an imperial placeholder with luxurious tastes who engendered little respect among his troops. Kuroda had served in England as a military observer during World War I. He spoke English with a British accent. He privately believed that Japan must seek an immediate peace lest it be destroyed by American bombers. To counter an

American invasion of the Philippines, he favored defending Luzon at the expense of all other islands.

Kuroda's penchant for playing golf and whiling away many hours reading volumes captured two years earlier by the Imperial Army from MacArthur's personal library sparked an investigation into his actions by the War Ministry's Personnel Bureau. His posh lifestyle did not help his case. He resided in a Manila mansion, where, it was salaciously claimed in Fourteenth Area Army circles, he lived with Japanese women from the headquarters secretarial pool. The investigating officer, Lieutenant Colonel Seiichi Yoshie, later told his American captors, "I obtained many statements substantiating the unfavorable stories in regard to Lt. Gen. Kuroda. The recommendation of all the staff was that [he] be relieved as soon as possible." It is difficult to imagine, especially in the intensely hierarchical Imperial Army, that the disgruntled talk of underlings could have led to the removal of a senior officer if Tokyo decision makers had not already determined upon this course of action. Fair or not, they sacked Kuroda on September 26.

His successor, fifty-nine-year-old General Tomoyuki Yamashita, arrived in Manila to take command on October 6. Arguably Japan's finest army-level commander, Yamashita exuded professional competence. Bullet-headed, stocky, personable, courteous, down-to-earth in manner and speech, and prone to sonic-level snoring, Yamashita hailed from Shikoku, the smallest of the home islands, where he grew up in a remote village as the son of a country doctor. A colleague once described him as "a strong character, clean and honest and of a kindly and gentle disposition." A longtime subordinate assessed him as "a commander of outstanding qualities." Blessed with a clever sense of humor, innate courage. and a keen ability to inspire the loyalty of subordinates, Yamashita's middle-class background marked him as different from the aristocrats who dominated the officer corps. He had fought against the Germans during World War I but then served multiple tours of duty in Germany as a military attaché during the Weimar Republic and head of a military mission during the Nazi era. As a new general in the 1930s, he had become a close friend of General Hideki Tojo. Yamashita had actually flirted with the ultranationalism that had begun to dominate the ranks of Imperial Army officers before eventually moderating his views to the point where he questioned the wisdom of continuing the war in China and pursuing war with the Western powers.

Most famously, Yamashita had commanded an undermanned Japanese force that outfought, outwitted, and outmaneuvered a poorly led British Commonwealth army to capture Singapore in February 1942, handing the British perhaps the most catastrophic defeat in their history. During the surrender negotiations, a weary and impatient Yamashita had famously ordered his interpreter to tell Lieutenant General Arthur Percival, his over-matched opponent, "I want to hear nothing from him except yes or no!" Percival meekly agreed to surrender unconditionally. The stunning victory earned Yamashita international fame and the daunting nickname "the Tiger of Malaya." By now his relationship with Tojo had soured, possibly as a result of Yamashita's more moderate outlook on the war. Instead of receiving a major command fighting against the Americans and Austra-lians in the Pacific, as one might expect for such a successful general, To-kyo sent him to Manchuria as commander of the First Area Army, where he had languished for two years keeping a wary watch on hollow Soviet armies while the war turned against Japan. Such wrongheaded neglect of a major asset was hardly unique to the Japanese. Yamashita's relegation to the war's sidelines paralleled, almost eerily so, Lieutenant General Eichel-berger's consignment by MacArthur to training duty in the wake of Eichel-berger's hard-earned victory at Buna in early 1943, in that instance mainly out of his superior's jealousy over publicity. MacArthur had eventually realized how much he needed Eichelberger, and the same was true for the Japanese in relation to Yamashita. By October 1944, with Tojo out of power and the country facing an existential crisis, Japan could no longer afford the luxury of keeping a star commander in the shadows, hence his transfer to the Philippines. The locals soon nicknamed the homely general "Old Potato Face."

Yamashita was hardly cheered by what he found. He knew few of his staffers, and most of them had little experience in the Philippines. The hur-ried nature of the effort to strengthen the archipelago's defenses, the shoe-string character to logistics, in addition to the inability to control the air and sea upon which Fourteenth Area Army depended for its very survival, hardly inspired much confidence. He later described the state of his com-mand as "unsatisfactory." Nonetheless he projected as much confidence as he could. In a speech to his staff at his Fort William McKinley headquar-ters just south of Manila, he said, "The battle we are going to fight will be decisive for Japan's fate. Each of us bears a heavy responsibility for our part in it. We cannot win this war unless we work closely and harmoniously together. We must do our utmost, setting aside futile recriminations from the past. I intend to fight a ground battle, regardless of what the navy and air force do. I must ask for your absolute loyalty, for only thus can we achieve victory." In a private conversation with José Laurel, the general predicted that he would some day demand MacArthur's surrender with the same "yes or no" manner in which he had dealt with Percival. Hearing of this years later, MacArthur wrote, with admirable restraint, about Yamashita, "He was an able commander, much like those I had known in the Russo-Japanese war, but, unlike them, he talked too much."

Privately, Yamashita might actually have agreed with MacArthur. To a trusted aide, Yamashita confided feeling a bit like he was about to fight another Minatogawa, a fourteenth-century Japanese internecine battle in which the losing commander knew ahead of time that he had little chance for victory but fought on anyway as an expression of loyalty and honor. Far too much an independent thinker to buy the fool's gold claims about the "Glorious Victory of Taiwan," he fully expected to fight a defensive battle in the Philippines. If somehow the Japanese did reverse the tides of war in the archipelago and at sea, then all the better, but as he indicated to his staff when he used the phrase "regardless of what the navy and air force do," he hardly counted on this best-case scenario. Yamashita saw no need to defend, at least in real depth, any part of the Philippines save Luzon, where he intended to fight a bruising battle of attrition amid the island's many jungles, mountains, and ridges. Like other intelligent Japanese commanders at this stage of the war, he eschewed any fantasies about repelling the Americans on their invasion beaches in favor of a bloody inland death struggle designed to sap the will of his opponents to pay the heavy price necessary for total victory. At Leyte, Yamashita envisioned fighting as nothing more than a holding action to conserve his main strength for the real showdown on Luzon.[3]

With no credible intelligence at his fingertips as to the actual timing of the imminent American Philippine invasion, Yamashita could not have known how little time he had to prepare. Even as he strategized, the American armada grew closer by the minute. At the vanguard, minesweepers cleared passages into Leyte Gulf, a stressful, dangerous, and absorbing task that led to the destruction of 227 mines, enough for the fleet to operate in these waters but not enough to eliminate the threat entirely. To protect against

the dangers of any remaining mines, troop ships were fitted with para-
vanes designed to snag the mines before they could explode and inflict
serious damage. Soldiers from the 6th Ranger Infantry Battalion seized the
small gateway islands of Suluan, Dinagat, and Homonhon against almost
no resistance. Underwater Demolition Teams reconnoitered the main
landing beaches on Leyte's northeast coast. The American invasion convoys safely approached Leyte Gulf on the evening of October 19, the night
before A-Day, the name chosen by MacArthur for invasion day, in order to
set it apart from Eisenhower's Normandy D-Day (the very existence of the
A-Day term yet another subtle reminder of the SWPA commander's enduring resentment against his onetime aide). Aboard the USS *Wasatch*,
Vice Admiral Kinkaid radioed MacArthur, "Welcome to our city." From
Nashville, MacArthur replied jovially, "Glad indeed to be in your domicile
and under your flag. As Ripley says believe it or not we are almost there."

Of that tense preinvasion evening, the general later wrote eloquently
that "the stygian waters below and the black sky above seemed to conspire
in wrapping us in an invisible cloak, as we lay to and waited for dawn before entering Leyte Gulf." Aboard the ships all around the famous general,
the troops seethed with anticipation. By now, they had all been briefed and
thoroughly prepared for practically any scenario. Most had little to do but
while away the last anticipatory hours. Aboard LST-745, Private Donald
Dencker of L Company, 382nd Infantry Regiment, 96th Infantry Division,
and the other rookies of his weapons platoon drew their mortar and small-
arms ammunition. The division, known as the "Deadeyes," had spent
nearly two years training for this first taste of combat. "The evening was
cool and refreshing. I wondered what was ahead for us and if I would stand
up to the stress of battle." Dencker lay down on his cot, muttered a private
prayer, and drifted off to sleep "while all around me were my comrades
talking in subdued tones." In direct contrast to Dencker's comfortable cot,
Lieutenant Gage Rodman, a new platoon leader with an otherwise combat-
experienced rifle company in the 7th Infantry Division, could scarcely
stand the heat of his transport ship a moment longer. In private notes, he
wrote of "sizzling decks, [a] steaming wardroom, and stifling quarters. I
could not get cool." Gathered with a small group in the galley aboard another ship, Lieutenant Phil Hostetter, a physician with the 24th Division,
assessed the general mood as "thoughtful, but not agitated or nervous. No
one was loud or boisterous. A small cluster of men, about 15, formed

around a poker game, a few playing the others watching." In the sick bay, sailors donated last-minute pints of blood while, elsewhere, chaplains lent a sympathetic ear to groups of contemplative soldiers.

Even as these men indulged humanitarian instincts, submachine gunners cut X marks on bullet cartridge heads in the hopes that their slugs might, upon striking an enemy body, split into fragments and cause massive damage. Other soldiers, in the recollection of Tech 5 Hanford Rants, a telephone lineman with an infantry battalion in the 24th Division, stood topside "all night, some weeping, some meditating, some cursing but all weighing their chances of getting through another campaign. It gets to be pretty emotional." Aboard another ship, Captain Warren Hughes, an antitank company commander in the 7th Division who had seen much combat on Attu and Kwajalein, felt awed by the menacing nature of his convoy. It reminded him of "the slinking approach of a black panther about to spring on an unsuspecting prey." On the deck of an attack transport that carried most of the 12th Cavalry Regiment, Brigadier General William Chase, the inspirational brigade commander who had contributed so much to the success of the Los Negros invasion in February, stood admiring the view, he wrote, "when I heard a loud scream and a splash. Sure enough one of the men had fallen overboard, a poor place indeed, what with sharks, Jap boats, floating mines, and our own numerous ships." Incredibly, Chase later heard that the lucky man was fished out of the water.

Untold thousands wrote pensive, idealistic last letters to loved ones that must have sent worried twinges through many homes. "I am going into battle with a free conscience, and faith in the fellows with me," PFC Wallace Jaep, a young rifleman in the 96th Division, told his family. "I have put myself in God's hands and trust in his will. The battle we are going into is a battle of liberation and I am proud and ready to do all in my power to free these people. If *doing all* means giving my life, I understand the reason clearly. And I shall be proud of the sacrifice. If the worst comes, there is no cause for mourning over something I am so eager to do." PFC Sidney Centilli, another 96th Division soldier about to experience his first taste of combat, reassured his family that, as a young, healthy man, his natural job was to protect them by fighting as a soldier. "Each of us is a representative of our family," he wrote of his fellow soldiers and himself; "the Japs and the Germans . . . threatened to destroy and degrade our families. We [are] young enough to be adaptive and capable of taking a lot of guff, old enough to take care of ourselves, and with no actual dependents. If one of us is sacrificed it will be a high price to pay . . . but it will well be worth it. It's all elemental, as simple as the division of labor in a bee hive."

More than any other soldier, General MacArthur felt the historical significance of this vast effort for which he had so long planned and prepared. Inside his stateroom on *Nashville*, he propped a picture of his wife, Jean, and young son, Arthur, atop a small writing desk and scrawled a short letter to her on ship's stationery. "Tomorrow we land. I am in good fettle and hope to do my part tomorrow and in the days that follow. Tell Arthur that we have more than six hundred ships and that as far as he can see in all directions there are nothing but ships. With all love . . . to you both. I'll be thinking of you tomorrow when I go in." He signed the letter "Sir Boss," Jean's pet name for him, inspired by a character in Mark Twain's novel *A Connecticut Yankee in King Arthur's Court*. Elsewhere on *Nashville*, General Kenney confided to his diary a prescient assessment of Operation King II's prospect for success. "We will get ashore OK and I hope the dumb Jap will try to defend the shoreline in strength—if he does we'll have airdromes soon. If he fights intelligently, holds the hills west of Dulag and southwest of Tacloban and counter-attacks after we land and delays the advance through the valley to the north coast of Leyte, we are in for trouble."[4]

On A-Day, radiant rays of sunshine beamed on the tranquil waters of Leyte Gulf, perfect weather for an invasion, and a true stroke of luck, considering what fickle nature had in store for the weeks ahead. The 24th Division's after-action report described the A-Day sea as "glassy calm." Assault troops who could successfully ward off nervous stomach pangs gorged themselves on a sumptuous breakfast heaped with generous quantities of rich food, the last many would enjoy for weeks and of course the last that some would ever eat. Lieutenant Jack Hogan, a 7th Division veteran of two previous invasions, savored a "'battle breakfast' steak and all the trimmings." Private Dencker eagerly consumed a "fine breakfast of powdered eggs, bacon, toast, pancakes, syrup, reconstituted milk and coffee." Full bellies or not, in the hundreds and then the thousands, they streamed carefully down cargo nets into LCVPs or packed aboard LVTs or piloted amtanks that circled and staged in formations like vehicular synchronized swimmers. Minute after monotonous minute they circled, waiting for the precise moment when they could head for the enemy coast, an agonizing, uncomfortable wait for their passengers. "My detachment and I are now on the water making those interminable circles before going in," Captain

George Morrissey, the surgeon for 1st Battalion, 34th Infantry Regiment, 24th Division, noted in his diary. "That's what takes the edge off your excitement." The absence of coral reefs and the almost impossible vastness of Kinkaid's fleet meant that the invaders could employ all manner of amphibious craft.

The individual soldiers themselves manifested the mind-boggling gobs of cargo produced by a prosperous nation and now transported across continent-size tracts of ocean, at such elaborate cost and effort, to this very place. The shoulders and joints of nearly everyone groaned under the weight of at least sixty pounds of gear; some hauled as much as ninety or one hundred. They were hobos of plenty who carried with them everything they owned, and they owned a lot—mess kits, shelter halves, tent poles, canteens, cartridge belts, mortar packboards, ropes, ponchos, K rations, Bibles, pencils, pens, writing paper, diaries, books, entrenching tools, pistols, rifles, submachine guns, machine-gun receivers, machine-gun tripods, machine-gun ammunition boxes or belts, mortar baseplates, mortar gun tubes, mortar rounds, communication wire, radios, rifle clips, bandoliers, grenades, helmets, spotted camouflage knapsacks, machetes, musette bags, first aid equipment, bazookas, flamethrowers, wire cutters, compasses, binoculars, shaving kits, cameras, combs, and family pictures. Nervously they huddled together, cloaked in the moist stench of diesel fumes mixed with sea spray, and waited to go in. Adjacent to Private George Brooks, a young rifleman in the rookie 96th Division, a soldier nervously fiddled with the safety switch on his M1 Garand so much that the weapon discharged, fortunately without inflicting harm on him or anyone else. "There was a black powder mark up the side of his face and a hole through his helmet. Nobody laughed." Some peeked at the Leyte coast in the nearing distance. Captain Charles Johnson, the Cannon Company commander of the 32nd Infantry Regiment, 7th Division, thought the island looked "green and beautiful but sickening."

Under the now standard umbrella of a massive supporting bombardment, the troop-laden craft, beginning at about 0935, migrated steadily westward, bound for Leyte's smoking, broiling beaches. To Brigadier General Chase, "it looked as though the entire beach were burning." Weirdly reminiscent of tornadic funnel clouds, numerous oily plumes of black smoke rose to the sky. Unlike most previous invasions, the Americans had this time dropped warning leaflets to the locals, urging them to move away from the coast and take shelter. In the meantime, the invaders inexorably approached Philippine soil. To a soldier from a follow-on wave who watched the landing craft from the vantage point of his ship, they "looked like a lot of race horses vaulting from the gates." The combined might of battleships, cruisers, destroyers, rocket-belching LCIs, carrier planes, and smaller supporting vessels created a wall of overwhelming noise. Private Bob Seiler of the 96th Division compared it to "a hundred Fourth of Julys, all at once." Captain Ray Tarbuck, a naval officer observing from the vantage point of USS *Blue Ridge*, the flagship of Rear Admiral Daniel Barbey, who presided over the northernmost landings, equated the steady bombardment "with the rumble of an earthquake. It is impossible to distinguish one explosion from another; it is just a roar." In the mile-long stretch of coastline where the 96th was scheduled to land—dubbed by planners as Orange and Blue Beaches—surface ships fired 2,720 shells in a 39-minute period. "It was a fearful chorus that heralded our coming," the division historian later wrote.

From 1000 to 1003, in most cases precisely on time, the leading waves hit their respective beaches, the largest synchronized troop landing to this point in the Pacific War, with thousands of soldiers and hundreds of amphibian vehicles setting foot on land at nearly the same time. Green coconuts shaken loose by the incessant shelling covered the beaches. More than a few hot, thirsty soldiers sliced them open and guzzled their milk. In a matter of minutes, the better part of four divisions splashed ashore, enough troops to make up two corps and one field army. In the view of one combat historian, the lightning landings left Krueger's Sixth Army "balanced like a giant with one foot ashore and one on a ship." Knowing that the Japanese had little capability of defeating separate beachheads in detail, the Americans boldly assaulted on two fronts separated thirteen miles from each other. In the north, Major General Franklin Sibert's X Corps, carried into position by Barbey's Northern Task Force, seized a mile and a half of coast with the 1st Cavalry Division on the right, near Tacloban, and the 24th Infantry Division to the south at Palo. Sibert had commanded the 6th Infantry Division in New Guinea successfully enough that Krueger had since tapped him for command of X Corps. Thirteen miles down the coast, the XXIV Corps, under Major General John Hodge and transported into position by Vice Admiral Ted Wilkinson's Southern Attack Force, hit their beaches, with the 96th Division in the north near San Jose, and the 7th Infantry Division to the south at Dulag, collectively landing over the span of less than two miles of Leyte seashore.[5]

Outnumbered and heavily outgunned at this point of contact, if not necessarily in the Philippines and its environs, the Japanese initially could do little besides harass the American fleet with individual air raids and pose whatever on-site resistance they could against the invaders. The vast majority of Americans landed unopposed, bothered at most by random mortar or sniper fire. For this majority, the intense heat and the marshy, boggy swamps that proliferated inland from many of the landing beaches inhibited their advance more so than did Japanese resistance.

For Lieutenant General Makino, the invasion could hardly have come at a more disadvantageous time. The day before, he had begun moving his headquarters from Tacloban to Dagami. With the move only partially completed, he was in anything but a good position to react to the invasion. When the Americans landed, he and many of his staff officers were on their way to Dagami, out of communication with anyone but themselves. His remaining headquarters troops at Tacloban fled or were killed in the face of the 1st Cavalry Division advance, abandoning or losing all communications equipment. This, in tandem with the preinvasion bombardment, reduced the 16th Division's communications to a Napoleonic standard. For two days, Makino remained out of touch with General Suzuki at 35th Army and Yamashita in Manila, leaving them in the dark as to the specifics of the US invasion. Makino did have elements of his division's three infantry regiments guarding some parts of the coast, either at the beaches or slightly inland. Battered by the bombardment, out of communication with higher authority, and massively outnumbered, they resisted gamely but posed no real threat to the overall security of the invasion. In this sense, Makino's 16th Division became a casualty of a doctrinal transition from beach to inland defense that unfolded too slowly to save his unit from becoming vulnerable to annihilation at the beachhead, even though many of his troops did retreat out of the range of the preinvasion bombardment rather than hold fast at the coast.

In a few spots, though, stranded groups of soldiers fought with characteristic ferocity. "Though life and death are separated by a thin sheet of paper, I will not die until I see a face of a Yankee," one of them scrawled in his diary. Perhaps the heaviest fighting unfolded at Red Beach, where the 19th and 34th Infantry Regiments of the 24th Division ran into prepared defenses manned by soldiers from Makino's 33rd Infantry Regiment. "Behind the narrow beach, flat marshy ground under palm trees and jungle growth extended inland to a wide swampy stream bed which angled to the southwest," the 24th Division after-action report noted. "Within this area a smaller stream had been converted into a wide and deep tank trap which paralleled the beach line for fifteen hundred yards. Fields of fire had been cleared for well camouflaged pillboxes which dotted the area." The bombardment had destroyed many of these defenses. In the recollection of one invading soldier, they looked "like monstrous teeth smashed by some mad dentist." All too many fortifications remained intact. The pillboxes were constructed primarily of palm logs and densely packed earth, undergirded by rocks and planks. Each pillbox measured twenty by thirty feet in size; well-concealed tunnels connected them. For three months prior to the invasion, the Japanese had forced the local men of nearby Palo to build these fortifications and other, similar works at Hill 522, the key cluster of high ground overlooking Red Beach. The Filipino men had worked in day and night shifts, with two daily meals of rice as their only compensation.

The Japanese defenders raked the invaders with wickedly accurate mortar, machine-gun, rifle, and 75-millimeter gun fire. Shells scored direct hits on four LSTs, setting one afire and forcing two others to retreat without disgorging tank and artillery units that might have helped silence the enemy guns. Another shell blew the ramp off a Higgins boat, sinking it and wounding three officers from division headquarters. Heavy machine-gun and shell fire laced through multiple waves of assault troops who now clustered together and took cover just beyond the waterline. Blood ran from the bodies of dead and wounded alike. Tech 5 Rants, the wireman, took cover ten feet away from the body of a man who had been cut into pieces by a direct hit of some kind. "There was no bottom half of him and he was stretched out, guts pouring from the bottom half, which was half in the water, and half out." Another soldier saw a dead American "head completely severed, veins, cords, breathing tube hanging out his neckline."

Redheaded Colonel Aubrey Newman, whose service with the division dated to the Pearl Harbor attacks, landed with the fifth wave and immediately recognized that he could not allow the soldiers to remain in place as stationary targets on the open beach. "Get the hell off the beach!" he bellowed. "Get up and get moving! Follow me." With a wave of his arm, he strode forward, straight at the sounds of the heaviest firing. Dozens and then hundreds followed, initiating or perhaps just reinforcing an intimate pillbox-to-pillbox battle amid the muck of rice paddies and marshes. "GIs started . . . crawling, jumping, running combat-style," Rants, who was only a few feet away from Newman, later wrote. "You run a little, roll over and try to take cover before moving again." Self-propelled guns destroyed several of the pillboxes, but, more commonly, small groups of foot soldiers assaulted them with grenades, small arms, and flamethrowers.

At the vanguard of the American attack, Captain Francis Wai, the regiment's assistant intelligence officer, personally took charge. Popular and respected throughout the regiment, Wai hailed from Hawaii and had once lettered in four sports at UCLA, including football as a quarterback for the 1937 and 1938 Bruin teams. He had joined the Army as a private in the fall of 1941 and earned a commission through officer candidate school, a rare Chinese-American in a predominantly white officer corps. Among the ranks of the 34th Infantry, it was said that Captain Wai had just found out that his wife had given birth to a baby, though he had not seen her in twelve months. "This really shook him and we knew he was going to fight with everything he had, even if he got killed in the process," one of the soldiers who knew him later commented. Three separate times, Captain Wai exposed himself to enemy fire long enough to allow his men to locate pillboxes and then led their subsequent assault and capture. Then, as a supporting squad laid down covering fire, Wai ordered Private Joe Hoffrichter, a flamethrower operator, to attack the next position. In this case, self-propelled fire had damaged the pillbox, possibly disorienting the defenders. Bending under the sixty-five-pound weight of his M1A1 flamethrower, Hoffrichter closed in to point-blank range and found an opening, when an enemy soldier inside attempted to clear a field of fire with his saber through packed dirt. "I placed the nozzle in the hole and shot three bursts into the bunker. The screams I heard were of intense agony. The machine guns were silenced and the stench of burning flesh drifted through the openings. I vomited on the spot." Four more times during the battle he sprayed his liquid fire inside pillboxes, setting the terrified enemy soldiers ablaze. Each time he vomited. "The last two bunkers left me with nothing but dry heaves." As a concession to the heaviness of the flamethrower, an Army observer had recommended "that large and strong men be picked to carry this weapon." He made no mention of how to alleviate the psychological toll of manipulating this horrifying apparatus. Though Hoffrichter survived the pillbox battle, Captain Wai's luck, perhaps predictably, ran out. As he led yet another assault, a machine gun opened up and stitched him. He took at least ten rounds in the chest and died instantly. Wai received a posthumous Distinguished Service Cross that was upgraded in 2000 to the Medal of Honor.

Ever so steadily the Americans cleared out the pillboxes and their supporting positions. "[Enemy] machine guns apparently fired down fixed, mutually supporting fire lanes, and opened up only when a target appeared within the fire lane," Captain William Hanks of the 19th Infantry wrote in a post-battle report. "The protecting riflemen were lavishly distributed around the machine gun positions, and seemed to be working in teams." The GIs worked around their firing lanes and killed them from behind or the flanks; seldom did they see a live enemy soldier. "The striking thing about it all is that not one of our men saw a Jap during the entire engagement," Hanks marveled.

The Japanese had made the mistake of evacuating Hill 522, temporarily abandoning their mortars, to escape the preinvasion bombardment and subsequent shelling from 24th Division artillery. Utilizing a covered trail, soldiers from the 19th Infantry quickly seized it. "The hill was very steep," the division after-action report chronicled. "Trails up its sides were winding. The men were already tired from a long day of activity and strain but they pushed steadily up the slope." They occupied some of the extensive warren of pillboxes, tunnels, and communications trenches only minutes before the Japanese attempted to return to the hill. "Some of the guys . . . started hollering that the Japanese were running up the other side of Hill 522 to meet us," PFC Eugene Welsh later said. In a sharp fight, the Americans drove them away, killing fifty Japanese soldiers and solidifying their control over the most important piece of terrain in the area, arguably even in the entire American Leyte beachhead. "Taking this position with its battery of mortars saved a lot of lives and equipment," Lieutenant Bruce Price, whose platoon helped secure the hill, later asserted. "The Japs had range cards marked with the position of logs anchored in the bay and on the beach." Major General Frederick Irving, the division commander, even went so far as to claim that "if Hill 522 had not been occupied when it was, we might have suffered a thousand casualties in the assault."[6]

All four divisions, more than 100,000 American troops, were now firmly ashore and with them an eye-popping 107,450 tons of supplies and equipment, with still more soldiers and freight arriving by the hour. "The beach was quickly organized to receive mobile loaded vehicles, exit roads were constructed over tank traps, and the development of dump areas for bulk cargo was initiated," Colonel Alexander Neilson, commander of the 532nd Engineer Boat and Shore Regiment, reported to a friend after the landings. In the course of A-Day, Sixth Army lost 49 soldiers killed, 6 missing, and 192 wounded; the Red Beach area fighting accounted for about half of these casualties. Krueger later opined that the landings "had been accomplished more easily than we had anticipated. The swamps in the rear of some of the beaches did make the establishment of supply dumps difficult, but it proved possible to disperse our supplies adequately enough for the time being."

The landings as a whole were successful enough to allow a special visitor to explore the beachhead for himself. Aboard *Nashville*, General MacArthur had spent the morning on the bridge, keenly watching the troops splash ashore. "From my vantage point, I had a clear view of everything that took place," he later wrote. During the voyage, his excitement at the prospect of returning to Philippines had been so palpable that, to one aide, he seemed "happy as a kid at a picnic." With the moment now so tantalizingly close, he saw no need to wait any longer than absolutely necessary. In the early afternoon, after a quick lunch, he decided to land at Red Beach, of all places. Clad in freshly washed and pressed khakis, wearing his distinctive braided cap and sunglasses, he boarded an LCM (Landing Craft Mechanized) with an entourage that included Sutherland, Kenney, Egeberg, and Lieutenant Gaetano Faillace, the SWPA photographer.

At the USS *John Land*, the LCM picked up Sergio Osmena, who had just ascended to the presidency of the Philippine government-in-exile after the August 1 death of Manuel Quezon, an old friend of MacArthur's. Osmena enjoyed no such intimacy with the SWPA commander; in fact, their only association had been adversarial. Osmena had ardently opposed MacArthur's prewar efforts to build up the Filipino armed forces, even going so far as to cut defense funds on the eve of the war. Though MacArthur was not the vindictive sort, he found it hard to forgive Osmena for the part he had played in eroding Fil-American readiness for war. Osmena had decided only reluctantly to participate in the Leyte invasion. Leery of MacArthur's almost mystical appeal to Filipinos and knowing that the general preferred others to head the Philippine government, Osmena anticipated that his power over his own country would pale in comparison with MacArthur's, at least as long as military operations continued. One historian aptly wrote of the new Philippine president, "Osmena's great dilemma was that he could neither compete with Quezon, a dead hero mourned by the people, nor with MacArthur, a living symbol already revered as a demigod." Back in Washington, Osemena's close friend Interior Secretary Harold Ickes, who loathed MacArthur with an intensity that might even have given Admiral King pause, had urged Osmena not to join the invasion. "The country will be entirely under military command, and you as a civilian leader will be powerless," Ickes told him accurately. "Your people will expect many things from you that you will be unable to give them." In the end, Osmena had agreed, at the personal urging of President Roosevelt, to participate—a wise decision, because his absence would have proven even more awkward than his presence.

Osmena and several members of his staff joined MacArthur's group aboard the LCM. With a pith helmet perched atop his head and a life belt wrapped around his waist, the president sat at the stern, near the engine housing of the craft, alongside MacArthur and Sutherland. In the distance, they could see the LSTs and other landing craft spewing smoke from where they had been hit earlier that morning. As the boat churned inexorably forward, MacArthur turned to Sutherland and exclaimed, "Well, believe it or not, Dick, we're here." Bill Dunn, a CBS News correspondent aboard the boat, fixed his gaze on the general and thought him "to be rather emotionally stirred, a rare instance for him."

All around them the waters bustled with landing craft. Vehicles, soldiers, and detritus choked the beach, making it difficult for the coxswain to find a place to land. One of MacArthur's aides radioed the beachmaster to inquire if he might provide a smaller craft that would allow the general to make a dry landing. Absorbed with the gargantuan task of creating order from the chaos of the landings, and imbued with the godlike authority that came as a small recompense for his difficult job, the young naval lieutenant had no patience for such niceties. "Let 'em walk," he radioed back. MacArthur's LCM came to rest on a sandbar and disgorged its distinguished passengers into knee-high water. With MacArthur in the lead, they waded resolutely forward. Lieutenant Faillace and other photographers scrambled ahead. "I rushed down past the general and all these high ranking officers went out front," he said. "I wanted a clean sweep so I could pan my movie camera as they walked onto shore." He and the others captured images of MacArthur and his group striding to the beach that later became famous. The expression on the general's face was incongruously grim for such a triumphant moment in his life, probably owing to his annoyance with the beachmaster at having to wade ashore. As quickly as he could, he forged through the water, "pressing the rest of us to keep up with him," Dunn recalled. MacArthur later wrote of the moment, "It took me only 30 or 40 long strides to reach dry land, but that was one of the most meaningful walks I ever took."

The area remained under intermittent sniper and mortar fire. With everyone else in tow, MacArthur strode along the beach and beyond, conversing with soldiers of all ranks, most of whom were stunned to see him in an area that remained under occasional though largely inaccurate fire. Trailing a few feet behind MacArthur, Kenney overheard one GI say to another, "Hey, there's General MacArthur!" The other GI did not even bother to look up, "Oh, yeah? And I suppose he's got Eleanor Roosevelt along with him." After examining several Japanese bodies and gleaning as much as he could about the tactical situation, MacArthur sat down on a log in a coconut grove and conversed quietly with Osmena. Soon, under a light drizzle, the general jotted a triumphant note to President Roosevelt. "The operation is going smoothly and if successful will strategically as well as tactically cut the enemy forces in two."

Word of MacArthur's presence swept through the ranks. Numerous curious soldiers gathered to watch Osmena and the general from a respectful distance. So many onlookers showed up that Dunn jovially wondered "just who was actually fighting the war!" A Sixth Army Signal Corps unit materialized with a radio transmitter mounted on a vehicle and set it up to broadcast to the entire archipelago. With Dunn acting as host, MacArthur took the microphone at about 1400 local time and broadcast a speech he had carefully written over several weeks, with the most recent input of Egeberg and Lehrbas, while aboard *Nashville*. "People of the Philippines: I have returned. By the grace of almighty God our forces stand again on Philippine soil—soil consecrated in the blood of our two peoples. At my side is your president, Sergio Osmena, worthy successor of that great patriot, Manuel Quezon, with members of his cabinet. The seat of your government is now firmly re-established. The hour of your redemption is here." MacArthur concluded with a fiery call to arms for the many guerrilla groups operating in the islands and anyone else who might feel inclined to help them. "Rally to me. Let the indomitable spirit of Bataan and Corregidor lead on. Strike at every favorable opportunity. For your homes and hearths, strike! For future generations of your sons and daughters, strike! In the name of your sacred dead, strike! Let no heart be faint. Let every arm be steeled. The guidance of divine God points the way. Follow in His name to the Holy Grail of righteous victory!" The speech was vintage MacArthur—self-centered, messianic, articulate, inspirational, and passionate, with an impeccable sense for the spirit of the moment. With this tough act to follow, Osmena took the microphone for about ten minutes to discuss his new civil government and his administration's plans for independence.[7]

Neither MacArthur nor Osmena lingered on Red Beach. Both returned to their ships within the hour. With Dunn's assistance, MacArthur reprised his speech for an American audience. SWPA headquarters issued a triumphant communiqué accurately outlining the course of current operations while declaring pointedly that "the commander in chief is in personal command of the operation." Over the following three days, as Krueger's divisions steadily pushed beyond their beachheads, MacArthur came ashore several more times at Tacloban and Dulag, leading to unfounded rumors of staged photo-op landings, and confusion among some veterans who saw him and conflated these appearances with the original landing on A-Day. Most importantly, he visited Tacloban on October 23, where four decades earlier he had once conducted surveys as a young engineer officer fresh out of West Point. The 1st Cavalry Division had secured the town and its adjacent airfield within twenty-four hours of landing on the northernmost American invasion beaches. Only a week earlier, the Japanese had forced the city's inhabitants to march in a contrived parade to celebrate the faux Japanese victory at Formosa. Now, on the steps of the bomb-damaged provincial capitol building, MacArthur convened with his senior commanders and Osmena for a ceremony to reinstitute the Philippine civil government. The stately columns of the building were intact, but inside, according to Captain Tarbuck's diary, "it is a shambles of papers and furniture . . . but has not been destroyed." A 1st Cavalry Division honor guard presented the colors of the United States and the Commonwealth of the Philippines. An impressed Tarbuck described the troopers as "dirty and tired, but efficient looking soldiers."

MacArthur and Osmena both spoke briefly. Sutherland read an official proclamation that outlined the authority of the new government and the ultimate Fil-American intention to "restore and extend to the people of the Philippines the sacred right of government by constitutional process under the . . . Commonwealth Government as rapidly as the several occupied areas are liberated and the military situation will otherwise permit." The ceremony lasted only a few minutes. Few, if any, locals even witnessed it, not out of indifference but rather from simple ignorance that it had taken place. In retrospect, though, this brief moment initiated a protracted, traumatic struggle for the political soul of the country, certainly during World War II against the Japanese occupiers and among the various Filipino factions vying for post-independence power, but also well into the postwar period when anticommunists, most notably the remarkable Ramon Magsaysay, successfully suppressed, through years of bitter struggle, a communist takeover that had once appeared all but inevitable.

On that happy October 23, few could have foreseen such a troubling and dramatic future for the Philippines. Though MacArthur certainly thought deeply about the political fate of the country—and envisioned no other acceptable outcome than a constitutional, pro-Western government in the American image—he focused for the moment on supporting guerrilla organizations that could assist with the immediate strategic goal of defeating the Japanese. After the ceremony, he decorated Colonel Ruperto Kangleon, a twenty-seven-year veteran of the Philippine Army, with the Distinguished Service Cross for his gallantry in forging a burgeoning guerrilla organization. Captured on Mindanao by the Japanese following the American surrender of the Philippines in May 1942, Kangleon had escaped by the end of that year and formed a guerrilla organization that tolerated no compromise or collaboration of any kind with the Japanese. Ruthless and idealistic, Kangleon had by October 1943 destroyed or incorporated every guerrilla cell on Leyte into his own, prompting SWPA headquarters to recognize him as the Leyte area commander. Kangleon's operatives stole Japanese weapons and equipment, harassed their patrols, and gathered intelligence information that they shared by radio and messenger with MacArthur's headquarters. SWPA gave Kangleon, mainly through clandestine submarine missions, over seventy tons of matériel in the summer of 1944. Financially, his organization was sustained by 50,000 dollars' worth of prewar currency as well as another 225,000 dollars' worth of counterfeit Japanese money.

By A-Day, Colonel Kangleon had organized his forces into a division-style outfit, with three subordinate regiments, a staff, and small-unit commanders. On paper, if not always in practice, Kangleon's 92nd Division mustered 3,190 local guerrillas, armed with a mixture of American and Japanese weapons, dispersed among barrios and heavily guarded hideouts all over the island. One guerrilla veteran later described his unit as "made up of men with previous military experiences, ones who had arms and ammunition . . . college students, high school kids and close relatives of . . .

guerrilla leaders." They represented a potent asset for MacArthur, not just as combat troops but more so as fifth columnists, guides, reconnaissance scouts, and political operatives.

The very existence and potency of the guerrillas represented the immutable fact that pro-American attitudes predominated among Leyte's population of nearly one million people (as well as nearly everywhere in the archipelago, too). Colonel Toshii Watanabe, a Japanese intelligence officer, claimed that the local bias in favor of the Americans stemmed from simple economics. "We had very little to offer the Filipinos in the way of bartering. Consequently, the number of Filipino inhabitants near Japanese Army posts gradually diminished, making difficult the collection of information regarding public sentiment." In reality, the Japanese cared little for the democratic notion of soliciting attitudes from locals. Their unpopularity stemmed from the repression they too often brought with them. Nor could they compete with the deep roots of a reasonably popular American presence. The fairly benevolent American colonial heritage, at least by the abysmal standards of imperialism, combined with the prospect of true independence and the frequency of Japanese brutality, all fostered pro-US attitudes. Most Filipinos had lived under martial law and with severe food restrictions for weeks or even months as the Japanese attempted to tighten their local control and prepare for an American invasion.

From the moment the Americans appeared off Leyte, excitement coursed through the local population. To the shock of the Americans, some civilians even rowed small boats out to meet ships. On land, hundreds enthusiastically greeted the GIs in liberation scenes similar to those playing out at nearly the same time in Europe. "We landed to be welcomed by natives who cried and cheered and prayed," PFC Ellis Moore, a radioman in the 383rd Infantry Regiment, 96th Division, wrote his family, using the common, almost dehumanizing term "native" that Americans of the time employed to describe locals all over the Pacific. "I never saw such a happy bunch of people." At Tacloban they converged on troopers of the 1st Cavalry Division with an almost ecstatic enthusiasm. "Everywhere we were greeted by Filipinos, literally hysterical with joy," awestruck *Yank* correspondent Ralph Boyce later wrote. "Some of the older ones who had been badly treated by the Japs saluted, crying, 'Welcome, Americans, welcome,' while tears rolled down their cheeks." A happy village leader told the Yanks, "We had to obey the Japanese to save our necks, but there was never any doubt, as you know, what our feelings were beneath." An excited, bare-footed priest exulted at the reopening of his church, "The bells, the bells, they are ringing again."

Happy civilians shook any GI hand they could and repeated over and over, "Thank you, sir." They sang and clapped. They flashed the V for Victory sign. They pressed bananas, papayas, and boiled eggs into the hands of the Americans, who reciprocated with C rations, K rations, chocolate bars, and massive numbers of cigarettes. One especially popular resident pilfered several cases of Japanese beer from a warehouse and handed out bottles to the troopers, who enthusiastically guzzled down their contents. In an encounter typical of many, a smiling young man offered Private Dencker, the mortarman, a container full of tuba, a sweet palm wine of nearly ubiquitous popularity throughout the archipelago. "Being brave—or foolish—in the name of Filipino-American friendship, I drank about half the Tuba," Dencker later wrote. "He drank the rest. The taste was not bad." The two young men shook hands and beamed at each other. Many, like Lieutenant William Bronnenberg of the 24th Division, found themselves almost transfixed by the exoticism they perceived in the Filipinos. "These people are part Spanish, English and Oriental," he asserted in a letter to his cousins. "They are a very good looking race of people. They are somewhat smaller in stature than we Americans but very strong. Truly many of the girls here are as cute as little dolls. They are small, have Spanish complexions and long jet black hair." Another soldier described the Filipinos as "very clean looking and . . . very honest and sincere in their dealings with us. The women wear neat looking dresses. The children are really cute and we can't help but like them."

The war had taken its toll, though. The Americans were troubled by the scrawny, impoverished appearance of many locals. "The Japs must have treated them miserably," PFC Moore, the radioman, commented sadly. "Most of them are wearing the rags they wore when the Japs came. They said the Japs took their food leaving them hardly enough to live on." With almost awestruck sympathy, Private Arthur Riehl wrote his mother that "there's nothing these people haven't sacrificed to the Japs. You just can't turn your back to things like that." One officer even speculated in a letter home that "if the Japs were to have continued their hold over these people for about two more years, the Filipinos would have almost become a lost or extinct race," due to mass starvation and outright killings. Private Otto

Woike of the 239th Engineer Combat Battalion was appalled at the sight of malnourished children silently begging for scraps near his unit's chow line. "These people appeared truly hungry. I tried to give that which I thought was still edible. The kids were not fussy. They wanted it all." In many of the GIs, almost all of whom were white at this stage of the campaign, the sympathy mixed with a prevailing assumption that framed the Filipinos as "natives" from a more primitive civilization, almost akin to contemporary racial attitudes, at least in some, about African-Americans. "It wasn't much to see," Tech 4 Howard Lumsden wrote revealingly of a local village to his parents; "looked like the negro section of a large southern city like Atlanta or Birmingham except that the streets aren't even paved."[8]

The wretched condition of many Filipinos hinted at the substantial humanitarian challenges that Sixth Army now faced on an island with poor infrastructure and a poverty-stricken population. Overburdened refugees, hauling children and possessions, began emerging from the ruins of combat-shattered villages or streaming from inland into American lines. "These people . . . had been without food or drink for many hours," the 24th Division Civil Affairs officer wrote in a descriptive report. "A number had been in foxholes during the naval bombardment of the island and were shaken up. Many of them carried all their worldly belongings on their heads or on bamboo poles across their shoulders. Upon their arrival immediate provisions were made for feeding them and supplying them with water." Within a day of the landings, the 24th Division alone was caring for two thousand refugees. Within three more days, about forty-five thousand people had come under the control of Krueger's forces. Overworked civil affairs sections provided bathing facilities and shelter, often in public buildings or churches. They distributed clothing, food, and water or helped refugees track down family members. The Americans disseminated 28,700 full rations and huge quantities of captured Japanese rice, fish, and condensed milk. Starting in Tacloban and spreading out as American units advanced, Sixth Army opened five hundred schools, many in war-damaged buildings. Civil affairs units even published their own mimeographed textbooks, illustrated by GI artists.

To maintain order and the political cohesion inherent in MacArthur's proclamation, troops disarmed anyone who did not belong to Colonel Kangleon's forces. "It was impossible to distinguish between the authentic guerrillas and the great majority who knew nothing of the enemy," Lieutenant Colonel Charles Young, the 1st Cavalry Division's civil affairs

officer, commented. In hopes of stabilizing the local economy, and minimizing black marketeering, finance sections established a new currency
known as the "Victory Peso." In an attempt to shelter Filipinos from the
fighting, soldiers enforced an evening curfew. Medical units found themselves treating a growing number of sick or injured civilians. "Besides being shaken up and sometimes wounded, they were also homeless,"
Lieutenant Phil Hostetter, a doctor who treated many of them, commented
sadly. In one typical instance, he bandaged a deep gash on the head of a
middle-aged woman while another nearby unit delivered a baby. Across
the entirety of the expanding Sixth Army front, local commanders did
whatever else they could for those in need. "Medical personnel were ordered to care for civilian patients to the extent permitted by military
needs," the Army Medical Corps historian wrote.

They found many more Filipinos affected by disease than by combat
wounds. A dizzying array of ailments from tuberculosis to syphilis plagued
the population. Infant mortality rates edged over 20 percent. A systematic
American check of Tacloban schoolchildren revealed that 45 percent were
afflicted with head lice. "I have seen the little kids picking each others' hair
for lice many times," one infantryman wrote to his family. "[The lice] in-
variably run to large families." Army medical technicians surveyed a group
of 282 civilians and found that 83 percent tested positive for some sort of
intestinal parasite. The high rates largely resulted from poor waste disposal
and lack of sewage facilities. Of 217 homes the technicians visited, only 73
were equipped with toilets. "The Filipino is very careful in his personal
body cleanliness, bathes frequently, looks neat," declared one medical survey report. "He does not give much attention to body waste disposal. Most
of the latrines are holes in the ground with a frame box on which the Filipino squats down to defecate. Some latrines have lids, but many do not.
Some homes have a slit in the floor of the house and then he squats over
the hole. The feces drops to the ground beneath the house." Attempts to
locate and organize local physicians and nurses to care for Filipinos came
to little; only the Americans had the resources and trained personnel to
dispense effective care. According to one Army post campaign report, "not
only was it necessary to care for the wounded but also a large number of
civilians required medical attention for both acute and chronic diseases. It
became necessary to divert a few Army hospitals to their care, and many
others treated lesser numbers." In all cases, they helped anyone they could,
though priority of care always went to wounded or sick Americans.[9]

As the Japanese were painfully aware, they could not prevent the Americans from landing and solidifying themselves on Leyte. But they could certainly do all in their power to destroy the American presence. Japanese commanders immediately activated the Sho plan, prompting a powerful enemy reaction by air, sea, and land. Hampered by bad weather, the 4th Air Army began launching raids against Kinkaid's fleet and the beachhead. On October 24 alone, the Japanese mustered a force of between 150 and 200 planes. They lost nearly half their aircraft to intense antiaircraft fire and American fighter opposition, but the raid signaled the troubling truth that the Americans did not fully control the skies over Leyte. Nor would they for many more weeks. As early as 1110 on October 18, in the wake of the Ranger landings and as the American invasion force had closed in on Leyte Gulf, Admiral Toyoda had issued the Sho Go order to his Combined Fleet, initiating the all-out naval engagement so coveted by the Imperial Navy. This, of course, resulted in the Battle of Leyte Gulf from October 23–26 when Kinkaid's Seventh Fleet absorbed powerful surface attacks from two Japanese strike forces that attempted to envelop the Leyte landing area from north and south. The Southern (or C) Force, under Vice Admiral Shoji Nishimura, was stymied with heavy losses at Surigao Strait in a classic nighttime surface engagement by an Allied force of six battleships, eight cruisers, twenty-eight destroyers, and over three dozen PT boats. Of seven ships that led the way for Nishimura, only one survived the battle. The others—two battleships, three destroyers, and a cruiser—were all sunk. The admiral himself lost his life when his flagship, the battleship *Yamashiro*, went down. To the north, a larger surface force, the Central Force under Vice Admiral Takeo Kurita, threaded its way through the narrow waters of the Sibuyan Sea and the San Bernadino Strait and, though diminished by American air and submarine attacks, advanced, like an unblocked rushing linebacker, along Samar's east coast with only three undergunned Allied task forces of escort carriers, destroyers, and other smaller ships standing between the Japanese and the Leyte beaches.

The Japanese had hoped to create just this kind of situation. To a great extent, Toyoda's Sho concept envisioned the necessity of drawing as much American naval hardware away from Leyte as possible. To that end, the third element of his combined fleet, Vice Admiral Jisaburo Ozawa's

Northern Force, put to sea from bases in southern Japan and headed in the general direction of Leyte. Northern Force (also called the Mobile Force) consisted of a fleet carrier, plus three light carriers, accompanied by a pair of battleships that had been partially converted into carriers, a trio of cruisers, and eight destroyers. On paper, the carriers formed the critical mass of the Imperial Navy's remaining aviation assets. In reality, the paucity of trained aviators and a shortage of aircraft—bitter fruits of the defeat a few months earlier in the Battle of the Philippine Sea—had rendered them hollow. Once the pride of the fleet, they were now consigned to duty as decoys to lure Admiral Halsey's Third Fleet away from Leyte and open the way for Kurita. After the war, Toyoda told American interrogators bluntly, "Admiral Kurita's mission was complete destruction of transports in Leyte Bay. In the orders there was no restriction to the damage he might take. Advance even though the fleet should be completely lost. The reason for my determination . . . was the fact that should we lose the Philippines . . . even though the fleet should be left, the shipping lane to the south would be completely cut off" from fuel and other supplies in the Dutch East Indies. "There would be no sense in saving the fleet at the expense of the loss of the Philippines." Vice Admiral Ozawa later said, "I expected complete destruction of my fleet, but if Kurita's mission was carried out, that was all I wished."

True to Halsey's aggressive nature, he famously took the bait, leaving the Seventh Fleet vulnerable to Kurita's advance, and himself open to criticism from generations of naval historians. Doubtless, Halsey erred badly, but his decision was every bit as much a symptom of the divided American command structure as from any failing on his part. Though Halsey lent aviation support to MacArthur for the Leyte battle, he was accountable to Admiral Nimitz, not the SWPA commander. Halsey and MacArthur got along well, but the admiral did not take orders from the general. Their agendas at Leyte were different. As always, Halsey viewed his main strategic objective as the destruction of the enemy's naval forces, not protecting the beachhead, as MacArthur might have wanted. When Ozawa presented himself as a target, Halsey acted accordingly. Fortunately for the Allies, when Kurita at Samar ran into unexpectedly ferocious resistance from the overmatched task forces, he lost his nerve and elected to retreat, snuffing out any chance of fulfilling Admiral Toyoda's vision for a naval victory. Halsey later disputed the notion that Kurita ever really had much of a chance to fulfill Toyoda's objective. "That Kurita's force could have leisurely and effectively carried out the destruction of shipping, aircraft, and supplies in Leyte Gulf was not in the realm of possibilities. Kurita would have been limited to a hit-and-run attack." Halsey's point had some merit, but Kurita's force, even in a hit-and-run mode, could still have inflicted heavy losses on the vulnerable LSTs, LCIs, and other transport-oriented ships then prevalent in the gulf, reversing, at least temporarily, the momentum of MacArthur's successful invasion. "Had the plan succeeded, the effect on the Allied troops on Leyte in all likelihood would have been calamitous, for these troops would have been isolated and their situation would have been precarious indeed," stated Krueger's Sixth Army post-battle report, succinctly summarizing the ground soldier's perspective on the affair. Alas, the notion fortunately remains forever moot.

As it was, the Battle of Leyte Gulf inflicted irreplaceable losses on the Imperial Navy and ceded control of Philippine waters to the Americans. The battle eliminated any chance that Japan's navy could positively influence the Leyte campaign, or any subsequent battles in the Philippines. Though victorious, the Americans were fortunate to dodge the consequences of a loosely dysfunctional command arrangement as well as risky operational decisions on Halsey's part and perhaps Kinkaid's, too, for deploying his surface forces too heavily in favor of protecting the southern approaches near Surigao at the expense of his northern forces near Samar. Some on the SWPA staff were inclined to blame Halsey for the near debacle, but MacArthur did not. When he heard several aides criticize the Third Fleet commander, he pounded on a table to get their attention and said, "That's enough. Leave the Bull alone. He's still a fighting admiral in my book." MacArthur fixed the blame on the divided command that had led Halsey and him to work at such cross-purposes. "Of all the faulty decisions of the war perhaps the most unexplainable was the failure to unify the command in the Pacific," he later assessed. "The principle involved is perhaps the most fundamental one in the doctrine and tradition of command. The failure to do so in the Pacific cannot be defended in logic, in theory, or even in common sense."[10]

Sho amounted to more than just an operational plan for strategic victory. It also alluded to a prevailing command-culture expectation for commanders to employ aggressive measures against the Americans, regardless of the prospects for ultimate success. General Yamashita came to the Philippines fully expecting to fight the decisive battle on Luzon, the only part of the archipelago he saw as strategically worthwhile. By contrast, Field

Marshal Terauchi and his staff wanted to fight with all possible strength wherever the Americans landed, for fear of allowing them to solidify air and naval bases that might make Luzon untenable. No matter where the Americans landed, whether Leyte or elsewhere, that would be the place to fight them. The argument about preventing a fatal American buildup did have some validity, though neither the field marshal nor his staff seemed to take into account Leyte's many inadequacies as a major base (the same largely held true for MacArthur and most of SWPA headquarters). Initially, the generals at Imperial General Headquarters in Tokyo agreed with Yamashita. But the fantastical Formosa victory—whose effect had by now become similar to that of a mirage for a thirsty refugee in a desert—had changed their perspective because of the belief that Halsey had suffered such losses that his carrier planes could not interfere with Japanese reinforcement convoys to Leyte. Optimism over Admiral Toyoda's prospects for success also shaped opinions in favor of Terauchi's concept.

By the time the Americans landed on A-Day, Tokyo had decided to embrace a showdown battle on Leyte. The army section of Imperial General Headquarters sent Colonel Ichiji Sugita, a staff officer, to Manila to inform the commanders. Field Marshal Terauchi was delighted with the new orders; Yamashita was less than thrilled. On October 21 the general and his like-minded staff met with Terauchi at Southern Army headquarters in Manila in hopes of persuading the field marshal to prevail upon Tokyo to change course. The levelheaded Yamashita did not buy the Formosa victory fantasies. He pointed to recent evidence of major air strikes from Halsey's carriers to make the argument that the job of shipping reinforcements securely to Leyte would be problematic. Even with safe passage, Yamashita doubted the troops could get to the island in time to destroy the Sixth Army. The massive reinforcement of Leyte promised to make Luzon less defensible and Fourteenth Area Army more vulnerable to follow-up American invasions elsewhere in the Philippines. The Tiger of Malaya urged his superior, with whom he generally got on well, to at least wait to see how Toyoda's Sho plan played out.

Terauchi remained noncommittal during the meeting but the next day made his intentions clear with a succinct message to Yamashita: "The providential hour has come for the total destruction of the proud enemy. The Fourteenth Area Army, in cooperation with naval and air forces, will muster all possible strength to totally destroy the enemy on Leyte." Terauchi and his aides brimmed with optimism over the imminent showdown with the Americans. "They seemed to believe that the Navy and the Air Force would, at any moment, destroy the American forces which had entered Leyte Gulf," Lieutenant General Akira Muto, Yamashita's trusted chief of staff, later commented.

Yamashita's staffers reacted with perplexed indignation and complained that the new mission was impossible. Yamashita would not let them indulge their own bitterness. He made it clear that the new orders emanated all the way from Tokyo, probably even the emperor himself, and that, as good soldiers, they must comply, regardless of their personal opinions. When word reached Lieutenant General Suzuki's 35th Army headquarters on Cebu, an ebullient mood swept through the ranks, in part owing to the assumption that the directive must mean the Americans had suffered major aerial and naval losses, but more so out of blind enthusiasm at variance with reality. "We had hopeful discussions of entering Tacloban by the 16th of November," Major General Tomochika, the chief of staff, later wrote with chagrin. "We were determined to take offensive after offensive and clean up landed American forces on Leyte island. We seriously discussed demanding the surrender of the entire American Army after seizing General MacArthur." An exuberant Suzuki told his chief of staff that he would insist upon "the capitulation of MacArthur's entire forces, those in New Guinea and other places as well as troops on Leyte." Clearly caught up in a moment of ecstatic self-deception, he added, "We don't even need all the reinforcements they are sending us." In a postwar letter to a Japanese journalist, a chastened Tomochika insightfully added, "The Japanese people were led to believe that strength through 'Yamato Damashi' (Yamato Spirit) was legendary. Our educational system was not founded on a scientific basis but was entirely based on this false concept." Too late, Tomochika grasped that the Japanese were far too prone to dismiss or disregard hard facts in favor of an almost spiritual mysticism. Many others would not survive to learn this lesson. The decision to stake Japan's future on an all-out struggle for Leyte, a place that offered the Japanese few advantages, qualified as a prime example of this tendency to embrace indulgent illusions.

In one respect, though, the notion of sending large numbers of reinforcements onto the island did make some sense. As long as the Americans failed to control the skies overhead, Fourteenth Area Army could find ways to land troops on Leyte. In that sense, island warfare proved similar to urban combat. Any attacking force that failed to seal off the battlefield

risked being worn down and defeated by attrition as the defenders reinforced themselves. This had almost happened two years earlier at Guadalcanal; the Japanese now attempted to make it a reality on Leyte. Between
October 23 and December 11, Fourteenth Area Army sent nine separate
convoys to Leyte, originating mainly from Luzon and Cebu, and managed,
in spite of intensive American air attacks, to land forty-five thousand
troops and ten thousand tons of matériel. The Americans sank an incredible 80 percent of the transport ships, yet almost all of them went down
close enough to the coast for large numbers of troops to stagger or swim
ashore, often minus weapons or equipment. In spite of the sinkings, the
majority of the new formations entered Leyte via dry landings. During
those weeks, 35th Army grew into a huge formation comprising five full
divisions, three independent mixed brigades, and at least one regiment-
size infantry formation. Suzuki himself arrived on November 1, Tomochika two days earlier. On A-Day the Japanese on Leyte had been heavily
outnumbered, doomed to eventual annihilation when the Americans
snuffed out Makino's 16th Division. The reinforcements changed that demoralizing dynamic. As Yamashita had anticipated, the Japanese could not
hope to equal or exceed American numbers on Leyte, at least while still
defending any other parts of the Philippines, but the reinforcements acted
as a blood transfusion of sorts for Japanese combat strength on the island
and now guaranteed the very sort of protracted battle MacArthur hoped
to avoid.[11]

The virulent nature of the increasingly costly battle set in, like a growing
malignancy, during the dying days of late October. The intensity of Japanese air attacks increased. "All of the antiaircraft guns in the area would
fire, and flak (shell fragments and spent bullets) would rain down on us,"
Major Thomas Clark, an engineer in X Corps, recalled of the numerous
raids. "We would lie down in slit trenches." Colonel Alexander Nielson, the
532nd Engineer Boat and Shore Regiment commander, eloquently described the sheets of bullets and other ordnance as "like feathers of fire in
the sky, as they wave back and forth following enemy planes. The heavens
are arched with streaks of fire as the tracers from the Navy ships meet
those from the guns ashore. Brilliant lights from flares, blinding flashes of
light from exploding bombs, and yellow domes of fire formed by burning
particles of phosphorous bombs light up the sky. Balls of flame streak

through the sky from time to time, as enemy planes gradually lose elevation until they finally crash into the sea in a great mass of flame."

The sandy soil at or near the beaches proved dangerously prone to cave-ins, especially for those who dug deep holes. "Foxholes dug in sand on the beach must not be over 3 feet deep unless they are revetted," an engineer group after-action report counseled. "Some men dug in 4 or 5 feet and when the beach was bombed some of the foxholes caved in. Some of the trapped men were dug out immediately and saved, but others died before they could be located in the dark." Enemy planes sank two LSTs and destroyed a warehouse at Tacloban. During the morning hours of October 26 alone, they raided the area sixteen separate times with a total of 150 planes. "They came in over the tops of the trees strafing and dropping fragmentation bombs as they flew the whole length of the strip," General Kenney later wrote. The bombs killed a dozen Filipinos and an American war correspondent. One of the most terrifying weapons, the kamikaze, had already come into play during the Battle of Leyte Gulf, and continued to plague Kinkaid's Seventh Fleet, exacting a particular toll on his escort carriers.

On October 27, Generals MacArthur and Kenney personally watched as thirty-four P-38 Lightning fighters from the 9th Fighter Squadron landed at the still crude, incomplete Tacloban airfield, the first Army Air Forces planes to touch Philippine soil since 1942. The two generals greeted the arriving pilots warmly. "About a quarter million people of all colours started yelling," Kenney noted in his diary, with effusive hyperbole, of the moment. Later that same day, MacArthur turned responsibility for all Leyte air operations over to Kenney's Far East Air Forces, thus releasing the Navy from the job. Halsey was only too happy to retire the logistically diminished Third Fleet to Ulithi and prepare plans to launch raids on Tokyo itself. But a few dozen overstretched fighters at Tacloban, assisted by bombers and fighters based hundreds of miles to the south at Morotai and elsewhere in the Southwest Pacific, could not begin to fulfill the mission of controlling the skies over Leyte. Three days of violent combat and enemy air raids whittled the operational strength of the 9th Fighter Squadron to twenty planes.

The stubborn, unrelenting Japanese aerial opposition proved to be only part of the problem. Out of necessity to maintain momentum for the sequence of operations that Nimitz and MacArthur had agreed upon at Oahu and thereafter, the SWPA commander had embraced the necessary evil of invading Leyte during the rainy season. The average monthly rainfall for this time of year measured at just under twelve inches, but Mother Nature apparently resolved to exceed even that high total. Starting on October 28 and over the following ten days, three typhoons hit Leyte, dumping nearly thirty-five inches of rain onto the island, turning the ubiquitous rice paddies, swamps, jungles, and roads into a sea of impassable mud. Powerful winds uprooted trees, or blew down buildings and tents. "From the angry immensity of the heavens floods raced in almost horizontal sheets," PFC Richard Krebs of the 24th Division later wrote vividly. "Palms bent low under the storm, their fronds flattened like streamers of wet silk. The howling of the wind was like a thousandfold plaint of the unburied dead." Major General Hodge, the XXIV Corps commander, later commented accurately that his men "were never dry from the time they got ashore until the battle was over." One of those men, Lieutenant Gage Rodman, graphically wrote to his parents that "the mud was knee deep and shiny, every low spot was a thin soup of dirt and water. The roads sank out of sight and trucks bogged down. The rice fields were nearly waist deep. We were wet all the time. Digging a foxhole amounted to digging a bath tub. I have laid in my hole afraid to go to sleep for fear I'd roll my head off my helmet and drown or at least inhale a lungful." The rain fell so sharply that the troops found themselves shivering, especially at night, in spite of the tropical temperatures. "Imagine, if you can, a night in the Philippines being cold," the historian of B Company, 381st Infantry, 96th Division, wrote plaintively. "Maybe you can't but it was colder than hell . . . with the wind blowing and rain all night, and everyone was just a little jumpy." Only by wrapping weapons, ammunition, and equipment in ponchos or underneath tarpaulins could they even hope to keep these vital implements clean. Otherwise they lived in a sea of sodden dirt. "I have never been so filthy before," Captain Morrissey, the physician, complained to his diary. "My HBT [Herringbone Twill] suit is coming apart at the knees and back."

The high winds, the suffocating rains, and the severe limitations of Leyte's loose, sandy soil made it nearly impossible for aviation and engineer units to make headway on constructing airfields and roads. "Mud is still mud no matter how much you push it around with a bulldozer," quipped Major General Ennis Whitehead, commander of the Fifth Air Force, the formation that made up the critical mass of Kenney's Far East Air Forces. As Lieutenant General Krueger later assessed, the heavy downpours, flooding, and mud "created havoc in [Sixth] Army headquarters, carried Treadway and other bridges out to sea, made it extremely difficult to establish dumps, hospitals . . . and inordinately delayed the construction of airdromes." The underdeveloped, unpaved roads limited mobility and degraded vehicles with vexing alacrity. "Passage of heavy Army vehicles and engineer equipment over the Leyte roads, none too good in the first place, soon churned them into elongated ribbons of deep, clinging mud which slowed all traffic to a crawl or stopped it completely at many points," SWPA's engineer historian later wrote. A Sixth Army after-action report testified that "the important supply roads rapidly deteriorated to become virtual quagmires and hindrances to offensive activities." Engineers spent most of their time and resources just clearing mud, extracting bogged vehicles, and keeping roads drained; meaningful improvements to the roads were generally out of the question. In addition to the horrendous conditions, the aftereffects of ruthless, deadly combat challenged the speed with which the engineers could work. "Hundreds of dead Japanese soldiers were lying everywhere," the unit history of the 339th Engineer Combat Battalion soberly complained. "The sight and smell of dead men were horrible and nauseating. Some were missing limbs, others [lay] on their backs, eyes bulging roundly; and others resembled weird figures as they were swollen stiff by flame throwers that had burnt them alive."[12]

Captured Japanese airfields were so substandard and degraded by the elements that American engineers essentially had to attempt to build new fields on top of them. None of the sites were more disappointingly deficient than Tacloban, where the Americans hoped to develop a major base for bombers and fighters, even though the field itself was confined to a narrow peninsula adjacent to the sea. Kenney immediately recognized Tacloban's shortcomings on his first visit the day after the invasion. "Two or three inches of coral on sandspit," he fumed disgustedly to his diary. "Flight strip about 125 feet wide and 4000 plus feet long. Some soft spots covered with light mesh which would roll up if one of our planes taxied over it. Will not take over three squadrons of fighters. Barely enough for a depot. Water table two feet below the surface—west half of point is swampy."

In fact, the airfield had more problems than even Kenney recognized. Engineers soon realized that in order to extend the main runway another two thousand feet to accommodate large enough numbers of American fighters, they must first rotate it ten degrees, a backbreaking, time-consuming job. Regular Japanese air attacks and the frequent rains only made the job that much more impossible. Attempts to defeat the mud and solidify the runways by pumping coral from the ocean floor yielded no results. To make matters worse, LST crewmen and shore parties had, for lack of finding any available storage space on the congested 1st Cavalry Division landing beaches, unloaded supplies onto the Tacloban strip. This, of course, hindered the work of the engineers, created confusion, and consumed valuable space on the already confining peninsula airfield. When Kenney saw what was happening, he blew his stack. He told Colonel David Hutchinson, one of the air commanders on-site, "to take his bulldozers and push back into the water anything . . . which interfered with getting an airdrome built." Many years after the war, Kenney even claimed that he gave Hutchinson orders to "set up some machine guns on the beach and fire at any son of a bitch who brought an LST in there."

These colorful measures had little impact, nor did a frantic attempt to levy Filipino labor as the liberation suddenly took on a slightly coercive character. Neither Tacloban nor any other field provided anything like the necessary support for the kind of forces Kenney intended to bring to bear but now simply could not. As a result, his land-based planes conducted little more than subsistence-level aerial operations during the campaign, falling far short of the goal of sealing Leyte off from the outside world. In the main, they were almost entirely absorbed in fighting off Japanese air attacks, providing supply drops for overextended ground troops, and bombing Japanese reinforcement convoys. Few planes were available to provide close air support for ground units in action. By November 10, a supplicant MacArthur had to admit this reality and ask Nimitz for renewed carrier support rather than risk losing control of the air altogether. The admiral graciously agreed to lend Halsey's carriers to him for two weeks and land-based Marine night fighter squadrons thereafter. Halsey was bitterly disappointed to cancel his Tokyo raids but loyally acceded. Grateful but chastened, MacArthur privately vowed to Kenney never to find himself in this situation again. "I'll undertake no more of these moves without my own Far East Air Force covering me." A frustrated General Krueger later told an Army historian that the objective of developing the airfields enough to gain control of the air "proved to be impossible because of terrific rains that flooded all level areas on the island. In consequence, we lacked the air support necessary . . . to support the operation. This was not the fault of the Allied Air Force . . . but mine."

Krueger was too hard on himself and even Mother Nature, too. As a potential base for sea and air forces, nothing could really turn the Leyte plow horse into a racehorse. The limitations presented by the island's climate, infrastructure, and prevailing conditions were simply too profound. Leyte had no major ports and could provide, at the cost of prodigious labor, only minor air and supply bases, at least by the standards of the hypermodern US military forces. Leyte's only value lay in its location at the midsection of the archipelago, an asset of transitory usage. Indeed, Krueger's engineer section had sensed Leyte's considerable limitations as early as two months before A-Day. Colonel Samuel Sturgis, the Sixth Army engineer, foresaw that "nearly all of the proposed sites for depots were located in rice paddies and swamps. There was very little available space that would not become a quagmire when the rains started." His executive officer, Colonel William Ely, a 1933 West Point graduate, felt especially strongly about Leyte's numerous deficiencies and the impossibility of developing it into a usable base, at least without committing many more engineers than the planners had envisioned. "I had a pretty strong disagreement with MacArthur's staff about the number of engineers that we needed to do the task that he wanted done on Leyte," he later said. These concerns led him to prepare a frank report in August urging the higher-ups to reconsider Operation King II altogether. "The construction mission cannot be satisfactorily accomplished with the engineer troops available, particularly during the first 90 days. Perhaps we can mud and muddle through . . . on a shoestring but the shoestring must be frayed by this time and if it broke we may lose our shirt as well as our shoe." From MacArthur on down, no one at SWPA seems to have taken these warnings to heed, at least not enough to reconsider invading Leyte. If they did take heed, they might well have judged that reorienting theater grand strategy to avoid Leyte in favor of some other operation (perhaps even risking Washington's support for MacArthur's return to the Philippines) would likely have presented even more headaches, at least at the planning level.[13]

Regardless, having bitten into the wormy Leyte apple, the Americans now had no choice but to consume it to the rotten core. Krueger's forces continued attacking westward, encountering scattered but stubborn Japanese resistance. The 7th Division had by the end of October plowed through a network of pillboxes and seized Dagami, where GIs fought grave to grave with Japanese infantrymen who had fortified the town cemetery by ghoulishly removing remains from crypts and taking shelter inside. "Enemy, hidden inside of the old stone crypts, waited until American troops passed and then [pulled] back the lids and opened fire," wrote Captain Denmark

Jensen, whose company of 75-millimeter self-propelled guns provided fire support in the Dagami area. The Americans had no choice but to move from headstone to headstone, killing their adversaries point-blank with "flamethrowers and vicious hand-to-hand fighting before the area could be cleared," the division after-action report summarized with chilling brevity. To the right of the 7th Division, the 96th Division advanced alongside, captured key stretches of high ground, and took an important supply depot at Tabontabon.

In X Corps, both the 1st Cavalry and 24th Infantry Divisions were pushing to the northwest, toward Leyte's northern coast. Their key objective was the north coast port of Carigara, where Spanish explorers had landed in 1569 and Christianized locals celebrated every July the Feast of the Triumph of the Holy Cross, marking the arrival of the Jesuits on Leyte. As the 1st Cavalry Division edged westward along the coastline at Carigara Bay, the 24th Division's 34th Infantry Regiment pushed north, often through torrential typhoon rains, along the main road that led from Jaro for ten miles into Carigara. They encountered mined roadblocks, pillboxes, and foxholes manned by newly arrived soldiers from the Imperial Army's 102nd Division. Swollen river waters flooded the road in multiple spots, eroding it, in the estimation of PFC Krebs, into "a ribbon of slime. The network of village paths [soaked] into a spiderweb of knee-deep mud." The 24th Division's engineers did the best they could to restore the road and suppress the floodwaters. "Dozers were used to divert the river away from the road and to build the road up again, using rock from [a] new channel," the division engineer reported after the battle. "A corduroy bypass was constructed and then rock was hauled from the river to fill over the original roadbed." Water would have proved a much greater impediment had not the 34th Infantry moved fast enough to capture a major steel bridge before the Japanese could destroy it. As machine gunners strode forward and fired short bursts from the hip, riflemen braved mortar fire to sprint onto the bridge. They discovered evidence of wires and explosives but were relieved to see that the structure was only slightly damaged.

Some of the heaviest fighting raged on October 30, just north of Jaro, where supporting American tanks had to blast Japanese defenders who dug underneath shacks that lined the road. Intense enemy mortar, artillery, and machine-gun fire pinned the attacking infantrymen in ditches and soggy fields on either side of the road. Colonel Aubrey Newman, the regimental commander who had led so boldly on A-Day, moved on foot to make contact with the most heavily engaged squads, the only place he felt he could truly appreciate the situation, "to gain that sixth sense that comes up there—not on the end of a phone, or reading a message." On the way, he glimpsed the corpse of a Japanese soldier who had recently been killed, in Newman's later recollection, "by a large shell fragment, for a piece of his skull the size of the palm of your hand had been smashed out." The colonel grimly gazed at "the black soup that had been his brain, which now boiled with the ceaseless pumping and writhing so characteristic of maggots. You can't erase things like that from memory."

The colonel made it to Lieutenant Lewis Stearns, commander of the lead platoon, and asked him, "What's the hold up here?" Stearns warned the regimental commander to take cover but he refused. Instead, he assured the young lieutenant, "I'll get the men going okay," and began walking forward on the road, expecting others to follow. Lieutenant Stearns called out to his troops, "Let's go! The colonel is here!" They got up and resumed the advance. At almost the same time, the Japanese peppered the area with mortar and artillery shells, one of which scored a direct hit on a nearby soldier, tearing him to pieces. Still, Newman and the others kept going: "As I took a step forward, another shell hit in almost exactly the same spot—lifting the poor body again. This time, instantly, I had a sudden feeling of alarm and knew I was hit in the abdomen." A large fragment tore a jagged hole in his belly, near his pistol belt. Lieutenant Stearns called for a medic. Together they pulled Colonel Newman into the ditch. He lay there badly wounded as the medic worked frantically to staunch the bleeding. "I had a sense of floating numbness—and I believed I was dying. I was no longer a leader. Just another burden to take care of. I had made a great mistake and become a casualty needlessly." Even in this state, Colonel Newman had the presence of mind to order Stearns to arrange for an artillery barrage that proved useful later when the Americans reorganized and attacked again, this time more successfully. Though the colonel urged the young lieutenant and the medic to leave him and take cover, they refused. They retrieved a jeep that evacuated him to a rear-area hospital and eventually off the island altogether, the beginning of a six-month hospital convalescence for the courageous regimental commander.

For two more days, the Americans lunged steadily forward under a shower of protective artillery. Major General Sibert's X Corps headquarters feared a major Japanese buildup in Carigara. Reconnaissance reports from guerrillas indicated the presence of between two and three thousand enemy soldiers. Before leading units from the two US divisions converged on the town during the morning of November 2, the Americans pummeled it with three thousand shells fired by artillery pieces from both of the divisions and corps. Once in Carigara, the lead troops found only shell holes and anticlimax. Local Japanese commanders had decided to withdraw their survivors to more defensible mountainous ground around Limon to the southwest. Lieutenant General Suzuki had planned to use Carigara as a jump-off point for a counteroffensive to recapture Tacloban, but the rapidity of the X Corps advance had eliminated this possibility. Moreover, the rapid American movement occurred as Suzuki was in the process of transferring his headquarters from Cebu to Leyte. He could thus have little impact on the tactical situation. Suzuki would now have to settle instead for holding the high ground, reinforcing and perhaps attacking on another day. The Americans knew none of this yet, only that they had captured a prime objective more easily than they had anticipated. A relieved Brigadier General Kenneth Cramer, the assistant division commander of the 24th, told a correspondent, "We must have broken their backs in [this] fight. It was a bloody go, and I thank God we didn't have to fight like that all the way."[14]

The moment of triumph soon evaporated, like morning mist in summertime, giving way to controversy. Lieutenant General Krueger grew increasingly concerned about the possibility that the Japanese might sail reinforcements across Carigara Bay and land them along Leyte's northern coast, splitting X Corps in two. By now, under the weight of ongoing operations, Sixth Army had become uncomfortably spread out. The 96th Division was driving to the island's midsection. The 7th Division was patrolling to clear out the sparsely defended southern portion of Leyte and also pushing for the west coast. The two divisions of X Corps were funneling from Baruga through Carigara to Pinamopoan along the north coast. The 1st Cavalry Division had also siphoned off units to secure the southwestern coast of Samar, an island located across narrow waters opposite Tacloban. Battle casualties, disease, and the entropy that eventuated from operating in appalling conditions had diminished Sixth Army's manpower. Krueger estimated that his army was understrength by 1,050 officers and 11,754 enlisted men, the near equivalent of an infantry division. He could expect few replacements anytime soon.

For logistical sustainment, Sibert's X Corps depended upon a combination of seaborne resupply runs by LCMs and the typhoon-degraded roads that led back to the east coast landing beaches, a tenuous umbilical cord. The Americans at this stage did not have a full grasp of Japanese intentions for land operations on Leyte. The abandonment of Carigara seemed to indicate a general withdrawal. As recently as October 31, MacArthur's headquarters, perhaps with a tinge of characteristic impatient triumphalism, had surmised that the enemy intended to evacuate the island. Ever since, the diverse Allied intelligence sources—Ultra decryption material, reconnaissance flights, guerrilla reports, radio intercepts, and frontline fighting—had slowly begun to detect the presence of the growing stream of reinforcements. An intercepted report of Lieutenant General Suzuki's arrival on November 2 provided a strong indication that the Japanese intended to fight hard for Leyte. After all, if the Japanese intended to abandon Leyte, why would they send an army commander there? As Krueger grew more aware that the Japanese were landing large numbers of troops at Ormoc, he could not help but wonder if they might do the same at Carigara Bay. To help him assess this possibility, he turned to Rear Admiral William Fechteler, one of Admiral Barbey's amphibious commanders. Fechteler told the Sixth Army commander that the Japanese were more than capable of landing troops at Carigara Bay without fatal interference from American air and naval forces. The admiral hastened to add his opinion that, in spite of this capability, he did not believe the Japanese would actually attempt any landings.

Krueger digested this information and weighed his options. With Sixth Army now butting into the spine of mountainous high ground that dominated the western neck of Leyte, he yearned to capture these hills and, from there, dash beyond, into the lowlands of the Ormoc Valley to take the key harbor of Ormoc, and snuff out Japanese resistance. He hoped to do this by means of northern and southern pincer movements launched by both of his corps. With the Japanese reinforcing seemingly by the minute, it was obvious to him that he must move quickly to capture any unattended high ground lest the enemy do it first. This meant continued attacks. But with Sibert's X Corps already stretched so thin along the Carigara Bay coast, could he risk overextending Sibert even more and possibly seeing the enemy split his forces in two with an amphibious coup de main, perhaps even cutting them off altogether in the western hills?

Basically, Krueger could take the risky option of pressing forward aggressively while flirting with the possibility of a serious reversal, or he could opt for the safety and security of holding in place to defend the north coast beaches of Carigara Bay, and then renew the offensive once he was sure the danger of a Japanese amphibious landing had passed. Here was a difficult circumstance whose decision revealed much about the nature of a general. Bold personalities like Grant or Patton or maybe even Eichelberger would have given little thought to potential enemy moves, much less consider halting offensive operations merely out of concern for what might happen. They would likely have accepted the risk of enemy landings at Carigara Bay as inherent to the fortunes of war while keeping their gaze fixed on the objective of quickly securing Leyte. Krueger was not wired this way. Circumspect and constitutionally incapable of recklessness, he could not embrace any course of action he viewed as needlessly risky. "A commander cannot afford to be rash," he once said. "I don't mean that he must be cautious. But rashness must be tempered with reasonable prudence."

Of course, one commander's rashness was another's audacity, and one's prudence another's timidity. In Krueger's case, he prioritized security over aggressiveness, an understandable if somewhat uninspiring course of action. As long as the possibility existed that the Japanese might inflict disaster upon him, he felt he must do all in his power to prevent this from happening. "I could not ignore the possibility of . . . a landing" on Leyte's north coast, Krueger wrote after the war. From November 4 to 6, he ordered Sibert to halt offensive operations in favor of defending the coast against an invasion that never came (though Yamashita did explore the possibility). The three-day respite allowed the Japanese to dig in and solidify control over most of the key ridgelines in northern Leyte. In particular, Krueger's halt provided breathing room for the Imperial Army's excellent 1st Division, newly arrived from Shanghai by way of Manila, to deploy into blocking positions on the high ground west and southwest of Carigara. Krueger correctly considered this full-strength, well-equipped unit to be among the four best divisions in the entire Imperial Army. To his later chagrin, he admitted that "it did more than any other enemy unit to prolong the Leyte operation." It is too much to say that if Krueger had opted to continue the X Corps advance, the Americans would have secured enough ridges to control all of northern Leyte and somehow end the battle within a few days; they would have had to fight and destroy the 1st Division and other newly arrived reinforcements regardless of who controlled which ridgelines. But the pause did allow the Japanese to gain control of much commanding terrain, guaranteeing that they could now inflict greater losses on the Americans, in both blood and time. Krueger had made the wrong decision albeit for many right reasons.

As a result, Leyte turned, throughout November and early December, into a nightmarish brawl for the endless muddy hills that anchored the island's mountainous western neck where defenders enjoyed nearly every advantage. Generally known as the Cordillera Range, it consisted of, according to a Sixth Army terrain study, "extinct volcanoes, of which the most prominent are the 4,426-foot Mount Majunag in central Leyte, the highest point on the island, and Mount Cabalian, which rises to 3,100 feet. Characterized by interlacing, knife-like spurs and ridges heavily overgrown with tropical foliage and cut by deep ravines, the Cordillera forms effectively a natural barrier between the eastern and western coastal areas of the island." An Armor School study added that "tropical rain, forests, tortuous and precipitous trails, an almost complete lack of roads in the modern sense, together with constant rain, made these mountains a tactical and logistical problem of almost insurmountable formidability." The 96th Division historian kvetched, with a detectible literary shudder, "The trails ran up and down in an endless series of ridges and gorges. The jungle was thick, providing ideal spots for Jap ambushes. The altitude was high—the clouds hung in a low mist, and it was usually raining. Altogether, it was about the least pleasant place one could imagine." The dogfaces of the 188th Glider Infantry Regiment found that all too many hills were so steep "that foot holds must be cut into the side of the hill and a soldier is forced to use his hands as well as his feet to keep from [falling] 40 to 100 feet." The chronic paucity of accurate maps, even in a former American colony, only added to the difficulties of fighting in the mountains. "This resulted in hills being shown which frequently did not exist and others sometimes as much as 2000 yards from their actual location," the authors of the armor study complained. The Americans improvised their own maps by registering artillery fire and then measuring distances by simple dead reckoning.[15]

With Japanese intentions for a showdown land battle painfully obvious now, the Americans rushed in their own reinforcements. The 32nd Infantry Division, victors of the pivotal Buna battle and other New Guinea fighting earlier in the war, arrived in mid-November to bolster X Corps, as did the 112th Cavalry Regiment, only a few months separated from its bloody debut at the Driniumor River fight on New Guinea. At XXIV Corps, Hodge received the brand-new, superbly trained 11th Airborne Division under dynamic, charismatic Major General Joe Swing, of whom a subordinate once wrote, "He is blunt where a contradiction of his principles is concerned and the compromise of these principles is not in him, no matter what the cost. He can be tactful and charming . . . but when he considers the cost of being so excessive, he will not bother to display either trait." From Breakneck Ridge in the north, where the 24th and 32nd Divisions attempted to envelop the newly fortified Japanese line, to Shoestring Ridge in the south, where the 7th Division manned an enclave on Leyte's west coast and fended off determined enemy counterattacks, and at many more anonymous places in between, Krueger's and Suzuki's soldiers fought with the kind of ametropic intimacy known only to mortal enemies. "Their howling is something that grabs your guts and twists them," a 24th Division machine gunner complained of the many Japanese infiltrators he cut down. Much of the fighting raged at close distance, in bunkers, foxholes, pillboxes, and half-flooded trenches. In an all-too-typical instance, one of Lieutenant Gage Rodman's men threw a white phosphorous grenade into a Japanese pillbox while the lieutenant knelt ten feet away with his carbine pointed at the aperture. "A Jap came running out swinging a long bayonet," Rodman wrote to a friend. "We saw each other at the same time at about six foot range. I snapped a shot at him and he went flat over like he'd hit a tree. The bullet went through from right eye to left ear, but he still hollered 'Banzai' and a lot of other stuff and tried to get up so I gave him three more. You are bloodthirsty." A small group of enemy soldiers got close enough to pitch grenades at a foxhole manned by PFC Whayland Greene, a new man seeing his first combat with the 32nd Division. Greene frantically looked around and spotted the man who threw the grenades. "I saw him about the same time he saw me. I was ready to fire just a second or two before he could get ready. I shot and killed him. It scared me real bad." Later, Greene could not stop thinking about his victim. "Every time I tried to close my eyes, I could see that Jap on his hands and knees. It was not because I felt sorry for him, but it was because it scared me so much."

Both sides ambushed the other with impunity. The victors typically finished off survivors with little compunction; the Americans took to pumping a bullet into the head of every Japanese body they found. "There was no place to take them and you're too busy," Tech Sergeant Edwin Sorenson, a paratrooper, later commented. "If you go by, they're going to shoot you." In foxholes half-filled with water and tinted red with lifeblood, GIs died anonymously during intimate attacks from Japanese infiltrators. "Here and there a lifeless head, a hand, a knee protruded from the . . .

holes," PFC Krebs of the 24th Division wrote sadly. "Corpses . . . resembled a congress of reptiles gazing motionless through mud-caked grass." The savagery could not snuff out all humanity, though. When PFC Calvin Lincoln's 2nd Battalion, 511th Parachute Infantry Regiment, surprised and annihilated an unsuspecting group of Japanese soldiers, he was stunned to come upon a badly wounded survivor who spoke perfect English. "He asked me . . . if I could get him a priest. I asked him, 'Where did you learn to speak such good English?' He said, 'I graduated from Catholic University in Washington.'" Lincoln and his buddies gave him last rites and a cigarette before he died. "It put a human face on the enemy. You thought they were animals and here he spoke perfect English and was more educated than I was. It makes you feel bad when you kill someone. I was only nineteen years old, and you can be swayed pretty easy in your thinking."

Like the relentless rumbling of angry storm fronts, attacks and counterattacks raged continuously along the pockmarked Cordillera front. "The action was fought along a razor back ridge with our forces gradually forcing the enemy to retreat, step by step, from prepared positions," stated the 7th Cavalry Regiment's action report of the fighting near Breakneck Ridge. "It was literally necessary to blast the enemy from his holes with artillery fire and 81mm mortars. In all the Japs had a total of four well-prepared positions with many pillboxes and bunkers on this ridge. Each one was uphill from our attacking troops and well concealed by the dense undergrowth." Both sides, but especially the Americans, used artillery in liberal quantities. In this single engagement for one ridgeline, supporting batteries fired over five thousand rounds.

Confined often to narrow jungle trails, commanders were forced to move their units in long columns that made them vulnerable to ambush, and difficult to control once the bullets flew. "The company had to move mostly in column and employing . . . human chains to ascend abrupt slippery sides of the gulches," Captain Kermit Blaney, a company commander in the 24th Division, later wrote of a typical unit movement in the Breakneck Ridge area. Amid this defender's paradise, a few well-prepared bunkers could hold up attacking units for days. "When hard pressed in one position [the Japanese] would evacuate to another position already prepared," summarized an Army Ground Forces observer. "When he reached his last prepared position he would shift from one to another, frequently occupying a previously abandoned location. He also frequently reoccupied positions from which he had been driven by artillery fire." Nor did a hard-fought breakthrough equate, for American units, to permanently gaining ground. "When penetrations of a Jap position have been made, great security must be exercised in flanks and rear, since the Jap does not hesitate to sacrifice riflemen and light MG's by sending them in to take position to fire in those areas," a 381st Infantry Regiment battle critique advised. "In particular, individual riflemen who have been bypassed will fire at supporting troops. These are erroneously referred to as 'snipers' and their marksmanship is derided. Derision is an error. They sacrifice accuracy for concealment, but once they have a victim in the firing lane, they usually get him." The ubiquity of heavy foliage and dug-in, prepared positions negated the effectiveness of the shells to the point where infantrymen did most of the killing and wounding in violent interpersonal fighting. "The third platoon assaulted and took the hill by sheer weight of firepower and guts," one officer wrote of an attack by a rifle company from the 19th Infantry Regiment, 24th Division. "Upon reaching the crest, they found that the Japs were dug in on the reverse slope of the hill and were firing on our men as they came across the crest. One squad, however, made short work of these Japs with a shower of hand grenades followed closely by tommy gun and BAR fire. In the face of this assault, the remaining Japs, in spite of their devotion to the emperor, screamed, panicked, and ran for dear life."

In marked contrast to most other combat units in the Army, the 11th Airborne employed multiple night attacks to attain objectives. "For one of the first times in Pacific warfare, the paratroopers departed from the custom of digging in for the night," the division's battle critique proudly boasted. "Operations after dark were conducted whenever the tactical situation warranted movement. Instead of squatting in foxholes and letting the Japs come to them, the 11th doughboys went after the Japs." Often as not, their tactics resulted in the surprise and destruction of opposing Japanese formations. With the exception of Shoestring Ridge, where Suzuki expended the better part of two infantry regiments in a vain attempt to eliminate a 7th Division enclave on the west coast that threatened the flank of Ormoc, Suzuki's vital port, the Japanese continued their penchant for piecemeal, wasteful local counterattacks. In the late afternoon or evening, under cover of closely coordinated mortar and artillery barrages, they shouted taunts of "Babe Ruth eats shit!" and "Death to Yankees!" and surged forward at the American foxholes. "We would light up the sky with flares, lighting the area like daytime," Private Norman Fiedler, a rifleman in the 96th Division, recalled. "We had our perimeter in the shape of a square with heavy machine guns placed at each corner and it was slaughter." A Sixth Army observer wrote of ineffectual "scattered uncoordinated counter-attacks with a platoon or company. These were broken up by our artillery and mortars."

Although the Japanese made no headway and clearly had no chance of fulfilling Suzuki's overly grand designs for chasing the Americans from Leyte and forcing MacArthur's surrender, the Sixth Army's pace of advance remained glacial. Steady losses to combat and disease, in addition to a paucity of replacements, eroded the size of frontline units, usually to around half strength. Seldom were there ever enough infantrymen to carry the terrific burden of the fighting, a common refrain here and at other American fighting fronts around the globe. Those who remained to do the fighting were not aggressive enough to suit Lieutenant General Krueger. "Infantry is the arm of *close combat*," he intoned severely in a Sixth Army circular. "It is the arm of *final* combat. Individual Japanese soldiers will remain in their holes until eliminated. Although the supporting arms are of great assistance, it ultimately becomes the task of small infantry units to dig them out." To do this, Krueger believed, they "must be aggressively led. There can be no hesitancy on the part of . . . leaders." In another memo, he made it clear that all his troops, no matter their job, must assume responsibility for attaining objectives. "It is essential that all units within and attached to the [infantry] division be imbued with the spirit that when necessary they shall take the same chances as the infantry." Increasingly frustrated and impatient, and deeply worried that his army had bogged down permanently in the mountains, Krueger told Sibert in one phone conversation, "Both the Chief [MacArthur] and I are rather chagrined by the progress made . . . up there. I want you to look into that personally and if necessary, take necessary action. I am afraid some of those regimental commanders are a little bit slow." Krueger's impatience with the stasis of his front might have contributed to the surprise relief on November 18 of Major General Frederick Irving, the popular commander of the 24th Division, in favor of the equally well regarded Major General Roscoe Woodruff, who had only just taken command of the Leyte garrison forces.[16]

Heedless of command changes, the immense difficulties and human cost of operating in Leyte's forbidding badlands yielded to no one. "Leyte was a hellhole," Private Fiedler bluntly commented. "Terrible rain, jungle conditions, heat and insects made living conditions at times unbearable."

The steamy heat sapped their energy. The heavy rain and resultant mud turned uniforms and other gear permanently wet and moldy; wet radios too often shorted out or proved ineffective due to the hills. Jungle rot ate away at skin, especially on constantly soaked feet. "It took quite a few years for my feet to clean up," Private Willis Winther, a machine gunner in the 96th Division, later recalled. Mosquitoes, ants, and other pests plagued them continually. Any water source seemed to contain swarms of leeches. "They . . . attached themselves to noses, eyelids, and every soft spot available," Lieutenant Robert Jackson later wrote. Jackson and others learned to burn the leeches off with lit matches or cigarettes. Even properly treated, they left distinctive marks on the skin. "They made a red spot like a cigarette burn everywhere they [bit]," said Private William Garbo, a rifleman with the 112th Cavalry.

At night, soldiers caught a few fitful hours of sleep in half-flooded or rocky foxholes. For weeks on end they existed in a confining world of ubiquitous filth. "The ground is a deep gooey churned mixture of mud, urine, fecal matter, garbage," Captain Morrissey, the physician, deplored in a diary entry. Private William Walter, a paratrooper, felt "like a pig in a pen, lying in the mud." The rotten stench of the decomposing dead from both sides permeated the forward areas like a fog. In some instances, the GIs slept or fought alongside the corpses. "I looked at their faces," PFC James Holzem of the 511th Parachute Infantry related after taking cover next to several maggot-ridden Japanese corpses. "The bodies were in different states of decomposition. It was absolutely horrible." The Americans attempted to police up and bury the remains of their own comrades, often after many days of decomposition. "You laid your poncho down, you got your trench shovel, and you took the parts of the body, moved them onto the poncho," Sergeant Werner Schlaupitz, an infantryman in the 24th Division, later recalled. "I can remember this friend of mine. I had to put his body on a poncho. And while I'm moving the body, the head . . . rolled off, so you had to get the head and put it back on the poncho." Another soldier was horrified to discover that the remains of his buddy had elongated grotesquely. "It seemed like he stretched out seven or eight feet." Once recovered and identified, they were buried in marked graves. Upon their commanders fell the traumatic job of writing to loved ones. "Arthur was a very liked member of this company," Captain William Bostwick, the C.O. of Headquarters Company, 1st Battalion, 511th Parachute Infantry Regiment, wrote to the mother of Lieutenant Arthur McLaughlin, who was killed near the village of Lubi. "He died among his friends and was fighting for them. Arthur suffered no pain. He died instantly when a bullet struck him in the chest. He will long be remembered by all of us."

The constant stress of close combat, the exhaustion inherent in digging foxholes or moving anywhere in the steep hill country, not to mention the unrelenting misery of the conditions, all wore the troops down to a state of perpetual fatigue. "The men looked 10 or 15 years older than their ages," Lieutenant Hostetter, the doctor, wrote of the surviving men in his battalion. "They spoke little and moved slowly. There was no joking or horseplay, yet they were considerate of each other. They had many physical conditions resulting from exhaustion, exposure, and poor nutrition." He became so concerned by their miserable condition that he ordered, against the express wishes of his battalion commander, a rest evacuation for several soldiers, including three company commanders. One graphic unit report described the troops as "bearded, mud-caked . . . exhausted and hungry. Their feet were heavy, cheeks hollow, bodies emaciated, and eyes glazed."[17]

The deeper that Krueger's divisions plunged into remote areas, the more difficult or even impossible became the job of supplying them properly, a situation strikingly similar to that of Merrill's Marauders in Burma, though on a far larger scale. After all, Sixth Army was the largest American ground formation employed so far in the war against Japan. MacArthur had anticipated that the size of his forces on Leyte and the complexities of operating there would require an extensive logistical network appropriate for the enterprise. Before the invasion, he had created a special Army Service Command (or ASCOM) to oversee this monumental job. He also understood that the issue of supply would become inextricably linked to engineering efforts, especially in relation to building and maintaining any semblance of a productive infrastructure to support the combat troops. Thus, to head up ASCOM, he chose Major General Hugh "Pat" Casey, his ranking SWPA engineer, a man who had escaped the Philippines with him over two years before and in whom his confidence was boundless. MacArthur viewed Casey as vitally important to the success of the Leyte operation, perhaps even more so than Krueger. Back at Hollandia, the night before boarding ship to invade Leyte, Casey had fallen into a hole and badly wrenched his back, to the point where he could barely stand or walk. Lieutenant Colonel Egeberg, the doctor, examined him and recommended he stay behind. "Doc, I don't think I have ever called anyone indispensable before, but at this time Pat Casey is indispensable to me and to this campaign. So you get him ashore and find some way in which he can work." Under Egeberg's close personal supervision, Casey was given liberal doses of codeine and aspirin to dull his intense pain, then corseted, strapped onto a stretcher, and hauled ashore. Holed up with his staff in a Tacloban house, and confined entirely to his stretcher, he ran ASCOM while his deputy, the equally hardy Brigadier General Leif "Jack" Sverdrup, roamed Leyte to implement Casey's vision.

They knew they could not rely on Leyte's troubled road net, where trucks and jeeps seemingly spent as much time bogged in mud as moving supplies. "The rain fell ceaselessly," Colonel Frank Gillette, the XXIV Corps supply officer later wrote. "Torrents came down the mountainsides, and there could always be seen long rows of engineers, soaked to the skin, working on the drainage ditches." A single division in action required the bare minimum of three hundred tons of supplies per day just to survive, much less fight for more than only a few days. The movement of those tonnages required a fleet of 240 two-and-a-half-ton trucks making daily round trips from the beaches to the front, a nearly impossible number of vehicles to keep in service. Resourceful as always, American commanders found other ways to transport the freight. In the water-soaked valleys and rice paddies of eastern Leyte, combat units made extensive use of DUKWs, tractors, LVTs, LCMs, and even trains of carabao, the main draft animal of the archipelago. The carabao presented a unique set of problems. "They were slow and required many animals with a driver for each animal," one American officer later wrote. "The drivers had to be fed and guarded. Trails were not secure from the enemy and were almost impassable for carabao anyway." In the recollection of Lieutenant Joseph Giordano, a platoon leader in the 11th Airborne Division, the animals could not function at all in the mountains. "They could not climb the vertical inclines, were too fat to squeeze through narrow cuts, and were too slow and noisy in the jungles."

The various innovations had little impact beyond perpetuating mere subsistence. Logistical shortfalls continued to sap Sixth Army of momentum. A state of barely controlled chaos reigned at hard-pressed, weather-stressed inland supply depots, many of which staved off Japanese air attacks and infiltration attempts. Congestion at the now remote landing beaches, where backlogs of unloaded cargo festered aboard ships, proved a problem here as elsewhere in the Pacific. From the second week of

November to the end of the month, the unloading rate declined from about twenty thousand tons of matériel per day to just under seven thousand tons a day. An Army Transportation Corps study found that shipping plans expected the average ship to disgorge twelve thousand tons a day, when in reality only half that made it ashore. "Shortage of trucks required unloading gangs to stand idle till cargo could be removed from the wharves," the author complained. "Dumps were so far from the wharves that some trucks could make only three trips a day. Heavy rains slowed truck movement on unsurfaced mountain roads, where trucks slid off the roads or across them."

If these rear areas were not necessarily secure from Japanese air attacks, neither were they safe from deadly mishaps. In one instance, soldiers carelessly heaped eighty tons of explosives, one thousand tons of ammunition, and tens of thousands of drums of gasoline into a dump measuring less than half a mile in size. One evening, something touched off a titanic detonation among the explosives, "sending a pressure wave that was strongly felt for miles," according to a postmortem report by the responsible ordnance battalion. In mere seconds, the explosion killed or badly wounded fifty-seven men, mostly at a nearby camp housing an ordnance company. Tents were obliterated; vehicles and other equipment were destroyed. The blast impulse registered at over one hundred pound-milliseconds per square inch, "7 times greater than that needed to rupture eardrums," according to one investigative report. Fortunately, the explosion somehow did not set off sympathetic detonations among the ammunition boxes or set the fuel drums on fire. Regardless, the investigating officer concluded that the accident represented "an example of a flagrant violation of all safety regulations for outdoor storage."

With vehicles largely unable to operate in the hills of the Corderilla, logisticians resorted to moving everything forward by way of perpetually exhausted carrying parties. "The trails were too steep and the terrain too rugged for even a pack train to have been practicable," a 1st Cavalry Division analytical report lamented. One 7th Division critique complained that "operating conditions were extremely poor since heavy rains made roads nearly impassable, while the lack of bridges necessitated a great deal of stream-fording." Round the clock, the long columns of hunched-over men slogged along muddy trails, hauling heavy crates of ammunition, rations, and jerry cans of water. To pick up the slack for the declining availability of American manpower as casualties and sickness eroded the ranks, civil affairs officers combed far and wide for local help. "Labor was vigorously recruited," one of the officers wrote. A typical infantry regiment needed at least 250 carriers to service its needs. "They work like devils for half a buck a day, carrying out the wounded and bringing up rations to the front," Tech 5 Don Boyd of the 32nd Division wrote to his family about the laborers.

Few Filipinos evinced much interest in earning these pittance wages to perform such hard and potentially dangerous work. Within a few weeks of the American landings, the majority of civilians had access, at the very least, to basic food, medicine, and shelter, mainly because of American subsidies. Some locals had even established prosperous businesses selling black market items, particularly alcohol, to the GIs. "Whiskey establishments in Tacloban have sprung up like mushrooms," one Filipino provincial official reported during the campaign. "With American soldiers as good customers, many people in Leyte have been able to accumulate millions of pesos in victory money from this lucrative whiskey-making industry." Nearly desperate for labor, the Americans begged, coerced, appealed to local patriotism and often sweetened the pot by trading food and souvenirs or simply paying more money. Sometimes, according to one US officer, "Simon Legree tactics had to be used to get the men to carry on when the going got tough." In all, the Army employed eight thousand laborers along the Sixth Army front, a barely adequate force.

Increasingly, forward infantry units and patrols were cut off behind enemy lines or isolated by rough terrain. "There was a general state of semi-starvation among us this morning," Captain Morrissey noted in his diary after his unit was cut off from its ground supply. "It was some fifty hours since our last real food and we had put quite a few miles on foot behind us." By design the airborne units spent long periods out of contact with their line of supply. "We planned . . . that the superb physical condition of the men would and should take up the slack of short supply," the division historian later wrote. "We tightened our belts by notches, and a lot of flesh we always thought we needed fell by the wayside. We began to shoot only when we saw the whites of their eyes. We were shorter of food than we had ever expected to be; our ammunition had to be counted by rounds rather than by clips; we suffered awaiting medical supplies from the skies which did not come; and we hated . . . the gods that made the weather, the pilots who wouldn't fly, and the powers that sent us into the mountains in the first place. Trails were sticky, treacherous mud paths.

Clothing became soaked and rotten, and mud sloshed over the tops of boots whose soles rotted after a few days of uncomfortable marching. The night air was penetratingly cold." Like Merrill's long-range formations in Burma, the 11th Airborne infiltrated behind Japanese lines on foot, but the division even parachuted an artillery battery and a forward aid station into place. Sergeant Bull Hendry, a paratrooper, remembered living on "one K ration meal each . . . and no rations for at least four more days." Another paratrooper, PFC Harry Swan, later commented that "it was miserable, raining, no shelter, no rations and no resupply at all. We were surrounded by the enemy, with no hope of getting out. We were paratroopers and we accepted it."

To sustain Swan's unit and many others, American commanders relied upon aerial resupply, much as they had in Burma. During a two-month period, the C-47s of the 11th Air Cargo Resupply Squadron parachuted 1,167,818 pounds of ammunition, food, medicine, weaponry, clothing, footgear, and other supplies to isolated units. Pilots flew anywhere from two to twelve hours per day, often in less-than-ideal weather. "On many days, a thick gray fog hugged the mountain areas, and the pilots had to circle to find an opening near the drop zone," Major Joseph Seay of the 11th Airborne Division later wrote. "Once under the ceiling, they made the drop and spiraled upward, hoping to break out on top before encountering a mountain peak." A Sixth Army analysis claimed minimal cargo loss rates between 10 and 35 percent. The aviators employed 2,776 parachutes, about 60 percent of which were recycled for renewed usage. Not surprisingly, their greatest beneficiaries were the troopers of the 11th Airborne Division, who received 388,570 pounds of matériel, about one-third of the Sixth Army total; the 7th Division, seldom out of contact, received only 4,200 pounds. Interestingly, another 91,054 pounds went to guerrilla formations.

Even these impressive tonnages did not fully meet the voracious needs of the forward-most fighting formations, no matter how lean they might have become. Several divisions augmented the C-47s by utilizing single-engine L-4 and L-5 liaison planes as aerial carriers. No one embraced this concept more enthusiastically than Major General Swing, the 11th Airborne commander who employed the planes so frequently that his troopers jokingly referred to him as the president of "Swing Airlines" presiding over an air fleet of "Biscuit Bombers." He wrote enthusiastically to General Peyton March, a former Army chief of staff and his father-in-law, "We've practically supplied ourselves with cub planes for over a month in the mtns." Though vulnerable to enemy fire and occasionally hampered by the bad weather, the small planes offered the advantage of speedy, efficient operations. Plus, they and their pilots were already under divisional control, unlike the C-47 units that answered to an Army Air Forces command structure. "It took the [liaison] planes only ten minutes to make the flight over the sharp-peaked mountains and drop the supplies," the 11th Airborne after-action report enthused. "L-5s carried a passenger who pushed the supplies over the side; in the L-4s the pilots did the work. Such fragile bundles as medical equipment were sent by parachute, but the rest, including rations and all kinds of ammunition and shells, were simply kicked out." Occasionally, all this falling matériel posed a danger to the troops as when a falling box killed a wounded man in an aid station and a mortar baseplate struck PFC Jack Jones on the head and killed him.[18]

The rugged terrain severely hampered the treatment and evacuation of wounded soldiers. Doctors at portable surgical hospitals and battalion aid stations bandaged, sewed, and bound up wounds as best they could with the limited medical supplies at their disposal. After treating a typical group of patients, Captain Morrissey told his diary that "the men's clothing and the mud are foul beyond description and are blown deeply into the wound by grenades. Grenades are getting to be the weapon of choice. How little most of the wounded asked for and how quiet most of them were as soon as night fell. Rain and blood soaked cut up clothes and dirty bandages to be burned every morning—all very smelly."

Ambulatory wounded trekked for enervating miles along slippery trails to reach clearing companies and evacuation hospitals. Soldiers dreaded the prospect of incapacitating wounds that might strand them far away from lifesaving medical care. For the many who could not walk, the only way out of the mountains was on a stretcher, a demoralizing, terrifying prospect. "When the American soldier is sure that he will receive prompt medical attention and evacuation if wounded, he will do a much better job under fire," Captain Dale Schweinler of the 32nd Division later wrote. "The tortuous evacuation trail over which the litters had to be carried a distance of six miles, tends to make the soldier extremely careful and unwilling to accept extra risk." A mere handful of casualties could absorb much of a small unit's manpower, at a minimum for a few hours, more commonly for a day or two. Lieutenant Richard Barnum, a platoon leader in the 511th Parachute Infantry, estimated that every stretcher evacuation case required eight soldiers, "four men to carry and four men for a relief. Platoons and

companies had to be taken from their combat duties to move these men."
The 1st Cavalry Division claimed that it took a staggering twenty-four carriers twelve hours to move one wounded man to the rear. As with carrying
supplies, the Americans collared numerous Filipino men to haul the
wounded. "Native litter bearers proved invaluable and should be utilized
whenever possible," recommended the 24th Division surgeon in an after-
action report. The 1st Cavalry Division employed two thousand local men.

The journeys were filled with misery for everyone involved. Delirious,
wounded men, sometimes in shock and often in pain, endured near torture
as their overburdened litter teams sloshed through the mud and attempted
to steady them down seemingly endless steep hills or precipices. "It required several hours to make the trip and the situation of organizing terrain to repel counterattacks was in most cases serious until the carrying
parties returned," Captain Kermit Blaney of the 24th Division recalled.
Regardless of their all-consuming exhaustion, commanders used them as
porters on the way back. "The parties carrying the wounded after leaving
the aid station were always instructed to pick up ammunition on their return trip. This was the main method of resupply." As always, the vast majority of wounded men survived, though the adverse evacuation situation
certainly made the fighting deadlier than it otherwise would have been.
"Adequate surgical care of patients was rendered difficult by the comparative isolation of certain forward units in the field, by the frequently long
litter carries from place of wounding to the installation providing emergency
surgery and by the difficult weather and terrain," declared one Medical
Corps study.

The close-quarters character of the fighting manifested itself in the nature of the casualties. As men blasted away at one another from close range,
small arms posed a greater hazard than was typical in modern combat. The
Sixth Army surgeon studied 519 patients who died of their wounds. Gunshots to the head, chest, or abdomen caused almost half the deaths. Fragmentation wounds from mortars, artillery shells, or grenades accounted
for most of the rest. Only one died from a bayonet wound. A XXIV Corps
study found that 53 percent of wounded men were hit by bullets, while
fragments injured just over 43 percent. The troubled isolation of treating
wounded men in the Cordillera hills hinted at future innovations in combat medical care. Paratroopers of the 11th Airborne Division rigged a few
L-4s with plywood litters for quick evacuation to hospitals. "Many a paratrooper who was caught by a mortar burst or had been hit in the stomach

with a sniper's bullet, was on the operating table fifteen miles away in less than 20 minutes," declared the division after-action report. Over two months, 44 men were evacuated in this fashion. One of them, Private Herbert Merritt, who had caught grenade fragments in the leg, remembered enduring a quick operation by a medic wielding a flashlight, after which fellow paratroopers loaded him into a plane. "I was stretched out behind the pilot. I was against his back." Even more resonant of the future, the 382nd Infantry Regiment of the 96th Division managed to acquire a small early-generation helicopter and use it to transport a pair of seriously wounded men to a hospital. "It would have required two or three days of arduous litter carrying over steep, rugged terrain to have taken them out," the unit after-action report exulted, before adding presciently, "Future study is strongly recommended for the use of the helicopter plane for this and similar missions."

Waves of disease also ate away at the ranks. "Leyte is an intern's paradise as far as disease is concerned," Major Frank Billings of the 118th General Hospital quipped to an Army interviewer. Throughout that fall, hospital admissions from sickness accounted for twice as many patients as combat wounds. The usual culprits were dysentery, malaria, and dengue fever. For the first time, schistosomiasis also made an appearance. Transmitted in Leyte's swamps and streams by parasitical larval worms released from snails, the disease caused severe abdominal pain, diarrhea, and bloody excreta. Unchecked, schistosomiasis could swell and destroy the liver. The 118th General Hospital alone documented at least two hundred cases. "Tactical considerations dictated the exposure of many of the troops to the disease," said Captain David Gage, a physician with the 124th Station Hospital. "Many of the men had to wade in the rice paddies, men on patrol, Engineer outfits, and Signal Corps men, setting poles and swinging lines, Aviation Engineers, laying their high test gasoline pipes." Others contracted schistosomiasis through recreational swimming. Eventually, Gage and the other medics prohibited all contact with freshwater streams, so much as this could be possible under combat conditions. For all washing and drinking, the medics instead mandated well water and chlorinated water.[19]

Back in Tacloban, General MacArthur had established his headquarters in a spacious, two-story, twelve-room stucco house formerly owned by Walter

Scott Price, a sixty-eight-year-old Philippine-American War veteran who had settled on Leyte after he left the Army, married a local woman, and earned a fortune from a variety of enterprises, particularly road construction. In 1942, the Japanese had apprehended Price and sent him to an internment camp for Allied civilians at Santo Tomas University in Manila. With Price incarcerated, they appropriated his comfortable house as an officers' club and headquarters before vacating it in the wake of the US invasion. MacArthur opened his headquarters in the house on October 26, immediately after the Navy's victory in the Battle of Leyte Gulf made his permanent presence on Leyte feasible. Within a few days, a vast network of SWPA headquarters sections followed the general to Tacloban, occupying nearby warehouses, office buildings, homes, and two pairs of prefabricated structures hastily erected by engineers. "Our communications center was located in what had once been an automobile repair shop," Major John McKinney, an officer in SWPA's sophisticated signals section, later wrote of one typical headquarters building. "It had a concrete floor and a roof that didn't leak, two enormous assets in Tacloban."

At the Price house, MacArthur settled into the master bedroom where Walter and his wife, Simeona, had once slept. A private shower room and porch, for the general's use only, adjoined the bedroom. From his new home MacArthur ran the campaign, seldom leaving the building. The lousy roads, deplorable conditions, and remoteness of the battle areas precluded any possibility of frontline visits. Indeed, when Major General Woodruff, the new commander of the 24th Division, wanted to visit one of his forward units, it took him three backbreaking hours slogging through mud "the consistency of thick pancake batter" just to get there and another three to get back to his headquarters. "It was a good thing I didn't realize what I was getting into," he wrote. "I think I was as tired as I have ever been. Although I thought I was in pretty good condition physically, I was quite stiff for three or four days." Any such similar journey for MacArthur, who was eleven years older than Woodruff, would simply have been out of the question. At Tacloban, the mere act of crossing the street could mean inundation in mud. "The rains came almost every day and the streets in this sleepy little town were ankle deep in mud," McKinney commented. "We had wooden sidewalks that kept us out of the mud as long as we stayed on one side of the street and kept within a single block. If we had to cross the street, we were in trouble."

MacArthur's distance from the fighting afforded him little security, an unhappy by-product of the ongoing contest for control of Leyte's airspace. The Japanese knew that MacArthur lived in the Price house and made repeated attempts to bomb it, subjecting the general to the most intensive bombardment—and by far the most danger—since his unhappy tenure on Corregidor almost three years earlier. With almost monotonous frequency, Japanese medium bombers and fighters raided the Price house and the surrounding blocks, usually at night, provoking a fierce response from American antiaircraft gunners and fighters. For some in the general's entourage, the experience reprised terrible memories from the unhappy days when the Japanese defeated MacArthur's forces in the Philippines. "Those who sweated out the events of Corregidor *were* different from those who did not," wrote the SWPA stenographer Paul Rogers, promoted by now to warrant officer after more than three years of serving the general. "All of us had given ourselves up for dead. We had no hope of salvation. When we were confronted with Tacloban, it was like being sent back to the tomb. It was not the bombs of Tacloban we suffered, but the reenactment of memories we had tried desperately to forget."

If MacArthur shared any of these emotions, he suppressed them well. He survived multiple near misses with scarcely any hint of concern, even as the bombs inflicted numerous military and civilian casualties throughout the area. Indeed, without any doubt, he faced more personal danger here and elsewhere during the war than any other American theater commander in World War II. During one conference with senior commanders, low-flying Japanese planes strafed the area, and antiaircraft batteries blasted at them furiously. "The noise was terrific but the Big Chief went right on talking," an approving Eichelberger wrote to Emma. He later added, "Since the Supreme Commander was deaf to the violence around him, the rest of us maintained the elaborate pretense that we couldn't hear any bombs falling either." On one occasion, enemy ordnance smashed through the ceiling and wall of a bedroom adjoining MacArthur's but did not explode. Another time, a pair of bullets shot by a strafing enemy fighter barely missed him as he stood shaving in front of a mirror; his only reaction was to ask an aide to dig one of the bullets out so that he could give it to his young son, Arthur, as a souvenir. MacArthur even came close to death from friendly fire when American antiaircraft shells hit the house; one American round zipped into his room and landed on a couch opposite his bed. MacArthur discreetly asked the antiaircraft commander to have his crews raise their guns a bit.

Always, he comported himself with a courageous, almost awe-inspiring calm. "He thought that nobody ever made a bullet which could kill him," Frederick Marquardt, a visitor from the Office of War Information, later marveled. "The man had complete courage, there's no question about that." To Turner Catledge, a war correspondent who observed him firsthand at Tacloban, "he seemed to be disdainful of air raids, refusing to interrupt a conversation or to rise from his bed to seek shelter during an attack." Sergeant Vincent Powers, an SWPA staffer who worked in a building immediately across the street from MacArthur's bedroom porch, often saw the general react to the raids with just this sort of contemptuous reserve. "Day and night he could be seen on his porch. Should the air alert sound, he would knock the glowing ashes from his pipe, stand by the rail in the center of the porch, peer into the sky, watching the red tracers and ninety mm's [millimeters] blast at the enemy. The raid over, he would resume his pacing."

Seemingly, every evening the raiders arrived as he ate dinner with an array of visitors, headquarters intimates, and subordinate commanders. "His was to preside at the dinner table with eight or ten generals and Larry [Lehrbas] and me," wrote Lieutenant Colonel Egeberg, the doctor who had by now become perhaps MacArthur's closest confidant. "The Japanese ritual was to try to bomb our house at that time." Heedless of the hair-raising sounds of screeching engines, whistling bombs, and strafing, MacArthur hardly batted an eye, eating or holding forth with a monologue as if hosting a dinner party, safe and secure in his home. With this example set, the others at the table could do little else but parrot MacArthur, though inwardly most wanted to flee in terror. "It was a terribly long wait," Egeberg recalled, "to see who would receive the bomb, our dinner table, our friends near us, or an empty street. Then the explosion, usually within a hundred yards, sometimes terrifyingly loud, sometimes muffled." In the wake of the raids, Egeberg often left the table to care for the wounded; everyone else stayed put, unless mercifully called away for some official duty.

Amid the frequent bombings and the dreariness of the long, bloody campaign, MacArthur enjoyed few pleasures beyond an occasional peaceful meal or some personal reading time. He received good news on December 16 of his promotion to five-star rank, along with Leahy, Marshall, Nimitz, King, Arnold, and Eisenhower. He was particularly satisfied to learn that Congress had afforded him seniority over Ike, against whom he continued to nurse a petty, jealous resentment. MacArthur employed a local silversmith to fashion a unique circular five-star emblem made from American, Dutch, Australian, and Filipino coins that embodied Allied partnership in the Pacific.[20]

The new five-star rank could not shield MacArthur from headaches created by the defiant machinations of his chief of staff. During the campaign, Lieutenant General Sutherland had been shuttling back and forth between Leyte and Hollandia, supervising the complex movements of SWPA headquarters to the Philippines. Behind MacArthur's back, and in direct defiance of his wishes, Sutherland instructed Brigadier General Sverdrup, the engineer, to build a cottage for WAC captain Elaine Bessemer-Clark, his Australian mistress, at Tanauan, site of a burgeoning base about a dozen miles to the south of Tacloban. An irritated Sverdrup, who had far more important matters to deal with than accommodating the comforts of Sutherland's girlfriend, related the news to Egeberg. The doctor reluctantly but promptly informed MacArthur, who refused to accept that his chief of staff could be so high-handed. Sutherland seized upon the breathing space afforded him by MacArthur's disbelief to make sure that Sverdrup's engineers completed the cottage.

Owing to MacArthur's seeming determination to look the other way, the chief of staff and Bessemer-Clark might well have continued on their merry way together had not Elaine, in characteristic passive-aggressive, self-defeating fashion, decided to telephone Lieutenant Colonel Lehrbas, the publicist, from her cottage and expressly make her presence in Leyte known. Lehrbas related the bombshell news to Egeberg, who once again found himself in the uncomfortable position of making it known to the general as they sat together on MacArthur's porch at the Price house. MacArthur was an even-tempered person, anything but prone to rage or mood swings. He seldom used profanity, and though self-centered in most all interactions, he almost universally treated others with courtesy and respect. But when he at last realized that Sutherland had indeed defied him, a fury descended over him. "What?!" he screamed, loud enough to startle several soldiers who were walking on the other side of the street. "Get me Dick!"

Egeberg eagerly retreated and had a clerk retrieve Sutherland. As nearby soldiers and the headquarters staff listened in shock, MacArthur exploded with rage against his chief of staff, dressing him down like a wayward cadet. "Dick Sutherland, I gave you an order. You disobeyed it. You are relieved of your command. You are under arrest." Enraged, MacArthur continued to berate Sutherland with explicit language that, in Egeberg's estimation, "any Missouri mule skinner would have envied. It was a violent, pent-up, end-of-the-rope loss of temper, and it continued for several minutes. The General ended by telling General Sutherland he was to have her out of Leyte in forty-eight hours." Listening from inside the Price house, a dazed Warrant Officer Rogers, similar to many other aides, found himself deeply upset by the altercation. "I do not think the explosion of a grenade in Sutherland's office would have caused more terror for me than the sight of MacArthur towering in rage over . . . Sutherland." When MacArthur calmed down, he eventually relented from the arrest and relief, but made absolutely sure that Bessemer-Clark left the Philippines immediately. "The lady was sent back to Australia with all the suddenness of [a] shot from the cannon," an SWPA staff officer later commented to D. Clayton James, MacArthur's greatest biographer. Lieutenant Colonel Rhoades, the pilot, drew the unenviable job of flying her home. "It is most distressing for me to admit a serious flaw exists in the character of someone I respect and admire," Rhoades told his diary of Sutherland, whom he considered to be a good friend. Rhoades dutifully transported Bessemer-Clark to Australia. Much to his consternation, Elaine soon unloaded her emotional turmoil onto him, perhaps because he represented a final link to Sutherland. In the privacy of his diary, Rhoades described her as "in a state of hysteria. I had no experience handling this kind of situation. She appeared to be afraid to allow me to leave her there alone. I tried to console her as best I could, but it was a horrible sight to watch a woman lose all of her dignity."

MacArthur's row with Sutherland represented the culmination of many months, maybe even years, of tension between the two. The chief of staff could not understand MacArthur's vociferous reaction to what he considered to be his own personal business. "What he did with his own private life should, in his opinion, have been his own affair," Rhoades later explained of opinions Sutherland had shared with him about his relationship with Bessemer-Clark. More important, Sutherland had been indispensable to MacArthur in the early stages of the war, when defeat loomed as a real possibility. When the fortunes of war improved, his influence with MacArthur had waned as the SWPA chief's prestige grew and his need for Sutherland's talents diminished. Either as a way to regain that influence or usurp his chief's power, Sutherland had foolishly resorted to defying him, a game he could not hope to win, but one that revealed the true nature of his conniving, ruthless character. MacArthur could never tolerate Sutherland's direct insubordination and the inherent challenge to his authority. The epic chewing-out was really about more than just MacArthur's reaction to Sutherland's ham-fisted attempts to bring Captain Bessemer-Clark along with him wherever he went. It actually marked a moment when MacArthur firmly and in the most unambiguous terms reaffirmed his authority over SWPA and all who served in it, even and especially Sutherland.

Officially, MacArthur kept Sutherland in place as chief of staff for the rest of the war, though he did privately approach an uninterested Eichelberger about the possibility of replacing Sutherland, whom he obviously no longer trusted. Outwardly, MacArthur treated Sutherland the same, as if the altercation had never taken place. In truth, though, Sutherland had become an administrative functionary, and no longer the true consigliere-style confidant he had once been. "He ended up a bitter and disillusioned soldier," Rhoades later commented of Sutherland. Warrant Officer Rogers sadly compared the deterioration of their once intimate partnership to "a marriage which slides down the skids into disaster, neither party understanding why or how, or knowing what to do about it." In day-to-day operational matters, MacArthur increasingly relied on Major General Richard Marshall, Sutherland's deputy. For confidential advice, he now tended to turn to Colonel Courtney Whitney, a former Army aviator and elitist Manila lawyer who had served since 1943 as an intelligence liaison to Filipino guerrilla organizations. Whitney was almost universally disliked at SWPA headquarters for his pomposity and predilection for underhanded scheming.[21]

MacArthur had little time to dwell on his broken relationship with Sutherland. The Leyte fighting still lingered on with no imminent end in sight. At the same time, he and his staff had to plan for the capstone invasion of Luzon, slated overoptimistically for December 20, an enormous undertaking and one almost wholly dependent on a positive outcome in the Leyte battle. In turn, MacArthur also intended on December 5 to invade lightly defended Mindoro, the seventh-largest island in the archipelago, located about 250 miles northwest of Leyte and 100 miles south of Manila, an ideal spot to position air bases in support of the Luzon operation. Vice Admiral Kinkaid adamantly opposed going ahead with these invasions until the Americans gained better command of the air. He understood the vulnerability of his ships to Japanese aerial attacks in the constricted waterways between Leyte and these objectives. So did Lieutenant General Kenney, who shared Kinkaid's concerns. In the face of such staunch opposition from his sea and air commanders, MacArthur reluctantly agreed to postpone the Mindoro invasion to December 15 and Luzon to January 9. Meanwhile, as the Japanese continued to resist stubbornly on Leyte, MacArthur cast about—almost with a pang of desperation—for some sort of knockout blow. Since mid-November, Lieutenant General Krueger had advocated the launching of an amphibious invasion at Ormoc, whose capture would outflank Lieutenant General Suzuki's front lines and deprive him of the port where most of his reinforcements arrived on the island. The postponements freed up shipping to fulfill Krueger's vision, though everyone understood that the invasion force would likely face formidable Japanese aerial, and perhaps naval, opposition.

To carry out the invasion, Krueger chose the 77th Infantry Division from deep on his bench. The original Leyte invasion plans had designated Major General A. D. Bruce's 77th, fresh from its fight on Guam, as the last of Krueger's reserve divisions. During the initial spasm of optimism following the Leyte landings, MacArthur, without the consent or knowledge of Krueger, had transferred the division to Nimitz's control, only to ask for it back when the battle grew much tougher. As a result, the Statue of Liberty soldiers experienced a dizzying Pacific Ocean travelogue that took them on a circuitous 6,111-mile odyssey. "Deep inside there was a feeling of utter loneliness and a gnawing fear that gripped the soul," Tech Sergeant Henry Lopez, a platoon sergeant in C Company, 307th Infantry Regiment, wrote of the journey in a history of his unit. Lopez and the rest of the division went from convalescing on Guam to boarding ships sailing east for New Caledonia, only to see them rerouted south to Seeadler Harbor on Manus as the unit came back under SWPA control. From there they sailed west to Leyte, where they landed in late November and, in most cases, spent their days unloading ships until Bruce received a warning order on the afternoon of December 1 for the Ormoc invasion. They marched to their embarkation points at Tarragona beach in eastern Leyte, a grueling, muddy process for many. Once at Tarragona, they hurriedly loaded vehicles, equipment, and supplies onto ships before the troops themselves boarded on the morning of December 6. In the estimation of Samuel Eliot Morison, the brilliant naval historian, the diminutive invasion armada "resembled that of the shore-to-shore amphibious operations that had taken place in the Southwest Pacific." Indeed, the Ormoc Attack Group, under the command of Rear Admiral Arthur Struble, consisted of eight attack transports, twenty-seven LCIs, twelve LSM assault vessels, and four LSTs escorted by a dozen destroyers, plus minesweepers and a few smaller supporting ships, enough to carry 269 vehicles, seven infantry battalions, a 105-millimeter artillery battalion, a battery of antiaircraft artillery, a chemical mortar company, plus supporting engineer, medical, and quartermaster formations.

Krueger planned to land the troops along a half-mile stretch of open beach at Deposito, about three miles south of Ormoc. Thanks to accurate aerial reconnaissance photographs and reports from Alamo Scouts who were operating with Filipino guerrillas near Ormoc, the Sixth Army commander and Bruce knew that the landing beaches were undefended, with little more than rear echelon enemy troops in the area. Other informal sources of information also added to their knowledge. "Our G-2 was especially active in rounding up for questioning a number of Filipinos who were familiar with the area," Bruce commented in a postwar lecture. Bruce's people were to land and unload two days' worth of supplies within a three-hour window, before the inevitable Japanese aerial counterattacks, and then drive for Ormoc as quickly as possible. At the same time, to siphon off as much Japanese combat power as possible, Krueger ordered the 7th Infantry Division to attack from its front line at Damulaan about sixteen miles south of Ormoc and ultimately link up with the 77th, while the 96th Division and the 11th Airborne supported the entire enterprise by continuing their westward push through the jungle. As the Ormoc Attack Group put to sea, an understandable mood of apprehension prevailed over the 77th Division soldiers. Many referred to their mission as the "Anzio of the Pacific," in reference to the abortive Allied attempt to unhinge the German line in Italy in early 1944 by launching an outflanking amphibious invasion.

At 0707 on the morning of December 7, three years to the day after the Japanese attacks on Pearl Harbor had started the war, the troops hit Deposito beach against no opposition. In the next two and a half hours, the entire force landed and completed the task of unloading vehicles and supplies, a coup de main that reflected the efficiency and adroitness of an army that, in tandem with its partners in the US Marine Corps, had indisputably become a world leader in amphibious operations. Encountering little Japanese resistance, Bruce wisely ordered an immediate advance north along Highway 2, a mediocre gravel and sand road, rather than simply hunker down, consolidate a beachhead, and wait for reinforcements as Allied commanders had done, with tragic consequences, at Anzio. He understood that the invasion had caught the Japanese off guard and he resolved to exploit their confusion. "The Ormoc landing came as a complete surprise," Major General Tomochika, the 35th Army chief of staff, later admitted to American interrogators. He and his boss Suzuki had mistakenly believed that mines and Japanese naval opposition along the southern coast of Leyte would keep LSTs and other invasion vessels out of those waters. Heavy Japanese losses in the ongoing Corderilla fighting probably played a role as well, since Suzuki could ill afford to siphon off troops from the front to defend against a notional invasion threat. Regardless, by nightfall on December 7, the 77th Division had secured the village of Ipil, about a third of the way to Ormoc.[22]

Unfortunately for the Americans, achieving the element of surprise hardly guaranteed an easy or rapid victory. Unbeknownst to MacArthur and Krueger, Yamashita had just given orders for a counterstroke of his own, timed by happenstance to coincide almost precisely with the Ormoc landings. "If the construction of the air bases on Leyte is permitted to continue, the communication between the Southern areas and the homeland will be cut and this would be a serious situation," he wrote to Suzuki. "We must annihilate the enemy's air power." To that end, he ordered surprise drops of a few hundred Japanese paratroopers at the American-controlled Buri and San Pablo airfields near the town of Burauen. While the airborne troops seized the fields and administered whatever damage they could to American aircraft and facilities, the 26th Division and 68th Independent Mixed Brigade were to punch through the American lines, link up with the paratroopers, and take permanent control of the bases. Bold in concept but problematic in execution, the drops did stun the Americans and lead to some sharp fighting December 6–10. But the relief forces had no hope of breaching US lines and capturing the airfields. The courageous, isolated enemy troopers destroyed some planes, inflicted minor damage to a few fuel and supply dumps, and plunged the Fifth Air Force into organizational chaos for a couple of days. But on a strategic level, their mission, known to its authors as the "Wa" operation, proved to be a dismal failure. Cut off and doomed, most of the enemy airborne soldiers were killed in a disjointed series of small-unit actions.

More troubling for the Ormoc invaders was the enemy aerial response and Yamashita's continued determination to reinforce Leyte. Bruce had no sooner gotten his soldiers ashore when, at 0934, Japanese planes initiated a series of violent attacks, including many by kamikazes, against Struble's ships. The raids persisted, on and off, for the next nine hours. Fifth Air Force P-38 Lightnings tore into the enemy planes, as did fire from antiaircraft batteries. They inflicted devastating losses on the attackers—the Japanese probably lost at least fifty aircraft in the course of the day—but they could not prevent them from threatening the ships. The Japanese sank the destroyer USS *Mahan* and inflicted fatal damage on the destroyer transport USS *Ward*, a venerable warship that had fired the first American shots of the war against a Japanese minisub south of Pearl Harbor on December 7, 1941. In a sad irony, Commander William Outerbridge, who had skippered *Ward* on that fateful day exactly three years earlier, but now served as captain of the USS *O'Brien*, found himself charged with the traumatic task of rescuing survivors from *Ward* and then sinking his old ship as she lay dead in the water.

During the days that followed, the Americans resupplied the 77th Division adequately with quick runs from Leyte Gulf to the beachhead, all in the face of more Japanese aerial resistance. Repeated Japanese attempts to land reinforcements in the Ormoc area added a surreal note to the battle. A convoy bearing five thousand soldiers of the 68th Independent Mixed Brigade was scheduled to land on December 7 in almost the same spot as the 77th Division invasion beaches. But these ships took such a pasting from Fifth Air Force planes that the convoy was forced to reroute and disgorge the surviving troops at San Isidoro harbor in northwest Leyte, where they reinforced the decimated 1st Division in its ongoing struggle against X Corps. Four nights later, fragments of another embattled convoy—the last the Japanese would send to Leyte—blundered into American vessels that were in the process of resupplying the beachhead. "We thought Ormoc was in our hands and that we could land there under the protection of our forces, but on landing discovered it was quite the opposite," one of the Japanese commanders later admitted. The Americans sank a destroyer, shot up several barges, and forced the surviving transport vessels to flee and haphazardly land whatever troops they could. Most of these newcomers were quickly annihilated by the advancing 77th Division.

An unopposed landing at Mindoro on December 15 by soldiers from the 24th Division, the 503rd Parachute Infantry Regiment, and the 2nd Engineer Special Brigade inflicted another body blow on the Japanese. The invaders quickly seized the useful port of San Jose and began constructing a pair of airfields. "No enemy ground activity was encountered by the Combat Team at any time," stated the 503rd's after-action report, with just the slightest hint of bored disappointment. The absence of ground opposition belied Japanese intentions to destroy the Mindoro beachhead. During the month that followed the invasion, enemy planes, including kamikazes, raided the area almost daily. "We fired at Jap planes day and night," Lieutenant Frederick Downs, an antiaircraft officer, later wrote to his sister about the intense fighting. The Americans counted 334 separate air raids, mainly against the supply convoys. American fighters shot down fifty-five enemy planes; antiaircraft batteries accounted for forty-eight others. The Imperial Navy even sallied a surface force of two cruisers, three destroyers, and three destroyer escorts off the coast to bombard the American perimeter, but with little effect.

In a sinister harbinger for future invasions, the kamikazes proved to be an especially potent weapon, sinking a pair of LSTs and damaging a destroyer. "For a time the destruction wrought by these suicide assaults created a serious problem, especially with regard to aviation gasoline and air force technical supplies," admitted a campaign history authored by MacArthur's staff. "Troops ashore were also subjected to sporadic and fatiguing night raids by hostile aircraft." The raiders could not and did not prevent the Americans from establishing firm control of Mindoro and developing the nascent fields into valuable air bases, ironically more useful to MacArthur's forthcoming Luzon operations than any bases on Leyte, mainly because of the latter's inherently poor infrastructure and inhospitable climate for modern aerial operations. Lest one wonder if MacArthur might well have skipped Leyte to focus primarily on Mindoro, the reality was that the Japanese in either instance intended to fight a decisive battle wherever the Americans landed.[23]

As the struggle for control of Mindoro played out, the 77th Division continued its relentless push for Ormoc. The hard-pressed Lieutenant General Suzuki reinforced his rear echelon troops with any units he could find, including much of the 12th Independent Infantry Regiment, about 80 wayward paratroopers, machine-gun teams from the Imperial Army's 30th Division, in addition to engineers and naval personnel, altogether comprising 1,740 men. On the morning of December 10, Major General Bruce's two leading regiments, the 306th and 307th, plunged into Ormoc following a ten-minute supporting barrage from artillery, chemical mortars, tank destroyers, and amtanks. Offshore, rocket-firing LCMs pounded the Ormoc pier. According to the vivid description of the 77th Division's after-action report, "the town was a blazing inferno of exploding WP [white phosphorus] and HE [high explosive] shells, detonating ammunition dumps, and blazing houses. A heavy pall of black smoke hung over the town. Every house . . . shielded a hole and several Japs. Our mortars, machine guns, and mobile artillery kept up a continuous barrage in front of the advancing troops." Clouds of gray dust from destroyed buildings mixed with the smoke to restrict visibility over "a scene of total destruction, of shambles, gutted buildings, and rubble," in the sad recollection of one combat soldier. Savage fights to the death raged in the ruins. Colonel Paul Freeman, a War Department observer, lamented that the "desperate house-to-house fighting necessitated the virtual destruction of the entire town." A Fourteenth Area Army staff officer dispatched by Yamashita to observe the fighting reported to the general that "Ormoc is a ruin of stone and steel with no living thing, not even a cat to be seen. Bodies are strewn along the roadside, burned black like statues, their rotting faces covered with flies. There is a terrible smell from these and from the bodies of many soldiers, all swollen up."

The 77th secured Ormoc by late afternoon at the cost of thirteen casualties, an incredibly low number considering the strategic importance of the prize and the heavy price ordinarily paid by attackers in urban combat. Close support from self-propelled artillery pieces probably saved many lives, but in the words of one officer, "The vigorous action of the infantry riflemen . . . was the deciding factor in clearing this town." An excited Bruce sent a pithy message to the 7th Division, the 11th Airborne, the XXIV Corps, and Sixth Army: "Have rolled two sevens in Ormoc. Come seven, come eleven. Bruce." The allusion to a winning dice throw and a desired linkup with the two nearest divisions in XXIV Corps reflected Bruce's mental creativity and prompted many knowing smirks around Sixth Army senior circles. Major General Hodge, the tough-as-gristle corps commander known more for his single-minded attention to duty than for his sense of humor, appreciated the progress if not necessarily Bruce's flamboyant phrase, the likes of which he equated with a vexing self-centered streak in the 77th Division commander. "I am a bit disappointed in Bruce," he confided in a letter to Lieutenant General Richardson. "He is brilliant as a tactician, but is a top line egotist, a publicity hound and is not as stable as he should be. He has a fine division and deserves all the credit in the world for it. They deserve all credit, but Bruce forgets that the stage was all set and the combined efforts of all elements of the XXIV Corps was behind the attack and that the 7th Division mopped up behind him and protected his flanks and rear and waited on him hand and foot." Hodge seemed not to realize nor care that Bruce's message had explicitly recognized the two divisions that most protected the flanks of his own.

In any event, the 77th and 7th Divisions linked up at Ipil the next morning to form a continuous front along Leyte's west coast and resume the advance, while X Corps pressured the Japanese in the north, to carry out Krueger's vision to crush Suzuki's outflanked formations to the east in the mountains and to the west in the Ormoc Valley. Some of the heaviest fighting took place at Cogon, a vital crossroads just north of Ormoc on Highway 2 at the Antilao River. "As long as this position remained Japanese, our troops could not use the highway to the North, even though the strong point was by-passed," explained the 77th Division after-action report. The Japanese made excellent use of this natural bottleneck by constructing concentric rings of sturdy pillboxes, supported by a seemingly endless number of dugout-style emplacements, most of which were six to eight feet deep, furnished with sleeping quarters, and covered by trapdoors or sheet metal. Tunnels even connected some of these positions. At the heart of this defensive spiderweb stood a fortified three-story concrete building that served as a citadel of sorts. "All manmade defenses were so well concealed by foliage and camouflage that they could seldom be detected more than a few yards away," explained the historian of the 305th Infantry Regiment. "The troops manning these defenses . . . were all well equipped soldiers, cunningly skillful, fanatically disciplined, and vigorously led." Colonel Freeman, the War Department observer who actually ended up leading a special task force to assault the citadel, later assessed the Japanese fortifications as "almost impregnable positions."

Bruce threw most of his division into the fray, enveloping and cutting off Cogon with his 306th and 307th Infantry Regiments. But this hardly mattered. As long as the Japanese controlled the town and the plateau it commanded, the Americans could not move vehicles and troops north on Highway 2. He had no choice but to send two battalions from the 305th straight into the heart of the enemy defensive network, where they fought pillbox to pillbox for nearly four days and warded off an untold number of Japanese counterattacks, in hellish heat and humidity, often in hand-to-hand duels to the death. At the height of the fighting, dozens of GIs fainted from heat exhaustion. Litter teams dragged them to an aid station a few hundred yards to the rear, laid them in the shade, and splashed them with cool water retrieved from nearby artesian wells. "After resting a while they would doggedly return to the lines to continue the fight," an Army historian later wrote. Their herringbone twill uniforms were perpetually soaked with an odoriferous mixture of sweat and moldy water, causing discomfort in the day and shivering at night.

The Americans pounded the pillboxes and the citadel with suffocating sheets of artillery fire; at times the pieces were located within a couple hundred yards of the leading troops. The citadel collapsed into shards of dusty ruins but remained a potent strong point. The artillery shells proved so overwhelming that some Japanese actually fled into American lines, where they were mercilessly mowed down or, in a few fortunate cases, taken prisoner. In addition to the artillery, Bruce brought to bear every weapon he could to support the vulnerable attacking infantrymen. "Some of the expedients we used were to bring M8s and M10s [self-propelled guns] forward to fire point blank into foxholes," Bruce later commented, "to run these vehicles over foxholes, using the escape hatches to drop grenades into them, to use armored bulldozers to either cover the holes or cut off the tops, while a captain fired into the holes with a rifle." The bulldozers often buried enemy soldiers alive. Bruce wanted to use tanks for close support but he had none available. As usual, terrified teams of riflemen and flamethrower operators had to assault each fortified hole, killing the recalcitrant Japanese defenders with any weapon at their disposal, an intimate viciousness of atavistic violence unforgettable to those who experienced it. "Facing a cold, ruthless foe who is approaching with bayonet pointed squarely at one's throat does cause chills of fear to play up and down one's spine," the 305th's historian, a personal participant, later reflected. "The final uprooting fell to the lot of the foot soldiers. It is always the lot of the dogface to be in at the kill. In vicious hand-to-hand fighting, supplemented by all the fighting tools at our disposal, we combed the area and tightened the ring, relentlessly killing the defiant enemy in our path." After six hours of ferocious combat on December 14, they captured the citadel, "which was literally packed with automatic weapons and riflemen," wrote Major Marshall Becker, an assistant operations officer. In the vicinity of the building, the Americans counted 633 dead Japanese, excluding those who had been buried by the bulldozers. Still, it took another day to snuff out the last Japanese resistance at Cogon and gain full control of the crossroads. By that time, the 305th had lost 82 killed and 296 wounded.[24]

The capture of Ormoc and Cogon, in tandem with continued pressure from X Corps against the northern portion of the Japanese front, proved too much for Suzuki's forces in the Ormoc Valley and to the east in the mountains. They continued to resist stubbornly but began to crumble. The stalemate broken, Hodge's XXIV Corps, with the 77th Division in the lead, leapfrogged ahead to Valencia and then northward to link up with Sibert's X Corps on December 21, trapping and dooming all enemy soldiers to the east. The many setbacks on Leyte finally convinced Japanese senior leaders, including Imperial General Headquarters in Tokyo and Field Marshal Terauchi, to cut their losses in favor of a new all-out struggle for Luzon. The field marshal had already in mid-November quietly moved his headquarters back to Saigon.

Yamashita took no pleasure in his vindication. Through multiple fragmented messages, he sadly informed Suzuki, the remnants of whose headquarters was on the move and often out of touch, that he could expect to receive no more reinforcements and supplies. Thirty-Fifth Army was on its own, charged with the thankless task of retiring to Leyte's west coast to fight the sort of delaying action that had become so commonplace now for the Imperial Army. "I cannot keep back tears of remorse for tens of thousands of our officers and men fighting on Leyte Island," Yamashita poignantly told Suzuki. "Help guard and maintain the prosperity of the Imperial Throne through eternal resistance to the enemy, and be ready to meet your death calmly for our beloved country." Suzuki's survivors consumed what remained of their rations and began living hungrily off the land, harassed at nearly every turn by guerrillas. "They just walked along, dumb, suffering from fatigue and starvation, dragging their numb legs along," an observer from Yamashita's headquarters wrote. "They were like sleepwalkers." The survivors who made it out of the mountains remained determined to fight on, just as their orders mandated. "We commanded a view of the Ormoc plains to the east and the Camotes Sea and the Island of Cebu to the west," Major General Tomochika recalled. "In order to subsist, we cultivated the land . . . and foraged. We also conducted raids on the enemy to obtain American rations." This provender, in addition to sweet potatoes, rice, and corn taken from Filipinos, proved sufficient to maintain unit integrity and satisfactory fighting resolve, making the 35th Army a still-dangerous adversary. "No one died of starvation and some units stored supplies enough for two to three months," a 35th Army post-battle report testified.

With the linkup of the Sixth Army front and a nice foothold established on Mindoro, General MacArthur no longer much concerned himself with the condition of the remaining Japanese on Leyte. His eyes were now firmly fixed on Luzon. For weeks he had waited impatiently for Krueger to wrap up the Leyte battle. MacArthur intended for Sixth Army to lead the Luzon invasion. Every day Krueger's forces persisted in fighting for Leyte distracted from and perhaps delayed that ultimate objective. At one point, while the fighting raged inconclusively at Cogon and elsewhere, an exasperated MacArthur even privately communicated to Eichelberger, according to the latter's diary, "dissatisfaction with W[alter] and stated he might have to relieve him. Said he had held him on over-age and expected him to be a driver. He said he wasn't worried about L[eyte] but was worried about conduct . . . on future operations if actions here were indicative."

The post-Ormoc victories evaporated the SWPA commander's dour ruminations, giving way instead to an impatient optimism. He understood as well as did the Japanese that their strategic position on Leyte was hopeless. As was his wont, though, he wrongly equated strategic victory with the end of Japanese resistance. To free up Sixth Army to prepare for Luzon, he had hoped back in November to turn over the Leyte battle to Eichelberger's newly created Eighth Army. Instead, he had to wait until well into December after the Ormoc invasion broke the stalemate and ended any chance for a Japanese strategic victory on Leyte. Finally, at the stroke of midnight on December 26, he turned responsibility for Leyte over to the Eighth Army. That same day, his headquarters issued a triumphant communiqué claiming victory and the complete destruction of Japanese forces on Leyte. "The Leyte-Samar campaign can be regarded as closed except for minor mopping-up. The enemy's ground forces participating in the campaign have been practically annihilated. General Yamashita has sustained perhaps the greatest defeat in the military annals of the Japanese Army." To Krueger, whom he had only recently considered relieving, he forwarded an upbeat congratulatory message: "This closes a campaign that has had few counterparts in the destruction of the enemy's forces with a maximum conservation of our own. It has been a magnificent performance on the part of all concerned."

Once again, the trite, disrespectful term "mopping up" failed to reflect stark realities. The curtain had not really closed on the Leyte fighting. Suzuki still had about fifteen thousand holdouts who continued to resist, just as Yamashita had envisioned. No one understood this better than Eichelberger, who quickly realized that he had inherited anything but a simple battlefield cleanup. Like an energetic dog straining on a leash, the newly minted army commander throughout the late summer and fall had eagerly yearned to get back into action. "Bob is impatient at being held in reserve," Brigadier General Clovis Byers, his chief of staff and close confidant, had written to Emma on December 9. Now Eichelberger bluntly compared his problematic new Leyte mission to being handed an unwiped baby. "I will take and try to perform any job that is given to me, but I will do it with my eyes wide open," he told Emma in one letter. He circulated all over the battlefront, visiting command posts, talking with soldiers, and occasionally observing the action from the vantage point of a liaison plane.

Along with thousands of his men, he came to resent the sweeping pronunciations of victory and especially the odious term "mopping up." "What mopping up!" he scoffed privately. "The bullets went up just as fast. We got everything they [the Japanese] could give us." In his memoir, he later added, "I am a great admirer of General MacArthur as a military strategist; his plans were always fundamentally sound. But I must admit that . . . I never understood the public relations policy that either he or his immediate assistants established. It seemed to me, as it did to many of the commanders and correspondents, ill advised to announce victories when a first phase had been accomplished. Too often . . . the struggle was to go on for a long time. Often these announcements produced bitterness among combat troops, and with considerable cause. The phrase 'mopping up' had no particular appeal for a haggard, muddy sergeant . . . whose platoon had just been wiped out in western Leyte." Indeed.

The fighting in the mountains, the jungles, and the muddy valleys of western Leyte continued to rage for nearly five months and, at various times, absorbed the efforts of eight American divisions. The soldiers who were fighting and dying to snuff out Japanese resistance cared little for the grandiloquent phrases of communiqués; they knew only that their lives were always on the line, regardless of how senior commanders characterized or eulogized the battles they fought. "MacArthur's communiques are inaccurate to a disgusting degree," Lieutenant Gage Rodman, the infantry platoon leader in the 7th Division, raged in a letter to his parents. "We who were on the spot knew we were only beginning to fight when he made his ridiculous announcement that our objective was secured." By Eichelberger's estimate, he lost at least 432 soldiers killed and 1,852 wounded in operations that the 11th Airborne historian described as fought "through mud and rain, over treacherous, rain-swollen gorges, through thick wet jungle growth, over slippery, narrow, root-tangled, steep, foot trails. It was bitter, exhausting, rugged fighting—physically, the most terrible we were ever to know." Not until May 1945 did the fighting peter out. About 1,200 Japanese, including Suzuki and Tomochika, escaped by boat to Cebu and other nearby islands. Only 828 surrendered. The vast majority of Japanese soldiers perished in place. At a minimum, the Japanese lost 50,000 dead in the ground fighting for the island. The US Army's official historian placed American ground losses at 3,504 killed, 12,000 wounded, and 89 missing. The Navy lost 2,500 sailors and aviators killed and wounded in the sea battles around the island.

In the end, neither side really got what it wanted out of Leyte. The Japanese Sho plan failed miserably. The intention to fight a showdown battle to reverse the tide of the war turned instead into a pointless bloodbath that forever wrecked the Imperial Navy as an offensive force, substantially diminished Japanese aerial power, and squandered tens of thousands of fine combat soldiers who might have more productively defended Luzon. The Americans found few if any useful bases on Leyte, nor much of any purpose for the place once the war moved on to other spots. At Leyte, they succeeded only in degrading the strength of Japanese combat forces, at significant cost to their own. For posterity's sake, Leyte amounted to little more than a protracted, deadly prelude to a more decisive campaign on Luzon and elsewhere in the archipelago.[25]

Epilogue

During the height of the Leyte campaign, as the fighting raged monotonously among the island's seemingly endless maze of muddy hills, two unusual visitors turned up at General MacArthur's headquarters in the Price house at Tacloban. PFC Ralph Merisiecki of Cleveland, Ohio, and his buddy PFC Charles Feuereisen, the son of Jewish immigrants who ran a grocery store in New York City, showed up uninvited at Price house. The two men were paratroopers from the 511th Parachute Infantry Regiment, 11th Airborne Division, who had recuperated from wounds and then temporarily gone to work loading aircraft that dropped supplies to their comrades who were still fighting in western Leyte. The privates and MacArthur hailed from different worlds. The troopers had experienced vicious, no-quarters combat, monsoon rains, steep hills, thick jungle, degrading mud, and the lean privation that came from fighting in marooned pockets beyond the front lines, where they had depended upon aerial resupply just to survive. In combat, they had blithely assumed that word of their unit's exploits was general knowledge in theater, and probably back home as well. But they were dismayed—perhaps even outraged—to read no mention of the 11th Airborne in SWPA communiqués. Once in Tacloban, they boldly resolved to ask the supreme commander himself about this omission.

MacArthur's circumstances were, of course, far more comfortable and certainly safer than the frontline world of the two paratroopers, though daily Japanese air raids endangered his life with vexing frequency. The rotten conditions on Leyte and the remoteness of the distant fighting had, in effect, penned MacArthur into a kind of lonely isolation. Every day, he followed the same routine, saw most of the same people, and attempted to run the battle from the oddly imperiled luxury of Price House. When Merisiecki and Feuereisen showed up and asked to meet with MacArthur, the first inclination of the general's aides was to claim that the great man was simply too busy to see them. But he happened to overhear the exchange and overruled his tenacious gatekeepers. Lieutenant Colonel Egeberg, the physician, ushered them into the general's office. Clearly yearning for some sort of outside contact, MacArthur greeted them with genial enthusiasm. The natural excitement of meeting face-to-face with the SWPA commander did not deter the two privates from bluntly asking why their outfit did not receive more official recognition for its fine combat record. Their complaint was common among many units in SWPA, where almost all publicity focused, by design, on the commander. MacArthur fielded their questions graciously. He showed them his situation map of the entire island where he highlighted the role of the 11th Airborne and explained that he did not mention them in his dispatches because he did not want the enemy to know of the division's presence. At his request, they pointed to the location of their company. He then asked them to convey to everyone, from division commander Major General Joseph Swing downward, his deep appreciation and awareness of the vital part the 11th Airborne was playing in the Leyte fighting. "With a mixed feeling of eminence and satisfaction, and with the feeling that their mission had been most successfully accomplished, the men departed," the division historian later wrote of the cordial meeting. "They had proved to themselves that their outfit was not forgotten; they had shown, at least to themselves, that the only way to find out things was to ask the man who knows."

Feuereisen and Merisiecki might have felt better when they left Price House, but in a larger sense, their concerns about the 11th Airborne Division's anonymity could just as well have applied to the army in which they served. Relatively overshadowed by the Marine Corps and the Navy—at least in terms of contemporary press coverage and latter-year posterity— the Army in the Pacific had matured into a professionally led citizen-soldier force of singular potency, flexibility, and complexity. Moreover, the unfortunate soldiers who had become POWs early in the war and now struggled desperately just to survive the depredations of Japanese captivity would hardly have recognized the Army they still served. At Leyte and elsewhere throughout the Pacific and portions of Asia, this army of nearly one million soldiers was carrying on the workaday, and sometimes terrifying, necessities of this existential war—logistics, engineering, construction, transportation, intelligence gathering, civil affairs, guerrilla operations, communications, medical care, strategic planning, amphibious warfare, and, most arrestingly, combined-arms modern combat on a

dizzying variety of terrain. From Kwajalein to Leyte, the Army had unleashed hammer blows against the Japanese and, in the space of less than
a year, advanced across many hundreds of miles of ocean, island, and continent to the verge of Japan's doorstep. Ultimate victory now loomed as a
distinct possibility, perhaps even a probability, and yet the greatest struggles were still to come.[1]

Acknowledgments

I can never hope to assign proper credit and thanks to all of the people who made this second volume of the victory in the Pacific Series possible, most of whom I have already thanked for their contributions to the first volume, but I beg the reader's indulgence for expressing my gratitude again here. So many people assisted me, in fact, that for every one I mention here, two or three others could probably lay claim to some role, especially because my research and writing occupied the better part of a decade. For those whom I have not mentioned, usually out of consideration for brevity, I offer my deep apologies and assurances that I have greatly appreciated your assistance. The input of so many knowledgeable, helpful people does not, of course, change the fact that I am solely responsible for any errors of commission or omission.

The dedicated military archivists at the National Archives and Records Administration embody professionalism and expertise, none more so than the dean of them all, Tim Nenninger, branch chief for Modern Military Records, who was kind enough to lead me to an incredibly rich vein of primary source material during my months in residence. The same was true for the remarkable staff at the United States Military History Institute (now known as the Army Heritage and Education Center), the leading repository of Army history and one of my favorite places on earth. Shannon Schwaller expertly processed my massive list of requests and, in the process, saved me a tremendous amount of time and consternation. Steve Bye always took the lead to access whatever I needed in a timely and efficient manner. During my visit to the Hoover Institution Archives at Stanford University, Carol Leadenham helped me find a fascinating array of firsthand material from among dozens of individual papers collections. This book is much the better for her assistance. Elizabeth Dunn and the staff at the David Rubenstein Rare Book and Manuscript Library on the campus of Duke University made General Robert Eichelberger's vast collection of correspondence, dictations, reports, musings, and photographs available to me in full. There is no way to overstate the importance of the Eichleberger papers, not only in bringing the general himself to life but also the story of the war as a whole.

In spite of many bureaucratic challenges, Susan Lintelmann and Suzanne Christoff of the United States Military Academy Library helped me access the library's vast array of individual papers collections, much of it from graduates who became prisoners of the Japanese. Genoa Stanford at the Donovan Research Library, Fort Benning, Georgia, made available to me an extensive assemblage of Infantry School papers from Pacific War veterans. Laura Farley at the Wisconsin Veterans Museum in Madison provided me with a fascinating group of letters and other firsthand accounts. Chris Kolakowski, who became the director of the museum as I was finishing this book, also was kind enough to share primary source material and useful personal wisdom with me. Mary Hope, senior archivist at the Army's Office of Medical History, Fort Sam Houston, Texas, and Carlos Alvarado, her assistant, made sure I had access to a rich trove of oral histories and interviews from Army nurses who served in the Pacific. Reagan Grau at the National Pacific War Museum in Fredericksburg, Texas, took the time and trouble to give me digital versions of hundreds of original oral histories from Army and Marine veterans. The stewards of the extensive oral history archive at the University of North Texas, J. Todd Moye and Amy Hedrick, worked hard to make a vast collection of individual accounts available to me in digital format.

The almost limitless collection of letters, diaries, interviews, and other primary source material at the National World War II Museum in New Orleans is a relatively underutilized archive. Lindsay Barnes and Nathan Huegen helped me tap into this remarkable resource both on-site during my visit and at distance as well. Frank Shirer at the US Army Center of Military History (CMH) in Washington, DC, went the extra mile to compile for me in digital format much of the American and Japanese institutional history of the war, from command reports to special studies to Japanese monographs and postwar interviews as well as fascinating, overlooked theater and battle histories, allowing me to bring a vividness and immediacy to the chapters that otherwise might not have been possible. I do not know that mere words can convey my appreciation to Frank. During my visit to CMH, Siobhan Blevins Shaw kindly helped me access even more of this insider's Pacific War.

The Eisenhower Library in Abilene, Kansas, might seem like an odd place to look for revealing source material from the American war with Japan. But a great many Army veterans of the war, from generals on down, donated their fascinating papers to this library, as did many units that fought in theater. In addition, Eisenhower's letters and writings from his purgatorial days as an aide to MacArthur offer a rich portrait of the SWPA commander and his proclivities. I am grateful to Kevin Bailey and Tim Rives for making my visit to Abilene so productive. At Fort Riley, just down the road from Abilene, Bob Smith, director of the Fort Riley Cavalry Museum, was kind enough to make a remarkable, and surprisingly under-utilized, collection of 112th Cavalry Regiment material available to me during my all-too-brief visit. The mecca for all things MacArthur is, not surprisingly, the MacArthur Memorial Archives and Museum in Norfolk, Virginia. Chris Kolakowski, who was director at the time of my visit, and Jim Zobel, the archivist, set new records for cordiality and helpfulness during my extensive visit. I was absolutely blown away by the richness of the MacArthur Memorial's Pacific War collections and especially by Chris's and Jim's unique level of expertise on the Army in the war. I would like to thank Jennifer Bryan and her staff at the United States Naval Academy Special Collections Library for helping me access a diverse blend of source material that allowed me to delve deeply into naval operations and the leadership of Admirals Nimitz, Spruance, and Halsey. During my year in residence at the Naval Academy as the Leo A. Shifrin Distinguished Chair of Military History, Rick Ruth and his colleagues in the History Department warmly welcomed me as one of their own. This book is much the richer for many, many wonderful conversations with my fellow department faculty members and the persistent enthusiasm of my midshipmen.

At the Association of the United States Army, the redoubtable Roger Cirillo, the muse of all modern Army historians, was kind enough to share, over the course of some long conversations, much knowledge and many productive suggestions. My good friend Kevin Hymel, another sage on the World War II Army, conducted the photo research and shared much good advice over the many years since I first shared my vision for the series with him over dinner at a restaurant in Portland, Maine. During the course of many conversations, Robert von Maier, the savvy editor of *Global War Studies* and director of the burgeoning think tank Brecourt Academic, helped shape my focus and enhanced my understanding of the vast and diverse assortment of topics covered by this series. The National

Endowment for Humanities (NEH) awarded this project a prestigious, and much-needed, Public Scholar Grant and I am deeply appreciative. The vital support and partnership of the NEH, especially with Mark Silver and his team, made possible a level of depth and complexity to the research that I otherwise could not have attempted.

Closer to home, the staff at the State Historical Society of Missouri worked hard to provide me with individual access to a fascinating archive of several thousand letters written by servicemen and women during the war. At Missouri University of Science and Technology, where I am a faculty member, the library and interlibrary loan staffs tirelessly fulfilled my dizzying range of requests for rare and not-so-rare books, articles, and dissertations. My colleagues in the Department of History and Political Science remain a daily source of inspiration and excellence: Diana Ahmad, Andrew Behrendt, Petra DeWitt, Larry "Legend" Gragg, Patrick Huber, Tseggai Isaac, Alanna Krolikowski, Michael Meagher, Justin Pope, Jeff Schramm, Kate Sheppard, all of our distinguished emeriti and especially our outstanding department chairs, Michael Bruening and Shannon Fogg. Another thank-you—of so many over the years—goes to Robin Collier, our world-class department administrative assistant and guiding light.

I would like to thank Chris Erichsen, a talented cartographer who prepared fine maps to meet an unforgiving deadline. In my view at least, Chris's maps have done much to illuminate my prose. Many thanks go to Brent Howard, executive editor at Dutton Penguin Random House, whose keen insight into good storytelling and good scholarship sets him apart from his peers. I greatly appreciate his belief in my work and the innumerable ways he continues to improve it with his relentlessly good judgment and unfailing professional eye. Michael Congdon, my sagacious agent and friend, helped guide and shape this work, so much so that, if not for his efforts, I do not believe it would have come to fruition. I greatly appreciate his wise counsel and especially his willingness to listen to my pessimistic diatribes about the remote chances for a Cardinal championship each upcoming baseball season.

I am especially grateful to friends and family, all of whom seem inexplicably resolved to put up with me, and all of whom have helped sustain me during the long gestation process for this book: Pat O'Donnell, Mitch Yockelson, Joe Balkoski, Paul Clifford, Paul Woodadge, Sean Roarty, Michael Roarty, Mike Chopp, Steve Loher, Steve Kutheis, Steve Vincent, John Villier, Jon Krone, Professor Dave Cohen, James Gavin McManus, the late

Tom Fleming, the late Russ Buhite, Dick Hyde, Charlie Schneider, Don Patton, Chris Ketcherside, Curtis Fears, Joe Ferraro, Don Rebman, Bob Kaemmerlen, Ron Kurtz, Joe Carcagno, all of my 7th Infantry Regiment Cottonbaler buddies, my numerous friends at the National World War II Museum, and many other friends than I have space to mention.

I'm extremely blessed to be part of a loving and supportive family. On the Woody side, I am very grateful to Nancy, Charlie, Doug, Tonya, David, Angee, and my nephews and nieces for many acts of kindness and a lot of laughs over the years. Ruth and Nelson, my mother- and father-in-law, are like bonus parents. I cannot ever repay them for all their love and support, though I can certainly continue to commend Nelson for his impeccable taste in baseball teams. A special thank-you to my elder siblings, Mike and Nancy, for a lifetime of support and friendship. The same goes for my brother-in-law John Anderson. My nieces Kelly and Erin are grown women now, and far smarter and more focused than I was at their age (or, let's be honest, even at my present age!). My teenaged nephew Michael is already taller than I am—which admittedly might not be saying much—but he is making us all proud with his intelligence and athleticism. Thank you all for many moments of affection and warmth. I have been blessed with incredible and supportive parents. Michael and Mary Jane McManus have given me such a great life that I could never possibly repay them, though I do try, probably ineffectively. Perhaps a simple and sincere thank-you will suffice. As always, my wife and soul mate, Nancy, has borne the greatest cross, enduring long absences and my deep absorption with this project. Naturally to her goes my deepest and most heartfelt thanks, not just for her enduring and true love, but for indulging my lifelong passion for words on paper. . . .

John C. McManus
St. Louis, Missouri

Notes

Prologue

1. Cole Kingseed, "The Pacific War: The U.S. Army's Forgotten Theater of World War II," *Army*, April 2013, 52; Maurice Matloff, *The United States Army in World War II, The War Department: Strategic Planning for Coalition Warfare, 1943–1944* (Washington, DC: Center of Military History, U.S. Army, 1990), 397–98; Louis Morton, *The United States Army in World War II, The War in the Pacific: Strategy and Command, the First Two Years* (Washington, DC: Center of Military History, United States Army, 2000), 538; "Army Battle Casualties and Nonbattle Deaths in World War II: Final Report, 7 December 1941–31 December 1946," 8–9, at www.ibiblio.org; Pacific War Encyclopedia, at www.pwencycl.kgbudge.com.

2. Company A, 162nd Infantry Regiment, History, 1940–1944, 21, Record Group 407, Entry 427, Box 9084, Folder 341-INF-163-0; 7th Infantry Division, Historical and Biographical Notes; Participation in Flintlock Operation, February 8, 1944, Record Group 407, Entry 427, Box 6115, Folder 307-0.1, National Archives and Records Administration II (NA), College Park, MD; Joseph Cribbins, oral history, Joseph Cribbins Papers, Box 1; Major General Charles Corlett memos, January 9, 1942, December 6, 1942; unpublished memoir, 212; Anonymous Briefing, Amphibious Operations on Kwajalein, all in Charles Corlett Papers, Box 1; Lieutenant Gage Rodman, letter to parents, March 6, 1944, Gage Rodman Papers, Box 5, all at U.S. Army Military History Institute (USAMHI), Carlisle, PA; Dean Galles, oral history, no date, AFC/2001/001/76663; Gerard Radice, oral history, September 2, 2006, AFC/2001/00173953, both at Veterans History Project, Library of Congress (LOC), Washington, DC; U.S. Army Center of Military History, *U.S. Army Campaigns of World War II: The Aleutians*, pamphlet, 23; William F. McCartney, *The Jungleers: A History of the 41st Infantry Division* (Washington, DC: Infantry Journal Press, 1948), 70–71; William C. Chase, *Front Line General: The Commands of William C. Chase: An Autobiography* (Houston, TX: Pacesetter Press, 1975), 43; Sy M. Kahn, *Between Tedium and Terror: A Soldier's World War II Diary, 1943–45* (Urbana and Chicago: University of Illinois Press, 1993), ix–xv, 41; Francis Catanzaro, *With the 41st Division in the Southwest Pacific: A Foot Soldier's Story* (Bloomington and Indianapolis: Indiana University Press, 2002), 30–31; Edmund G. Love, *The Hourglass: History of the 7th Infantry Division in World War II* (Washington, DC: Infantry Journal Press, 1950), 105–112; www.first-team.us website. Another converted cavalry unit, the 112th Cavalry Regiment, had landed on December 15, 1943, at Arawe, near Cape Gloucester.

3. Office of the Provost Marshal General, Report on American Prisoners of War in the Philippines, November 19, 1945, Record Group 389, Entry 460A, Provost Marshal Records, Box 2135; Military Intelligence Division, Prisoners of War in Taiwan, Record Group 389, Entry 460A, Provost Marshal Records, Box 2122, Taiwan Prisoner of War Camp Folder; Captain John Mamerow, POW Report on Fukuoka #17, April 12, 1946,

Record Group 389, Entry 460A, Provost Marshal Records, Box 2125, Fukuoka #17 Folder; Lieutenant Colonel Harold Johnson, diary, December 10, 1943, and January 13, 1944, Record Group 407, Philippine Archives Collection, Box 135, Folder 2, all at NA; Michael Campbell, questionnaire, WWII Veterans Survey #9728; unpublished memoir, 122–24, John Olson Papers, Box 2; General Harold Johnson, senior officer oral history, January 27, 1972, Harold K. Johnson Papers, Series VI, Oral Histories, Box 201, Folder 2, all at USAMHI; Major Michael A. (Buffone) Zarate, "American Prisoners of Japan: Did Rank Have Its Privilege?" Master's Thesis, U.S. Army Command and General Staff College, 1991, 170–72, Combined Arms Research Library (CARL), Fort Leavenworth, KS; Lester I. Tenney, *My Hitch in Hell: The Bataan Death March* (Washington, DC: Potomac Books, 1995), 154–55; Lewis Sorley, *Honorable Warrior: General Harold K. Johnson and the Ethics of Command* (Lawrence: University Press of Kansas, 1998), 68–71; Jonathan M. Wainwright, *General Wainwright's Story* (Westport, CT: Greenwood Press, 1945), 219–21; Duane Schultz, *Hero of Bataan: The Story of General Jonathan M. Wainwright* (New York: St. Martin's Press, 1981), 373–75. Another copy of Johnson's POW diary can be accessed in the Louis Morton Papers, Box 7, and the Harold K. Johnson Papers, Series I, Personal Correspondence, Box 89 at USAMHI.

4. Joseph W. Stilwell, *The Stilwell Papers,* ed. Theodore H. White (New York: William Sloane Associates, 1948), 185, 273–78; Barbara W. Tuchman, *Stilwell and the American Experience in China, 1911–1945* (New York: Macmillan, 1970), 419–25; Gordon S. Seagrave, *Burma Surgeon Returns* (New York: W. W. Norton, 1946), 94; Lieutenant General Joseph Stilwell, diary, December 1943–January 1944, www.hoover.org.

5. Major General Oscar Griswold, letter to Lieutenant General Leslie McNair, March 29, 1944, Record Group 337, Entry 58A, Box 9, NA; Major General Oscar Griswold, Informal Report on Combat Operations in the New Georgia Campaign, January 18, 1944, William Howard Arnold Papers, Box 2; Major General Oscar Griswold, diary, November 24, 1943; Hugh M. Milton II, "My Most Unforgettable Character," appended at the end of the diary in Oscar Griswold Papers, Box 1, all at USAMHI; John Miller, *The United States Army in World War II, The War in the Pacific, Cartwheel: The Reduction of Rabaul* (Washington, DC: Office of the Chief of Military History, Department of the Army, 1959), 268. Griswold entry, www.findagrave.com.

6. Lieutenant General Walter Krueger, Biographical Sketch; Colonel Walter Krueger, Junior, letter to Dr. Walther Nardini, October 12, 1976; General George Decker, letter to Mr. Ben Decherd, January 21, 1961, all in Walter Krueger Papers, Box 1; Lieutenant General Walter Krueger, letter to Colonel Fay Brabson, April 30, 1943, Fay Brabson Papers, Box 6, all at USAMHI; General Walter Krueger, Responsibilities in a Joint Operation, lecture, Armed Forces Staff College, April 18, 1947, 24; General Walter Krueger, letter to Major General Orlando Ward, 1951, both in Walter Krueger Papers, Box 12; Commander R. W. MacGregor, letter to General Walter Krueger, August 31, 1964; Roy Miller, letter to Dr. William Leary, May 20, 1989, both in Walter Krueger Papers, Box 40, all at United States Military Academy Library Archives (USMA), West Point, NY; Major General Charles Willoughby, interview with Dr. D. Clayton James, July 30, 1971, Record Group 49, Box 4, D. Clayton James Collection, Douglas MacArthur Memorial Archives (DMMA), Norfolk, VA; General Arthur Collins, oral history, 1975–1976, Arthur Collins, Box 1, USAMHI; Arthur Collins, "Walter Krueger: An Infantry Great," *Infantry,* January–February 1983, 14–19; William M. Leary, ed., *We Shall Return: MacArthur's Commanders and the Defeat of Japan* (Lexington: University Press of Kentucky, 1988), 60–70; Kevin C. Holzimmer, *General Walter Krueger: Unsung Hero of the Pacific War* (Lawrence: University Press of Kansas, 2007), 1–2, 9–61, 101–103; General Walter Krueger, *From Down Under to Nippon: The Story of Sixth Army in World War II* (Washington, DC: Combat Forces Press, 1953), 29–30; Dwight

D. Eisenhower, *Crusade in Europe* (New York: Doubleday, 1948), 11; Jean Edward Smith, *Eisenhower in War and Peace* (New York: Random House, 2012), 164–65; Daniel Barbey, *MacArthur's Amphibious Navy: Seventh Amphibious Force Operations, 1943–1945* (Annapolis, MD: United States Naval Institute, 1969), 27; Stephen R. Taaffe, *MacArthur's Jungle War: The 1944 New Guinea Campaign* (Lawrence: University Press of Kansas, 1998), 36–37. Krueger was one of only two foreign-born US Army generals of his time. The other was Ben Lear, who was born in Canada.

7. Lieutenant General Robert Eichelberger, Dictations, July 6, 1955, Box 74, Robert Eichelberger Papers; Lieutenant General Robert Eichelberger, Dictations, March 25, 1955, and April 14, 1961, Box 73, Robert Eichelberger Papers; Lieutenant General Robert Eichelberger, letters to Emma Eichelberger, December 29, 31, 1943, January 7, 1944; Brigadier General Clovis Byers, letter to Emma Eichelberger, Feburary 9, 1944, Box 8, Robert Eichelberger Papers; Lieutenant General Robert Eichelberger, Memo for Mr. Ellis Skyring, The American Occupation of Rockhampton, Box 68, Robert Eichelberger Papers, all at David Rubenstein Rare Book and Manuscript Library, Duke University (DU), Durham, NC; Lieutenant General Robert Eichelberger, Memo for Emmalina, October 22, 1943, Record Group 41, Box 2, Folder 9, Robert Eichelberger Papers; Frank Britton, interview with Dr. D. Clayton James, July 28, 1971, Record Group 49, Box 1, D. Clayton James Collection; Willoughby interview, all at DMMA; Cole Kingseed, "Restoring the Fighting Spirit," *Army*, March 1996, 49–53; Robert L. Eichelberger, *Our Jungle Road to Tokyo* (New York: Viking Press, 1950), xiii–xxvi, 97–99; Jay Luvaas, ed., *Dear Miss Em: General Eichelberger's War in the Pacific, 1942–1945* (Westport, CT: Greenwood Press, 1972), xiv, 3–24; Paul Chwialkowski, *In Caesar's Shadow: The Life of General Robert Eichelberger* (Westport, CT: Greenwood Press, 1993), 1–91; John F. Shortal, *Forged by Fire: Robert L. Eichelberger and the Pacific War* (Columbia: University of South Carolina Press, 1987), 1–74; Harold Riegelman, *Caves of Biak: An American Officer's Experiences in the Southwest Pacific* (New York: Dial Press, 1955), 171–72; Taaffe, *MacArthur's Jungle War*, 83–84; Barbey, *MacArthur's Amphibious Navy*, 27; Leary, *We Shall Return*, 155–68. For more information on Eichelberger's background, his actions in the Buna campaign, and its aftermath, see the first volume of this series, *Fire and Fortitude*.

8. Brigadier General Charles Willoughby, Press Briefing, November 17, 1943, Record Group 200, Entry 19810 (A1), Richard Sutherland Papers, Box 57, NA; Brigadier General Charles Willoughby, "The Return of MacArthur," Charles Willoughby Papers, Box 2, Folder 2-3, Hoover Institution Archives (HIA), Stanford University, Palo Alto, CA; Dr. Paul Rogers, letter to Brigadier General Legrand "Pick" Diller, October 30, 1984, Record Group 46, Box 1, Folder 4, Paul Rogers Papers, DMMA; General Robert Eichelberger, Dictations, September 14, 1959, Box 73, Robert Eichelberger Papers, DU; John McCarten, "General MacArthur: Fact and Legend, *American Mercury*, January 1944, 7–18; Sidney Huff, with Joe Alex Morris, *My Fifteen Years with General MacArthur: A First-Hand Account of America's Greatest Soldier* (New York: Paperback Library, 1964), 9–11; Wilkinson is quoted in Michael Schaller, *Douglas MacArthur: Far Eastern General* (New York: Oxford University Press, 1989), 74; D. Clayton James, *The Years of MacArthur*, vol. 2, *1941–1945* (Boston: Houghton Mifflin, 1975), 369–74; Walter R. Borneman, *MacArthur at War: World War II in the Pacific* (New York: Little, Brown, 2016), 330–38; Douglas MacArthur, *Reminiscences* (New York: Da Capo, 1964), 182–84; George C. Kenney, *General Kenney Reports: A Personal History of the Pacific War* (Washington, DC: Office of Air Force History, 1987), 332–34; Paul Rogers, *The Bitter Years: MacArthur and Sutherland* (New York: Praeger, 1990), 61–62; Leary, *We Shall Return*, 1–20; Taaffe, *MacArthur's Jungle War*, 7–8; Morton, *Strategy and Command*, 538. The James biography remains the best-researched, most original and important biography of MacArthur. Also see Arthur Herman, *Douglas MacArthur:*

American Warrior (New York: Random House, 2016); William Manchester, *American Caesar: Douglas MacArthur, 1880–1964* (New York: Dell, 1978); and Frazier Hunt, *The Untold Story of Douglas MacArthur* (New York: Devin-Adair Company, 1954). For more information on MacArthur's actions during the first two years of the war, including his abortive attempt to secure the presidency of the United States, see *Fire and Fortitude*. MacArthur's personal life belies the oft-asserted myth that divorce was always fatal to the careers of World War II officers. In addition to MacArthur, two other phenomenally successful soldiers, Matthew Ridgway and James Gavin, were divorcés.

1. Flintlock

1. Admiral Chester Nimitz, letter to Professor E. B. Potter, February 26, 1957, MS-335, Box 1, Folder 1, E. B. Potter Papers; Admiral Raymond Spruance, letter to Professor E. B. Potter, December 1, 1964, MS-335, E. B. Potter Papers, Box 1, Folder 17, both at Special Collections and Archives Department, Nimitz Library, U.S. Naval Academy (USNA), Annapolis, MD; Rex Knight, "Commander's Calculated Risk," *World War II*, January 1994, 51–52; Noel Busch, "Admiral Chester Nimitz," *Life*, July 10, 1944, 82–92; Walter R. Borneman, *The Admirals: Nimitz, Halsey, Leahy, and King—The Five-Star Admirals Who Won the War at Sea* (New York: Little, Brown, 2012), 53–65, 348–52; Samuel Eliot Morison, *History of United States Naval Operations in World War II*, vol. 7: *Aleutians, Gilberts and Marshalls, June 1942–April 1944* (Boston: Little, Brown, 1951), 203–208; Robert L. Sherrod, *On to Westward: War in the Central Pacific* (New York: Duell, Sloan and Pearce, 1945), 227; Philip A. Crowl and Edmund G. Love, *United States Army in World War II, The War in the Pacific: Seizure of the Gilberts and Marshalls* (Washington, DC: Office of the Chief of Military History, Department of the Army, 1955), 168–70; Henry Shaw, Bernard Nalty, and Edwin Turnbladh, *History of United States Marine Corps Operations in World War II*, vol. 3: *Central Pacific Drive* (Washington, DC: Historical Branch, G-3 Division, Headquarters, U.S. Marine Corps, 1966), 120–22; Robert D. Heinl and John A. Crown, *The Marshalls: Increasing the Tempo* (Washington, DC: Historical Branch, G-3 Division, Headquarters, U.S. Marine Corps, 1954), 9–12; Holland M. Smith and Percy Finch, *Coral and Brass* (New York: Charles Scribner's Sons, 1949), 141–42; Norman V. Cooper, *A Fighting General: The Biography of Gen. Holland M. "Howlin' Mad" Smith* (Quantico, VA: Marine Corps Association, 1987), 137–38; Nimitz entries at www.militarymuseum.org and www.history.navy.mil and www.pacificwarmuseum.org; information on the fleet is from www.fleetorganization.com. Holland Smith claimed in his memoirs that he supported Nimitz's proposal from the beginning. But the historical record proves this to be either a falsehood or a mistaken recollection. The best single biography of Nimitz is E. B. Potter, *Nimitz* (Annapolis, MD: Naval Institute Press, 1976).

2. Colonel Syril Faine, Army Ground Forces Observer, "Operations of the 7th Infantry Division (Reinforced) in the Marshall Islands," February 24, 1944, Record Group 337, Entry 15A, Box 52, Folder 71, NA; Corlett, unpublished memoir, 211, Anonymous Briefing, both at USAMHI; Headquarters, United States Fleet, "Amphibious Operations, The Marshall Islands, January–February, 1944," CARL; Knight, "Commander's Calculated Risk," 54–55; Wesley F. Craven and James L. Cate, eds., *The Army Air Forces in World War II*, vol. 4: *The Pacific: Guadalcanal to Saipan, August 1942–July 1944* (Washington, DC: Office of Air Force History, United States Air Force, 1983), 302–310; Crowl and Love, *Seizure of the Gilberts and Marshalls*, 166–82, 193–218; Morison, *History, vol. 7: Aleutians, Gilberts and Marshalls*, 214–15, 211–24, 234–35; Shaw et al., *Central Pacific Drive*, 122–31, 136–41; Heinl and Crown, *The Marshalls: Increasing the Tempo*, 20–34.

3. Colonel S. L. A. Marshall, "Notes on Various Aspects of Operation Flintlock," Record Group 319, Entry 62, Box 4, Records of the Office of the Chief of Military History, Seizure of the Gilberts and the Marshalls; Major General Charles Corlett, Comments on Manuscript, January 18, 1948, Record Group 319, Entry 62, Box 6, Records of the Office of the Chief of Military History, Seizure of the Gilberts and the Marshalls; 7th Infantry Division, Participation in Flintlock Operation, all at NA; Major General Charles Corlett, letters to Commandant, U.S. Marine Corps, November 29, 1952, and June 14, 1953, Charles Corlett Papers, Box 1 (this box also contains another copy of his comments on manuscript); Ernest Bears, personal account, *Hourglass Newsletter*, 1993, 12; World War II Veterans Survey, Maurice H. Reeves, #4115, both at USAMHI; United States Army Forces in the Central Pacific Area (USAFICPA), Participation in the Kwajalein and Eniwetok Operations, 44, 90–94, 104–107, 131–32, 370.2, U.S. Army Center of Military History (CMH), Washington, DC; Brigadier General David Ogden, Amphibious Operations, lecture before the Engineer School, Fort Belvoir, VA, March 15, 1949, 31, Record Group 117, Box 2, Folder 1, A. M. Neilson Papers, DMMA; "Amphibious Operations, the Marshall Islands," CARL; Transport Division 4, "Action Report: Kwajalein Atoll, Marshall Islands," 1, February 4, 1944, World War II Battle Action and Operations Reports, Box 11, Folder 4, USNA; Major Clark Campbell, "The Operations of the First Battalion (Reinforced), 184th Infantry, 7th Infantry Division, in the Capture of Kwajalein Atoll, 31 January–6 February 1944 (Personal Experiences of a Battalion Operations Officer)," Advanced Infantry Officers Course, 1947–1948, The Infantry School, 6–8, Donovan Research Library (DRL), Fort Benning, GA; Major General Archibald Arnold, "Preparation for a Division Amphibious Operation," *Military Review*, May 1945, 3 (Arnold had been promoted to two-star general and division command by the time he wrote this article); Worrall Carter, *Beans, Bullets, and Black Oil: The Story of the Fleet Logistics Afloat in the Pacific During World War II* (Washington, DC: Department of the Navy, 1953), 115–26; Morison, *History, vol. 7: Aleutians, Gilberts and Marshalls*, 343–51; Crowl and Love, *Seizure of the Gilberts and Marshalls*, 187–89. Many of the intelligence photographs were fresh, almost real-time images, taken only a few days before the invasion.
4. Captain James Doyle, USN, Oral History, March 30, 1944, Record Group 38, Entry P11, Box 8, Records of the Chief of Naval Operations, World War II Oral Histories and Interviews, 1942–1945, 3; Colonel S. L. A. Marshall, letter to Bob and comments on manuscript, January 7, 1948, Record Group 319, Entry 62, Box 6, Records of the Office of the Chief of Military History, Seizure of the Gilberts and the Marshalls; 7th Infantry Division, Participation in Flintlock Operation; Corlett comments on manuscript, all at NA; "Amphibious Operations Marshall Islands," CARL; Joint Expeditionary Force, Task Force 51, "Report of Amphibious Operations for the Capture of the Marshall Islands," February 25, 1944, MS-416, World War II Battle Action and Operations Reports, Box 13, Folder 4; Transport Division 4, Action Report: Kwajalein, both at USNA; Bears, personal account, *Hourglass Newsletter*, 12; Anonymous Briefing; Hughes, unpublished memoir, 4–5, all at USAMHI; George Eddy, "Planning for Kwajalein," *Army*, July 1996, 50; S. L. A. Marshall, *Island Victory: The Battle for Kwajalein Atoll* (Lincoln: University of Nebraska Press, 2001), 7–19; S. L. A. Marshall, *Bringing Up the Rear: A Memoir*, ed. Cate Marshall (Novato, CA: Presidio Press, 1979), 78–79; Love, *The Hourglass*, 113–20; Crowl and Love, *Seizure of the Gilberts and Marshalls*, 219–32; Morison, *History, vol. 7: Aleutians, Gilberts and Marshalls*, 253–61.
5. Lieutenant Colonel S. L. A. Marshall, Gilberts and Marshalls Campaign, Invasion of Porcelain (Kwajalein) Island, notes, 3–4, Record Group 319, Entry 62, Box 4, Records of the Office of the Chief of Military History, Seizure of the Gilberts and the Marshalls (the planners code-named Kwajalein Porcelain Island); 7th Infantry Division,

Participation in Flintlock Operation, both at NA; Sergeant T. S. Blish, "The 708th Amphibian Tank Battalion and Its Part in the Kwajalein Campaign"; Lieutenant Paul Leach, "Tanks on Kwajalein Atoll," both at 314.7, CMH; Joint Expeditionary Force, Task Force 51, "Capture of the Marshall Islands," 25, USNA; Sgt. Merle Miller, "Marshalls Massacre," *Yank*, March 31, 1944, 10; Marshall, *Island Victory*, 20–21; Morison, *History, vol. 7: Aleutians, Gilberts and Marshalls*, 89–90, 260–62; Crowl and Love, *Seizure of the Gilberts and Marshalls*, 188–89, 232–37; Love, *The Hourglass*, 120–27.

6. Allied Translator and Interpreter Section (ATIS), Defects Arising from the Doctrine of "Spiritual Superiority" as Factors in Japanese Military Psychology, Research Report, October 10, 1945, 10, quoting from ATIS Bulletin, No. 882, 7, Record Group 165, Entry 79, Box 339, Report #76; Marshall, Invasion of Kwajalein Notes, 5–8, 30, 41–47, and Marshall notes on Engineers, all at NA; Leach, "Tanks on Kwajalein Atoll," CMH; Love, *The Hourglass*, 123–35; Crowl and Love, *Seizure of the Gilberts and Marshalls*, 163, 243–47; Marshall, *Island Victory*, 20–34, 42–51; "The Flamethrower in the Pacific," 554–55, at www.history/army.mil.

7. Major General Archibald Arnold, letter to Lieutenant General Leslie McNair, March 20, 1944, Record Group 337, Entry 58A, Box 9; Marshall, Invasion of Kwajalein Notes, 31; Faine, "Operations of the 7th Infantry Division in the Marshall Islands," 9, all at NA; Hughes, unpublished memoir, 6, USAMHI; Task Group 58.1, "Action Against the Maloelap and Kwajalein Atolls," March 1, 1944, MS-416, World War II Battle and Operations Reports, Box 13, Folder 6, USNA; Major General A. V. Arnold, "Kwajalein Atoll—An Interim Report," *Field Artillery Journal*, September 1944, 595–96; Crowl and Love, *Seizure of the Gilberts and Marshalls*, 189–90, 249–51.

8. The Infantry School, "Infantry-Engineer Team at Kwajalein, Part Nine," 36–41, Dwight D. Eisenhower Library (EL), Abilene, KS; War Department, Military Intelligence Service, "Soldier's Guide to the Japanese Army," November 15, 1944, 11, MS1427, Box 7, Folder 7, Center for the Study of War and Society, Special Collections, University of Tennessee–Knoxville (SCUTK); Combat Lessons, Number 9: Rank and File in Combat, 41, CARL; Leach, "Tanks on Kwajalein Atoll," CMH; Marshall, Invasion of Kwajalein Notes, 32–34, G2 Notes, 4–5, NA; Campbell, "Operations of the 1st Battalion, 184th Infantry," 17–18, 26, DRL; Corlett, unpublished memoir, 215–17, USAMHI; William Chickering, "Mop-Up on Kwajalein," *Time*, February 21, 1944; Richard Wilcox, "Kwajalein," *Life*, February 21, 1944; Sgt. Fred Baxter, "Infantrymen Who Fought in Makin Battle Summarize the Lessons They Learned," *Yank*, February 11, 1944, 1; Marshall, *Island Victory*, 47–51; Crowl and Love, *Seizure of the Gilberts and Marshalls*, 183–84.

9. Lieutenant Colonel S. L. A. Marshall, 17th Infantry in the Burton and Clifton Invasions, Record Group 319, Entry 62, Box 4, Records of the Office of the Chief of Military History, Seizure of the Gilberts and the Marshalls; Captain Franklin Sherman III, Oral History, June 2, 1944, Record Group 112, Entry 302, Surgeon General, Inspections Branch, Box 219, Interview Number 74; 106th Infantry Regiment, Comments on the Eniwetok Operation, May 31, 1944, Record Group 407, Entry 427, Box 7316, Folder 327-INF-106-0.3.0; Marshall G2 notes, all at NA; Statistics of the Pacific Campaigns, OPRST 050; Army Ground Forces, Battle Casualties: A Study, September 25, 1946, OPRST Pacific 704; USAFICPA, Participation in the Kwajalein and Eniwetok Operations, 139–40, all at CMH; Dean Galles, interview with Christin Seifert, August 12, 2007, AFC/2001/001/76663, LOC; Administrative History of Medical Activities in the Middle Pacific, Office of the Surgeon, the Marshalls Campaign, U.S. Army Forces Middle Pacific, Office of the Surgeon Collection, Box 1, Block 18b; Hughes, unpublished memoir, 7; Corlett, unpublished memoir, 219–20, all at USAMHI; Miller, "Marshalls Massacre," *Yank*, 10–11; S. L. A. Marshall, *Battle at Best* (New York: Jove Books,

1963), 173–200; Alvin P. Stauffer, *The United States Army in World War II, The Quar-
termaster Corps: Operations in the War against Japan* (Washington, DC: Center of
Military History, United States Army, 2004), 254; Mary Ellen Condon-Rall and Albert
E. Cowdrey, *United States Army in World War II, The Medical Department: Medical
Service in the War Against Japan* (Washington, DC: Center of Military History,
United States Army, 1998), 227–33; Marshall, *Bringing Up the Rear*, 77; Marshall, *Island Victory*, 69–103; Shaw et al., *Central Pacific Drive*, 179–80, 636; Morison, *History,
vol. 7: Aleutians, Gilberts and Marshalls*, 278, 304; Love, *The Hourglass*, 164–94; Crowl
and Love, *Seizure of the Gilberts and Marshalls*, 283–301, 364–65.

10. Major General Charles Corlett, letter to Major General Orlando Ward, February 18,
1952, Record Group 319, Entry 62, Box 6, Records of the Office of the Chief of Military
History, Seizure of the Gilberts and the Marshalls, NA; Lieutenant Colonel S. L. A.
Marshall, Conversations with Division Commander, Memo, June 12, 1944, 2-3.7 BJ,
CMH; "Holland Smith: Old Man of the Atolls," *Time*, February 21, 1944; Holland
Smith entry in Pacific War Online Encyclopedia at www.pwencycl.kgbudge.com;
Harry Gailey, *Howlin' Mad vs the Army: Conflict in Command, Saipan 1944* (Novato,
CA: Presidio Press, 1986), 86–101; Cooper, *A Fighting General*, 139–45; Smith and
Finch, *Coral and Brass*, 146–51; Sherrod, *On to Westward*, 256–57; Morison, *History,
vol. 7: Aleutians, Gilberts and Marshalls*, 256–57; Marshall, *Bringing Up the Rear*, 74–
78. Cooper's Holland Smith biography was originally a 1974 dissertation at the University of Alabama. The tone of Smith's postwar memoir was critical, self-aggrandizing,
and vituperative, stirring up much postbellum animosity among both his Army and
Navy colleagues. For a more complete account of his actions during the Gilbert campaign and his tension with Ralph Smith, see the first volume in this series, *Fire and
Fortitude*.

11. Historical Review, Statistical and Evacuation Section, Surgeon's Office, Central Pacific Base Command, Vertical Files, Box 20, Folder 311; Corlett, unpublished memoir,
222, both at USAMHI; Army Ground Forces, Battle Casualties Study, CMH; Marshall, *Island Victory*, 108–114; Marshall, *Bringing Up the Rear*, 80–81.

2. Acceleration

1. Major General Richard Marshall, interview with Dr. D. Clayton James, July 27, 1971,
Record Group 49, Box 3; Brigadier General Bonner Fellers, interview with Dr. D.
Clayton James, June 26, 1971, Record Group 49, Box 2; General George Kenney, inter-
view with Dr. D. Clayton James, July 16, 1971, Record Group 49, Box 3, all in D. Clay-
ton James Collection; Major General George Kenney, diary entries, January
1–February 23, 1944, Record Group 54, Box 1, George Kenney Papers, all at DMMA;
Miller, *Cartwheel*, 316–21; William Frierson, *The Admiralties: Operations of the First
Cavalry Division, 29 February–18 May, 1944* (Washington, DC: Center of Military
History, United States Army, 1990), 4–7; MacArthur, *Reminiscences*, 157; Kenney, *General Kenney Reports*, xi–xviii, 357–60; Leary, *We Shall Return*, 15; Craven and Cate,
Army Air Forces in World War II, vol. 4, 557–58; Taaffe, *MacArthur's Jungle War*,
56–58; Borneman, *MacArthur at War*, 280; James, *Years of MacArthur*, vol. 2, 379–80;
Manchester, *American Caesar*, 346–51.

2. Brigadier General Charles Willoughby, biographical information, circa 1950, Charles
Willoughby Papers, Box 1, Folder 1-1, HIA; Brigadier General Charles Willoughby,
interviews with Dr. D. Clayton James, August 28, 1967, and July 30, 1971, Record
Group 49, Box 4; Rear Admiral Raymond Tarbuck, interview with Dr. D. Clayton
James, September 4, 1971, Record Group 49, Box 4; Dr. Roger Egeberg, interview with
Dr. D. Clayton James, June 30, 1971, Record Group 49, Box 2; Fellers, Kenney inter-
views, all in D. Clayton James Collection, DMMA; Edward J. Drea, *MacArthur's*

ULTRA: Codebreaking and the War Against Japan, 1942–1945 (Lawrence: University Press of Kansas, 1992), 16–18, 101–103; Roger O. Egeberg, *The General: MacArthur and the Man He Called "Doc"* (Washington, DC: Oak Mountain Press, 1993), 41; Miller, *Cartwheel*, 320–21; Taaffe, *MacArthur's Jungle War*, 58.

3. General Walter Krueger, letter to Colonel Frank Kowalski, March 27, 1957, Walter Krueger Papers, Box 13, USMA; Lt. Col. Gibson Niles, "The Operations of the Alamo Scouts (Sixth U.S. Army Special Reconnaissance Unit) . . . Advanced Reconnaissance of Los Negros Island, 27–28 February 44, Prior to Landing by the First Cavalry Division in the Admiralty Islands," Advanced Infantry Officers Course, 1947–1948, 4–12, DRL; Lance Zedric, "Prelude to Victory: The Alamo Scouts," *Army*, July 1994, 48–50; "Walter O. Pierce, Surprise Visit," *Recon*, February/March 2018, 9; Lieutenant Colonel Frank Sackton, "Southwest Pacific Alamo Scouts," *Armored Cavalry Journal*, January /February 1947, 55; Larry Alexander, *Shadows in the Jungle: The Alamo Scouts Behind Japanese Lines in World War II* (New York: NAL Caliber, 2009), 56–83; Frierson, *The Admiralties*, 17; Miller, *Cartwheel*, 322; Taaffe, *MacArthur's Jungle War*, 59–60; Holzimmer, *General Walter Krueger*, 134–35; Krueger, *From Down Under to Nippon*, 29–30, 49; Alamo Scouts entry in Pacific War Encyclopedia, at www.pwen cycl.kgbudge.com; other pertinent information at www.alamoscouts.com. Though Krueger's command at this time was officially called the Alamo Force, it would soon transition to its ultimate identity as Sixth Army. For clarity of narrative throughout this book—and to avoid confusion—I refer to it as Sixth Army.

4. Colonel Marion Carson, "Defense of Beachhead, Los Negros Island," 3, Record Group 337, Entry 15A, Box 57, Folder 178; Headquarters Alamo Force/Sixth Army, Conference Report, Manus Island Operation, Reconnaissance in Force, February 25, 1944, Record Group 338, Entry P50487, Box 3, Folder 7; Major Julio Chiaramonte, comments on manuscript, 1953, Record Group 319, Entry 49, Box 3, Records of the Office of the Chief of Military History, Cartwheel: The Reduction of Rabaul, all at NA; Kenney diary, February 28, 1944, DMMA; Barbey, *MacArthur's Amphibious Navy*, 150–53; Leary, *We Shall Return*, 208–224; Chase, *Front Line General*, 38–50; Drea, *MacArthur's ULTRA*, 102–103; Miller, *Cartwheel*, 322–25; Frierson, *The Admiralties*, 17–20; Kenney, *General Kenney Reports*, 360–61; Holzimmer, *General Walter Krueger*, 135–37; Krueger, *From Down Under to Nippon*, 48–49; Taaffe, *MacArthur's Jungle War*, 60; www.first-team.us. Sources differ as to whether McGowen got to Chase's ship by boat or plane. I personally think the former is more likely.

5. General Clyde Eddleman, oral history, circa 1975, Clyde Eddleman Papers, Box 2, USAMHI; Gaetano Faillace, interview with Dr. D. Clayton James, Record Group 49, Box 2, D. Clayton James Collection; Dr. Roger Egeberg, oral history, September 23, 1982, Record Group 32, Oral History #26; Kenney diary, February 26, 1944, all at DMMA; Noel Busch, "MacArthur and His Theater," *Life*, May 8, 1944; Douglas MacArthur, *Reports of General MacArthur*, vol. 1: *The Campaigns of MacArthur in the Pacific* (Washington, DC: Center of Military History, 1966, 1994), 136–38; Hunt, *Untold Story of Douglas MacArthur*, 318; Borneman, *MacArthur at War*, 347–52; Taaffe, *MacArthur's Jungle War*, 59; Manchester, *American Caesar*, 393–95; James, *Years of MacArthur*, vol. 2, 382–83; Krueger, *From Down Under to Nippon*, 49; Egeberg, *The General*, 24–25. Faillace was MacArthur's main photographer and he accompanied him on this operation.

6. Carson, "Defense of Beachhead," 2–4, NA; Task Unit 76.1.3, Destroyer Squadron 5, "Landing Operations on Los Negros Island, 29 February, 1944," March 7, 1944, MS-416, World War II Battle and Operations Reports, Box 14, Folder 2, USNA; "1st Cavalry Division in the Admiralty Islands," *Cavalry Journal*, November–December 1944, 3–4; Charles Rawlings, "They Paved Their Way with Japs," *Saturday Evening Post*, October 7, 1944, 14–15, 42–43; Corporal Bill Alcine, "Landing on Los Negros," *Yank*, April 14,

1944, 2–3; Frierson, *The Admiralties*, 22–31; Miller, *Cartwheel*, 325–28; Chase, *Front Line General*, 48–51; Taaffe, *MacArthur's Jungle War*, 62–63.

7. Chiaramonte, comments on manuscript, NA; Faillace, Egeberg, oral histories, DMMA; Cribbins oral history, USAMHI; Busch, "MacArthur and His Theater," *Life*, 100–102; Rawlings, "They Paved Their Way with Japs," *Saturday Evening Post*, 44; Taaffe, *MacArthur's Jungle War*, 64; Egeberg, *The General*, 26–36; Chase, *Front Line General*, 51–52; James, *Years of MacArthur*, vol. 2, 384–86; Manchester, *American Caesar*, 395–97; Borneman, *MacArthur at War*, 352–54. McGowen and his Alamo Scout team resented media reports of Lieutenant Henshaw as the first man ashore at Los Negros. After all, they had landed there a full two days earlier.

8. Chiaramonte, comments on manuscript; Carson, "Defense of Beachhead," 4–5, 14, both at NA; Mr. Sam Harris, interview with Ms. Virginia Roberts, September 29, 2002, Nimitz Education and Research Center, National Museum of the Pacific War (NMPW), Fredericksburg, TX; Sergeant Lawrence Baldus, diary, February 29, 1944, Record Group 103, Box 1, Folder 5, Lawrence R. Baldus Papers, DMMA; Rawlings, "They Paved Their Way with Japs," *Saturday Evening Post*; Alcine, "Landing on Los Negros," *Yank*, 3–4; Frierson, *The Admiralties*, 32–36, 53–55; Miller, *Cartwheel*, 333–36; Chase, *Front Line General*, 52–53. Harris was wounded in the battle and had to be evacuated.

9. Carson, "Defense of Beachhead," 8–12, NA; Combat Lessons Number 5, Rank and File in Combat, 73–74, CARL; "McGill Loses Life as He Battles 200 Drink-Crazed Japs, Slays 105," MS1608, Box 13, Folder 19, SCUTK; Baldus diary, March 2, 1944, DMMA; Rawlings, "They Paved the Way with Japs," *Saturday Evening Post*; Alcine, "Los Negros Landing," *Yank*, 4; Edward F. Murphy, *Heroes of WWII* (New York: Ballantine Books, 1990), 175; Miller, *Cartwheel*, 333–37; Frierson, *The Admiralties*, 43–50, 55–57; Krueger, *From Down Under to Nippon*, 55; Drea, *MacArthur's ULTRA*, 104. Army Air Forces sources claim that their planes dropped barbed wire to Chase, but all ground unit sources unanimously say they never had any barbed wire. McGill's Medal of Honor citation claims that his body was surrounded by 105 enemy corpses that he killed personally. Given the paucity of firepower available to him, I find this highly unlikely. Henshaw, in an interview with Rawlings, claimed that he actually saw a depleted McGill leave the front line and retreat after hours of desperate fighting only to be killed by friendly machine-gun fire. If true, this would undoubtedly be a controversial matter. After the passage of so many decades and the death of almost everyone involved, Henshaw's claims can probably never be proven. Henshaw actually drowned a couple of weeks after the battle while trying to save the lives of several troopers who had blundered into deep water. The McGill family was originally from Knoxville, Tennessee. During my days as a PhD student at the University of Tennessee, I came to know McGill's brother Wesley, a Navy veteran of World War II, quite well.

10. 1st Cavalry Division, Techniques Developed in Mopping Up Operation, October 26, 1944, Record Group 337, Entry 15A, Box 60, Folder 269; Major General Innis Swift, letter to Brigadier General Edwin Patrick, April 11, 1944, and Anonymous Imperial Japanese Army soldier, diary, March 22, 23, 30, 1944, in Record Group 338, Entry PP50487, Box 2, Folder 2; Carson, "Defense of Beachhead," 17–18; Chiaramonte, comments on manuscript, all at NA; Cribbins oral history, USAMHI; Major General Innis Swift, letter to Lieutenant General Walter Krueger, March 8, 1944, Walter Krueger Papers, Box 8, USMA; 7th Cavalry Regiment, Historical Report, Admiralty Islands Campaign, 7th Cavalry Regiment Records, Box 498; 8th Cavalry Regiment, History of the Admiralty Islands Campaign and Lieutenant William Koski, "Combat Patrols on Number Four Road, Manus Island," 8th Cavalry Regiment Records, Box 504; 12th Cavalry Regiment, History of the Admiralty Islands Campaign, 12th Cavalry

Regiment Records, Box 505, all at EL; "1st Cavalry Division in the Admiralty Islands, Part II," *Cavalry Journal*, January/February 1945; "1st Cavalry Division in the Admiralty Islands, Part III," *Cavalry Journal*, March/April 1945; Miller, *Cartwheel*, 340–48; Frierson, *The Admiralties*, 58–143; Chase, *Front Line General*, 60; Krueger, *From Down Under to Nippon*, 53; Holzimmer, *General Walter Krueger*, 140. It is important to note that Chase thought highly of MacArthur, but not necessarily his staff and their planning process. Another similarity with Vietnam can be found in the American tendency to overestimate enemy deaths. The kill ratios recorded in many of the records cited here defy rational belief.

11. Marshall interview, DMMA; MacArthur, *Reports*, vol. 1: *Campaigns in the Pacific*, 139–43; Miller, *Cartwheel*, 348–49; Frierson, *The Admiralties*, 144–49; MacArthur, *Reminiscences*, 187–88; Craven and Cate, *The Army Air Forces in World War II*, vol. 4, 568–74; Drea, *MacArthur's ULTRA*, 104–105; Taaffe, *MacArthur's Jungle War*, 74–76; Krueger, *From Down Under to Nippon*, 53–55; Borneman, *MacArthur at War*, 354–55; James, *Years of MacArthur*, vol. 2, 386–87.

3. Consolidation

1. 3rd Marine Division, After Action Report, Bougainville, November–December 1943, Record Group 127, Box 6, World War II Area Geographic Files, Folder A5-2; XIV Corps Report of Operations on Bougainville Island, 15 December 1943–30 April 1944, Record Group 407, Entry 427, Box 4014, Folder 214-0.3; 37th Infantry Division, AAR, Bougainville Campaign, 1 November 1943–31 March 1944, Record Group 407, Entry 427, Box 8602, Folder 337-0.3; United States Army Forces in the South Pacific Area, Headquarters, Service of Supply, Final History, Service Command, Record Group 494, Entry 398, U.S. Army Forces, Middle Pacific, Box 69, Folder 1; Colonel William Long, letter to Major General A. C. Smith, March 24, 1954, Record Group 319, Entry 49, Box 3, Records of the Office of the Chief of Military History, Cartwheel, the Reduction of Rabaul; Griswold letter to McNair, March 29, 1944, all at NA; Corporal Stanley Jones and Corporal Francis Saunders, "The Bougainville Campaign," chapters 1, 4, and 5, particularly 199–201, 243–79, 8-5.7 BD cyl; Major General Oscar Griswold, "Bougainville: An Experience in Jungle Warfare," 1–7, 17–22, 38–47, 8-5.7 BE, both at CMH; Edward Sears, unpublished memoir, 1, MS1881, Box 24, Folder 4, SCUTK; Captain John Guenther, "The Second Battle of Bougainville," *Infantry Journal*, February 1945, 8–10; Captain John Guenther, "Artillery in the Bougainville Campaign," *Field Artillery Journal*, June 1945, 330–31; Lieutenant Howard Haines, "Three Months on Bougainville," *Field Artillery Journal*, July 1944, 444–45; Lieutenant Colonel William Shimonek, "Shop Talk from Bougainville," *Chemical Warfare*, June/July 1944, no pagination; Command and General Staff School, "Medical Problems in Jungle Warfare and the Pacific Area," 8; Captain Francis D. Cronin, *Under the Southern Cross: The Saga of the Americal Division* (Washington, DC: Combat Forces Press, 1951), 129–39; Harry A. Gailey, *Bougainville 1943–1945: The Forgotten Campaign* (Lexington: University Press of Kentucky, 1991), 120–31, Ellis is quoted on page 129; Miller, *Cartwheel*, 266–71, 351–55; Craven and Cate, *The Army Air Forces in World War II*, vol. 4, 247–67. For a thorough account of the Marine seizure of the beachhead at Bougainville, see pages 207–269 of Henry Shaw and Douglas Kane, *History of U.S. Marine Corps Operations in World War II*, vol. 2: *Isolation of Rabaul* (Washington, DC: Historical Branch, G3 Division, Headquarters, U.S. Marine Corps, 1963). For an excellent treatment of the invasion and subsequent naval battles, see Samuel Eliot Morison, *History of United States Naval Operations in World War II*, vol. 6: *Breaking the Bismarcks Barrier, 22 July 1942–1 May 1944* (Boston: Little, Brown, 1968), 279–322.

2. Allied Translator and Interpreter Section, #1502, Detailed Instructions on Participation in TA Operation, Record Group 165, Entry 79, Box 285, ADVATIS, Current

Translations #157; Americal Division, AAR, 21 December 1943–29 April 1944, Record Group 407, Entry 427, Box 4802, Folder 300-0.3; XIV Corps AAR; 37th Division AAR, all at NA; Lieutenant General Haruyoshi Hyakutake, Report to the Throne: War Situation in Southeast Area, no date, located in Translation of Japanese Documents, Volume IV, 8-5.1 AD1 V4, CY1; Griswold, "Experience in Jungle Warfare," 50–65, 70–78; Jones and Saunders, "The Bougainville Campaign," 290–302, the Japanese sergeant is quoted on page 302, all at CMH; Cletus Schwab, memoir, no pagination, World War II Veterans Survey, no number; Major General William "Duke" Arnold, speech, no date, 8, William Howard Arnold Papers, Box 1, both at USAMHI; Yukio Kawamoto, Interview with Mr. Terry Shima, no date, AFC/2001/001/07420, LOC; Guenther, "Second Battle of Bougainville," *Infantry Journal*, 10; John R. Walker, *Bracketing the Enemy: Forward Observers in World War II* (Norman: University of Oklahoma Press, 2013), 77–79; Miller, *Cartwheel*, 356–58; Gailey, *Bougainville*, 137–48; Morison, *History, vol. 6: Breaking the Bismarcks Barrier*, 428; Cronin, *Under the Southern Cross*, 141–42. For more information on Hyakutake's difficult experiences on New Guinea and Guadalcanal, see *Fire and Fortitude*, the first book in this series.

3. Americal Division, Report of Operations, 21 December 1943–29 April 1944, Record Group 407, Entry 427, Box 4802, Folder 300-0.3; Lieutenant Kermit Holt, Oral History, October 17, 1944, Record Group 38, Entry P11, Box 13, Records of the Chief of Naval Operations, World War II Oral Histories and Interviews, 1942–1945; XIV Corps Report of Operations; 37th Infantry Division, AAR, all at NA; Jones and Saunders, "Bougainville Campaign," 316–20, CMH; Stanley Frankel, "'Hell' 700: The Key to the South Pacific," *Infantry*, May–June 1994, 26; Stanley Frankel, "Battle of Bougainville: Hell on Hill 700," *World War II*, September 1997, 43–44; Guenther, "Second Battle of Bougainville," *Infantry Journal*, February 1945, 10; Charles H. Walker, *Combat Officer: A Memoir of War in the South Pacific* (New York: Ballantine Books, 2004), 91–92; John Walker, *Bracketing the Enemy*, 80; Cronin, *Under the Southern Cross*, 148; Gailey, *Bougainville*, 149–50; Miller, *Cartwheel*, 358–59.

4. Sergeant E. R. Birnberg, "History of Bougainville," Record Group 407, Entry 427, Box 8741, Folder 337-INF-145-0.1; Major General Oscar Griswold, "Combined Infantry-Tank Operations in the Jungle," 9, Record Group 337, Entry 15A, Box 53, Folder 98; XIV Corps Report of Operations; 37th Infantry Division, AAR; Griswold letter to McNair, all at NA; Major General Oscar Griswold, Extracts from Overseas Reports, D793.52.G881 du, DRS; Griswold, "Experience in Jungle Warfare," 87–94; Jones and Saunders, "Bougainville Campaign," 321–25, both at CMH; Frankel, "'Hell' 700," *Infantry*, May–June 1994, 27–30; Guenther, "Artillery in Bougainville Campaign," *Field Artillery Journal*, June 1945, 333; John Kennedy Ohl, *Minuteman: The Military Career of General Robert S. Beightler* (Boulder, CO: Lynne Rienner Publishers, 2001), 137; Gailey, *Bougainville*, 150–55, 168; Miller, *Cartwheel*, 359–64.

5. 182nd Infantry Regiment, History, January–March 1944, Record Group 407, Entry 427, Box 4985, Folder 300-INF-182-0.2, and Report of Operations, 21 December 1943–29 April 1944, Record Group 407, Entry 427, Box 4986, Folder 300-INF-182-0.3; 129th Infantry Regiment, Medical Report, Bougainville, Record Group 407, Entry 427, Box 337-INF-129-MD-0.3; Lieutenant Sherman Davis, Medical Department Activities in the Bougainville Campaign, 6, Record Group 494, Entry 398, U.S. Army Forces, Middle Pacific, Box 79, Folder 10; Major Martin Taliak, 8th General Hospital, Surgery, South Pacific Area, 21–23, Record Group 494, Entry 398, U.S. Army Forces, Middle Pacific, Box 80, Folder 5; Major John Aldes, Orthopedic Surgery South Pacific Area, Record Group 112, Entry 31, Surgeon General, Administrative Records, Box 239; Lieutenant Colonel Richard Shackelford, Oral History, Record Group 112, Entry 302, Surgeon General, Inspections Branch, Box 219, Interview 75; Long letter to Smith, all at NA; Arnold speech, 13, USAMHI; Jones and Saunders, "Bougainville Campaign,"

371–405; Griswold, "Experience in Jungle Warfare," 96–136, both at CMH; William Trubiano, interview with Mr. Richard Misenhimer, December 30, 2003, NPMW; Morris Weiner, interview with Mr. David Winer, November 11, 2013, AFC/2001/001/91318, LOC; Combat Lessons Number 9: Rank and File in Combat, 29–30, CARL; Captain Leonard Savitt, "With the Americal Division at Bougainville," *Military Surgeon*, October 1944, 259–60; Cronin, *Under the Southern Cross*, 152–67; Gailey, *Bougainville*, 156–61; Miller, *Cartwheel*, 364–72. Trubiano was a member of a carrying party and shared the anecdote about the locals who would not work under fire.

6. 129th Infantry Regiment, Narrative History, Bougainville, Record Group 407, Entry 427, Box 8729, Folder 337-INF-129-0.1; Birnberg, "History of Bougainville"; Long letter to Smith; Griswold letter to McNair; XIV Corps Report of Operations; Americal Division, AAR; 37th Infantry Division, AAR, all at NA; Griswold, "Experience in Jungle Warfare," 129–39, CMH; Keiji Fujii, interview with Mr. James Tanabe, December 4, 2003, AFC/2001/001/18090, LOC; Charles Henne, "The Bougainville Experience," 65–69, xix; Yukio Kawamoto, veterans questionnaire, World War II Veterans Survey #5465; the captured diary with the automatic artillery comment is mentioned in Fernando Vera, unpublished memoir, 12; World War II Veterans Survey #8629, all at USAMHI; Frankel, "'Hell' 700," *Infantry*, May–June 1994, 31–32; Guenther, "Second Battle of Bougainville," *Infantry Journal*, February 1945, 13–15; Guenther, "Artillery in the Bougainville Campaign," *Field Artillery Journal*, June 1945, 334; Eric Bergerud, *Touched with Fire: The Land War in the South Pacific* (New York: Penguin Books, 1996), 518–19; Morison, *History, vol. 6: Breaking the Bismarcks Barrier*, 429–30; Gailey, *Bougainville*, 165–66; Miller, *Cartwheel*, 375–78. Fujii was a Japanese-American typist who typed up the translation of the diary that provided so much valuable intelligence. An African-American coast artillery battalion participated in the effective bombardment, thus becoming the first black combat support unit to engage the Japanese in the South Pacific.

7. POW Interrogation #100118 in ATIS Significant Items 1–75, Record Group 496, Entry 134, Box 651, Records of General Headquarters, SWPA/USAFP, ATIS Administrative Records, 1942–1945; Pacific Warfare Board Report, Battle Experiences Against the Japanese, Number 17, July 10, 1945, Record Group 337, Entry 15A, Box 70, Folder 484; Tech 4 Robert Webb, Report on Scouting, no date, Record Group 407, Entry 427, Box 4986, Folder 300-INF-182-0.3.0; Americal Division, Lessons Learned from Bougainville Operations, April 15, 1944, Record Group 407, Entry 427, Box 4805, Folder 300-4; Company C, 182nd Infantry Regiment, Mom Hill Operations, August 26, 1944, Record Group 407, Entry 427, Box 4997, Folder 300-INF-182-7.03; Company L, 182nd Infantry Regiment, AAR, October 20, 1944, Record Group 407, Entry 427, Box 4997, Folder 300-INF-7.03; 37th Infantry Division, Lessons Learned from Bougainville Campaign, Record Group 407, Entry 427, Box 8602, Folder 337-0.3; 93rd Infantry Division, Summary of Operations in World War II, March 1946, Record Group 497, Entry 427, Box 11329, Folder 393-0.1, all at NA; Arthur Johnson, interview with Eugene Green, March 25, 2005, AFC/2001/001/34912, LOC; Jones and Saunders, "Bougainville Campaign," 405–444, CMH; Captain Jack Tucker, "Bougainville Pay-Off," *Infantry Journal*, March 1945, 15–16; Gailey, *Bougainville*, 184–85, 190–93; Cronin, *Under the Southern Cross*, 168–91. Bougainville's isolation was further solidified by Halsey's decisive seizure in February–March of the adjacent Green Islands. A New Zealand battalion did most of the fighting.

8. Soldier Attitude Surveys, Negro Study, 1942–1943, Record Group 330, Entry 92, Records of the Secretary of Defense, Box 4, S32; General George Marshall to Lieutenant General Millard Harmon, March 18, 1944; Major General Oscar Griswold, letters to Lieutenant General Millard Harmon, March 31, April 3, 1944; Major General Oscar Griswold, letter to Major General A. J. Barnett, Chief of Staff, U.S. Army Forces in the

South Pacific, May 6, 1944; Barnett, Report on Combat Activities of the 1st Battalion, 24th Infantry and the 25th Regimental Combat Team at Bougainville, May 9, 1944; Major General Oscar Griswold, Report on 1st Battalion, 24th Infantry Regiment and 25th Regimental Combat Team, May 10, 1944, all in Record Group 407, Entry 427, Box 11340, Folder 393-INF-25-7-0.1; Rowe's stories are in 93rd Infantry Division Press Clippings, Record Group 407, Entry 427, Box 11330, Folder 393-0.15; 93rd Infantry Division Summary of Operations in World War II, all at NA; *Command of Negro Troops*, War Department Pamphlet, 12–14, February 29, 1944; Walter White, memo, February 12, 1945, 25th Infantry Regiment, Lessons Learned on Bougainville; Captain George Little, Psychiatric Report on Front Line Conditions of the 25th CT, May 8, 1944, all in Leonard Russell Boyd Papers, Box 1; Brigadier General Leonard Boyd, letter to Commanding General, XIV Corps, Misconduct Before the Enemy, May 8, 1944; Brigadier General Leonard Boyd, letter to Major General J. E. Hull, May 17, 1944, both in Leonard Russell Boyd Papers, Box 2; 25th Infantry Regiment, History, Leonard Russell Boyd Papers, Box 3, all at HIA; Jones and Saunders, "Bougainville Campaign," 444–52, CMH; William McLaughlin, questionnaire, World War II Veterans Survey #207, USAMHI; Major Paul von Liles, "The Operations of the 1st Battalion, 24th Infantry in the Battle at Empress Augusta Bay, Bougainville, Solomon Islands, 19–24 April 1944, Personal Experiences of a Corps Headquarters Observer," Advance Infantry Officers Course, 1947–1948, DRL; Stephen Lutz, "The 93rd Infantry Division: The Only African-American Division in the Pacific Theater," *WWII Quarterly*, Spring 2017; John Kennedy Ohl, "The Fight Near Hill 250: K Company at the Battle of Bougainville," November 17, 2015, at www.warfarehistorynetwork.com; Ulysses Lee, *United States Army in World War II: The Employment of Negro Troops* (Washington, DC: Office of the Chief of Military History, United States Army, 1966), 138, 497–517; Mary Penick Motley, ed., *The Invisible Soldier: The Experience of the Black Soldier, World War II* (Detroit: Wayne State University Press, 1975), 76, 84–92; Robert F. Jefferson, *Fighting for Hope: African American Troops of the 93rd Infantry Division in World War II and Postwar America* (Baltimore: Johns Hopkins University Press, 2008), 157–89; Bryan Booker, *African Americans in the United States Army in World War II* (Jefferson, NC: McFarland & Company, 2008), 172–84; Gailey, *Bougainville*, 169–83. The ill-fated patrol involved K Company, 25th Infantry Regiment.

9. United States Army Forces in the South Pacific Area, Headquarters, Service of Supply, Final History, Service Command, NA; Private Gordon Rose, letter to Mother, August 3, 1944, Folder 2544, Accession #553, World War II Letters Collection 68, State Historical Society of Missouri (SHSM), Columbia, MO; Jones and Saunders, "Bougainville Campaign," 280–83; Griswold, "Experience in Jungle Warfare," 24–27, both at CMH; Gailey, *Bougainville*, 186–87; Cronin, *Under the Southern Cross*, 214–15. Soon after writing to his mother, Rose went missing in action during a patrol. He remains unaccounted for to this day. For a full list of the World War II American MIAs, see www.dpaa.mil. General Hyakutake suffered a stroke in early 1945 and yielded command to General Kanda, who surrendered to the Australians at the end of the war.

4. Informed Boldness

1. Edward Drea, "MacArthur's Greatest Secret," *Military History Quarterly*, Autumn 2002, 16–23; Edward Drea, "Hardly Reckless," *Army*, April 1994, 51–52; Edward Drea, "Ultra Intelligence and General Douglas MacArthur's Leap to Hollandia," *Intelligence and National Security*, April 1990, 323–33; Drea, *MacArthur's ULTRA*, 108–113. In a January 2016 Facebook post, the National Cryptologic Museum at Fort Meade, MD, shared information about the capture and deciphering of the code books.

2. Brigadier General Bonner Fellers, interview with Dr. D. Clayton James, June 26, 1971, Record Group 49, Box 2, D. Clayton James Collection; Kenney diary, March 9, 1944,

both at DMMA; Drea, "MacArthur's Greatest Secret," 20–22; Drea, "Ultra Intelligence and . . . Leap to Hollandia," 337–40; Thomas E. Griffith Jr., *MacArthur's Airman: General George C. Kenney and the War in the Southwest Pacific* (Lawrence: University Press of Kansas, 1998), 156; Taaffe, *MacArthur's Jungle War*, 77–78; Kenney, *General Kenney Reports*, 369; Borneman, *MacArthur at War*, 360–65; Drea, *MacArthur's ULTRA*, 97–98; James, *Years of MacArthur*, vol. 2, 443–45.

3. SWPA G2 Monthly Summary of Enemy Dispositions, March 31, 1944, Record Group 3, Box 17, Folder 2, Records of Headquarters, SWPA, 1942–1945; Rear Admiral Raymond Tarbuck, interview with Dr. D. Clayton James, September 4, 1971, Record Group 49, Box 4; Rear Admiral Felix Johnson, interview with Dr. D. Clayton James, Record Group 49, Box 3, both in D. Clayton James Collection; Kenney diary, March 26–27, 1944, all at DMMA; General Douglas MacArthur, letter to Professor E. B. Potter, July 28, 1959, MS-335, EB Potter Papers, Box 2, Folder 4; Mrs. Catherine Nimitz, letter to Professor E. B. Potter, MS-335, E. B. Potter Papers, Box 1, Folder 11; Admiral Chester Nimitz, letter to Mrs. Catherine Nimitz, December 4, 1944, MS-236, Box 1, Folder 1, Chester Nimitz Papers, all at USNA; William D. Leahy, *I Was There: The Personal Story of the Chief of Staff to Presidents Roosevelt and Truman Based on His Notes and Diaries Made at the Time* (New York: McGraw-Hill, 1950), 230; E. B. Potter, *Nimitz*, 290–92; James, *Years of MacArthur*, vol. 2, 397–402; Borneman, *MacArthur at War*, 365–68; Taaffe, *MacArthur's Jungle War*, 78, 97–99; Kenney, *General Kenney Reports*, 377. As a midshipman at the US Naval Academy in the early twentieth century, Nimitz had witnessed firsthand the toxic effect on morale of open disputes between senior officers when Rear Admirals Winfield Scott Schley and William Sampson, and their adherents, became involved in a protracted, vitriolic mass media controversy over their actions in the recently completed Spanish-American War. According to Nimitz's biographer, Potter, the effect on the future admiral "seems to have been nothing less than traumatic. He made a vow then and there that, if ever he was in a position to prevent it, there would be no washing of the Navy's dirty linen in public." See page 53 of Potter's book *Nimitz*.

4. I Corps, History of the Hollandia Operation, Record Group 407, Entry 427, Box 2517, Folder 201-0.3; 24th Infantry Division, Tanahmerah Historical Report, Record Group 407, Entry 427, Box 6611, Folder 324-0.3, both at NA; Seventh Amphibious Force, Report of Tanahmerah Bay–Humboldt Bay Aitape Operation, May 6, 1944, MS-416, World War II Battle Action and Operations Reports, Box 15, Folder 9, USNA; Brigadier General Charles Willoughby, Press Briefing, September 4, 1944, Charles Willoughby Papers, Box 7, USAMHI; Brigadier General Charles Willoughby, "The Return of MacArthur," Charles Willoughby Papers, Box 2, HIA; Kenney diary, March 29–April 3, 1944, DMMA; Hollis Peacock, unpublished memoir, no pagination, World War II Veterans Survey #3444, USAMHI; Lieutenant Colonel Cornelius Lang, "The 24th Infantry Division Artillery in the Southwest Pacific Operations 1 Oct '41 to 15 Aug '45: Personal Experience of an Organic Field Artillery Battalion Commander," School of Combined Arms, Regular Course, 1946–1947, Ft. Leavenworth, KS, 8, CARL; 21st Infantry Regiment, self-published history, 11–17, copy in author's possession; Drea, "MacArthur's Greatest Secret," *Military History Quarterly*, 23; Drea, "Hardly Reckless," *Army*, 53; Karl C. Dod, *The United States Army in World War II, The Corps of Engineers: The War Against Japan* (Washington, DC: Office of the Chief of Military History, U.S. Army, 1966), 527–29; Robert Ross Smith, *United States Army in World War II, The War in the Pacific: The Approach to the Philippines* (Washington, DC: Office of the Chief of Military History, Department of the Army, 1953), 16–38; Charles Willoughby and John Chamberlain, *MacArthur: 1941–1951* (New York: McGraw-Hill, 1954), 181–85; Holzimmer, *General Walter Krueger*, 144; Samuel Eliot

Morison, *History of United States Naval Operations in World War II*, vol. 8: *New Guinea and the Marianas, March–August 1944* (Boston: Little, Brown, 1968), 61–66; Craven and Cate, *The Army Air Forces in World War II*, vol. 4, 590–600; Griffith, *MacArthur's Airman*, 160–64; Kenney, *General Kenney Reports*, 373–76, 379–82; McCartney, *Jungleers*, 74–77; Taaffe, *MacArthur's Jungle War*, 80; Catanzaro, *With the 41st Division in the Southwest Pacific*, 50. During World War II, the Army often augmented infantry regiments with a range of combined arms attachments for an amphibious invasion. In these instances, the invading regiment became known as a regimental combat team (RCT).

5. Lieutenant General Robert Eichelberger, letters to Emma Eichelberger, March 1944; Lieutenant General Robert Eichelberger, Dictations, Hollandia, 1948, in Boxes 8 and 68, Robert Eichelberger Papers, DU; I Corps, History of the Hollandia Operation, NA; 2nd Battalion, 186th Infantry Regiment, "LST to Hollandia," by Dr. Hargis Westerfield and Unnamed E Company 186th Infantryman, at www.jungleer.com; John F. Shortal, "Hollandia: A Training Victory," *Military Review*, May 1986, 41–45; Barbey, *MacArthur's Amphibious Navy*, 160–61; Luvaas, *Dear Miss Em*, 90–99; Eichelberger, *Road to Tokyo*, 100–104; Chwialkowski, *In Caesar's Shadow*, 90–95; Shortal, *Forged by Fire*, 75–78.

6. Lieutenant General Robert Eichelberger, letters to Emma Eichelberger, April 18–21, 1944, Robert Eichelberger Papers, Box 2, Folder 4, USAMHI; Brigadier General Clovis Byers, letter to Marie Byers, April 17, 1944, Clovis Byers Papers, Box 9, Folder 9-9, HIA; A Company, 163rd Infantry Regiment, History, 22, Record Group 407, Entry 427, Box 9084, Folder 341-INF-163-0, NA; I Company, 186th Infantry Regiment, "Our Hard Luck at Hollandia," by Dr. Hargis Westerfield with Sergeant Emerson Koenig, at www.jungleer.com; Major General Hugh J. Casey, *Engineers of the Southwest Pacific, 1941–1945*, vol. 4: *Amphibian Engineer Operations* (United States Army Forces in the Far East, 1959), 265; Catanzaro, *With the 41st Division in the Southwest Pacific*, 39; Eichelberger, *Our Jungle Road to Tokyo*, 104; McCartney, *Jungleers*, 74; Reigelman, *Caves of Biak*, 102; Willoughby and Chamberlain, *MacArthur*, 183; James, *Years of MacArthur*, vol. 2, 450; Egeberg, *The General*, 49–51; Borneman, *MacArthur at War*, 370–71.

7. E Company, 163rd Infantry Regiment, History, 6, Record Group 407, Entry 427, Box 9084, Folder 341-INF-163-0; I Corps, History of the Hollandia Operation; 24th Infantry Division, Tanahmerah Historical Report, all at NA; Lieutenant General Robert Eichelberger, letter to Emma Eichelberger, April 22, 1944, Robert Eichelberger Papers, Box 2, Folder 4, USAMHI; Seventh Amphibious Force, Report of Tanahmerah Bay–Humboldt Bay Aitape Operation, USNA; K and F Companies, 162nd Infantry Regiment, "Hollandia: Our Landings," by Dr. Hargis Westerfield . . . with K Company's Charles Brockman and F Company's Chester Young, at www.jungleer.com; Arthur Veysey, "Hollandia Taken by Yanks," *Chicago Tribune*, April 25, 1944; Morison, *History, vol. 8: New Guinea and the Marianas*, 36–37, 68–86; Smith, *Approach to the Philippines*, 53–59, 68–71; McCartney, *Jungleers*, 78; MacArthur, *Reminiscences*, 190; Barbey, *MacArthur's Amphibious Navy*, 170.

8. Sixth Army, Combat Notes, Number 3, September 15, 1944, Record Group 337, Entry 15A, Box 71, Folder 491; 162nd Infantry Regiment, Report of Operations, 12 March–10 May 1944, Record Group 407, Entry 427, Box 9080, Folder 341-INF-162-0.3; I Corps, History of the Hollandia Operation; 24th Infantry Division, Tanahmerah Historical Report, all at NA; Colonel Aubrey "Red" Newman, diary, April 1944, Aubrey S. Newman Papers, Box 3; Newman, Speech, Recollections, letter to Mr. Benny Fowlkes, October 30, 1986, Boxes 1 and 2, Aubrey S. Newman Papers, all at USAMHI; Lang, "24th Infantry Division Artillery in SWPA," 10, CARL; D Company, 163rd Infantry

Regiment, Unit History, at www.jungleer.com; Lieutenant Colonel John Clarke, "The Longest 12 Miles on Earth," *Chemical Warfare*, January/February 1945, 47–48; Major General Hugh J. Casey, *Engineers of the Southwest Pacific, 1941–1945*, vol. 7: *Engineer Supply* (United States Army Forces in the Far East, 1947), 120; Casey, *Engineers*, vol. 4: *Amphibian Engineer Operations*, 271–74; Smith, *Approach to the Philippines*, 55–61; Eichelberger, *Our Jungle Road to Tokyo*, 107–109; Taaffe, *MacArthur's Jungle War*, 86–87.

9.   Lieutenant General Robert Eichelberger, Dictations on MacArthur, November 12, 1954, Robert Eichelberger Papers, Box 1, Folder 1; Eichelberger letter to Emma, April 22, 1944, both at USAMHI; Eichelberger, Dictations Hollandia, DU; 24th Infantry Division, Tanahmerah Historical Report, NA; Faillace interview, DMMA; "M'Arthur Lands at Hollandia During Attack," *Boston Globe*, April 24, 1944; "New MacArthur Invasion: Yanks Leap 500 Miles," *Chicago Tribune*, April 24, 1944; Krueger, *From Down Under to Nippon*, 64–65; Holzimmer, *General Walter Krueger*, 147; Barbey, *MacArthur's Amphibious Navy*, 172–73; Shortal, *Forged by Fire*, 81–82; James, *Years of MacArthur*, vol. 2: 450–54; Borneman, *MacArthur at War*, 372–75; Egeberg, *The General*, 50–54; Eichelberger, *Our Jungle Road to Tokyo*, 106–107; Taaffe, *MacArthur's Jungle War*, 87–88.

10.   Captain Wilbur Hayden, 116th Medical Battalion, Training Suggestions and Notes, 2–4, Record Group 112, Entry 31, Surgeon General, Administrative Records, Box 75; Sixth Army, Combat Notes, Number 3; Corporal Nobuhiro Kawabe, "A Message to My Comrades in Arms in the South Pacific," Record Group 496, Entry 134, Box 648, Records of the GHQ, SWPA/USAFP, ATIS Administrative Records, 1942–1945; I Corps, History of the Hollandia Operation; 24th Infantry Division, Tanahmerah Historical Report, all at NA; William LeGro, World War II Veterans survey, no number, USAMHI; Lieutenant General Robert Eichelberger, letter to Lieutenant General Walter Krueger, May 5, 1944, Walter Krueger Papers, Box 9, USMA; Julius Siefring, interview with Ms. Adelma Siefring, no date, AFC/2001/001/41633, LOC; Bill Campbell, interview with Mr. Floyd Cox, April 21, 2000, NMPW; 116th Medics at Hollandia by Dr. Hargis Westerfield and George Jackson, at www.jungleer.com; 21st Infantry Regiment, self-published history, 23, copy in author's possession; Captain Robert Smith, "Logistics vs. Tactics: The 24th Infantry Division at Tanahmerah Bay, Dutch New Guinea," *Military Review*, June 1949, 19; Haruka Taya Cook and Theodore F. Cook, *Japan at War: An Oral History*, (New York: New Press, 1992), 273–74; Smith, *Approach to the Philippines*, 62–78; Eichelberger, *Our Jungle Road to Tokyo*, 114–15; Catanzaro, *With the 41st Division in the Southwest Pacific*, 46. The Japanese diary is included with the Tanahmerah Historical Report, pages 154–55.

11.   "Report on 649th Ordnance Ammunition Company," 1–3, Brigadier General Clovis Byers, letter to Colonel Gus Broberg, October 10, 1044, both in Clovis Byers Papers, Box 3, Folder 3-2, HIA; I Corps, History of the Hollandia Operation, NA; 532nd Engineer Boat and Shore Regiment, The Hollandia Fire and Lake Sentani, by Dr. Hargis Westerfield; 41st QM Company: Those Indispensable Quartermasters, by Dr. Hargis Westerfield and Colonel Henry Cary; 41st Military Police Platoon: Soldiers and Policemen by Dr. Hargis Westerfield with Colonel Paul Wendell, Sergeant Lewis Clark and other MPs; 116th Engineer's New Guinea Campaign: Road-Building. Firefighting, Combat by Dr. Hargis Westerfield, all at www.jungleer.com; Lee, *Put 'Em Across: A History of the 2nd Engineer Special Brigade, 1942–1945* (Fort Belvoir, VA: Telegraph Press, 1946), 76–78; Casey, *Engineers*, vol. 4: *Amphibian Engineer Operations*, 274; McCartney, *Jungleers*, 80; Eichelberger, *Our Jungle Road to Tokyo*, 110–11; Kahn, *Between Tedium and Terror*, 114; Smith, *Approach to the Philippines*, 78–80.

12.   Lieutenant General Robert Eichelberger, letter to Emma Eichelberger, May 9, 1944, Robert Eichelberger Papers, Box 2, Folder 4, USAMHI; Lieutenant General Robert Eichelberger, letters to Lieutenant General Walter Krueger, April 29, May 16, 1944;

Lieutenant General Walter Krueger, letter to General Douglas MacArthur, June 9, 1944, all in Walter Krueger Papers, Box 9; General Clyde Eddleman, letter to Dr. William Leary, no date, Walter Krueger Papers, Box 40; General Walter Krueger, The Commander's Appreciation of Logistics, Army War College lecture, January 3, 1955, Walter Krueger Papers, Box 12; Mr. E. R. Vadeboncoeur, WSYR Radio, Syracuse, New York, "Dispatches From the Southwest Pacific," May 22, 1944, Carter McLennan Papers, Box 1, all at USMA; Brigadier General Clovis Byers, letter to Marie Byers, May 17, 1944; Brigadier General Clovis Byers, letter to Mrs. Emma Eichelberger, May 30, 1944, both in Clovis Byers Papers, Box 9, Folder 9-9; Lieutenant General Robert Eichelberger, letter to Mrs. Marie Byers, June 1, 1944, Clovis Byers Papers, Box 4, Folder 9-9, all at HIA; 339th Engineer Combat Battalion, "This Is an Engineer's War," 9, Record Group 15, Box 2, Folder 20, Contributions from the Public Collection, DMMA; Dr. James Masterson, "United States Army Transportation in the Southwest Pacific Area, 1941–1947," 516, 2-3.7 AZ C1, CMH; Lieutenant General Robert Eichelberger, letter to Lieutenant General Leslie McNair, May 17, 1944, Record Group 337, Entry 58A, Box 9; Rear Admiral Daniel Barbey, letter to Major General Orlando Ward, January 12, 1951, Record Group 319, Entry 54, Box 6, Records of the Office of the Chief of Military History, The Approach to the Philippines; I Corps, History of the Hollandia Operation, all at NA; Seventh Amphibious Force, Report of Tanahmerah Bay-Humboldt Bay Aitape Operation, USNA; Rod Paschall, "MacArthur's Ace of Spades," *Military History Quarterly*, Spring 2006, 76; Dod, *The Corps of Engineers: The War Against Japan*, 531–32; Casey, *Engineers*, vol. 7: *Engineer Supply*, 124; Riegelman, *Caves of Biak*, 116–17; Krueger, *From Down Under to Nippon*, 66–69; Eichelberger, *Our Jungle Road to Tokyo*, 113–14; Chwialkowski, *In Caesar's Shadow*, 97; Smith, *Approach to the Philippines*, 82–83; Taaffe, *MacArthur's Jungle War*, 98–103. During the construction phase, a fire broke out among captured Japanese matériel, causing several million more dollars of wastage.

5. "From New Guinea No One Returns Alive"

1. Colonel William Leaf, letter to Colonel Al Clark, January 3, 1947, Record Group 319, Entry P47, Box 1, Records of the Office of the Chief of Military History, American Forces in Action, The Admiralties, Operations of the 1st Cavalry Division; 37th Field Hospital, Quarterly Report, June 1944, Record Group 112, Entry UD1012, Surgeon General, HUMEDS, Box 69, both at NA; Lieutenant Colonel Charles Ritchie, "Quartermastering—Australia to Tokyo, 14 December 1943 to 11 August 1946: Personal Experiences of a Base and Intermediate Section Quartermaster," School of Combined Arms Regular Course, 1946–1947, Fort Leavenworth, KS, 7, CARL; Masterson, "United States Army Transportation in the Southwest Pacific Area," 435–41, 495, CMH; 339th Engineer Combat Battalion, "This Is an Engineer's War," 9, DMMA.

2. United States Army in the South Pacific Area, Services of Supply, History of the South Pacific Base Command, RG494, Entry 398, U.S. Army Force, Middle Pacific, Box 69, Folder 3; Lieutenant Colonel Milton Cloud, Oral History, July 8, 1944, Record Group 112, Entry 302, Surgeon General, Inspections Branch, Box 219, Interview Number 85; Captain Matthew Mendelsohn, Oral History, April 8, 1944, Record Group 112, Entry 302, Surgeon General, Inspections Branch, Box 219, Interview Number 67; Lieutenant William Shaw, Oral History, Record Group 112, Entry 302, Surgeon General, Inspections Branch, Box 219, Interview Number 90, all at NA; Captain Frederic Cramer, diary, June 21, 1944, Frederic Cramer Papers, Box 1; Joseph Steinbacher, unpublished memoir, 30, Joseph Steinbacher Papers, Vertical Files, Box 42, Folder 8; Robert Jackson, unpublished memoir, 27, World War II Veterans Survey #3849; LeGro survey, all at USAMHI; Sergeant Paul Kinder, letters to Ruth and Sam, August 10 and September 15, 1944, Folder 1632, Accession #1711; Tech Sergeant Leslie Robertson, letter to Bill,

June 12, 1944, Folder 2512, Accession #3047, both at SHSM; Lieutenant Colonel Maxwell Berry, letter to wife, April 4, 1944, unpublished memoir, 31, World War II Participants and Contemporaries Collection, Maxwell Berry Folder, EL; John McKinney, unpublished memoir, no pagination, Record Group 15, Box 29, Folder 13, Contributions from the Public Collection, DMMA; Masterson, "United States Army Transportation in the Southwest Pacific Area, 258–59, 285–89, CMH; Taaffe, *MacArthur's Jungle War*, 106.

3. Pacific Warfare Board Report, Battle Experiences Against the Japanese, Tips on Sanitation, Number 18, July 19, 1945, Record Group 337, Entry 15A, Box 72, Folder 519; Major Whitman Newell and Major Theodore Lidz, "The Toxicity of Atabrine to the Central Nervous System," Record Group 112, Entry 31, Surgeon General, Administrative Records, Box 210; 17th Malaria Survey Unit, Residual Effect of Diesel Oil on Incidence of Adult Malaria Mosquitoes, Base B, August 3, 1944, Record Group 212, Entry 31, Surgeon General, Administrative Records, Box 212; Major William Davis, Oral History, August 2, 1944, Record Group 112, Entry 302, Surgeon General, Inspections Branch, Box 219, Interview Number 80; Major Henry Gwynn, Oral History, May 23, 1944, Record Group 112, Entry 302, Surgeon General Branch, Box 219, Interview Number 73; Major Donald Patterson, Oral History, December 14, 1944, Record Group 112, Entry 302, Surgeon General, Inspections Branch, Box 220, Interview Number 116; Major John Schwartzwelder, Oral History, September 11, 1944, Record Group 112, Entry 302, Surgeon General, Inspections Branch, Box 220, Interview Number 95; Cloud oral history, all at NA; Denton Crocker, "Malaria Survey and Malaria Control Detachments in SWPA in World War II," unpublished paper, 2–3, Denton W. Crocker Papers, Vertical Files, Box 61, Folder 1, USAMHI; Robertson letter to Bill, June 12, 1944, SHSM; Mary Ellen Condon-Rall, "The Role of the U.S. Army in the Fight against Malaria, 1940–1944," *War & Society* 13, no. 2 (1995): 91–111; Clarke, "Longest 12 Miles on Earth," *Chemical Warfare*, 48; Eichelberger, *Our Jungle Road to Tokyo*, 43; Condon-Rall and Cowdrey, *Medical Service in the War Against Japan*, 208, 265–67.

4. Allied Geographical Section, SWPA, "You and the Native: Notes for the Guidance of Members of the Forces in their Relations with New Guinea Natives," 1–3, Charles V. Trent Papers, Box 1; Lieutenant Colonel Stewart Yeo, letter to father, May 5, 1944, Stewart Yeo Papers, Box 1; Private Joseph Adams, letter to wife, July 2, 1944, Joseph Q. Adams Papers, Box 1, all at USAMHI; Lieutenant Howard McKenzie, letter to Lelah and Howard, June 5, 1944, Folder 2128, Accession #286; Lieutenant John Harrod, letter to mother, April 1944, Folder 1238, Accession #2435; Tech Sergeant Leslie Robertson, letter to Bill, July 24, 1944, Folder 2512, Accession #3047; Kinder letter, September 15, 1944, all at SHSM; Allen Douglas, unpublished memoir, 422–23, World War II Participants and Contemporaries Collection, Allen Douglas Folder, EL; War and Navy Departments, Washington, DC, "A Pocket Guide to New Guinea," 11, copy in author's possession; Taaffe, *MacArthur's Jungle War*, 108–109. For an insightful discussion of relations between American soldiers and the New Guinea population, see the relevant portions of Peter Schrijvers, *Bloody Pacific: American Soldiers at War with Japan* (New York: Palgrave Macmillan, 2010).

5. Lieutenant General Richard Sutherland, Interview with Dr. Louis Morton, November 12, 1946, Louis Morton Papers, Box 2; Lieutenant General Robert Eichelberger, letter to Emma Eichelberger, December 27, 1944, Robert Eichelberger Papers, Box 2, Folder 4, both at USAMHI; General Robert Eichelberger, letter to Mr. Reuben Robertson, July 17, 1961, Record Group 15, Box 15, Folder 19, Contributions from the Public Collection; Mrs. Natalie Carney, letter to Dr. Paul Rogers, circa 1983, Record Group 46, Box 1, Folder 3, Paul Rogers Papers, both at DMMA; Brigadier General Clovis Byers, letter to Major Jerry O'Sullivan, June 5, 1944, Clovis Byers Papers, Box 3, Folder 3-6, HIA; Eichelberger letter to McNair, NA; William Dunn, "MacArthur's Mansion and Other

Myths," *Army*, March 23, 1973, 39–41; John F. Day, *An Officer in MacArthur's Court: The Memoir of the First Headquarters Commandant for General Douglas MacArthur in Australia* (Fremont, CA: Robertson Publishing, 2014), 379–82; George Kenney, *The MacArthur I Know* (New York: Duell, Sloane and Pearce, 1951), 92–93; Paul P. Rogers, *The Bitter Years: MacArthur and Sutherland* (New York: Praeger, 1990), 80–85, 91–92, 146–51; Weldon F. "Dusty" Rhoades, *Flying MacArthur to Victory* (College Station: Texas A&M Press, 1987), 283–85, 522–23; Willoughby and Chamberlain, *MacArthur*, 187–88; Barbey, *MacArthur's Amphibious Navy*, 229; Kenney, *General Kenney Reports*, 421; Luvaas, *Dear Miss Em*, 186; Krueger, *From Down Under to Nippon*, 69; Egeberg, *The General*, 59. For more information on Sutherland's actions earlier in the war, see *Fire and Fortitude*, the first volume in this series. With Sutherland's cooperation, Kenney and Major General Richard Marshall, the deputy chief of staff, also arranged for their Australian girlfriends, Beryl Spiers Stevenson and Louise Mowatt, to get WAC commissions and duty at GHQ in New Guinea. Stevenson and Mowatt were much better liked around headquarters and kept a lower profile than Bessemer-Clark. It seems that Elaine's uniquely toxic personality contributed much to the tensions that ultimately flared between MacArthur and Sutherland.

6. Imperial Japanese Army, "Hygiene in the Tropics for Medical Officers," October 1, 1943, #1189, 70, Record Group 165, Entry 79, Box 279, ADVATIS, Current Translations, 107–108; Lieutenant Uchimura, 41st Division, diary entry, no date, #1123, Record Group 165, Entry 79, Box 278, ADVATIS, Current Translations, #102, both at NA; SWPA G2 Summaries, May 31, June 30, 1944, Record Group 3, Box 17, Folder 2, Records of Headquarters, SWPA, 1942–1945, DMMA; Millard Gray, "The Aitape Operation," *Military Review*, July 1951, 44–46; Edward Drea, "Defending the Driniumor: Covering Force Operations in New Guinea, 1944," Combat Studies Institute, U.S. Army Command and General Staff College, Ft. Leavenworth, KS, 14–29; Smith, *Approach to the Philippines*, 145–51; Taaffe, *MacArthur's Jungle War*, 188–90; Drea, *MacArthur's ULTRA*, 67, 143–48; Willoughby and Chamberlain, *MacArthur*, 190–91; Krueger, *From Down Under to Nippon*, 69–70; Holzimmer, *General Walter Krueger*, 168–69.

7. Major General Charles Hall, Biography, Record Group 407, Entry 427, Box 3568, Folder 211-0.1; 128th Infantry Regiment, AAR, 28 June–25 August 1944, Record Group 407, Entry 427, Box 8038, Folder 332-INF-128-0.3; 124th Infantry Regiment, Historical Record, Aitape Campaign, Record Group 407, Entry 427, Box 7775, Folder 331-INF-124-0.3; Uchimura diary entry, all at NA; Brigadier General Johnnie Elmore, interview with Dr. D. Clayton James, June 25, 1971, Record Group 49, Box 2, D. Clayton James Collection, DMMA; 112th Cavalry Regiment, Historical Report, June 21–August 25, 1944, 12th Cavalry Regiment Records, Box 507, EL; 112th Cavalry Regiment, Historical Report, Summary of Lessons Learned, August 30, 1944, Records of the 112th Cavalry Regiment; Major General Charles Hall, letter to Lieutenant General Walter Krueger, June 30, 1944, both in Records of the 112th Cavalry Regiment, John Dunlap Collection, Box 8; Mr. Ben Moody, letter to Dr. Edward Drea, January 16, 1992, Records of the 112th Cavalry Regiment, Box 4, all at United States Cavalry Museum (USCM), Fort Riley, KS; Major General William Gill, Oral History, no date, William Gill Papers, Box 1, USAMHI; Mr. Claire Ehle, interview with Mr. Mik Derks, November 25, 2002, Wisconsin Veterans Museum (WVM), Madison, WI; Mr. Ben Moody, interview with Mr. Glenn Johnston, October 8, 2003, #1559; Mr. William Garbo, interview with Mr. Glenn Johnston, November 24, 2003, #1566, both at University of North Texas Oral History Collection (UNT), Denton, TX; Drea, "Defending the Driniumor," 61–69; Krueger, *From Down Under to Nippon*, 71–72; Smith, *Approach to the Philippines*, 134–51; Taaffe, MacArthur's Jungle War, 193–96; Drea, *MacArthur's ULTRA*, 144–51. The Napoleon Bonaparte quote can be found at www .Napoleon-series.org.

8. General Walter Krueger, letter to Major General Orlando Ward, January 2, 1951; Brigadier General Clarence Martin, comments on manuscript (Martin was Gill's assistant division commander and for a time commanded the Driniumor front; he also previously served as Eichelberger's intelligence officer); Colonel Edward Starr, letter to Major General Orlando Ward, August 21, 1951; Major Edward Becker, Comments on Aitape, November 13, 1950, all in Record Group 319, Entry 54, Box 6, Records of the Office of the Chief of Military History, The Approach to the Philippines; Sixth Army, Combat Notes, Number 3; 128th Infantry Regiment, AAR; 124th Infantry Regiment, Historical Record, Aitape Campaign; Uchimura diary entry, all at NA; Brigadier General Julian Cunningham, letter to Major General William Gill, July 30, 1944; Major General Charles Hall, letter to Lieutenant General Walter Krueger, July 16, 1944, both in Records of the 112th Cavalry Regiment, Box 8; Mr. Judson Chubbuck, interview with Mr. John Dunlap, no date, Records of the 112th Cavalry Regiment, Box 1; 112th Cavalry Regiment, Historical Report, EL; 112th Cavalry Regiment, Historical Report, Summary of Lessons Learned, all at USCM; Mr. James Chennault, interview with Ms. Shelly Henley, March 16, 1994, no number; Mr. Charles Brabham, interview with Mr. Glenn Johnston, September 9, 2003, #1553; Garbo, Moody interviews, all at UNT; Mr. William Garbo, Oral History, no date, NMPW; Staff Sergeant Milton Sutherland, letter to brother and sister, July 28, 1944, Folder 2931, Accession #2595, SHSM; Brigadier General Charles Willoughby, Press Briefing, September 4, 1944, Charles Willoughby Papers, Box 7; Lieutenant Colonel Stewart Yeo, letter to father, July 15, 1944, unpublished memoir, 10, Stewart Yeo Papers, Box 1; Gill, Oral History; Steinbacher, unpublished memoir, 18–19, all at USAMHI; Marion Hess, "Destruction on the Driniumor," *World War II*, July 1999, 46–52; Gray, "The Aitape Operation," *Military Review*, July 1951, 49–62; Major Edward Logan, "The Enveloping Maneuver of the 124th Infantry Regiment East of the Driniumor River, Aitape, New Guinea, 31 July–10 August 1944, Personal Experience of a Regimental S-2," Advanced Officers Course, 1946–1947, 18–23, 30–37, DRL; Drea, "Defending the Driniumor," 69–132; Harry A. Gailey, *MacArthur's Victory: The War in New Guinea, 1943–1944* (Novato, CA: Presidio Press, 2004), 239–41; Smith, *Approach to the Philippines*, 152–205; Taaffe, *MacArthur's Jungle War*, 196–209; Krueger, *From Down Under to Nippon*, 72–74; Holzimmer, *General Walter Krueger*, 173–76; Cook and Cook, *Japan at War*, 276. According to Gray and Drea, there were two Afua villages within about fifteen hundred meters of each other.
9. Sixth Army, Conference Report, Wakde-Sarmi and Biak Island Operations, May 9, 1944, Record Group 338, Entry P50487, Box 3, Folder 7; History of the Tornado Task Force, 6th Infantry Division, 12 June–18 July 1944, Record Group 407, Entry 427, Box 6036, Folder 306-0.3; 158th Infantry Regiment, Sarmi-Wakde Operation, 10 May–21 June 1944, Record Group 407, Entry 427, Box 16986, Folder INRG-158-0.3; Major Paul Shoemaker, Affidavit, June 4, 1944, Record Group 319, Entry 54, Box 6, Records of the Office of the Chief of Military History, The Approach to the Philippines; Krueger letter to Ward, all at NA; General George Decker, Oral History, 1972, George Decker Papers, Box 1; General Bruce Palmer, Oral History, 1975–1976, Bruce Palmer Papers, Box 1; Brian Machmer, "Vanishing Warriors: The Plight of the Native Americans of the 158th Infantry Regimental Combat Team Before and After World War II," unpublished paper, Bloomsburg University, 1–9, World War II Veterans Survey #3897, all at USAMHI; Japanese Monograph Number 14, Second Area Army Operations in the Western New Guinea Area, May 1944–January 1945, 8-5.1 AC14, CMH; Anthony Arthur, *Bushmasters: America's Jungle Warriors of World War II* (New York: St. Martin's Press, 1987), 3–9, 100–104; Smith, *Approach to the Philippines*, 212–36; Taaffe, *MacArthur's Jungle War*, 119–31; Gailey, *MacArthur's Victory*, 190–96; Dod, *The Corps of*

Engineers: The War Against Japan, 534–36; *Put 'Em Across*, 84–86; Holzimmer, *General Walter Krueger*, 154–55.

10. Colonel Sidney Mashbir, letter to Major General Orlando Ward, November 15, 1950; Colonel J. Prugh Herndon, letter and statement to Commanding General, Base F, USASOS, July 28, 1944; Sworn Statement, July 29, 1944; Lieutenant Colonel Wilson Wood, Affidavit, June 10, 1944; Shoemaker Affidavit; Colonel J. Prugh Herndon, Recommendation for Reclassification Board Action, May 31, 1944; Brigadier General Edwin Patrick, Statement, May 31, 1944; Major Joy Bogue, Affidavit, June 25, 1944; Colonel J. Prugh Herndon letter to Major General Orlando Ward, November 8, 1950, all in Record Group 319, Entry 54, Box 6, Records of the Office of the Chief of Military History, The Approach to the Philippines; 158th Infantry Regiment, Sarmi-Wakde Operation, all at NA; Ramon "Ray" Acuna, Oral History, no date, NMPW; Machmer, "Vanishing Warriors," 9–11, USAMHI; Arthur, *Bushmasters*, 104–107, 114–28, 219–20; Smith, *Approach to the Philippines*, 238–52; Taaffe, *MacArthur's Jungle War*, 133–35.

11. 158th Infantry Regiment, Noemfoor Operation, June–August 1944, Record Group 407, Entry 427, Box 16986, Folder INRG-158-0.1; 158th Infantry Regiment, Sarmi-Wakde Operation, both at NA; Mr. Walter Mauzaka, letter to Mr. Hal Braun, March 26, 1984; Mr. Hal Braun, letter to Mr. Walter Mauzaka, circa 1984, World War II Veterans Survey #3527, USAMHI; Acuna oral history, NMPW; Japanese Monograph Number 14, CMH; Douglas MacArthur, *Reports of General MacArthur*, vol. 2: *Japanese Operations in the Southwest Pacific* (Washington, DC: Center of Military History, 1966, 1994), 280–81; Arthur, *Bushmasters*, 128–48; Smith, *Approach to the Philippines*, 257–62, 397–424; Taaffe, *MacArthur's Jungle War*, 177–87; Gailey, *MacArthur's Victory*, 245–50; Krueger, *From Down Under to Nippon*, 89–90, 106–113; Holzimmer, *General Walter Krueger*, 156–57, 170–71. For more information on the airborne drop and instances of cannibalism, see Patrick K. O'Donnell, ed., *Into the Rising Sun: In Their Own Words, World War II's Pacific Veterans Reveal the Heart of Combat* (New York: Free Press, 2002), 126–31.

12. 20th Infantry Regiment, The Battle of Lone Tree Hill, 14–26 June 1944, Record Group 407, Entry 427, Box 6101, Folder 306-INF-20-0.3; 37th Field Hospital, Quarterly Report, June 1944, Record Group 112, Entry UD1012, Surgeon General, HUMEDS, Box 69; History of the Tornado Task Force, both at NA; Charles Hanks, unpublished memoir, 8, Charles F. Hanks Papers, Vertical Files, Box 7, Folder 88; Frank Caudillo Survey, no number; Carlie Berryhill World War II Veterans Survey #4014; Minor Hara, World War II Veterans Survey #6782, all at USAMHI; Mr. Murven Witherel, Interview with Mr. Richard Misenhimer, June 22, 2011, NMPW; Captain Raymond Hensley, letter to mother, August 13, 1944, Folder 1302, Accession #2444, SHSM; Mr. Frank Caudillo, letter to author, circa 1999, copy in author's possession; Japanese Monograph Number 14, CMH; Smith, *Approach to the Philippines*, 262–79; Taaffe, *MacArthur's Jungle War*, 136–43; Gailey, *MacArthur's Victory*, 203–207; Holzimmer, *General Walter Krueger*, 163–64.

13. "Operations of the Yuki Group in the Biak Island and Sarmi Areas," October 1944, Translation of Japanese Study by Lieutenant Guilfoyle, Record Group 319, Entry 54, Box 7, Records of the Office of the Chief of Military History, The Approach to the Philippines, NA; Japanese Monograph Number 14, CMH; Seventh Amphibious Force, Biak Operation Report, June 13, 1944, MS-416, World War II Battle Action and Operations Reports, Box 16, Folder 10, USNA; Major Roger Lawless, "The Biak Operation, Part I," *Military Review*, May 1953, 53–60; Edward Drea, "A Tale of Too Many Chiefs," *World War II*, December 2006, 42–44; MacArthur, *Reports*, vol. 2: *Japanese Operations in the Southwest Pacific*, 282–83; *Put 'Em Across*, 86–87; Morison, *History*, vol. 8: *New Guinea and the Marianas*, 103–108; Drea, *MacArthur's ULTRA*, 135; Smith,

Approach to the Philippines, 280–85, 299–303; Taaffe, *MacArthur's Jungle War*, 144–48. The anonymous correspondent was quoted in *Put 'Em Across*. He mistakenly described Biak's size as one thousand square miles. It is actually closer to one hundred.

14. 162nd Infantry Regiment, Report of Military Operation, Biak Island, 15 May–19 August 1944, Record Group 407, Entry 427, Box 9080, Folder 341-INF-162-0.3; "Operations of the Yuki Group in the Biak Island and Sarmi Areas," both at NA; Japanese Monograph Number 14, CMH; GHQ, Southwest Pacific Area, Communique, May 28, 1944, USAMHI; Seventh Amphibious Force, Biak Operation Report, USNA; Sergeant Floyd West Letters, E Company, 162nd Infantry, at www.jungleer.com; Lawless, "The Biak Operation, Part I," *Military Review*, 60–61; Drea, "A Tale of Too Many Chiefs," *World War II*, 44; McCartney, *Jungleers*, 102–106; Catanzaro, *With the 41st Division in the Southwest Pacific*, 57–58; Taaffe, *MacArthur's Jungle War*, 148–50; Smith, *Approach to the Philippines*, 290–99.

15. 41st Infantry Division, Japanese Tactics, Biak Operation, September 12, 1944, 2, Record Group 337, Entry 15A, Box 81, Folder 717; 603rd Tank Company, After Action Report, August 28, 1944; Colonel Harold Haney, letter to Major General Orlando Ward, November 20, 1950, both in Record Group 319, Entry 54, Box 6, Records of the Office of the Chief of Military History, The Approach to the Philippines; 162nd Infantry Regiment, AAR, all at NA; Japanese Monograph Number 14, CMH; William Cooley, Oral History, AFC/2001/001/10204, LOC; Thomas Smith, I Company, 162nd Infantry Regiment, personal account; M Company, 162nd Infantry Regiment, Machine Gunners in the Parai Defile; Charles Brockman, K Company, 162nd Infantry Regiment, personal account; Lewis Weiss, G Company, 162nd Infantry Regiment, personal account; Charles Solley, I Company, 186th Infantry Regiment, personal account, all at www.jungleer.com; Colonel Cecil Helena, oral history, circa 1990, Cecil Helena Papers, Vertical Files, Box 35, Folder 11, USAMHI; Major Roger Lawless, "The Biak Operation, Part II," *Military Review*, June 1953, 48–52; Drea, "A Tale of Too Many Chiefs," *World War II*, 44–45; "Americans Take Ridges on Biak," *Boston Globe*, June 3, 1944; MacArthur, *Reports*, vol. 2: *Japanese Operations in the Southwest Pacific*, 285–86; Catanzaro, *With the 41st Division in the Southwest Pacific*, 64–65; McCartney, *Jungleers*, 107–110; Taaffe, *MacArthur's Jungle War*, 150–52; Smith, *Approach to the Philippines*, 305–316.

16. Biak Climatic Data, May–June 1944, Headquarters, Air Weather Service, Record Group 112, Entry 31, Surgeon General, Administrative Records, Box 232; E Company, 163rd Infantry Regiment, History, 4; 162nd Infantry Regiment, AAR, all at NA; Mr. Lewis Turner, HQ, 186th Infantry Regiment, personal account; G Company, 186th Infantry Regiment, Company History, both at www.jungleer.com; Major Herbert Gerfen, "Task Force Operation," *Quartermaster Review*, September–October 1945, 47–48; Richard Austin, ed., *Letters from the Pacific: A Combat Chaplain in World War II* (Columbia: University of Missouri Press, 2000), 77–79; Taaffe, *MacArthur's Jungle War*, 159–61; Catanzaro, *With the 41st Division in the Southwest Pacific*, 65; McCartney, *Jungleers*, 110.

17. Lawless, "The Biak Operation, Part II," *Military Review*, 55–58; Craven and Cate, *The Army Air Forces in World War II*, vol. 4, 637; Kenney, *General Kenney Reports*, 404; Griffith, *MacArthur's Airman*, 170–73; MacArthur, *Reports*, vol. 2: *Japanese Operations in the Southwest Pacific*, 290; Smith, *Approach to the Philippines*, 346–64; Morison, *History, vol. 8: New Guinea and the Marianas*, 117–33; Taaffe, *MacArthur's Jungle War*, 152–57; Gailey, *MacArthur's Victory*, 217–18; McCartney, *Jungleers*, 111.

18. Major General Horace Fuller, letters to Lieutenant General Walter Krueger, June 9, 13, 1944, Record Group 319, Entry 54, Box 6, Records of the Office of the Chief of Military

History, The Approach to the Philippines; General Douglas MacArthur, message to Lieutenant General Walter Krueger, June 14, 1944; Lieutenant General Walter Krueger, letters to General Douglas MacArthur, June 5, 8, 1944, all in Record Group 200, Entry 19810 (A1), Richard Sutherland Papers, Box 34; Krueger letter to Ward; E Company, 163rd Infantry Regiment History, 7, all at NA; Eddleman, oral history, 19, USAMHI; Nick Wheeler, D Company, 186th Infantry Regiment, personal account, at www.jun gleer.com; Smith, *Approach to the Philippines*, 326–40; Krueger, *From Down Under to Nippon*, 101; Riegelman, *Caves of Biak*, 138; Taaffe, *MacArthur's Jungle War*, 164.

19. I Corps, History of the Biak Operation, 15–27 June 1944, Record Group 407, Entry 427, Box 2514, Folder 201-0; Lieutenant General Robert Eichelberger, Background on Biak Operation, April 4, 1948, and February 10, 1949; Letter to Dr. Samuel Milner, December 19, 1951; Major General Horace Fuller, Letter to the Soldiers of the 41st Infantry Division, June 16, 1944, all in Record Group 319, Entry 54, Box 6, Records of the Office of the Chief of Military History, The Approach to the Philippines, all at NA; Lieutenant General Robert Eichelberger, letter to Emma Eichelberger, June 14, 1944, Robert Eichelberger Papers, Box 2, Folder 4; General Robert Eichelberger, Dictations, July 29, 1957, Robert Eichelberger Papers, Box 1, Folder 9, both at USAMHI; Lieutenant General Robert Eichelberger, Diary, June 14–15, 1944, Box 1, Robert Eichelberger Papers; Lieutenant General Robert Eichelberger, Background for the Biak Operation, 1948, 1949; Biak Battle for the Caves, Box 68, Robert Eichelberger Papers, all at DU; General Clovis Byers, interview with Dr. D. Clayton James, June 24, 1971, Record Group 49, Box 2, D. Clayton James Collection, DMMA; 41st Division Headquarters: General Fuller and His Barber; General Fuller's Resignation by Dr. Hargis Westerfield, both at www.jungleer.com; Eichelberger, *Our Jungle Road to Tokyo*, 136–42; Luvaas, *Dear Miss Em*, 125–27; Chwialkowski, *In Caesar's Shadow*, 98–99; Shortal, *Forged by Fire*, 86–88; Riegelman, *Caves of Biak*, 158–59; Taaffe, *MacArthur's Jungle War*, 163–69. In Eichelberger's postwar reflections, he claims that Fuller was intoxicated when the two met on Biak.

20. Lieutenant General Robert Eichelberger, Background on Biak Operation, 1948–1949; "Operations of the Yuki Group in the Biak Island and Sarmi Areas," both at NA; Japanese Monograph Number 14, CMH; Eichelberger, Background for Biak Operation, 1948–1949, DU; Drea, "A Tale of Too Many Chiefs," *World War II*, 46–47; Eichelberger, *Our Jungle Road to Tokyo*, 142–48; Shortal, *Forged by Fire*, 89–90; Chwialkowski, *In Caesar's Shadow*, 99–100.

21. Sixth Army, Combat Notes, Number 2, August 15, 1944, 8, Record Group 407, Entry 427, Box 1998, Folder 106-3.01; Extracts from Operations Reports on Reduction of Japanese Cave-Type Fortifications, May 2, 1945, 9, Record Group 337, Entry 15A, Box 68, Folder 426; ATIS, Japanese Reactions to Allied Leaflets, Research Report, December 1, 1945, Record Group 165, Entry 79, Box 339, Report #93, Part I; 603rd Tank Company, AAR; Shaw, oral history; 41st Infantry Division, Japanese Tactics, Biak Operation, 3, 7, 21; I Corps AAR, all at NA; Combat Lessons Number 8, 13, CARL; Douglas, unpublished memoir, 462, EL; Japanese Monograph Number 14, CMH; Arthur Merrick, World War II Veterans Survey #1847 in Hargis Westerfield, Folder 3; Lieutenant General Robert Eichelberger, letter to Emma Eichelberger, June 23, 1944, Robert Eichelberger Papers, Box 2, Folder 4; McCool, unpublished memoir, 37–38, all at USAMHI; Paul Austin, interview with Mr. Floyd Cox, September 18, 2004, NPWM; "A Jap Officer in Defeat on Biak" by Dr. Hargis Westerfield; Solley, personal account, both at www .jungleer.com; Colonel Harold Riegelman, Cave Defenses, Biak, June 22, 1944, Box 16, Robert Eichelberger Papers, DU; "Bazookas on Biak," *Infantry Journal*, March 1945, 18–21; "Jap Ambushes," *Infantry Journal*, May 1945, 27–28; McCartney, *Jungleers*, 123; Riegelman, *Caves of Biak*, 153–55; Eichelberger, *Our Jungle Road to Tokyo*, 152;

Japanese diarist quoted in Kahn, *Between Tedium and Terror*, 155–56. The Imperial Japanese Army sources maintain that Kuzume died on July 2. The original claim that he committed ritual hara-kiri on June 22 came from a POW interrogation.

22. 92nd Evacuation Hospital, Historical Report on Biak Operation, August 21, 1944, Record Group 112, Entry UD1012, Surgeon General, HUMEDS, Box 84; Sixth Army, Combat Notes, Number 2; E Company, 163rd Infantry Regiment, History, 12; Shaw oral history, all at NA; Sergeants Charles Pearson and Roy Bennett, personal account, Biak, June 1944, World War II Veterans Survey #1857, Hargis Westerfield Folder, no number; LeGro survey, both at USAMHI; Colonel William Shaw, "The Use of Medical Units in an Amphibious Landing in the S.W.P.A.," *Military Surgeon*, September 1945, 177–84; Robert Windlinx, "Into Battle on Biak," *World War II*, June 2005, 55–56; Austin, *Letters from the Pacific*, 75, 87.

23. Major General Jens Doe, letter to Major General Orlando Ward, December 4, 1950, Record Group 319, Entry 54, Box 6, Records of the Office of the Chief of Military History, The Approach to the Philippines; Sixth Army, Combat Notes, Number 3, both at NA; Lieutenant General Robert Eichelberger, letters to Emma Eichelberger, June 20, 22, 23, 30, 1944, Robert Eichelberger Papers, Box 2, Folder 4; Dictations, 1957, both at USAMHI; Lieutenant General Robert Eichelberger, Diary, June 25, 1944; Lieutenant General Robert Eichelberger, Dictations, Formation of Eighth Army, 1949, 1–2, Box 68, Robert Eichelberger Papers; Background for Biak Operation, 1948, 13, all at DU; Masterson, "United States Army Transportation in the Southwest Pacific Area," 448–49, CMH; Eichelberger, *Our Jungle Road to Tokyo*, 156–58; Chwialkowski, *In Caesar's Shadow*, 101–104; Shortal, *Forged by Fire*, 95–96; McCartney, *Jungleers*, 184; Holzimmer, *General Walter Krueger*, 166–67, 179–83; Luvaas, *Dear Miss Em*, 135; Smith, *Approach to the Philippines*, 388–96; Taaffe, *MacArthur's Jungle War*, 174–76. As MacArthur's signals chief, Akin was in a position to read the SWPA commander's communications, including those in relation to Eighth Army, so he knew firsthand that Eichelberger would command the new formation. In the 1957 dictation, Eichelberger attributed the slow pace of the 41st Division advance at Biak in early June to the fact that Fuller never visited the front.

6. Galahad and Machiavelli

1. Major General Frank Merrill, interviews with Mr. Charles Romanus and Mr. Riley Sunderland, April 20, 26, 1948, Record Group 319, Entry 75, Box 9, Records of the Office of the Chief of Military History, Stilwell's Mission to China; Captain James Hopkins, oral history, September 27, 1944, Record Group 112, Entry 302, Surgeon General, Inspections Branch, Box 220, both at NA; Historical Section, China-Burma-India Theater, "History of the China-Burma-India Theater 21 May 1942–25 October 1944," 8-6.1 AA4; Historical Division, "History of the Northern Combat Area Command, Volume I," 43, 8-6.2 AE V1, both at CMH; Lieutenant Colonel Henry Kinnison IV, "The Deeds of Valiant Men: A Study in Leadership, the Marauders in North Burma, 1944," 10–13, U.S. Army War College, Class of 1993, digital version; Major John Gaither, "Galahad Redux: An Assessment of the Disintegration of Merrill's Marauders," 13–16, Master's Thesis, U.S. Army Command and General Staff College, 1975; Gary Bjorge, "Merrill's Marauders: Combined Operations in Northern Burma in 1944," 1–9, Combat Studies Institute, U.S. Army Command General Staff College, no date, all at CARL; George Gordon Bonnyman, interview with Dr. Kurt Piehler and Mr. Tim Bracken, April 20, 2000, University of Tennessee Special Collections Library, Repository for the Center for the Study of War and Society, University of Tennessee–Knoxville (SCUTK); Historical Division, War Department, "Merrill's Marauders: February–May, 1944," U.S. Army Center of Military History, 1990 edition, 8–12; Charles Romanus and Riley Sunderland, *The United States Army in World War*

II: China-Burma-India Theater, Stilwell's Command Problems (Washington, DC: Office of the Chief of Military History, Department of the Army, 1956), 28–36; Gerald Astor, *The Jungle War: Mavericks, Marauders, and Madmen in the China-Burma-India Theater of WWII* (New York: John Wiley & Sons, 2004), 70; James H. Stone, ed., *Crisis Fleeting: Original Reports on American Military Medicine in India and Burma in the Second World War* (Washington, DC: Office of the Surgeon General, Department of the Army, 1969), 305–321; Donovan Webster, *The Burma Road: The Epic Story of the China-Burma-India Theater in World War II* (New York: Farrar, Straus and Giroux, 2003), 81–110; Charlton Ogburn Jr., *The Marauders* (New York: Harper & Brothers, 1956), 11–16, 42, 61–62. Background information on Wingate can be accessed at www.zionism-israel.com, www.jewishvirtuallibrary.org, and www.arlingtoncem etery.net. Information on Merrill's background can be found at www.marauder.org and www.ww2gravestone.com.

2. 5307th Composite Unit (Provisional) War Diary, January 1944, 8-6.2 AE V19, CMH; Lieutenant General Joseph Stilwell, Comments on the Chiang Couple, October 12, 1943, Record Group 319, Entry 75, Box 9, Records of the Office of the Chief of Military History, Stilwell's Mission to China, NA; Brigadier General Frank Dorn, Thoughts on Stilwell, no date, Frank Dorn Papers, Box 4, Folder 15, HIA; Lieutenant General Joseph Stilwell, diary, May 19, August 9, 1944, www.hoover.org; Dr. James Hopkins, Interview with Mr. Kenneth Thompson, September 20, 2003, NMPW; Morris Factor, Gene Santoro, "A Hard Look Back at Burma: Conversation with Morris Factor," *World War II*, November/December 2013, 21; Scott McMichael, "Common Man, Uncommon Leadership: Colonel Charles N. Hunter with Galahad in Burma," *Parameters*, Summer 1986, 46; George McGee, "*The History of the 2nd Battalion, Merrill's Marauders*," self-published, 1987, 14–24; Historical Division, "Merrill's Marauders," 14–17; Charles N. Hunter, *Galahad* (San Antonio, TX: Naylor Company, 1963), 10; Logan E. Weston, *The Fightin' Preacher* (Cheyenne, WY: Vision Press, 1992), 118; Romanus and Sunderland, *Stilwell's Command Problems*, 39–41; Stilwell and White, *Stilwell Papers*, 292–93; Astor, *The Jungle War*, 169–70; Ogburn, *The Marauders*, 45–48, 53–56.

3. Combined Chiefs of Staff, Sextant Conference Proceedings, CCS Conference Proceedings, Box 2, EL; "History of the China-Burma-India Theater," CMH; Brigadier General Frank Dorn, letter to Major General Wendell Coats, Chief of Information, Department of the Army, May 7, 1969, Frank Dorn Papers, Box 6, Folder 4; Brigadier General Frank Dorn, letter to Mr. John Hart, August 3, 1960, John Hart Papers, Box 1, both at HIA; Lieutenant General Joseph Stilwell, diary, December 1943, October 1, 19, 1944, www.hoover.org; Historical Division, "Merrill's Marauders," 16–20; Frank Dorn, *Walkout: With Stilwell in Burma* (New York: Thomas Y. Crowell Company, 1971), 75–79; Tuchman, *Stilwell and the American Experience in China*, 400–414; Stilwell, *Stilwell Papers*, 242–67; Mitter, *Forgotten Ally*, 306–314, 336; Romanus and Sunderland, *Stilwell's Command Problems*, 9–10, 56–75, 130–44, 200–203.

4. Colonel William Peers, letter to Mr. Riley Sunderland, June 12, 1950, Record Group 319, Entry 75, Box 7, Records of the Office of the Chief of Military History, Stilwell's Mission to China, NA; Major General Ernest Easterbrook, letter to Mr. John Hart, July 26, 1960; Colonel S. L. A. Marshall, letter to Mr. John Hart, October 22, 1960, both in John Hart Papers, Box 1, HIA; Richard Johnston, Interview with Mr. Bill Alexander, February 17, 1999, #1351, UNT; U.S. Office of War Information, "How to Get Along with the Kachins, Shan and Burmans: A Brief Guide to the Peoples of North Burma," 1, 4, Hiram Boone Collection, #2002.210, National World War II Museum (WWIIM), New Orleans, LA; Mr. John Egan, interview with Ms. Sheila Dyer, August 27, 2005, AFC/2001/001/30282, LOC; 5307th Composite Unit (Provisional), War Diary, February 8, 13–18, 21, 1944, CMH; Major Randall Wenner, "Detachment 101 in the

CBI: An Unconventional Warfare Paradigm for Contemporary Special Operations,"
39–41, School of Advanced Military Studies, U.S. Army Command and General Staff
College, 2010; Gaither, "Galahad Redux," 17–19, both at CARL; Kinnison, "The Deeds
of Valiant Men," 18–21; Lieutenant Colonel William Peers, "Guerrilla Operations in
Northern Burma," *Military Review*, June 1948, 10–12; McGee, "History of the 2nd
Battalion, Merrill's Marauders," 33, 39; William R. Peers and Dean Brelis, *Behind the
Burma Road: The Story of America's Most Successful Guerrilla Force* (Boston: Little,
Brown, 1963), 141–47; Hunter, *Galahad*, 19; Stilwell and White, *Stilwell Papers*, 256,
278–80, 293; Ogburn, *The Marauders*, 77. McGee on page 39 of his book and Ogburn
on pages 87–88 both mention that Stilwell did meet with a small group of 5307th officers and made a good impression on them.

5. Mrs. Helen Landis, clipping from *Pittsburgh Press*, November 25, 1944, letter to Colo-
nel Ernest Easterbrook, December 27, 1944, Record Group 407, Entry 427, Box 17055,
Folder INRG-475-0.3; Lieutenant Colonel Marcel Crombez, Report of Army Ground
Forces Special Representative in China, Burma and India, February–April 1944, 8,
Record Group 337, Entry 15A, Box 53, Folder 99, both at NA; Roy Matsumoto, Ques-
tionnaire, Record Group 15, Box 70, Folder 8, Contributions from the Public Collec-
tion, DMMA; Tech Sergeant Dave Richardson, letter to Staff Sergeant Don Cooke,
April 20, 1943 [*sic*], George Burns Collection, Box 3, USAMHI; Colonel Logan Weston,
USA (ret.), personal account in *Burman News*, November 1992, Merrill's Marauders
Association Papers, Box 1, HIA; Historical Division, "History of Northern Combat
Area Command," 87–89; 5307th Composite Unit (Provisional), War Diary, February
26, March 5–6, 1944, both at CMH; Dave Richardson, oral history, May 4, 1993,
NMPW; Roy Matsumoto, Interview with Mr. John de Chadenedes, September 6,
2008, Densho Digital Archive, at www.ddr.densho.org; Werner Katz, Interview with
Ms. Sheila Dyer, August 27, 2005, AFC/2001/001/29918; Bernard Jezercak, Interview
with Mr. John Hayes, July 11, 2012, AFC/2001/001/84603; Roy Matsumoto, Interview
with Mr. Terry Shima, August 29, 2005, AFC/2001/001/53181, all at LOC; Lieutenant
General Joseph Stilwell, diary, March 6, 1944, www.hoover.org; McGee, "History of
the 2nd Battalion, Merrill's Marauders," 57–58; Historical Division, "Merrill's Marauders," 31–45; Hiroshi Fuwa, "Japanese Operations in the Hukawng Valley," *Military Review*, January 1962, 51–58; Sergeant Dave Richardson, "Behind Jap Lines in
Burma with Merrill's Marauders," *Yank*, June 9, 1944; Romanus and Sunderland,
Stilwell's Command Problems, 148–59; Weston, *The Fightin' Preacher*, 79–99, 128–35;
Ogburn, *The Marauders*, 39–40, 107–134; Astor, *The Jungle War*, 194; Stilwell and
White, *Stilwell Papers*, 282. Background on Weston can be found at www.ma
rauder.org. Richardson obviously misdated his letter for 1943 instead of 1944. He
could not have written his description in 1943 because Operation Albacore had not
begun yet.

6. Japanese Monograph Number 134, Burma Operations Record, 64–66, A-5.1 AC 134;
5307th Composite Unit (Provisional), War Diary, March 7, 1944, both at CMH; Joe
Robinson, Interview with Mr. Paul Zigo, no date, AFC/2001/001/24008, LOC; Lester
Sherry, Ralph Pollock, personal accounts, in *Burman News*, May 1991, Merrill's Ma-
rauders Association Papers, Box 1, HIA; Gaither, "Galahad Redux," 21–25; Bjorge,
"Merrill's Marauders," 24–25, both at CARL; George Johnston, "Our Strangest Tank
Unit," *Saturday Evening Post*, July 29, 1944; Historical Division, "Merrill's Maraud-
ers," 43–45; Hunter, *Galahad*, 45; Romanus and Sunderland, *Stilwell's Command
Problems*, 153–59; Stilwell and White, *Stilwell Papers*, 283. The Chinese suffered 802
dead, 1,479 wounded, and 530 lost to disease and other causes during this part of the
campaign. For a fascinating, honest contemporary report on the experiences of an
American liaison officer with a Chinese unit, see Captain Paul L. Tobey, letter to

Sarah, July 10, 1944, Record Group 319, Entry 75, Box 7, Records of the Office of the Chief of Military History, Stilwell's Mission to China, NA.

7. Peers letter, NA; Lieutenant General William Peers, Oral History, circa 1977, William R. Peers Papers, Box 1, USAMHI; 5307th Composite Unit (Provisional), War Diary, March 19, 28, 31, April 1–3, 1944; Japanese Monograph Number 134, Burma Operations Record, 66–69, both at CMH; Matsumoto questionnaire, DMMA; Matsumoto interview, LOC; Kinnison, "The Deeds of Valiant Men," 52–80; Wenner, "Detachment 101 in the CBI," 36–38; Gaither, "Galahad Redux," 21–29; Bjorge, "Merrill's Marauders," 25–29, all at CARL; McGee, "History of the 2nd Battalion, Merrill's Marauders," 71–105, 127–28; Historical Division, "Merrill's Marauders," 47–86; Fuwa, "Japanese Operations in the Hukawng Valley," *Military Review*, 58–59; O'Donnell, *Into the Rising Sun*, 101–103; Hunter, *Galahad*, 72; Peers, *Behind the Burma Road*, 146–47; Ogburn, *The Marauders*, 30–31, 180–81, 189–205; Astor, *The Jungle War*, 244–46; Romanus and Sunderland, *Stilwell's Command Problems*, 175–91. Information on Lieutenant Osborne's background and adventures in the Philippines can be accessed at www.findagrave.com and in his self-published book *Voyage into the Wind*. In the decades after the war, at Marauder reunions, Matsumoto's buddies often told him and their family members that his actions at Nhpum Ga had saved their lives. He was inducted into the Ranger Hall of Fame in 1993.

8. ATIS, Japanese Reactions to Surrender Leaflets, Research Report, December 1, 1945, 58, Record Group 165, Entry 79, Box 339, Report #93, Part I; Captain James Hopkins, Medical Study of the 5307th Composite Unit (Provisional), and Preliminary Report of Physical and Mental Condition of Men and Officers of the 3rd Battalion, both in Record Group 319, Entry P73, Box 1, Records of the Office of the Chief of Military History, American Forces in Action, Merrill's Marauders, all at NA; 5307th Composite Unit (Provisional), War Diary, March 30, April 2–3, 5, 11–12, 1944; Japanese Monograph Number 134, Burma Operations Record, both at CMH; John "Red" Acker, personal account in *Burman News*, May 1992, Merrill's Marauders Association Papers, Box 1 (Acker was in charge of the two pack howitzers that supported the 3rd Battalion advance), HIA; Hopkins Interview, NMPW; McMichael, "Common Man, Uncommon Leadership," *Parameters*, 47; Fuwa, "Japanese Operations in the Hukawng Valley, *Military Review*, 57; James H. Stone, "The United States Army Medical Service in Combat in India and Burma, 1942–1945," PhD Dissertation, Yale University, 1947, 149–50; McGee, "History of the 2nd Battalion, Merrill's Marauders," 115, 120, 129; Historical Division, "Merrill's Marauders," 88–91; Stone, *Crisis Fleeting*, 327–31; O'Donnell, *Into the Rising Sun*, 100, 104; Weston, *The Fightin' Preacher*, 149; Ogburn, *The Marauders*, 207–219, 227; Astor, *The Jungle War*, 243; Hunter, *Galahad*, 72, 81; Romanus and Sunderland, *Stilwell's Command Problems*, 34–35, 189–91. Hopkins's original report on the health of the 3rd Battalion is reproduced verbatim in Stone's book.

9. Field Marshal Shunroku Hata, Comments, circa 1952, Record Group 319, Entry 76, Box 11, Records of the Office of the Chief of Military History, Stilwell's Command Problems; Lieutenant Colonel Charles Lutz, Report on Combat Efficiency of the Chinese Army, February 27, 1944, Record Group 319, Entry 76, Records of the Office of the Chief of Military History, Stilwell's Command Problems; Major General Claire Chennault, letter to Major General O. C. Smith, March 30, 1954, Record Group 319, Entry 77, Box 8, Records of the Office of the Chief of Military History, Time Runs Out in CBI, all at NA; Colonel Thomas Taylor, letter to Lieutenant General Albert Wedemeyer, December 13, 1944, Albert Wedemeyer Papers, Box 87, Folder 9, HIA; Lieutenant General Joseph Stilwell, diary, April 3, 1944, www.hoover.org; Japanese Monograph Number 133, "Burma Operations Record, Outline of Burma Area Line of

Communications, 1941–1945," 12–21, 8-5.1 AC133; Japanese Monograph Number 134, 79–93, both at CMH; William Slim, *Defeat into Victory* (New York: David McKay Company, 1961), 233–36; Jonathan Fenby, *Chiang Kai-shek: China's Generalissimo and the Nation He Lost* (New York: Carroll & Graf Publishers, 2003), 416–23; Mitter, *Forgotten Ally*, 318–25; Tuchman, *Stilwell and the American Experience in China*, 437–42, 457–59; Stilwell and White, *Stilwell Papers*, 285; Romanus and Sunderland, *Stilwell's Command Problems*, 191–94, 198–99, 316–28. In 1950, the remains of Wingate and the other men were disinterred and transported to the United States, where they were buried in a mass grave at Arlington cemetery. Thus, the eccentric Chindit commander is one of the few Britons buried, albeit without the consent of his family, on American soil. For more information, see his entry at www.arlingtoncemetery.net. The most vocal advocate of Chennault's strategic outlook was Joseph Alsop, a cousin of President Roosevelt who served as an aide to the Fourteenth Air Force commander. Alsop blamed Stilwell for Ichi-go's success in weakening the Nationalists and accelerating the eventual communist takeover of China. An ardent anticommunist and influential postwar columnist, Alsop thought of Stilwell as a Neanderthal who understood little to nothing about modern warfare, especially airpower. See, for instance, his letter to Mr. John Hart, dated January 27, 1960, in which he disparaged Stilwell as "an almost total military incompetent. I have always been convinced that Stilwell plunged into the Burma campaign because, with his old fashioned military ideas, his limited experience, his total contempt of modern staff work, and other limitations, he could think of nothing else to do except to start a fight to open a road." (John Hart Papers, Box 1, HIA). Alsop was apparently ignorant, even a decade and a half after World War II, of Stilwell's orders from the Joint Chiefs to open the supply road through Burma. Most of Stilwell's staff officers and aides defended his strategic concepts in their postwar writings. The general and his intimates often contemptuously referred to Alsop as "All-Slop."

10. Captain Edward Fisher, Headquarters, United States Army Forces, India-Burma Theater, "History of Northern Combat Area Command, China-Burma-India Theater," 143–48, 8-6.2 AE V2 CYI; 5307th Composite Unit (Provisional), War Diary, April 20, 1944, both at CMH; Classified Memos, "Supply of the Chinese Army in India and Combat Forces in Burma" and "Narrative of the Chinese Army in India," no pagination, no dates, both in Haydon Boatner Papers, Box 4, HIA; Gaither, "Galahad Redux," 36–39; Kinnison, "The Deeds of Valiant Men," 90–97, both at CARL; Historical Division, "Merrill's Marauders," 93–97; Ogburn, *The Marauders*, 220–27; Romanus and Sunderland, *Stilwell's Command Problems*, 223–26.

11. Major John Grindlay, Oral History, April 29, 1944, Record Group 112, Entry 302, Surgeon General, Inspections Branch, Box 219, Interview Number 58; Major General Howard Davidson, letter to Major General A. C. Smith, November 4, 1953, Record Group 319, Entry 77, Box 8, Records of the Office of the Chief of Military History, Time Runs Out in CBI; Crombez Report, 10, all at NA; Historical Section, United States Army Forces, India-Burma Theater, History of Northern Combat Area Command, Appendix 7, Medical Department Units Assigned to NCAC, 1943–1945," mixed pagination, 8-6.2 AE V10; "History of Northern Combat Area Command, Appendix 9, Miscellaneous Topics, 1943–1945," mixed pagination, 8-6.2 AE V12; "History of Northern Combat Area Command, Appendix 6, History of Air Dropping, February 1943–February 1945," 22–23, 26–27, 8-6.2 AE V9; Fisher, "History of Northern Combat Area Command," 147–48; 5307th Composite Unit (Provisional), War Diary, April 28–May 10, 1944, all at CMH; Colonel Robert Parvin Williams, unpublished memoir, no pagination, Robert Parvin Williams Papers, Box 1, Folder 11, HIA; Gaither, "Galahad Redux," 39–42; Kinnison, "The Deeds of Valiant Men," 98–100; Captain Fred

Lyons as told to Paul Wilder, circa 1945, "Merrill's Marauders in Burma," located at www.cbi.org; Historical Division, "Merrill's Marauders," 98–105; Michael Gabbett, *The Bastards of Burma: Merrill's Marauders and the Mars Task Force Revisited* (Albuquerque: Desert Dreams, 1989), 31; Weston, *The Fightin' Preacher*, 151–55; Ogburn, *The Marauders*, 231–33; Romanus and Sunderland, *Stilwell's Command Problems*, 225–26.

12. Lessons Learned from the Salween Campaign, by U.S. Army Liaison Officers, December 20, 1944, Record Group 319, Entry 76, Box 5, Records of the Office of the Chief of Military History, Stilwell's Command Problems, NA; Colonel Reynolds Condon, Opinions of the Chinese Army, March 21, 1944, Frank Dorn Papers, Box 1, Folder 30, HIA; Lieutenant General Joseph Stilwell, diary, May 1, 17, 1944, www.hoover.org; Historical Section, Headquarters, United States Army Forces, India-Burma Theater, "History of Northern Combat Area Command, Appendix 2, Siege of Myitkyina," 7–17, 8-6.2 AE V5 Pt 1; 5307th Composite Unit (Provisional), War Diary, May 16–17, 1944, both at CMH; Captain Dale Brown and Major Scott McMichael, undated correspondence, circa 1980s; Mr. Riley Sunderland, Commentary on Major Scott McMichael's Article in *Parameters*, McMichael Response, Spring 1987, all in Scott McMichael Papers, Box 1, USAMHI; Borje, "Galahad Redux," 80–85; Kinnison, "The Deeds of Valiant Men," 100–107, both at CARL; McMichael, "Common Man, Uncommon Leadership," *Parameters*, 52–54; Historical Division, "Merrill's Marauders," 105–12; Stilwell and White, *Stilwell Papers*, 291–99; Hunter, *Galahad*, 98–106; Romanus and Sunderland, *Stilwell's Command Problems*, 228, 310–14, 329–60. Some historians, most notably McMichael, have claimed that the British 36th Infantry Division was combat ready and available to reinforce Stilwell's forces at Myitkyina and could have taken the town, preventing the siege, if not for the anglophobic general's refusal to accept help, apparently out of sheer jingoism and a desire for Myitkyina to remain exclusively a Chinese-American victory. However, this is patently false and unfair. Stilwell did inquire about the availability of the 36th Division and found out that it would not be ready until early June, well after the opportunity passed to grab Myitkyina quickly. For evidence of his inquiry, see Joseph W. Stilwell, *Stilwell's Personal File: China, Burma, India, 1942–1944*, vol. 4, ed. Riley Sunderland and Charles F. Romanus (Wilmington, DE: Scholarly Resources, 1976), 1743, and Sunderland's personal commentary cited above. The underlined and capitalized passages in the Condon memo are in the original.

13. Listing of Casualties of 5307th Composite Unit Through June 4, 1944, Record Group 319, Entry P73, Box 1, Records of the Office of the Chief of Military History, American Forces in Action, Merrill's Marauders, NA; Headquarters Myitkyina Task Force, Medical Service in the Myitkyina Campaign, August 15, 1944, Haydon Boatner Papers, Box 2, HIA; Lieutenant General Joseph Stilwell, diary, May 30, 1944, www.hoover.org; Stone, "The United States Army Medical Service in Combat in India and Burma," 192–94; Historical Section, Headquarters United States Army Forces, India-Burma Theater, "History of Northern Combat Area Command China-Burma-India Theater and India-Burma Theater," 8-6.2 AE V1 CY1, 155; Fisher, "History of Northern Combat Area Command," 156, and Inclosure #5; "History of Northern Combat Area of Command, Siege of Myitkyina," record of July 14, all at CMH; Robinson interview, LOC; Mr. Howard Garrison, letters to Major Scott McMichael, July 2, 1986, and February 4, 1987, Scott McMichael Papers, Box 1, USAMHI; Corporal Ferdinand Stauch, "Men, the Commanding General," *Ex-CBI Roundup*, November 1952, 13; Al Hemingway, interview with Mr. Frank Rinaldi, "Brilliant Feat of Arms," *World War II*, November 1993, 32; James Stone, "Surgeons in Battle: The Mobile Surgical Hospital in Burma 1943 to 1945," *Military Surgeon*, October 1949, 311–20; Historical Division, "Merrill's Marauders," 114; Seagrave, *Burma Surgeon Returns*, 127; Condon-Rall and

Cowdrey, *Medical Service in the War Against Japan*, 302–311; Stilwell and White, *Stilwell Papers*, 301; Hunter, *Galahad*, 125, 130; Weston, *The Fightin' Preacher*, 163–67; Ogburn, *The Marauders*, 250–52, 260–61, 279.

14. Fisher, "History of Northern Combat Area Command," 158, CMH; Brigadier General Theodore Wessels, letters to Major General Orlando Ward, 1951; interview with Mr. Riley Sunderland, July 19, 1948, Record Group 319, Entry 75, Boxes 7 and 9 respectively, Records of the Office of the Chief of Military History, Stilwell's Mission to China; Lieutenant General Albert Wedemeyer, letter to Sutherland [*sic*] and Romanus, April 21, 1950, Record Group 319, Entry 75, Box 7, Records of the Office of the Chief of Military History, Stilwell's Mission to China; Corroborating Statements by Ten Officers Who Served Under Brigadier General Haydon Boatner, October, 1944, Record Group 319, Entry 75, Box 6, Records of the Office of the Chief of Military History, Stilwell's Mission to China, all at NA; Brigadier General Haydon Boatner, letter to Brigadier General James Collins, circa 1973; Critique of *Stilwell and the American Experience in China* by Barbara Tuchman, both in Haydon Boatner Papers, Box 1; Mrs. Charles Hunter, letter to Major Scott McMichael, July 28, 1986, Scott McMichael Papers, Box 1, all at USAMHI; Brigadier General Frank Dorn, letter to Mr. John Hart, August 3, 1960, notes for Hart, circa 1960–1961; Colonel David Barrett, letter to Mr. John Hart, July 4, 1962, all in John Hart Papers, Box 1, HIA; Major Robert Waters, "The Operations of the 88th and 89th Regiments (30th Chinese Division) at Myitkyina, Burma, 26 May–8 August 1944, Personal Experiences of an American Liaison Officer," no date, 34; Major John Dunn, "Operations of the 3d Battalion, 5307 Composite Unit (Provisional) in the Battle of Myitkyina, Burma 27 July–3 August 1944, Personal Experiences of a Company Commander," Advanced Infantry Officers Course, 1947–1948, 9, both at DRL; Borje, "Galahad Redux," 75–82; Kinnison, "The Deeds of Valiant Men," 102–116, both at CARL; Lloyd Kessler, "From Construction to Combat," *World War II*, March 2001, 55; McMichael, "Common Man, Uncommon Leadership," *Parameters*, 53–56; Hunter, *Galahad*, 140, 164; Romanus and Sunderland, *Stilwell's Command Problems*, 242–45. McMichael argued for Hunter's importance and shed light on the disgraceful treatment he received by the Army hierarchy. Hunter grew disillusioned with Stilwell and criticized him throughout his memoir. McGee, the 2nd Battalion commander, admired Stilwell and dissented from Hunter's critique, even arguing in his own memoir, "History of the 2nd Battalion, Merrill's Marauders," that the latter exaggerated his own combat record and overall contributions.

15. Hideo Fujino, unpublished memoir, I, 95, 106, 111, 370.04; "History of Northern Combat Area Command, Siege of Myitkyina," 66, June 27 entry, Appendix; Japanese Monograph Number 134, 166–87, all at CMH; "Supply of the Chinese Army in India and Combat Forces in Burma," no pagination, HIA; Colonel Husayasu Maruyama, postwar interrogation, Haydon Boatner Papers, Box 1; Brigadier General S. C. Godfrey, CBI Air Service Command, Advantages of Air Transport, October 20, 1944, Vertical Files, Box 12, Folder 194, both at USAMHI; Corporal Harold Seadler, letter to brother, August 1, 1944, Folder 2669, Accession #2565; Lieutenant Robert Jones, letter to family, July 1944, Folder 1517, Accession #2461, both at SHSM; Waters, "Operations of the 88th and 89th Regiments," 31; Dunn, "Operations of the 3d Battalion, 5307th Composite Unit," 31, both at DRL; Lieutenant General Joseph Stilwell, diary, August 4, 1944, www.hoover.org; Fuwa, "Japanese Operations in Hukawng Valley," *Military Review*, 60–63; Kessler, "From Construction to Combat," *World War II*, 57–59; Won-loy Chan, *Burma: The Untold Story* (Novato, CA: Presidio Press, 1986), 83; Stilwell and White, *Stilwell Papers*, 311–13; Tuchman, *Stilwell and the American Experience in China*, 473–74; Romanus and Sunderland, *Stilwell's Command Problems*, 253–54.

16. Brigadier General Frank Dorn, letters to Mr. John Hart, July 20, August 3, 1960; Colonel David Barrett, Thoughts on John Hart Book, March 2, 1962, all in John Hart Papers, Box 1, HIA; Ambassador Clarence Gauss, Message to Sec State Number 2932, Sep 4, 1944; Vice President Henry Wallace, Summary Report to President Franklin Roosevelt, July 10, 1944, both in Foreign Relations Series of the United States (FRUS) at www.history.state.gov; Jay Taylor, *The Generalissimo: Chiang Kai-shek and the Struggle for Modern China* (Cambridge: Belknap Press of Harvard University Press, 2009), 280–84; Mitter, *Forgotten Ally*, 337; Tuchman, *Stilwell and the American Experience in China*, 464–78; Romanus and Sunderland, *Stilwell's Command Problems*, 374–84. In conversations with Americans, both Joseph Stalin and Vyacheslav Molotov described the CCP as a sort of "communist light" organization with few similarities to their own Soviet brand of communism. There is no way to tell how much influence, if any, these claims had on American perceptions of Mao's organization; nor is there any way to know if the Soviets deliberately misled their American allies. President Roosevelt chose Wallace to go to China primarily to get him out of the country in advance of the upcoming Democratic Party convention. Wallace had lost the confidence of many Democrats, including Roosevelt, and the president intended to dump him from the ticket. Ultimately, Senator Harry Truman supplanted Wallace as FDR's running mate.

17. Major General Patrick Hurley, letter to Major General Orlando Ward, January 11, 1952, Record Group 319, Entry 76, Box 11, Records of the Office of the Chief of Military History, Stilwell's Command Problems, also see his letter to Major General R. W. Stephens, December 15, 1956, in Record Group 319, Entry 77, Box 9, Records of the Office of the Chief of Military History, Time Runs Out in CBI; Madame Chiang Kai-shek, Interview with Mr. Charles Romanus and Mr. Riley Sunderland, June 21, 1949, Record Group 319, Entry 75, Box 9, Records of the Office of the Chief of Military History, Stilwell's Mission to China, all at NA; Lieutenant General Albert Wedemyer, letter to Mr. John Hart, January 8, 1960; Mr. Frank McCarthy, letter to Mr. John Hart, February 4, 1964, both in John Hart Papers, Box 1, HIA (McCarthy was Marshall's aide and in a position to comment on the relief); Lieutenant General Joseph Stilwell, diary, September 7, 15, 19, October 19, www.hoover.org; Combined Chiefs of Staff, Proceedings, Octagon/Quebec Conference, CCS Conference Proceedings, 1941–1945, Box 3; General Dwight Eisenhower, letter to General Joseph Stilwell, May 12, 1945, DDE Pre-Presidential Papers, 1916–1952, Box 111, both at EL; for more information on Stilwell's first recall crisis in the fall of 1943, and Mei-ling Soong's vital role in saving him, see *Fire and Fortitude*, the first volume in this series, 486–88; Taylor, *The Generalissimo*, 292–95; Fenby, *Chiang Kai-shek*, 423–31; Stilwell and White, *Stilwell Papers*, 330–39, 345–46; Tuchman, *Stilwell and the American Experience in China*, 475–509; Romanus and Sunderland, *Stilwell's Command Problems*, 413–33, 443–72. I have shared excerpts only from Roosevelt's ultimatum and Hurley's recommendation letter.

7. Hell on Land and at Sea

1. Anonymous Imperial Japanese Army soldier, diary, Dec 6–7, 1941, #713, Record Group 165, Entry 79, Box 273, ADVATIS Current Translations, #62-64; Office of the Provost Marshal, Report on American Prisoners of War in the Philippines, November 19, 1945, Record Group 389, Entry 460A, Provost Marshal Records, Box 2135; U.S. Army, Military Intelligence Division, Prisoners of War in the Philippine Islands, 8, September 20, 1944, Record Group 389, Entry 460A, Provost Marshal Records, Box 2135; ATIS, Information Bulletin, Japanese Violations of the Laws of War, April 29, 1944, Record Group 165, Entry 79, Box 314, Bulletin #10, all at NA; Imperial Japanese Army pamphlet, *To Win the War, You Need Only Read This*, 10, Record Group 2, Personal Files,

Box 5, Folder 4, Records of HQ, USAFFE, DMMA; Zarate, "American Prisoners of Japan: Did Rank Have Its Privilege?," 228, CARL; Arthur Thomas, Interview with Mr. Roger Mansell, May 15, 2000, Roger Mansell Papers, Box 22, Folder 19, HIA; Charles Roland, "Allied POWs, Japanese Captors and the Geneva Convention," *War & Society*, October 1991, 83–101; John E. Olson, O'Donnell, *Andersonville of the Pacific: Extermination Camp of American Hostages in the Philippines*, self-published 1985, 129–57; Geneva Convention rules and Imperial Japanese Army regulations on the treatment of prisoners are reproduced in full at E. Bartlett Kerr, *Surrender and Survival: The Experience of American POWs in the Pacific, 1941–1945* (New York: William Morrow, 1985), 329–38. The Provost Marshal report is also available at 4-4 EB C1, CMH. For more information on the brutal treatment of POWs during the Bataan Death March and at Camp O'Donnell, see www.mansell.com and *Fire and Fortitude*, the first volume in this series.

2. U.S. Army Military Intelligence Division, Prisoners of War in Taiwan, October 20, 1944, Record Group 389, Entry 460A, Provost Marshal Records, Box 2122, Taiwan Prisoner of War Camps Folder, NA; *Philippine Postscripts*, March 1944, CARL; Lieutenant Colonel Joseph Chabot, Interview with Dr. D. Clayton James, July 2, 1971, Record Group 49, Miscellaneous File, Part I, DMMA; American Red Cross, *Prisoners of War Bulletin* 1, no. 4: 3, Ivor Williams Collection, #2009.153.021, WWIIM; Colonel Michael Quinn, Diary, November 30, 1944, Jonathan Wainwright Papers, Box 5, USAMHI, also see page 254 of his self-published book; *Time*, May 8, 1944; Van Waterford, *Prisoners of the Japanese in World War II* (Jefferson, NC: McFarland & Company, 1994), 204, 253; Wainwright, *General Wainwright's Story*, 216–53; Schultz, *Hero of Bataan*, 369–84.

3. Captain John Olson, letters to mother, April 2, April 30, May 11, June 4, November 10, and no date, 1944, John Olson Papers, Box 1; Campbell, unpublished memoir, 121–32, both at USAMHI; Provost Marshal, Report on American Prisoners of War in the Philippines, 131, NA; Zarate, "American Prisoners of Japan: Did Rank Have Its Privilege?," 183–84, CARL; Donald Knox, ed., *Death March: The Survivors of Bataan* (New York: Harcourt, Brace, Jovanovich, 1981), 359, 370–71; Kerr, *Surrender and Survival*, 176–77; Waterford, *Prisoners of the Japanese in World War II*, 201. For more information on Olson's life and career, see www.philippine-scouts.org.

4. Mamerow, POW Report on Fukuoka 17, NA; Dr. Thomas Hewlett, "Di Ju Nana Bunysho Nightmare Revisited," in *The Japanese Story: American Ex-POW Inc.*, National Medical Research Committee, Packet #10, circa 1980, 74–78, John Olson Papers, Box 1, USAMHI; Dr. Lester Tenney, interview with Mr. Mike Farrar, June 10, 2012, AFC/2001/001/86613, LOC; Zarate, "American Prisoners of Japan: Did Rank Have Its Privilege?," 183–84, CARL; Peter Maas, "They Should Have Their Day in Court," *Parade*, June 17, 2001, 4–5; Tenney, *My Hitch in Hell*, 144–69; Knox, *Death March*, 364, 399, 419; Fukuoka Number 17 documents and information at www.mansell.com.

5. Camp Conditions Report, Philippine Islands; U.S. Army, Military Intelligence Division, Prisoners of the War in the Philippine Islands, September 20, 1944; Hospital at Cabanatuan Prison Camp and Japanese Atrocities from a Medical Standpoint, all in Record Group 389, Entry 460A, Provost Marshal Records, Box 2135; Notes on the Feeding of American Military Personnel Interned in Cabanatuan Prison Compound #1, Record Group 112, Entry 31, Surgeon General, Administrative Records, Box 213; Major Cecil Sanders, History of Cabanatuan Camp Library, Record Group 407, Philippine Archives Collection, Box 143, Folder 4; Major Elbridge Fendall, diary, June 1, June 28, September 21, 1944, Record Group 407, Philippine Archives Collection, Box 129, Folder 14; Lieutenant Philip Meier, diary, March 1, 1944, Record Group 407, Philippine Archives Collection, Box 136, Folder 13; Mrs.Vazques de Amusategui, unpublished memoir, 106, Record Group 407, Philippine Archives Collection, Box 143A,

Folder 8; Provost Marshal, Report on American Prisoners of War in the Philippines, 50–57; Johnson diary, December 10, 1943, February 11, August 5, September 26, 1944, all at NA; General Harold Johnson, oral history, January 27, 1972, USAMHI; Major General Chester Johnson, "West Point's Tragic Loss Honored by Memorials at Cabanatuan," 10, Armand Hopkins Papers, Box 2, USMA; Zarate, "American Prisoners of Japan: Did Rank Have Its Privilege?," 102–105, CARL; Martin Blumenson, "Harold K. Johnson: Most Remarkable Man," *Army*, August 1968, 19–22; Betty Jones, *The December Ship* (Jefferson, NC: McFarland & Company, 1992), 90–93; Kerr, *Surrender and Survival*, 196–98. A copy of the Johnson diary can also be found at the USAMHI in the Harold K. Johnson Papers, series I, Personal Correspondence, Box 89.

6. Lieutenant Colonel Jack Schwartz, Statement, "Surviving the Sinking of the Oryoku Maru, December 1944," September 14, 1945, Record Group 407, Philippine Archives Collection, Box 147; Johnson diary, October 16, 1944, both at NA; Lieutenant Colonel E. Carl Engelhart, unpublished memoir, 207–15, E. Carl Engelhart Papers, Box 1; Major Dwight Gard, POW notebook; Major Eugene Jacobs, "Diary of a Hell Ship Journey," *Medical Opinion and Review*, November 1970, 67–69, both in Dwight Gard Papers, Box 1; Major General Alva Fitch, oral history, Alva Fitch Papers, Box 1; Johnson, oral history, January 27, 1972, all at USAMHI; Captain Harry Mittenthal, Statement on POW Conditions, Philippines and Japan, 4–6, Harry Mittenthal Papers, Folder 1; Lieutenant Colonel Armand Hopkins, unpublished memoir, 74–76, 95, Armand Hopkins Papers, Box 1, both at USMA; Zarate, "American Prisoners of Japan: Did Rank Have Its Privilege?," 146, CARL; Headquarters, Eighth Army, Office of the Staff Judge Advocate, United States versus Junsaburo Toshino, Shushuke Wada et al., May 4, 1948, copy in author's possession; George Weller, "Yanks Go Mad on Agony Ship," *Chicago Daily News*, November 9, 1945; George Weller, "Death Cruise: Yanks Bomb Yanks," *Chicago Daily News*, November 13, 1945; Gregory Michno, *Death on the Hellships: Prisoners at Sea in the Pacific War*, 258–60; Kerr, *Surrender and Survival*, 217–18, 224; Sorley, *Honorable Warrior*, 75; James, *Years of MacArthur*, vol. 2, 557; Knox, *Death March*, 349–52; Waterford, *Prisoners of the Japanese in World War II*, 163; Information on *Oryoku Maru* ship and passengers at www.mansell.com and www.west-point.org /family/japanese-pow; text of MacArthur speech at www.emersonkent.com; Toshino's shooting victim in the galley was Lieutenant William Brewster.

7. Schwartz, Statement, NA; Mittenthal, Statement on POW Conditions, 11; Johnson, "West Point's Tragic Loss," 15, both at USMA; Johnson, oral history, January 27, 1972; Johnson, interview with James; Jacobs, "Diary of a Hell Ship Journey," 70–74; Engelhart, unpublished memoir, 219, all at USAMHI; Eighth Army, United States versus Toshino, Wada et al.; George Weller, "Death Cruise: From Agony on Hell Ship to Terror at Sea," *Chicago Daily News*, November 14, 1945; George Weller, "Death Cruise: Sun Burns Naked G.I.s," *Chicago Daily News*, November 15, 1945; George Weller, "Death Cruise: Merry Chree-eestmas," *Chicago Daily News*, November 16, 1945; Knox, *Death March*, 354; Kerr, *Surrender and Survival*, 226–28; Michno, *Death on the Hellships*, 261; Sorley, *Honorable Warrior*, 75–76, 80; POW roster at www.west-point .org/family/japanese-pow. Engelhart spoke Japanese, so he often functioned as a translator.

8. Major Arthur Peterson, diary, January 21, 1945, Record Group 15, Box 87, Folder 12, Contributions from the Public Collection, DMMA; Schwartz, Statement, NA; Major John Duffy, letter to Dr. Samuel Gordon, May 1, 1950, Albert Svihra Papers, Box 1; Mittenthal, Statement on POW Conditions, 21; Johnson, "West Point's Tragic Loss," 16–17; Hopkins, unpublished memoir, 96–97, all at USMA; Johnson, oral history, January 27, 1972; Johnson, interview with James; Jacobs, "Diary of a Hell Ship Journey," 76; Engelhart, unpublished memoir, 227, all at USAMHI; Eighth Army, United States versus Toshino, Wada et al.; George Weller, "Death Cruise: Thirst Kills Yanks,"

Chicago Daily News, November 20, 1945; George Weller, "Death Cruise: Hell Ship Ends Trip," *Chicago Daily News*, November 21, 1945; Blumenson, "Most Remarkable Man," *Army*, 21–22; Dominic J. Caraccilo, ed., *Surviving Bataan and Beyond: Colonel Irvin Alexander's Odyssey as a Japanese Prisoner of War* (Mechanicsburg, PA: Stackpole Books, 1999), 209; Knox, *Death March*, 356–57; Kerr, *Surrender and Survival*, 236–37; Sorley, *Honorable Warrior*, 78–79; POW roster at www.west-point.org/family/japanese-pow; Major Walter Kostecki, Statement, at www.mansell.com; Michael Hurst, "The Story of the Bombing of the Enoura Maru," at www.powtaiwan.org. In 1948, both Toshino and Wada were found guilty of war crimes. Toshino was executed by hanging and Wada sentenced to life at hard labor.

8. Triumph and Travesty

1. Territory of Hawaii, Office of the Military Governor, Memorandum to Lieutenant General Robert Richardson, May 26, 1944; Mr. John McCloy, letter to Lieutenant General Robert Richardson, May 17, 1944; Lieutenant General Robert Richardson, letter to Mr. John McCloy, June 16, 1944, all in Robert Richardson Papers, Box 74; Sergeant John Thorburn, letter to Major General Ralph Smith, June 4, 1946, Ralph Smith Papers, Box 7; Lieutenant Colonel William Van Antwerp, unpublished memoir, 1, Ralph Smith Papers, Box 1, all at HIA; Sharon Lacey, "Smith vs. Smith," *World War II*, May/June 2011, 59–62; David Lippman, "Saipan 1944: Smith vs. Smith, Part One," at www.avalanchepress.com; Francis A. O'Brien, *Battling for Saipan* (New York: Ballantine Books, 2003), 31–32; Philip A. Crowl, *United States Army in World War II, The War in the Pacific: Campaign in the Marianas* (Washington, DC: Office of the Chief of Military History, Department of the Army, 1960), 37–39; Gailey, *Howlin' Mad vs the Army*, 35–52.

2. Captain Edmund Love, "The Battle for Saipan, Part 1," 2–6, 8-5.3 BC pt1, CMH; "Operation Forager: The Battle of Saipan, 15 June–9 July 1944," at www.history.navy.mil; Carl W. Hoffman, *Saipan: The Beginning of the End* (Washington, DC: Historical Branch, G-3 Division, Headquarters, U.S. Marine Corps, 1950), 1–2, 13–25; Shaw et al., *Central Pacific Drive*, 231–44; Edmund G. Love, *The 27th Infantry Division in World War II* (Nashville: Battery Press, 1949), 112–17; James H. Hallas, *Saipan: The Battle That Doomed Japan in World War II* (Guildford, CT: Stackpole Books, 2019), 10–14; Carter, *Beans, Bullets, and Black Oil*, 137–41; Harold J. Goldberg, *D-Day in the Pacific: The Battle of Saipan* (Bloomington and Indianapolis: Indiana University Press, 2007), 10–26; the Roosevelt quote about King is recounted in James and William Belote, *Typhoon of Steel: The Battle of Okinawa* (New York: Harper & Row, 1970), 6; Morison, *History, vol. 8: New Guinea and the Marianas*, 157–65, 353–55, 407–411; Crowl, *Campaign in the Marianas*, 33–41. For the sake of simplicity, in this chapter, I will refer to Holland Smith as commander of the V Amphibious Corps, though obviously he played a dual role as commander of the Northern Troops and Landing Force.

3. Van Antwerp, unpublished memoir, 6, HIA; "Holland M. Smith, General, USMC," at www.history.navy.mil; "Holland McTyeire Smith," at Pacific War Encyclopedia, www.pwencyl.kgbudge.com; "Old Man of the Atolls," *Time*, February 21, 1944; Lacey, "Smith vs. Smith," *World War II*, 60–61; Smith and Finch, *Coral and Brass*, 22–63, 137–40; Cooper, *A Fighting General*, 11–70, 154–55; Gailey, *Howlin' Mad vs the Army*, 20–34; McManus, *Fire and Fortitude*, 527–31. Smith held the Navy in no less esteem. His memoir is rife with barbs, veiled and otherwise, against the sea service.

4. Private Charles Richardson, letter to Ms. Althea Blackman, circa 1944, Folder 2477, Accession #2552, SHSM; "Pearl Harbor Ablaze Again: The West Loch Disaster, 21 May 1944," at www.history.navy.mil; Morison, *History, vol. 8: New Guinea and the Marianas*, 171; Crowl, *Campaign in the Marianas*, 47–48; Hoffman, *Saipan: The Beginning of the End*, 32–34; Hallas, *Saipan*, 42–49.

5. Saipan Garrison Plan for the First Expeditionary Force, May 19, 1944, 370.2; Japanese Monograph Number 48, Central Pacific Operations Record, Volume 1, 21, 8-5.1 AC48; Love, "The Battle for Saipan, Part 1," 12–15, all at CMH; ATIS, Enemy Publications, Combat Regulations for Island Garrison Forces (Shubi) Provisional Study of Island Defense, December 25, 1943, Record Group 165, Entry 79, Box 213, #415; Lieutenant Colonel John Lemp, Observer Report on Marianas Operation, July 11, 1944, 3–6, Record Group 337, Entry 15A, Folder 102, both at NA; Van Antwerp, unpublished memoir, 8–9, HIA; Haruko Taya Cook, "The Myth of the Saipan Suicides," *MHQ*, Spring 1995, 12–13; D. Colt Denfield, *Hold the Marianas: The Japanese Defense of the Mariana Islands* (Shippensburg, PA: White Mane Publishing, 1997), 14–32; John Toland, *The Rising Sun: The Decline and Fall of the Japanese Empire, 1936–1945*, vol. 2 (New York: Random House, 1970), 607–613; Cook and Cook, *Japan at War*, 282; Morison, *History, vol. 8: New Guinea and the Marianas*, 149–69; Crowl, *Campaign in the Marianas*, 50–70; Shaw et al., *Central Pacific Drive*, 245–47, 258; Hoffman, *Saipan: The Beginning of the End*, 9, 13, 26–30; Goldberg, *D-Day in the Pacific*, 22–38; Love, *27th Infantry Division in World War II*, 117–19; Hallas, *Saipan*, 25–26, 31, 55–57. Good information on the sinking of the *American Maru* can be accessed at www.combinedfleet.com and www.wrecksite.edu.

6. Report of Canadian Officers Attached to the 27th Infantry Division, U.S. Army for the Saipan Operation, 15 June–9 July 1944, 2–3, Record Group 337, Entry 15A, Box 56, Folder 164; 106th Infantry Regiment, Forager (Saipan) Comments, 24, Record Group 407, Entry 427, Box 7315, Folder 327-INF-106-0.3, both at NA; Tech 3 Vincent Donnolo, diary, May 31, June 3, 1944, 314.81 Diary Donnolo; Love, "The Battle for Saipan, Part 1," 8–11, both at CMH; Charles Hilbert, unpublished memoir, 35–37, WWIIM; Major Max LaGrone, "The Operations of the Second Regiment (Second Marine Division) on Saipan-Tinian, 15 June–1 August 1944, Personal Experience of a Regimental S-4," Advanced Officers Course, 1946–1947, The Infantry School, General Section, 4, DRL; E. A. Red Butler, unpublished memoir, 10–11, copy in author's possession courtesy of Mrs. Ann Butler; Sherrod, *On to Westward*, 31–37; Morison, *History, vol. 8: New Guinea and the Marianas*, 172–73; Love, *27th Infantry Division in World War II*, 117; Goldberg, *D-Day in the Pacific*, 50; Hoffman, *Saipan: The Beginning of the End*, 34; O'Brien, *Battling for Saipan*, 72–74.

7. Task Force 58, Operations in Support of the Capture of the Marianas, September 11, 1944, MS-416, World War II Battle and Operations Reports, Box 23, Folder 1, USNA; Sergeant Tarao Kawaguchi, diary, June 11, 1944, Record Group 112, Entry 31, Surgeon General, Administrative Records, Box 67, NA; United States Strategic Bombing Survey (Pacific), Naval Analysis Division, *Interrogations of Japanese Officials*, vol. 2 (Washington, DC: Government Printing Office, 1946), 429; James D. Hornfischer, *The Fleet at Flood Tide: America at Total War in the Pacific, 1944–1945* (New York: Bantam Books, 2016), 93–94, 97–98, 137; Bruce M. Petty, ed., *Saipan: Oral Histories of the Pacific War* (Jefferson, NC, and London: McFarland & Company, 2002), 32; Goldberg, *D-Day in the Pacific*, 53; Cook and Cook, *Japan at War*, 282–83; Morison, *History, vol. 8: New Guinea and the Marianas*, 165–66, 174–79, 183–84; Denfield, *Hold the Marianas*, 45–47; Hallas, *Saipan*, 67–69, 81–83; Crowl, *Campaign in the Marianas*, 72–78; Hoffman, *Saipan: The Beginning of the End*, 35, 42. The other ship that suffered casualties was the destroyer USS *Braine* with three killed and fifteen wounded. For corroboration, see page 7 of the ship's history at www.ibiblio.org/hyperwar/USN/ships/DD/DD-630_Braine.html.

8. Task Group 52.17, Action Report, Bombardment of Saipan Island, 14 June–9 July 1944, MS416, World War II Battle Action and Operations Reports, Box 18, Folder 7, USNA; First Lieutenant Russell Gugeler, "Army Amphibian Tractor and Tank Battalions in the Battle of Saipan, 15 June–9 July 1944," January 9, 1945, 3–27, 8-5.3 BA c1; Japanese

Monograph 48, 39–40, both at CMH; 4th Marine Division, Operations Report, 15 June–9 July 1944, Record Group 127, Box 328, World War II Area Geographic Files, Folder A14-1; 2nd Marine Division, Summary of Action, Record Group 127, Box 334, World War II Area Geographic Files, Folder A16-3; Lemp, Observer Report on Marianas Operation, 14–15; Kawaguchi diary, June 15, 1944, all at NA; Sergeant Frank Madzey, in collaboration with Sergeant Jack Sprechman, "Of the Amtanks on Saipan," 1, World War II Participants and Contemporaries Collection, Jack Sprechman Folder, EL; Major Howard Hooker, "Amphibian Tank Battalion on Saipan," 15, Instructor Training Division, Advanced Officers Class #1, May 1, 1948, the Armor School, Fort Knox, KY, CARL; LaGrone, "Operations of the Second Regiment," 7, DRL; Seaman William Schmidt, letter to parents, June 14, 1945, Folder 2633, Accession #2558; Private Charles Harvey, letter to Aunt Sue and Andy, July 22, 1944, Folder 1252, Accession #1194; Sergeant Charles Kohler, letter to parents, September 6, 1944, Folder 1663, Accession #2784; Richardson letter, all at SHSM; Butler, unpublished memoir, 29–30; the lieutenant is quoted in "Forgotten Battalions: Amphibian Tanks in the Pacific War," at www.worldoftanks.com; S. E. Smith, ed., *The United States Marine Corps in World War II*, vol. 2: *Battering the Empire* (New York: Ace Books, 1969), 615–18; Shaw et al., *Central Pacific Drive*, 261–87; Hallas, *Saipan*, 86–87, 91–95, 135–43; Petty, *Saipan: Oral Histories of the Pacific War*, 46, 123; Crowl, *Campaign in the Marianas*, 79–96; Hoffman, *Saipan: The Beginning of the End*, 50–73; Denfield, *Hold the Marianas*, 48–58; Sherrod, *On to Westward*, 45; Morison, *History, vol. 8, New Guinea and the Marianas*, 181; Love, *27th Infantry Division in World War II*, 127; Toland, *Decline and Fall of the Japanese Empire*, vol. 2, 614. For more information on casualties for the 1st Infantry Division in the Normandy invasion, see pages 291–92 of my book *The Dead and Those About to Die, D-Day: The Big Red One at Omaha Beach* (New York: NAL Caliber, 2014).

9. Hoffman, *Saipan: The Beginning of the End*, 77–79; Morison, *History, vol. 8: New Guinea and the Marianas*, 213–21; Smith and Finch, *Coral and Brass*, 164–65; Hornfischer, *Fleet at Flood Tide*, 178–211. In addition to their naval losses, the Japanese lost fifty land-based planes in the battle. In the midst of the one-sided victory, Mitscher and Spruance conflicted. The former was aggressive by nature, highly focused on destroying enemy planes and ships; the latter was cautious and circumspect, with a better grasp of the higher strategic purpose of Operation Forager. In this context, Spruance understood that the Fifth Fleet's main job was to protect the landings, not necessarily risk all to sink Japanese ships and destroy their planes.

10. 27th Infantry Division, Battle for Saipan, 17 June–6 August 1944, Record Group 407, Entry 427, Box 7208, Folder 327-0.3; Lemp, Observer Report on Marianas Operation, 20, both at NA; James Warthen, unpublished memoir, 3; Hilbert, unpublished memoir, 37, both at WWIIM; Love, "The Battle for Saipan, Part 1," 35–40, Tech 3 Vincent Donnolo, diary, June 17, 1944, both at CMH; Van Antwerp, unpublished memoir, 21–23, 28, HIA; Love, *27th Infantry Division in World War II*, 124–59; Hoffman, *Saipan: The Beginning of the End*, 84–96; O'Brien, *Battling for Saipan*, 95–96; Morison, *History, vol. 8: New Guinea and the Marianas*, 178; Crowl, *Campaign in the Marianas*, 98–117. For more information on the death of Colonel Gardiner Conroy, see the first volume in this series, *Fire and Fortitude: The U.S. Army in the Pacific War, 1941–1943*.

11. Captain Frank Olander, letter to Captain Edmund Love, May 7, 1947, Record Group 319, Entry 62, Box 6, Records of the Office of the Chief of Military History, Seizure of the Gilberts and the Marshalls; Report of Canadian Officers, 4, both at NA; Lieutenant Colonel Coudert Nast, Civil Affairs Report, 2, 27th Infantry Division G1 Material, CARL; Captain Roy Appleman, "Army Tanks in the Battle for Saipan," 22–25, 8-5.3 BB c1; Japanese Monograph Number 48, Central Pacific Operations Record, Volume I; Tech 3 Vincent Donnolo, diary, June 22, 1944, all at CMH; Major ER Werner

McCabe, "The Operations of the 27th Infantry Division on Saipan Island, Marianas Group, Central Pacific, 16–24, June 1944, Personal Experiences of the Aide to the Division Commander," Advanced Infantry Officers Course, 1948–1949, 13, USAMHI; Van Antwerp, unpublished memoir, 35, HIA; Kohler letter, SHSM; Matthew Hughes, "War Without Mercy? American Armed Forces and the Deaths of Civilians During the Battle for Saipan, 1944," *Journal of Military History*, January 2011, 93–123; Captain Edmund Love, "The 27th's Battle for Saipan," *Infantry Journal*, September 1946, 10; Sharon Tosi Lacey, *Pacific Blitzkrieg: World War II in the Central Pacific* (Denton: University of North Texas Press, 2013), 137–38; Craven and Cate, *The Army Air Forces in World War II*, vol. 4, 689–91; Goldberg, *D-Day in the Pacific*, 148; Sherrod, *On to Westward*, 82; Denfield, *Hold the Marianas*, 59–61, 70; Smith and Finch, *Coral and Brass*, 168–71, italics in original; Petty, *Saipan: Oral Histories of the Pacific War*, 38; Hoffman, *Saipan: The Beginning of the End*, 101; Crowl, *Campaign in the Marianas*, 148–61; Love, *27th Infantry Division in World War II*, 189–94; Hallas, *Saipan: The Battle That Doomed Japan in World War II*, 283–84; Gailey, *Howlin' Mad vs the Army*, 140–48. The majority of the "Japanese" civilians who came into American custody were actually from Okinawa.

12. 27th Infantry Division, Battle for Saipan; Lemp, Observer Report on the Marianas Operation, 28, both at NA; Major Martin Nolan, "The Operations of the 3d Battalion, 165th Infantry (27th Infantry Division) in the Assault of the Eastern Slopes of Mt. Topotchau Hill Mass, Saipan, Mariana Islands, 24–28 June 1944, Central Pacific Theater (Personal Experiences of a Battalion Operations Officer)," Advanced Infantry Officers Course, 1948–1949, 9; Captain Charles Hallden, "The Operations of Company L, 3rd Battalion, 106th Infantry (27th Infantry Division) in the Battle of Death Valley, Saipan, 23 June–28 June 1944, Western Pacific Campaign (Personal Experiences of a Company Commander)," Advance Infantry Officers Class No. I, 1947–1948, 33, both at DRL; McCabe, "The Operations of the 27th Infantry Division on Saipan," 22, USAMHI; Major William Allen IV, "Sacked at Saipan," School of Advanced Military Studies, United States Army Command and General Staff College, Ft. Leavenworth, KS, 15, CARL; Captain Edmund Love, Memo for Commanding General, 27th Infantry Division, September 27, 1944, Gerard W. Kelley Papers, Box 1; Van Antwerp, unpublished memoir, 50, 56, both at HIA; Major General Sanderford Jarman, Memo for the Record, June 23, 1944, 319.1 Buckner Board; Colonel Geoffrey O'Connell, Memorandum for General Richardson, July 12, 1944, 314.7, both at CMH; Sharon Lacey, "Smith vs. Smith," *World War II*, May/June 2011, 65; Edmund Love, "Smith Versus Smith," *Infantry Journal*, November 1948, 10; Robert Sherrod, "The Saipan Controversy," *Infantry Journal*, January 1949, 19; Love, "The 27th's Battle for Saipan," *Infantry Journal*, 12; Shaw et al., *Central Pacific Drive*, 313–14; Love, *27th Infantry Division in World War II*, 222, 236–46; Crowl, *Campaign in the Marianas*, 180–201; Sherrod, *On to Westward*, 88–89; Gailey, *Howlin' Mad vs the Army*, 176–78, 181–89.

13. Proceedings of the Buckner Board, August 4, 1944 (the original report is misdated to July 4), Ralph Smith Papers, Box 7, HIA; Lieutenant General Simon Bolivar Buckner, diary, April 24, 1945, Simon Bolivar Buckner Papers, Box 1, EL; Vice Admiral Richmond Kelly Turner, Memo, August 18, 1944; Lieutenant General Holland Smith, Memo, August 28, 1944, both in Record Group 127, Box 334, World War II Area Geographic Files, Folder A16-3, NA; Brigadier General Roy Blount, letter to Lieutenant General Robert Richardson, November 15, 1948, underline in original, Robert Richardson Papers, Box 36, HIA; Lieutenant General Robert Richardson, Editorial, reprinted on page 28 of Sherrod, "The Saipan Controversy," *Infantry Journal*; Ray Richards, "Army General Relieved in Row over High Marine Losses," *San Francisco Examiner*, July 8, 1944, 1; Love, "Smith Versus Smith," *Infantry Journal*, 6–12; Cooper, *A Fighting General*, 207, 216; Smith and Finch, *Coral and Brass*, 176–79; Crowl,

Campaign in the Marianas, 192; Gailey, *Howlin' Mad vs the Army*, 219–21. Holland Smith believed that Ralph Smith had defied him by issuing orders to 27th Division units that were supposed to remain under corps control, and he pointed to this as a reason for relieving him. In reality, Ralph Smith did not deliberately defy his corps commander. This minor issue instead resulted from a miscommunication on Holland Smith's part. The corps commander undoubtedly knew this by the time he wrote his memo, but he probably mentioned the supposed disobedience of orders as a way to build his overall case for firing Ralph Smith.

14. Colonel Russell Ayers, After Action Report, 20–26 June 1944, 106th Infantry Regiment, Russell Ayers Papers, Box 1, USMA; Colonel Albert Stebbins, Narrative Account of Operations of the 27th Infantry Division during the Period 16–26, June 1944, July 14, 1944, Record Group 407, Entry 427, Box 7316, Folder 327-INF-106-0.3.0; Extracts from Operations Reports on Reduction of Japanese Cave-Type Fortifications, May 2, 1945, 16, Record Group 337, Entry 15A, Box 68, Folder 426; 27th Infantry Division, Battle for Saipan; Kawaguchi diary, June 29, 1944, all at NA; Love, "The Battle for Saipan, Part I," 294–95; Appleman, "Army Tanks in the Battle for Saipan," 37–39; Donnolo diary, June 27, 1944, all at CMH; Historical Review, Statistical and Evacuation Section, Surgeon General's Office, Central Pacific Base Command, 16, Vertical Files, Box 20, Folder 311, USAMHI; Hilbert, unpublished memoir, 49, WWIIM; Kohler letter, SHSM; Felix Giuffre, "Remembering Father Brunet," *Orion Gallivanter*, June 1992, 8; John O'Brien, "Saipan," *Orion Gallivanter*, June 1991, 5; Love, "The 27th's Battle for Saipan," *Infantry Journal*, 13; Cook and Cook, *Japan at War*, 287; Goldberg, *D-Day in the Pacific*, 164–65; Toland, *Decline and Fall of the Japanese Empire*, vol. 2, 638–39; Denfield, *Hold the Marianas*, 81; Love, *27th Infantry Division in World War II*, 254–55, 324–25; Crowl, *Campaign in the Marianas*, 211–13, 230–32.

15. Major General George Griner, Statement, July 12, 1944; Major Takashi Hirakushi, "The Last Days of Lieutenant General Saito," July 14, 1944, both in Record Group 127, Box 334, World War II Area Geographic Files, Folder A16-3; Kawaguchi diary, July 5, 7, 1944, all at NA; Cook, "The Myth of the Saipan Suicides," *MHQ*, 14–15; Love, "The 27th's Battle for Saipan," *Infantry Journal*, 15; Don Jones, *Oba: The Last Samurai: Saipan 1944–1945* (Novato, CA: Presidio Press, 1986), 54–56; Cook and Cook, *Japan at War*, 288–89; Toland, *Decline and Fall of the Japanese Empire*, vol. 2, 604; Smith and Finch, *Coral and Brass*, 175; Denfield, *Hold the Marianas*, 87–88; Morison, *History, vol. 8: New Guinea and the Marianas*, 336–37; Love, *27th Infantry Division in World War II*, 331; Hallas, *Saipan: The Battle That Doomed Japan in World War II*, 365–67; Gailey, *Howlin' Mad vs the Army*, 202–204. Neither Hirakushi nor any other survivor actually witnessed the suicides of Saito, Igeta, and Nagumo. As a result, we are unlikely to know the precise circumstances of how they actually ended their lives. Hirakushi merely asserted that Saito almost certainly observed the proper hara-kiri ritual.

16. 27th Infantry Division, Battle for Saipan, NA; Japanese Monograph Number 48, Central Pacific Operations Record, Volume I; Love, "The Battle for Saipan," Part II, 862–72; Donnolo diary, July 7, 1944; Appleman, "Army Tanks in the Battle for Saipan," 100–110, all at CMH; Sergeant Victor Mazzeo, Statement, no date, also signed by Sergeant Anton Sandles, Private Louis Pavona, PFC Guianto Chianchiano, PFC Roy Ogle, and PFC Steward Loyd, Robert Richardson Papers, Box 36; Van Antwerp, unpublished memoir, 115, 119–20, both at HIA; Administrative History of Medical Activities in the Middle Pacific, Office of the Surgeon, the Marianas Campaign, Phase I, the Capture of Saipan, 32, U.S. Army Forces Middle Pacific, Office of the Surgeon Collection, Box 2, Block 18d, USAMHI; Dr. Robert West, letter to Congressman Brad Sherman, July 7, 1997, and April 28, 1998; Captain Edmund Love, sworn statement, October 17, 1969; Dr. Eugene Saberski, sworn statement, March 22, 1969; Colonel

Miles Bidwell, sworn statement; Mr. Stephen Burns, sworn statement, August 6, 1969, all in Captain Benjamin Salomon Medal of Honor packet, U.S. Army Awards and Decorations Branch, Fort Knox, KY, copy in author's possession courtesy of Mr. Bradley Hunt; John C. McManus, "Ben Salomon's Battle," *World War II*, October 2020, 40–49; Lieutenant Colonel William Van Antwerp, "Warning of the Banzai Attack," Captain Frank Olander, Statement, and Mr. Ben Salomon Sr., letter to Captain Edmund Love, listed respectively on pages 20–21, 23, and 24 of Sherrod, "The Saipan Controversy," *Infantry Journal*; Cook, "Myth of the Saipan Suicides," 15, *MHQ*; Love, "The 27th's Battle for Saipan," 15, *Infantry Journal*; Major General Patrick Sculley, "At the Intersection of Character and Circumstance," unpublished story of Captain Ben Salomon, copy in author's possession, and e-mail exchanges, September–October, 2019; Edmund G. Love, *War Is a Private Affair* (New York: Harcourt, Brace, 1959), 160–71; O'Brien, *Battling for Saipan*, 229, 238, 245; Love, *27th Infantry Division in World War II*, 437–38, 454–56; Petty, *Saipan: Oral Histories of the Pacific War*, 138; Toland, *Decline and Fall of the Japanese Empire*, vol. 2, 642–43; Crowl, *Campaign in the Marianas*, 256–59. For confirmation that the 1929 Geneva Convention allows medics to use weapons to defend themselves and their patients, see www.ihl-databases.icrc.org/. According to John Toland, the area where the Japanese staged for the attack was still littered with hundreds of empty liquor bottles in 1969.

17. 31st Field Hospital, Report of Activities in the Saipan and Tinian Mission, August 16, 1944, 3–7, Record Group 112, Entry UD1012, Surgeon General, HUMEDS, Box 69; 106th Infantry Regiment, Forager Comments; Griner statement, July 12, 1944, 3–5; 27th Infantry Division, Battle for Saipan, all at NA; Major James Bartholomees, "Operations of the 773rd Amphibian Tractor Battalion (Attached to the 27th Division) in the Operation on Tanapag Plans, Saipan, 7–8 July 1944, Western Pacific Campaign (Personal Experiences of a Battalion Executive Officer)," Advanced Infantry Officers Course, 1947–1948, 11, DRL; Van Antwerp, unpublished memoir, 104, 112, 123, HIA; Donnolo diary, July 7 and 11, 1944, CMH; Kohler letter, SHSM; Robert Cypher letter, *Orion Gallivanter*, December 1990, 8; Lieutenant Colonel Oakley Bidwell, G1 Report, 4, CARL; Van Antwerp statement in Sherrod, "The Saipan Controversy," *Infantry Journal*, 21; Shaw et al., *Central Pacific Drive*, 342; Hoffman, *Saipan: The Beginning of the End*, 233; Sherrod, *On to Westward*, 133, 140; Crowl, *Campaign in the Marianas*, 261; Gailey, *Howlin' Mad vs the Army*, 214. Like so many other aspects of the Saipan battle, the body count of dead Japanese in the wake of the attack became a point of controversy between the Army and the Marines, mainly because of Holland Smith's skepticism over the size of the assault and the fighting acumen of the 27th Division. As a result, Griner personally supervised the count and prepared an estimate of how many Japanese his soldiers killed versus nearby Marine units. To explore the documentation over this issue, see Major General George Griner, memo to the Commanding General, Northern Troops and Landing Force, July 13, 1944, Memo to Northern Troops and Landing Force, July 16, 1944, Major General Harry Schmidt, memo to Major General George Griner, July 15, 1944, and Lieutenant Colonel Oakley Bidwell, memo to Commanding General, 27th Infantry Division, July 12, 1944, all at Robert Richardson Papers, Box 73, HIA. This correspondence was made available by the Hoover Institution only in 2016. The Marine Corps official historians Shaw and Hoffman accepted and cited the numbers compiled by Griner and his staff.

18. Soldier Attitude Surveys, Hospital Survey, January 1945, 3, Record Group 330, Entry 92, Records of the Secretary of Defense, Box 20, S193, NA; Captain James Rooney, Report of Medical Inspector, Saipan Operation, 1–6; Major Albert Pattillo, Report of Activities of the Division Psychiatrist during Saipan Operation, 1–3, Bidwell G1 Report, 4, all at CARL; Major Max LaGrone, "The Operations of the Second Regiment (Second Marine Division) on Saipan-Tinian, 15 June–1 August, 1944, (Personal

Experiences of a Regimental S-4)," Advanced Officers Course, 1946–1947, 14, DRL; Butler, unpublished memoir, 247–48, copy in author's possession; Cook, "Myth of the Saipan Suicides," 16–18, *MHQ*; Condon-Rall and Cowdrey, *Medical Service in the War against Japan*, 240; Sherrod, *On to Westward*, 147, 246–47; Crowl, *Campaign in the Marianas*, 265; Toland, *Decline and Fall of the Japanese Empire*, vol. 2, 653-62; Hallas, *Saipan: The Battle That Doomed Japan in World War II*, 430–41, 444–45. The emperor did not ask Tojo to join the jushin until February 1945.

19. Admiral Chester Nimitz, letter to Admiral Ernest King, October 27, 1944; Admiral Ernest King, letter to General George Marshall, November 6, 1944; General George Marshall, letter to Admiral Ernest King, November 22, 1944; Griner statement, all in Record Group 127, Box 334, World War II Area Geographic Files, Folder A16-3, NA; Major General George Griner, letter to Lieutenant General Robert Richardson, September 30, 1944, Charles Nast Papers, Box 1, USAMHI; Major General George Griner, "Combat Service Under the Command of Lieutenant General H. M. Smith, USMC," October 11, 1944; Major General Sanderford Jarman, statement, September 6, 1944; Major General Ralph Smith, statement, August 28, 1944; Brigadier General Redmond Kernan, statement, August 16, 1944, all at 370.2 27th Infantry Division, CMH; Sergeant John Thorburn, letter to Major General Ralph Smith, December 27, 1944, Ralph Smith Papers, Box 7; Lieutenant Edmund Love, Memo to Commanding General, 27th Infantry Division, September 27, 1944, Gerard W. Kelley Papers, Box 1; Major General George Griner, letter to the editor of *Time* magazine, September 28, 1944; Lieutenant Edmund Love, "Facts Relating to Article in Time Magazine, 18 September 1944," September 30, 1944, both in Robert Richardson Papers, Box 36; Colonel Gerard Kelley, letter to Congressman James Fay, October 9, 1944, Gerard W. Kelley Papers, Box 1 (Kelley also wrote letters to Brigadier General William Donovan, the head of the OSS, and Lieutenant General William Haskell); Captain John Gaddis, letter to Major Hugh Lytle, July 21, 1944; Censorship Intercepts from 27th Infantry Division Mail, 1944–1945, both in Robert Richardson Papers, Box 73, all at HIA; "The Generals Smith," *Time*, September 18, 1944, 68 (Sherrod did not have a byline but he wrote the article); Sherrod, "The Saipan Controversy," *Infantry Journal*, 23; Love, "Smith Versus Smith," *Infantry Journal*, 13; Ray Boomhower, *Dispatches from the Pacific: The World War II Reporting of Robert Sherrod* (Bloomington: Indiana University Press, 2017), 156–60, 168; Shaw et al., *Central Pacific Drive*, 352; Smith and Finch, *Coral and Brass*, 179; Cooper, *A Fighting General*, 215–16; Love, *27th Infantry Division in World War II*, 668–70; Gailey, *Howlin' Mad vs the Army*, 218, 234–42. The controversy took on a new life after the war when Holland Smith, against the heartfelt advice of friends and colleagues, ripped the 27th Division and the Army in his postwar memoir as well as in an article entitled "My Troubles with the Army on Saipan," published in the *Saturday Evening Post*, November 13, 1948. Smith's writings provoked a strident interservice quarrel between the Marine Corps and the Army. Richardson published a rebuttal in the December 11, 1948, issue of the *Saturday Evening Post*. Griner published one in *Infantry Journal*. Adherents of the 27th, and the division association, wrote editorials and lobbied the War Department for an official statement repudiating Holland Smith's criticisms. By this time, the Marine general had become a hated pariah to them. In an angry letter to Ralph Smith on August 22, 1949, Edmund Love described Holland Smith as "the most ignorant, and at the same time, deliberate liar who ever wore the stars of a General officer." Love and other friends of Ralph Smith, who by now had retired from the Army, urged him to make a public statement to set the record straight. True to form, he refused. "I have felt my best position was to remain silent," he wrote to his old friend Colonel Truman Smith on November 15, 1948; "It's hard to win a contest with a skunk." The letters can be found in the Ralph Smith Papers, Boxes 1 and 7, respectively at HIA. Ralph Smith kept quiet about his relief and

the other controversies for over forty years. Only in the 1980s, during a series of private interviews with historian Harry Gailey, did he discuss the topic.

9. Right Way and Wrong Way

1. Task Group 53.2, Guam After Action Report, August 29, 1944, 3, MS-416, World War II Battle Action and Operations Reports, Box 22, Folder 2, USNA; William Morgan, oral history, William Morgan Collection, AFC/2001/001/30140, LOC; Harry A. Gailey, *The Liberation of Guam, 21 July–10 August 1944* (Novato, CA: Presidio Press, 1988), 67–70; Major O. R. Lodge, *The Recapture of Guam* (Washington, DC: Historical Branch, G-3 Division, Headquarters, U.S. Marine Corps, 1954), 16–28; Carter, *Beans, Bullets and Black Oil*, 137–48; Shaw et al., *Central Pacific Drive*, 422–23; Crowl, *Campaign in the Marianas*, 299–312; Morison, *History, vol. 8: New Guinea and the Marianas*, 343–45. Holland Smith made sure that the 27th Division did not participate in the Tinian operation.

2. Captain Randy Seligman, letter to Lieutenant Mary Jane Anderson, June 7, 1944, Mary Jane Anderson Papers, Vertical Files, Box 29, Folder 447, USAMHI; Men Who Were There, *Ours to Hold It High: The History of the 77th Infantry Division in World War II*, ed. Max Myers (Washington, DC: Infantry Journal Press, 1947), 29–43; Donald O. Dencker, *Love Company: Infantry Combat Against the Japanese, World War II: Leyte and Okinawa* (Manhattan, KS: Sunflower University Press, 2002), 47–48; Charles O. West, *Second to None: The Story of the 305th Infantry in World War II* (Washington, DC: Infantry Journal Press, 1949), 100–106, and also see pages 37–90 for background on the division's many training cycles; Crowl, *Campaign in the Marianas*, 315–19; Gailey, *Liberation of Guam*, 79.

3. Major General Andrew Bruce, Biography, Record Group 407, Entry 427, Box 9789, Folder 377-0; Sergeant James MacGregor Burns, Informal notes from interview with Major General Andrew Bruce, Record Group 319, Entry P57, Box 1, Records of the Office of the Chief of Military History, American Forces in Action, Guam, Operations of the 77th Division, both at NA; Sergeant A. R. Gunner, letter to Lieutenant General Andrew Bruce, circa 1951, Andrew Bruce Papers, Box 7; Brigadier General Edwin Randle, letter to Mrs. Roberta Bruce, August 5, 1969, Andrew Bruce Papers, Box 1; Major General Andrew Bruce, letter to Major Robert Murphey, April 6, 1944; Captain Paul Leach, letter to Major General Andrew Bruce, January 30, 1946, both in Andrew Bruce Papers, Box 10; Anonymous United States Navy Officer, letter to Major General Andrew Bruce, January 16, 1945, Andrew Bruce Papers, Box 6; Sister Matilde Romero, Mother Superior, letter to Major General Andrew Bruce, September 13, 1945, Andrew Bruce Papers, Box 8, all at USAMHI; General Roy Geiger, Biography, Reference Branch Files, United States Marine Corps History and Museums Division, (USMCHD), Quantico, VA; General Roy Geiger, Lieutenant General Andrew Bruce, biographies at www.arlingtoncemetery.net; General Roy Geiger, biography at www .findagrave.com; "Lieutenant General Andrew Davis Bruce," at www.uh.edu/adbruce /about; *Ours to Hold It High*, 30–31, 39; West, *Second to None*, 106. After the war, Sergeant Burns earned fame as a leading biographer of Franklin Roosevelt.

4. Major L. A. Gilson, letter to Major O. R. Lodge, February 11, 1952; Vice Admiral Richard Connolly, letter to Commandant of the Marine Corps, November 12, 1952, Record Group 127, U.S. Marine Corps History and Museums Division, Publication Background Files, Recapture of Guam, Box 12, Folders 8 and 5 respectively (underline in original Connolly letter); Lieutenant Colonel Takeshi Takeda, letter to Brigadier General J. C. McQueen, Marine Corps Historical Center, February 20, 1952, Record Group 127, Box 68, Folder 17; Task Force 53.2, After Action Report; Task Force 53.4, After Action Report; Task Force 53.3.1, After Action Report; Task Force 53.4.2, After Action Report, Record Group 127, Box 49, Folders 3, 5, 6 and 8 respectively; 3rd Marine

Division, D3 Comments on Naval Gunfire Support, Annex C, Record Group 127, Box 50, Folder 9, all at NA; Lieutenant Colonel Takeshi Takeda, "The Outline of Japanese Defense Plan and Battle of Guam Island," October 4, 1946, Box 1, Folder 11, Lester Dessez Papers, Gray Research Center, USMCHD; Major General Haruo Umezawa and Colonel Louis Metzger, "The Defense of Guam," *Marine Corps Gazette*, August 1964, 37–39; I. E. McMillan," Naval Gunfire at Guam," *Marine Corps Gazette*, September 1948, 52–56; John C. McManus, *Grunts: Inside the American Infantry Combat Experience, World War II Through Iraq* (New York: NAL Caliber, 2010), 19–23; Lodge, *Recapture of Guam*, 7–9, 106; Shaw et al., *Central Pacific Drive*, 441–49; Morison, *History, vol. 8: New Guinea and the Marianas*, 12, 378–79; Crowl, *Campaign in the Marianas*, 330–42; Petty, *Saipan: Oral Histories of the Pacific War*, 80–81, 87–89; Gailey, *Liberation of Guam*, 37–41, 64–65.

5. 3rd Marine Division, Report on Guam Operations, August 8, 1944; AAR, Record Group 127, Box 50, Folders 8 and 9 respectively; 1st Provisional Marine Brigade, Unit Reports, July 21–22, 1944, Record Group 127, Box 57, Folder 13; 305th Infantry Regiment, Operation Report on Forager, August 16, 1944; 306th Infantry Regiment, Inclosure #1 to Operations Reports, no date, both in 77th Infantry Division, Comments on the Forager (Guam) Operation, Record Group 407, Entry 427, Box 9789, Folder 377-0.3, all at NA; UDT Team #4, AAR, Guam Operation, August 15, 1944, MS-416, World War II Battle Action and Operations Reports, Box 20, Folder 7, USNA; Committee 8, Officers Advanced Course, "Armor in Operation Forager: A Research Report," 121–22, The Armored School, May 1949, Fort Knox, KY, located in DRL; Japanese Monograph Number 48, Central Pacific Operations Record, Volume I, CMH; Ernest Schichler, unpublished memoir, 4, World War II Veterans Survey, no number; Richard Forse, World War II Veterans Survey #3173, both at USAMHI; Henry D. Lopez, "*From Jackson to Japan: The History of Company C, 307th Infantry, 77th Division, in World War II*," self-published, 1977, 73, copy in author's possession; Historical Division, War Department, *Guam: Operations of the 77th Division, 21 July–10 August 1944* (Washington, DC: Center of Military History, United States Army, 1990), 21–41, a book written by James MacGregor Burns, based on the material he gathered as a combat historian; Robert A. Arthur and Kenneth Cohlmia, *The Third Marine Division*, edited by Robert T. Vance (Washington, DC: Infantry Journal Press, 1948), 143–49; Smith, editor, *United States Marine Corps in World War II*, vol. 2, 645; McManus, *Grunts*, 16, 22–32; Morison, *History, vol. 8: New Guinea and the Marianas*, 379–80; West, *Second to None*, 109–12; Shaw et al., *Central Pacific Drive*, 458–78; Crowl, *Campaign in the Marianas*, 344–45; Lodge, *Recapture of Guam*, 37–64; *Ours to Hold It High*, 63; Gailey, *Liberation of Guam*, 87–112.

6. 3rd Marine Division, Report on Guam Operations; AAR; Bruce interview notes; Takeda letter, 11, all at NA; General Allen Turnage, biography, Reference Branch Files, USMCHD; Lieutenant General Andrew Bruce, letter to General Lemuel Shepherd, October 31, 1952; letter to Major General A. C. Smith, February 11, 1955; General Lemuel Shepherd, letter to Lieutenant General Andrew Bruce, November 4, 1952, all in Andrew Bruce Papers, Box 8; Captain Randy Seligman, letter to Lieutenant Mary Jane Anderson, September 20, 1944, Mary Jane Anderson Papers, Vertical Files, Box 29, Folder 447, all at USAMHI; 706th Tank Battalion, After Action Report, 21 July—9 August 1944, CARL; Carl Coker, e-mail to author, March 5, 2008; Lieutenant Colonel Max Myers, "'Lookit Those Old Buzzards Go!'" *Saturday Evening Post*, January 11, 1947, 71; Robert "Pepper" Martin, "Notes from Guam," *Marine Corps Gazette*, October 1944, 19–20; Umezawa and Metzger, "The Defense of Guam," *Marine Corps Gazette*, 42–43; Historical Division, *Guam*, 61–70; *Ours to Hold It High*, 76–81; West, *Second to None*, 112; Shaw et al., *Central Pacific Drive*, 503–517; Lodge, *Recapture of*

Guam, 78–88; Arthur and Cohlmia, *Third Marine Division*, 152–59. For an in-depth account of the Japanese July 25–26 attack, see pages 36–51 of my book *Grunts*.

7. Major General Andrew Bruce, Participation in the Guam Campaign, September 26, 1944, Record Group 407, Entry 427, Box 9789, Folder 377-0; 307th Infantry Regiment, Report on Forager, 3; 305th Infantry Regiment, Operation Report on Forager, 8; Lieutenant Colonel John Ivins, Surgeon, 77th Infantry Division, Operation Report, August 15, 1944; 36th Field Hospital Report of Activities During Guam Operations Between 24 July 1944, and 14 August 1944, all in Comments on the Forager Operation, all at NA; Task Group 53.2, AAR, 3, USNA; Administrative History of Medical Activities in the Middle Pacific, Office of the Surgeon, the Marianas Campaign, 19, U.S. Army Forces Middle Pacific, Office of the Surgeon Collection, Box 2, Block 18d; Richard Spencer, unpublished memoir, 14, World War II Veterans Survey, no number; Schichler, unpublished memoir, 2, all at USAMHI; Tech Sergeant Virgil Fruckey, poem, Folder 959, Accession #2662, SHSM; United States Army in the Central Pacific Area, Participation in the Marianas Operation, 370.2, CMH; Bush is quoted in Paul Borja, "Liberators Meet the Liberated," at www.nps.gov; Major General A. D. Bruce, "Administration Supply, and Evacuation of the 77th Infantry Division on Guam," *Military Review*, December 1944, 6–8; *Ours to Hold It High*, 84–91, 125; Crowl, *Campaign in the Marianas*, 383–85; Gailey, *Liberation of Guam*, 154–61. For more information on S. L. A. Marshall's ratio of fire, see his book *Men Against Fire: The Problem of Battle Command* (Norman: University of Oklahoma Press, 2000 reprint). He was a pioneering combat historian, a dedicated soldier, and a fine writer, but he presented no evidence to support his somewhat absurd contentions.

8. 2nd and 3rd Battalions, 305th Infantry Regiment, Operations on Guam, September 9, 1944, Record Group 407, Entry 427, Box 9895, Folder 377-INF-305-0.3; Staff Sergeant James MacGregor Burns, Report of Historian of the 77th Infantry Division on Guam, October 23, 1944, Record Group 319, Entry 77, Box 6, Records of the Office of the Chief of Military History, Time Runs Out in CBI; Major James Doyle, G1 Operations Report, August 16, 1944, in Comments on the Forager Operation; Bruce, Participation in Guam Campaign, all at NA; Lieutenant General Andrew Bruce, Comments on "The Recapture of Guam," October 31, 1952, Andrew Bruce Papers, Box 8; Captain Randy Seligman, letter to Lieutenant Mary Jane Anderson, September 10, 1944, Mary Jane Anderson Papers, Vertical Files, Box 29, Folder 447, both at USAMHI; Takeda, "Outline of Japanese Defense Plan," 4, USMCHD; 706th Tank Battalion, AAR, CARL; Japanese Monograph, Number 48, Central Pacific Operations Record, Volume I, CMH; Bruce, "Administration, Supply and Evacuation," *Military Review*, 3; Historical Division, *Guam*, 75–101, 127–31; *Ours to Hold It High*, 89–123; Crowl, *Campaign in the Marianas*, 386–434; West, *Second to None*, 113–15; Lodge, *Recapture of Guam*, 159; Gailey, *Liberation of Guam*, 161–87. The cave in which the Americans found sixty bodies might well have been the location of Obata's headquarters.

9. 36th Field Hospital, AAR, in Comments on the Forager Operation, NA; Captain Nathaniel Saucier, letter to Mrs. J. H. Spear, February 13, 1945; Captain Lee Cothran, letter to Mrs. Mary Lee Spear, September 2, 1944, both in Connie Davis Collection, #2010.054, NWWIIM; Spencer, unpublished memoir, 13; Sergeant Alfred Cauley, Major Harry Cutting, Statements on the death of Colonel Douglas C. McNair, August 14, 1944, Major General Andrew Bruce, letter to Colonel Ralph Mace, October 14, 1946; Major General Andrew Bruce, letter to Mrs. Freda McNair, August 14, 1944; Major General Andrew Bruce, letter to Mrs. Clare McNair, August 14, 1944, all in Andrew Bruce Papers, Box 10, USAMHI; "Douglas C. McNair, 1928," at www.westpoint.aog .org; Eugene Wright, "The Jap Fighting Man," *Infantry Journal*, February 1945, 47; Umezawa and Metzger, "The Defense of Guam," *Marine Corps Gazette*, 43; *Ours to*

Hold It High, 112, 123–25; Crowl, *Campaign in the Marianas*, 416, 436–37; Denfield, *Hold the Marianas*, 204; Shaw et al., *Central Pacific Drive*, 531–33; Lodge, *Recapture of Guam*, 164–65; Morison, *History, vol. 8: New Guinea and the Marianas*, 400–401; Gailey, *Liberation of Guam*, 187. Holland Smith, in his capacity as the ranking American ground commander in the Marianas, made two brief visits to Guam during the latter stages of the battle. True to form, he comported himself with ignorant brusqueness. Without understanding anything about the ferocity of Japanese resistance in the wake of W Day, including the all-out assault on July 25–26, he leveled criticism at Geiger over the supposed slowness of the operation. Surprisingly, this time Smith directed much of his invective at the 3rd Marine Division and not at a specific Army unit. For his latter-year thoughts on the Guam battle, see pages 215–18 in Smith and Finch's *Coral and Brass*.

10. General Douglas MacArthur, letter to General George Marshall, June 18, 1944, Record Group 46, Box 2, Folder 14, Paul Rogers Papers; Dr. Roger Egeberg, interview with Dr. D. Clayton James, June 30, 1971, Record Group 49, Box 2, D. Clayton James Collection, both at DMMA; General George Marshall, letter to General Douglas MacArthur, June 24, 1944, Record Group 200, Entry 19810 (A1), Richard Sutherland Papers, Box 40, NA; General Robert Eichelberger, Dictations, September 14, 1959, 2, Box 73, Robert Eichelberger Papers; General Robert Eichelberger, letter to Major General Clovis Byers, October 23, 1959, Box 22, Robert Eichelberger Papers; Brigadier General Clovis Byers, Memo for Lieutenant General Robert Eichelberger, December 4, 1945, Box 16, Robert Eichelberger Papers, all at DU; Smith, *Approach to the Philippines*, 11–12; James, *Years of MacArthur*, vol. 2, 522–25; Borneman, *MacArthur at War*, 377–79; Kenney, *The MacArthur I Know*, 156.

11. Weldon "Dusty" Rhoades, Oral History, no date, Record Group 32, Oral History #38, DMMA; Lieutenant General Robert Eichelberger, interview with General MacArthur in the presence of Brigadier General Clovis Byers, "General MacArthur's Own Story of his Conference in Honolulu with President Roosevelt and the Navy," conducted on December 20, 1947, Robert Eichelberger Papers, Box 1, USAMHI (with MacArthur's approval, Eichelberger took handwritten notes of their conversation and later had them typed up); Lieutenant General Robert Richardson, letter to General George Marshall, August 1, 1944, Robert Richardson Papers, Box 74, HIA; President Franklin Roosevelt, Daily Log, July 21–26, 1944, at www.fdrlibrary.marist.edu; Honolulu weather data for July 26, 1944, accessed at www.weatherunderground.com; The 81st Wildcat Division Historical Committee, *The 81st Infantry Wildcat Division in World War II* (Washington, DC: Infantry Journal Press, 1948), 59; Ian W. Toll, *Twilight of the Gods: War in the Western Pacific, 1944–1945* (New York: W. W. Norton, 2020), 45–50, 60–67; Leahy, *I Was There*, 249–50; MacArthur, *Reminiscences*, 198–99; Rhoades, *Flying MacArthur to Victory*, 249, 256–57; Luvaas, *Dear Miss Em*, 155–56; James, *Years of MacArthur*, vol. 2, 527–32; Borneman, *MacArthur at War*, 394–99; Manchester, *American Caesar*, 424; E. B. Potter, *Nimitz*, 184–90. Apparently, there were only two sizable open-top cars on Oahu, a bright red vehicle that belonged to the fire chief and a larger car owned by the woman who ran a prosperous house of prostitution in Honolulu. Though the fire chief's vehicle was smaller and less comfortable, General Richardson prudently chose it to transport his distinguished visitors.

12. General Douglas MacArthur, Answers to Questions Submitted by Dr. Louis Morton, February 8, 1954, Record Group 10, Box 119, Folder 11, General Douglas MacArthur Private Correspondence; President Franklin Roosevelt, letter to General Douglas MacArthur, August 9, 1944; General Douglas MacArthur, letter to President Franklin Roosevelt, August 26, 1944, both in Record Group 15, Box 23, Folder 23, Contributions from the Public Collection; Rhoades oral history, all at DMMA; Fleet Admiral Chester Nimitz, letter to Midshipman Etheridge King, December 7, 1953, MS-335, E. B.

Potter Papers, Box 1, Folder 14, USNA; Eichelberger, "General MacArthur's Own Story," USAMHI; President Franklin Roosevelt, Daily Log, July 26–28, 1944, at www .fdrlibrary.marist.edu; MacArthur, *Reminiscences*, 101, 197–98; James, *Years of MacArthur*, vol. 2, 530–35; Schaller, *Far Eastern General*, 16–18, 84–88; Luvaas, *Dear Miss Em*, 156; Toll, *Twilight of the Gods*, 70–82; Manchester, *American Caesar*, 166, 424–28; Leahy, *I Was There*, 250–51; Rhoades, *Flying MacArthur to Victory*, 260–61. MacArthur claimed to Eichelberger that, at some point during the Oahu meetings, Pa Watson, one of Roosevelt's key aides, took the general aside and offered him any administration position he wanted, including secretary of war, in exchange for supporting the president's reelection bid. Toll placed the main conference among Roosevelt, Leahy, Nimitz, and MacArthur on the morning of July 28, but most other sources claim it occurred the previous evening after dinner.

13. Proceedings, Octagon/Quebec Conference, CCS Conference Proceedings, 1941–1945, Box 3, EL; SWPA Planning Conference Notes, August 10, 16, 1944, Record Group 29c. Box 1, Folder 4, Richard J. Marshall Papers; SWPA G2 Monthly Summary of Enemy Dispositions, July 31, 1944, and September 30, 1944, in Record Group 3, Box 18, Folders 1 and 3, respectively; Mrs. Natalie Carney, letter to Dr. Paul Rogers, circa 1983, Record Group 46, Box 1, Folder 3, Paul Rogers Papers; Major General Richard Marshall, letter to General Douglas MacArthur regarding the Octagon Conference, September 28, 1944, Record Group 29-e, Box 1, Folder 4, Richard J. Marshall Papers; Lieutenant General George Kenney, diary, September 16, 1944, all at DMMA; SWPA, Staff Study on Formosa versus Luzon, September 21, 1944, Record Group 200, Entry 19810 (A1), Richard Sutherland Papers, Box 57; Major General Richard Marshall, letter to General Douglas MacArthur, September 8, 1944; Major General Richard Marshall, Memo for General Douglas MacArthur, October 7, 1944, both in Record Group 200, Entry 19810 (A1), Richard Sutherland Papers, Boxes 40 and 57, respectively (these communications apprised MacArthur of the status of grand strategy talks in Washington), all three sources at NA; Joseph Alexander, "What Was Nimitz Thinking?," *United States Naval Institute Proceedings*, November 1998; Robert W. Coakley and Richard M. Leighton, *United States Army in World War II, The War Department: Global Logistics and Strategy, 1943–1945* (Washington, DC: Center of Military History, United States Army, 1989), 412–16; M. Hamlin Cannon, *United States Army in World War II, The War in the Pacific, Leyte: The Return to the Philippines* (Washington, DC: Center of Military History, United States Army, 1954), 8–9; Robert Ross Smith, *United States Army in World War II, the War in the Pacific: Triumph in the Philippines* (Washington, DC: Center of Military History, United States Army, 1963), 12–17; Bill D. Ross, *A Special Piece of Hell: The Untold Story of Peleliu* (New York: St. Martin's Paperbacks, 1991), 135; Fleet Admiral William Halsey and Lieutenant Commander J. Bryan III, *Admiral Halsey's Story* (New York: Whittlesey House, 1947), 199–202; E. B. Potter, *Bull Halsey* (Annapolis, MD: Naval Institute Press, 1985), 277–79; MacArthur, *Reports*, vol. 2: *Japanese Operations in the Southwest Pacific*, 309–311; Smith, *Approach to the Philippines*, 453–54; Drea, *MacArthur's ULTRA*, 157–59; Borneman, *MacArthur at War*, 407, 410–17; Rogers, *The Bitter Years*, 156–66; Rhoades, *Flying MacArthur to Victory*, 285; Kenney, *General Kenney Reports*, 432; Kenney, *The MacArthur I Know*, 159–61; James, *Years of MacArthur*, vol. 2, 539–41; E. B. Potter, *Nimitz*, 191–92. Though the Japanese were caught off guard by the successful Morotai invasion, they responded with numerous air raids and by landing a regimental-size force on the island. Sharp ground fighting raged in late 1944 and early 1945 as the Americans foiled several enemy counterattacks. The Japanese never seriously challenged the security of the American base, nor did they interfere with Allied aerial operations. Similar to many other places in the Pacific, the Japanese survivors on Morotai hung on until the end of the war, when they eventually surrendered. The monumental argument between

Sutherland and MacArthur over Bessemer-Clark occurred when MacArthur returned to Hollandia from the Morotai invasion and discovered her presence.

14. Lieutenant James Wickel, Interrogation of Lieutenant General Sadae Inoue, May 23, 1947, 8; Lieutenant James Wickel, Interrogation of Colonel Takuchi Tada, May 24, 1947, 3, both in Rex Beasley Papers, Box 1, Folder 1, USAMHI; Edward Drea, "Warriors to the End: The Japanese Defense of Peleliu," *World War II*, December 2003, 54–57; Bobby Blair and John Peter DeCioccio, *Victory at Peleliu: The 81st Infantry Division's Pacific Campaign* (Norman: University of Oklahoma Press, 2011), 18–20; Harry A. Gailey, *Peleliu 1944* (Annapolis, MD: Nautical & Aviation Publishing Company of America, 1983), 36–41; Frank O. Hough, *The Assault on Peleliu* (Washington, DC: Historical Branch, G-3 Division, U.S. Marine Corps, 1950), 193; James H. Hallas, *The Devil's Anvil: The Assault on Peleliu* (Westport, CT: Praeger, 1994), 11, 19–20; Ross, *A Special Piece of Hell*, 121–26; Smith, *Approach to the Philippines*, 459–63; McManus, *Grunts*, 55–57.

15. III Marine Amphibious Corps, Operation Report, Record Group 127, Box 298, Folder 1; 81st Infantry Division, Operation Report, Capture of Angaur Island, 17 September–22 October 1944, 16, Record Group 407, Entry 427, Box 10334, Folder 381-0.3, both at NA; "Highlights in the History of the 81st Infantry Division," August 15, 1945, Charles Ryder Papers, Box 10, EL; Brigadier General Harold Deakin, Oral History, 48; General Oliver Smith, Oral History, 130, both at USMCHD; Major Nelson Drummond Jr., "The Palau Campaign," chapter 2, 16, 2-3.7 AA.P CY1; Japanese Monograph Number 49, Central Pacific Operations Record, Volume II, April–November 1944, both at CMH; Major General William Rupertus biographical entry, www.arlingtoncemetery.net; Drea, "Warriors to the End," *World War II*, 56; George W. Garand and Truman R. Strobridge, *History of United States Marine Corps Operations in World War II*, vol. 4: *Western Pacific Operations* (Washington, DC: Historical Division, Headquarters, U.S. Marine Corps, 1971), 79; George McMillan, *The Old Breed: A History of the First Marine Division in World War II* (Washington, DC: Infantry Journal Press, 1949), 230–41; E. B. Sledge, *With the Old Breed at Peleliu and Okinawa* (New York: Oxford University Press, 1990), 31; Blair and DeCioccio, *Victory at Peleliu*, 30–31; Smith, *Approach to the Philippines*, 494–99; 81st *Wildcat Division in World War II*, 15–17, 65–66; Gailey, *Peleliu 1944*, 58–63; McManus, *Grunts*, 66–78. Locals generally refer to Babelthaup as Babeldaob. To avoid confusion, I have opted to utilize the Western-oriented spelling.

16. Underwater Demolition Team 10, Action Report, Angaur Island, October 1, 1944; Transport Division 32, Action Report, Palau-Ulithi Operation, September 29, 1944, MS-416, World War II Battle and Operations Reports, Box 23, Folders 9 and 7, respectively, USNA; Lieutenant Colonel P. L. Elliott, Observers Report on 81st Infantry Division, Stalemate Operation, 30 August–25 September 1944, October 2, 1944, 5–6, DRL; Japanese Monograph Number 49; Drummond, "The Palau Campaign," Chapter 5, 3–9, Chapter 6, 41–50, both at CMH; 81st Infantry Division, Capture of Angaur Island, 17–39, NA; Lieutenant Bob Guitteau, unpublished memoir, 21–23, NWWIIM; John Walker, "The Beach Approach," *Time*, October 2, 1944; 81st *Wildcat Division in World War II*, 66–79, 85–90; Gailey, *Peleliu 1944*, 105–112; Blair and DeCioccio, *Victory at Peleliu*, 33–47; Smith, *Approach to the Philippines*, 461–61, 499–508.

17. Colonel Benjamin Venable, letter to Major General Orlando Ward, November 16, 1951, Record Group 319, Entry 54, Box 6, Records of the Office of the Chief of Military History, The Approach to the Philippines; 81st Infantry Division, Capture of Angaur Island, 39–49, 89, both at NA; Elliott, Observers Report on 81st Infantry Division, 6–7, DRL; Drummond, "The Palau Campaign," Chapter 5, 24; Chapters 6 and 7, no pagination, CMH; "Invasion of Palau 81st Infantry Division WWII Pacific Campaign," at www.youtube.com; Blair and DeCioccio, *Victory at Peleliu*, 58–73; *81st*

Wildcat Division in World War II, 98–99; Smith, *Approach to the Philippines*, 517–23; Gailey, *Peleliu 1944*, 112–13.

18. Major General Paul Meuller, diary, September 1944, Record Group 319, Box 305, Folder 6, Records of the Army Staff, Records of the Office of the Chief of Military History, History Division, Approach to the Philippines; Major General Paul Mueller, Comments on Manuscript, circa 1951; Major Nelson Drummond, Comments on Manuscript, both in Record Group 319, Box 306, Folder 4, Records of the Army Staff, Records of the Office of the Chief of Military History, History Division, Approach to the Philippines; I Company, 322nd Infantry Regiment, History and Unit Critique, Angaur Operation, Record Group 407, Entry 427, Box 10389, Folder 381-INF-322-9-0.4; 322nd Infantry Regiment, Casualty Report, Angaur Island, Fall 1944, Record Group 407, Entry 427, Box 10387, Folder 381-INF-322-1.16; Sergeant Major Masao Kurihara, Interrogation Notes, Record Group 127, Box 6, Folder 2, United States Marine Corps History and Museums Division, Publication Background Files, Assault on Peleliu; Venable letter to Ward; 81st Infantry Division, Capture of Angaur Island, 65–66, 86–90, all at NA; Anonymous Japanese Soldier, diary, October 11, 1944, and 322nd Infantry Regiment, Supplement to Periodic Report #32, October 1944, both in Rex Beasley Papers, Vertical Files, Box 59, Folder 10; Lyle McCann, World War II Veterans Questionnaire #5333, both at USAMHI; Japanese Monograph Number 49, 90; Drummond, "The Palau Campaign," Chapter 5, 52, Chapter 7, 20–27 and no pagination, both at CMH; Guitteau, unpublished memoir, 24–26, NWWIIM; Captain Jerry Keaveny, "Operations of Company A, 322nd Infantry (81st Infantry Division) in the Cleanup Phase of the Capture of the Island of Angaur, 11–22 October 1944 (Western Pacific Campaign), Personal Experience of a Company Commander," Advanced Infantry Officers Course, 1949–1950, 14–15, DRL; Craven and Cate, *The Army Air Forces in World War II*, vol. 4, 309–311; 81st *Wildcat Division in World War II*, 99–134, 309; Blair and DeCioccio, *Victory at Peleliu*, 105–17; Gailey, *Peleliu 1944*, 112–15; Smith, *Approach to the Philippines*, 522–31. Similar to the Japanese, Communist troops in both Korea and Vietnam learned to fight at close quarters with the Americans as a means of negating their firepower. In the introduction to *Fire and Fortitude*, the first volume of this series, I shared the moving correspondence of 81st Infantry Division next of kin who lost family members during the Angaur fighting. To Major General Mueller's eternal credit, he conscientiously wrote to the family members and shared as many details as possible about the deaths of their loved ones at Angaur.

19. 1st Marine Division, Special Action Report, Annex A, Infantry, 1–2, Annex B, Intelligence, 29–30, Record Group 127, Box 298, Folder 19; 1st Marine Regiment, After Action Report, Record Group 127, Box 299, Folder 4; History, Record Group 127, Box 300, Folder 5; Lieutenant Colonel Spencer Berger, "Comments . . . on Preliminary Draft of Marine Corps Historical Monograph, Palau," no date, Record Group 127, Box 6, Folder 1, United States Marine Corps History and Museums Division, Publication Background Files, Assault on Peleliu; Colonel William Wachtler, letter to Commandant, March 1, 1950; Colonel William Coleman, letter to Commandant, no date, Record Group 127, Box 6, Folders 3 and 1, respectively, United States Marine Corps History and Museums Division, Publication Background Files, Assault on Peleliu, all at NA; Deakin, Oral History, 55; Smith, Oral History, 142, both at USMCHD; George Peto, interview with the author, April 25, 2008; George Peto, "Battle for Peleliu," 3, copy in author's possession; Joseph Alexander, "'Everything About Peleliu Left a Bad Taste,'" *Leatherneck*, September 2004, 29–33; Jon Hoffman, "The Truth about Peleliu," *United States Naval Institute Proceedings*, November 2002; Richard C. Kennard, *Combat Letters Home: A U.S. Marine Corps Officer's World War II Letters from Peleliu, Okinawa and North China, September 1944 to December 1945* (Bryn Mawr, PA: Dorrance & Company, 1985), 17, 31; Garand and Strobridge, *History*, vol. 4: *Western Pacific*

Operations, 219; Hough, *Assault on Peleliu*, 73–93; Ross, *Special Piece of Hell*, 264–68; Gailey, *Peleliu 1944*, 132–35; McManus, *Grunts*, 79–92. In these passages, I am using the term "Umurbrogol" to refer to all of Peleliu's high ground that contained fortified caves. The Marine Corps refers to its regiments, not its divisions, with a distinct numerical shorthand. For instance, the term "1st Marines" refers to the 1st Marine Regiment, not the 1st Marine Division. I have utilized that terminology.

20. 81st Infantry Division, History of Operations, Record Group 127, Box 300, Folder 4; 321st Infantry Regiment, After Action Report, Record Group 407, Entry 427, Box 12324, Folder 8; 1st Marine Regiment, History, all at NA; Major General William Rupertus, letter to 1st Marine Division, October 13, 1944, Roy Geiger Papers, Box 5, Folder 101, Gray Research Center, USMCHD; Colonel Robert Dark, letter to wife, October 24, 1944, Robert Dark Papers, Box 1, HIA; Sergeant Thomas Climie, unpublished memoir, 22, World War II Veterans Questionnaire #10149, USAMHI; Peto, "Battle for Peleiu," 3; Drea, "Warriors to the End," *World War II*, 60; *81st Wildcat Division in World War II*, 139–55; George McMillan, *The Old Breed*, 318; Kennard, *Combat Letters Home*, 31; Gailey, *Peleliu 1944*, 137–45; Ross, *Special Piece of Hell*, 277; Blair and DeCioccio, *Victory at Peleliu*, 128–52; Smith, *Approach to the Philippines*, 532–43, 549–55; McManus, *Grunts*, 92–96.

21. 323rd Infantry Regiment, After Action Report; Terrain and Intelligence Summary; Medical Report #4, 13, all in Record Group 407, Entry 427, Box 12338, Folder 7; 81st Infantry Division, History of Operations; 321st Infantry Regiment, AAR; Extracts from Operations Reports on Reduction of Japanese Cave-Type Fortifications, 17; Venable letter to Ward, all at NA; E Company, 323rd Infantry Regiment, History, 4; Administrative History of Medical Activities in the Middle Pacific, Office of the Surgeon, the Palaus Campaign, 35, both at USAMHI; Lieutenant General Robert Richardson, letter to General George Marshall, May 27, 1945, Robert Richardson Papers, Box 74, HIA; Private David Poteet, letter to family, February 4, 1945, Folder 2365, Accession #2274, SHSM; Committee 14, Armored Officers Advanced Course, the Armored School, 1949–1950, Fort Knox, Kentucky, May 1950, "Armor in Angaur-Peleliu Campaign," 105; Captain Pierce Irby, "The Operations of Company 'L,' 321st Infantry (81st Infantry Division) in the Capture of the Island of Peleliu, 23–29 September 1944 (Western Pacific Campaign), Personal Experiences of a Company Commander," Advanced Infantry Officers Course, 1948–1949, 26, both at DRL; Drea, "Warriors to the End," *World War II*, 60; *81st Wildcat Division in World War II*, 179–201; Hough, *Assault on Peleliu*, 163–82; Smith, *Approach to the Philippines*, 559–75; Garand and Strobridge, *History*, vol. 4: *Western Pacific Operations*, 248–65, 285–88; Hallas, *The Devil's Anvil*, 279–82; McManus, *Grunts*, 100–102. Technically, the highest-ranking Japanese officer at Pelelieu was Major General Kenjiro Murai, whom Inoue had dispatched there a few months before the battle, probably to buttress Nakagawa's authority with naval officers who outranked him. Though the exact command relationships remain opaque after so many decades, there is no doubt that Nakagawa controlled the tactical battle. Like Nakagawa, Murai committed suicide in November and was posthumously promoted to lieutenant general. William Rupertus had more health problems than just a broken ankle. It is probable that he was also suffering from a heart condition and this might well have affected his dismal performance during the battle. Sadly, he died on March 25, 1945, of a heart attack.

10. The Ugly Midsection

1. General Headquarters, Southwest Pacific Area, Communique, September 15, 1944, USAMHI; Rhoades, *Flying MacArthur to Victory*, 290; Borneman, *MacArthur at War*, 414; James, *Years of MacArthur*, vol. 2, 489. For an excellent in-depth treatment of the American-Australian wartime partnership in the Southwest Pacific, see Peter J. Dean,

MacArthur's Coalition: US and Australian Military Operations in the Southwest Pacific Area, 1942–1945 (Lawrence: University Press of Kansas, 2018).

2. Sixth Army, Report of Leyte Operation, 20 October–25 December 1944, 24–25 (AAR), Record Group 407, Entry 1113, Philippine Archives Collection, Box 1478, NA; United States Army Forces in the Pacific Ocean Areas, Participation in the Western Carolines and Central Philippines, 17, 161–62, 175–77, 241–43, 370.2; Major General Yoshiharu Tomochika, "The True Facts of the Leyte Operation," 12, 8-5.4 AA14c1, both at CMH; Samuel Eliot Morison, *History of United States Naval Operations in World War II*, vol. 12: *Leyte, June 1944–January 1945* (Boston: Little, Brown, 1958), 64–85, 93–109, 114–17, 415–29; Milan Vego, *The Battle for Leyte: Allied and Japanese Plans, Preparations, and Execution* (Annapolis, MD: Naval Institute Press, 2006), 25–28, 134–42; Stanley L. Falk, *Decision at Leyte* (New York: W. W. Norton, 1966), 75–78; E. B. Potter, *Bull Halsey*, 280–85; Halsey and Bryan, *Admiral Halsey's Story*, 207–208; Carter, *Beans, Bullets, and Black Oil*, 239–42; Cannon, *Leyte*, 36–37, 41–42; Day, *An Officer in MacArthur's Court*, 387–88; Krueger, *From Down Under to Nippon*, 151–52; Barbey, *MacArthur's Amphibious Navy*, 237; MacArthur, *Reminiscences*, 214; James, *Years of MacArthur*, vol. 2, 545. China-based medium and heavy Army Air Forces bombers participated in strikes against Formosa but played only a small role, mainly because of fuel and supply problems, stemming mostly from Ichi-go.

3. Japanese Monograph #4, Philippine Operations Record, Phase III, July–November 1944, Preparations made by the 14th Area Army for the Military Operations in the Philippines Islands, no pagination, 8-5.1 AC4; Major General Yoshiharu Tomochika, Interrogation, 6, in HQ, Eighth Army, Staff Study of the Japanese 35th Army on Leyte, 8-5.4 AA16c1, both at CMH; Imperial Japanese Army, Officer's Duty Roster with Efficiency Reports, Kaki 655 Force, 20th Infantry Regiment, 16th Division, ADVATIS #1511, Record Group 165, Entry 79, Box 286, ADVATIS, Current Translations, #164-165, NA; U.S. Army Center of Military History pamphlet, *The U.S. Army Campaigns of World War II: Leyte*, 10; John Deane Potter, *The Life and Death of a Japanese General* (New York: Signet Books, 1962), 11, 15–106; Max Hastings, *Retribution: The Battle for Japan, 1944–45* (New York: Vintage Books, 2007), 121–23; Cannon, *Leyte*, 45–54; Falk, *Decision at Leyte*, 34–55, 71; Drea, *MacArthur's ULTRA*, 158–60; Morison, *History*, vol. 12: *Leyte*, 67; James, *Years of MacArthur*, vol. 2, 548; MacArthur, *Reminiscences*, 221; Toland, *Decline and Fall of the Japanese Empire*, vol. 2, 668–69. Cannon places the Kuroda relief on September 23 and the arrival of Yamashita on October 9, as did Yamashita himself in his witness testimony during his postwar trial for war crimes. Contemporary US Army sources, especially unit after-action reports and planning documents, routinely blamed the Imperial Army's 16th Division for the Bataan Death March, but in truth the unit was probably not involved to any substantial degree. See Falk, *Decision at Leyte*, page 70, and *Bataan: The March of Death* by the same author.

4. Amphibious Group Three, Report of Participation in Amphibious Operations for the Capture of Leyte, October 26, 1944, 6, MS-416, World War II Battle and Operations Reports, Box 26, Folder 1, USNA; Phil Hostetter, unpublished memoir, 92, World War II Participants and Contemporaries Collection, Philip Hostetter Folder, EL; Lieutenant Gage Rodman, diary/contemporary memoir, December 30, 1944, Gage Rodman Papers, Box 6; Hughes, unpublished memoir, 5, both at USAMHI; Sixth Army, AAR, 31, NA; PFC Wallace Jaep, letter to family, no date, Folder 1445, Accession #459; PFC Sidney Centilli, letter to mother, no date, Folder 472, Accession #2350, both at SHSM; General Douglas MacArthur, letter to Jean MacArthur, October 19, 1944, Record Group 10, Box 7, VIP Correspondence; Kenney diary, October 19, 1944, both at DMMA; Gerald Astor, *Crisis in the Pacific: The Battles for the Philippine Islands by the Men Who Fought Them* (New York: Dell, 2002), 325–26; Rogers, *The Bitter Years*, 196;

Cannon, *Leyte*, 54–58; Dencker, *Love Company*, 60; MacArthur, *Reminiscences*, 214; Chase, *Front Line General*, 62. The Sixth Army report claimed that the sweepers destroyed 224 mines.

5. Leyte Historical Report of the 24th Infantry Division Landing Team, 20 October 1944–25 December 1944 (AAR), 6, CARL; Captain George Morrissey, diary, October 20, 1944, World War II Veterans Survey in Carl Brand Folder, #9725, USAMHI; W. T. Dean Jr., "The Liberation of Leyte, Volume 2," 18, 2-3.7 AV v2; USAPOA, Participation in the Western Carolines and Central Philippines, both at CMH; Captain Charles Johnson, "Operations of Cannon Company, 32nd Infantry Regiment (7th Infantry Division), on Leyte, P.I., 20–25 October 1944 (Leyte Campaign), Personal Experiences of a Cannon Company Commander," 8, DRL; Annette Tapert, *Lines of Battle: Letters from American Servicemen, 1941–1945* (New York: Times Books, 1987), 195–96; Orlando R. Davidson, J. Carl Willems, and Joseph A. Kahl, *The Deadeyes: The Story of the 96th Infantry Division* (Washington, DC: Infantry Journal Press, 1947), 21; Dencker, *Love Company*, 61; Astor, *Crisis in the Pacific*, 350; Chase, *Front Line General*, 63; Cannon, *Leyte*, 60–80; Morison, *History*, vol. 12: *Leyte*, 117–50; Tarbuck's account is reproduced in Barbey, *MacArthur's Amphibious Navy*, 245.

6. XXIV Corps, Operation Report, Battle of Leyte, Philippine Islands, 20 October–25 December 1944 (AAR), February 28, 1945, Record Group 337, Entry 15A, Box 59, Folder 251; Captain William Hanks, "Combat Report on Leyte Operation," Record Group 337, Entry 15A, Box 65, Folder 378; Information from Combat Reports and Reports Submitted by Observers of Combat Operations in the Western Pacific, April 12, 1945, 33, Record Group 337, Entry 15A, Box 61, Folder 296; Sixth Army, AAR, 32–38, all at NA; 24th Infantry Division, AAR, 2, 6–10, CARL; Dean, "The Liberation of Leyte, Volume 2," 64–68, CMH; Tracy Derks, "MacArthur's Return," *World War II*, September 2000, 30–34; Jaeson "Doc" Parsons, "The Invasion of Leyte and the Heroism of Captain Francis B. Wai," at www.sofrep.com; Jan Valtin, *Children of Yesterday: The 24th Infantry Division in the Philippines* (New York: Reader's Press, 1946 original, 2014 reprint), 22; Falk, *Decision at Leyte*, 93–94; Cannon, *Leyte*, 85–130; Astor, *Crisis in the Pacific*, 327–28, 333, 336–38. Jan Valtin was the pen name for PFC Richard Krebs, a German-born soldier who served with the 24th Infantry Division. For more information on the remarkable Captain Francis Wai, see www.findagrave.com and www.ww2research.com. Colonel Newman's actions on Red Beach were markedly similar to those of Colonel George Taylor of the 1st Infantry Division during D-Day on Omaha Beach. Though the latter battle was bloodier and more difficult, the positive effect of their actions was much the same.

7. Colonel Alexander Neilson, letter to Frank, December 4, 1944, Record Group 117, Box 1, Folder 3, A. M. Neilson Papers; General Douglas MacArthur, letter to President Franklin Roosevelt, October 20, 1944, Record Group 15, Box 23, Folder 23, Contributions from the Public Collection; Faillace interview, all at DMMA; Sixth Army, AAR, 34, NA; General Douglas MacArthur, Proclamation, October 20, 1944, Bonner Fellers Papers, Box 15, Folder 5, HIA; Joseph Connor, "Shore Party," *World War II*, January/February 2017, 41–43; William Dunn, "MacArthur's Mansion and Other Myths," *Army*, 42; Astor, *Crisis in the Pacific*, 338–41; Krueger, *From Down Under to Nippon*, 158–59; MacArthur, *Reminiscences*, 215–17; Rogers, *The Bitter Years*, 175; Cannon, *Leyte*, 78–84; Borneman, *MacArthur at War*, 427–30; James, *Years of MacArthur*, vol. 2, 514–17, 554–57; Manchester, *American Caesar*, 448–53; Kenney, *General Kenney Reports*, 448; Kenney, *The MacArthur I Know*, 164–65. Today on Red Beach, at roughly the same spot where MacArthur landed, seven life-size bronze statues of the general, President Osmena, and their entourage commemorate the famous photograph taken by Faillace.

8. General Headquarters, Southwest Pacific Area, Communique, October 20, 1944; PFC Ellis Moore, letter to family, October 22, 1944, World War II Veterans Survey, no number, both at USAMHI; General Headquarters, Southwest Pacific Area, Proclamation, October 23, 1944, Bonner Fellers Papers, Box 15, Folder 5, HIA; PVT Herbert "Bud" Rogers, letter to mother, January 28, 1945, Folder 2534, Accession #1642; Private Arthur Riehl, letter to mother, December 2, 1944, Folder 2484, Accession #1652; Lieutenant William Bronnenberg, letter to cousins, December 3, 1944, Folder 334, Accession #723; Lieutenant Malcolm McLew, letter to family, no date, Folder 2080, Accession #492; Tech Four Howard Lumsden, letter to parents, March 18, 1945, Folder 1819, Accession #1365, all at SHSM; Colonel Toshii Watanabe, Narrative, 12, in Eighth Army, Staff Study of the Japanese 35th Army on Leyte, CMH; General Headquarters, United States Army Forces, Pacific, Military Intelligence Section, General Staff, "The Guerrilla Resistance Movement in the Philippines," 1–5, CARL; Otto Woike, unpublished memoir, 70, WWIIM; John Whitman, "They Remained: Filipino Guerrillas in World War II," *MHQ*, Winter 2002, 59; Sergeant Ralph Boyce, "Philippines Advance," *Yank*, November 24, 1944; Falk, *Decision at Leyte*, 88–89; Barbey, *MacArthur's Amphibious Navy*, 250–51; Dencker, *Love Company*, 74–75; Toland, *Decline and Fall of the Japanese Empire*, vol. 2, 679; Valtin, *Children of Yesterday*, 50; Cannon, *Leyte*, 16–20.

9. Headquarters, Base K, U.S. Army Services of Supply, Health Survey of Leyte Troops and Civilians, February 23, 1945, 2–6, Record Group 112, Entry 31, Surgeon General, Administrative Records, Box 213; "Medical Aspects of the Leyte-Samar Campaign," 9, Record Group 319, Entry 55, Box 4, Records of the Office of the Chief of Military History, Leyte, the Return to the Philippines, both at NA; 24th Infantry Division, AAR, 146, CARL; W. T. Dean Jr., "The Liberation of Leyte, Volume 3," 7, 36, 2-3.7 AV v3, CMH; Hostetter, unpublished memoir, 99, EL; Lieutenant Gage Rodman, letter to parents, November 8, 1944, Gage Rodman Papers, Box 5, USAMHI; Condon-Rall and Cowdrey, *Medical Service in the War Against Japan*, 320–23; Cannon, *Leyte*, 203–204.

10. General Douglas MacArthur, Answers to Questions Submitted by Morton, 6, DMMA; Sixth Army, AAR, 43, NA; United States Strategic Bombing Survey (Pacific), Naval Analysis Division, *The Campaigns of the Pacific War* (Washington, DC: Government Printing Office, 1946), 283–87; United States Strategic Bombing Survey (Pacific), *Interrogations of Japanese Officials*, vol. 2, 219, 316; Morison, *History*, vol. 12: *Leyte*, 159–316; Falk, *Decision at Leyte*, 125–215; Vego, *The Battle for Leyte*, 255–99; Cannon, *Leyte*, 86–92; Manchester, *American Caesar*, 458–59; E. B. Potter, *Bull Halsey*, 286–307; Kenney, *The MacArthur I Know*, 170. Australian ships participated in the Battle of Surigao Strait. A follow-on force of three cruisers and four destroyers under VADM Kiyohide Shima had little impact on the Surigao Strait battle, withdrew, and then was pummeled by American air strikes.

11. Major General Yoshiharu Tomochika, letter to Mr. Keisuke Saito, October 2, 1945, in Eighth Army, Staff Study of the Japanese 35th Army on Leyte; Tomochika, "True Facts of the Leyte Operation," 13–15, both at CMH; MacArthur, *Reports*, vol. 1: *Campaigns in the Pacific*, 223–25; Nathan N. Prefer, *Leyte 1944: The Soldiers' Battle* (Philadelphia and Oxford: Casemate, 2012), 334–36; Wesley F. Craven and James L. Cate, eds., *The Army Air Forces in World War II*, vol. 5: *The Pacific, Matterhorn to Nagasaki, June 1944 to August 1945* (Washington, DC: Officer of Air Force History, 1983), 375–79; J. D. Potter, *Life and Death of a Japanese General*, 110–14; Morison, *History*, vol. 12: *Leyte*, 349–54; Falk, *Decision at Leyte*, 104–108; Toland, *Decline and Fall of the Japanese Empire*, vol. 2, 715–16; Kenney, *General Kenney Reports*, 470–71; Cannon, *Leyte*, 93–94, 101–102.

12. Thomas Clark, unpublished memoir, 24; B Company, 381st Infantry Regiment, History, 3, Ron Van der Bussche Collection, #2005.175, both at WWIIM; Combat Lessons

Number 9, Rank and File in Combat, 47, CARL; 339th Engineer Combat Battalion, "This Is an Engineer's War," 12; Neilson letter to Frank; Kenney diary, October 27, 1944, all at DMMA; Lieutenant Gage Rodman, letter to parents, February 21, 1945, Gage Rodman Papers, Box 5; Morrissey diary, October 29, 1944, both at USAMHI; Major General John Hodge, letter to Major General Orlando Ward, June 28, 1951, Record Group 319, Entry 55, Box 4, Records of the Office of the Chief of Military History, Leyte, the Return to the Philippines; Sixth Army, AAR, 45, both at NA; General Walter Krueger, "The Commander's Appreciation of Logistics," Army War College Lecture, 25, Walter Krueger Papers, Box 12, USMA; Major General Hugh J. Casey, *Engineers of the Southwest Pacific, 1941–1945*, vol. 1: *Engineers in Theater Operations* (United States Army Forces in the Far East, 1947), 490–91; Kenney, *General Kenney Reports*, 465; Craven and Cate, *The Army Air Forces in World War II*, vol. 5, 372; Valtin, *Children of Yesterday*, 150.

13. General Walter Krueger, letter to Major General Orlando Ward, August 15, 1951, plus Additional Comments on Manuscript, Record Group 319, Entry 55, Box 4, Records of the Office of the Chief of Military History, Leyte, the Return to the Philippines, NA; Kenney interview with James; Kenney diary, October 20–21, 1944, both at DMMA; Lieutenant General William Ely interview, at www.witnesstowar.org; Casey, *Engineers*, vol. 4: *Amphibian Engineer Operations*, 482–85; Dod, *The Corps of Engineers: The War Against Japan*, 585–86; Craven and Cate, *The Army Air Forces in World War II*, vol. 4, 372; Kenney, *General Kenney Reports*, 455; James, *Years of MacArthur*, vol. 2, 568–69; Cannon, *Leyte*, 35–36.

14. 7th Infantry Division, Operations Report, King II (Leyte) Operation, 20 October 1944–10 February 1945 (AAR), Record Group 407, Entry 427, Box 6115, Folder 307-0.3; XXIV Corps, AAR; Sixth Army, AAR, 38–40, all at NA; Eighth Army, Staff Study of Operations of the Japanese 102nd Division on Leyte and Cebu, 8-5.4 AA4 C1; Lieutenant Russell Gugeler, The 7th Infantry Division in the Invasion of Leyte, 314.7; Dean, "The Liberation of Leyte, Volume 3," no pagination, all at CMH; Aubrey "Red" Newman, unpublished memoir, 4–8, Aubrey S. Newman Papers, Box 2, USAMHI; 24th Infantry Division, AAR, 32–34, 118, CARL; Captain Denmark Jensen, "The Operations of Cannon Company, 17th Infantry (7th Infantry Division) During the Advance on Dagami, Leyte Island, 23–29 October 1944 (Leyte Campaign), Personal Experience of a Company Commander," Advanced Infantry Officers Course, 1948–1949, 34, DRL; Davidson, Willems, and Kahl, *The Deadeyes*, 35–55; Love, *The Hourglass*, 233–35; Astor, *Crisis in the Pacific*, 417–21; Valtin, *Children of Yesterday*, 79, 109–111; Falk, *Decision at Leyte*, 228–39; Cannon, *Leyte*, 144–83.

15. 188th Glider Infantry Regiment, History of the King II (Leyte) Operation, 21 November–25 December 1944 (AAR), 1, Record Group 407, Entry 427, Box 6558, Folder 311-INF-188-0.3; Sixth Army, AAR, 5; Krueger letter to Ward and Comments, 3, all at NA; SWPA, G2 Monthly Summary of Enemy Dispositions, October 31, 1944, Record Group 3, Box 18, Folder 4, Records of Headquarters, Southwest Pacific Area, 1942–1945, DMMA; General Walter Krueger, Biographical Sketch, Walter Krueger Papers, Box 1, USAMHI; General Clyde Eddleman, Comments, Walter Krueger Papers, Box 40, USMA; "Armor on Leyte: A Research Report Prepared by Committee 16, Officers Advanced Course, the Armored School, 1948–1949," Fort Knox, KY, May 1949, 8, copy in author's possession; Ronald H. Spector, *Eagle Against the Sun: The American War with Japan* (New York: Vintage Books, 1985), 513–14; Falk, *Decision at Leyte*, 244–47; Leary, *We Shall Return*, 74–76; Holzimmer, *General Walter Krueger*, 195–99; Drea, *MacArthur's ULTRA*, 169–72; Krueger, *From Down Under to Nippon*, 166–70; Davidson, Willems, and Kahl, *The Deadeyes*, 59. Most US Army sources referred to Majunag as Mahonag. Eddleman was Krueger's operations officer.

16. 11th Airborne Division, History, Record Group 407, Entry 427, Box 6545, Folder 311-0.1; 381st Infantry Regiment, Comments, Criticisms, Recommendations and Lessons Learned, 3, Record Group 407, Entry 427, Box 11544, Folder 396-INF-381-0.3; Sixth Army, Mistakes made and Lessons Learned in K-1 (Leyte) Operation, November 25, 1944, Record Group 319, Entry 55, Box 4, Records of the Office of the Chief of Military History, Leyte, the Return to the Philippines; Pacific Warfare Board, Battle Experiences Against the Japanese, Number 16, July 18, 1945, 1, Record Group 337, Entry 15A, Box 58, Folder 216; Night Operation in Pacific Ocean Areas, March 18, 1945, Record Group 337, Entry 15A, Box 60, Folder 270; Colonel Harvey Shelton, "Extracts of Observer Report in the Pacific Areas," 1, Record Group 337, Entry 15A, Box 57, Folder 192; 7th Infantry Division, AAR; Hanks, Combat Report on Leyte Operation, all at NA; 24th Infantry Division, AAR, 39–52, CARL; Lieutenant General Walter Krueger, telephone conversation with Major General Franklin Sibert, November 22, 1944, transcript in Thomas F. Hickey Papers, Box 1; Lieutenant Gage Rodman, letter to Bill, November 24, 1944, Gage Rodman Papers, Box 5, both at USAMHI; Headquarters, Army Ground Forces, Lessons Learned from the Leyte Campaign, May 16, 1945, 6, .353, CMH; 7th Cavalry Regiment, Historical Report, Operations on Leyte Island (AAR), 10, 7th Cavalry Regiment Records, Box 498, EL; Major General Edward Sebree, letter to Lieutenant General Joseph Swing, August 19, 1960, Joseph Swing Papers, Box 1, USMA; Captain Kermit Blaney, "The Operations of Company L, 21st Infantry (24th Infantry Division), South of Pinamopoan (Breakneck Ridge), Leyte Island, P.I., 5–15 November 1944 (Leyte Campaign), Personal Experiences of a Company Commander," Advanced Infantry Officers Course, 1948–1949, 17, DRL; Whayland Green, unpublished memoir, no pagination, MS1881, Box 11, Folder 16, SCUTK; Patrick O'Donnell, "Angels' Nightmare on Leyte," *World War II*, March 2002, 35–37; Major General Edward Sebree, Research Memorandum, "Leadership at Higher Levels of Command as Viewed by Senior and Experienced Combat Commanders," U.S. Army Leadership Human Research Unit, Presidio at Monterey, California, 32–33, copy in author's possession; Valtin, *Children of Yesterday*, 143–44; Astor, *Crisis in the Pacific*, 455–56; Cannon, *Leyte*, 240. In the telephone conversation with Sibert, Krueger was specifically referring to the 32nd Infantry Division and its commander, Major General William Gill.

17. Willis Winther, oral history, AFC/2001/001/53141; Werner Schlaupitz, oral history, AFC/2001/001/48925, both at LOC; Robert Jackson, unpublished memoir, 25, World War II Veterans Survey, #3849; Morrissey diary, November 20, 1944, both at USAMHI; Hostetter, unpublished memoir, 144, EL; Captain William Bostwick, letter to Mrs. McLaughlin, December 3, 1944, Schulte Collection, #2009.224; Robert Jackson, unpublished memoir, 25, both at WWIIM; 24th Infantry Division, AAR, 59, CARL; Garbo oral history, NMPW; O'Donnell, "Angels' Nightmare on Leyte," *World War II*, 34, 38; Astor, *Crisis in the Pacific*, 455; Cannon, *Leyte*, 244–52.

18. Joint Army-Navy Storage Board, Report on Base in the Philippines Area, December 10, 1944, Record Group 334, Entry 15, Records of Interservice Agencies, Box 2, Folder 27; 511th Parachute Infantry Regiment, History, Leyte Campaign, 18 November–27 December 1944 (AAR), Record Group 407, Entry 427, Box 6562, Folder 311-INF-511-0.3; 188th Glider Infantry Regiment, AAR; 11th Airborne Division, History; 7th Infantry Division, AAR, all at NA; 24th Infantry Division, AAR, 149, CARL; 170th Ordnance Battalion, Base K Ammunition Depot, "Explosion Flattens Camp," 1–2, January 17, 1945, in Captain Frederic Cramer diary, Frederic Cramer Papers, Box 1; Lieutenant Colonel Henry Burgess, letter to Mr. William Breuer, May 13, 1985, William Breuer Papers, Box 4; Morrissey diary, November 12, 1944, and Additional Notes, all at USAMHI; Tech 5 Don Boyd, letter to Mom and All, December 10, 1944, Folder 291,

Accession #2337, SHSM; Major General Joseph Swing, letter to General Peyton March, December 24, 1944, Joseph Swing Papers, Box 1, USMA; Major Joseph Giordano, "The Operations of Company 'G' 187th Glider Infantry Regiment (11th Airborne Division) in the Breakthrough to the Ormoc Corridor, 22–23 December 1944 (The Leyte Campaign), Personal Experience of a Platoon Leader," Advanced Infantry Officers Course, 1947–1948, 8; Lieutenant Richard Barnum, "The Operations of the 3rd Battalion, 511th Parachute Infantry (11th Airborne Division) in the Advance through the Mahonag-Anas Pass to the West Coast of Leyte, 27 November–25 December 1944 (The Leyte Campaign), Personal Experience of a Mortar Platoon Leader," Advanced Infantry Officers Course, 1948–1949, 13, 24, both at DRL; Masterson, "United States Army Transportation in the Southwest Pacific Area," 788–90, CMH; Colonel Frank Gillette, "Supply Problems on Leyte," *Military Review*, April 1945, 65–66; Major Joseph Seay, "The 11th Airborne Division in the Leyte Mountain Operation," *Military Review*, October 1949, 20–22; 1st Cavalry Division, "1st Cavalry Division in the Leyte Campaign," *Cavalry Journal*, November/December 1945, 2–5; Elmer Lear, "Agriculture and Food During Leyte's Liberation," *Leyte-Samar Studies*, Issue #2, 1978, 13; Harry Swan, "The Paratrooper Mortarman in the Battle of Leyte," *Winds Aloft*, January 1990, 21–22; Colonel Edward H. Lahti, Memoirs of an Angel, self-published, 1994, 61, copy in author's possession courtesy of Mr. Rick Britton; Edward M. Flanagan Jr., *The Angels: A History of the 11th Airborne Division, 1943–1946* (Washington, DC: Infantry Journal Press, 1948), 47, 55; Egeberg, *The General*, 80–81; Dod, *The Corps of Engineers: The War Against Japan*, 570–76; Stauffer, *The Quartermaster Corps: Operations in the War Against Japan*, 274–77; Craven and Cate, *The Army Air Forces in World War II*, vol. 5, 383–84; Cannon, *Leyte*, 204–205, 308–311.

19. 382nd Infantry Regiment, Character of Hostile Opposition during the Leyte Island Operation from 20 October–25 December 1944, 4, Record Group 407, Entry 427, Box 11554, Folder 396-INF-382-0.3; Major Frederick Billings, Chief, General Medical Service, oral history, March 29, 1945, Record Group 112, Entry 302, Surgeon General, Inspections Branch, Box 321, Interview Number 141; Captain David Gage, 124th Station Hospital, oral history, February 15, 1945, Record Group 112, Entry 302, Surgeon General, Inspections Branch, Box 221, Interview Number 135; 11th Airborne Division, AAR; "Medical Aspects of the Leyte-Samar Campaign," 4, all at NA; Army Ground Forces, Battle Casualties, Study, 12, CMH; 24th Infantry Division, AAR, 137, CARL; Mr. Herbert Merritt, interview with Mr. Richard Misenhimer, June 17, 2005, NMPW; Major Dale Schweinler, "Operations of Company F, 126th Infantry, 32nd Infantry Division on the Ormoc Road, Leyte Island, 1–24 December 1944," Advanced Infantry Officers Course, 1948–1949, 30; Morrissey diary, November 28, 1944, Additional Notes, both at USAMHI; Blaney, "The Operations of Company L," 23; Barnum, "The Operations of 3rd Battalion, 511th Parachute Infantry," 31, both at DRL; "1st Cavalry Division in the Leyte Campaign"; Cannon, *Leyte*, 195–98; Condon-Rall and Cowdrey, *Medical Service in the War Against Japan*, 324–30.

20. Frederic Marquardt, oral history, no date, Record Group 32, Oral History #34; Turner Catledge, interview with Dr. D. Clayton James, March 25, 1971, Record Group 49, Miscellaneous File, Part II; Dr. Paul Rogers, letter to Dr. Roger Egeberg, circa 1981, Record Group 46, Box 1, Folder 7, Paul Rogers Papers; McKinney unpublished memoir, no pagination, all at DMMA; Roscoe Woodruff, unpublished memoir, 60–61, Roscoe Woodruff Papers, Box 1, EL; Sarwell Meniano, "Tacloban's Price Mansion Brings Back World War II Memories," Philippine News Agency, October 18, 2019, at www.pna.gov.nh; Joseph P. McCallus, *The MacArthur Highway and Other Relics of American Empire in the Philippines* (Washington, DC: Potomac Books, 2010), 53–58; Manchester, *American Caesar*, 461–66; Rogers, *The Bitter Years*, 195–99; Borneman, *MacArthur at War*, 446–52; Egeberg, *The General*, 87–88; Luvaas, *Dear Miss Em*, 172;

Eichelberger, *Our Jungle Road to Tokyo*, 177; Flanagan, *The Angels*, 62–63; James, *Years of MacArthur*, vol. 2, 584–91. Among other American theater commanders, only Joseph Stilwell during his famous trek out of Burma and the siege of Myitkyina, faced any real personal danger, though not nearly to the same degree as MacArthur.

21. Lieutenant General Robert Eichelberger, diary, June 3, 1945, Box 1, Robert Eichelberger Papers, DU; Dr. Paul Rogers, letter to Dr. Roger Egeberg, circa 1982, Record Group 46, Box 1, Folder 5, Paul Rogers Papers, also in the same record group see Rogers's correspondence with Mrs. Natalie Sutherland Carney, Brigadier General LeGrande "Pick" Diller and Lieutenant Colonel Weldon "Dusty" Rhoades, DMMA; Rogers, The *Bitter Years*, 211–17, 236–38; Egeberg, *The General*, 90–93; Borneman, *MacArthur at War*, 452–55; Manchester, *American Caesar*, 468–70; Rhoades, *Flying MacArthur to Victory*, 333–35, 523; James, *Years of MacArthur*, vol. 2, 596–98. During this same time, Sutherland also dealt with severe blood pressure and tooth decay problems that necessitated, in January 1945, medical treatment in Australia, where he was briefly reunited with Elaine before he eventually returned to the Philippines. After the war, MacArthur finally accepted Sutherland's resignation and tapped Major General Paul Mueller, the commander of the 81st Infantry Division, to replace him.

22. 77th Infantry Division, After Action Report, Leyte (AAR), 6–8, Record Group 407, Entry 427, Box 9790, Folder 377-0.3; Lieutenant General A. D. Bruce, letter to Major General Orlando Ward, August 16, 1951, and Lecture, "The Operations of the 77th Division in Leyte," Command and General Staff College, January 19, 1951, 3, Record Group 319, Entry 55, Box 4, Records of the Office of the Chief of Military History, Leyte, the Return to the Philippines; Sixth Army AAR, 62–72; XXIV Corps AAR, all at NA; Lieutenant Paul Leach, History of the 77th Infantry Division at Ormoc/Leyte, 77th Infantry Division World War II Veterans Collection, Box 1; previously cited Bruce lecture in Andrew Bruce Papers, Box 11, both at USAMHI; Eighth Army Staff Study of the Japanese 35th Army on Leyte, 10, CMH; Major Marshall Becker, "Operations of the 77th Infantry Division (XXIV Corps) in the Ormoc Corridor, Leyte Island, 7 December 1944–5 February 1945 (Southern Philippines Campaign), Personal Experience of a Division Assistant G-3," Advanced Infantry Officers Course, 1947–1948, 14, DRL; Lieutenant Colonel Delbert Bjork, "Waterborne Envelopments: The 77th Infantry Division at Ormoc," *Military Review*, March 1951, 49–57; "The Fall of Ormoc on Leyte," *Military Review*, August 1945, 51–53; Captain Thomas Doherty, "Raid at Ormoc: An Alamo Scout Mission During WWII," *Infantry*, June–August 2011, 42–44; Lopez, "From Jackson to Japan," 101; Lance Q. Zedric, *Silent Warriors of World War II: The Alamo Scouts Behind Japanese Lines* (Ventura: Pathfinder Publishing of California, 1995), 160–73; Alexander, *Shadows in the Jungle*, 190–217; Krueger, *From Down Under to Nippon*, 179–82; Morison, *History*, vol. 12: *Leyte*, 377; Holzimmer, *General Walter Krueger*, 200–202; *Ours to Hold It High*, 152; Cannon, *Leyte*, 275–84. At Ormoc, as elsewhere in the Pacific, Alamo Scouts played a vital reconnaissance role. At Leyte, and several other islands, they were already functioning as important liaisons to guerrilla groups, almost similar to Special Forces of a later era. When they were not performing these missions, they served as personal bodyguards for General Krueger.

23. 503rd Parachute Infantry Regiment, Historical Report on the Mindoro Operation, February 1, 1945, 503rd Parachute Infantry Regiment Records, Box 1533, EL; Japanese Monograph #6, Philippine Operations Record, Phase III, June 1944–August 1945, 106–107, 8-5.1 AC6; Tomochika, "True Facts of the Leyte Operation," 23; Dean, "The Liberation of Leyte, Volume 3," no pagination, all at CMH; Sixth Army, AAR, 71–79; XXIV Corps, AAR, both at NA; LSM Group 4, Action Report, Ormoc, December 9, 1944, MS-416, World War II Battle and Operations Reports, Box 31, Folder 5; Task Unit 78.3.5, Action Report, Amphibious Landing . . . in Ormoc Bay, December 22, 1944, MS-416, World War II Battle and Operations Reports, Box 32, Folder 2, both at

USNA; Lieutenant Frederick Downs, letter to Mrs. G. W. Jeffries, September 29, 1945, Folder 748, Accession #2399, SHSM; Samuel Eliot Morison, *History of United States Naval Operations in World War II*, vol. 13: *The Liberation of the Philippines—Luzon, Mindanao, The Visayas, 1944–1945* (Annapolis, MD: Naval Institute Press, 2012 reprint), 17–51; MacArthur, *Reports*, vol. 1: *Campaigns in the Pacific*, 251; Craven and Cate, *The Army Air Forces in World War II*, vol. 5, 378–88, 392–400; Morison, *History*, vol. 12: *Leyte*, 379–93; Prefer, *Leyte 1944*, 220–33; Krueger, *From Down Under to Nippon*, 199–207; *Ours to Hold It High*, 162–64; Falk, *Decision at Leyte*, 271–85, 290–91, 296; Cannon, *Leyte*, 294–305, 317–18; Smith, *Triumph in the Philippines*, 43–54. For information on the USS *Ward*, see www.history.navy.mil and www.warfarehistory network.com. Outerbridge retired as a rear admiral in 1957. The most prominent casualty of the Mindoro invasion was USS *Nashville*, MacArthur's erstwhile maritime home. A kamikaze plane crashed into the cruiser, inflicting serious damage, killing 133 and wounding another 190. Among the dead was Admiral Struble's chief of staff.

24. 77th Infantry Division, Lessons Learned in the Leyte Campaign, May 16, 1945, Record Group 337, Entry 15A, Box 58, Folder 204; 77th Infantry Division, AAR, 16–17; Leach, History of the 77th Infantry Division at Ormoc/Leyte; Bruce lecture, "The Operations of the 77th Division at Leyte," 13, 18–19, all at NA; Major General John Hodge letter to Lieutenant General Robert Richardson, December 28, 1944, Robert Richardson Papers, Box 74, HIA; Colonel Paul Freeman, "Observers Report, 77th Infantry Division in the Ormoc Area of West Leyte during the Period 7–18 December 1944," December 20, 1944, 3, and Appendix A, 1, Andrew Bruce Papers, Box 6, USAMHI; Japanese Monograph #6, 98–99, 106–8; Dean, "The Liberation of Leyte, Volume 3," no pagination, both at CMH; Becker, "Operations of the 77th Infantry Division in the Ormoc Corridor," 26, DRL; Bjork, "Waterborne Envelopments," *Military Review*, 56–62; "The Fall of Ormoc on Leyte," *Military Review*, 54–56; Lopez, "From Jackson to Japan," 115; *Ours to Hold It High*, 156–59; J. D. Potter, *Life and Death of a Japanese General*, 115–16; West, *Second to None*, 129–33; Cannon, *Leyte*, 284–93.

25. Report of the Commanding General Eighth Army on the Leyte-Samar Operation, 7–18, 9-2.8 AA; Headquarters, Army Ground Forces, Lessons Learned from the Leyte Campaign; Japanese Monograph #6, 120–24; Tomochika, "True Facts of the Leyte Operation," 27–29, 31–33, all at CMH; General Headquarters, Southwest Pacific Area, Communique, December 26, 1944; Lieutenant Gage Rodman, letter to parents, January 4, 1944 [*sic*], Gage Rodman Papers, Box 5, both at USAMHI; XXIV Corps, Operation Report, Battle of Leyte, 26 December 1944–10 February 1945, Record Group 337, Entry 15A, Box 60, Folder 272; XXIV Corps, AAR; Sixth Army, AAR, 84, all at NA; Lieutenant General Robert Eichelberger, diary, December 13, 1944, Box 1, Robert Eichelberger Papers; letters to Emma Eichelberger, January 1945, Box 9, Robert Eichelberger Papers; Dictations, 1949, Box 68, Robert Eichelberger Papers, all at DU; Brigadier General Clovis Byers, letter to Emma Eichelberger, December 9, 1944, Clovis Byers Papers, Box 3, Folder 3-4, HIA; Joe H. Camp Jr., *32 Answered: A South Carolina Veteran's Story*, self-published, 2015, 351–56; Luvaas, *Dear Miss Em*, 170; Flanagan, *The Angels*, 33; Falk, *Decision at Leyte*, 308–319; Prefer, *Leyte 1944*, 337; J. D. Potter, *Life and Death of a Japanese General*, 121–22; Cannon, *Leyte*, 361–70; Holzimmer, *General Walter Krueger*, 202–207; Eichelberger, *Our Jungle Road to Tokyo*, 181–82; James, *Years of MacArthur*, vol. 2, 602, claims that Eighth Army lost seven hundred killed but provides no source for this contention. Eighth Army records estimate Japanese strength at twenty-five thousand as of December 26. Ironically, and perhaps even sadly, Eighth Army after-action reports employed the term "mopping up." Even Eichelberger himself used it in his own book. Camp's book is an excellent history of the 32nd Infantry Division through the eyes of many veterans.

Epilogue

1. Seymour "Sy" Brody, "Jewish Heroes and Heroines in America, World War II to the Present: P.F.C. Charles Feuereisen, A Hero Talks with MacArthur," at www.seymour brody.com; Flanagan, *The Angels*, 62–63, 169; James, *Years of MacArthur*, vol. 2, 584–91. After the war, Feuereisen became heavily involved in veterans' affairs. He served as president of the 11th Airborne Division Association, president of the New Jersey Allied Veterans Council, and national president of the Jewish War Veterans of the U.S.A. For more information on Feuereisen's postwar activities, see October 10, 1984, remarks by the Honorable Robert C. Torricelli on page 31746 of the *Congressional Record* at www.govinfo.gov.

Selected Bibliography

Archives and Manuscript Collections

Abilene, KS. Dwight D. Eisenhower Library (EL).
Annapolis, MD. Special Collections and Archives, United States Naval Academy (USNA).
Carlisle, PA. United States Army Military History Institute (USAMHI).
College Park, MD. National Archives and Records Administration, II (NA).
Columbia, MO. State Historical Society of Missouri Research Center (SHSM).
Denton, TX. University of North Texas Oral History Collection (UNT).
Durham, NC. David Rubenstein Rare Book and Manuscript Library, Duke University (DU).
Fort Benning, GA. Donovan Research Library (DRL).
Fort Leavenworth, KS. Combined Arms Research Library (CARL).
Fort Riley, KS. United States Cavalry Museum (USCM).
Fort Sam Houston, TX. Army Nurse Corps Collection, Army Medical Department Center of History and Heritage (AMEDD).
Fredericksburg, TX. Nimitz Education and Research Center, National Museum of the Pacific War (NMPW).
Knoxville, TN. University of Tennessee Special Collections Library, Repository of the Center for the Study of War and Society (SCUTK).
Madison, WI. Wisconsin Veterans Museum (WVM).
New Orleans, LA. National World War II Museum (WWIIM).
Norfolk, VA. Douglas MacArthur Memorial Archives (DMMA).
Palo Alto, CA. Hoover Institution Archives, Stanford University (HIA).
Quantico, VA. United States Marine Corps History and Museums Division (USMCHD).
San Diego, CA. Special Collections Library, San Diego State University (SDSU).
Washington, DC. Library of Congress, Veterans History Project (LOC).
Washington, DC. U.S. Army Center of Military History (CMH).
West Point, NY. United States Military Academy Library Archives (USMA).

Books

81st Wildcat Division Historical Committee. *The 81st Infantry Wildcat Division in World War II*. Washington, DC: Infantry Journal Press, 1948.
Alexander, Larry. *Shadows in the Jungle: The Alamo Scouts Behind Japanese Lines in World War II*. New York: NAL Caliber, 2009.
Anders, Leslie. *The Ledo Road: General Joseph W. Stilwell's Highway to China*. Norman: University of Oklahoma Press, 1965.
Appleman, Roy E., James M. Burns, Russell A. Gugeler, and John Stevens. *United States Army in World War II, The War in the Pacific, Okinawa: The Last Battle*. Washington, DC: U.S. Army Center for Military History, 1948.
Arthur, Anthony. *Bushmasters: America's Jungle Warriors of World War II*. New York: St. Martin's Press, 1987.

Arthur, Robert A., and Kenneth Cohlmia. *The Third Marine Division.* Edited by Robert T. Vance. Washington, DC: Infantry Journal Press, 1948.

Astor, Gerald. *Crisis in the Pacific: The Battles for the Philippine Islands by the Men Who Fought Them.* New York: Dell, 2002.

———. *The Jungle War: Mavericks, Marauders, and Madmen in the China-Burma-India Theater of WWII.* New York: John Wiley & Sons, 2004.

Austin, Richard, ed. *Letters from the Pacific: A Combat Chaplain in World War II.* Columbia: University of Missouri Press, 2000.

Barbey, Daniel. *MacArthur's Amphibious Navy: Seventh Amphibious Force Operations, 1943–1945.* Annapolis, MD: United States Naval Institute, 1969.

Bergerud, Eric. *Touched with Fire: The Land War in the South Pacific.* New York: Penguin Books, 1996.

Black, Robert. *Rangers in World War II.* New York: Ballantine Books, 1992.

Blair, Bobby, and Peter DeCioccio. *Victory at Peleliu: The 81st Infantry Division's Pacific Campaign.* Norman: University of Oklahoma Press, 2011.

Booker, Bryan. *African Americans in the United States Army in World War II.* Jefferson, NC: McFarland & Company, 2008.

Boomhower, Ray. *Dispatches from the Pacific: The World War II Reporting of Robert Sherrod.* Bloomington: Indiana University Press, 2017.

Borneman, Walter R. *The Admirals: Nimitz, Halsey, Leahy, and King—The Five-Star Admirals Who Won the War at Sea.* New York: Little, Brown, 2012.

———. *MacArthur at War: World War II in the Pacific.* New York: Little, Brown, 2016.

Cannon, M. Hamlin. *United States Army in World War II, The War in the Pacific, Leyte: The Return to the Philippines.* Washington, DC: Center of Military History, United States Army, 1954.

Caraccilo, Dominic J., ed. *Surviving Bataan and Beyond: Colonel Irvin Alexander's Odyssey as a Japanese Prisoner of War.* Mechanicsburg, PA: Stackpole Books, 1999.

Carter, Worrall. *Beans, Bullets, and Black Oil: The Story of Fleet Logistics Afloat in the Pacific During World War II.* Washington, DC: Department of the Navy, 1953.

Casey, Hugh J. *Engineers of the Southwest Pacific, 1941–1945. Vol. 1, Engineers in Theater Operations.* United States Army Forces in the Far East, 1947.

———. *Engineers of the Southwest Pacific, 1941–1945. Vol. 7, Engineer Supply.* United States Army Forces in the Far East, 1947.

———. *Engineers of the Southwest Pacific, 1941–1945. Vol. 4, Amphibian Engineer Operations.* United States Army Forces in the Far East, 1959.

Catanzaro, Francis. *With the 41st Division in the Southwest Pacific: A Foot Soldier's Story.* Bloomington and Indianapolis: Indiana University Press, 2002.

Chan, Won-loy. *Burma: The Untold Story.* Novato, CA: Presidio Press, 1986.

Chase, William C. *Front Line General: The Commands of William C. Chase: An Autobiography.* Houston, TX: Pacesetter Press, 1975.

Chwialkowski, Paul. *In Caesar's Shadow: The Life of General Robert Eichelberger.* Westport, CT: Greenwood Press, 1993.

Coakley, Robert W., and Richard M. Leighton. *United States Army in World War II, The War Department: Global Logistics and Strategy 1943–1945.* Washington, DC: Center of Military History, United States Army, 1989.

Condon-Rall, Mary Ellen, and Albert E. Cowdrey. *United States Army in World War II, The Medical Department: Medical Service in the War Against Japan.* Washington, DC: Center of Military History, United States Army, 1998.

Cook, Haruko Taya, and Theodore F. Cook. *Japan at War: An Oral History.* New York: New Press, 1992.

Cooper, Norman V. *A Fighting General: The Biography of Gen. Holland M. "Howlin' Mad" Smith.* Quantico, VA: Marine Corps Association, 1987.

Craven, Wesley Frank, and James Lea Cate, eds. *The Army Air Forces in World War II*. Vol. 4, *The Pacific: Guadalcanal to Saipan, August 1942–July 1944*. Washington, DC: Office of Air Force History, United States Air Force, 1983.

———. *The Army Air Forces in World War II*. Vol. 5, *The Pacific, Matterhorn to Nagasaki, June 1944–August 1945*. Washington, DC: Office of Air Force History, 1983.

Cronin, Francis D. *Under the Southern Cross: The Saga of the Americal Division*. Washington, DC: Combat Forces Press, 1951.

Crowl, Philip A. *United States Army in World War II, The War in the Pacific: Campaign in the Marianas*. Washington, DC: Office of the Chief of Military History, Department of the Army, 1960.

Crowl, Philip A., and Edmund G. Love. *United States Army in World War II, The War in the Pacific: Seizure of the Gilberts and Marshalls*. Washington, DC: Office of the Chief of Military History, Department of the Army, 1955.

Davidson, Orlando R., J. Carl Willems, and Joseph A. Kahl. *The Deadeyes: The Story of the 96th Infantry Division*. Washington, DC: Infantry Journal Press, 1947.

Davis, Russell. *Marine at War*. Boston: Little, Brown, 1961.

Day, John F. *An Officer in MacArthur's Court: The Memoir of the First Headquarters Commandant for General Douglas MacArthur in Australia*. Fremont, CA: Robertson Publishing, 2014.

Dean, Peter J. *MacArthur's Coalition: US and Australian Military Operations in the Southwest Pacific Area, 1942–1945*. Lawrence: University Press of Kansas, 2018.

Dencker, Donald O. *Love Company: Infantry Combat Against the Japanese, World War II: Leyte and Okinawa*. Manhattan, KS: Sunflower University Press, 2002.

Denfield, D. Colt. *Hold the Marianas: The Japanese Defense of the Mariana Islands*. Shippensburg, PA: White Mane Publishing, 1997.

Dixon, Chris. *African Americans and the Pacific War, 1941–1945: Race, Nationality, and the Fight for Freedom*. Cambridge: Cambridge University Press, 2018.

Dod, Karl C. *United States Army in World War II, The Corps of Engineers: The War Against Japan*. Washington, DC: Office of the Chief of Military History, United States Army, 1966.

Dorn, Frank. *Walkout: With Stilwell in Burma*. New York: Thomas Y. Crowell Company, 1971.

Drea, Edward J. *MacArthur's ULTRA: Codebreaking and the War Against Japan, 1942–1945*. Lawrence: University Press of Kansas, 1992.

Egeberg, Roger O. *The General: MacArthur and the Man He Called "Doc."* Washington, DC: Oak Mountain Press, 1993.

Eichelberger, Robert L. *Our Jungle Road to Tokyo*. New York: Viking Press, 1950.

Eisenhower, Dwight D. *Crusade in Europe*. New York: Doubleday, 1948.

Falk, Stanley L. *Decision at Leyte*. New York: W. W. Norton, 1966.

Fenby, Jonathan. *Chiang Kai-shek: China's Generalissimo and the Nation He Lost*. New York: Carroll & Graf Publishers, 2003.

Flanagan, Edward M., Jr. *The Angels: A History of the 11th Airborne Division 1943–1946*. Washington, DC: Infantry Journal Press, 1948.

Frierson, William C. *The Admiralties: Operations of the 1st Cavalry Division, 29 February–18 May 1944*. Washington, DC: Center of Military History, United States Army, 1990.

Gabbett, Michael. *The Bastards of Burma: Merrill's Marauders and the Mars Task Force Revisited*. Albuquerque: Desert Dreams, 1989.

Gailey, Harry A. *Peleliu 1944*. Annapolis, MD: Nautical & Aviation Publishing Company of America, 1983.

———. *Howlin' Mad vs the Army: Conflict in Command, Saipan 1944*. Novato, CA: Presidio Press, 1986.

———. *The Liberation of Guam, 21 July–10 August 1944*. Novato, CA: Presidio Press, 1988.

———. *Bougainville 1943–1945: The Forgotten Campaign*. Lexington: University Press of Kentucky, 1991.

———. *MacArthur's Victory: The War in New Guinea, 1943–1944*. Novato, CA: Presidio Press, 2004.

Garand, George W., and Truman R. Strobridge. *History of United States Marine Corps Operations in World War II*. Vol. 4, *Western Pacific Operations*. Washington, DC: Historical Division, Headquarters, United States Marine Corps, 1971.

Gibney, Frank, ed. *Senso: The Japanese Remember the Pacific War*. Translated by Beth Cary. Armonk, NY: M. E. Sharpe, 1995.

Goldberg, Harold J. *D-Day in the Pacific: The Battle of Saipan*. Bloomington and Indianapolis: Indiana University Press, 2007.

Green, Bob. *Okinawa Odyssey*. Albany, TX: Bright Sky Press, 2004.

Griffith, Thomas E., Jr. *MacArthur's Airman: General George C. Kenney and the War in the Southwest Pacific*. Lawrence: University Press of Kansas, 1998.

Hallas, James H. *The Devil's Anvil: The Assault on Peleliu*. Westport, CT: Praeger, 1994.

———. *Saipan: The Battle That Doomed Japan in World War II*. Guildford, CT: Stackpole Books, 2019.

Halsey, William F., and J. Bryan III. *Admiral Halsey's Story*. New York: Whittlesey House, 1947.

Hardee, David L. *Bataan Survivor: A POW's Account of Japanese Captivity in World War II*. Edited by Frank A. Blazich Jr. Columbia: University of Missouri Press, 2016.

Hastings, Max. *Retribution: The Battle for Japan, 1944–45*. New York: Vintage Books, 2007.

Heinl, Robert D., and John A. Crown. *The Marshalls: Increasing the Tempo*. Washington, DC: Historical Branch, G-3 Division, Headquarters, United States Marine Corps, 1954.

Herman, Arthur. *Douglas MacArthur: American Warrior*. New York: Random House, 2016.

Historical Division, War Department. *Guam: Operations of the 77th Division, 21 July–10 August 1944*. Washington, DC: Center of Military History, United States Army, 1990.

Hoffman, Carl W. *Saipan: The Beginning of the End*. Washington, DC: Historical Branch, G-3 Division, Headquarters, United States Marine Corps, 1950.

Holzimmer, Kevin C. *General Walter Krueger: Unsung Hero of the Pacific War*. Lawrence: University Press of Kansas, 2007.

Hornfischer, James D. *The Fleet at Flood Tide: America at Total War in the Pacific, 1944–1945*. New York: Bantam Books, 2016.

Hough, Frank O. *The Assault on Peleliu*. Washington, DC: Historical Branch, G-3 Division, United States Marine Corps, 1950.

Huff, Sidney, with Joe Alex Morris. *My Fifteen Years with General MacArthur: A First-Hand Account of America's Greatest Soldier*. New York: Paperback Library, 1964.

Hunt, Frazier. *The Untold Story of Douglas MacArthur*. New York: Devin-Adair Company, 1954.

Hunter, Charles N. *Galahad*. San Antonio, TX: Naylor Company, 1963.

James, D. Clayton. *The Years of MacArthur*. Vol. 2, *1941–1945*. Boston: Houghton Mifflin, 1975.

Jefferson, Robert F. *Fighting for Hope: African American Troops of the 93rd Infantry Division in World War II and Postwar America*. Baltimore: Johns Hopkins University Press, 2008.

Jones, Don. *Oba: The Last Samurai: Saipan 1944–1945*. Novato, CA: Presidio Press, 1986.

Kahn, Sy M. *Between Tedium and Terror: A Soldier's World War II Diary, 1943–45*. Urbana and Chicago: University of Illinois Press, 1993.

Kennard, Richard C. *Combat Letters Home: A U.S. Marine Corps Officer's World War II Letters from Peleliu, Okinawa and North China, September 1944 to December 1945.* Bryn Mawr, PA: Dorrance & Company, 1985.

Kenney, George C. *The MacArthur I Know.* New York: Duell, Sloane and Pearce, 1951.

———. *General Kenney Reports: A Personal History of the Pacific War.* Washington, DC: Office of Air Force History, 1987.

Kerr, E. Bartlett. *Surrender and Survival: The Experience of American POWs in the Pacific, 1941–1945.* New York: William Morrow and Company, 1985.

Knox, Donald, ed. *Death March: The Survivors of Bataan.* New York: Harcourt, Brace, Jovanovich, 1981.

Krueger, General Walter. *From Down Under to Nippon: The Story of Sixth Army in World War II.* Washington, DC: Combat Forces Press, 1953.

Lacey, Sharon Tosi. *Pacific Blitzkrieg: World War II in the Central Pacific.* Denton: University of North Texas Press, 2013.

Leahy, William D. *I Was There: The Personal Story of the Chief of Staff to Presidents Roosevelt and Truman Based on His Notes and Diaries Made at the Time.* New York: McGraw-Hill, 1950.

Leary, William M., ed. *We Shall Return: MacArthur's Commanders and the Defeat of Japan.* Lexington: University Press of Kentucky, 1988.

Lee, Robert C. *Put 'Em Across: A History of the 2d Engineer Special Brigade, 1942–1945.* Fort Belvoir, VA: Office of History, US Army Corps of Engineers, 1988.

Lee, Ulysses. *United States Army in World War II: The Employment of Negro Troops.* Washington, DC: Office of the Chief of Military History, United States Army, 1966.

Lodge, Major O. R. *The Recapture of Guam.* Washington, DC: Historical Branch, G-3 Division, Headquarters, United States Marine Corps, 1954.

Love, Edmund G. *The 27th Infantry Division in World War II.* Nashville: Battery Press, 1949.

———. *The Hourglass: History of the 7th Infantry Division in World War II.* Washington, DC: Infantry Journal Press, 1950.

———. *War Is a Private Affair.* New York: Harcourt Brace, 1959.

Luvaas, Jay, ed. *Dear Miss Em: General Eichelberger's War in the Pacific, 1942–1945.* Westport, CT: Greenwood Press, 1972.

MacArthur, Douglas. *Reminiscences.* New York: Da Capo, 1964.

———. *Reports of General MacArthur.* Vol. 1, *The Campaigns of MacArthur in the Pacific.* Washington, DC: Center of Military History, 1966, 1994.

———. *Reports of General MacArthur.* Vol. 2, *Japanese Operations in the Southwest Pacific.* Washington, DC: Center of Military History, 1966, 1994.

Manchester, William. *American Caesar: Douglas MacArthur 1880–1964.* New York: Dell, 1978.

Marshall, S. L. A. *Battle at Best.* New York: Jove Books, 1963.

———. *Bringing Up the Rear: A Memoir.* Edited by Cate Marshall. Novato, CA: Presidio Press, 1979.

———. *Island Victory: The Battle for Kwajalein Atoll.* Lincoln: University of Nebraska Press, 2001.

Matloff, Maurice. *United States Army in World War II, The War Department: Strategic Planning for Coalition Warfare, 1943–1944.* Washington, DC: Center of Military History, United States Army, 1990.

McCallus, Joseph P. *The MacArthur Highway and Other Relics of American Empire in the Philippines.* Washington, DC: Potomac Books, 2010.

McCartney, William F. *The Jungleers: A History of the 41st Infantry Division.* Washington, DC: Infantry Journal Press, 1948.

McLaughlin, John J. *General Albert C. Wedemeyer: America's Unsung Strategist in World War II*. Philadelphia and Oxford: Casemate, 2012.

McManus, John C. *Grunts: Inside the American Infantry Combat Experience, World War II Through Iraq*. New York: NAL Caliber, 2010.

———. *The Dead and Those About to Die: D-Day: The Big Red One at Omaha Beach*. New York: NAL Caliber, 2014.

———. *Fire and Fortitude: The US Army in the Pacific War, 1941–1943*. New York: Dutton Caliber, 2019.

McMillan, George. *The Old Breed: A History of the First Marine Division in World War II*. Washington, DC: Infantry Journal Press, 1949.

Men Who Were There. *Ours to Hold It High: The History of the 77th Infantry Division in World War II*. Edited by Max Myers. Washington, DC: Infantry Journal Press, 1947.

Miller, John. *United States Army in World War II, The War in the Pacific, Cartwheel: The Reduction of Rabaul*. Washington, DC: Office of the Chief of Military History, Department of the Army, 1959.

Mitter, Rana. *Forgotten Ally: China's World War II, 1937–1945*. Boston: Mariner Books, 2013.

Morison, Samuel Eliot. *History of United States Naval Operations in World War II*. Vol. 7, *Aleutians, Gilberts and Marshalls, June 1942–April 1944*. Boston: Little, Brown, 1951.

———. *History of United States Naval Operations in World War II*. Vol. 12, *Leyte, June 1944–January 1945*. Boston: Little, Brown, 1958.

———. *History of United States Naval Operations in World War II*. Vol. 6, *Breaking the Bismarcks Barrier, 22 July 1942–1 May 1944*. Boston: Little, Brown, 1968.

———. *History of United States Naval Operations in World War II*. Vol. 8, *New Guinea and the Marianas, March–August 1944*. Boston: Little, Brown, 1968.

Morton, Louis. *United States Army in World War II, The War in the Pacific: Strategy and Command, the First Two Years*. Washington, DC: Center of Military History, United States Army, 2000.

Motley, Mary Penick, ed. *The Invisible Soldier: The Experience of the Black Soldier, World War II*. Detroit: Wayne State University Press, 1975.

Murphy, Edward F. *Heroes of WWII*. New York: Ballantine Books, 1990.

O'Brien, Francis A. *Battling for Saipan*. New York: Ballantine Books, 2003.

O'Donnell, Patrick K., ed. *Into the Rising Sun: In Their Own Words, World War II's Pacific Veterans Reveal the Heart of Combat*. New York: Free Press, 2002.

Ogburn, Charlton, Jr. *The Marauders*. New York: Harper & Brothers, 1956.

Ohl, John Kennedy. *Minuteman: The Military Career of General Robert S. Beightler*. Boulder, CO: Lynne Rienner Publishers, 2001.

Peers, William R., and Dean Brelis. *Behind the Burma Road: The Story of America's Most Successful Guerrilla Force*. Boston: Little, Brown, 1963.

Petty, Bruce M., ed. *Saipan: Oral Histories of the Pacific War*. Jefferson, NC, and London: McFarland & Company, 2002.

Potter, E. B. *Nimitz*. Annapolis, MD: Naval Institute Press, 1976.

———. *Bull Halsey*. Annapolis, MD: Naval Institute Press, 1985.

Potter, John Deane. *The Life and Death of a Japanese General*. New York: Signet Books, 1962.

Prefer, Nathan N. *Leyte 1944: The Soldiers' Battle*. Philadelphia and Oxford: Casemate, 2012.

Radike, Floyd W. *Across the Dark Islands: The War in the Pacific*. New York: Ballantine Books, 2003.

Rhoades, Weldon E. "Dusty." *Flying MacArthur to Victory*. College Station: Texas A&M Press, 1987.

Riegelman, Harold. *Caves of Biak: An American Officer's Experiences in the Southwest Pacific*. New York: Dial Press, 1955.

Rogers, Paul P. *The Bitter Years: MacArthur and Sutherland*. New York: Praeger, 1990.

Romanus, Charles F., and Riley Sunderland. *United States Army in World War II, China-Burma-India Theater: Stilwell's Command Problems*. Washington, DC: Office of the Chief of Military History, Department of the Army, 1956.

Ross, Bill D. *A Special Piece of Hell: The Untold Story of Peleliu*. New York: St. Martin's Paperbacks, 1991.

Schaller, Michael. *Douglas MacArthur: Far Eastern General*. New York: Oxford University Press, 1989.

Schrijvers, Peter. *Bloody Pacific: American Soldiers at War with Japan*. New York: Palgrave Macmillan, 2010.

Schultz, Duane. *Hero of Bataan: The Story of General Jonathan M. Wainwright*. New York: St. Martin's Press, 1981.

Seagrave, Gordon S. *Burma Surgeon Returns*. New York: W. W. Norton, 1946.

Shaw, Henry, and Douglas Kane. *History of United States Marine Corps Operations in World War II*. Vol. 2, *Isolation of Rabaul*. Washington, DC: Historical Branch, G-3 Division, Headquarters, United States Marine Corps, 1963.

Shaw, Henry, Bernard Nalty, and Edwin Turnbladh. *History of United States Marine Corps Operations in World War II*. Vol. 3, *Central Pacific Drive*. Washington, DC: Historical Branch, G-3 Division, Headquarters, United States Marine Corps, 1966.

Sherrod, Robert L. *On to Westward: War in the Central Pacific*. New York: Duell, Sloan and Pearce, 1945.

Shortal, John F. *Forged by Fire: Robert L. Eichelberger and the Pacific War*. Columbia: University of South Carolina Press, 1987.

Sledge, E. B. *With the Old Breed: At Peleliu and Okinawa*. New York: Oxford University Press, 1990.

Slim, William. *Defeat into Victory*. New York: David McKay Company, 1961.

Smith, Holland M., and Percy Finch. *Coral and Brass*. New York: Charles Scribner's Sons, 1949.

Smith, Jean Edward. *Eisenhower in War and Peace*. New York: Random House, 2012.

Smith, Robert Ross. *United States Army in World War II, The War in the Pacific: The Approach to the Philippines*. Washington, DC: Office of the Chief of Military History, Department of the Army, 1953.

Smith, S. E., ed. *The United States Marine Corps in World War II*. Vol. 2, *Battering the Empire*. New York: Ace Books, 1969.

Sorley, Lewis. *Honorable Warrior: General Harold K. Johnson and the Ethics of Command*. Lawrence: University Press of Kansas, 1998.

Spector, Ronald H. *Eagle Against the Sun: The American War with Japan*. New York: Vintage Books, 1985.

Stauffer, Alvin P. *United States Army in World War II, The Quartermaster Corps: Operations in the War Against Japan*. Washington, DC: Center of Military History, United States Army, 2004.

Stilwell, Joseph W. *The Stilwell Papers*. Edited by Theodore H. White. New York: William Sloane Associates, 1948.

———. *Stilwell's Personal File: China, Burma, India, 1942–1944*. Vol. 4. Edited by Riley Sunderland and Charles F. Romanus. Wilmington, DE: Scholarly Resources, 1976.

Stone, James H., ed. *Crisis Fleeting: Original Reports on American Military Medicine in India and Burma in the Second World War*. Washington, DC: Office of the Surgeon General, Department of the Army, 1969.

Taaffe, Stephen R. *MacArthur's Jungle War: The 1944 New Guinea Campaign*. Lawrence: University Press of Kansas, 1998.

Taylor, Jay. *The Generalissimo: Chiang Kai-shek and the Struggle for Modern China*. Cambridge: Belknap Press of Harvard University Press, 2009.

Tenney, Lester I. *My Hitch in Hell: The Bataan Death March*. Washington, DC: Potomac Books, 1995.

Toland, John. *The Rising Sun: The Decline and Fall of the Japanese Empire, 1936–1945*. Vol. 2. New York: Random House, 1970.

Toll, Ian W. *Twilight of the Gods: War in the Western Pacific, 1944–1945*. New York: W. W. Norton, 2020.

Tuchman, Barbara W. *Stilwell and the American Experience in China, 1911–1945*. New York: Macmillan, 1970.

United States Strategic Bombing Survey (Pacific), Naval Analysis Division. *The Campaigns of the Pacific War*. Washington, DC: Government Printing Office, 1946.

United States Strategic Bombing Survey (Pacific), Naval Analysis Division. *Interrogations of Japanese Officials*, vol. 2. Washington, DC: Government Printing Office, 1946.

Valtin, Jan. *Children of Yesterday: The 24th Infantry Division in the Philippines*. New York: Reader's Press, 1946 original, 2014 reprint.

Vego, Milan N. *The Battle for Leyte: Allied and Japanese Plans, Preparations, and Execution*. Annapolis, MD: Naval Institute Press, 2006.

Veterans Administration, Office of Planning and Preparation. *POW: Study of Former Prisoners of War*. Washington, DC: Government Printing Office, 1980.

Wainwright, Jonathan M. *General Wainwright's Story*. Edited by Robert Considine. Westport, CT: Greenwood Press, Publishers, 1945.

Walker, Charles H. *Combat Officer: A Memoir of War in the South Pacific*. New York: Ballantine Books, 2004.

Walker, John R. *Bracketing the Enemy: Forward Observers in World War II*. Norman: University of Oklahoma Press, 2013.

Waterford, Van. *Prisoners of the Japanese in World War II*. Jefferson, NC: McFarland & Company, 1994.

Webster, Donovan. *The Burma Road: The Epic Story of the China-Burma-India Theater in World War II*. Farrar, Straus and Giroux, 2003.

Wedemeyer, Albert. *Wedemeyer Reports! An Objective, Dispassionate Examination of World War II, Postwar Policies, and Grand Strategy*. New York: Henry Holt & Company, 1958.

West, Charles O. *Second to None: The Story of the 305th Infantry in World War II*. Washington, DC: Infantry Journal Press, 1949.

Weston, Logan E. *The Fightin' Preacher*. Cheyenne, WY: Vision Press, 1992.

Willoughby, Charles A., and John Chamberlain. *MacArthur, 1941–1951*. New York: McGraw-Hill, 1954.

Zedric, Lance Q. *Silent Warriors of World War II: The Alamo Scouts Behind Japanese Lines*. Ventura: Pathfinder Publishing of California, 1995.

Index

Note: Page numbers in *italics* indicate maps.

About the Author

John C. McManus is an award-winning professor, author, and military historian, and a leading expert on the history of the American combat experience. He is the Curators' Distinguished Professor of U.S. Military History at Missouri University of Science and Technology, and recently completed a visiting professorship at the U.S. Naval Academy as the Leo A. Shifrin Chair of Naval and Military History. His critically acclaimed books on World War II include *Fire and Fortitude, Deadly Sky, September Hope*, and *The Dead and Those About to Die*.